Rebellion at Coranderrk

Aboriginal History Incorporated

Aboriginal History Inc. is a part of the Australian Centre for Indigenous History, Research School of Social Sciences, The Australian National University, and gratefully acknowledges the support of the School of History and the National Centre for Indigenous Studies, The Australian National University. Aboriginal History Inc. is administered by an Editorial Board which is responsible for all unsigned material. Views and opinions expressed by the author are not necessarily shared by Board members.

Contacting Aboriginal History

All correspondence should be addressed to the Editors, Aboriginal History Inc., ACIH, School of History, Research School of Social Sciences, ANU RSSS Building, The Australian National University, Canberra ACT 2600, or aboriginalhistoryinc@gmail.com.

WARNING: Readers are notified that this publication may contain names or images of deceased persons.

Rebellion at Coranderrk

DIANE E. BARWICK

Editors
LAURA E. BARWICK AND
RICHARD E. BARWICK

ANU PRESS

For Patricia Croft
and
Shirley Andrew Rosser
friends & editors

Published by ANU Press and Aboriginal History Inc.
The Australian National University
Canberra ACT 2600, Australia
Email: anupress@anu.edu.au

Available to download for free at press.anu.edu.au

ISBN (print): 9781760466497
ISBN (online): 9781760466503

WorldCat (print): 1437516471
WorldCat (online): 1437628739

DOI: 10.22459/RC.2024

This title is published under a Creative Commons Attribution-NonCommercial-NoDerivatives 4.0 International (CC BY-NC-ND 4.0) licence.

The full licence terms are available at
creativecommons.org/licenses/by-nc-nd/4.0/legalcode

Cover design and layout by ANU Press. Cover image: A street in Coranderrk, 1889, Chronicle / Alamy Stock Photo.

This book is published under the aegis of the Aboriginal History editorial board of ANU Press.

This edition © 2024 ANU Press and Aboriginal History Inc.

Contents

List of Figures	ix
Foreword to the 2024 Edition	xi
Author's Preface	xix
Editors' Preface	xxi
Introduction: Of History and Happenstance	1
1. Kulin and Ngamajet	9
2. The Years Before	25
3. A New Beginning	37
4. Mr Green's Way	51
5. Proprietors for the First Decade	65
6. The Board Takes Control	79
7. Loss of a Good Master	95
8. The Threat of Removal	111
9. Who Owns the Land?	129
10. Cause for Rebellion	147
11. Mrs Bon Intervenes	165
12. A Brief Victory	189
13. Final Defeat	209
14. The End of the Story	231
15. Dispersal	269
Appendix 1: The History of Farm Development at Coranderrk	281
Appendix 2: Membership of the Boards	285
Bibliography	289
Index	297

List of Figures

Diane MacEachern – BA (First Class Hons) Graduation, University of British Colombia, Canada, 1959.	xiv
Diane Barwick, PhD student, fieldwork, Melbourne, 1961.	xiv
Diane Barwick, PhD graduation, The Australian National University, Canberra, April 1964.	xiv
Richard Barwick, BSc graduation, Victoria University Wellington, New Zealand, 1953.	xiv
Richard Barwick, PhD student working on the Australian skink *Egernia cunninghami*, The Australian National University, Canberra, 1962.	xv
Diane and Richard Barwick, 1962.	xv
'New Zealander Studies Zoology in Canberra', *Christchurch Press*, 9 February 1963.	xvi
Dr Diane Barwick, Emeritus Professor W.E.H. (Bill) Stanner, Dr H.C. (Nugget) Coombs and Professor Wang Gungwu examine Volume 1 of *Aboriginal History* at the launch, Canberra, 1977.	xvii
Diane and Richard Barwick with their daughter Laura, Vancouver, Canada, 1973.	xvii
Stage coach on the road to Coranderrk, near Lilydale, Victoria 1889.	xxii
Map 1: The Aboriginal clans of Central Victoria.	11
Wayside Inn on the road to Coranderrk.	23
Map 2: Locations of stations and reserves established by the Victorian Board for the Protection of Aborigines.	24
Dindarmin – Malcolm, leader of the Jajowrong, aged approximately 67 years.	30
The first houses at Coranderrk, c. 1867.	49
John Green (1828–1908) and Mary Smith Benton Green (1837–1919).	52
Lilydale, Victoria, on the way to Coranderrk.	56
Beembarmin – Tommy Farmer of Mount Franklin, c. 1867.	67
Maria Wonga, Simon Wonga's wife, c. 1876.	70
Robert Wandin (1854–1908), nephew of William Barak at 11 years of age, c. 1876.	70
Back cottage, Coranderrk, 1868.	73
John and Elizabeth Charles, c. 1876, with children William and Henry.	86
Mrs Louisa Briggs with her children (rear: William, Sarah, Jack [John Jr], Mrs Lizzie Briggs Charles; front: Caroline, Ellen, Louisa and grandson William Charles).	87
The hop gardens at Coranderrk, c. 1877–1878.	89
The dwellings at Coranderrk, c. 1886.	101
Birdarak – Tommy Bamfield with his children David and Betsy.	107
The hop kiln at Coranderrk.	113

James Edgar.	121
A cricket match at Coranderrk, c. 1879.	128
William Parker (1847–1886), his wife Mary and children.	137
Jemmy Barker with his wife Jeannie (Rowan) and their children, Aaron and Israel, c. 1876.	142
Coranderrk pioneers Martin and Matilda Simpson, later 'native missionaries' at Maloga Mission.	158
William Barak (1818/24–1903) with his second wife Annie and their son David.	161
Mrs Ann Briggs (1824–1884).	166
Deardjoo Warramin – Tommy Avoca (1834–1894).	169
Annie Hamilton and her infant son.	179
William and Annie Hamilton and children.	179
Alfred Morgan, c. 1876.	184
David Barak (1867–1881), son of William and Annie; he died of consumption in August 1881.	192
Birdarak – Thomas Bamfield and his wife Eliza with their children, Betsy and David, c. 1876 (lady on left is not identified).	202
Bella Lee and Lizzie, and their infants.	214
Tommy Dunolly (1856/57–1923), woman on left unidentified, on right Eda Brangy.	214
Daniel Matthews and his wife Janet of the Maloga Mission.	228
Mrs Lily Hamilton Harris (right) and daughters with Mrs Jessie Hamilton Dunolly, c. 1876.	238
Emily Hall and Jemima Burns Wandin Dunolly.	239
Mrs Caroline Malcolm Ferguson Morgan (1845–1889) and sons Marcus (left), John (in front), Caleb (on mother's knee), and Augustus (right), c. 1876.	246
Annie Mclellan Reece Manton and her daughters, Maryann Mclellan (left) and Charlotte Reece, c. 1876.	247
Betsy Bamfield Foster (1870–1898) and David Bamfield (1868–1885).	263
Cottages at Coranderrk, c. 1891.	273
'Throwing boomerangs at Coranderrk, the Aborigines station, Victoria'.	278
Histogram to show the periods of tenure of the individual Board members.	288

Acknowledgments

Most of the photographs published in this book are from collections previously held at the Museum of Victoria, principally from the Charles Walter and Frederick Kruger albums, and now held at the State Library of Victoria. These appear on pages 30, 49, 52, 56, 67, 70, 73, 86, 87, 89, 101, 107, 113, 121, 128, 137, 142, 158, 161, 166, 169, 179, 184, 192, 202, 214, 238, 239, 246, 247, 263 and 273. The editor is deeply grateful for the assistance provided in sourcing these images for publication. Other illustrations are from original material that was in the author's possession at the time of her death. Family photographs (pages xiv–xvii) have been added by the editor.

Foreword to the 2024 Edition

The publication of *Rebellion at Coranderrk* in 1998, after my mother, Diane Barwick's death in 1986, was the final publication of a personal and professional collaboration between my parents that lasted for more than 25 years. It reflected the enduring love and respect my father had for my mother, and his determination that her scholarship should be recognised. Her death hit him very hard, and the years of work that went into the final publication of the Rebellion manuscript was, in truth, a labour of love.

My father, Richard Essex (Dick) Barwick, an influential vertebrate zoologist, palaeontologist, artist, Antarctic explorer and Aboriginal-rights activist, died peacefully in Canberra on 10 November 2012. He was born in Christchurch, New Zealand, on 1 September 1929. He attended Victoria University College (later Victoria University of Wellington) where he took a bachelor's degree in 1956, followed by an MSc (Hons) in 1957, and then worked as a junior lecturer. He was the biologist and artist on three Antarctic expeditions, including one with Sir Edmund Hillary. Barwick Valley in the Antarctic was named for him. In 1959 he applied for a lectureship at Canberra University College. The college became part of The Australian National University (ANU), where he enrolled for a PhD in reptile ecology and physiology and took up residence at University House. Shortly after, he was appointed to the Zoology Department at ANU. My father retired as a reader in Zoology at ANU in 1992, continuing on as a visiting fellow in the Research School of Earth Sciences until his death.

Living at University House was to transform his life. In October 1960, my mother came to Australia from Canada to study for her PhD in anthropology and, on her first day at ANU, Dad glanced down the communal breakfast table at University House and asked his neighbour 'Who is that attractive new student?' My mother was similarly struck, and romance blossomed.

My mother grew up in remote areas of Vancouver Island, Canada, and spent much of her early life in the bush. Despite her having successfully undertaken fieldwork in very remote First Nations communities in Canada, the Australian academic patriarchy of the time saw female students as 'not suitable' for remote fieldwork. Finding her first choices of fieldwork areas (the Papua New Guinea highlands and remote Northern Territory) blocked, she accepted an offer from Professor John Barnes to work on a project in regional and metropolitan Victoria.

My mother was welcomed into the Aboriginal community in Victoria with great kindness, generosity and warmth. She felt a great deal of kinship with members of the community and, in many ways, they reminded her of the communities that she had grown up in in Canada. In particular, Aboriginal Elder Aunty Ellen Atkinson took pity on a 21-year-old woman, 8,200 miles from her home and family in Canada, navigating the stress of a PhD.

Aunty Ellen's accounts of the past shaped my mother's research for more than 25 years, fuelling her conviction that ethnography must be contextualised and complemented by historical scholarship, and that this should centre the voices and lived experience of Aboriginal and Torres Strait Islander Australians.

However, Aunty Ellen's influence on my mother's life was deeper than that. In writing about Aunty Ellen, my mother recalled:

> At first, our conversations were limited to the topics appropriate between strangers, I was shy and afraid of being impertinent; she was kind yet implacable in her skilful management of interviews … But our relationship changed, just because I was a young girl without relatives and needed help. Her people have, I think, a special kindness for waifs and strays bereft of family, perhaps because their own identity is based on kinship ties. Several men of the district told me that as lonely youngsters during the depression years, they had been sheltered by Aboriginal families just as I was befriended and protected. When I turned to Aunty Ellen for advice and emotional support, she showed me the fondness of a grandmother, calling me 'my girl' and expressing anxious concern about my finances, my diet, and the suitability of my fiancé. My own mother could not have bettered Aunty Ellen's inquisition about his habits.[1]

Indeed, my parents' love and respect for Aunty Ellen was so great that my father formally asked both her *and* my grandparents for their blessing to marry my mother. Aunty Ellen, a shrewd judge of character, gave her blessing, telling my mother, that he was 'a kind and gentle man, and would make a good father'. That, and my father's willing adoption of a stray kitten my mother had rescued, later known as 'Sir Garfield' Barwick, reinforced her certainty that she had met the right man. They married on 14 April 1961.

Due to commitments of study and teaching, my parents spent the first couple of years of their married life apart, with Mum working in Victoria, and Dad in Canberra. My father would drive to see her every weekend he could in a somewhat disreputable Triumph Herald. My mother completed her PhD in 1964, and my father in 1965.

While collaboration between an anthropologist and a herpetologist/vertebrate palaeontologist might seem unusual, it was founded on shared interests. Dad was a talented artist and photographer. Since his first days at Victoria University, he had had a keen interest in history, archaeology, and anthropology. He had spent a lot of time surveying in remote parts of New Zealand as a student and had made friends with several Elders in the local Māori community, learning as much Te Reo as he could so he could converse more freely with them. He was a founding member of the New Zealand Archaeological Association in the early 1950s. He was also an early champion of cross-disciplinary research, and collaborated with both archaeologists and anthropologists, including co-supervising several biological anthropology students. This fascination with anthropology and archaeology, along with his interest in ethnographic art, led to a number of collaborations with my mother.

My mother's role as editor of the *Aboriginal History* journal led to Dad having a close involvement with the journal. A skilled scientific illustrator, he became the journal's unpaid designer and artistic adviser in 1977, designing the logo, advising on layout and typography, taking and developing photographs, and preparing maps and illustrations. Some of my earliest memories are of sitting in Aboriginal History Board meetings.

In 1986, my mother died unexpectedly of a cerebral haemorrhage, struck down while writing. It was a devastating loss for Dad. However, he was determined that my mother's research not be lost. He spent a great deal of time assembling her papers and editing and publishing a number of her unfinished manuscripts.

---

1   Diane Barwick, 'Aunty Ellen the Pastor's Wife', in *Fighters and Singers: The Lives of Some Aboriginal Women*, ed. I. White, D. Barwick and B. Meehan (Sydney: Allen & Unwin, 1985), 175–99.

FOREWORD TO THE 2024 EDITION

In 1997, Dad and I painstakingly digitised the typewritten *Rebellion at Coranderrk* manuscript – an enormously slow process with the technology of the time. We then prepared the book for digital publication, with Dad taking the design lead. This included layout and ensuring that the photographs and illustrations reproduced in it were as high quality as possible. It was very important to him to produce a book that reflected my mother's intentions. This was their last collaboration, something that Dad felt deeply. To be true to both their wishes, this edition has retained the format of the first edition.

Rebellion at Coranderrk tells of speaking truth to power. It was an honour and enormously moving to be able to launch the first edition at Healesville, with the descendants of the people described in this book, and with Aunty Ellen's kin. One young girl from the local primary school came up to us to tell us how brave and strong she thought the people of Coranderrk were in the face of so much injustice, and how glad she was to hear their story because it would help keep her strong and proud, and give her courage to speak out. I hope that it does the same for all who read it.

In truth, Dad's collaboration with Mum did not really end there. Over the next few years, after the publication of the first edition, Dad and I worked with Ann McCarthy, Gavan McCarthy and the University of Melbourne to catalogue my mother's papers and to set up the Diane Barwick Collection with the State Library of Victoria.

Dad's involvement in *Aboriginal History* also continued, with him contributing more than 30 journal and monograph covers before his death. This 35-year commitment reflected his passion for social justice for First Nations Australians, one shared with my mother.

One of the last conversations I had with my Dad, the day before his death in November 2012, was about his desire to see a new edition of *Rebellion at Coranderrk* released. I'm glad to see this last wish fulfilled.

When my mother wrote in the 1985 author's preface 'My greatest debt is to my husband Richard Barwick who has supported my work for half a life time' she was speaking only of the 25 years of their marriage. My father spent the following 26 years supporting her work too. More than half *his* lifetime. I feel very blessed to have not only their extraordinary scholarship as an example but also their deep and abiding love for each other.

My mother would be most amused to know that my 13-year-old son, Sebastian (now the same age that I was when my mother passed away), has frequently reassured me that 'doing research and writing is more important than making meals'.

Laura Barwick
Canberra, 2022

Diane MacEachern – BA (First Class Hons) Graduation, University of British Colombia, Canada, 1959.

Photographer: unknown [possibly R. MacEachern].

Diane Barwick, PhD graduation, The Australian National University, Canberra, April 1964.

Photographer: R.E. Barwick.

Diane Barwick, PhD student, fieldwork, Melbourne, 1961.

Photographer: R.E. Barwick.

Richard Barwick, BSc graduation, Victoria University Wellington, New Zealand, 1953.

Photographer: unknown [possibly J. Barwick].

FOREWORD TO THE 2024 EDITION

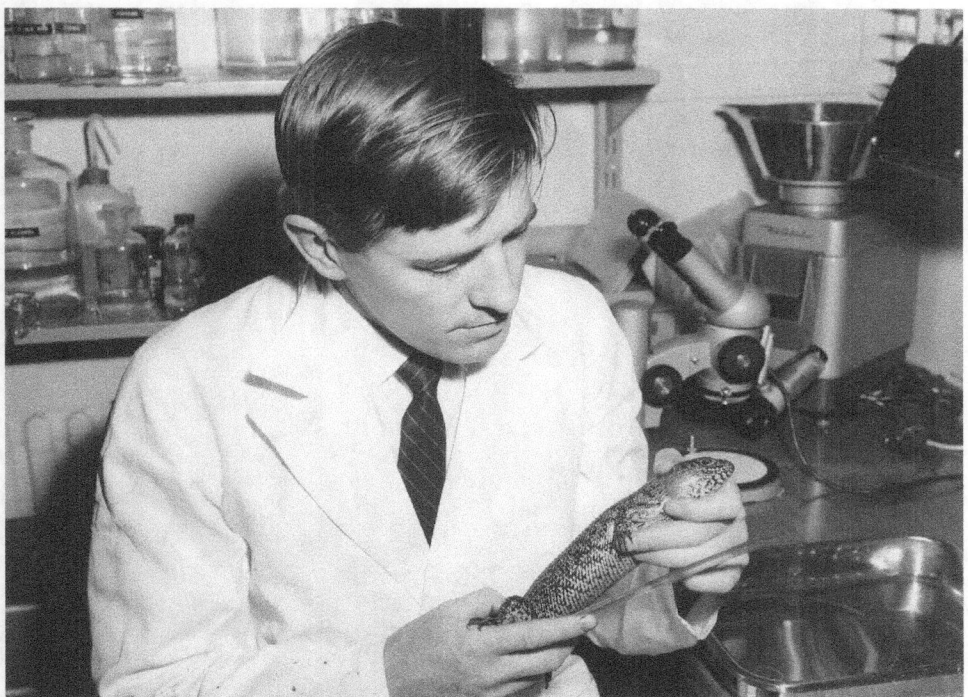

Richard Barwick, PhD student working on the Australian skink *Egernia cunninghami*, The Australian National University, Canberra, 1962.
Source: Australian News and Information Bureau. Photographer: W. Pedersen.

Diane and Richard Barwick, 1962.
Notes: 'Mr and Mrs Barwick in their lounge of their apartment at ANU. They are looking at native carving from Mozambique'. University House, The Australian National University, Canberra, 1962.
Source: Australian News and Information Bureau. Photographer: W. Pedersen.

NEW ZEALANDER STUDIES ZOOLOGY IN CANBERRA

Marriage To Vancouver Girl

[By GEOFF DE FRAGA, for the Australian News and Information Bureau]

CANBERRA.

A New Zealander in Australia to study lizards for his Ph.D. in zoology has married a Vancouver girl studying the Australian aborigines for her Ph.D. in anthropology.

He is Richard Barwick, of Ohiro road, Wellington. His wife, Diane, was formerly Diane McEachern, of Smith avenue, South Barnaby, B.C. They are both studying at the Australian National University, Canberra.

Diane has found that life with a zoologist husband has taken a little getting used to. There was the time, for instance, after they returned to Canberra from their honeymoon, when she was horrified to find two black snakes in the refrigerator—dead specimens, of course, but still —. Again, later on, there was the time when she found a brace of frogs in the bath.

Richard, with scientific reasonableness, found it hard to understand her protests. After all, he had been pretty understanding when she wanted to go off and live with aborigines down on the banks of the Murray, and when she wanted to work with them in a canning factory. And he felt he had taken it pretty well when, on their first anniversary, they realised that they had had only five months together.

But those days are over now, those days of field research, and Richard and Diane Barwick are well established in the academic life of Australia's federal capital.

Richard met Diane at University House on her second night in Canberra. That was more than two years ago. She had graduated B.A. with honours from the University of British Columbia in 1959 then, after studying museum planning at the Provincial Museum of Victoria, B.C., she took a job with the University's Department of Anthropology.

Aborigines And Their History

Her department chief, a New Zealander who had studied at Canberra's Australian National University drew her attention to the scholarship offered, and Diane applied and was accepted in mid-1960.

She has devoted most of her research into assimilation and integration of Australia's aborigines to the south-eastern mainland State of Victoria. "The records here are marvellous," she pointed out. "It's possible to trace most of the families back to their first contact period with Europeans, over 150 years ago. And over the last 10 years, with all restrictive education now a thing of the past, the progress has been quite remarkable."

The path that led Richard Barwick from his home in Ohiro road, Wellington, to marriage with Diane in Canberra was just as unusual. After graduating M.A. from Wellington University (his thesis was on lizards), he taught there, and then took a job teaching zoology at the Australian National University, where he is also working for his Ph.D. (on lizards, of course). While in New Zealand, he spent three seasons in the Antarctic, on Victoria University of Wellington expeditions.

To identify individual Canberra lizards, whose ecology, feeding habits and movements he studies closely, he paints their slaws with nail-lacquer. He has a small colony of them on a farmer's property not far out of Canberra.

"He's terribly fond of them," said Diane. "When he's got to cut one up and empty out the stomach contents to see what it's been eating, he goes and catches a stranger from another area."

But marriage to a zoologist has not lessened Diane's horror of lizards. "I wouldn't go within ten yards of the beastly things," she said.

Another responsibility of Richard's is that of deputy warden at Bruce Hall, where 150 graduates of both sexes are in residence. It is the only mixed residential university hall in Australia. He will finish his Ph.D. in another 14 months. And then —to Vancouver to meet his in-laws. Then probably California.

"And some day, perhaps," said Diane, "it might be rather fun to run a museum together. He's deeply interested in museum decor. He paints, too—mainly zoological illustrations."

She pointed to a framed water-colour of six different sorts of frogs.

"He did them in the bathroom."

'New Zealander Studies Zoology in Canberra', *Christchurch Press*, 9 February 1963.
Note: The date at the top was written by Diane Barwick.
Source: Laura Barwick.

FOREWORD TO THE 2024 EDITION

Dr Diane Barwick, Emeritus Professor W.E.H. (Bill) Stanner, Dr H.C. (Nugget) Coombs and Professor Wang Gungwu examine Volume 1 of *Aboriginal History* at the launch, Canberra, 1977.

Note: The cover was designed by Dr Richard Barwick.

Photographer: R.E. Barwick.

Diane and Richard Barwick with their daughter Laura, Vancouver, Canada, 1973.

Photographer: unknown [possibly R. MacEachern].

Author's Preface

With the permission of the Victorian Aborigines Welfare Board, I examined the records of its predecessor, the Board for the Protection of the Aborigines, in 1966–67. These papers have since been lodged in the Australian Archives at Brighton, Victoria, but my citations refer to their uncatalogued state. I must also thank the librarians of the La Trobe Library and the State Library of Victoria, Melbourne; the Mitchell Library Sydney; the National Library, Canberra; and the Australian Institute of Aboriginal Studies Library for access to documents in their care. I am indebted to the Museum of Victoria for permission to publish photographs from the Charles Walter and Frederick Kruger albums in their collection, and to Mr John Green Parkinson for information on the family of John Green.

My research from 1965–72 was supported by the Department of Anthropology and Sociology, Research School of Pacific Studies of The Australian National University. Completion of the final manuscript was made possible by a one-year fellowship in the same university's Department of History, Research School of Social Sciences. The staff and students of that department and their colleagues in the *Australian Dictionary of Biography* generously shared their knowledge and much laughter.

This book owes much to the help of my friends Diane Bell, Phillip Boas, Patricia Croft, Philip Felton, Neil Gunson, Luise Hercus, Alick and Merle Jackamos, Isabel McBryde, Nell Millist, D.J. Mulvaney, Marie Reay, Shirley Andrew Rosser, Marlies Robinson, C.D. Rowley, F.B. Smith, C.T. Stannage, W.E.H. Stanner, C.M. Tatz, N.B. Tindale, James Urry, John Waiko, Sally Weaver, Alan West and Nancy Williams.

My greatest debt is to my husband Richard Barwick who has supported my work for half a life time, and to my daughter Laura Barwick who constantly assures me that making books is more important than making meals.

Diane Barwick
Canberra, 1985

Editors' Preface

Rebellion at Coranderrk was revised twice by Diane before it was accepted by the Australian National University Press after the usual referee procedures. With the closure of the Australian National University Press after Diane's death the manuscript was returned to the family. Subsequently, the typed manuscript was edited for publication at our request by Shirley Andrew Rosser. The book was then submitted to two Australian publishers who rejected it on the basis of its perceived commercial prospects.

In the intervening period the nature of publishing has changed dramatically with the development of electronic publishing. The original typescript has been converted to an electronic format and prepared for desktop publication. This has required many minor modifications to the form of the book. We have attempted to keep these to a minimum as editorial changes can gravely distort the authors' intentions. *Rebellion at Coranderrk* is essentially a continuing life work, that would have been further refined and polished had Diane lived, and any errors are as much the result of the editors' ignorance as the author's death.

In the editorial process we have been greatly helped by Philip Felton, Michael Hanslip, Isabel McBryde, Mary Morris, Peter Read, Gaye Sculthorpe, Tikka Wilson and Maribelle Young.

Publication of *Rebellion at Coranderrk* has been substantially assisted by Aboriginal Affairs Victoria and the Australian Academy of the Humanities. We and *Aboriginal History* wish to thank Mr A.V. Cahir, Director, Aboriginal Affairs Victoria, for their generous subsidy. The Museum of Victoria has helped with illustrative material. We are greatly indebted to them for this support.

Diane refused to overlook injustice and prejudice, and fought against them all her life, often to her professional cost. She had a profound compassion and empathy for the people of Coranderrk, whose descendants she regarded as kin.

The publication of this book is an attempt to rectify some of the injustices of the past two hundred years, and to prevent similar occurrences in the future. The 'rebellion' at Coranderrk is reflected in current political events. *Rebellion at Coranderrk* is a parable for today.

Laura Barwick
Richard Barwick
Canberra, 1998

Stage coach on the road to Coranderrk, near Lilydale, Victoria 1889.
Source: The *Illustrated News*, 12 January 1889, engraving by Melton Prior.

Introduction: Of History and Happenstance

> Afterwarde, there were some whose remembrance is gone, they came to nought and perished as though they had never ben, and became as though they had never ben borne, yea, and their children also with them.
>
> Nevertheless these are lovyng menne, whose righteousnesse shall never be forgotten, but continue by theyr posteritie.
>
> Their children are an holy good herytage: theyr seede endured salt in the covenant.
>
> For theyr sakes shall their chyldren and seede continue for ever, and their prayse shall never be put downe.
>
> Their bodies are buried in peace, but theyr name liveth for evermore.
>
> Ecclesiasticus 44:9–13[1]

A century ago an Aboriginal community in Victoria campaigned for recognition of their right to occupy and control the small acreage they had farmed for 25 years. But others wanted to develop this tract. Government spokesmen denied that the occupants had inherited any rights to this land and declared that, anyway, they were not really Aborigines. This book is about the 'rebellion' at Coranderrk Aboriginal Station between 1874 and 1886. It describes how Coranderrk families fought to keep their land and how they finally lost it. To explain why they fought I must begin with the years before, to show what this 'miserable spadeful of ground' meant to them, and how they came to be there.

Finally I sketch what ultimately happened to show the consequences of their defeat. As a result of their protests their home was 'permanently preserved for Aboriginal purposes'. But nothing now remains except their cemetery.

The title chosen for my account is justified by contemporary opinion. Dismayed officials repeatedly used the term rebellion to describe Aboriginal tactics in openly resisting and defying lawful authority. It was a rebellion without violence – a paper war. The Coranderrk people used strikes, petitions and deputations to protest the policy decisions of the Board for the Protection of the Aborigines, the statutory authority which administered Aboriginal affairs for the Victorian government from 1860 to 1957. Using contemporary records, and evidence from an earlier period unknown to or ignored by incumbent officials, it is possible to reconstruct the events of that decade.

Coranderrk Aborigines had genuine grievances. They complained of the mismanagement of their farm and the proposed sale of their land, and they asked for reinstatement of the one European official who understood their wish for self-determination. Because earlier reserves had been alienated they distrusted the Board's ability to resist the lobbying of Europeans who coveted the land at Coranderrk. Their complaints provoked an extraordinary series of investigations, including a Royal Commission and a Parliamentary Board of Inquiry, as well as numerous Parliamentary debates and unprecedented press coverage. Although Board spokesmen publicly blamed 'outside interference', they were well aware that 'incitement' did not

---

1   Bishop's Bible Translation, 1578.

explain the fervour and duration of the well-organized protests. In fact there was internal disagreement about the policy imposed by new Board members. Some members upheld the justice of the complaints, as did a score of eminent colonists who made independent inquiries during the troubled years.

The Board members who had resolved to sell Coranderrk were ignorant of the past and the residents' claims to the land. Their statements were biased by concern for their own reputations as authors of the disputed policy. In their eyes maintenance of European dignity and authority, and discipline of a 'childlike race', were essential goals of effective management. They interpreted Aboriginal demands for self-determination as insubordination.

They could not amend their decisions without a humiliating abandonment of their claim to expertise. They used the authority granted by special legislation and the powers of police and courts to control the protests. They denied the truth of the complaints, ridiculed the leaders as mere trouble-makers rebelling against necessary discipline and, finally, argued that the Aborigines were ignorant pawns misled by 'agitators' whose criticisms must be ignored in order to maintain 'law and order'.

Their allegations of subversion provided an acceptable explanation of Aboriginal distrust and discontent, served as rationale for greater administrative control, and distracted public attention from the actual content of their policies and the proven negligence of their administration. Other Aboriginal communities protested Board decisions just as ardently. However they had no local champions and their protests did not win press attention.

The fate of Coranderrk became a public issue largely because its residents were able to make a direct appeal to sympathetic politicians in Melbourne. The support of Graham Berry, who was the responsible Minister or opposition leader for much of this decade, and the interest of two Melbourne newspapers (organs of the radical and conservative factions in colonial politics) made their grievances a test case for issues of contemporary political importance. Yet in the end the Board retained power as no government wanted direct responsibility for the contentious administration of voteless Aborigines.

Much of the contemporary documentation of the Coranderrk rebellion was self-serving propaganda, aimed at refuting challenges by press, public and Parliament. It was intended to protect the reputations of Board members and the jobs of their staff. Then and later it was accepted as a reliable account of what had occurred. The Coranderrk people perceived and remembered events differently. Their tales of how they were driven from Coranderrk and how this land was lost influenced the way in which subsequent generations responded to the planning by later officials who knew nothing of the past.

The 'rebellion' at Coranderrk is not mentioned in any history of Victoria. I first heard of it in 1960 from a daughter of participants who recalled how her family had 'battled for years' to keep Coranderrk but had been forced to leave their home. She said the old people had told her that 'John Green who was manager, he helped the people'. It had happened well before her birth in 1894 and we were both more interested in talking about current protests.

Yet because I had heard only criticism of the many nameless officials who had ruled the lives of Aboriginal communities I asked why this manager was remembered kindly. She explained that 'John Green was a good man, the old ones said – a father and a brother to his people at Coranderrk. They were loyal to him when there was trouble with the Board, back in my father's time'. My acquaintance with her community had just begun and I was too ignorant of their past to ask the questions which might have tapped her knowledge. To my lasting regret I was unable to ask her for more detailed recollections. She and most others of her generation had died before I saw the documents written by and about their parents – the contemporary records of how they had fought for Coranderrk.

INTRODUCTION

My research task in 1960 was an anthropological study of contemporary life – not the recording of oral history. Yet within weeks Mrs Ellen Campbell Atkinson and other members of Victorian Aboriginal communities had taught me that past decisions had present consequences. Their memories had not been obliterated with each change of policy or administrative personnel. I could not understand modern conditions without examining the aims and effects of past policies.

During the 1960s many Victorian Aborigines were concerned about the loss of reserves which had been the homes of their ancestors, and were bitterly frustrated because they were not consulted about government programs intended for their benefit. They were campaigning to regain the use of land at Cumeroogunga, the New South Wales Aboriginal reserve on the Murray River where many families had found refuge after their exile from Coranderrk. They were also protesting the forced dispersal of families from Lake Tyers, the last of six Victorian Aboriginal stations. Earlier generations had successfully farmed these reserves until, as Mrs Atkinson said, 'the government sent the half castes off and gave our land to white men to use'. The Aboriginal people who were called 'half castes' (because they had some European ancestry) were denied the right to define their own identity when an 'absorption' policy was implemented in the 1880s. Until 1957 they were excluded from the definition of Aborigines in Victorian legislation. Officials were empowered to decide which persons were 'legally white' and thus ineligible to live on Aboriginal reserves or receive assistance.

This policy ignored Aboriginal loyalties, the extent of European prejudice and the restricted employment opportunities available in rural areas. Consequently most of the children, grandchildren and great-grandchildren of the exiles had spent much of their lives camping on the rubbish tips of country towns. Inevitably they recalled the past when an 'assimilation policy' was introduced by a new Aborigines Welfare Board in 1957. The newly appointed Board members and their staff were genuinely puzzled at the mistrust and resentment evoked by their well-intentioned decisions. Government spokesmen ridiculed Aborigines' pleas to occupy and farm the old reserves. They declared that the maintenance of separate communities was contrary to the aim of assimilation and insisted that the protests were merely the result of interference by 'agitators'.

Observation of these modern disputes stimulated my interest in the political processes involved in policy formulation and the role of pressure groups including the Aboriginal people themselves and their sympathisers. But annual reports, the only public documents, gave little information on policy formulation. As files were closed an observer could not accurately assess the flow of information within the bureaucratic structure or evaluate the decision-making roles of public servants, Board members, the responsible Minister, Cabinet and Parliament.

Analysis of policy and administration and studies of the history of indigenous communities were respectable topics for anthropological inquiry in Canada largely because of the work of H.B. Hawthorn, my first teacher. In Australia however, the theoretical concerns of social anthropology were rather different and such studies were also discouraged by governmental attitudes to research. Certainly the pioneers of Australian anthropology and their students had recorded the effects of administration on Aboriginal communities. Most of them had publicly criticised past policy and had worked with or on behalf of Aboriginal friends to bring about reforms.[2] Few studied Administration per se. There was a substantial body of research on social change but, for a variety of good reasons, little commentary on the reaction of specific communities to the management styles of the missionaries and administrators who served as agents of imposed change. The published literature tended to present generalised descriptions of 'traditional'

---

2   See bibliography in Weaver 1981 for a listing of Canadian Studies: see Barwick, Urry and Bennett 1977, and Stanner and Barwick 1979 for bibliographic information on Australian anthropology.

practice set in the undated 'ethnographic present'. This was both a device for protecting the anonymity of sources and a convenience for the construction of theory. Reliance on this convention discouraged the development of biography, ethno-history and political anthropology.

My interest in Victorian policy and administration was partly antiquarian: I was impressed with the historical and genealogical knowledge revealed in the reminiscences of older Aborigines and simply wanted to know more about events they had mentioned. As I was preoccupied with present-day anthropological concerns and lacked training in historical research techniques most of my discoveries about the past were the result of serendipity rather than science.

I searched newspapers, located the published government reports and avidly read the histories of Victoria. Information proved scanty. The available literature described the Aboriginal past in a curiously generalised and depersonalised fashion. Colonists' reminiscences gave negligible information about the Indigenous people whose land and labour were the source of their wealth. Local histories typically offered a few paragraphs of garbled description of tribe and territory plus, perhaps, a note on the last 'fullblood' survivor, as prologue to the achievements of Europeans. Aborigines did figure in descriptions of the expansion of the pastoral industry written by economic and social historians but disappeared once they were 'no longer a serious problem to the squatters'.[3]

The few published histories of Aboriginal administration were generalised accounts of the earliest period of frontier administration, largely because the relevant records were available in public archives. The documentation for later periods was either lost or inaccessible in confidential government files unread even by the present custodians. The enduring dilemma of Aboriginal administration remained the concern of Aborigines, anthropologists and administrators until late in the 1960s, when the influence and example of W.E.H. Stanner and C.D. Rowley stimulated new research by historians, anthropologists and political scientists.[4] Both these scholars encouraged my unfashionable concern with the past and made me aware of the complexity of Aboriginal administration.

In 1966–67 I was able to examine the rediscovered archives of the Board. The records were sadly incomplete;[5] but the detailed documentation of affairs at Coranderrk revived my interest in writing a full account of those long ago protests. There were urgent practical reasons for careful analysis of official records of the past. False stereotypes were serving as rationale for present policies. As Rowley has pointed out, the lack of detailed historical studies had helped to 'bowdlerise the role of settlers and governments' and encouraged administrators to assume that current planning operates in a historical vacuum.[6] Moreover, a kind of pseudohistory which characterised past policy as segregation and deplored the maintenance of separate communities on reserves had become accepted by many concerned Australians. This stereotype was being used to justify the forcible dispersal of such communities to achieve the current policy of assimilation. False generalisations about the past deprived current generations of pride in their places of origin and the achievements of their forebears.

This kind of pseudohistory also challenged their hopes for self-determination. In Victoria several communities felt a strong attachment to the remaining reserves and wished to continue farming. Their pleas were rejected because a government adviser had reported that all previous farming experiments had 'entirely failed' and had declared that Aborigines 'are not agriculturists by inclination'. Descendants believed that earlier generations had farmed the reserves successfully until the land was resumed for use by Europeans.

---

3   Serle 1963:2.
4   See Stanner 1969; Rowley 1970, 1971a, b.
5   Deverall 1878.
6   Rowley 1970:7–9.

My analysis of the Board records substantiated those beliefs that farming had ended because of policy decisions; it also revealed that the stereotype of failure had originated in Board propaganda aimed at justifying the sale of Coranderrk and other reserves.[7] It seemed to me that a study of Coranderrk had considerable relevance for modern 'land rights' protests throughout Australia. Denial of the authenticity of Aboriginal protest was still a characteristic reaction of administrators when answering criticism of their policies. A curious paternalism, perhaps a vestige of the old belief that Aborigines were a 'childlike race' requiring authoritarian control and protection, still encouraged government spokesmen to suggest that Aborigines were prone to exploitation by 'stirrers'. Officials still cast doubt on their capacity to organize themselves, under sustained leadership, for economic enterprises or political action.

A detailed study of the rebellion at Coranderrk was also of potential interest for anthropological theory. The data might make possible some conclusions about political process in administrative decision-making. There were no studies of the operation of 'protection boards' which had controlled Aboriginal policy in south-eastern Australia for up to a century. The records provided sufficient evidence of the opinions of the Coranderrk people for a case study of how station residents had reacted to the personalities and powers of Board employees who actually administered – and often reinterpreted – official policy. Despite the popular belief that residents of controlled settlements were cowed victims of authoritarian oppression, the records and oral history suggested that they had on occasion managed their managers with considerable finesse.

In 1972 I completed a study of the 'rebellion'. It was an anthropological analysis of decisions made in the past – not a history of Coranderrk. It was accepted for publication yet I remained dissatisfied with my understanding of those events long ago and my depiction of the participants. My generalised account suggested that the Board was monolithic and its decisions were apolitical and often inexplicable. My own observations of decision-making by committees and the economic and political considerations which were shaping modern policy made me realise that I had distorted some past reality. The decisions of the Board and Coranderrk people had to be explained in their contemporary political and economic context. The outcome of the dispute over Coranderrk was, only in the most general sense, the result of attitudes about 'race relations'. The participants had acted in particular ways because of differing beliefs about land use, justice and power.

There are many generalised accounts of the history of race relations and policy development in Victoria.[8] My aim is rather to provide an anthropological analysis of the dispute over Coranderrk. Events are described in fine detail to show the 'curious concatenation of circumstances, intrigues, personal aims and faction cross currents'[9] which contemporaries perceived as part of the decision-making process. It is necessary to describe as fully as possible the perceptions of the individuals who took part in order to show how their conflicting beliefs shaped the outcome of the protests. This book attempts to explain the discrepancy between the perceptions of those at Coranderrk and the administrators. The residents of Coranderrk were not Europeans, nor yet 'Aborigines'. They were members of specific clans, influenced by inherited rights and obligations, by the beliefs and conventions of their own society, and by their individual experience of the consequences of European intrusion. I make no apology for including innumerable names and much biographical detail in my narrative. There is no other memorial to the Kulin[10] clans who tried to build their own 'blackfellows' township' at Coranderrk and little record of their dealings with the Europeans who helped and hindered them. By piecing together scraps of evidence about the background, personality

---

7   McLean 1957: Barwick 1971 (see portion reprinted as Appendix 1).
8   Barwick 1963, 1972; Blaskett 1979; Christie 1979; Foxcroft 1941; Long 1970; Massola 1970, 1975; Rowley 1970, 1971a.
9   Deakin 1957:77.
10 A description and discussion of the Kulin nation is provided in Chapter 1.

and behaviour of individuals I can draw some conclusions about how and why the Coranderrk leaders and European officials misunderstood each other. But my conclusions depend on deduction from partial evidence, on art as well as science.

No living person can fully understand the sentiments of people who lived a century ago. The most I can do is outline the political and economic circumstances to which the people of Coranderrk responded as men and women of their own time, and draw attention to certain features of indigenous culture (as explained by their leaders to amateur ethnographers)[11] which apparently influenced what they said and did. Reconstruction of their beliefs is not a simple matter as their culture had been transformed, by choice as well as necessity, within the lifetime of these elders. Survivors of the Kulin clans had abandoned the old patterns of residence and land use long before they assembled at this farming village, yet indigenous concepts of political authority and responsibility for land still functioned in this new setting. Europeans saw only the superficial transformation of Kulin life and were oblivious of the continuity: this error was the real cause of the crisis at Coranderrk.

The evidence for Kulin behaviour and motivation is of course defective: I must rely on the incomplete archives of the Board, other government records and contemporary newspaper accounts. These include few first-hand statements as only a minority of the Kulin adults could write. Their surviving documents are mostly public records of public decisions, signed by the men who had authority to speak for the owning clan. The letters and petitions reveal little about dissenting opinion or the achievement of consensus. Most of the recorded observations were written by Europeans who were ignorant of the past of the Coranderrk people and had decided views about their future. Their preconceptions influenced their observations. Moreover, much of the documentation was compiled by alien officialdom for specific contemporary purposes and cannot be assessed simply as the idiosyncratic testimony of individuals. Formal conventions shape the language and content of public records such as minutes, reports and official correspondence. Documents produced in an official capacity are 'a cross between testimony and social bookkeeping'.[12] Their evaluation requires some understanding of the bureaucratic structure which produced them, and some assessment of the public role and private interests of the writers.

Any study of administration must take account of the ambitions and jealousies of individuals, the flow of information behind the scenes, the persuasive or protective intent of internal memoranda and public statements. If, as the anthropologist Weaver suggests in her study of modern policy making, all documents are forms of strategy, part of the political process in administration, then the use of documents in the contemporary context must be clarified.[13] This goes far beyond Berkhofer's statement that 'the historian needs to know the political processes that produced the data' in order to interpret or evaluate the reliability of sources.[14] The role and perspective of the author, the timing, occasion and expected audience, the intent and consequences of disseminating particular information are as much part of the evidence as the actual contents of the document. These things were known to contemporaries and were implicitly part of the decision-making process. Therefore I have tried wherever possible to weave such information into my narrative, to suggest what information was available to which participants and to indicate how reportage shaped contemporary opinion.

---

11 A.W. Howitt (MS; 1904) recorded William Barak's information on Kulin clans and tribes between 1881 and 1902; Smyth's (1878) compendium includes data collected by John Green from 1861 to 1874, and by William Thomas from 1839 to 1867.
12 Dibble 1964:218.
13 I am greatly indebted to Sally Weaver (personal communication, 1980) for sharpening my awareness of the crucial problems of intent and political process when analysing official documents. Her stimulating study of the 'hidden agenda' in the making of modern Canadian Indian policy explains the necessity of exploring the use of documentation as political strategy. She notes that: 'Interviews provided necessary data on the unofficial arguments and events, as well as clarification of the contents of documents and their use. The interviews also allowed me to decide whether the documents' contents were, in fact, the substance of the arguments or whether they were, in addition, "strategy statements" designed to elicit responses other than the contents might suggest.' (Weaver 1981:x–xi).
14 Berkhofer 1971:367.

INTRODUCTION

Although I am primarily concerned to explain why the Coranderrk people acted as they did in a particular decade of the nineteenth century, my study is necessarily also a kind of political and administrative history. The development of this district of Victoria and the colonial government's responsibility for Aboriginal affairs are part of the story. To explain the course and outcome of the protests I must examine contemporary economic conditions and the political preoccupations, racial attitudes and religious beliefs of European colonists. Political disputes over landownership and use, friction between radical and conservative interests, and denominational conflict all had some bearing on events. For my sketch of the political issues of the time I have drawn heavily upon Serle's[15] histories of the colony, and relevant biographies in the *Australian Dictionary of Biography*. Other reference works, biographies, histories, newspapers, church and Parliamentary records and the membership lists of various societies and charities were of use in identifying European participants and explaining their opinions, antagonisms and alliances.

The fate of Coranderrk was determined by the conflicting interests of two racial groups. Yet individuals made the decisions. Their fears and vanities, sectarian affiliations, economic interests, notions of morality and justice, and their personal and political loyalties influenced events. Victorian Aboriginal policy was not the unanimous, anonymous creation of faceless employees of a monolithic government department. Policy resulted from largely *ad hoc* decisions of a handful of laymen appointed to a semi-executive Board. Members presented their views with varying effectiveness and from a variety of motives. Their planning was constrained by what was financially and politically possible. Voting on specific issues was influenced by their interests, enmities – even their absences from meetings. Their secretary, a senior clerk virtually independent of the public service hierarchy, shaped decision-making by his own control of information. He and his subordinates at Coranderrk – manager, teacher, dormitory matron, overseer, hopmaster – could reinterpret policy as they implemented it. Political responsibility for Aboriginal affairs was allotted to a busy senior Minister who could ignore or overrule Board opinion in order to satisfy government priorities, placate other departments and their Ministers, silence opposition criticism or win needed votes for the local member. Cabinet and Parliament had the ultimate authority to withhold or delay the funding and legislation needed for policy implementation.

At every level policy decisions could be influenced by interested critics. Politicians, public servants, philanthropists, reformers, clergymen, journalists, competing land-users and former members and employees of the Board pressed their own views. Some offered unsolicited advice, some had been recruited by the Coranderrk Aborigines. The sympathisers were sometimes motivated by a particular ideology, more often by sympathy with the frustration of Aborigines they had come to know as friends. In this political manoeuvring the 20 or so families who made Coranderrk their home were not ignorant pawns. They enlisted, even manipulated, Europeans for their own purposes. Their leaders relied on an ancient political authority derived from responsibility for land; they proved that a new kind of community was capable of concerted and purposeful action to defend that land.

---

15 Serle 1963, 1971.

Chapter 1
KULIN AND NGAMAJET

> ... there were head men called ngurungaeta. If a man was sensible and spoke straight and did no wrong to anyone the people would call him ngurungaeta and listen to him and obey him. Billibillary the father of my cousin was a ngurungaeta, so was also Capt. Turnbull at Mt Macedon and Billy Lonsdale and Mr De Villiers in Western Port ... Captain Turnbull made my father and Billibillary ngurungaeta. Billibillary made Bungarim ngurungaeta and I am ngurungaeta from my father ... Beside each of the ngurungaeta there was the man to whom he gave 'his words'. Beside Captain Turnbull was my father's brother Jack Wortherly. Beside my father his uncle Winberi. Beside Billibillary was Bungarim.
>
> William Barak [1882][1]

Between 1853 and 1874 the *ngurungaeta* of the clans which owned the Yarra River region encouraged survivors of other Kulin clans – owners of all the land stretching from the Barwon and Loddon rivers in the west to the Broken and Tarwin rivers in the east – to make a new home for themselves at Coranderrk. In 1875 officials decided to sell this reserve and move 'the blacks' to a distant site somewhere on the colony's Murray River boundary. It was for their good. It was administratively convenient. Above all it was demanded by politicians who said this land could be used more profitably.

The Kulin (their word for 'men') demanded recognition of their right to this land. Their resistance outraged the Europeans who had occupied Kulin land for 40 years but remained ignorant of the laws governing Kulin land tenure and inheritance. Administrators would not acknowledge that the last of the Wurundjeri-balluk *ngurungaeta*, William Barak (Beruk, c. 1824–1903), and the younger men from related clans to whom he gave 'his words' had the right to determine how this land was used and who should live there. These leaders had an obligation to protect the owners of this land plus all children born on it and those authorized visitors who could claim access to its resources.

Barak explained, and the official records confirm, that Kulin clans were governed by senior men, one or several of whom represented the component patrilineages in the formal office of clan-head designated by the title *ngurungaeta*. A clan-head was also considered the group's rightful representative in external affairs. All *ngurungaeta* were men of distinguished achievement; certain of them were so eminent that their influence was acknowledged by all clans comprising a *-(w)urrung* and sometimes by all clans of a region. Protectorate officials who saw daily evidence of their leadership in the early 1840s had no doubt that Billibellary was the 'paramount chief' of the Melbourne region while Munangabum held sway as 'chieftain over most of the Jajowrong people'. Officials used the words respect and obedience to characterize the loyalty shown to all clan-heads; reverence was the term used to describe the reception accorded to two

---

1   Howitt MS:5, 33, 34. I have adopted Stanner's term 'clan-head' to describe the representative role or office designated by the title *ngurungaeta* which A.W. Howitt translated as Headman. (As the author worked in close collaboration with W.E.H. Stanner this usage was probably in personal communication; see also Williams 1985:247, 1986:99. S. A-R.)

aged and famous *ngurungaeta* who visited Jajowrong and Woiworung assemblies: one was leader of the Peeruk-el-moom-bulluk clan of Wathaurung and the other was clan-head of the Mogullumbuk from beyond the Kulin pale.

Information on Kulin clan-heads is scanty because most of them died a few years after Europeans began to occupy their lands. The censuses and genealogical information recorded by Protectorate officials, unseen by A.W. Howitt, in fact confirm what Barak told him: in the 1830s and 1840s the *ngurungaeta* of the southern Kulin clans were closely linked by kinship ties resulting from inter-marriage (in part because prominent men acquired more wives and thus more children to be deployed in politically advantageous marriages). These records also confirm Barak's statements suggesting that a *ngurungaeta* was 'made' by other men — the men of his own patriline and clan and the leaders of other clans with whom they maintained certain relationships. Although genealogical seniority was important in clan government and a *ngurungaeta* could confidently name a particular son or brother as heir, hereditary succession was not automatic. Aspirants had to prove their competence and — as Barak indicated — win endorsement from the established clan-heads of the region. It was their support which enabled younger men to acquire religious knowledge, wives and *entrée* to the political forums where opinions, oratorical skills and influence were tested.

Although Europeans could not perceive political authority among Aborigines, the Kulin had a shrewd comprehension of the nuances of power in the society which had overwhelmed their own. When officials would not heed their protests Barak and his aides enlisted the help of other Europeans perceived to be sympathetic and influential. The Kulin had not conceded their sovereignty when the European intruders they called *Ngamajet* occupied their land.

The unwelcome visitors knew they were called *Ngamajet* but did not know why. Unlike their hosts they were poor linguists, dull of ear and slow to learn the speech and customs of strangers. 'Ammijaic', 'Amydeet', 'horn-mer-geek' was what they wrote, using a skill new to the Kulin.[2] Barak was an old man when he told one of them the meaning: 'White men were called by us "*Ngamajet*" — this word is also used to mean the bright red colours at sunset'. Because Howitt did not fully understand, Barak patiently explained that *ngamat* was the place where the sun goes down and the sky, the sunset, was where a dead man's *murup* or spirit went: 'when he comes back he is *Ngamajet*. This is the Westernport belief'.[3] In Barak's boyhood the red-faced intruders — dead men returned — had claimed all the land of the Kulin and their neighbours.

Howitt himself was old when his summary of Barak's account of the Kulin was published in 1904. He misunderstood and muddled some of Barak's statements and omitted much information contained in the original notes collected in 1881–1901. Howitt's idiosyncratic and inconsistent use of the terms 'nation', 'tribe', 'clan' and 'horde', and his inaccurate rendering of Barak's statements about 'class' (moiety) affiliation have discouraged modern researchers attempting to link Howitt's published findings with other nineteenth-century records. Yet his original notes prove that he grasped Kulin concepts which no *Ngamajet* had previously understood. His records of how Barak used the word *kulin* and other words ending in *-(w)urrung*, *-balluk* or *-(w)illam* make plain what contemporary officials never understood: how Barak and other Kulin perceived rights to land and why they fought for Coranderrk.

---

2   Haydon 1846:169; Howitt 1904:442–6, Morgan 1967:64; de Labilliere 1878:II 72; Smyth 1878:II 123.
3   Howitt MS:24, 63. Belief that Europeans were the returned spirits of their own dead was widespread among Australian Aborigines. English-speaking Kulin used the term 'jump-up-white-fella' to signify death during the early decades of European occupation (Giglioli 1875:791; [Kerr] 1872:25; Legislative Council 1858–59:60).

1. KULIN AND NGAMAJET

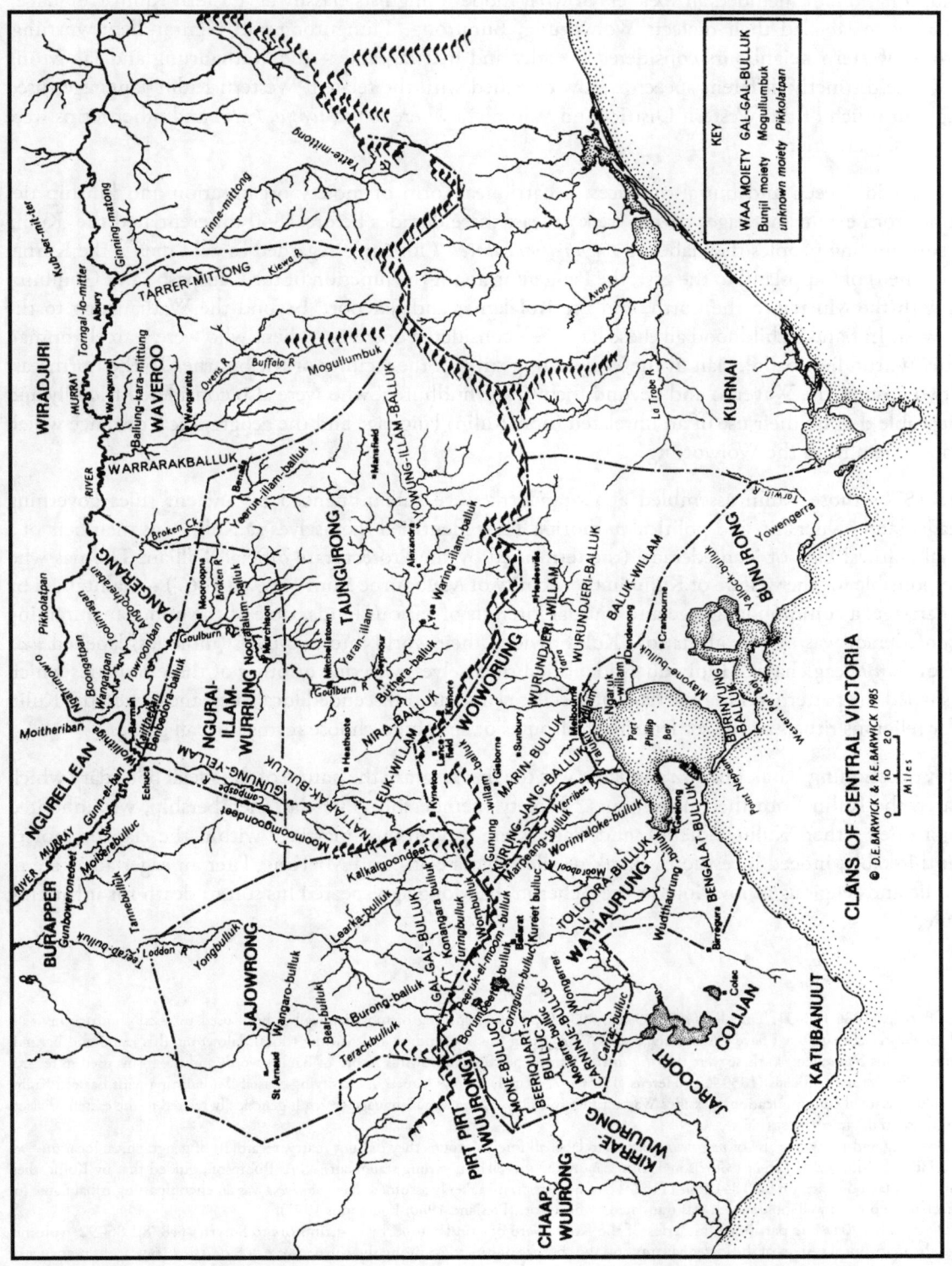

Map 1: The Aboriginal clans of Central Victoria.
Source: From Barwick, 1984.

The vast area – roughly equal to Tasmania – owned by the intermarrying clans whom Barak identified as Kulin is indicated on the map of central Victoria (Map 1). Howitt called this regional cultural bloc 'the Kulin nation'. It included all speakers of what modern linguists classify as 'Eastern Kulin Language': the clans who labelled their dialects Woiworung, Bunurong, Taungurong and Ngurai-illam-wurrung, plus those western neighbours considered friendly and marriageable – the Wathaurung and Jajowrong clans whose distinctly different speech is now classified with the related 'Western Kulin' languages used throughout much of the Western District and Wimmera where *mara, wotjo, kulin* and other terms were used to designate 'men'.[4]

Similarities in speech and burial practices, a patrilineal form of moiety organisation and kinship ties resulting from extant marriages dating back at least three decades before 1840 differentiated the 'Kulin' from surrounding peoples they labelled *meymet/mainmeet*[5] ('foreign', 'regarded as wild men'); the Kurnai (*ganai* – men) of Gippsland to the east, the Pangerang about the junction of the Campaspe and Goulburn rivers with the Murray to the north, and the Kolakgnat and 'Jarcoort' beyond the Wathaurung to the south-west. In Barak's childhood all these had been considered enemies – aliens who were scarcely human – by his Wurundjeri-balluk clan of the Woiworung tribe in the vicinity of Melbourne. To the north-east were two groups, the Waveroo and beyond them the Dhudhuroa, who were also considered friendly and marriageable despite their use of an unrelated (non-Kulin) language and the geographical distance which separated them from the Woiworung.

In the 1870s those Kulin assembled at Coranderrk were still influenced by ancient rules governing marriage, land ownership and political authority. They identified themselves as Kulin – as members of a regional cultural bloc or 'confederacy' (the term used by the Protectorate official William Thomas who was responsible for the welfare of Kulin in the vicinity of Melbourne from 1839 to 1867) – maintained by intermarriage, a common language and mutual interests of various kinds. One of the bonds maintaining this confederacy was moiety affiliation: Kulin divided their world into two parts (moieties) labelled *waa* 'crow' or *bunjil* 'eaglehawk'. Individuals identified themselves with one or other of these moieties which both shaped the patterned intermarriage of specific clans and transcended local allegiance when the Kulin met for religious rituals or the settlement of disputes or simply to choose teams for ball games.

Howitt, questioning Barak in 1882 and later, was the first to grasp the nature of the social boundary which separated the Kulin from their neighbours.[6] Moiety membership, like clan membership, was inherited through one's father. Kulin moieties, and clans, were exogamous: marriage within the clan or moiety was unthinkable, indeed incestuous. Barak recalled that a clan-head Mr King, later an eager advocate of economic and religious innovations at the Acheron, had long ago speared his son to death for infringing this rule.[7]

---

4 See Barwick 1984:100–31. Tindale's (1974:131–3, 203–9) preferred spelling of most names has been used to assist comparisons with his well-known tribal map, but I have retained the names Woiworung (his Wurundjeri and Kurung tribes), Jajowrong (his Jaara) and Ngurai-illam-wurrung (his Ngurelban) as these were the *–(w)urrung* names specified in Howitt's record of Barak's words and the forms used in records compiled by Protectorate officials (1839–49). Hercus (1969:5–7, Map 1) follows Capell in classifying coastal Wathaurung with Eastern Kulin; Dixon (1980, personal communication) classifies Wathaurung (his H2) as a separate language which is genetically related to the eastern dialects (H1) and those to the north-west (H3).
5 Woiworung and Jajowrong use of *meymet/mainmeet* to label all foreign groups they did not marry, regardless of geographical location, was noted by Howitt (MS:1) and Parker (Morrison 1967a: 52 quotes an 1841 Jajowrong statement). G.A. Robinson, guided first by Kulin, then Kolakgnat then Jarcoort men on his 1841 tour of the Western District, mistakenly assumed that *mainmeet* was an encompassing tribal name for the alien clans whose unintelligible speech was translated by his escort (Presland 1980; Lourandos 1977).
6 Howitt MS, 1904. The patrilineal moieties of the Kulin were not understood by contributors to Smyth's (1878:I 86–92) volume, although the matrilineal system of the lower Murray and the absence of moieties among the Kurnai were noted. After 16 years as manager of Coranderrk Joseph Shaw was flabbergasted when told the principles of Kulin social organisation; he had assumed all Aborigines were the same as those he had known on the lower Murray 40 years before (Shaw to John Mathew, 25 June 1898, Box 3, Mathew Papers, Australian Institute of Aboriginal Studies Library).
7 Howitt MS, 1904:255–6.

William Thomas had been aware that the Kulin clans formed an intermarrying confederacy and perceived the political importance of the resulting 'social compact'. However he never grasped the moiety principle which directed the choice of spouses. Neither did John Green, the first manager of Coranderrk, although he understood that past marriages had created kinship ties between members of distant clans and that the Kulin forbad marriage between persons who could trace links of common ancestry:

> There were relationships created outside through intermarrying, and they could not marry when we would say there was only one hundredth part of blood in the veins. They knew of it and would not marry. It was one great conflict that we had at the Station to get the old people to consent to the marriage of some of the young people. They would count blood where we could not count it.[8]

Mothers were consulted about their children's marriages but betrothal arrangements were made by fathers with their older brothers and uncles (the senior men of their clan). Spouses were acquired by a formalized 'sister-exchange' with a clan of the opposite moiety. Such marriages occurred between member clans within a 'tribal' area, but it was preferable to choose a spouse from a distant location so that the localities and economic opportunities of present and future generations extended beyond family and neighbourhood.

Barak had to use European names for clan localities when he explained this to Howitt[9] but Kulin clans were still identified by the country they owned, even if Europeans had dispossessed them half a century before. Barak used the example of his own clan of eastern Woiworung, of the *waa* moiety. They gave wives to, and took them from, the Woiworung and Bunurong clans about Dandenong, Mordialloc and Mount Macedon (all *bunjil*), but not those about Cranbourne and the Werribee River which were *waa* like themselves. They married with the Geelong clan of Wathaurung which was *bunjil*, but not some other Wathaurung clans inland of their own moiety. They also arranged marriages with the Taungurong clans about the junction of the Yea and Goulburn rivers, about Seymour and that which owned the area between Benalla and Mansfield, but not with the Taungurong clans about Kilmore and Alexandra for they too were *waa*. Barak's own mother Tooterrie had come from the Ngurai-illam-wurrung clan about Murchison and women from his clan had gone there, for they were *bunjil*. Barak's clan had also arranged marriages with certain Jajowrong clans of the opposite moiety, notably that of old Malcolm around Mount Blackwood, but not the Gal-gal-bulluk who were *waa*.

Since every Kulin clan arranged marriages with reciprocating clans in other localities the Kulin were held together by a network of kinship ties. The Kulin clans formed an enclave, surrounded by groups with different patterns of social organisation. This fact explains much that puzzled European observers in the 1840s, and is essential to an understanding of the internal politics of the Coranderrk community decades later. Yet Kulin boundaries were permeable. They were maintained, and breached, for political reasons.

Individuals might also choose to emphasise a narrower 'tribal' or district loyalty. Within the Kulin bloc clusters of adjacent clans which shared a common dialect or manner of speaking and some degree of mutual political and economic interest because of their geographical continuity distinguished themselves by a 'language' name with the suffix *-(w)urrung* (meaning mouth or speech). The strength of such 'tribal' allegiances, however, depended on a number of things including the disposition of neighbouring clans. The cell-like structure and political autonomy suggested by the term tribe is an inappropriate description of the *-(w)urrung* groupings named by Barak.

---

8   Legislative Council 1858–59:68; Royal Commission 1877:85–6; Howitt 1904:252–7. Many Victorian Aborigines still consider marriage between first or second cousins improper, saying this is 'the old law'.
9   Howitt MS. Studies of the distribution of various forms of social organisation note, but do not attempt to explain, the existence of named patrilineal moieties in this 'small isolate region of southcentral Victoria' (Elkin 1964: 95–8; Berdnt and Berndt 1977: 44–5, 52–8).

After resettlement at Coranderrk the pioneer residents continued to use the *-(w)urrung* names – Bunurong, Woiworung, Wathaurung, Taungurong, Ngurai-illam-wurrung and Jajowrong – which indicated their district of origin and something of their history. However the deliberate maintenance of speech differences to demarcate district loyalties or comply with mythological sanctions had less importance. Eastern Kulin dialects were mutually intelligible, most Kulin were multi-lingual, and etiquette demanded that residents of a territory should use the language of its owners. Yet neither dispossession nor migration had altered the importance of clan and moiety membership.

The discreteness of the *-(w)urrung* groupings had always been limited by any traceable genealogical tie, or same clan or moiety membership – either *waa* or *bunjil*. (In modern anthropological terminology each territorial patrician was also a localised moiety segment whose members were recruited by a rule of patrifiliation.) Clan members had to find spouses either within or outside their own *-(w)urrung* grouping but preferably at some distant locality. District loyalties were thereby extended and trade with more remote areas was made possible by the resulting web of kinship ties uniting all Kulin clans in a far-flung confederacy.

The basic unit of Kulin society was a named localised patrilineal descent group (clan) whose members had a historical, genealogical and religious identity. Clan territories were defined by ritual and economic responsibilities. Clan names were distinguished by the suffixes *-balluk* or *-bulluk* meaning people and *-(w)illam* meaning dwelling place (*-bulluk* or *-goondeet* and *-lar* were the Jajowrong equivalents). The clan names recorded by Protectorate officials and mentioned by Barak half a century later are listed in Barwick 1984 and shown in their approximate location on the map. The base map was that published in 1878 by Smyth – draftsman and surveyor before he became Secretary for Mines – because it shows the rivers before most of them were dammed or diverted in irrigation schemes. Gazetteers of pastoral stations were used to check localities in the 1840s.[10]

Nineteenth-century European observers ignored or were bewildered by the various levels of Kulin social identity because they did not grasp the underlying principles. A few perceived dialect and language differences and labelled the populations thus distinguished as 'tribes' and 'nations' but most used the label tribe to designate the small named groups occupying particular localities. The names they recorded were those of land-owning clans, yet clans as such were apparently invisible to Europeans because all members did not live together permanently as an observable residential unit on their jointly owned estate. Clan lands were exploited by a 'band'[11] composed of a core of male clan members, their wives, sons and unmarried daughters and other relatives whose rights of access were acquired by descent or marriage. These relatives were most commonly the husbands, children (and grandchildren) of daughters who had married into distant clans yet retained and transmitted various rights to use and care for the land and resources of their natal clan. Near kinsmen of women married to men of the owning clan were able to visit this territory and use its resources, and members of associated clans of the same moiety also had certain rights of access.

---

10   Map 1 and Barwick 1984 rely on the original notes of interviews with Barak rather than the inaccurate published summary (Howitt MS, 1904:41–4, 88–9, 126–7). Barak's information clarifies and is confirmed by the unpublished records of Protectorate officials. These manuscripts were not available to Tindale whose account of the 'problem area' between Melbourne, Echuca and Albury (1974:131–3, 203–9) is thus influenced by the erroneous conclusions published by Howitt and R.H. Matthews. Linguistic clues to the distinction between *-(w)urrung* and *-balluk* (tribe and clan) were in fact published by E.S. Parker in 1854 (see Smyth 1878:I 40–1; Morrison 1967b); William Thomas recognised that marriage maintained a 'confederacy' among five clans near Melbourne but as he scarcely travelled beyond this region he remained unaware of its full extent and was apparently oblivious of the principle of moiety exogamy (Legislative Council, Victoria, 1858–59:68).

11   See Stanner (1965; 1969:157–61) for an account of the distinction between clan and band. I am indebted to Nancy Williams and to the late W.E.H. Stanner for advice on analysis of the ethnographic evidence for this region.

During the course of a year the families and individuals entitled to make use of a specific clan estate were sometimes together, sometimes dispersed, sometimes journeying to other areas to fulfil the religious and family obligations of responsible adults in Kulin society. Over a lifetime a person might successively join bands in different localities, utilising various rights to make lawful use of land owned by others. But clan membership was fixed at birth. Each person inherited clan (and moiety) membership from his or her father and retained that membership until death. The patrilineal clans so recruited were stable units owning particular territories: their members' sense of identity derived from their own recognition, and public acceptance, of their inherited responsibility for that land. Available records suggest that social identity beyond the clan level was situational, but this scanty evidence is so flawed by observers' errors and misconceptions that we have only hints of how the Kulin, alive in the 1840s, perceived social boundaries and used language and other devices to maintain or cross such boundaries.

The land tenure system of the Kulin permitted individuals to make claims on various relatives in order to use land outside their own clan estate. Individuals born on the land of another clan had lifelong access rights but did not acquire clan membership. Visitors who had no entitlement could also seek formal permission from clan-heads for temporary access to their land. The safety of all approved visitors was guaranteed. The system worked because 'one basic principle was rarely violated – the host must not suffer because of his guests: his land must not be depleted by the visitors; he must not be worse off than those enjoying the fruits of his land'.[12] Reciprocity was the guiding principle of land and resource management.

Europeans, who did not grasp this concept and merely noticed the fluctuating size and variable membership of observed groups without understanding the principles of recruitment, were prone to assume that Aborigines were nomads incapable of the responsibilities of owners and proprietors. By the time officials of the Port Phillip Protectorate made their first censuses and amateurish ethnographic inquiries in 1839, band composition had been affected by the movements of individual refugees driven from their own territories by predatory squatters. Although the Kulin population had already been grievously reduced by introduced disease and European violence, the protectors constantly heard complaints of hunger resulting from the destruction of game and vegetable foods. The direction and extent of a band's travels for subsistence purposes were now shared by the demands of Europeans and their stock.

John Batman's 1835 'treaties' with the leaders of clans near Melbourne show that he – or perhaps his escort of Aborigines from the Sydney region – did understand that named land-owning groups were the basic political units of Kulin society. The colonists who followed Batman were quickly made aware that Kulin *ngurungaeta* had authority over their own clans and often had influence over distant groups. For a few years after 1835 Europeans had to negotiate with these leaders and were able to rely on their goodwill. But when the squatters outnumbered the Kulin they sneered at the tattered dignity of landless chiefs. The next generation, eager to forget that the European occupation of Victoria was accomplished by carnage rather than courage, also forgot the generosity of the Woiworung, Bunurong and Wathaurang clans: within their territories, as Chief Protector Robinson noted in 1840, 'half the runs had been shown by the natives'. These Kulin honoured their pledge to live in amity with the greedy and deceitful strangers; their recompense for sharing their land was destruction and an undeserved reputation for treachery. Their dispossession did not take long for the intruders came by sea to Melbourne and also overland across the Murray River and through Kulin territory to the coast.

The first wave of colonists occupied Bunurong, Woiworung and Wathaurung territory in 1835: within six years almost 12,000 Europeans had dispossessed these clans and expropriated the territories of most of the Taungurong, Jajowrong and Ngurai-illam-wurrung clans. By 1843 the lands held by the Kulin from time immemorial, and those of their neighbours, were being denuded by 100,000 cattle and 1,500,000 sheep.

---

12 Kolig's (1977:62) statement, derived from fieldwork in the Kimberley, fittingly summarises Kulin sentiment and practice as reported by Barak.

REBELLION AT CORANDERRK

By 1851 the new colony of Victoria was occupied by 77,345 Europeans, 391,000 cattle and 6,590,000 sheep. The new proprietors did not enumerate the surviving Kulin, although they made a careful tally of the 59 Europeans and several thousand head of stock killed by Aborigines between 1835 and 1850.[13]

By the time Coranderrk Aboriginal station was formed in 1863 over half a million Europeans had usurped all the habitable land in Victoria. No more than 250 Kulin remained. Most of them made their home at Coranderrk and fought to keep it because this 4,850 acre (1,963 ha) reserve was the only land left to them. Billibellary's son, Simon Wonga (Wonga, c. 1824–1875), and nephew, William Barak, the *ngurungaeta* who invited other Kulin to share their land at Coranderrk, had seen the first *Ngamajet* arrive in Wurundjeri-balluk territory. Their fathers had offered the strangers hospitality and protection. But the *Ngamajet*, if men at all, were mannerless men. The few granted sanctuary in 1835 had returned with others of their kind who did not return to their own country when the seasons changed. They stayed on Kulin land and called it their own.

Barak and other residents of Coranderrk reacted to official policy decisions of the 1860s and 1870s as Kulin and as individuals whose opinions and expectations had been shaped by their particular experience of European intruders. Death and dispossession had discouraged the maintenance of many of their own beliefs and practices, and the survivors had selected and adopted some of the alternative patterns offered by European culture. For a generation they had adapted to the demands of the European economy. At the end of the 1850s the Kulin clans and their leaders sought to negotiate better terms for this accommodation. They took the initiative in seeking land where the old and sick could find refuge; they asked for what would today be called technical assistance so their children could acquire new skills in their own communities. They had little choice, of course.

Between 1851 and 1861 the European population of Victoria had climbed to 540,000 while the Aboriginal population had decreased from 3,000 to about 2,000. By 1863 there were only 1,920 survivors and half of them were adult males. Some communities had no children.[14] The estimated Aboriginal population of Victoria before 1835 was at least 11,500. Sex and age ratios were already grossly distorted when the first enumerations were made by Protectorate officials between 1839 and 1843. The intruders had brought disease to the Kulin before any of them set foot on Kulin land. The pockmarked faces of many members of the coastal clans had been noticed by Europeans who surveyed Port Phillip Bay and built the first official settlement on Kulin land in 1803. The Europeans who arrived between 1835 and 1839 remarked on the number of aged, scarred victims among all the Kulin tribes.[15]

The Wathaurung, Bunurong and Woiworung clans around Westernport and Port Philip bays had suffered the depredations of *Ngamajet* intruders ever since 1798.[16] The first whaleboat party did no harm but the crew of a brig stole food and a canoe in 1801. The brig returned in January 1802. The intruders who first spoke to a Kulin group showed some sensitivity to local etiquette which required visitors to indicate their peaceful intent by holding aloft a 'green bough' as a symbol when entering the territory of a foreign clan.[17] Young Lieutenant Bowen apparently was acquainted with a similar convention among the communities of coastal New South Wales. When his boat approached a group of Bunurong men they dropped their fur cloaks and signalled the *Ngamajet* to undress. Bowen, with commendable aplomb, walked ashore naked carrying 'a root of fern'. He offered his involuntary hosts a tomahawk, some bread and the ducks

---

13 Presland 1977:4; E.S. Parker, Periodical Reports 29 February and 3 August 1840; William Thomas Papers; Series 1963:231, 282; Nance 1981:540.
14 For details of the population decline among Victorian Aborigines see Barwick 1971.
15 Bonwick 1883:15, 28; Bride 1898:209; Curr 1886–87:I 216–18; Grieg 1928:112; Haydon 1846:23; [Kerr] 1872:16; McCrae 1912:122.
16 Unless specifically stated the details of early European intrusions in Kulin territory are drawn from the contemporary accounts published by de Labilliere 1878 and Bonwick 1883.
17 Smyth 1878:II 154.

he had just stolen from their territory. The old leader, 'besmeared with red oaker' and noticeably more suspicious than the young men with him, signalled the boat party to move a mile down the beach where the men were joined by three women with children. This encounter remained cordial until the naked boat crew displayed bad manners by approaching 'somewhat near' and were loudly rebuked. The frightened intruders fired to protect their retreat.

On the brig's third visit a month later the crew took quantities of timber, swans and shellfish from Bunurong territory, then sailed round to Port Phillip Bay for a four-week stay. Bowen was leader of the boat party which accosted 20 men and boys whose laden baskets suggested they were on an expedition to collect gum. News of the previous encounter must have reached them for Bowen found they disbelieved his explanation that the guns were merely walking sticks. Yet cordial relations were cemented by an exchange of gifts and 'dancing on both sides'. Again he had unwittingly complied with Kulin etiquette: 'When visitors came to meetings from some distant place they danced and the hosts looked on; for it was for them to dance and make friends with each other, being from a distance'.[18] Later the Kulin became annoyed when a second boat party from the brig obstinately demanded their cloaks and weapons in exchange for European food and clothing. The intruders fired repeatedly, killing at least two of the 18 Kulin, because they reportedly detected a hidden man armed with a spear. Just before sailing away on 12 March 1802 the brig's captain took 'possession' of the port in the name of his King. In English law all of the Kulin were thereby dispossessed.

This meretricious claim to title by right of 'first discovery' would prevail against any claim made by the French ship which visited the following month. Captain Millius[19] spent a few hours pursuing a party of Kulin men whose faces were painted with white ochre, an indication that they were mourning the death of a close relative and perhaps were messengers carrying the news from their own clan-head to another. The Kulin forbad Millius to approach until he undressed. Amused by his dancing and singing, they took his shoes and garments and urged him to follow. He soon gave up because his feet were hurting.

Scarcely two weeks later a British sloop visited. The crew climbed the hill called *wonga* (Arthur's Seat) but the Kulin they saw eluded pursuit. A few days later, in Wathaurung territory across the bay, a boat party shared food with three men who were already familiar with the use of guns.

Nine months later a schooner brought more intruders intending to survey possible settlement sites. Boat parties gave food and trifles to three groups they met when camping in Bunurong territory. They also encountered some Wathaurung during their month's visit.

In October 1803 some 300 convicts, a military guard and 16 free settlers arrived to occupy Bunurong land for seven months. Unarmed Kulin at first approached eagerly and were given food but after they protested the theft of timber near *wonga* the fearful carpenters retreated to the settlement complaining that 'four hundred' men had threatened them. The environmental damage caused by their building and clearing and the massive theft of game and waterfowl soon became known to neighbouring clans.

The meetings of boat parties with Kulin around the bay were at first friendly, but all knew the use of guns and the Europeans had to keep these hidden. Finally a boat party surveying Wathaurung territory provoked violence. They gave beads and blankets to three visitors, but when some 40 Kulin (who carried their supposed 'chief') took some tools from the boat the crew immediately assumed they intended to 'plunder' European property. The crew reported they had killed one and wounded several of the 'two hundred' Kulin who subsequently assembled. Fear of Kulin retaliation for such murders was one motive for abandoning the settlement soon afterward. Two of the three convicts left behind were in fact

---

18 Barak gave this explanation of inter-clan rituals when Howitt questioned him about William Buckley's observations (Howitt MS:57).
19 Scott 1917:15–17; Howitt MS: 56.

sheltered by Wathaurung clans. One was soon killed for improper behaviour towards women but William Buckley was protected as the reincarnation of the recently deceased 'Murrangalk'. Barak remembered that 'Buckley's friends were at Geelong, Bacchus Marsh, Werribee, Mordiallock [sic – Wardy Yalloak River?]. I know this because they told me this. His lot were the Geelong tribe – Wudthowrung'.[20]

The government abandoned schemes for occupation of Kulin territory because known coastal sites seemed unsuitable for cultivation but other Europeans who were not under official restraint continued to intrude on the coastal clans. Sealing and whaling ships established shore-based camps, and whaleboats crewed by escaped convicts and deserting seamen readily made the passage from the Bass Strait islands. Their efforts to obtain Tasmanian women by negotiation and kidnapping had already had severe demographic consequences; now they sought women from the Australian coast. No official notice was taken of their depredations although a Sydney newspaper's report that a schooner crew had escaped after killing the 'chief' who forbad them to bring guns ashore in 1815 also mentioned 'numerous previous accounts' of conflict between intruders and Port Phillip Aborigines.

By 1826 sealers had established permanent camps on the uninhabited islands in Westernport Bay. Fourteen men removed by a French corvette in November were reportedly well acquainted with the 'amiable natives'. Weeks later an official party from Sydney found that the seven remaining sealers had several Kulin women. The new arrivals, some 40 convicts and soldiers sent to demonstrate that the British claimed Kulin land by 'possession', remained for 16 months. They were removed because the distant British government had decided that a claim of 'prior discovery' was sufficient legal cause for 'keeping out the French ... whether our establishments be continued there or not'.[21] The intruders did not make inquiries about land ownership at the Kulin camps they visited in Bunurong territory, but seemed interested in the fact that the Kulin were using tin pots, some woollen cloth and iron shaped into tomahawks.

By this time some inland clans had also seen strangers traversing their lands. Eight intruders with bullock carts and horses crossed Taungurong and Woiworung territory and arrived among the Wathaurung by December 1824. They had not seen any Kulin but were frightened because unseen people continuously set fire to the country ahead of them. They retreated the day after their arrival at the coast because they found the Wathaurung aggressive. No more came overland for 12 years but the coastal clans were troubled because the intruders who came by sea were kidnapping Kulin women.

Protectorate officials were later told of two raids during the 1820s. One party captured at Port Phillip escaped but two women were killed and others walked with a limp years later. The *ngurungaeta* of four Woiworung and Bunurong clans reminisced about their attack on sealers at Westernport who wounded visitors to a tent camp.[22] In 1833 a sealing schooner made another raid near Arthur's Seat. A Tasmanian woman enticed a party of Woiworung and Bunurong women and children to board a whaleboat but one escaped in the struggle that followed. Seven women, two young girls and two lads were taken to the Bass Strait islands. The mother of the girls had already discovered that the *Ngamajet* were like other men:

---

20 Howitt MS. Buckley lived until 1835 with two intermarrying Wathaurung clans whom early colonists called 'the Barrabools': the Wudthaurung-bulluk around Geelong and the Bengalat-bulluk to the south. The former married with the Wurundjeri-balluk (Woiworung) and the latter with the Yallukit-willam (Bunurong) and with other Wathaurung clans according to the rule of moiety exogamy. None of these Kulin clans married the unrelated Kolakngat and '*mainmeet*' (strangers) to the west, considered hostile. Because Buckley's hosts were outliers of the Kulin bloc constantly fighting with these alien neighbours, his reminiscences are an unreliable guide to pre-contact levels of conflict within Kulin society (Morgan 1967; Bonwick 1883:220–63; Presland 1977:3; Mulvaney 1976:77; Cannon 1982:176–85).
21 Labilliere 1878:I 247.
22 James Dredge, Journal 16 June 1841; Gunson 1968:17; William Thomas, Journal 9 February 1840. The *ngurungaeta* named were Billy Lonsdale, De Villiers, Budgery Tom and Old George or Tuolwing (see Barwick 1984:117–24).

her elder daughter born in 1820 or 1821 was the child of a European. Neither she nor this daughter would agree to be repatriated from the islands in 1837 but her granddaughter Louisa Briggs played a prominent part in the later campaign to save Coranderrk.[23]

The next intrusion was that by John Batman in May 1835. He arrived at Port Phillip to 'purchase' Kulin land for a partnership composed of Tasmanian officials and wealthy pastoralists. He was accompanied by three European servants and seven 'Sydney' Aborigines he had employed for some years to assist in deporting Tasmanian Aborigines from their lands. They landed first at Indented Head in Wathaurung territory. After finding a recently deserted winter camp of seven 'large huts' they followed the owners' tracks up the river and met 20 heavily burdened women who were obviously moving camp. Twenty-four children were with them but they indicated that their men had gone ahead. The women had no fear of the Sydney men, two of whom could 'partially understand them'. These men might have had some contact with the Port Phillip captives in Tasmania but both parties must have relied on hand signs rather than speech. This form of language, particularly well developed in Australia, was used whenever individuals were subject to speech taboos and in dealings with speakers of foreign languages. The women willingly returned to the coast with Batman but when they saw his ship seemed fearful that another kidnapping was planned. They were reassured when the strangers departed after giving them handkerchiefs, mirrors, bead necklaces, sugar, apples, one tomahawk and a blanket each. In return they gave baskets, spears and a wooden bucket. Batman had impertinently inspected one of their net bags: it contained tools hafted in the indigenous fashion but the materials were fragments of cartwheel tyre and iron hoops.

Batman's party surveyed the bay for a week, deliberately avoiding other Kulin camps so that word of their peaceful intention might spread, then made their way up the Saltwater River and overland to the Plenty River. The Sydney men wore 'native dress', probably the fur cloaks used in winter throughout south-eastern Australia. The party carried gifts intended for the chiefs who would be asked to sign the parchment treaties carefully drafted by a former Attorney General of Tasmania. He had instructed Batman in the ritual of enfeoffment, an archaic but still valid legal conveyance which had to be conducted on the land to be transferred: 'the giving of feudal possession, known as livery or seisin, was affected by the handing over of part of the soil, a twig of a tree, or some other small part of the property as symbolic of the whole'.[24]

Eventually Batman's party met a family which was not surprised by the strangers' presence: the Sydney men learned that their earlier encounter with the women of another 'tribe' was well known. The man seemed to understand Batman's request, relayed by his escort, to be taken to the 'chiefs' (Kulin etiquette required that strangers entering another clan's territory should seek permission from the responsible clan-head and elders). Batman, unaware that visitors conventionally paced their journey so as to arrive a few hours before sunset, was worried by the guide's circuitous route and alarmed when challenged by eight armed men. After his escort presented them with gifts they led the intruders to their bark dwellings. Batman's journal records that he found 45 people in this Woiworung winter camp; his later report says 55. Twenty were men. The names he recorded suggest that he interrupted a meeting of the Wurundjeri-balluk clan-heads assembled with their aides and messengers to discuss some matter requiring action – possibly his own arrival. Within 24 hours Batman's party persuaded eight senior men to take part in his ritual of enfeoffment and secured their names for his 'treaties', which purported to be agreements for the cession of some 500,000 acres (202,347 ha) of land in the area owned by Woiworung and Bunurong clans and another 100,000 acres (40,469 ha) in Wathaurung territory.

---

23 G.A. Robinson, Journal 1836–37, v12, pt2, 26 December 1836; Haydon 1846:119; J. Dredge, Journal 16 June 1841; Barwick 1985; Cannon 1982:52–5.
24 Billot 1979:116; Bonwick 1883:174–219; Howitt 1904:71–2, 309–10; Hopton 1960:109–11.

On the first night the Sydney men danced for their hosts, as etiquette demanded. Next morning, after each of the leading men had at Batman's request, 'delivered to me a piece of the soil', Joe Bungett reinforced this ritual bond by cutting on a tree, out of sight of the women, a symbol used by his own clansmen in religious rites. The 'principal chief' immediately showed his understanding of its significance by pointing to his own mouth: tooth evulsion was an element of male initiation ceremonies among the Kulin as it was in the Sydney area. The symbolic design he then reluctantly revealed was copied by Batman on the paper treaties dated 6 June 1835. He had already made a formal presentation of the goods brought as 'compensation' for his supposed purchase, but it is unlikely that his party actually carried the £200 worth of flour, blankets, knives, scissors, mirrors, handkerchiefs and clothing specified on the two treaties which also promised much larger amounts as 'yearly rent or tribute'.

Batman reported that the three 'principal chiefs' were brothers, all bearing the name Jagajaga. Two were six feet tall and the third a little shorter; each seemed to have two wives and several children with them in the camp. His journal indicates that the three formed a hierarchy of authority and mentions that the two most senior deliberately emphasised their personal bond with him by presenting their own fur cloaks and various weapons as he made his hasty departure.

Five of the Sydney men remained at the Indented Head camp with Batman's European servants who, on 23 June, persuaded some Wathaurung men to 'make there [sic] mark on a tree' after which one 'made signs for me to give them some paper and a pencil' and 'drew out a most extraordinary mark which filled half a sheet'. One of the five named was the Wudthaurung-bulluk *ngurungaeta* Wolmudging or Coralcurke (murdered 16 months later by employees of one of Batman's partners). Another partner, J.H. Wedge, arrived on 7 August. He found 46 Wathaurung peaceably settled at the camp and learned that several of the Sydney men had already been promised wives.

Also in the camp was the convict 'Murrangalk' who had abandoned his Bengalat-bulluk allies in July to resume his identity as William Buckley.[25] He won a pardon with his tale of placating two men, 'each having a coloured cotton handkerchief fastened to the end of his spear', who supposedly sought allies for an attack when refused tomahawks 'although presents were made to the tribe near Indented Heads'. Wedge, formerly Assistant Surveyor General of Tasmania, soon learned that Wolmudging and Culgorine (another who had placed his mark on paper at Indented Head) had left to protect a boy accused of theft and were entirely friendly, as was the powerful clan-head Murradonnanuke of the You Yangs district whom Buckley feared.[26] Two days after his arrival Wedge had written worriedly to his partners reporting Buckley's opinion that the Aborigines 'are divided and wander about in families, and there is no such thing as chieftainship among them'; he had urged secrecy 'as it may affect the deed of conveyance if there should be any validity in it'. Wedge quickly learned that Buckley was useless as adviser or intermediary and came to respect the authority of the *ngurungaeta*. This and subsequent letters demanded that they be recompensed as the treaties had pledged (albeit with the cheapest possible goods) but his partners never did provide the 'yearly rent or tribute' promised. Indeed, the various Wathaurung clans received no compensation for trespass. Early in 1836 two servants transporting goods from Indented Head to the Werribee River were killed by a northern Wathaurung clan. Both Wolmudging and Batman's newly arrived competitor J.P. Fawkner believed they 'mistook the provisions for those which had been promised to them and unjustly withheld'.[27]

---

25 Hopton 1960:123; Bonwick 1883:173–219, 421; Cannon 1982:55–61.
26 Morgan 1967:84–5; Bonwick 1883:232–6, 249–73. When questioned by Howitt (MS:4–6) about this report Barak pointed out that the material of the messengers' spears was the essential clue to their intentions. A hide apron hung on a reed spear was the signal for peaceful assemblies; the same apron on the jagged ironbark 'war spear' was used to summon allies to attack a common enemy.
27 These documents, quoted a century later to ridicule Batman's treaties, in fact suggest that he and Wedge believed they had established a firm alliance with specific *ngurungaeta* and were confident that Kulin groups would make further treaties with Europeans (Hopton 1960:119–20, 131; Christie 1979:25–9). See also Bride 1969:19, 34, 39: Cannon 1982:40–1.

1. KULIN AND NGAMAJET

On Batman's return a newspaper had immediately dubbed him 'the Tasmanian Penn': this reference was clear to most colonists, who were familiar with the practice of making treaties in other colonies and well aware that the British Government had long countenanced private treaties of purchase. Batman's partners, all wealthy businessmen or senior government officials, quickly concocted a leasing account of his transaction, emphasising that their planned settlement venture would greatly benefit the Port Phillip Aborigines.

The Lieutenant Governor of Tasmania expressed sympathy for this enterprise conducted by some of his closest associates but warned that their treaty 'would appear to be a departure from the principle upon which a Parliamentary sanction without reference – to the aborigines has been given to the settlement of Southern Australia, as part of the possessions of the Crown'. He referred the problem to his superior in Sydney (whose commission enjoined him to protect Aborigines 'in the free enjoyment of their possessions'), delicately suggesting an argument that would protect both men from possible criticism: he questioned the political capacity of Aborigines to conduct land dealings recognisable in English law. Governor Bourke, already determined not to incur the cost of protecting more unauthorised sheep runs, immediately proclaimed the treaties void and rebuked the perpetrators as intruders upon the 'vacant lands of the Crown'.

This preposterous assertion had long been an accepted legal fiction. For 47 years the British Government had sent colonists to Australia without explicitly ordering any official to investigate the inhabitants' system of land tenure and negotiate treaties of cession. No colonist had previously attempted to pay compensation before occupying land. Batman's peaceful dealings with the Kulin were an embarrassment. Officials in Sydney and London exchanged a flurry of letters while Batman's influential backers consulted London lawyers. Executive or legal recognition of Batman's treaties would challenge a Crown Title based on 'discovery and settlement' of land declared 'waste and uncultivated' and thus cast doubt upon all previous real estate transactions in the Australian colonies. Officialdom had reason to fear embarrassment: reformers in the House of Commons had just begun an inquiry into the condition of Indigenous peoples in all British colonies.[28]

This Select Committee expressed astonishment in their 1837 report that governments had always ignored the claims of Australian Aborigines as 'sovereigns or proprietors of the soil' and had taken their land without the assertion of any other title than that of force. They also disapproved of private purchases and declared it 'inexpedient' to entrust treaty making to local legislators because of their proven cupidity. In discussing the Australian colonies the report acknowledged that 'in the recollection of many living men every part of this territory was the undisputed property of the Aborigines' – but lamely concluded that the 'debt owed to the natives' for this unjust encroachment could only be repaid by 'charging the land revenue of each of these provinces with whatever expenditure is necessary for the instruction of the adults, the education of their youth, and the protection of them all'.[29]

Parliamentary, executive and legal opinion discouraged recognition of Batman's treaties. His partners apparently had little hope of success (some perhaps thought them a deliberate fraud) and were careful to ask for a Crown grant should their 'purchase' not be recognised. Most colonists, then and later, ridiculed the treaties on the ground that Australian Aborigines had no chiefs. Few tried to discover what Batman's negotiation had meant to the Kulin.

---

28   Bonwick 1883:210–11, 216, 331–423. See also McCulloch 1961, Lester and Parker 1973 and Christie 1979 for discussions of the title issue. Batman's treaties and the 'purchase' made by J.P. Fawkner were the first formal attempts to recognise native title in Victoria but many other colonists felt some concern about the morality of their occupation. Immigrants such as E.M. Curr (1883:244) and the Rev. David Mackenzie (Andrews 1920:33) reportedly paid some compensation to the owners of their holdings in the Murray region.

29   See Lester and Parker 1973 and extracts in Cannon 1982:61–71.

The terms of the written treaties were fraudulent in that the Woiworung, Bunurong and Wathaurung men with whom Batman dealt could not have understood that the words 'Give, Grant, Enfeoff and Confirm unto the said John Batman, his Heirs and Assigns' meant a sale of their clan territories. Such an abdication of religious and other responsibilities was quite literally unthinkable to the Kulin. The men Batman met perceived his intentions in Kulin terms — strongly developed concepts of sharing rights in, and use of, territory — the Tanderrum ceremony.

This ceremony was a formal procedure whereby approved strangers were guaranteed the host clan's protection as well as giving and receiving allegiance and access to each other's resources. By handing their guests token portions of foliage, water and available foods of their estate the owners signified 'that as long as they are friendly, and under such restrictions as their laws impose, they and their children may come there again without fear of molestation; the presents of boughs and leaves and grass are meant to show that these are theirs when they like to use them'.[30]

The names and boundaries recorded on Batman's treaties confirm that he concluded an alliance with representative leaders of this region. But he misinterpreted the meaning of the Tanderrum ritual they performed. The Sydney Aborigines who in fact conducted this piece of frontier diplomacy were presumably familiar with similar ceremonies confirming alliances between distant clans. The boundaries indicated in the treaties and on Batman's map so nearly fit the territories of the Wurundjeri-balluk and the Yalukit-willam and those of the two clans near Geelong whom they married (the map labels the intervening area Dutigalla — which George Augustus Robinson learned later was the name of the woman Batman's party first met) that the interpreters and owners must have achieved some mutual comprehension-whatever they thought of Batman's intentions.[31]

Batman and his 'foreign' escort had approached slowly — correct behaviour for visitors seeking permission to enter the territory of strangers. Their prior gifts to the women they met in Wathaurung territory (some of them were wives obtained from the Yalukit-willam and Wurundjeri-balluk at Melbourne) were probably perceived as an attempt to enlist intermediaries as propriety demanded. Previous *Ngamajet* visitors had revealed such ignorance of the observances of civility that Batman's circumspection was reassuring. His hosts could ill afford to reject any friendly alliance. The Wurundjeri-balluk and other Woiworung and Bunurong clans to the east had suffered severe losses in recent raids by the Kurnai of Gippsland, and the southern Wathaurung were always threatened by the alien Katubanuut, Kolakgnat and Jarcoort.

Although Batman's entourage behaved with appropriate decorum his puppyish eagerness to perform the enfeoffment ritual and rapid departure afterwards must have seemed uncouth. But his medieval English purchase procedure inadvertently resembled, and must have suggested knowledge of, the Tanderrum ceremony. However, he had been instructed to procure such tokens from the owners as to make his purchase valid in English law and would have been unconcerned with the Kulin laws that made hospitality contingent on good faith.

---

30 Smyth's (1878:I 134–5) description is based on a late generalised account by William Thomas; the ceremony is named in his own brief summary (Thomas [1852/54] in Bride 1969:34–5). Thomas' journals provide eye-witness accounts for several such ceremonies when Billibellary welcomed distant clans during the 1840s; his contemporary notes of these, and gift exchange ceremonies with friendly clans, suggest the formal speeches emphasised that alliances could be binding for generations, and perhaps in perpetuity (William Thomas Papers).
31 Smyth 1878:I 135; Bonwick 183:173–219. The treaties were subject to contemporary ridicule because Batman's report (but not his journal) claimed he had walked the boundaries — an impossible feat in the time he specified. Other evidence suggests how the owners might have given Batman's treaty an accurate understanding of their territories. In 1845 Yanem Goona or Old Man Billy, a prisoner transferred from Portland who understood neither English nor any kind of the Kulin dialects, seized paper and pen from William Thomas and drew an accurate map 'marking, the water courses' of the area between Melbourne and his country west of the Avoca River, over 150 miles away. Thomas commented that Aborigines' accurate knowledge of far distant localities probably arose from their 'long and dangerous journeys in search of Mambulla' (i.e. the 'kidney fat' of alien clansmen blamed for deaths attributed to sorcery) (William Thomas, Journal, 1 and 15 August 1845; Smyth 1878:I 445–6).

1. KULIN AND NGAMAJET

The men Batman met in this winter camp near the Plenty River were custodians of the law. Some of them had authority to represent their clans: they were *ngurungaeta*. Barak, an 11-year-old witness of Batman's negotiation, recalled it when discussing the authority structure of Kulin society with Howitt half a century later. His account explains their role in 1835 and that of the leaders of the 'Coranderrk rebellion' a generation afterward. His evidence is independently corroborated by the records of Protectorate officials notably the daily journals kept from 1839 to 1867 by William Thomas, official Guardian of Aborigines in the Melbourne region.

Wayside Inn on the road to Coranderrk.
Source: The *Illustrated London News*, 12 January 1889, engraving by Melton Prior.

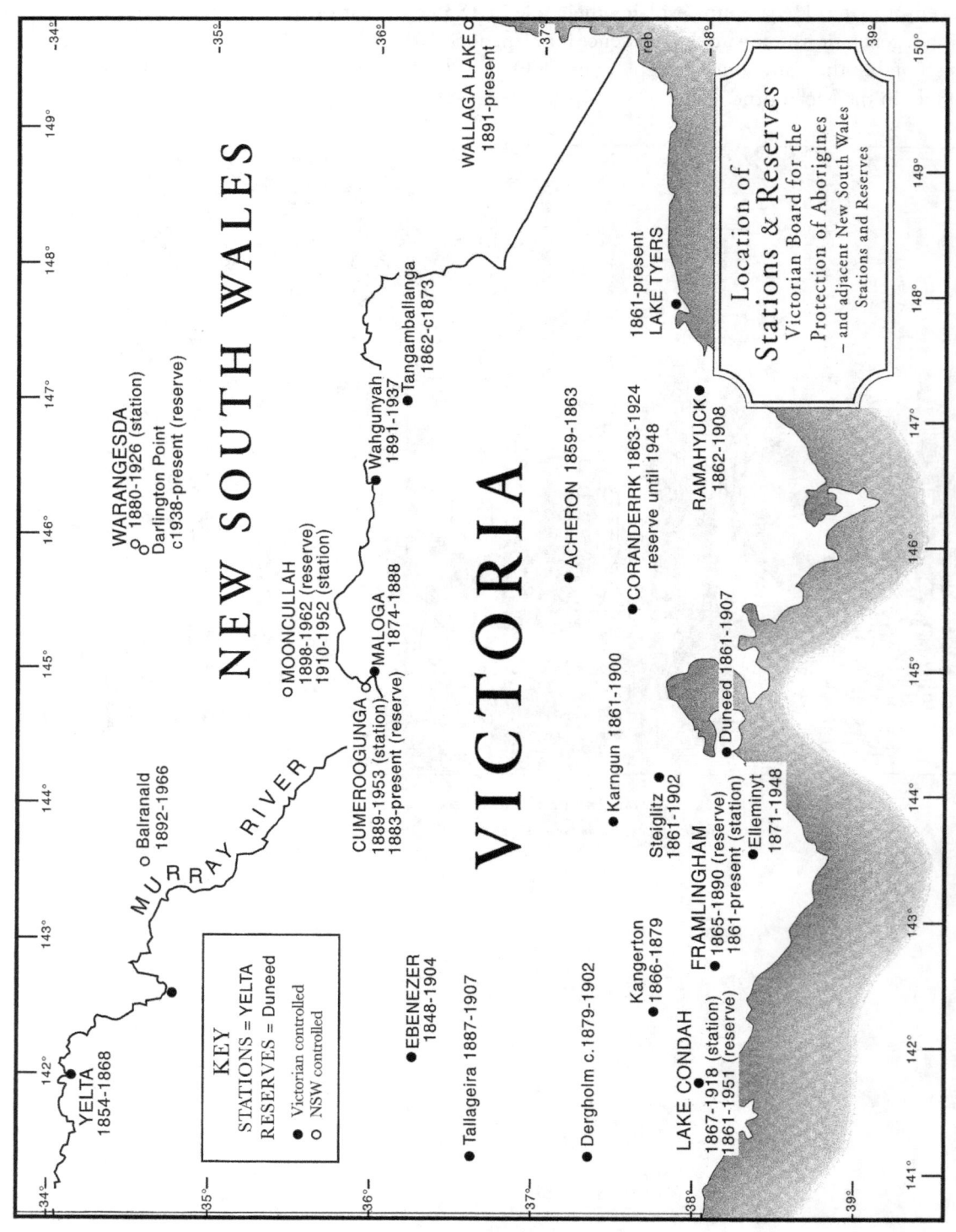

Map 2: Locations of stations and reserves established by the Victorian Board for the Protection of Aborigines.

Note: Contemporary Aboriginal spellings of place names differ in some cases from official spellings of the names of the stations.

Chapter 2
THE YEARS BEFORE

> Appointed as I have been by Her Majesty's Government specially, to watch over 'the rights and interests of the natives', and to 'protect them from any encroachment and injustice' I feel it my duty respectfully but firmly to assert the right of the aborigines to the soil and its indigenous productions, until suitable compensation be made for its occupation, by reserving and cultivating a sufficient portion for their maintenance.
>
> E.S. Parker 1840[1]

Decisions about the siting and use of Coranderrk Aboriginal Station were made between 1860 and 1863 by a handful of men who did not understand each other's views of the past. The ideas of the Europeans who planned a central refuge and school for Aboriginal children were shaped by their perceptions of the 'failure' of earlier schools and farming settlements. Most of the planners were immigrants of the 1850s who had no knowledge of church or government ventures since 1836. The opinions of those who had been in Victoria when the Port Phillip Protectorate operated from 1839 to 1849 were shaped by the hearsay reports of an antagonistic press. Only William Thomas and the Kulin themselves remembered that previous experiments had failed because of the lack of land and rations and the appointment of unsuitable staff. Only they recalled how greedy pastoralists had opposed the establishment of reserves and how these scraps of land had finally been lost.

The last 20 years, 1839 to 1859, were all that Europeans could remember. But the attitudes of the Kulin who came to Coranderrk, and particularly those of the Woiworung clan-heads Simon Wonga and William Barak who invited other Kulin to come to their land and build a farming township where their children could be trained, were shaped by all that had happened since Europeans arrived and by the laws of their own society.

The five Protectorate officials appointed in 1839 could do little to protect the Kulin and their neighbours from the avarice of thousands of European immigrants. G.A. Robinson's four subordinates were allocated districts covering most of Victoria. They received little support from either the government, courts, police or press in their efforts to control the violent inclinations of squatters greedy for land. Many of the early arrivals were former convicts from Tasmania or New South Wales who feared and despised the Aboriginal inhabitants and were prepared to exterminate them.

The 'better class' immigrants were scarcely more sympathetic. Protectorate officials could not effectively implement the more humane views of distant British reformers because they could not acquire sufficient land as hunting ground for the various clans and tribes and anyhow could not keep them isolated. The Protectorate scheme was of little benefit to the Kulin because staff salaries, building expenses and

---

1   E.S. Parker, Periodical Report, 1 April 1840.

stock purchases consumed most of the allotted funds.[2] Policy forbad the issue of rations in sufficient quantities to enable the Kulin to give up hunting. The four assistant protectors who tried to form depots between 1839 and 1843 complained that the intermittent supply of little clothing, food and medicine did not enable any Kulin group to settle permanently. Yet the government, press and influential pastoralists blamed the incompetence of these few officials and the wandering propensities of the Kulin. The legislators in Sydney tried to end the Protectorate in 1843 but, in the end, cut its budget by three-quarters so that no longer were rations issued nor school teachers employed. Only the station serving the Jajowrong survived; other Kulin were dependent on employment offered by pastoralists and farmers.

Kulin economy required undisturbed possession of large tracts of land; so did the European pastoralists. Violent encounters occurred all over the colony when pastoralists drove the owning clans from the sources of food and water which had been their undisputed possession for thousands of years. Fearful and angry Europeans often exaggerated the threat offered by the Aboriginal 'enemy', alleging unprovoked attacks by 200, 400 or even 600 armed warriors when justifying detected murders or demanding punitive raids by police. Many murders were openly discussed and condoned as a justified defence of European interests. Many more were concealed by Europeans who felt some shame about the massacre of unarmed women and children or were reluctant to admit that Aboriginal reprisals had been provoked by their own mistreatment and more particularly by their use of Aboriginal women.[3] But after 1843 the Kulin died mainly from introduced diseases to which they had no acquired resistance and for which their own doctors, and European doctors of the time, had no effective remedies.[4]

Protectorate officials quickly became aware that the 'tribes' of the Kulin area had more than speech in common. Robinson and William Thomas witnessed gatherings of up to 800 men, women and children who met at Melbourne for ceremonies, trade, marriage arrangements and the settlement of disputes, and knew that large assemblies met elsewhere in Kulin territory. Robinson, a fair linguist who had spent many years with Tasmanian Aborigines, soon grasped the fact that Kulin from widely separated districts were acquainted. In January 1840 he met Ngurai-illam-wurrung on the Campaspe River who asked after the Bunurong man Derrimut and other friends in Melbourne as well as Taungurong acquaintances in the Goulburn Valley. He found their language like that of the Woiworung 'with slight deviation'.[5] Thomas, too, was soon aware that Kulin dialects were mutually intelligible and their speakers formed an intermarrying 'confederacy'. (Intermarriage enabled individuals to travel in safety far beyond the territory occupied by their own 'tribes'.)[6]

The Wathaurung clans in the vicinity of Geelong and the Werribee River had suffered in William Buckley's time from raids by their western neighbours whose language and social organisation were very different. This area was densely settled by Europeans and the Wathaurung had no resident official to protect their interests. There were 173 Wathaurung on the Geelong sheep run in 1837, and altogether 375 persons were enumerated in Wathaurung territories in that year. In 1842 only 118 remained; by 1853 there were 34 survivors. Only 15 were alive in 1863. The Wathaurung clans had a little food and medicine while Assistant Protector C.W. Sievewright was based at Geelong for 15 months to February 1841, but few Kulin accompanied him to the depots briefly maintained at Keilumbete and Terang in 1841 and none

---

2   A few contemporaries such as Haydon (1846:92) understood that the Protectorate system failed because of the denial of food, and this judgment is confirmed by various historians (Bossence 1965; Corris 1968; Foxcroft 1941; Nelson 1966).
3   Blaskett 1979, Carris 1968 and Christie 1979 examine 'frontier violence' in some detail.
4   Barwick 1971; Curr 1883.
5   Presland 1977:14.
6   Legislative Council, Victoria 1858–59:68.

2. THE YEARS BEFORE

went to the depot formed at Mount Rouse in 1842. These sites far to the west were within the territory of unrelated tribes (who used the word *mara* for man). Sievewright was suspended in June 1842 and never reinstated. Only a part-time medical officer supervised Mount Rouse until it was closed in 1849.[7]

The Methodist Church began the Buntingdal mission station near Colac in 1838 but it was on the territory of the Kolakgnat whom the Kulin did not marry. Because of their obvious hostility the missionaries discouraged Wathaurung clans from visiting at the end of 1839 and forbad them entry from March 1843. Squatters had been removed to make this reserve and were always antagonistic to the mission. Government support for Buntingdale ended in 1844, but the missionaries secured a pastoral lease of the land and relied on gifts to continue. Government surveyors arrived in 1848 to arrange for disposal of the leased land. Since supporters could not pay the price asked the mission had to close.[8]

Thus there was no reserve within the territory of the Wathaurung and Kurung clans during the Protectorate period or later (Map 2). Some did join their Woiworung neighbours at the depot established by Assistant Protector Parker near Sunbury (where Bungarim was the responsible clan-head) in September 1839. At the end of 1840 many followed Parker to Tarringower near Mount Macedon, within the territory of the Gunung-willam-balluk clan of Woiworung headed by the influential Captain Turnbull. But when Parker, seeking a reserve site with greater agricultural potential, moved to the Loddon River in 1841 few Woiworung and a minority of the Kurung-jang-balluk and Wathaurung clans joined his Mount Franklin station. It was located in the territory of the Learka-bulluk, one of 13 Jajowrong clans whose speech and marital alliances linked them more closely to their neighbours in north-western Victoria than with speakers of the Eastern Kulin language. Indeed this clan (led by Munangabum who was recognised as *Neyernneyernneet*, or chieftain over most of the Jajowrong people by 1843), the Gal-gal-bulluk around Kyneton (whose clan-head Booringurmin or King Bobby was aide to the Woiworung leader Captain Turnbull), and four more Jajowrong clans were on bad terms with their Taungurong neighbours in 1841 although they married and were friendly with adjacent Woiworung, Kurung-jang-balluk and Wathaurung clans.

By 1843 Parker was acquainted with 670 Aborigines, including 247 identified as Jajowrong. An 1852 enumeration listed 142 members of Jajowrong and Ngurai-illam-wurrung clans living in the district but only 116 were counted in 1858. In 1863, 38 survived in the goldfields area.[9] Their reserve was originally 41,073 acres (16,622 ha) but only 122 acres (49 ha) were available for Jajowrong use after 1850. In 1852 Lieutenant Governor La Trobe approved a land grant of ten acres (4 ha) for two men who wished to farm for themselves. Their crops were worth £100 in 1853 and their grant was extended to 21 acres (8.5 ha). Two more farmers acquired grants but both were dead by 1852. Their children and some orphans attended the government school at Mount Franklin until it was closed in 1864 when only one of the farmers was alive.[10]

Kulin clans on the Campaspe, Goulburn, Broken and Delatite rivers had even less benefit from the Protectorate. Assistant Protector James Dredge began a depot at Mitchelltown on the territory of a Taungurong clan in May 1839 but it lasted only 11 months. He was appalled by the hostility of Europeans near this busy Goulburn River crossing and resigned when it was obvious that government policy was ineffective. In November 1840 his successor William LeSouef re-established the Goulburn station at what

---

7   Sievewright was charged with misappropriation of government property. His colleagues Parker and Dredge also questioned his sexual morality (Corris 1968:95–6). For population data see Smyth 1878:I 41; Bride 1969:115, 310–11; Legislative Council, Victoria 1853; Barwick 1971; Corris 1968; Great Britain 1844:279.
8   Nelson 1966:100–14; see also Corris 1968; Benson 1935.
9   Parker MS 1841, and 1843 census in Great Britain 1844:312–16; Legislative Council, Victoria 1853, 1858–59:19; Barwick 1971.
10 BPA – Report on Mount Franklin, April 1864, by William Thomas and John Green. For histories of this station see Foxcroft 1941; Nelson 1966; Morrison 1967a, b.

is now Murchison, within the territory of Barak's mother, Tooterrie's clan of Ngurai-illam-wurrung. Up to 200 Ngurai-illam-wurrung and Taungurong visited but the lack of rations and LeSouef's brutality discouraged permanent settlement on this reserve of 50 square miles (80 km2). Average attendance doubled to 80 from late 1843 when LeSouef was dismissed on charges of harsh treatment and misappropriation of government property.[11] Residents were then harvesting 47 acres (19 ha) of grain and vegetables. Rations were not issued after 1843 and the depot was supervised only by a part-time medical dispenser until it closed in 1849. Pressure from neighbours soon reduced the reserve area and the last remnant became a police paddock. The homeless clans of this region were now wholly dependent on seasonal employment by pastoralists. A few Ngurai-illam-wurrung and Taungurong, probably those who had kinship ties with certain Jajowrong clans, left their country for the one remaining government refuge at Mount Franklin but there was no land and no food there either. In 1841 an estimated 600 Aborigines occupied this region; in 1845 Chief Protector Robinson enumerated 302 members of nine clans in the vicinity of the Goulburn River; in 1863 there were 95 survivors scattered throughout this area.[12]

Woiworung and Bunurong clans in the vicinity of Melbourne were quickly dispossessed by large numbers of European immigrants. Assistant Protector William Thomas estimated that the two tribes had included 350 persons in 1836; 292 were counted in 1838; only 207 were listed in Thomas' census of November 1839. He reported that none died at the hands of Europeans after 1839 yet only 59 survived by 1852. In 1863 he enumerated 22 Woiworung and 11 Bunurong, including some non-Kulin wives brought from Gippsland after 1847.[13]

European schemes to transform the Aborigines inevitably focussed on those nearest Melbourne. The pre-eminent Woiworung clan-head Billibellary supported most of the innovations adopted by the Woiworung and Bunurong in the early years. Two of his sons were among the 18 boys who attended the government's Yarra Mission School taught by George Langhorne from 1836 to 1839. He also cooperated in recruiting a few young men as constables in 1837–39 and Thomas relied on his support when the government resolved to form a Native Police Corps in 1842. Billibellary himself enrolled with several of his sons and near kinsmen, but soon there were few young men left in these two tribes and recruiting from distant areas was necessary before the corps was finally disbanded in 1853.

In a reminiscence Thomas explained why the force collapsed. When Billibellary learned:

> that the Police were employed to kill and capture other blacks he did all he could to break up the corps – one after another deserted, it was only kept up by recruiting or kidnaping [sic] from other tribes.[14]

Early entries in the journal William Thomas kept from January 1839 show that already the Woiworung and Bunurong had trouble obtaining game and vegetable food in the vicinity of Melbourne and were suffering from introduced diseases. Europeans objected when Aborigines entered fenced paddocks to hunt and so both tribes were forced to subsist by begging and cutting bark and firewood for the intruders. By March 1840 Thomas was convinced that the various Aboriginal groups moved about from necessity but he was forbidden to supply adequate rations to enable them to settle. He divided his time between Billibellary's clan of Woiworung, camped on the Yarra two miles (3.2 km) above Melbourne, and the Bunurong camp at Arthur's Seat. In August he learned that the Bunurong had been driven from this

---

11 Bossence 1965:52; Christie 1979:96; Great Britain 1844:279–80. See also Parris 1950; Massola 1958.
12 Curr 1886–87:524; Robinson 1846:193; Barwick 1971.
13 Smyth 1878:132; William Thomas, Census 20 November 1839. The teacher Langhorne's 1889 letter published in the *Argus* 28 April 1906 said that 'the Wawarongs of Melbourne, the Watowrongs of Geelong and Borawongs of Western Port … numbered in 1837 about 1000, or 1200'.
14 William Thomas to Redmond Barry, 21 October 1861. For information on the Native Police see Bride 1969:65–83; Bridges 1971; Great Britain 1844. The ethnocentric Kulin felt no solidarity with the matrilineal Mara-speakers and willingly joined punitive expeditions to the Western District, but Billibellary would not tolerate attacks on other Kulin.

2. THE YEARS BEFORE

refuge by the authorities, and recorded in his journal the bitter complaints of Benbow and Ningerranow about their 'present usage' and their reminiscence of how they had saved the first Melbourne residents from attack by the 'Barrabool'.

Thomas searched in vain for a suitable reserve site, rejecting the first choice of the Woiworung and Bunurong because it was only eight miles (12.8 km) from Melbourne. In October 1840 he formed a depot at Narre Warren on the Dandenong Creek within the territory of an eastern Woiworung clan. At first up to 150 visited but only those who cooperated in planting nine acres (3.6 ha) of wheat and two acres (0.8 ha) of vegetables were given rations. The collection of vegetable food was women's work in Kulin society and no doubt the senior men and skilled hunters thought such tasks unrewarding and humiliating. Moreover the scanty ration could not appease their hunger for meat. By the end of 1841 Narre Warren was often deserted despite Thomas' use of the Native Police to coerce attendance. Europeans occupied the small reserve and had to be removed. After Thomas left the site in 1843 it became the Native Police camp. Many Bunurong were reluctant to settle there, presumably because they were of the same moiety as the owning clan and thus had no inherited occupation rights resulting from intermarriage. The lack of food discouraged permanent occupation by any of the people who had legitimate rights to occupy this land.

Narre Warren had no school until August 1841 and it was closed at the end of 1842. Billibellary sent a daughter and his young son Tommy Munnering to the school but not his eldest and favourite son Wonga. Thomas, who had first met Wonga in 1839, could never persuade him to attend and found that Billibellary 'was so attached to his son that he used no coercion to compel him',[15] although he sent his younger children to any available school between 1836 and 1846.

Thomas was denied permission to provide food for the Woiworung and Bunurong at their camps near Melbourne after 1843 and could do little teaching or preaching because of his court duties in Melbourne. He grew more and more sympathetic to Kulin complaints about their dispossession by Europeans. In September 1844 he was irate about the condition of Billibellary who was very ill: 'poor fellow he is forced to beg about though a King for his large family'. A month later he was disgusted to learn that wealthy colonists had sent Billibellary hunting for lyre birds and paid him only sixpence although they were worth £1 each. Two months later he was touched when Billibellary insisted he should not pay for the *miam* the Kulin built for him and criticised official treatment of Thomas: 'no good governor no give marminarta tent'. But Thomas shared the ethnocentric arrogance of his countrymen: on 20 December 1844 his journal recorded that he had spent the evening talking to the old men 'of the laws of the white men and when they take a country they will have their laws obeyed'. A month later Billibellary's brother-in-law Ninggollobin 'Captain Turnbull', head of the Mount Macedon clan, was wrongly gaoled for a murder committed by another. Thomas took Billibellary to the gaol and was greatly moved by his grief-stricken exclamation: 'Oh, that whiteman had never come …'.[16]

Throughout the 1840s the Woiworung and Bunurong clans still attempted to maintain their religious obligations. Other Kulin clans tried to join them for initiations and other ceremonies but travel grew increasingly difficult. Europeans always tried to disperse large assemblies because they were fearful for their own safety. In April 1845 Thomas warned the Kulin in Melbourne that if they did not keep to the roads instead of crossing fenced properties the police would remove them.

In January 1845 Thomas had noted that the two tribes had no children under the age of five; he expected they would soon be extinct. For years they had resisted his preaching, saying they would listen if they had food. He forbad them to enter Melbourne on Sundays and they were consequently hungrier than

---

15   Redmond Barry, 21 October 1861 (Thomas Papers); for accounts of Narre Warren see Crawford 1966; Nelson 1966; Bridges 1966; Foxcroft 1941.
16   William Thomas, Journal, 16 January 1845; Thomas in Bride 1969:73.

usual. In January 1846 the Melbourne Baptist Church hired Edward Peacock, formerly at Narre Warren, as teacher for their Merri Creek school. They fed some 20 boys and girls but the government would do nothing for the adult Kulin. Thomas was embarrassed and sympathetic when he came empty-handed to preach and they told him 'You get us flour like Peacock for the children and we will hear you'.

In June 1846, at the government's orders, Thomas removed the valuables from the *miams* in the Bunurong camp then wrecked and burnt them. He ordered the 51 residents to disperse. He also ordered the 120 residents of the Woiworung camp on the Yarra to depart. For the first time he had to call police to force them to leave their camps. They were almost 'maniacal' in their grief and anger. Thomas knew that they were already distressed because their clan-head Billibellary was dying. But he had to enforce government orders.

Billibellary died on 9 August 1846. Thomas feared that the Merri Creek school would soon collapse as it had been supported by Billibellary's authority. Billibellary's son Tommy Munnering and a few others did remain a few months longer but the European head of the Native Police sent men to enlist the bigger boys during this period and soon only small children remained. Very few Kulin attended thereafter although the Bungeleen family, who were Kurnai from Gippsland, remained until the school finally closed in 1850.

In December 1846 Thomas lamented that he had to order the Kulin to move their camps every time a European objected: 'Poor fellows, they are now compelled to shift almost at the will and caprice of the whites'. Their hardship was intensified because there was no bark left in the district and they were now compelled to build 'mud huts'.

Dindarmin – Malcolm, leader of the Jajowrong, aged approximately 67 years.

2. THE YEARS BEFORE

The Yeerun-illam-balluk clan of Taungurong of the Devil's, Delatite and Broken rivers (who moved south to take refuge with a friendly squatter) regularly intermarried with Billibellary's clan; his elder daughter married a man from there in 1845. Thus all members of these distant clans had rights of access to each other's territories and individuals visited freely. Thomas witnessed the 'ceremony of mutual friendship' when 130 of this 'Devil's River clan' came to Melbourne in March 1847. They presented skins and spears; the Woiworung gave them handkerchiefs and other European goods, 'all new'. Unlike Batman and other Europeans, they and their descendants continued to fulfil the obligations of reciprocity: a son of their clan-head was one of the aides to whom the last Woiworung clan-head Barak gave his words in the 1870s.

Old Boronuptune, 'brother' to Billibellary, had tried to fulfil the role of clan-head at this ceremony probably because Wonga, oldest of Billibellary's three surviving sons, was only 23 and not married. Thomas spoke scathingly in the same month of another 'brother' Malcolm: the 'would-be chief of the Yarra who bye the bye has lately turned a regular drunkard'. Neither claimant could influence his own and neighbouring clans as Billibellary had. By the 1850s Wonga became a worthy successor to his father but there were few Woiworung and Bunurong left.

Disease ravaged them, particularly the influenza epidemic which began in June 1847. The 'Devil's River' people and the 136 'Goulburns' (other Taungurong clans with whom the Woiworung intermarried) took the infection home with them. Thomas wept with the Woiworung and Bunurong as they carried their sick away on sheets of bark or on their backs because the government had again ordered that their camps be moved farther from Melbourne. Many had died by October and they were in great fear that 'sickness is coming all about like long time ago'. The oldest man among them gave Thomas 'a strange account of many years ago when die die die after illness'. Within the month the epidemic had spread to the Goulburn and Murray rivers. Thomas learned that many were dying and confided to his journal his bitterness about the government's total neglect of the epidemic.[17]

In November the Woiworung who had survived the epidemic retreated to camp in the Yarra Ranges 40 miles (64 km) from Melbourne and took their children from the Merri Creek school to save them from infection.[18] Thomas visited on 3 December but found none would return to the school. At the same time he made his first visit to the Goulburn depot, 107 miles (171 km) from Melbourne, and gave prayerful thanks that this reserve had survived the Europeans' demands. Ever since 1843 he had vainly petitioned for secure homes where the Woiworung and Bunurong could settle without interference. He was always told no land was available for Aborigines.

In 1848 Thomas' private journal was full of complaints about the cruelty of various European employers in exploiting the Woiworung and Bunurong workers who saved their harvests. The wealthy entrepreneur Hugh Glass was a particular offender; when Thomas questioned him he said he would never employ another Aboriginal while a Bunurong clan-head said the Kulin would not do his reaping again.[19] In September Thomas noted that residents of the Woiworung camp were 'regularly going to work' like Europeans. When Thomas made a Sunday visit one man insisted on paying him for the shoes he had brought and told him how good it was that 'God give one day to sit down all day'.

---

17 William Thomas, Journal 2–26 October 1847.
18 Nelson (1966:230–5) and Christie (1979:143) ignore the epidemic, suggesting that the Merri Creek school collapsed because the old men opposed it and removed the boys for initiation. They rely on Thomas' official reports, which naturally blamed the Aborigines' peculiarities rather than government neglect of the epidemic and official orders to vacate the camps.
19 William Thomas, Journal, 10 March and 21 June 1848.

Thomas' journal entries for 1849, however, were mostly concerned with Europeans' complaints about the proximity of Kulin camps and his efforts to fulfil orders to move them further into the bush. In January members of one camp asked him 'where were they to go, why not give them a station'. On 29 February Benbow's clansmen came to beg Thomas for 'a country to locate themselves upon'; Thomas told the Woiworung and Bunurong of 'Earl Grey's humane despatch' and said that as a result they might 'soon have a country'. Grey had suggested establishing more reserves, large enough for cultivation, where the Aborigines could obtain rations and attend school. On 20 March Benbow resolved to see Superintendent La Trobe to ask for a country for the Bunurong. Thomas tried to dissuade him but Benbow insisted he 'would send up his brass plate (meaning as a card)'. He stood outside all day but was not admitted.

Week by week Thomas was forced to disperse one camp after another although all pleaded to stay a little longer as they could find work in Melbourne but there was no more bush food. Thomas could not answer their incessant question – where were they to go? The Woiworung could retreat to the northern portion of their territory and many found refuge in the Yarra Ranges at an ancient camp site on the Yering run occupied by the Ryrie brothers. But the coastal Bunurong clans had long since been dispossessed of all clan territory.

In 1845 Woiworung and Bunurong had kidnapped women from the western Kurnai but by 1847 the Wurundjeri-balluk and the Jato-wara-wara division of the Brataualung at Anderson's Inlet had reconciled their disparate marriage rules and begun to make sister-exchange betrothals. These Kurnai, once at enmity with their Kulin neighbours, now visited their allies in Melbourne. No Kurnai had received any aid whatsoever after 10 years of Protectorate care. Thomas sent them away with their sick but on 29 July 1849 received a petition:

> the Gippsland blacks thro' mine beg of me to urge a spot for them by the River Tarrer where they may get food and medicine when sick and stay that their children shall come to the school.

The Bunurong who introduced them said these Kurnai wanted 'a country for cultivation' within their own territory. Thomas pleaded with the government to relieve the destitute state of the tribes near Melbourne by granting them flour as they could no longer obtain bush food. At the end of 1849 the government instead dismissed the Protectorate staff. A Select Committee in distant Sydney had opposed Earl Grey's scheme to expand the Protectorate system because it meant that Europeans would have to give up land for Aborigines. The local decision not to spend anything more on Aborigines was in the end over-ruled by pressure from London so that the Native Police Corps and the schools at Merri Creek and Mount Franklin were maintained for a few more years.[20] From 1851 Victoria became a separate colony but the squatters who dominated the appointed Legislative Council were busy defending their tenure of land by pastoral licences against the growing pressure of immigrants wanting small holdings to farm. The schemes for Aboriginal reserves won little sympathy.

William Thomas was the only Protectorate official retained, mainly because he was needed as an interpreter for court cases involving Aborigines. He became Guardian of the Aborigines for the two counties nearest Melbourne and later the county of Evelyn was added as many of the Woiworung preferred to camp in the Yarra Ranges where Coranderrk was eventually formed. It was not until 1852 (as a result of a bargain with La Trobe who wanted the Kulin kept out of Melbourne) that Thomas was able to obtain land for their use and was authorised to issue occasional supplies of food and clothing to the aged and ill. By June 1852 he secured 832 acres (367 ha) at Mordialloc, a favourite camping place of the Bunurong, and 1908 acres (772 ha) on the Yarra at Warrandyte. The Warrandyte site was part of Barak's father's country, but the

---

20   See Foxcroft 1941 and Christie 1979 for details of this decision.

European who acquired this station in 1839 shot some Woiworung for 'potato thefts' on 8 January 1840. Perhaps this was why Barak and his nearest relatives preferred the camp a half mile from the homestead at Yering (sold by the Ryries in 1850 and subsequently owned by Swiss immigrants, including the sympathetic Paul de Castella and Guillaume de Pury).[21] When the Warrandyte district was a major goldfield during the early 1850s the reserve was rarely occupied as farmers eagerly employed the able-bodied workers. William Thomas, unable to visit because of his court duties, requested neighbours to issue a pair of blankets annually and keep a small supply of flour, sugar and tea for the needy. But expenditure on this depot was small as the Woiworung workers could maintain their dependents. Both Thomas, as Guardian of the Aborigines, and the teacher retained at Mount Franklin were now responsible to the Lands Department. The Commissioners of Crown Lands were empowered to assist needy Aborigines in other districts but little was spent on provisions and blankets. A third of the annual vote usually reverted to Treasury and of the £11,323 actually expended from 1851 to 1858 over half was paid in salaries. Only £11/10/1 was spent in medical care over the decade, while the Aboriginal population of the colony declined by one-third.[22]

The Kulin had made a substantial contribution to the pastoral industry during the 1840s and their labour became essential in the labour shortage that followed the gold rush of 1851. Pastoralists eagerly hired them for shepherding, sheep washing and stockkeeping from the early 1840s. The Kulin could bargain for just payment for harvesting tasks, wood splitting, bark stripping and fencing. They refused to work for those who exploited them. By the 1850s they were usually paid at the same rate as Europeans for shearing and reaping, at least in the areas closest to Melbourne. By 1858 Thomas could report that the Woiworung and Bunurong were 'apt and ready' as farm labourers and were 'welcomed at all times at the farms on the River Plenty, and wherever they go'.[23]

In the hinterland the Kulin had no protection from employers who exploited them by paying in liquor and offal instead of cash and the recognised rations. And they had no secure home except for the remnant of reserve at Mount Franklin and the two reserves near Melbourne. The few able-bodied were supporting the dependent sick and aged. Pastoralists and farmers offered only seasonal work and expected the Kulin to support their families by reverting to subsistence hunting when their labour was not needed. Most complained of the hunting dogs kept by the Kulin and few allowed workers to make permanent camps on their stations.

Subsistence hunting was no longer possible as a full-time economic alternative and the Kulin grew increasingly resentful of the humiliations they suffered as wandering beggars dependent on the tolerance of Europeans for food and a camping place in their own country. In the goldfield areas and expanding townships, begging and prostitution were the only source of income for many who would not leave their clan territory for work elsewhere or were not fit enough to work.

A dozen children at Mount Franklin and the two Bungeleen boys in Melbourne received some schooling but the rest of the Kulin remained illiterate. Some of the clan remnants despaired and died one by one of drink, disease and mistreatment. Others like the Woiworung and some of the Taungurong clans, were held together by young leaders prepared to bargain for their rights. After 20 years experience of farming tasks they believed they had the skills to farm for themselves. They wanted the children to read and write. They wanted some of their land back and sympathetic teachers to help.

---

21 O'Donnell 1917:125–6; Cranfield 1956:1, 3; Massola 1975:15, 101.
22 Legislative Council, Victoria 1858–59:31; Victorian Hansard, Session 1859–60:204.
23 Legislative Council, Victoria 1858–59:29, 35, 39.

European attitudes hardened during the 1850s. The squatters did not publicise their dependence on Aboriginal labour or praise the skills of their workers: if Aborigines were equal to European labour they would have to be paid equally. Newcomers to the colony during the 1850s saw only the miserable camps and found it easy to condemn the Aborigines as drunken and diseased and to assert that they were too lazy to work. (Much the same things were said about the poor Irish immigrants in a colony dominated by English and Scots.) The reputed failure of the Protectorate stations and the difficulties of the Moravian and Anglican missions established for the western neighbours of the Kulin in the 1850s did not encourage increased expenditure once Victoria obtained its own Parliament in 1856.[24]

There was a widespread feeling of guilt about the dispossession of the Aborigines, accentuated perhaps by the questions of newcomers who knew that land rights of Maoris and North American Indians had been recognised and wondered at the peculiarities of colonial policy in Australia. In addition the incredible prosperity brought by the gold rush meant the government could no longer argue that it could not afford to make some recompense to the original inhabitants.

The Jajowrong farmers allotted land at Mount Franklin in 1852 had considerable success under the supervision of the former Protectorate official E.S. Parker who published a defence of Aboriginal interests in 1854. A few sympathetic churchmen also prepared a report on new ventures in the neighbouring colony of South Australia in 1856 when the current owner-editor of the *Argus* (a fairly radical newspaper until his departure in 1858) publicly reproached an unsympathetic government and Parliament. In the same year William Thomas found some senior Lands Department officials sympathetic to his plea that land be reserved as refuges. The Surveyor General asked him to draft a plan to supply the needs of all Aborigines in the colony. Parliament, however, refused to increase funds for Aboriginal welfare and no action was taken on Thomas' January 1857 submission or the petition sent to Parliament by local Church of England officials later in the year.

One member of the Legislative Council was sympathetic. The research necessary for Thomas McCombie's 1858 history of Victoria, and his correspondence with individuals and groups concerned to protect 'native races' likely to become extinct, had made him aware of the alarming mortality of the Aborigines. In October 1858 he secured appointment of a Select Committee to examine conditions throughout the colony. Like most of the 65 colonists who answered his questionnaires McCrombie believed that real 'civilisation' of the Aborigines was impossible; indeed his circulars pointed out that his ethnographic queries might not all be applicable to 'a race deemed so low in the scale of civilisation'.[25] He was the only one of the eight appointed Legislative Council Select Committee members who attended all 10 meetings and with three others he drafted the final report.

Only 28 of the 46 replies to McCombie's question about the capacity of Aborigines to receive instruction said they were equal to other races; 20 replies said they were incapable of benefiting from teaching. Most respondents opposed the reservation of land for them and many asserted that all relief measures would be a waste of money. Yet the main witnesses, the former Protectorate officials Thomas and Parker and the Moravian missionaries who had begun a mission station in the Wimmera after squatters forced closure of an earlier mission on the Murray, could disprove these assertions from their own experience.

The Select Committee members had no understanding of Aborigines' attachment to their own place and people and had thought to solve the problem by putting all the survivors together on one reserve. Thomas and other witnesses had insisted the clans would not leave their own territories and would pine away if forcibly removed. The Select Committee's report, presented to Parliament in January 1859, recommended

---

24 For a detailed survey of European attitudes see Christie 1979; Rowley 1970, 1971a.
25 Victorian Parliamentary Debates, Session 1868:684. The questions were copied from circulars he had received from the British Association for the Promotion of Science and the Ethnographical Society of Paris. See Urry 1972 for a discussion of such questionnaires.

that separate reserves, large enough for the development of agricultural and pastoral pursuits, should be set aside for the various 'tribes' in their home areas. The report recommended supervision by missionaries and agreed that supplies should be distributed to all needy Aborigines. It was essentially Thomas' scheme. But there was already doubt that suitable reserves could be obtained because of the continuing flood of British migrants seeking gold or land to farm. Thomas had argued that no relief scheme could succeed unless the reserves were of sufficient size and quality so that Aborigines could support themselves by cultivation. He insisted that their land must be permanently protected against intrusion by covetous Europeans. Finally he demanded that reserve residents must be fed adequately whether they worked or not so that their homes would become a secure refuge. That much he had learned from the failure of the Protectorate.

None of these requirements, however, were met during the 1860s and 1870s. Greedy colonists opposed reservation of land and lobbied for access to the little that was reserved. They criticised the cost of maintaining Aborigines on the allotted tracts of poor quality land and urged their dispersal as a useful labour force for the colony. The Aboriginal farmers had little funding for development, inadequate rations and no wages. They had to work elsewhere to obtain cash for their needs and then were criticised for their failure to cultivate the reserve.

Chapter 3
A NEW BEGINNING

> ... it is our first duty to supply them with food and shelter; to protect them as far as possible from contact with the debased amongst our own people; and to provide instruction for the children, black and half-caste ... How hopeless soever may be their condition, the people of this country must still perform their duty, nor grumble at a rent charge of some six thousand or seven thousand pounds a year for nearly fifty-six million acres of the richest lands in the world.
>
> Richard Heales 1862[1]

On 28 February 1859 the two surviving sons of Billibellary appeared at William Thomas' home on the Merri Creek where their father had died in 1846. Simon Wonga was now 35, his brother Tommy Munnering nine years younger. Thomas had known them for 20 years and they were welcomed. He was concerned that Munnering, who had attended the Narre Warren and Merri Creek schools and also served in the Native Police, appeared near death from consumption. Thomas had no trouble understanding the Woiworung; he had used their dialect for years and they spoke fair English. Indeed, he had recently told the Select Committee that all of the Woiworung and Bunurong spoke English well and pronounced it 'far better than half the Scotch or Irish emigrants'.[2]

But they had to interpret for the five Taungurong men they had brought with them, who belonged to three neighbouring clans of the upper Goulburn River. They were the former policeman Bearringa or Tall Boy, a celebrated doctor who had cured Wonga's blindness when treatment in the European hospital failed; Murrum-Murrum or Simon; Parnegean, known as Charley King, son of the Yowung-illam-balluk clan head; young Kooyan or Peter Hunter; and Burruppin or Jemmy Webster Jr, who had spent much time with the Woiworung.[3]

Thomas invited them all to eat and to sleep the night in his kitchen and on the verandah because he wanted to hear news of their people. He rarely visited the Kulin now because of his court duties and they were kept out of Melbourne by government edict. He had done his best for them and was proud that they were making their own way and were well thought of by their European employers. He particularly admired Wonga, who had proved his fitness to carry his father's responsibilities as clan head and now cared for all the Woiworung and the clans with whom they married. Wonga had learned a good deal about the Europeans' way of doing business: as so many of them could not be trusted he made it a practice to bargain in advance, to make a contract for the work they wanted and the price to be given.[4] He wanted a new kind of contract now.

---

1   BPA – Annual Report 1862:15.
2   Munnering died in Melbourne Hospital of 'pneumonia and phthisis' on 7 November 1860 (Smyth 1878:I 266). Legislative Council, Victoria 1858–59:68.
3   William Thomas to Commissioner of Lands and Survey, 28 February 1859; Smyth 1878:I 463.
4   BPA – Annual Report 1861:17.

Next morning Wonga took Thomas aside and explained that the Taungurong men had come as a deputation to ask his intercession with the government which now controlled their land. Wonga told him:

> Marminarta, I bring my friends Goulburn Blacks they want a block of land in their country where they may sit down, plant corn, potatoes, etc. – and work like white men.

Thomas reasoned with him alone for an hour, the Goulburn men in the distance looking on anxiously. Thomas saw no hope for the scheme: no European believed that the Kulin should have land to live on in their own way and few were willing to give land and money to Kulin who wished to settle and grow crops – to use land in the European way. But Wonga was persuasive and at last Thomas proposed to question the men through him 'and insisted on his not deceiving me in the interpretation'. They talked for two hours about the particular tract of land they wanted and their plans for using it.[5]

Convinced that the Taungurong clans 'intended to cultivate and in a measure to 'locate there', Thomas promised to do his utmost to secure the land they wanted. He took them to the Lands and Survey Office and found the Surveyor General very encouraging. Thomas left a letter for the absent Minister and took the men home for another night. He was increasingly sure that their scheme was practical and was hopeful of government interest. McCombie's motion to petition the Governor to set aside reserves and provide funds for food, clothing, buildings and staff salaries had been passed by the Legislative Council a month earlier, even though some members had protested that Aborigines could not be civilised and opposed a money grant.[6] Thomas subsequently interviewed the Minister, Charles Gavan Duffy, an Irish reformer who perhaps recognised the parallel between the plight of the Kulin and his landless compatriots. Duffy fixed a date for the Taungurong to be heard by himself and the responsible Board of Land and Works.

On 4 March 1859 the deputation, with Wonga as interpreter, accompanied Thomas to interview the board members, all prominent citizens concerned about productive use of land. The Surveyor General, perhaps primed by Thomas, led the deputation to explain their plans for cultivation. Through Wonga, they assured him that although they must hunt for meat 'some would always stop and turn up ground and plant potatoes and corn'. Thomas thought the deputation succeeded because of Wonga's 'diplomacy'.[7]

The Board agreed that the men could select the land they wanted. Thomas had to wait for the Minister's written authorisation for its selection and survey and his promise that some 4,500 acres (1,821 ha) would be reserved. Then the deputation set off with Thomas and Wonga.

After some days of travel through the Yarra Ranges they reached the land they wanted, just below the junction of the Acheron and Little rivers and near one of their sacred sites, a hill known to colonists as The Cathedral. Thomas and the men chopped some trees to mark the boundaries and departed to collect the members of their clans who were scattered on pastoral properties or camped near the townships of Mansfield, Yea and Alexandra. Thomas waited for the district surveyor to measure the proposed Acheron reserve – it covered 4,688 acres (1,897 hectares) – and made his way back to Melbourne. On his return journey he met groups of Taungurong:

> wending their way to their Goshen, greeting me; the Aged Men assuring me that 'they would cultivate and set down on the land like white man'.[8]

---

5   All details of the initial interview and quoted speech come from William Thomas' letter to Redmond Barry, 21 October 1861.
6   Victorian *Hansard*, Session 1858–59:747–3.
7   Melbourne *Herald* 8 March 1859, quoted by Christie (1979:158); William Thomas to Redmond Barry, 21 October 1861 (Thomas Papers).
8   All details of the formation of Acheron Station come from the 'Acheron File' in the BPA Archives, unless otherwise indicated.

Duffy had resigned in Thomas' absence and although the Treasurer, George Harker, was personally sympathetic, he could not provide increased funding for implements and draught animals to enable the Taungurong to begin farming. Thomas used the remaining few hundred pounds from his meagre budget to buy food.[9] On 30 March he hired Robert and Emily Hickson, who were already known to many Taungurong, to go to Acheron Station as superintendent and teacher at 10 shillings a day. Hickson reported on 24 April that he had only enough flour to feed 36 persons but more families were assembling daily. The Kulin had no tools for another nine months and could do little but build shelters for themselves and make a start at fencing and clearing. By August the women were producing and selling baskets to purchase food and tools. In December Thomas sent, at the request of the five women who had made them, five baskets to the Governor in Melbourne. The Kulin principle of reciprocity was still maintained.

Eighty Kulin settled between April and December 1859. The firstcomers, whom Hickson called 'the Goulburns', belonged to the Waring-illam-balluk and Yowung-illam-balluk clans whose territories encompassed Yea and Alexandra. By July survivors of the Yeerun-illam-balluk or 'Devil's River' clan had joined them. Whenever the scanty provisions of flour and sugar sent by Thomas were exhausted the Acheron families had to disperse for subsistence hunting. By the end of 1859 Thomas had no money for more food. All able-bodied men reluctantly left to hire themselves to pastoralists. Only 40 women, children and aged or sick men were left on their 'reserve'.

Acheron Station, 34 miles (54 km) beyond Yea, was almost inaccessible because the roads beyond Kilmore were poor. Drays took a week to bring supplies from Melbourne. Because Thomas could not leave his court duties in Melbourne to supervise this community he advised the government to vest the reserve in local trustees. In June 1859 he had recommended appointment of Peter Snodgrass, who represented this region in the Legislative Assembly, and three more prominent pastoralists in the vicinity of Yea. He then told the Acheron superintendent Hickson to deal direct with Snodgrass and merely forward quarterly reports on progress. By the time Thomas learned that the trustees had never been gazetted, Snodgrass had dispossessed the Acheron people.

Meanwhile, Thomas did what he could to obtain money for the station by persuading the government to act on the Select Committee's report. On 19 July 1859, he again interviewed Duffy, now Lands Minister. He was asked to prepare a comprehensive scheme of guardianship for the colony. His paper, printed the next day, stressed his dismay at the disappointment of these intelligent and industrious Aborigines, 'inured to civilised labor', who could not develop their station for lack of funds.[10] He proposed the formation of 22 reserves (of no more than 6,000 acres [2,428 ha] each) in the most closely settled districts where ration depots would be maintained by trustworthy pastoralists and magistrates. In the most remote districts five very large tracts should be set aside, he argued, under the supervision of missionaries and boards of trustees. He insisted that the government must remove squatters from the vicinity, compensating them if necessary, and not let their interests prevail over the Aborigines' needs. He now believed every reserve must be chosen by the Aborigines themselves: all previous failures could be blamed on the choice of sites in which they took no interest. Thomas calculated that £10,000 in the next Estimates would cover all expenditure and future costs would be negligible as the Aborigines could support themselves on their own lands.

But this government, already in difficulties over Duffy's land reform measures, fell six weeks later. It was December 1859 before the new Treasurer proposed a total expenditure of £2,250, including £1,000 for the maintenance of Aboriginal stations. Men from Acheron had been waiting at Thomas' home until funds

---

9   Government expenditure on Aborigines in 1858 was £983; in 1859 it was £1,795, including Thomas' salary of £600 and the £150 paid to the Mount Franklin teacher (Christie 1979:208; Legislative Council, Victoria 1858–59:31).
10   William Thomas to Commissioner of Lands and Survey, 20 July 1859.

became available for the eight bullocks and dray of food and tools he had promised them. On 24 January 1860, they triumphantly drove their dray home to their station. By March they were ploughing their land. Hickson informed Thomas of their delight and gratitude but asked in vain for more food. It was never possible to supply the beef Hickson thought necessary to encourage the workers and compensate them for the time they had formerly spent hunting.[11] But at the end of February two sympathetic members of Parliament forced this ministry to increase expenditure on Aboriginal welfare.

Richard Heales and Dr Thomas Embling (who had provided information for the 1858 Legislative Council Select Committee) condemned the government's continuing neglect and on Heales' motion the Legislative Assembly voted to double the appropriation to £5,000.[12]

The Legislative Assembly then appointed a Select Committee in March 1860 with Heales as chairman and Embling and Snodgrass were members. Their brief report, adopted in May, recommended that a 'sufficient quantity of land' be set aside under local trustees in every district and that a 'central board' of gentlemen resident in Melbourne be appointed to oversee all expenditure. The latter idea came from Embling whose motion asking the Governor to appoint such a committee had lapsed when the Select Committee was appointed. Embling (a prominent reformer who belonged to many groups lobbying the government in defence of minority interests) was probably motivated by distrust of the pastoralists in the Legislative Council who had, so far, defeated all at attempts at land reform.[13]

Of course the idea was not new: in the 1830s sympathisers had suggested that committees of churchmen and philanthropists should join with government officials to supervise Aboriginal welfare, and boards including prominent laymen had been appointed to control health, land use and education since 1856.[14] The only legal authority for such a committee was the Governor's commission which instructed him to protect the Aborigines. The incumbent Governor, Sir Henry Barkly, appointed a 'Central Board to Watch Over the Interests of the Aborigines' on 21 May 1860. Magistrates and prominent pastoralists in various districts were also appointed to form 'Local Committees' to assist the Central Board.

The Board had seven members all of whom were prominent and respected colonists but few had ties to the squatter establishment or much knowledge of the condition of Aborigines in the hinterland.[15] The least active recruit, Anglican merchant Stephen George Henty (1811–1872), was the only member of the Legislative Council. In 1836 he had joined family members already occupying the country of the Mara tribes of the Western District where he became a prominent storekeeper and pastoralist. His attendance was always poor and he was asked to resign in 1871 to make way for new members.

Three (Heales, Langlands and Embling) were members of the Legislative Assembly representing Melbourne electorates. All were prominent opponents of state aid for the churches. (This probably explains why Board composition was carefully non-sectarian.)

The Congregationalist coach builder and radical politician Richard Heales (1822–1864) who immigrated in 1842 was appointed President. He recruited the two other English-born Assembly members who shared his working-class background and radical views. All three were temperance advocates, champions of education and land reforms and leaders of the 'eight hour day' movement.

---

11   William Thomas, Correspondence 1860, 30 January 1860.
12   Victorian Hansard, Session 1859–60:610, 674–5.
13   Victorian Hansard, Session 1859–60:389, 688, 706, 1169.
14   Macard 1964:27–9.
15   Biographical information on Board members and other Victorian colonists is derived from the *Australian Dictionary of Biography*, Serle 1963, 1971, Thomson and Serle 1972, and earlier references such as Henderson 1936, 1941, Menell 1892, Percival and Serle 1949 and Sutherland 1888.

3. A NEW BEGINNING

The Baptist iron-founder Henry Langlands (1794–1863) who arrived in the colony in 1847 was now its largest employer of labour. He had been interested in the Merri Creek school and the subsequent education of the Bungeleen children and was concerned that Aborigines should have opportunities for education.

The Congregationalist physician Thomas Embling (1814–1893) was much less moderate and, indeed, was considered a radical eccentric because of his ardent championship of social reforms and his sympathy for Chinese immigrants. He arrived in 1851 and as a bush doctor had employed (and travelled for two years with) Aboriginal assistants in north-western Victoria. He respected their capacity to learn new ways and was determined that they should acquire land and be treated as equals. Embling lost his Parliamentary seat in 1867 and could not attend Board meetings from 1868 when he was resident of the Western District. While there he served as unpaid medical officer to the Board's Framlingham station until 1871 and throughout the 1870s cared for many Coranderrk patients sent to the various Melbourne hospitals.[16] He did not formally resign when requested in 1871 but he was no longer listed as a member after 1872.

The other three (Sumner, Jennings and Macredie) were not then members of Parliament although Sumner served in the Council for a decade from 1873. The merchant–importer Theodatus Sumner (1820–1884), son of a Methodist minister, became a pastoralist on his arrival in 1842 but by 1855 was a partner in a firm of wholesale merchants supplying pastoralists. He was the appointed vice-president of the Board from 1861 to 1869 and was elected vice-chairman in 1871–72. He was listed as a member until his death although he did not attend after 1875.

The Anglican solicitor Henry Jennings practised in Victoria from 1849 until his death in 1885. He was presumably appointed because of his legal skills but soon became the unofficial representative of the Church of England Mission Committee on the Board. He resigned in 1883 still defending the interests of the Coranderrk people against the decisions of newcomers to the Board.

The Anglican business man and philanthropist William Macredie (1813–1891) served on the Board for 31 years. After extensive travel in North and South America, he had joined his squatter brothers in Victoria in the early 1850s but soon settled in Melbourne and became manager of an insurance company and later partner in a firm of woolbrokers and stock and station agents. He had become (like Sumner's business partner) a trustee of the Moravian mission property in the Wimmera just before the Board was established. He later represented unofficially the interests of the two Moravian mission stations.

These Board members and their successors were a tightly knit circle of prominent gentlemen involved in most of the charitable activities of Melbourne, supporters of its hospitals, and of the Old Colonists Association and the Zoological and Acclimatisation Society. Only Embling was acquainted with the individual Kulin who made their home at Coranderrk.

When the Board was created by the reformer Heales he chose as secretary a 30-year-old Lands Department official who was an agnostic, somewhat radical in his political allegiance and already one of the colony's best known scientists. Robert Brough Smyth, the son of a mining engineer, accepted reluctantly and was appointed on 7 June 1860. He had immigrated in 1852, worked briefly on the western goldfields and as a carter, then he joined the Crown Lands Office where he soon became acting chief draughtsman and later director of meteorological observations. Since 1858 he had been secretary of the government's Board of Science which was dissolved in 1860 when its task of recommending goldfields policy was ended.[17]

---

16   Royal Commission 1877:107; Serle 1963:255.
17   Hoare 1974:26–33.

Smyth's knowledge of Lands Department procedures and his acquaintance with its staff were useful. But he was autocratic, hot-tempered and impatient of colleagues he considered less efficient than himself – and few could equal his mania for work. Smyth served without pay for eight years and then received £100 a year for expenses. Since he earned £750 annually as Secretary for Mines from the end of 1860 he could afford the occasional visit to Coranderrk. Apparently he rarely, if ever, visited the other five stations, four of them managed by missionaries supervised by two church committees. Smyth's colleagues so valued their secretary's services that they had him appointed a voting member in 1863 – a privilege not granted to his successors.

The Central Board members drafted their own commission in June 1860 but found that amendments by the Lands Minister limited their executive power: they could only 'advise' the government on annual appropriations and 'recommend' the appointment and removal of officers. They had, however, full authority to control expenditure of allotted funds. The commission approved by the Governor-in-Council on 18 June 1860 required the Board to report annually on the condition of the Aborigines, providing population statistics and details of expenditure. All administrative arrangements were left to the discretion of the members and their secretary. But the Lands Minister's amendment had seriously curtailed their power to acquire land: they could only 'recommend' reservation of sites for Aboriginal use and this defeated the policy suggested by Thomas.

Board members had been told that they would be granted a commission subject to the political responsibility of the Lands Minister but no Minister was named in the commission and during July the Board somehow became responsible to the Chief Secretary. This was probably arranged by Heales but Lands Minister Duffy, who had previously promised the Board every facility 'to carry out its views', was thereafter uncooperative. In any case, powerful interests opposed the granting of land to Aborigines and there was increasing pressure on available Crown land as the population of Victoria climbed from half to three-quarters of a million between 1861 and 1871. Every application for a reserve was delayed or opposed by the Lands Minister, his board, department officials or competing applicants.

In formulating Board policy the members relied initially on the advice of the former Guardian William Thomas whose services were transferred from the Lands Department. After lengthy discussion and consideration of the replies to circulars Smyth had sent to interested colonists, the Board endorsed Thomas' scheme of providing refuges in their homeland for each 'tribal' group. But the Board never secured sufficient land to enable the Aborigines to support themselves by cultivation and be free of annoyance from their European neighbours.

The government and the Board relied on pastoralists and magistrates in rural districts for information on local conditions. The Board did not have the staff to supervise the scattered Aboriginal population. The government wished to encourage benevolent effort at no cost. But communications were still poor and the scattered members of the Local Committees appointed in May 1860 found it almost impossible to meet. At the Board's request, the more conscientious members were re-appointed as 'Honorary Correspondents' in August. Many more, usually prominent pastoralists and justices who had long employed Aborigines or shown a sympathetic interest in their welfare, were later appointed on the Board's nomination.[18] Their duties were to report regularly on the number and condition of Aborigines in their vicinity and make an annual distribution of blankets (and after 1864, clothing) to the aged and sick who could not support themselves. Scanty rations of flour, sugar, tea and tobacco were issued sparingly and only to those in extreme need.

---

18   At the end of 1861 there were 39 correspondents, who maintained 23 depots. Under the 1869 Act they became 'Local Guardians'. From 1876 to the end of the 1890s some 14 depots were maintained, but after this stores were issued mainly by local police. The Victorian Board's minimal use of police contrasts with usage in other colonies.

3. A NEW BEGINNING

The seven worthy gentlemen who volunteered their time to watch over the interests of the Aborigines in 1860, and who framed the legislation for their protection, were genuinely concerned about the social and moral issues of contemporary race relations. They had to design policies without any information on comparable problems and administrative remedies, and had to fight the inertia and greed of their fellow colonists to implement those policies. Their belief in the potential of Aborigines to adapt to their middle-class version of the good life when offered opportunities for European-style schooling, housing and employment was a positively radical viewpoint. Scholars and churchmen were still inclined to believe that this race was 'not perfectible' and most of the pastoralists sympathetic enough to reply to the circulars of the 1858 Legislative Council Select Committee had insisted that education and training were in vain, and reserves unnecessary. What information Board members had on race relations overseas was limited and not reassuring. The press was full of accounts of native wars and rebellions in Asia, Africa and North America; there was some alarm at the likely consequences of Mr Lincoln's policies; and for years there had been shocking accounts of Maori uprisings in New Zealand. Except for the pious and biased accounts of missionaries in various church journals, which tended to emphasise the intransigence of the 'natives' in order to win sympathy and raise funds, there was little information available on the administration of indigenous minorities in British colonies. The Board in fact had no precedents. Theirs was the first attempt to draft protective legislation in Australia – the first legislation for Canadian Indians did not appear until 1865 and welfare legislation for New Zealand Maoris was delayed until 1867.

The legislation framed by the Board between 1861 and 1863, but not passed as the *Aborigines Act* until 1869, was intended to be benevolent. The provisions were those considered necessary by Thomas, who had seen the Woiworung and Bunurong dwindle from 300 to 30 in two decades, and by Smyth, whose tour of all goldfields in the colony had acquainted him with the extent to which Aborigines everywhere were being mistreated. Some legal flourishes were added by Henry Jennings. Their legislation outlived its usefulness and its provisions were used repressively by later Board members and their staff, yet in the contemporary context of violence and ill-will the 1869 Act was beneficial. In attempting to regulate residence, employment and access to liquor, the authors aimed to curb the nastier propensities of Europeans rather than limit the civil liberties of Aborigines.

Meanwhile the residents at Acheron had been working enthusiastically from February to May 1860 but then had to disperse again because supplies were exhausted. Thirteen 'Seymours'[19] (survivors of the Buthera-balluk clan) had now joined the Acheron Taungurong and four Woiworung had also arrived to visit friends and relatives. But there was much sickness and only 19 of the 65 Acheron residents were able-bodied men. Superintendent Hickson reported they had fenced 17 acres (7 ha), grubbed, cleared and ploughed this area and planted five acres (2 ha) of wheat and an acre and a half (0.6 ha) of vegetables. They were currently planting 10 acres (4.1 ha) of potatoes.

Thirteen young men and eight children had attended school until supplies ran out when they left to find work or subsist by hunting. Delays in forwarding supplies left residents 'in great want', Hickson complained, because they had no other food or income while working their property. There were no quarrels between the assembled clans, all showed great interest in farming and already the Taungurong considered their station 'a place of rest and comfort, especially the aged and sick'. Hickson informed Thomas that the reserve could support 1,500 sheep and the Taungurong would produce their own flour and vegetables after this year.[20]

---

19 Howitt MS, 1904. Curr (1886:566–73) apparently relying on LeSouef's memories of 34 years earlier, locates the 'Bootherboolok' wrongly on his map. See discussion of LeSouef's involvement with the Kulin in Chapter 7.
20 BPA – Acheron File is the source for all correspondence cited unless otherwise stated.

The Taungurong had waited and worked for 13 months; three months later they lost their chosen land. Thomas' choice of trustees had been unwise. Snodgrass, whose father had been acting Governor of New South Wales, was one of the first to bring cattle overland to Taungurong territory. He was one of the colony's most popular 'gentlemen squatters'. He was also implicated in the corrupt dealings of Hugh Glass, the powerful squatter who controlled secret funds raised by certain pastoralists to bribe members of Parliament who could influence the allocation of land. Glass used Snodgrass as a 'paymaster'; he also employed the son of the Lands Minister, Duffy, and a son of the Surveyor General.[21]

After the Lands and Works Department district surveyor had conducted the initial survey of Acheron with Thomas in March 1859 he had advised his superiors in July that the site was unsuitable for Aborigines. He said that local pastoralists were strongly opposed to its reservation as the hunting dogs of the Taungurong would endanger their pastoral operations. He did not name them: one was certainly the impoverished squatter Stephen Jones who held the grazing lease of Mohican Station which adjoined the Taungurong 'reserve'. In May and July 1859 Jones had offered to sell his property, including buildings, sheep, cattle and horses, to the government for £1,500 for use as an Aboriginal station. The Surveyor General favoured the purchase on learning that Snodgrass thought this small sheep station ideal for training Aborigines. But the government did not intend to re-purchase leased land for Aboriginal use. When this ploy failed, Jones' agents then demanded compensation for general devaluation of the property and alleged destruction of sheep. Snodgrass was suggested as a reliable witness for Jones' claim. The area chosen by the Taungurong included part of the pastoral lease of one sympathetic 'trustee' who made no objection and had accommodated Thomas while he waited for the surveyor. But the eastern half of the area surrounded the pre-emptive Taungurong selection while the western portion was part of the pastoral empire of Hugh Glass who had cheated Bunurong and Woiworung employees back in 1848.

At the end of 1859, the Lands Board did approve gazettal of the proposed reserve and four trustees but the cautious incumbent Minister withdrew the papers pending further inquiry about the sentiments of European occupiers. As they did not reply, the Lands Board again recommended reservation in March 1860. Instead the government, anxious to placate the squatters, placed £1,000 on the Estimates on 1 May 1860 as compensation to Jones for 'loss of sheep and damage' to Mohican Station.

Thomas, learning of this in the next day's Gazette, advised his Lands Department superiors to use the sum instead to purchase the area as additional hunting ground for the Taungurong. The Minister, apparently dubious about his department's dealings, sent a surveyor to investigate. The surveyor reported two weeks later that Jones' station was valueless as no European would occupy it. It was uninhabited; there were no sheep and the few wild cattle were not worth mustering though there were four good huts worth £300. He recommended its acquisition for the Aborigines as the selector objected to the proposed reserve surrounding his farm. Meanwhile Hugh Glass had also demanded compensation for 'damage' to the portion of his run occupied by the Taungurong. On 29 May Hickson replied to Thomas' queries asserting that Glass' allegations were false.

At the first meeting on 7 June, the new Board was presented with the opinions of both surveyors and Snodgrass, Glass and Thomas. Since £1,000 had already been allotted by the government, the Board approved the purchase of Mohican Station, assuming this was an addition to the Acheron reserve. Three weeks later, when Snodgrass asked him to supply the names of the other 'trustees' (who had never met) Thomas learned how Snodgrass had usurped control. Meanwhile, Snodgrass had interviewed the Lands Minister and Treasurer to expedite payment for Jones and had completed the legal transfer, ostensibly to the trustee, on 28 June. The purchase price was to cover several thousand sheep but Jones' agents amended

---

21   Kiddle 1961:249–62. See also Sayers in Legislative Assembly, Victoria 1956:102; Sayers 1969:215; Cannon 1978:122–3. When Snodgrass died in 1867 Parliament voted funds for his family (Thomson and Serle 1972:196).

the contract to cover 'stock' and by the time Lands Department officials noticed nothing could be done. For £1,000 the government acquired four huts, a few wild cattle and a grazing lease on 16,000 acres (6,475 ha) of Crown land in high cold country so useless no European would settle there.

Snodgrass insisted the Taungurong must settle there. Delayed by much sickness, they had just completed their winter *willams* of bark and were comfortably settled on their chosen ground at Acheron. Without consulting the Board or Guardian, Snodgrass ordered Hickson to move the Taungurong and all government property to the Mohican homestead five miles (8 km) south. Half the stores were removed at the end of August and Hickson was to vacate the 'reserve' by 19 September. Glass was still asking compensation for damages and in August had complained to the Board about the delay in removing the Taungurong from the 'best part' of his run. The Board, unaware that Acheron Station had never been reserved, replied that they intended to retain possession of all Aboriginal reserves in the colony.

Thomas knew nothing of this forcible transfer until Taungurong deputations again walked down seeking his help. He reported their distress to the Board on 5 October:

> The Goulburn blacks have waited twice upon me complaining that they have been ordered to remove from the land they had settled on and selected, which I had promised them ever should be theirs – I fear it will be long if ever they are satisfied with their removal, they say 'that it is not the country they selected. it is too cold and blackfellows soon die there'.

Still believing that Mohican Station was intended to supplement the original acreage, Thomas urged the Board to seek gazettal of the Acheron reserve:

> or else it will soon be taken up by others after the labor the blacks have bestowed upon it – and altercations may arise between them and the settlers as the Goulburn blacks will ever consider that as their Reserve.

Three days later he received Hickson's quarterly report which described the removal on 19 September. Hickson reported that the Taungurong were so 'disgusted and disappointed at leaving the reserve and all they had done on it' that none would consent to drive the dray loaded with stores to the Mohican site. Indeed, in their 'disappointment and passion', 48 had left their home 'in a body'. Hickson had tried to persuade them to remain and care for the crops but they refused unless he stayed with them. The Woiworung who suffered Glass' bullying more than 20 years earlier, had presumably warned their hosts that they must have a European witness in their dealings with him.

Thomas forwarded Superintendent Hickson's report to the Board and expressed his own anger and anxiety about the 'iniquitous' behaviour of Snodgrass:

> Never did a finer opportunity offer itself – In fact the Upper Goulburn blacks have surpassed all in patience I ever met with – disappointed from April 1859 to March 1860 yet thro' the whole time hanging about their own favored selected spot – and as soon as money was voted for the Implements &c, two of them (waiting at my residence) drove the team and Implements from Melbourne to their adopted land, set to work immediately, and have ploughed and fenced in crops …

> My impression is that this settlement after all will prove an utter failure – not thro' any act of the Aborigines, but through being forced miles from the spot they cherished and which I assured them Government would most sacredly retain for them.

On 18 November Hickson wrote directly to Thomas: when he went to check on the crops five days earlier he had found Glass and his partner there. They claimed possession of Acheron 'reserve' as part of their run and had installed a shepherd in the government hut. Subsequently Hickson received a letter from Snodgrass ordering him to meet the nearest 'trustee' (who had declined to interfere) to decide what part of the reserve should be returned to the squatters. Hickson had just returned to the reserve and found the fences deliberately broken and the wheat and potato crops totally destroyed by cattle. Glass had ordered him to remove the government bullocks but the fencing on Jones' station was so decayed there was no secure paddock for them.

Appalled that the trustee he had chosen to protect the Taungurong had handed over their land to the squatters, Thomas immediately begged the Board to intervene, warning that 'This, the fate of Aboriginal industry is enough to deter Aborigines from ever after having confidence in promises held out to them'.

Thomas now obtained copies of all Hickson's earlier reports to Snodgrass. He learned that this 'trustee' had been well aware in August that the new site was unsuitable because there was no arable land and the Taungurong believed it too cold. Hickson had suggested moving Jones' huts to the reserve and had urged the trustees to visit but had no reply. Hickson's October 1860 report to Snodgrass pointed out that only two men, four old women and two children had settled at Jones' station. Before the move, an average of 50 had been settled at the reserve and they never left their chosen home unless driven by hunger when provisions were exhausted. Their desertion was due to anger that 'Glass & Nash were to have their portion of the Reserve restored to them, the only part frequented by the Blacks, and where all their improvements were made'.

Hickson's next report to Snodgrass in December 1860 begged for medicines and monthly visits by a doctor: six had died in an earlier influenza epidemic and there was continuing sickness but patients could not travel 34 miles (54 km) to the doctor at Yea. Hickson had not been able to form a regular school until 27 November 'for want of a house, Books, stationary, Primers &c.' Most of the young people had come to Jones' Mohican station now that it was summer and 10 children plus eight youths and six girls over the age of 15 were so 'anxious to gain information' that they sat for six hours of instruction each day in the renovated stable. He was still seeking Snodgrass 'permission to return to the Acheron reserve where there was more arable land and enough grass to keep 30 cows. He emphasised that milk was needed for the children and invalids and the younger men had taken great interest in the cows and shown themselves 'very good milkmen'. Jones' station was 'cold wet scrubby mountainous country' which had no resources except game and a few wild cattle.

As Snodgrass had not replied to the Board's queries in mid-December their secretary sought information from the Lands Department about the trustees' powers. They learned there were no trustees – and no reserve as the previous Lands Minister had withdrawn the application for gazettal.

Because the Board's President, Richard Heales, had become Premier and Chief Secretary on 26 November 1860 the members hoped for major reforms in Aboriginal welfare. But Heales' minority government was unpopular not only with pastoralists because of its land policy but with the public service because it had to make massive cuts in salaries, and with business interests because it had to impose new taxes to cover the deficits of its predecessors. It lasted only 12 months.

No major reforms were implemented and the accession of this 'democratic' government in fact hardened a basic division in political allegiance which was 'based on wealth, economic class and, to some extent, social origins'.[22] From 1861 to 1871 Victorian governments were uneasy coalitions which had to balance the competing interests of radical reformers, urban entrepreneurs and pastoralists. The Board, dependent on Parliamentary support for funds and on the Lands Minister and his board to obtain reserves, was affected by this political context. In 1860 the Board had £5,000 to spend and in 1861 little more as their requested budget had been halved. The pleas of various Kulin groups for land, tools and teachers were delayed or ignored.

---

22   Serle 1963:301.

3. A NEW BEGINNING

In January 1859 the Kurung-jang-bulluk and related clans in the vicinity of Bacchus Marsh and Moorabool River had asked for blankets like those Governor Barkly had recently given to the Wathaurung remnants assembled at Geelong. A month later they asked for a reserve. The site was fixed by September and on the Board's recommendation 640 acres (259 ha) were reserved by the Governor in June 1860. Three months later the friendly squatter who had forwarded previous requests reported that 34 men, women and children had assembled at Bacchus Marsh and were 'anxious to proceed to the reserve on the Little River'. He estimated that £150 worth of bullocks and tools would enable them to support themselves. However the Board, only now discovering the real extent of Aboriginal need from the questionnaires sent out by the Select Committee in 1858, could afford to send them just a little food and clothing.[23] This reserve was never developed because the Kurung had to disperse for wage employment to feed their dependents.

Many Kulin were anxious to farm for themselves but the only ones to benefit immediately from Board funds were two Jajowrong who had jointly farmed a land grant at Mount Franklin since 1852. The Board granted a hundred guineas for seed wheat, working bullocks and tools to enable the last of the Wornbulluk clan, Dicky (Yerrebulluk, c. 1827–1862) and Tommy Farmer (Beembarmin, c. 1831–1880) of the Gal-gal-bulluk clan, to 'cultivate and sow the land which is indeed their own'.[24]

The young Woiworung leader Wonga also had ambitions for his own people. He found Thomas sympathetic:

> Wonga, having seen his friends the Goulburn Tribe comfortably provided for – in 1860 waited upon me again and said he had looked out a spot for the few blacks left in his tribe – I stated that there was a fine reserve for the Yarra tribe which I had for many years secured for them on both sides of the Yarra River – he said, 'Yes Marminarta you very good but black fellow no tell you to look out that one country – I want like you get'em Goulburn blacks where black fellows likes'.[25]

From the beginning the Board's main priority was a central school. It had to be central because there were few children in any camp and self-appointed advisers (citing the failure of the Merri Creek school) argued that Aboriginal children must be removed from their parents and home districts. In September 1860 the Board sought reservation of five acres (2 ha) on the Merri Creek to serve as a school and refuge for the aged and sick. This was opposed by the unsympathetic deputy Surveyor General and refused by the Lands Board in October. The Central Board asked them to reconsider and meanwhile sent Thomas and the educated Kurnai lad Thomas Bungeleen to the Warrandyte reserve to report on the Woiworung. But they had gone to Wonga's chosen site.

A year later Thomas reminisced about how he and 'another gentleman' (Bungeleen) had made their way up the Yarra Ranges to Yering where Woiworung had camped for generations. Indeed, a generation had grown up since Thomas last visited the area where they had gone after Billibellary's death. Finding the site ideal for cultivation and well away from squatters, Thomas was enthusiastic about Wonga's scheme to form a school and refuge here. He arranged:

> with Wonga and another black & Revd Mr Green of the Upper Yarra (who had taken much interest in the Aborigines) to form a deputation for the Central Aboriginal Board – Mr R Brough Smyth Secretary received our deputation graciously, and after questioning Wonga suggested that I should officially bring the desire of the Yarra Blacks before the Central Board.[26]

---

23 Mordaunt McLean to William Thomas, 6 January 1859–September 1860 (Thomas Papers). See also p.37.
24 BPA – Annual Report 1861:6; Legislative Council, Victoria 1858–59:19; Charles Judkins to William Thomas, 25 February 1862; Great Britain 1844:312.
25 William Thomas to Redmond Barry, 21 October 1861.
26 William Thomas to Redmond Barry, 21 October 1861.

The fourth member of this deputation was Wonga's cousin Barak, the only other surviving clan-head of the Woiworung and the young Scottish lay preacher Green's most enthusiastic convert.

Thomas sent the Board a sketch of the spot 'that the chief of the Yarra tribe claimed they would like to settle' and reported the 'anxiety of Mr Green to teach the Aborigines there' on 19 November 1860. Two days later he wrote again of this site and the need for a training school on the Yarra. Thomas' proposals were deferred and instead the Board made plans in December 1860 to inspect a site chosen by the deputy Surveyor General for the planned refuge and school. Europeans still could not accept Kulin opinions about land.

This time however the Woiworung would not give up and, as well as the weary old Guardian William Thomas, they had a new ally, John Green, who was appointed as Local Guardian in January 1861. Again in January and April Thomas urged the Board to provide a school for the children at Wonga's site on the Upper Yarra. In July stores were sent to Yering for their use and Mary Green had begun a school for four Woiworung children. In August the Lands Board wrote that it would not sanction any reserves within 25 miles (40 km) of Melbourne. This ruled out the old Merri Creek and Warrandyte sites. On 21 October 1861, William Thomas summarised for an influential acquaintance the history of Wonga's efforts in 'improving the condition of his race' over the last three years. He, Wonga and Green had again formed a deputation to the Board secretary, and he now had:

> no doubt but eventually Wonga's persevering efforts will be crowned with success, and an Aboriginal training school for half cast [sic] and pure Aboriginal children will be formed on Wonga's selected spot.[27]

From 1860 to 1862 Thomas was also trying to defend the interests of the Bunurong. The few survivors were strongly attached to the Mordialloc reserve, their main camp for 25 years where all the recent dead were buried. In 1860 Thomas had defeated a petition 'signed by a host of Chinamen and two or three interested whites' to sell this reserve and throughout 1861 he sought the Board's support to prevent its alienation as commonage for European neighbours. The secretary remonstrated with the Lands Board insisting no reserve should be cancelled without Board approval.

The occupation and selection of Crown land was the most bitterly disputed political issue of the 1860s and disputes over land policy had already caused ministries to lose office in 1859 and 1860. Licence moneys for pastoral leases were a major source of revenue and the many squatter members of the Legislative Council and Assembly formed a strong lobby opposing alienation or subdivision of pastoral holdings. Almost no one favoured the allocation of land for Aborigines. Moreover, the radical political leanings of many Board members made them distrusted by other members of Parliament and senior public servants. The fortunes of the various Kulin clans who pleaded for land, and money to develop it, would depend on the resolution of the political battle over land use in the colony.

The Board's policy was scarcely one of segregation: after 17 years of Board control 581 of the 1,077 surviving Aborigines were still outside stations living without government or police supervision in some part of their homelands.[28] By 1877 the Kurnai tribes of Gippsland lived on two mission stations, Ramahyuck and Lake Tyers, within their own territory; the tribes of the Wimmera and Lower Murray had their own Ebenezer Mission at Lake Hindmarsh; and two separate settlements, Framlingham and Lake Condah, were maintained in the Western District because the various Mara-speaking Gunditjmara and Kirrae-wurrung clans still preferred their own place. At Coranderrk, Barak, the last clan-head of the Woiworung, shared his estate with the survivors of the clans with whom his people had always intermarried together

---

27 William Thomas to Redmond Barry, 21 October 1861.
28 Royal Commission 1877:70.

with Kulin kinsmen who were similarly linked by past marriages, and, also the few survivors of the Kurnai clan with whom Barak began to make marriage alliances in 1847. In 1877 fewer than a dozen adults were strangers without an ancient claim to hospitality and, by Kulin law, their children born at Coranderrk acquired access rights to this clan's land for their lifetime.

The Board's policy had two aims: to provide large acreages, tools and teachers so that Aborigines could farm for themselves and their children could gain new skills; and to provide for the conservative elderly who wished to live and die in their own clan territory but might be persuaded to send their children to a new life in what they themselves called 'the blackfellows' township'. The Board's tolerance of the old people's preferences invited charges of neglect, while their support for costly communities – particularly the secular station at Coranderrk which included many 'half castes' – offended many interest groups.

After the Board's experience with Snodgrass (and some other pastoralists who used government rations for their own benefit when appointed local Guardians) they needed first-hand reports on rural conditions from someone they could trust. Neither Thomas, now old and ill, still serving as court interpreter nor Smyth, who did the Board's work in his spare time with the aid of a Mines Department clerk, could undertake the constant journeys of inspection required to provide the Board with the accurate information they needed to plan expenditure.

A lengthy search for a suitable General Inspector resulted in the temporary appointment, on 8 August 1861, of 33-year-old John Green whom the Board considered 'fully qualified by experience and character'.[29] The implementation of Board policy from then until 1875 largely depended on information and advice provided by this stubborn Scottish preacher.

The first houses at Coranderrk, c. 1867.

---

29   BPA – Annual Report 1861:6.

Chapter 4
MR GREEN'S WAY

> If any do not like Coranderrk, they can go away, and come back by-and-by. This place (Coranderrk) is very good. It is better to live here than to go about and drink. The Government has gathered us from the drink.
>
> (Translation from Woiwurru 1863)[1]

John Green (1828–1908) and Mary Smith Benton Green (1837–1919) sailed from Scotland the day after their marriage on 24 August 1857. Soon after their arrival Green began work as a Presbyterian lay preacher – a 'bush missionary' to the Europeans on the goldfields around Anderson's Creek, Doncaster and Lilydale.[2] During 1860 he rode over regularly to hold services for the young Woiworung couples camped at Yering, who were much the same age as himself and his wife. His wife accompanied him and their babies played together. The Scottish couple shared the puritanical views of their church but they had some sensitivity to the cultural and linguistic differences of minority groups and, perhaps, little sympathy for English ethnocentrism. Green's chapel was supported by the donations of a small population of mostly Irish Presbyterian miners and selectors and his income was little more than that the Woiworung men earned as farm labourers. The Greens, too, were used to farm tasks, but they cared deeply about schooling. The Woiworung clan-heads listened to their views because there were four children in their camp and they had a responsibility to plan for their future.

Neither Wonga nor the Wathaurung woman Maria he had married before 1851 had attended a European school. They were still childless but were rearing a young girl Currie. In 1837 Wonga's cousin Barak had spent a few months at Langhorne's Yarra Mission school on the land which became Baron von Mueller's Melbourne Botanic Gardens. He had one of the Coranderrk school children write his reminiscence of this in 1888: 'we heard our minister Mr Lanon. We got a schoolroom in the German garden and the Schoolmaster's name Mr Smith. We was singing up Hallalooler'.[3] Barak's two infant daughters had died but he had hopes of more children from his young wife Lizzie acquired in a sister-exchange betrothal from the Brataualung clan of Kurnai. His sister Borat (c. 1838–1871) was at Port Albert with her Kurnai husband, Andrew (Pondy-yaweet), and had an infant son as well as an older 'half caste' son Wandoon (Robert Wandin, 1855–1908) born at Steele's Flat.[4] They too would attend school if the Board would help to get a building and a teacher.

---

1 Translation by John Green (Smyth 1878:I 112).
2 Personal communication, John Green Parkinson; *Healesville Guardian* 4 September 1908.
3 Barak MS 1888; *Argus* 28 November, 12 and 19 December 1931; Selby 1935:89.
4 William Thomas, census of the Aborigines of Gippsland, 31 December 1860; Howitt MS.

REBELLION AT CORANDERRK

Although Barak was Green's first Christian convert his influence was severely tested before he undertook to 'reform his life'. He was sceptical of Green's views about drinking and Sabbath-keeping, but he refused the European who pressed him to go on a Sunday hunting expedition; the whole community was impressed with 'the Lord's power' when the Sabbath-breaker was accidentally shot. Barak was not only an initiated man but had some training in the arts of the *wirrarap* (doctors and sorcerers). This was usual among clan heads although he later told A.W. Howitt that 'some *ngurungaeta* are doctors, not all – I am not'. Barak abandoned his attempt to kill a Kurnai visitor by sorcery when Green substituted a lock of his own hair for that of the victim; he explained he 'could not manage to get a white man made sick'.[5] He gave up drinking and began to explore Green's Christian beliefs with scholarly curiosity.

John Green (1828–1908) and Mary Smith Benton Green (1837–1919).

---

5   Smyth 1878:I 464–5; Howitt MS; *Revival Record*, (23), February 1862.

4. MR GREEN'S WAY

In 1858 William Thomas had written despairingly of the lack of interest in Christianity among the Woiworung and Bunurong, but Rev. Robert Hamilton was impressed by the enthusiasm in Wonga's camp when Green brought him there to preach in June 1861.[6]

Green had hopes that this influential friend and sponsor, who had a special interest in mission work on the goldfields and was a member and later convener of the Heathen Missions Committee (subsequently Chinese and Aborigines Missions Committee) of the local Presbyterian Church, would assist the Woiworung. He knew that this church was planning a mission station in Gippsland to be supervised by a Moravian missionary who had worked in the Wimmera. But the church committee found that local congregations had little enthusiasm for Aboriginal missions and donations were small. As the church would not help and the Board still delayed, Mary Green began a school for the Woiworung children at Yering early in 1861. She and her infant children were there alone when Green began the journeys of his inspection after his temporary appointment as General Inspector, at £25 a month, in August.

The first problem for the new General Inspector was the Acheron station. After the forced removal to Jones' station in August 1860 Hickson sent copies of all his reports to both Snodgrass and Thomas. In March 1861 the Board had learned that the pseudo-trustees had never visited and this, together with evidence from Hickson and Thomas showing that all difficulties were due to the supposed transfer, caused the Board to insist that the Lands Department gazette the original reserve and reject Snodgrass' demand that Hickson be dismissed because his 'character was an annoyance'. Snodgrass resigned.

Thereafter Hickson reported to the Board secretary. Some 30 Taungurong had joined him at Jones' station over the summer months, and with the help of a European labourer they had fenced 15 acres (6.1 ha) and planted seven and a half acres (3 ha) of wheat and potatoes and one and a half acres (0.6 ha) of garden, but there was scarcely enough grass for their 41 cattle. Hickson had earlier reported to Thomas his problems with strangers constantly coming to 'tempt away' his best workers to serve as guides, assistant bullock drivers and stockmen; at the end of March 1861 he had only two men able to work and they were too disheartened to do so. Thomas informed the Board that this had been a 'perennial problem' on all previous settlements. There were only 28 Taungurong at Jones' through the winter, mostly the old and sick, and when others returned in the spring Hickson soon complained that the men were taken away to shear.

Whole families were asked to go and strip bark for neighbouring pastoralists. One of them was a former 'trustee' and when Hickson refused his request for six shearers, because other workers had threatened to leave the station, this pastoralist angrily asserted that it was Board policy to encourage Aborigines to accept employment with settlers.

Green was sent to investigate the state of the station early in October 1861.[7] There were four Woiworung among the 35 settled with Hickson but 51 Taungurong still refused to move to Jones' station. Green praised the residents' crops and their care of the cattle and informed the Board that:

> They are all very cleanly, they wash themselves and dress for prayers each morning. The men with few exceptions are very lazy. The women are good workers at what they can do. They make their own dresses, and have made a large number of baskets for a present to the Governor for the food and clothing which they have got.[8]

---

6   Legislative Council, Victoria 1858–59:67; Royal Commission 1877:22–3; Hamilton 1888:238–9, 321–5.
7   On 2 September Hickson had reported that a daughter of the selector had borne a child to the Taungurong 'Davy' employed by her father. Neighbours had complained to Thomas, who was dismayed by this unprecedented occurrence. Green confirmed that the girl still wished to marry 'Davy' although the child had died, but David Hunter accompanied his brothers to Coranderrk, married, and died there in 1867.
8   John Green, 18 October 1861 (BPA – Acheron File).

He was less impressed with the Hicksons who had done little teaching and were tactless in their dealings with the Taungurong. He said they had been faithful servants and might do well elsewhere but the neighbouring pastoralists constantly criticised them and had tried to prejudice the Taungurong against them. At the end of his eight-day visit Green gave Smyth 'the blacks opinion on the whole matter':

> They do not like Mr and Mrs Hickson. They say, that they are no good for black fellow and black Lubra, Hickson to [sic] proud. They say, Governor very good to black fellow and black Lubra – give them plenty food and clothing. They say that this station 'no good, to [sic] cold, plenty work, no wheat, nor potatoes.' They say, old station very good, plenty hot, plenty work, plenty wheat, potatoes and cabbages, plenty everything. They say, if the Governor give them the old station that by and by black fellow need no more things from him; Black fellow by them himself. They want to get liberty to ride in wild unbranded cattle that are on this station [for meat].

Green's inquiries proved that Snodgrass' forcible transfer had been disastrous: Jones' Mohican station was useless for grazing (the 16,000 acres [6,475 ha] could not support 200 cattle and were not worth fencing). The 40 arable acres (16 ha) would scarcely repay seed and labour and Jones' buildings were worth less than £30. Asserting that the Kulin could make Acheron self-supporting within two years, Green advised an immediate return to the 'reserve', which was good grazing country and included 1,000 acres (405 ha) suitable for cultivation.

Throughout 1861 the Board had been protesting delays in gazetting reserves and resumptions of some approved earlier. Smyth had written to the Lands Minister, his Board of Land and Works and Chief Secretary Heales, the Central Board's president. The Lands Board did not reply to their March request for gazettal of the Acheron reserve for eight months, then simply queried the number of Aborigines involved. On 4 November the Board asked 'by what right and with what object' such inquiries were made. They also accepted Green's arguments for a return to the Acheron reserve and ordered him to take charge and report on the cost of re-establishing the station.

On 23 November Green reported that the necessary buildings would cost £85 plus £192 for implements and stock. He also advocated a European staff of five costing £140 a year. He assured the Board that a hundred Kulin, 'including my blacks on the Yarra who say they will go with me', had promised to settle if given their original site.

Altogether there were 29 children ready for school and 45 young men and women eager to attend. But Heales' government had fallen on 14 November and a new Lands Minister (Duffy once more) would not gazette any reserves unless the Board answered his Department's queries. Smyth was ordered to reply that the Board's commission from the Governor justified their request for gazettal of all needed reserves. The Board informed Duffy that the Woiworung and Taungurong would form one station at Acheron.

The powerful squatter Hugh Glass exerted political pressure once again, complaining to the Lands Minister and the Board about new damage to his run: Green had marked off home sites in 'his' best paddock. Two days later the Board of Land and Works said it could not consent to the reservation of Glass' station as Jones' station provided land enough for the Aborigines.

Smyth immediately sent a detailed account of how the Taungurong and the Board had been deceived by Snodgrass and asked the Lands Minister to reconsider. Heales, Embling and Macredie were somewhat more moderate in their interview with Duffy on 30 December. They told him the purchased land was useless but said they were unwilling to provoke the hostility of neighbours. They asked him to pledge approval for any land Green could secure by negotiation with Glass. Duffy agreed to reserve any site 'not destructive of the interests of the settlers'.[9]

Because of these events the Board's first report, published near the end of 1861, was a piece of political propaganda. It complained of the reduction of funds – the £5 per head requested for provisions and medical care had been halved – and suggested that any attempt to instruct Aborigines 'would be futile so long as they were allowed to starve'. The Board stressed the necessity of forming a school near Melbourne where large numbers of Aboriginal and 'half caste' children could be trained as servants; if neglected they might become as idle and depraved as the worst Europeans. The Board members, like most other colonists, distinguished between people of wholly Aboriginal descent and 'half castes' of partly European ancestry. Many who gave evidence to the 1858 Legislative Council Select Committee had favoured differential treatment: the 'fullbloods' should be protected and maintained while the 'half castes' supported themselves by working for settlers.

This first Board report announced that it had:

> a serious duty to interfere at once to prevent their growing up amongst us with the habits of the savage, as they possess the instincts, powers of mind, and altogether different constitution of the white man.[10]

John Green was one of the few who considered that people of wholly Aboriginal ancestry were as intelligent and capable as 'half castes' and Europeans. He insisted that 'half castes' had no inherent superiority; their only advantage was that they met with less prejudice from Europeans. The evidence he presented in annual reports and at later inquiries was ignored.

The Kulin themselves made no distinction: the 'half castes' were their children, born of their women on their land. Girls were usually betrothed before puberty. Any child born to a Kulin wife was her husband's child – which of course was English law also. Yet European guilt and prurience encouraged public interest in the numbers and origins of the 'half castes' and this imposed distinction in the end drove the Kulin from Coranderrk. The Board's view that persons of mixed race belonged with the Europeans was in fact a liberal attitude for the 1860s when arguments concerning Negro slavery in the United States were much in the news. Indeed, the parallel had been made explicit in the 1858 Select Committee report which concluded that the mental powers of the Aborigines were equal to other races and 'perhaps superior to the Negro, and some of the more inferior divisions of the great human family'.[11] But the attitudes of most Europeans in Victoria were less enlightened, and the mental capacity and morality of the 'half castes' were the focus of official inquiries in 1877 and 1881. (The Melbourne press still published articles and letters opposing intermarriage in the middle of the twentieth century.)

---

9   BPA – Minutes 30 December 1864.
10 BPA – Annual Report 1861:11. 'Half castes' were not distinguished in the Board's first complete enumeration in 1863, but analysis of the returns shows that there were 200 in a population of 1,920; in an 1877 enumeration there were 293 in an Aboriginal population of 1,067 (Barwick 1971:292–5).
11 Legislative Council, Victoria 1858–59:v.

Lilydale, Victoria, on the way to Coranderrk.
Source: The *Illustrated London News*, 12 January 1896, engraving by Melton Prior.

The Board's first report also listed recommendations which were not so much principles of well-considered policy as political statements about urgent problems. By July 1861 Heales' reform government was losing ground in its battle with the pastoralists and urban conservatives and the Board wanted land and funds. The report insisted that colonists had an obligation to provide 'permanent' reserves wherever numbers warranted and that necessary food and clothing must be supplied as of right to those whose land had been taken. This of course was a reproof to the majority of the European population who denied that Aborigines had any entitlement to compensation. The Board recommended that all Aborigines except 'educated' workers employed by Europeans should be 'confined' to their reserves and prohibited from visiting towns and goldfields and urged the formation of settlements supervised by missionaries where some residents could be taught to farm while others supported themselves by hunting and fishing.[12] The Board also sought to have their commission amended by new legislation giving the Governor power to make orders about the residence and maintenance of Aborigines and the custody of orphaned and deserted children. All of these recommendations were remedies for the Board's current problems with Europeans who took away workers and abandoned them, kept children as servants in unsavoury circumstances, paid workers in drink and mistreated those camped near European settlements. There was no conscious principle of racial segregation. Board members had neither the imagination nor the funds to invent a policy of apartheid.

Indeed, the Board envisaged that Aborigines could and would be trained to protect themselves from Europeans and would take their place as self-supporting labourers in colonial society. Members assumed this would be achieved on a community rather than individual basis, for they were well aware of the Aborigines' loyalties and the extent of European prejudice. There was no notion of individual assimilation in 1861. Thomas had warned the 1858 Select Committee of the pitiable state of those Aborigines reared

---

12 BPA – Annual Report 1861:10.

4. MR GREEN'S WAY

in isolation by Europeans. They had no family ties, few friends among those they equalled in education and training and no hope of marriage.[13] During the 1850s he had tried to help the Aboriginal tailor Charles Nevers and others separated from their own kind by such philanthropic experiments. Indeed, he and the Board members were currently concerned about Thomas Bungeleen, the Kurnai lad educated at Merri Creek and other Melbourne schools. Bungeleen had disliked his training as a seaman but proved an excellent draughtsman in the Mines Department under Smyth. Yet he found acceptance only in 'low company' as his fellow officers would not associate with him after hours. Like all the others, he died young.[14]

The policy framed by these Board members, and their successors, was in fact never a coherent articulated set of principles guiding administration. Rather it was succession of *ad hoc* decisions constrained by budget limitations and individual members' beliefs about the nature of Aboriginal and European society and what seemed to them morally right and administratively possible. Morality had prevailed for the Woiworung: 1,200 acres (486 ha) of their land was at last gazetted for a school in January 1862. Wonga had taken Thomas up for a week's visit in November to see Mary Green's school for six Woiworung children and his enthusiastic reports to Smyth had been used to persuade officialdom.[15] The Taungurong, however, would have to settle for what was possible.

In the first week of 1862 the Board asked Hickson to resign. He was offered three months notice but left at the end of January, angry at being told he was unsuitable and at the 'impertinence' of the Taungurong who would not obey him once Green told them he no longer had authority. Green was there to locate the new reserve Duffy had promised but it was hopeless: no lease-holder would give up a portion of his run. He had to compromise, choosing a new homestead site five miles (8 km) north but still within the boundaries of the purchased property. Green came again to take charge on 13 February but when he warned that Jones' station was useless the Board resolved to break it up; correspondents could issue supplies to any Taungurong who preferred to remain in the district.

But by this time Green's family and all the Woiworung were walking to the Acheron station. Green had secured Board permission to cut a new track through the bush in a direct line from Yering to the headwaters of the Goulburn River – to 'benefit the miners' who were now moving into this district in search of gold.[16]

On 13 March they arrived. There were 55 Taungurong and Woiworung camped at the new location with Mary Green and her children (left in the care of Wonga and Barak) when Green set off for a two-month tour of Gippsland. Bitterly resenting Glass' repossession of their chosen home, and frustrated by the continuing shortage of food and tools, the Taungurong had little heart for this third attempt at clearing, fencing and building homes for themselves.

At the end of April Thomas complained to the Board secretary that Green should not leave his wife so much alone: he was 'too sanguine and confident in the blacks' and the Greens would not be safe with them until they had 'permanently secured their confidence'. This was partly due to the envy of his successor: he had protested that at 68 he was still capable of inspecting for the Board but Green was appointed

---

13 Legislative Council 1858–59:40.
14 Bungeleen was placed in Thomas' charge on 15 March 1861; his fate is described by Green (Royal Commission 1877:84), and in Board reports (BPA – Annual Report 1861:8, 1862:14, 1864:12, 1866:18).
15 William Thomas to Smyth, 30 November 1861.
16 BPA – Minutes 4 November 1861. Massola (1975:12, 14) reports local European belief that the pack-horse track to Woods Point was originally blazed by two Englishmen, suggesting it was used by Green's party only when they left Acheron for Coranderrk. He published two photographs from the La Trobe library labelled 'The Yarra Tribe Starting for the Acheron, 1862' and 'Celebrating the First Service on Arrival'; the latter seems to include Jajowrong brought to Coranderrk in 1864; the number of children assembled and their apparent ages suggest that this photograph was taken at the same time as Green's own Coranderrk album of 1867 (the Charles Walter photographs now in the National Museum of Victoria).

and his own salary was reduced from £600 to £450 in 1862. Thomas admired and was concerned for Mary Green but his letter was also a criticism of Green's egalitarian attitude to the Kulin and his method of encouraging them to manage their affairs for themselves. Thomas warned the Board secretary that Aborigines 'need to fear you as well as love you before you are safe'.[17] Smyth, something of a despot in his own Mines Department, also disapproved of Green's use of what would today be called 'community development' techniques. Green did hire a servant, Thomas Harris, as a result of their reproaches but he never would treat the Kulin as anything but free men and women equal to himself in all but knowledge of European ways. He eventually lost his job because he upheld this principle; his son and namesake later died in New Guinea because he shared his father's beliefs.[18]

On 5 May 1862 Green wrote to Thomas reporting that the Taungurong and Woiworung were getting on well together at the new camp site on Jones' station, but all said it was too cold for them. He was as discouraged as they: most of the Kulin were sick; so were his three children; even his horses were failing from the cold. Barak's 20-year-old wife Lizzie had died and so had the Woiworung child 'Little Mr Green'. On the same day he wrote advising the Board it would be 'folly to spend sixpence more' on the place as cultivation could never repay expenses. Only 43 Kulin remained there: 'a good many of the blacks had left a few days after I left for Gippsland. Those that have left do not like this place. My Yarra blacks do not like it either, but while I remain here they will also remain'.

He advocated removal to the reserve on the Yarra, confident that 'the greater part of the Goulburn blacks would settle down with the Yarra blacks as the Yarra blacks has done with them'. But their Woori Yalloak reserve was already unsuitable – miners' tracks crossed it and two public houses had been built nearby. On 6 June 1862 Green informed the Board that the Kulin at Jones' station had agreed to give the new location a 'fair trial' for a year. He and his servant Harris were working with them, building huts and fencing. He said he urgently needed £30 to purchase bullocks before they could begin farming but did not requisition clothing as the men still had money earned by working for neighbours. He warned that clothing would have to be supplied when they worked full-time on their own station and had no cash income.

On 11 July Green informed Thomas the Board had decided he was to establish the new school; he said the Woiworung and his wife were glad to be returning to the Yarra. A month later he was authorised to select another reserve but the Watts River site he chose with the Woiworung clan-heads was not gazetted for five months. On 26 September he wrote to tell Thomas the 69 Kulin with him had not yet been instructed to move although the parents had consented to send all 24 children to the new school. Mary Green was already teaching 15 children and eight young men and women. Green praised Simon Wonga who was very helpful especially when disputes occurred. These were usually settled by a 'court of four magistrates' (the four clan-heads at the station) who had recently decided no man should have more than one wife. The only man with two wives was the Yowung-illam-balluk 'magistrate' Mr King (Moornalook, c. 1806–1867) and he had given one to a younger man. The court had also agreed that no woman should be married without her own consent and that of her parents or nearest kinsman. Green's letter closed with a report that Wonga was 'almost a Christian'; his cousin Barak had been for some time 'a real Christian'.

---

17 William Thomas to Smyth, 12 March and 26 April 1862; BPA – Annual Report 1861:6.
18 John Green Jr. (1865–1897), an Assistant Resident Magistrate commended by his superior Monckton as the best man the New Guinea administration ever possessed, was renowned for his fearlessness, linguistic skills, and 'faculty of gaining a native people's confidence'. He was killed in 1897 by Binandere tribesmen who had asked him to disarm his police escort to show his trust. His reputation as a just man was not forgotten: in 1976 the Doepo clan of Datama village, Ioma, Northern Province, named their progress association 'Misi Giriri [Mr Green] Association' (Monckton 1921:77–82; *Age*, 26 February 1897; Barereba 1964; Waiko 1970; John Waiko, personal communication).

In fact the delay in moving was occasioned by uncertainty about the site, future funding and Green's own position. The Board's first published report had said an inspector was necessary to supervise correspondents and missionaries. This roused antagonism and Green's reports on his tours of Gippsland and the Western District in 1862 roused more, for he had questioned the honesty of certain pastoralists entrusted with supplies. There was some competition for appointment as correspondents because such depots tethered Aboriginal workers to the locality and assured employers of a convenient labour force. The Board publicly upheld their inspector. But Heales' successor as Premier and Chief Secretary, the landowner John O'Shanassy whose run near Echuca relied on local Aboriginal labour, challenged Green's appointment in August 1862.[19]

On 2 September Heales, Langlands and Jennings interviewed O'Shanassy, Minister responsible for the Board. He agreed to retain Green on a temporary basis and arrange a pension for William Thomas. He approved, with minor amendments, Smyth's draft of a Bill for the protection of Aborigines. But he said Board plans for a central school must await the next Estimates. At the end of the month, they asked for £8,600; they got £6,500 and after battle in Parliament Heales obtained £400 more. They cut costs to save for school buildings so they would not have to defer for another year their plan to 'rescue the half caste children from a life of infamy'.[20] Again a letter from Mary Green to William Thomas was used to win government sympathy: she had written reporting she was alone while Green toured the Murray, had only three weeks food left and hoped soon to move to the Yarra as she feared for the children in her school, 'exposed to so much vice for want of a proper place to put them'.[21]

The 1858 Select Committee had been told of the Bunurong leader Derrimut's despair as the immigrants built homes on his land – 'you haves all this place, no good have children' and Thomas had fought every European move to interfere with the Bunurong camp at Mordialloc. When he visited in November 1862 Derrimut angrily asked why he 'let white man take away Mordialloc where black fellows always sit down'. The Lands Board had approved its sale and surveyors were already dividing it into allotments. The Bunurong feared they would soon see 'ploughs furrowing up the bones of their ancestors'. Thomas knew their dead had been buried there since 1839 and protested to the Central Board about the 'cruelty' of the survey department. He begged Smyth to intervene, knowing he was a protege of the Surveyor General: 'he would not rob the blacks of land but Mr Hodgkinson [his deputy] would sell every portion they "doted" on and remove the whole race to Phillip or French Island'. When Smyth protested he was told the area had never been gazetted as an Aboriginal reserve and was a common for European use. The Lands Board had again made a decision to alienate land occupied by Aborigines without consulting the Central Board.[22]

The Board saved for the school buildings by reducing the rations issued throughout the colony. The policy enunciated in a December 1862 circular to all correspondents, and published in the 1863 annual report, specified that 'able and healthy blacks should be encouraged to provide, as far as possible, for their own and the wants of their families'.[23] This was both necessary, because the Parliamentary vote was inadequate, and proper in the minds of the self-made men who composed the Board. The underlying philosophy was that of the British poor laws which demanded that the indigent, for the good of their souls, support themselves and their kin by working for their food. As a historian describing similar

---

19 BPA – Minutes 11 and 25 August 1862; BPA – Annual Report 1863:4, 7–10; 1864:11. See Daniel Mathews Papers and Cato 1976 for information on O'Shanassy's run.
20 BPA – Annual Report 1863:3–4, 6.
21 William Thomas to Robert Brough Smyth, 21 November 1862.
22 Thomas to Smyth, November 1862; Legislative Council, Victoria 1858–59:12, Thomas to Surveyor General 19 June 1863.
23 BPA – Annual Report 1863:5.

policies for indigenous North Americans has pointed out, nineteenth-century officials 'not yet exposed to doctrines of social welfare' thought that there was 'something obscene about grown men and women drawing rations'.[24]

Board staff were influencing policy also. The 1861 annual report had merely recommended medical aid in 'certain cases', noting that the Board's Inspector would investigate correspondents' reports that Aborigines would not go to European doctors. Smyth's December 1862 circular instructed correspondents to call doctors at Board expense whenever necessary. It specified that the central school was also to be a refuge where the sick could obtain medical aid. Green had apparently acquired some medical knowledge before he left Scotland and, to the end of his days, was consulted by Europeans in the vicinity of Coranderrk.[25] His ministrations were surely as effective as those of Dr Embling who recommended a 'soap and sugar plaster' for nearly every ailment suffered by Aborigines at the Board's second station.[26]

But Board policy was subject to challenge in Parliament, and within a month of receiving the circular one of the Board's correspondents gave notice of a motion for a Legislative Assembly Select Committee 'to inquire into the best means of improving the present condition of the Aborigines'. On 5 February 1863, he named himself, Snodgrass and another correspondent plus the Premier, the Leader of the Opposition (Heales) and three others, one of them Barak's teacher in 1837. At least one missionary was called to give evidence but no report was ever submitted to Parliament. The main burden of the mover's dissatisfaction, it would seem from the Premier's reply, was his belief that pastoral employers rather than police magistrates should be responsible for disbursing funds. The Board had previously asked this correspondent to make inquiries about a nearby pastoralist who paid workers in liquor. He did not reply for five months and then asked to be excused from investigating the case.[27] Green had obtained this information on his tour of the Murray and found more evidence of misappropriation of supplies on a second tour of the Western District in 1863. Presumably, the evidence silenced Parliamentary critics, for there was almost no comment on Board administration for four years. Green's permanent appointment as General Inspector, at £300 a year including travelling expenses, was subsequently confirmed.

The longest-serving Moravian missionary later recalled that this Select Committee, chaired by Heales, had instructed the Lands Minister, Duffy, to grant the reserves required. He believed he was the only witness examined about the proposed school; he had favoured the plan and the site and recommended Green as its superintendent.[28] In fact the Board had authorised expenditure of £350 for buildings and instructed Green to bring the Kulin to the Yarra on 26 January before the Select Committee was appointed. Green himself recalled that he accepted the Inspector's post on condition he was allowed to collect orphaned children on his tours and 'make a home for them'.[29]

After four years of struggle and disappointment the home the Taungurong deputation had asked for was abandoned. Thomas felt great bitterness that the government had broken its 'covenant' with them and condemned the 'villainy' of the transaction with Jones: the Taungurong had lost their Acheron reserve and their faith in European promises 'all because a needy broken down squatter owed for £800 to two merchants, I believe, one in the upper House, one in the lower, his station was bought by Government – £1000 – the blacks ordered there'.[30]

---

24 Hagan 1976:161.
25 *Healesville Guardian*, 4 September 1908; this obituary comments that he was remembered with 'grateful kindliness' for his care of the sick.
26 Barwick 1971:307.
27 Victorian *Hansard*, 4 December 1862, 5 February 1863; BPA – Minutes 11 August 1862, 26 January, 2 March, 14 July 1863.
28 Royal Commission 1877:37; Coranderrk Inquiry 1881:45. Marcard (1964:29) suggests that appointment of this Select Committee is evidence that the Board was not intended to draft and guide official policy. It seems more probable that it was motivated by spite but Heales shrewdly used the opportunity to achieve Board aims.
29 BPA – Minutes 26 January 1863; Royal Commission 1877:130.
30 William Thomas, 'Notes to self' for Report of 30 June 1863 (Thomas Papers).

4. MR GREEN'S WAY

The 3,000 acre (1214 ha) Watts River reserve had been gazetted in December 1862, when the Woori Yalloak site was cancelled, but Kulin occupation was again contested by a pastoralist in the Upper Yarra district. Fearing that neighbours' hostility would become a chronic hindrance here as it had at the Acheron, the Board cancelled tenders for buildings and resolved to seek yet another locality. But the Greens and their four children (including a new baby), the Woiworung families and the younger Taungurong – 40 in all – were already walking to the new reserve on the track they had blazed a year earlier. They travelled at a pace the children and the cattle could manage and were frequently delayed by accidents to the one overburdened dray. In March 1863 they formed a new home at an old camping place in Wurundjeri-balluk territory. Their chosen site, where the Coranderrk (Badger) Creek joined the Yarra, adjoined the contested tract that had been reserved for them. Both areas were part of an out-station of the Yering run occupied by the Ryrie brothers until 1850. Wonga and Barak had frequented this district since their childhood.[31]

Sir Henry Barkly, Governor of Victoria from December 1856 to September 1863, showed no particular interest in Aborigines until 1859 when he presided over a distribution of blankets at Geelong. The Kulin, however, had for years been told that the Queen had explicitly commissioned the Governor to protect Aborigines and were apparently aware that his formal consent was required for the reservation of land.[32] The leaders of the camp at Coranderrk Creek originated the idea of attending the Governor's public levee, open to all gentlemen, on 24 May 1863. The whole colony was celebrating the recent marriage of the Prince of Wales as well as the Queen's birthday and the Kulin decided they too would send gifts to equip Prince Albert for his role as a married man. Learning two days beforehand of their plan to walk to Melbourne with weapons for the Prince and rugs and baskets for the Queen, Smyth hastily sent for William Thomas to help draft and translate a loyal address in the express hope that this would win sympathy for the Aborigines from the 'Home Government'. Wonga gracefully presented the written address with a speech in Woiwurru. Wonga, Barak, two more Woiworung and two Bunurong men, eight men and five boys from various Taungurong clans and one man of the 'Pangeran tribe' formed the deputation. They spoke good English. They had a few words with their host, Sir Henry Barkly, about their need for land.

The reservation of 2,300 acres (931 ha) for their use on 30 June 1863 was probably coincidental. Gazettal of this first portion of the Coranderrk reserve was perhaps hastened by the fact that Heales, the Board's president, had replaced Duffy as Lands Minister in a new coalition government three days earlier. But the timing of this decision, whatever its cause, encouraged the Kulin to believe in the efficacy of deputations to men who could influence governments. Subsequently, the Coranderrk people were sent copies of the Queen's letter assuring them of her protection. These letters helped to establish their belief, still voiced by descendants in the 1970s, that Coranderrk was the direct gift of the Queen and Sir Henry Barkly and belonged to them and their heirs in perpetuity.[33]

But the sale of the Mordialloc reserve was announced a week later. Thomas had written privately begging the new Lands Minister, Heales, to intervene and had sent Green to protest to the survey office, but in vain.[34] The Bunurong lost the last of their territory. Derrimut, half-crazed with grief, drank himself to

---

31 Guillaume de Pury had held this land 1855–1858. The pastoralist W. Nicholson strongly protested reservation of any part of his Dairy station (Aveling 1972:16–19; Massola 1975:14; BPA – Annual Report 1864; BPA – Minutes, 30 March 1863).
32 As yet the only land reserved for Kulin use was the acreage gazetted in June 1860 by the Governor – not, as later, by the Governor-in-Council – for the Kurung clans.
33 BPA – Annual Report 1863:11; 1864:12, 20.
34 Thomas' private notes for his June 1863 report cryptically comment: 'determination of Survey office, Mr. Green bashed or threatened with police to drive him off'.

death within the year. The 'saviour of Melbourne' was only 53. The two young Bunurong men who found wives at Coranderrk reared families there, but nine old men and women remained near Mordialloc and Cranbourne where the last of them died in 1877.

The Jajowrong at Mount Franklin sent their gifts to the Queen independently with two letters penned by young Ellen, daughter of the farmer Dicky who had died in 1862 'as most Aborigines do, of disease of the lungs'.[35] Ellen had made a crocheted collar for the Queen and a doily for the wife of the departing Governor. The collar was specifically mentioned in the Queen's reply which asked Ellen to make known the Queen's interest in their welfare. Mount Franklin was the centre of a goldfields area and the teacher complained that the 'diggings and the drink were a curse'. Jajowrong parents took their children from the school when they went away to work. Thomas, sent to report in February, urged the Board to replace the disgraceful school building and develop this station. But Smyth had toured the goldfields too and saw no hope of protecting the Jajowrong from mistreatment; on 7 July 1863 the Board accepted his recommendation to move the Jajowrong to the new central school.

On 28 July 1863 Green wrote from 'Coranderrk Aboriginal Station'[36] to report that all of the Woiworung and many Taungurong were happily settled and all liked the site. He described their eager development of their new home:

> When the Board came to the conclusion that it would be better to abandon the Acheron Station and establish one on the Yarra, so strong was the desire for improvement by this time among the young men belonging to the Goulburn, that they all at once consented to leave, and go to the Yarra. After the young men consented, all the old ones consented also. And in the month of Feb'y when I started to proceed to the Yarra all the young men and two old ones started with me, and others sent their children as a token that they would soon follow. It is now four months since we arrived, and during that time there has been only one case of drunkness [sic] and not one of them have ever left the station without my leave. They have nearly finished nine bark huts. In the course of one week or so they will all be living in huts instead of their Willams; they have also during that time made as many rugs, which has enabled them to buy boots, hats, coats &c, &c, and some of them has even bought horses.

There had been no sickness and all had consented to be vaccinated. All attended prayers twice daily and kept the Sabbath 'better than many of the Europeans'. The children were obedient and 'easily learnt' and would make great progress when their school was built if they were 'properly managed'. Green had no doubt that the Kulin would support themselves and their children within two years – if 'properly managed'. Green not only emphasised this point but spelt out his meaning:

> My method of managing the blacks is to allow them to rule themselves as much as possible. When there is any strife among them this is always settled at a kind of court, at which I preside.

Nineteenth-century Victorian officials generally believed that Aborigines were a 'childlike race' requiring authoritarian direction and paternalistic control. Green was the only one of the succession of managers who took charge of the six Aboriginal stations who ever entrusted full responsibility for discipline to the residents. He was almost unique in treating the Kulin as 'free and independent men and women'

---

35 William Thomas to Smyth, 20 February 1863; 17 August 1863; Ellen (1849/50-1874) was married at Coranderrk to the Brataualung man Thomas Arnott (Mayyurn 1843/44-1893) of Port Albert. Their three children died of tuberculosis.
36 The Woiworung name for the flowering 'Christmas Bush' (*Prostanthera lasianthos*) was Coranderrk, and this became the name of a stream where it was abundant. It was renamed Badger's Creek during the 1860s but the Aboriginal settlement on this stream retained the name of Coranderrk (BPA – Annual Report 1864:5, Shaw 1949:13).

who would work well if well led but would not be driven.[37] He considered them equal to Europeans in intelligence and superior in honesty and truthfulness; there were no locks at Coranderrk for eight years until strangers came.

He disapproved of coercion and insisted that the only effective method of bringing about change was by example and explanation. He believed that:

> They are very proud and sensitive, and you can work a great deal upon their pride: in that way you can make them see that it is disgraceful to take what they have not earned.

From 1863 all men (and by 1865 all adults) participated in the court which laid down rules of conduct and punished offenders by administering fines, withdrawing privileges or imposing the ultimate sanction of banishment. Because work at Acheron station had been continually disrupted by neighbours' attempts to hire the able-bodied men, the Kulin soon ruled that none could work elsewhere without the consent of this general assembly. Moreover, those who went shearing or took other employment off Coranderrk must hand over their wages to Green who acted as their banker. He found that 'compulsion would make them kick against it, but if they get a voice in it themselves, and they once pass it as a law of their own, they would stick to it'.

Green chaired these assemblies when he was at home. When he spoke and argued he usually relied upon his moral authority as a respected leader, in the traditional manner of the *ngurungaeta*, rather than his externally imposed powers as manager. No resident could leave Coranderrk 'without the sanction of all upon the station' and Green described his own role at such an assembly when a newcomer wished to leave:

> … I asked the aborigines to give their views first, and they said, 'Oh well, he can go; all right'. I said he should go, so I stood up and said, 'You can go, that is the way here. You are a smart young man, Jimmy, and you have a nice smart wife; here you have a capital home, everything is your own here, but whenever you go away over to the station there you will be standing up at the door, "Please ma'am a drop of cold tea, any cold meat". "Get away you dirty fellow". And now, Jimmy, are you a man there now?' Jimmy saw his position at once, and he said, 'I will not go' … he did not like the picture of himself being driven away asking for bread.[38]

Extracts from his journals show their sanctions for drunkenness:

> 13/4/65 Had a long court today, about Buckley, Locket, Dick [Richards], Davey [Hunter], and Andrew drinking a bottle of grog; and there was a law made (this day) that every one should be fined 5s. for the first offence; for the second offence 10s.; for the third offence, if any young man he would forfeit all right to a wife from among the young women on the station – (it was a rule that none could get married to any of the young women until they had been two years on the station) – and for married men £1.
>
> – Agreed to by all the Aborigines on the station, 110 in all.
>
> 4/5/65 Had court today about drunkenness; several were fined 15s. viz., Timothy, Jemmy Webster [Jr], Dick, Morgan, Johnny Webster, and Jemmy Barber [Barker].[39]

---

37 Royal Commission 1877:82, 85–6; Coranderrk Inquiry 1881:128.
38 Royal Commission 1877:86.
39 Royal Commission 1877:81.

But Green did try to impose his own notions of morality, as another diary entry shows:

> 5/2/66 Jemmy Webster [Jr] was ordered to leave the station today, for lying with Harriet, and for threatening to stick Simon, when he reproved him for his wickedness. I told all that were not going to stand to the right way that they would have to leave with him. But all said that they were going to stand on the side of right.

There were only two extramarital liaisons at Coranderrk between 1863 and 1875: in this first case, all of the men resolved the offender should be sent away until he was willing to marry the woman. They detected the second case, when a European teacher seduced a girl after promising to marry her, and insisted on his dismissal.[40]

The sophistication of the Kulin at Coranderrk and their determination to manage their own affairs amazed and annoyed other officials. And it impressed visitors, notably the Royal Commissioners who visited in 1877: their report commented that the Coranderrk residents' 'bearing and demeanour form a contrast with those of the natives on all the other stations'.[41] Green's method of management had made the difference; but it roused the antagonism of other Europeans determined to impose their notions of discipline on the Kulin.

---

40   Royal Commission 1877:87; Coranderrk Inquiry 1881:134.
41   Royal Commission 1877:xi.

Chapter 5
PROPRIETORS FOR THE FIRST DECADE

> Bad white men have nearly killed all our men and women … Before the white people came to our country we were all very happy together; but when they came they gave us grog, and it made us mad. Then we became unhealthy, and began to die off.
>
> At that time there were a great many men, women, and children, but now there are but few of us. But since we began to settle and live in our own houses, we have improved much. We are now happier, and glad to see so many children about us. Some are coming home; they are now tired of the bush.
>
> (Translation from Woiwurru 1863)[1]

Green had listed the names of the 117 surviving members of Woiworung, Taungurong and Ngurai-illam-wurrung clans in his July 1863 letter to the Board. Within a year 67 were settled at Coranderrk. By June 1865 there were 107 Kulin there. The dormitory held 34 children whose parents were not present, and others lived in the new dwellings. Two clan heads who had founded Acheron station, Mr King of the Yowung-illam-balluk and Baundaurrong (Mr Cotton, c. 1806–1871) of the Waring-illam-balluk and their wives walked to Coranderrk with the children and young men in 1863 to see that all was well.[2] Yet they and a handful of Taungurong elders always preferred to spend much of their time in their own country about Yea, Alexandra and Mansfield. Most of them died there.

By this time there were few aged Taungurong and none had apparently shown opposition to the new religion introduced by Green. Christian burial was universal from 1861 and by 1864 the old men were 'much pleased' that a 'fine coffin' was made for every funeral.[3] Old Jemmy Webster (Wildgung, c. 1806–1874), father of one of the 1859 deputation members, had accepted Green's teaching because he believed Green was his deceased brother reincarnated:

> He clung to Mr Green as to his real brother, and always took up his abode as near as possible to him, displaying the utmost confidence and esteem, and invariably telling him where he was going when he went to fish or hunt. When he spoke of matters which had occurred in his brother's lifetime he expected Mr Green to join in the conversation, as if he knew all about the events. To all Mr Green's protestations of ignorance he would reply in the most serious manner: 'you no 'member – you forget – you not tumble down (die) yet. That long time before you tumble down.' When Mr Green spoke in his hearing of what was revealed

---

1   Translation by John Green (Smyth 1878:I 111–12).
2   Mr King's son Charley King died soon after the 1859 deputation and his daughter Kitty in 1861 but his widowed daughter Sarah and her sons Henry and William Nash lived out their brief lives at Coranderrk. Baundaurrong was childless by 1861.
3   John Green to William Thomas, 23 June 1864 (Thomas Papers).

in Scripture concerning the unseen world, Jamie implicitly believed, and his assurance was confirmed that his brother had come from the dead, and was simply relating what he had seen and heard in another world.[4]

His sons, Jemmy Jr (Burruppin, 1835–1879) and John Webster (Banadruk, 1837–1876), remained ardent supporters of Green to the annoyance of later managers.

Another influential Taungurong ally was Tommy Bamfield (Birdarak, c. 1844–1893) who succeeded his father Baalwick as clan-head of the Yeerun-illam-balluk and in maturity became Barak's chief aide. Tommy (also known by the surnames Mansfield and Michie and nicknamed Punch for his exceptional girth) had been born at Benalla but Baalwick led the survivors of this clan to John Bon's Wappan run near Mansfield after 1846. Most of this 'Devil's River' group had joined the Acheron community in 1860 but Bamfield maintained a lifelong friendship with Bon's widow, Mrs Anne Fraser Bon (1837–1936), who felt a special responsibility for this 'young King of the Broken River tribe' entrusted to her care by 'his mother the Chiefess'. Bamfield, a famous shearer, continued to visit Wappan each year at shearing time and Mrs Bon's home in Melbourne became a refuge for Coranderrk people. This friendship had considerable importance in saving Coranderrk because the socially prominent widow was an ardent philanthropist who had considerable influence in political, medical and Presbyterian church circles in Melbourne.[5]

Between 1864 and 1866 most survivors of the Jajowrong, Kurung and Wathaurung clans joined their Kulin neighbours at Coranderrk. After his second tour of the goldfields Smyth complained of the filth and disorder at the Mount Franklin school and urged that the children and any adults willing to leave be transferred. When the Board cautiously asked local correspondents if they objected Parker strongly opposed closure of the settlement he had begun in 1841, asserting that the Jajowrong would not join enemy tribes. Yet when Thomas and Green visited in March 1864 only two parents refused to let their children go.[6] Parker had never understood how the rules of clan and moiety exogamy cut across the clan and dialect affiliations which he had discovered in his enumerations of the Jajowrong and their neighbours during the 1840s.

Many Mount Franklin people had kinsmen among the Woiworung and Taungurong at Coranderrk, and the decision to move was strongly supported by the Taungurong woman Eliza (Biebie, c. 1833–1886) who for years had acted 'like a mother' to the children at this school. William Thomas was delighted to hear this 'amiable widow' of the farmer Dicky haranguing other Mount Franklin people to 'leave of that beastly drink'. Green too was impressed, informing the Board that Eliza was 'sharp, shrewd, industrious, able to look after her own; as civilised and as careful as any white woman, and as domesticated'.[7]

Eliza, who had believed all members of her Nira-balluk clan of the Kilmore district dead, found her mother and brother at Coranderrk when she, four Jajowrong adults and seven children arrived on 20 April 1864. The letters written by her daughter Ellen did much to reassure the Jajowrong left behind, who voluntarily brought all the children to Coranderrk within the year although some parents returned to their own country after satisfying themselves that the youngsters would be safe at Coranderrk in the care of the Greens and their Kulin relatives.[8]

---

4   Hamilton 1888:App. E.
5   Sutherland 1888:524–5; Anne F. Bon to Chief Secretary, CSIC 82/X4907, 29 May 1882.
6   BPA – minutes 4 December 1863; E.S. Parker to Smyth, 28 January 1864; Green to Smyth, 4 March 1864.
7   BPA – Green to Smyth, 5 March 1864; Thomas to Smyth, 20 February 1863.
8   Morrison 1967a:98; Green to Thomas, 23 June 1864 (Thomas Papers).

5. PROPRIETORS FOR THE FIRST DECADE

Beembarmin – Tommy Farmer of Mount Franklin, c. 1867.

The land grant at Mount Franklin was already deserted as the last of the four owners had sought work on the goldfields when his bullocks died. Tommy Farmer soon brought his wife Norah from Carngam to Coranderrk where he became ploughman. Although the head of Farmer's Gal-gal-bulluk clan had served as aide to Captain Turnbull (maternal uncle of Wonga and Barak's father)[9] two decades earlier, this clan and Barak's clan were of the same moiety and thus Farmer had no claim through intermarriage and descent to reside at Coranderrk and had little influence. He was frequently absent on protracted visits to the former Protectorate employee who had reared him and remembered him as 'a smart smal [sic] boy and clean of a discerning mind and quick at asking questions'.[10] The adjacent Wurrung-hura-gerung-bulluk clan of Jajowrong had made marriages with Barak's clan but the two surviving men, Peter Werry (Weragoondeet) and Harry Nelson (Karkom), were dead before the Coranderrk community was seriously threatened.

One child from the Mount Franklin school, Tommy Dunolly (1856–1923), had been taken to Coranderrk before July 1863, probably by his mother Harriet and Jajowrong stepfather Jemmy Warren (Corownang). They brought Dunolly's half-brother John Charles (c. 1849–1884) to the dormitory in 1864 but it was not until 1866 that they settled at Coranderrk with Dunolly's elder sister 'Ellen of Carngham' (c. 1846–1921) who subsequently married the Taungurong elder Dick Richards (Wyerdierum, 1838/39–1907) of Kilmore. All three of Harriet's 'half caste' children were prominent in the long fight to prevent the closing of Coranderrk but Dunolly had a special role: from the late 1870s this lad was one of the three spokesmen to whom the clan-head Barak 'gave his words' and Barak told A.W. Howitt that he intended to name Dunolly as a *ngurungaeta*.

---

9   Howitt 1904:310, MS:54.
10 BPA – James Bodkin to A.M.A. Page, 13 July 1879.

The only elder among the 20 Jajowrong who had settled at Coranderrk by 1866 was the celebrated *wirrarap* Malcolm (Dindarmin c. 1813–1869), who brought his wife and 'half caste' daughter Caroline (1844–1889). She also was prominent in the troubled years.

The next to come were the inland clans of Kurung and Wathaurung. In 1865 the Board's correspondent at Carngham reported that the survivors of the Mount Emu, Mount Cole, Ballarat and Wandyallock clans travelled separately in small bands of 10 or 12 people, subsisting by making rugs, baskets and nets for sale and occasionally working for pastoralists. They had asked for a reserve near Chepstowe 'where they might make a paddock, and grow wheat and potatoes, and erect permanent residences'. The correspondent reported that the site had game and water, and the young men were 'very anxious about it' now that they had heard of Coranderrk. He had recommended the removal of seven youths, with their parents' consent, early in the year. After the children boarded the train the parents of four had decided to follow them on foot:

> The parents remained at Coranderrk for upwards of four months, and then returned to inform the tribe of the comfort and happiness they had witnessed in the blackfellows' township, as they called it. On hearing their story, which was very interesting, the king made up his mind to take the whole tribe, and go to see the blackfellows' township.[11]

Balybalip (c. 1823–1881), known as Billy Phillips or 'King Billy of Ballarat' and his family remained at Coranderrk; the Kulin did not force him to give up his second wife in accordance with their new rule.

By 1866 most of the surviving Kulin had been gathered in except for the few old Wathaurung at Geelong and Bunurong at Mordialloc, and one family of Ngurai-illam-wurrung finally brought from Murchison in 1874. The Kulin clans were all together for the first time since the great meetings in Melbourne during the 1840s. There is no evidence to show whether they tried to revive and continue the old religion: the Board's correspondence and Green's diaries for this period have vanished and in any case Europeans were usually oblivious of Aboriginal belief. But it seems unlikely. Wonga and Barak had gone through the basic initiation ritual at puberty but Kulin religious ceremonies had been disrupted by the end of the 1840s.[12] In Wonga's mind, at least, Coranderrk was to be a Christian community. He made this plain in a speech to the Taungurong early in 1865 (although the occasion, Green's birthday, may have influenced his sentiments):

> Mr Green and all the Yarra blacks and me went through the mountains. We had no bread for four or five days. We did this to let you know about the good word. Now you have come to the Yarra. I am glad.[13]

A flourish of marriages followed. The mortality of the 1850s and dispersal on pastoral stations had made it difficult for the surviving members of Kulin clans to find spouses. Now they set about forming new ties in the old way. Then they validated the alliances with a new kind of ceremonial. Green's friend Rev. Robert Hamilton had maintained his interest in the Kulin since 1861 and made regular visits once Coranderrk was established. From 1865 to 1874 he solemnised every marriage in the Presbyterian form. The first wedding occurred on 26 January 1865, when old Malcolm's daughter Caroline married John Ferguson, a Taungurong from Kilmore who had been a member of the 1863 deputation to the Governor's

---

11 BPA – Annual Report 1866:13. In July 1868 there were still 42 adults at Carngham, but all of their children were at Coranderrk. They never were granted a reserve.
12 Barak was initiated by the Woiworung clan heads Captain Turnbull, Billibellary and Billy Lonsdale (Howitt MS:8). The last great intertribal assembly near Melbourne was held in 1852, for Thomas interrupted attempts by the Kurnai and Wathaurung to recruit the Acheron folk in 1860 and 1861.
13 Rev. Robert Hamilton, in *Illustrated Australian News* of 25 August 1865, quoted in Massola (1975:13).

levee. On 25 February there was a double wedding: Eliza married the suitor Peter Werry who had followed her from Mount Franklin, and Barak remarried. With the consent of the Presbyterian General Assembly Hamilton conducted the first baptism, of 27 adults instructed by Green, in September 1865. The Kulin pioneers always clung to the Presbyterian form of worship, to the chagrin of later Anglican managers; in 1881, seven years after he left Coranderrk many still preferred to 'call themselves Scotchmen' and drive in to Green's chapel at Healesville on Sundays.[14]

Although there were only 22 Woiworung left in 1863, Wonga and Barak were the undoubted leaders of the Coranderrk community: this was proper, for they represented the land-owning clan. In his annual report for 1864 Smyth commended both leaders:

> Wonga and Barak, who had made homes for themselves at Coranderrk, are very intelligent men, and in their behaviour would compare favourably with the better class of other races.

Wonga was pre-eminent until his death. Thomas, Green and Smyth acknowledged that he had 'much influence for his people' and warmly praised his upright character, 'always gentle and courteous manner' and his skill as a great orator in his own language.[15] But he was childless when his wife Maria died in 1875, for their son, young Simon, had already been buried at Coranderrk. Wonga's mother had been a sister of Captain Turnbull, Mount Macedon clan-head, and Wonga's 'speaker' was a young Taungurong man who bore Turnbull's name. Ninggullabull or Jemmy Barker (1834–1880) was presumably related through his own maternal kin.[16] Barak's father's mother, Barla, was also a sister of captain Turnbull so he and Wonga were cousins. Wonga was the sole survivor of Billibellary's family after 1860, but Barak had a brother, the childless Harry Miller (Jellebyook c. 1837–1876) whose first wife was dead by 1870. He and his second wife Maggie, widow of the Woiworung Tommy Hobson, both died in the home of his sister Borat's son, Robert Wandin in 1876. After Borat's Kurnai husband had died she married the Bunurong Adam Clarke (Mongara, c. 1830–1870) but Wandin was the only one of her five children who lived to adulthood. He later married Jemima Burns (1855–1944), one of the Pangerang 'half castes' brought to Coranderrk in 1866 and was to be its last resident. Their 10 children kept the Woiwurru language alive in the twentieth century.[17]

The widower Barak's remarriage in February 1865 was an innovation – not because it was conducted by Presbyterian ritual with 60 Kulin and 40 Europeans as witnesses – but because it was the first union of a Woiworung with one of the matrilineal tribes to the west, beyond the Kulin pale. His wife Annie (Ra-gun, c. 1846–1881) came from Bumbang Station, below Euston on the Murray River. She had been abandoned in Melbourne by the squatter who had employed her as nurse girl for a year and who had praised her competence at every household task.[18] The Board, unable to afford her fare home, sent her to Coranderrk with her consent. She bore Barak one child, David, who, like his mother, died of tuberculosis in 1881.

---

14 Hamilton 1888:238–40; Coranderrk Inquiry 1881:44, 137.
15 Smyth 1878:I 9–10, 78; BPA Annual Report 1861.
16 The Woiworw1g had several sources of personal names: Wonga was named for his birthplace, but Barak's name was bestowed by a paternal relative, who named him 'after a son of his' (Howitt MS; Smyth 1878:I 55–58.
17 Hercus 1969:192–3; *Riverine Herald*, 4 April 1866.
18 Smyth to Thomas 27 June and 8 July 1863 (Thomas Correspondence).

Maria Wonga, Simon Wonga's wife, c. 1876. **Robert Wandin (1854–1908), nephew of William Barak at 11 years of age, c. 1876.**

Reconciliation of the Kulin marriage rule with that of their non-Kulin neighbours to the north-east was easy because they too had patrilineal moieties. Barak's clan had always exchanged wives with *bunjil* clan of Kwatkwat about Wangaratta,[19] despite the language difference. So too with the eastern Pangerang clans; Barak recalled that his clan had obtained wives from the clan above Benalla and the eastern Pangerang also married with Taungurong clans. These kin ties created their entitlement to live at Coranderrk. A Pangerang man had taken part in their deputation to the Governor in 1863 and the Kulin accepted responsibility for the Pangerang children brought to the dormitory between 1866 and 1870 by the Echuca merchant Daniel Matthews.[20] The few surviving Minyambuta to the east of the Taungurong were also considered marriageable despite the language difference: the Woiworung had welcomed these 'Mogullumbitch' when they came with their aged clan head – to Melbourne in 1845.[21]

The Kurnai of Gippsland fought with their Kulin neighbours until the mid-1840s. Their speech and their marriage rules were different. They too emphasised patrilineal descent, and their local groups obtained spouses from other localities, but the Kurnai had no moiety or other 'class' divisions.[22] Population decline caused by European intrusion encouraged the Woiworung and Bunurong to negotiate marriages with the western most Brataualung clan of Kurnai in 1847. In the 1850s Barak and his sister Borat were betrothed

---

19 Howitt MS, 1904:257; see also Curr 1883:231–4; Tindale 1974:207.
20 Matthews frequently visited Coranderrk and had ambitions to begin a similar refuge for the totally neglected Aborigines of New South Wales; he brought a dozen children here before he opened the Maloga Mission on his own land across the Murray in 1874 (Daniel Matthews, letter to *Age*, 29 May 1866; BPA – Annual Report 1871:5; Cato 1976; Barwick 1972).
21 William Thomas, Journal 20 March–18 April 1845; Thomas 1858:57, Bride 1969:98; Smyth 1878:I 136–7; Tindale 1974:204, 206; Great Britain 1844:281.
22 Howitt 1904:134–5, 171, 257, 272–4. Howitt suggests that elopement rather than betrothal was the norm for Kurnai marriage, but Elkin (1976:212) concludes that this may have been a consequence of the severe depopulation that occurred in this region by the 1870s.

to members of this clan. Because of the kinship ties formed by these marriages some Brataualung accepted the hospitality of the Woiworung at Coranderrk from 1863 instead of joining the rest of the Kurnai at two distant mission stations in eastern Gippsland.

The Kulin were ethnocentric: only they were truly human. Thomas had commented in the 1840s on their antipathy to the few Aborigines from Echuca and the Western District who came to Melbourne. The Kulin felt no solidarity with the distant clans whom they rarely met and did not marry. When Coranderrk was founded in 1863 no marriages linked the Kulin with the Mara-speaking clans of the Western District, the Wotjo-speakers of the Wimmera or the various tribes on the Murray River below Echuca. The matrilineal moieties of the Western District were elaborated on the Murray as section and subsection systems, while an intermediate form prevailed in the Wimmera.[23] Few people from western Victoria ever came to Coranderrk and those few had a claim because of their membership of, or links to, Kurung and Jajowrong clans on the margin of the Kulin area. Wonga probably organised the only exchange with the distant Mara-speaking clans of the Lake Condah district: his 'speaker' Jemmy Barker acquired a wife from that area in 1867 and a girl from Barker's Taungurong clan was married in 1870 to the Lake Condah man 'John Green' and returned there with him. The innovation was not repeated.

Aside from Barak's bride Annie, the Woiworung had no contact with the people of the lower Murray until 1872 when officials brought some Burapper from Mount Hope to Coranderrk. They were outsiders who had no kin ties here and no legitimate claim to Kulin hospitality. In Barak's youth the Woiworung had believed the Murray River clans at and below Echuca were dangerous sorcerers, unfriendly to the Kulin.[24] Probably the feeling was reciprocal, for when Green first visited the camp at Mount Hope in July 1870 the women and children consented to come but then hid from him. But the station owner wanted them removed because of mistreatment by his men and Green was notified that they wished to go to Coranderrk in January 1872; he escorted the women south and their male relatives and friends soon made their own way to Coranderrk.

During his absence in Gippsland a month later all 15 resolved to return to Mount Hope, stating that their rations were insufficient, but in the end decided to remain at Coranderrk.[25] As these Burapper men married the women they had followed, they could not be incorporated into the Kulin group by marriage. The social distance between them and the pioneers was accentuated when a later manager appointed them to jobs formerly held by Kulin who were still loyal to Green. But because these newcomers were 'half castes', a distinction important to Europeans, they interpreted the resulting hostility as 'caste' antagonism, rather than a dispute between Kulin who had rights on this land and newcomers who did not.

The Kulin had certain expectations about Coranderrk. It was to be their own farm and township where they managed things themselves: Green and other officials were to be helpers rather than guardians. They had enough of European bosses on the pastoral stations. As a matter of principle Green agreed, but he was driven by his own desire to reform and Christianise the Kulin and to rescue the neglected children he saw on his tours of inspection. The Board members wanted a successful school which would vindicate their beliefs about the capacity of Aborigines and enable them to obtain greater funds from Parliament for similar establishments. The farm was a lesser priority although the Board's bargaining power would be increased if the Kulin could support themselves. Smyth was by conviction an agnostic and was mainly concerned with the physical welfare of the Aborigines; but he was a proud man, always determined to

---

23   Howitt 1904:51–5, 120–9; Elkin 1976. The border clans of Jajowrong had worked out the equivalence of their own moieties with the matrilineal moieties or section systems of their western neighbours but other Kulin groups to the east and south rarely or never met clansmen from the Wimmera and Lower Murray before European intrusion (Howitt MS:66).
24   Howitt MS.
25   This pastoralist asked that the male workers be returned but the men refused (BPA – Annual Report 1871:5; Secretary's Letter Book: 8 January, 2 and 14 March 1872; Coranderrk Inquiry 1881:135; Royal Commission 1877:26–9, 83).

excel, and took a proprietary interest in the success of the Board's secular experiment at Coranderrk. At the end of six years the Board members were congratulating themselves on the Kulin achievement: 22 children equalled the performance of Europeans of their age in the 'Common Schools', the adults had 70 acres (28 ha) under crops, the population decline had been arrested and the Aborigines had been transformed without help from any church.

The Coranderrk school building, with attached dormitories for orphans and other children whose parents were not resident, was completed in December 1863. The Board secretary then sent out a circular to correspondents, asking about orphaned or abandoned children who should be brought in and any others their clansmen would willingly surrender. Their 1864 annual report admitted that the response was poor as the Kulin and their neighbours were kind to their children, reluctant to give them up and 'jealous of any interference with them by the whites'. The Board's 1864 and 1866 annual reports pleaded for legislation enabling them to take charge of children and young women neglected by their relatives or kept by pastoralists and publicans for immoral purposes, and to protect Aboriginal workers from employers who treated them 'rather as slaves than servants' and frequently abandoned them in Melbourne, penniless and far from home.[26]

Green and the Kulin experienced two new pressures from 1865: a Melbourne doctor was employed to make quarterly reports on sanitary conditions and prescribe for the sick; and the first of a series of unsatisfactory teachers arrived. Until September 1867 John and Mary Green did most of the teaching, assisted by senior pupils as was the fashion of the time. She taught the women and children for three hours daily, and he conducted a two-hour evening class for the working men. Almost every adult was illiterate, as only the exceptional pastoral employer gave Aboriginal workers or their dependents any instruction. But the Kulin were eager to learn: 11 children and 18 adults could read and write 'a fair round-hand' by July 1865, and by the time Green left in 1874, 30 adults and 37 children could read and write. Rev. Hamilton reported that many wished to learn 'that they might peruse the bible'; they also wanted to read newspapers, and to be able to write to distant relatives and former employers in order to arrange shearing contracts and holiday visits.[27] Eventually most adults could read but the complex skill of writing was much more difficult and many adults had to rely on the dormitory children who had more opportunity for tuition.

Green attacked the persistent prejudice that Aborigines were 'incapable of instruction', repeatedly reporting that there was no difference between 'blacks' and 'half castes' who were equally quick to learn. He found them equal to European students of the same age and as easy to teach as Europeans.[28] But despite the proofs supplied by Green and later teachers that Coranderrk children were as 'intelligent as the average class of white children', Europeans clung to the comfortable prejudice that this race was 'not perfectible' and thus, of course, required to be kept under discipline by Europeans.[29]

Green had promised the Kulin that Coranderrk would be their home forever if they worked to make it a productive farm. Building, fencing, clearing and cultivation proceeded during the 1860s with a speed Smyth considered 'truly astonishing'. The men, 'anxious to make the station self-supporting', organised themselves into four companies and managed the farming tasks with little supervision.

---

26 BPA – Annual Report 1864:10,12; 1866:17–18.
27 Royal Commission 1877:23; BPA – Annual Report 1866:5.
28 BPA – Annual Report 1865, 1869; Royal Commission 1877:84; Coranderrk Inquiry 1881:128.
29 Royal Commission 1877:79, 84, 92; Giglioli 1875:794.

5. PROPRIETORS FOR THE FIRST DECADE

Back cottage, Coranderrk, 1868.

Indeed, Green was absent for three to six months of each year inspecting the stations and ration depots while Mary Green was busy with her own large family and the care of up to 40 children in the dormitory.[30] Subsequent manager's wives received £50–100 a year to act as dormitory matrons and teach sewing but Mary Green was not paid although she also had charge of the school until a satisfactory teacher was appointed in 1867. Green paid his servant Thomas Harris until January 1866, when the Board hired him as farm overseer at £50 a year. Although teachers at other stations earned £100–150 a year and the four missionary managers had £200 a year from their churches, Green's annual salary remained fixed at £300 including travelling expenses. In 1872 he warned the Board that he would have to give up his post as he 'could not make ends meet' and was at last granted 10 shillings a day for expenses when he was actually on tour.[31]

The pioneers' affectionate loyalty was coupled with respect: they always used the title Mr Green. But Thomas Harris was called Tom and the men regarded him as 'quite one of themselves'. This scarcely literate labourer, Green's private servant since 1862, was overseer until 1883. He married Lily Hamilton, one of the Taungurong 'half castes' in 1870, and thus became brother-in-law to two of the leading men, Barak's speaker Tommy Dunolly and Willie Hamilton. No other staff member was equally esteemed. Help was needed to free Green for his duties as Inspector but the Kulin would not easily accept other supervisors. The first 'master' appointed to take charge of Coranderrk left after a month because the men refused to work under him and threatened to abandon the station if he was not removed.[32] Eight teacher

---

30 Several of the Green's seven sons and five daughters died in a diphtheria epidemic soon after they left Coranderrk in 1874 and only four daughters survived their parents.
31 BPA minutes, 6 September and 3 October 1872.
32 BPA – Minutes, 2 June 1865.

managers and dormitory matrons hired by Smyth between 1865 and 1873 were all dismissed within months when investigations proved that Green's complaints of their drunkenness, incompetence, immorality or dishonesty were fully justified.

Agricultural development was more rapid and intensive than at the other five stations but not because the Board initially provided much more capital. To secure stock, seeds and implements Green had to use his own salary and the savings Kulin men brought home from shearing and harvesting as well as the income from baskets, weapons and skin rugs made by the women and aged men. The small income from crops and crafts paid for improvements, clothing and the many household necessities not provided by the Board. The pioneers saw a direct return for their work and were contented. Their freedom under Green to manage the farming and their investment of savings as well as labour encouraged them to feel they really were proprietors.

In the beginning, the only horses they had were their own. There were few tools and no building or fencing materials except what they cut on the reserve. The Board could not afford to stock Coranderrk, so the men were ordered to hunt two days a week to supplement the scanty and intermittent beef ration obtained from their few cattle and to accumulate skins for the manufacture of rugs.

Since the Sabbath was kept with Presbyterian rigour, this left only four days a week for farm tasks. The male labour force of 20 to 30 men – perhaps half of them really able-bodied – was less than a quarter of the total population. They were hindered by sickness, poor diet and the chronic shortage of tools and draught animals. In shearing and harvesting seasons as many as 14 left to work for neighbours: the cash wages they earned were needed to support their own families, the dependent aged and the 'orphan' children in the dormitory.

The whole region was densely forested in the 1860s and the Coranderrk reserve was covered with large timber and thick scrub. Only the river flats were suitable for cultivation and most of the recently extended 4,850 acre (1,963 ha) reserve consisted of ranges covered with scrub which could not support many cattle. The heavy work of clearing, grubbing, suckering, ring barking, burning brush and seeding better grasses to support stock could be only a part-time occupation. Only 170 acres (69 ha) of improved pasture had been sown by the time Green left and no more clearing was done until after 1881. Cutting, carting and erecting post and rail fencing were also necessarily intermittent occupations: while the Board paid no wages the men were better off working at cultivation tasks which brought an immediate income. The necessary subdivision and garden fencing was quickly constructed but only four miles (6.4 km) of boundary fencing had been completed by 1872. The adjoining land had been surveyed and offered for selection by 1870. The European population increased rapidly as farmers occupied these allotments and the township of Healesville began to grow. Their trespassing stock soon threatened the station's meat supply but Green's request for wages and materials to enable the Kulin to complete the boundary fence was refused for lack of funds. No more fencing was done until 1883.

Through the 1850s cattle were on all accessible land in the region: Europeans derived their income from producing fat cattle for the Melbourne market, a lucrative business once the gold rush had increased the population.[33] Pastoral development would have been more suitable for the locality and labour force. The Board, lacking funds for stock and fencing, could never extend the reserve to provide sufficient carrying capacity to produce enough meat for the resident population, or a surplus for sale. Europeans in the Healesville district tried, but soon abandoned, grain production and dairying: both were uneconomic. By the end of the 1880s, the main industries were beef cattle, hops and timber cutting.[34]

---

33   Aveling (1972:17) notes that the region was too wet for sheep and there were none in the Lilydale district by 1856.
34   Sutherland 1888:402.

5. PROPRIETORS FOR THE FIRST DECADE

The other small farmers in the Lilydale and Healesville districts also found clearing was slow work. The virgin soil was initially fertile and needed only spading or shallow ploughing for good yields of grain and potatoes. Wheat and oats were the major money earners in the 1850s but soil exhaustion due to overcropping without fallowing, low prices and the difficulty of getting crops to market had discouraged grain production by 1861; the appearance of rust in the Lilydale area in 1863 meant an end to wheat growing. European farmers deserted their holdings to take new selections under the 1865 Land Act and Chinese market gardeners moved onto the river flats[35] – but the Kulin had nowhere else to go.

Grain cultivation was initially chosen because it required only seed, use of a plough, much manpower and the least capital investment. The Board hoped that local wheat production would save cartage costs on flour which was the staple of the ration. The Board did not take into account local climatic conditions or the health of the workers. This subsistence level of production, on small acreages, with no storage facilities or transport to mill or market, and no market except the local coaching company, meant that the Coranderrk people risked much labour for little return. Moreover, grain cultivation could employ only a small number of the strongest men for the brief ploughing and harvesting periods precisely the seasons when they could earn needed cash from other employers. But the Kulin liked growing wheat: Tommy Farmer was always disappointed at the unsuitability of the locality and complained that Coranderrk 'will not grow me wheat and wheat is a valuable thing to grow bread'.[36] By 1867 all their flour came from their own wheat, ground at the Lilydale mill.[37] The pioneers were proud that their station could produce grain, vegetables and meat, and openly dissatisfied when these crops were replaced by hops, for which they could see no use. The Kulin had 10 acres of wheat in 1864 and 70 acres (28 ha) by 1868. This steadily increased to 161 acres (65 ha) in 1872 but thereafter grain cultivation was limited to 10–20 acres (4–8 ha) for the subsistence needs of their stock because of the demands of hop cultivation.

By 1866 game was scarce, despite the extension of the reserve. In 1877 men could 'hunt all day without seeing any' game and preferred to sell their catches of fish for cash. After 1871 the demands of hop cultivation halved their hunting days. The meagre meat ration always caused discontent: in 1865 the 104 residents averaged less than a pound (450 g) a week. By 1871 the regular workers received a pound a day, other men six pounds (2.7 kg) a fortnight and the women and children little or none. They had driven five cattle from the Acheron; with natural increase and purchases they had 216 in 1869 and some 525 by 1873. But the Board rarely allowed Green to buy a few sheep or cattle for killing. In fact, the Board rations had been reduced after the move to Coranderrk. In 1863 adults were allowed six and a half pounds (2.9 kg) of flour a week and men received one and a half (675 g) pounds of sugar, women one pound and children half a pound (225 g), with four ounces (112 g) of tea weekly for each adult and two ounces (56 g) per child. From 1864 to 1875 'working men' subsisted on five pounds of flour (2.25 kg)], one pound of sugar and two ounces of tea weekly, less than half the ration given European shepherds in the 1840s.[38] Women and the aged had less and children only half rations. The Board had ruled that the able-bodied must support themselves and their families and at first gave the basic ration only to the sick, aged and orphaned children. Yet it was immediately obvious that workers and their families must be rationed so they could stay home to develop their station. The Board had so little money in the early years that supplies were intermittently exhausted and the men had to seek work elsewhere. In 1865 residents voluntarily pooled their savings of £14/11/0 to buy flour for the dormitory children.

---

35 Aveling 1972:26–28.
36 Royal Commission 1877:31.
37 BPA – Annual Report 1869:23–24.
38 Kiddle 1961:59.

Most families had their own neat gardens of vegetables, fruit and flowers by 1868, and this was liberally supplemented during Green's tenure by potatoes, vegetables, fresh fruit and home-made jam from the station garden. After his departure, little attention was paid to food production. This too became a serious grievance. In this district, dairying was always difficult in the cold winters but in the summer there was milk for all. Yet cheese and butter production likewise ceased with Green's departure.

The Board provided materials and some European labour for the original school and dormitories of 1863 and the brick store and dormitories of 1867, but Green, Harris and the Kulin men had to provide their own dwellings. The traditional bark shelters (called *willam* by the Woiworung and *miam* by their western neighbours) were almost immediately replaced by bush huts of slabs and bark identical to those of European selectors. In 1864 a carpenter was hired for 10 months to teach the use of tools and afterwards Green proudly estimated the value of their first 15 cottages at £400. Without help, they cut and carted materials, first slabs and bark, later palings and sawn hardwood, and erected the 32 cottages and five other buildings completed by 1874. Repairs, extensions and improvements were negligible due to lack of time and money for a decade from 1872, and the condition of their homes became a major grievance. The green timber shrank and warped, making the early dwellings damp and draughty without constant maintenance. The Board gave them no help while an endless stream of newcomers was housed. Despite medical evidence that poor housing encouraged poor health the Board declined to pay for improvements after resolving upon abandonment of the station in 1875.

The annual cost to the Board averaged £5 per resident through the 1860s, and £10 in the 1870s. But the Coranderrk people themselves raised their living standard by their 'canny' expenditure of income from crafts and the wages they brought home. Visitors repeatedly commented that their homes and furnishings were equal to those of 'English workingmen' and superior to many selectors in the district. Green's successor, manager of Coranderrk in 1874–75, recalled that:

> They spent their money very suitably. The Hawkers used to come to the station and offer their goods. Some of them have taken away as much as £60 or £80 at one time.[39]

Surviving photograph albums of 1867 and 1877 and photographs owned by descendants prove that the Coranderrk people dressed with remarkable elegance. The women sold their baskets, eggs and fowls to visiting pedlars for fashion books, dress lengths and trimmings and then paid itinerant photographers to record their finery. Most of their furniture was home-made but they eagerly saved to buy sofas, chiffoniers and rocking chairs, curtains and wallpaper, clocks for the mantlepiece, pretty ornaments and tea cups, sewing machines and perambulators, spring carts and harness and guns, as well as all the utilitarian bedding, dishes, cutlery, candles and kerosene lamps not supplied by the Board. In addition to spending large sums in the Healesville shops they ordered furniture and other goods from Melbourne, and the manager in 1877 complained that 'there is no end to their propensity for good dress when they have the money'.[40] They also spent their money on novels and newspapers although the station had a library of 'improving works'. The illustrated weeklies contained engravings of stirring events and portraits of Her Majesty to decorate their walls; the Melbourne daily newspapers, the *Age*, and *Argus*, were their main source of information on Board decisions.

Rugs made from wallaby and possum skins, once worn as cloaks, took a fortnight's stitching but had a ready sale in 1865 at 20 to 35 shillings each. These and other indigenous manufactured goods – nets, weapons, bags and baskets – were a spare-time industry for the women and the aged. The sale of such crafts supplemented the income from crops by an average of £100 a year to 1874 but lessened later as materials grew scarce. For outside employment, the men usually received the same rates as Europeans.

---

39 Royal Commission 1877:19.
40 Royal Commission 1877:112.

Despite deductions, a gang of six could bring home as much as £114 from six weeks' shearing. The total extent of their private earnings was certainly known to Green, who acted as their banker, but he did not inform the Board of their business. When subsequent managers were asked to discover this information they ruefully reported that the men refused to say – and had threatened to leave the station or take court action if any attempt was made to control their earnings.

Green encouraged residents to keep chickens, ducks and other poultry for use and sale. When his successors forbad this as a 'community nuisance' it was another grievance for the pioneer families. Initially, the clan heads Wonga, Barak, Bamfield and some others had a few cattle of their own and the horses they possessed were used for station work. The leading Woiworung and Taungurong men in fact gained a steady income in Green's time by breeding and breaking horses; in 1868 they owned 32 horses but when private grazing on the reserve was forbidden by Green's successor in 1875 the number was reduced to 14. A year later they owned five horses. Ostensibly the ban was occasioned by a shortage of feed; in fact, the Board hoped that lack of transport would discourage outside employment and prevent contact with sympathisers in Melbourne. By 1881 the ban was lifted but by then only Barak, his nephew Wandin and his aide Bamfield owned a few head of stock. The ban was re-imposed in 1882 largely to punish these leaders.

Details of farm production, expenditure and income from 1863 to 1924 appear in Appendix I and Barwick 1972, but these financial details do not explain the fate of Coranderrk. Local lobbying for land alienation, government and Parliamentary attitudes toward land use and the future of Aborigines, and the Board's lack of political power after 1864 were the main forces that directed farm development at Coranderrk.

In July 1863 the Board secretary Smyth became a voting member and the pastoralist John Mackenzie of Wyuna, long a correspondent, replaced the deceased Langlands. The Board's president, Heales, died in June 1864. The political influence of their president was clearly critical and the members nominated the wealthy Scottish businessman and pastoralist James MacBain (1828–1892). He represented the Wimmera region in the Legislative Assembly until 1880, then joined the Legislative Council.

He employed Kulin shearers on his station near Kilmore, was prominent in Presbyterian church affairs, and was considered an 'honourable old Tory' by all factions in Parliament. Dr Embling lost his Parliamentary seat at the end of 1867, moved to the Western district and did not attend meetings after April. With the loss of the reformers Heales, Langlands and Embling the Board became increasingly conservative and Aboriginal affairs became an apolitical matter.

The Board was able to secure the original Coranderrk reserve only because pastoralists had no particular interest in the river flats along the Yarra and before 1863 there was little pressure on land in this district. However once selectors moved in and hop cultivation proved rewarding the area of rich agricultural land on the reserve was coveted by neighbours, who persistently sought its alienation. The 2,450 acres (992 ha) reserved in 1863 was an insufficient area for cattle breeding because of the poor quality of most of the land. Green urged the Board to acquire the adjoining 3,000 acres (1,214 ha), the reserve which had been the first choice of the Woiworung, when the pastoralist who had opposed its reservation became willing to sell early in 1865. The Board could not pay the £2,510 asked, but eventually agreed to seek government approval for an extension.[41]

The Lands Department did not reply. Renewing their application 14 months later, the Board discovered that the Lands Minister J.M. Grant, a former member of Heales' cabinet who gained fame as a radical reformer, had not yet seen their request for extension of Coranderrk. His Department was instead preparing to grant portions of the existing reserve to many Europeans who had applied under a clause

---

41   BPA – Minutes, 3 January and 28 April 1865.

REBELLION AT CORANDERRK

of the 1865 Land Act which allowed selection within 30 miles of a goldfield. The survey was actually under way. Coranderrk was saved for the Kulin only because the new member who held the seat of Evelyn from 1866 to 1874 was persuaded to intervene. He was also persuaded to seek an extension of 2,400 acres (971 ha), approved by Lands Minister Grant, on 24 July 1866.[42]

But no Kulin were enrolled as voters[43] and the local member subsequently paid more heed to his constituents' sentiments. In eight Parliamentary speeches between 1867 and 1870, he insisted the Coranderrk 'half castes' should be forced into service and complained that 'the old blacks persuaded them not to go' when he and others tried to hire them. He demanded that the reserve be resumed for European settlement.[44]

Up to 1872 the Board and their secretary Smyth supported and publicly praised their zealous and indefatigable General Inspector Green. Smyth worked closely and amicably with him for more than a decade, gave him full responsibility for the selection of reserve sites and relied on his judgment for most decisions about the secular administration of the six Aboriginal stations and up to 40 ration depots. Smyth also gave Green a free hand at Coranderrk. Year after year the published reports testified to the success of Green's method of encouraging the Kulin to manage their own affairs:

> the progress made in education and the amount of labour performed on the farm are truly astonishing and reflect the highest credit on Mr Green ... the order and general management of the station reflect much credit on the tact and industry of the superintendent.[45]

But when Europeans coveted this land, Smyth and the Board were immediately willing to give it up for profit, regardless of the residents' attachment. When this failed, the Board drove residents to make the station profitable. The Kulin, who wanted to work for themselves, not for European masters, began to rebel.

---

42 BPA – Minutes, 16 June and 13 July 1866. There is disparity in the records of the figures between the area surveyed and the area gazetted, see Felton 1981.
43 The Board's next Inspector discouraged enrolment of Aborigines, 'even if legal', when the missionary P.A. Hagenauer recommended this in 1878.
44 Victorian Parliamentary Debates, Sessions 1867–1870.
45 BPA – Annual Report 1866:4, 6.

Chapter 6
THE BOARD TAKES CONTROL

> It must be remembered that Coranderrk is the principal station; the feeble and the sick are sent to it; destitute Aboriginal children and half castes are gathered together there; and it would be unreasonable to require the few healthy and strong men to support a large number who can contribute nothing to their own support.
>
> Robert Brough Smyth 1870[1]

The Board was strongly criticised in Parliament in March and April 1867 because it had asked for an expanded appropriation for buildings, largely for a new station at Lake Condah to be supervised by the Anglican mission committee. The member representing Evelyn, the district where Coranderrk was located, focussed his attack on the number of 'half castes', insisting they be removed and made of service to the country. He and others also criticised the amount of land 'laying waste' for Aboriginal reserves.[2]

The threat of revocation was therefore in Smyth's mind when he and Board member Mackenzie visited Coranderrk in November. Smyth's report, intended for publication, noted that the costly new school and dormitory completed in May would remain a valuable property whatever changes might be made. As usual he rode about unescorted and visited every household: he was impressed by the residents' good health, the women's tasteful decoration of their homes and care of their children and the state of the stock, fencing and crops. From the men's 'shouts as they drove the oxen and turned the plough' he concluded that they worked willingly and took pleasure in it. But he thought the work of grain cultivation heavy and monotonous. He urged the Board to develop crops which would pay better; now that the roads were improving fruit and vegetables could be grown for the Melbourne market with some expenditure on irrigation and special transport.

Smyth considered it 'humiliating' that Coranderrk was not self-supporting after nearly five years. He suggested that the labour of women and children could be used in market gardening, reminding the Board that he had advised this when Coranderrk was first planned. He opposed the idea of apprenticing 'blacks and half castes' off the station as European prejudice was too great for them to win acceptance and anyhow he doubted their capacity for self-reliance. He thought:

> It would be well to confine Mr Green almost entirely to the duties of his office, Inspector of stations, or appoint him manager at Coranderrk, and get some other person to act as Inspector. He should continue to live at Coranderrk, as his influence among the blacks is considerable; and it appears to have been always used, as far as I can learn, beneficially.[3]

---

1   BPA – Annual Report 1871:8.
2   Victorian Parliamentary Debates, Session 1867:695, 816–8.
3   BPA – Annual Report 1869:18–20.

However, local pressure for alienation and the Lands Minister's lack of sympathy discouraged plans for development. The Board rejected Smyth's 1867 scheme even though he argued that expenditure on this valuable property could be recouped in compensation if the land was taken. They also rejected his recommendation that Green should hand over all income from crops and crafts to the Treasury as recompense for the government's 'bounty' instead of spending it on clothing and other goods for residents. Green convinced them that this direct reward taught the Kulin the value of their farm work and that the women and the aged had a right to profit from the crafts made in their spare time. Yet at Smyth's insistence Green now had to obtain Board approval to spend station income.[4]

The pioneer families resented Green's insistence on distributing goods according to need which meant that the penniless newcomers to the station got more than the workers who supported them. They were already annoyed by Green's destruction of their hunting dogs at the doctor's order when an epidemic of 'low fever' (probably typhoid) prostrated his family, the overseer Harris and most of the Kulin during 1867. Their court still regulated station affairs but the Board had rejected their written rules submitted by Green in July 1867 and forbad Green to enforce them without Board consent.[5]

In March 1868 several men left Coranderrk and sent a letter of complaint to Smyth. Jemmy Barker was demanding wages and Green had reproached him for laziness. Many had left the station during 1867 for fear of infection and the work was in disarray because of the resulting shortage of labour and the sickness of the Greens and Harris. In June Wonga, Barker and Barak led the first and last protest against Green's management. They came to Melbourne to tell Smyth they wanted the right to sell the potato crop and manage the profits for themselves. Smyth and Mackenzie did not go up to investigate until October when Green was away on his delayed inspection tour. They found that residents were satisfied now that Green supported their court's decision to give the best workers a larger share.

In an August Parliamentary debate the local member had demanded information on all aspects of the Board's administration and asked for population figures which distinguished the 'half-castes'. The Board president, MacBain, did not make this distinction in his detailed account of the stations. J.M. Grant, Lands Minister from 1864 to 1869, publicly supported the local member's criticisms, reporting that the people of the district wanted the acreage reduced by nine-tenths as Coranderrk could support a hundred European families. He told Parliament that all reserves were too large and their residents should be forcibly dispersed and made of use to the colony.[6]

Smyth's published report on his next visit in May 1869 warmly praised the work of Green and the teacher and the 'order, cleanliness and cheerfulness' of the Kulin. He had examined everything 'in company with the principal men' and was delighted; but the real business of his visit was not revealed to the public or to the Kulin.[7] Their tenure was still threatened. In response to continuing local agitation the Surveyor General had recommended the resumption and sale of half the reserve in January 1869. The Board had urged the Lands Minister not to consent but in April Smyth learned of further attempts to secure Coranderrk and the Board resolved to seek another reserve 'in some locality not likely to be invaded by settlers'.[8]

---

4   BPA – Minutes 23 November 1867.
5   BPA – Annual Report 1869:20; Coranderrk Inquiry 1881:136.
6   Victorian Parliamentary Debates, Session 1868:752–3.
7   BPA – Annual Report 1869:20–21.
8   BPA – Minutes 16 and 28 April 1869.

6. THE BOARD TAKES CONTROL

Smyth had gone to tell Green that 'influences were being brought to bear' upon Board and government and both they and Lands Minister Grant were inclined to give way, for they would be handsomely paid for all improvements if they gave up Coranderrk. Admitting that the Board knew they could not move the Kulin without Green's help, Smyth urged him to persuade them to go to the 'Big Swamp' near Westernport. Green refused to move them from their home, explaining that he would act only 'if I could assure them that it was for their good to do so, because I could speak to them as men and brothers'.[9] The Board then appealed to Grant to forbid revocation.

Green's July 1869 annual report was dispirited although the Kulin had worked steadily and well to clear and fence another 50 acres (20 ha) and build new homes. The value of their crops was £645 but most of the produce had been consumed. He had bought the Kulin goods worth £106 and regretted that he had too little income to reward the best workers adequately; there had been much trouble with some 'lazy' workers who got less and some had demanded all cash income from crops 'to do with it as they like'. He urged the Board to allow them a regular cash wage and meat ration. His report did not make public the underlying reasons for discontent: not only had the men discovered the teacher's seduction of one of their girls but Smyth had recently hired European labourers to clear their land at a cost of £85.[10] The population had been reduced by epidemics of typhoid fever in 1867 and whooping cough in 1868 – not by deaths, but by the departure of many Kulin to avoid infection, like the old Taungurong who went home to Yea saying there was 'too much sick' at Coranderrk.[11]

The long-awaited legislation was introduced to Parliament in August after the Board approved amendments to the final Bill. There was negligible discussion of the Board's need for increased powers: MacBain merely explained that there were many attempts to interfere with the 'rights of Aborigines' and the Board had no authority to punish offenders. One amendment, allowing appointment of local committees to supervise the stations, was sponsored by the hostile member for Evelyn who as usual argued that 'half castes' should be trained to work for their living. The *Aborigines Act* 1869 received royal assent on 11 November. It changed the Board's title to the 'Board for the Protection of the Aborigines' but the same members continued. The position of President lapsed as the responsible Minister, the Chief Secretary, became *ex officio* chairman. Since he did not attend, the vice-chairman elected by members (MacBain from 1869 to 1871) was the effective chairman of the Board. Smyth and Jennings drafted, and the Board approved, the Regulations gazetted in February 1871. Smyth immediately implemented the requirement that European employers could not hire Aborigines unless a temporary work certificate signed by a station manager or local guardian had been issued. This was abandoned after three years as too troublesome, and only used occasionally by Smyth's successors as a device to control workers. The power to prescribe an individual's residence by Order-in-Council was not used until 1872, and then primarily to force Europeans to release children and young girls, but occasionally to control men who resisted station discipline.[12] The Board's new powers made little difference to Green who preferred persuasion to coercion when he was instructed to bring in women and children from rural camps. He knew that the Kulin court at Coranderrk would simply approve the departure of any reluctant residents.

---

9   Coranderrk Inquiry 1881:132.
10   BPA – Annual Report 1871:14–15; BPA – Minutes 9 June, 7 and 27 July 1869.
11   BPA – Annual Report 1871:22.
12   From 1872 to 1935 the Governor-in-Council approved 61 orders and made five rescinding orders: 67 adults and 58 children were ordered to reside at specific Aboriginal stations; five adults were sent to institutions for medical reasons, and 11 children were transferred to the care of the Children's Welfare Department. Of the 25 orders made from 1875 to 1883 nine were used to restrain adults from leaving their stations, and most of the rest were obtained to force Europeans to give up children and women living in unsavoury circumstances.

The local member renewed his criticisms of the Kulin and Green in Parliament on 18 November 1869, six weeks after a new government took office. He was answered by the Board's former president now vice-chairman, MacBain, who strongly criticised the actions of unnamed neighbours who 'coveted the fine piece of land in the possession of the Aborigines', and told the House that the former Lands Minister (Grant) had promised the Board he would allow no interference with this reserve.[13]

Things looked more hopeful in January 1870. In his inspection report Smyth[14] informed the Board that:

> The men are still anxious and uncertain respecting their tenure of the land. They feel they may be turned away at any time, and I hope the Central Board will make an effort to get a grant of the land now reserved for the use of the Aborigines. This, more than anything else, would give contentment and ensure the happiness of these people.

He also advised the Board to approve their 'just request' for wages, explaining that:

> Many of the men are good labourers, and they are now so thoroughly domesticated that they show an earnest desire to get profit from their labours. The most industrious feel that they are giving their time and their work not only for the partial support of themselves and their families, but also for the benefit of the large number of females and children who are incapable of labour, and they wish to get some remuneration.

Noting that they had little time to hunt or fish, Smyth also advised spending £100 on stock for a regular meat supply since 'strong industrious willing men (some of whom work as hard or harder than ordinary Europeans) should be well fed'. Wages and meat must be provided immediately, Smyth insisted, to reward the workers for their industry and perseverance. But 10 months passed before the Board allowed Green a small monthly sum to purchase meat until the station herd built up.[15] The Kulin had worked harder than ever since 1867 and expanded the cultivated area from 70 to 130 acres (28 to 48 ha) and built six new huts at their own expense. Green and Smyth had tried to vary the crops, adding maize, tobacco, flax and an orchard of stone fruits as well as a large vegetable garden. Mary Green and the Kulin women had begun cheese production as well as making butter for sale and the new piggery proved profitable. Their efforts were inevitably defeated by the Board's failure to provide capital for irrigation, storage and transport of their produce, or money for fencing and stock. Moreover, now that the 1869 Act authorised forcible removal to the stations, an increased population (mostly aged, sick and dependent children) meant that there was less surplus for sale.

Throughout 1870 the Kulin and Green had disputes with Mr and Mrs Burril Johnson, the teacher manager and dormitory matron chosen by Smyth and MacBain. Johnson complained incessantly about his exclusion from the residents' court, which only Green attended; about Green's absences to conduct the funerals of Healesville residents during a diphtheria epidemic; and about the authority exerted by Mary Green who had no paid position. Green also made serious charges about them, and in July MacBain and Smyth brought the district police magistrate to investigate. The couple were immediately dismissed and the Board advised Green that he was 'exonerated' of all charges against him.[16] The Johnsons' gossip was a useful weapon for the local member who told Parliament on 23 November that the Board should be relieved of control so that local committees could train the Aborigines for employment off the stations. He asserted that the manager, 'formerly an itinerant preacher, was now the largest cattle proprietor in the neighbourhood'. MacBain declared false the statement that Green used Coranderrk for his own profit, reporting that he, Smyth and the magistrate had found no fault with Green's management. MacBain

---

13   Victorian Parliamentary Debates, Session 1869:2314–15.
14   BPA – Annual Report 1871:8.
15   BPA – Annual Report 1871:8–9; BPA – Minutes 14 November 1870.
16   BIL – Coranderrk, Burril Johnson to Smyth, 1 May 1870; BPA – Minutes 14 January, 3 June, 7 July, 20 September 1870.

6. THE BOARD TAKES CONTROL

said he hoped the government would not succumb to the tactics being used by Europeans who coveted Coranderrk. He received unsolicited support from W.M.K. Vale, the radical barrister who had been vice-president of the Board of Land and Works from 1866 to 1868, and a new member, the conservative lawyer Robert Ramsay. Both had visited Coranderrk, both praised Green's management, and both insisted that the attacks on him inside and outside Parliament were entirely without foundation, maliciously concocted by neighbours who coveted the Aboriginal reserve.[17]

The member for Evelyn said no more about Coranderrk; indeed there was little Parliamentary discussion of Aborigines until 1876, when he lost his seat. The local campaign to secure Coranderrk continued but changed its form. Smyth was a land owner in the district: both he and Green had purchased adjoining residential allotments in the township of Healesville in 1865, perhaps to have a voice in local politics if a Roads Board was formed, and in October 1869 he, Green and Harris applied for adjoining blocks on the north-eastern boundary, in order to protect the reserve from less sympathetic neighbours. From 1870 to 1873 Smyth was approached privately by many neighbours and Healesville residents who asked his aid in obtaining leases of the reserve or making other arrangements to alienate portions of it.[18]

Smyth had adequate funds to develop his purchase but Green had a struggle to make improvements and stock his land within three years to meet the selection requirements. He had only a few hours a week free for fencing and clearing, as he still rode about the district on Sundays to hold Presbyterian services for Europeans. He placed his eldest son William, born in 1858, on the block to meet requirements.[19] Smyth and the founding members of the Board had no objection to Green's private venture, knowing that he was utterly scrupulous and had used his own salary to subsidise the farming at Coranderrk. Moreover he needed to make provision for his large family. For years he had paid agistment fees to two neighbours for his own stock but when they strayed onto the unfenced reserve jealous Europeans were quick to complain, for the Kulin stockmen regularly impounded their trespassing stock. Nevertheless while Green farmed in the vicinity he was always liable to charges that he used his official position for private profit and thus in danger of becoming an embarrassment to the Board.

Green's report for December 1870 still hoped that Coranderrk would be self-supporting within two years and commended the industry of the Kulin but admitted that the continued insecurity of tenure and lack of wages had discouraged them:

> I was in hopes that before this time to have this station self-supporting, but have failed to succeed. This is owing a good deal to the bad influence of Europeans, who tell them that they are only working for the Government, and it (the station) will be sold. But this evil will be partly remedied when they are paid for the amount of work they do.[20]

Early in January 1871 five young Kulin refused to work and left Coranderrk to call attention to the inadequate supply of meat and clothing. The leaders were Wonga's Taungurong aide Bamfield and Johnny Phillips, son of the old Kurung clan head from Ballarat. Green reported he gave the best workers a pound (450 g) of beef per day and the rest of the residents half that. When he asked the Board to visit only Smyth and the Anglican mission committee representative Jennings, who had never visited before, came up. They spent two days on their inquiry, interviewing the men at a general assembly in Green's absence. All of the men complained of the lack of wages, citing Smyth's own recommendation in the previous annual report. He and Jennings strongly supported the justice of their complaints and urged the Board to supply immediately the stock and plants needed for development, provide all workers with the clothing

---

17 Victorian Parliamentary Debates, Session 1870:279–81.
18 BPA – Minutes 11 July 1873.
19 Personal communication, Department of Crown Lands and Survey, 6 June, 1, 5 and 30 July 1968.
20 BPA – Annual Report 1871:15.

and household necessities they lacked, and grant regular wages on a scale to be fixed by Green.[21] The Board did not approve the recommendations. Smyth's December 1871 inspection report, also intended for publication, criticised the decision and pointedly commented that his scheme was approved by the members who had seen the station.[22] Besides Smyth himself only Mackenzie, Jennings and MacBain had ever visited Coranderrk.

There was more criticism of Green in 1871 but it came from another quarter, and united Smyth and Green. By the end of the year Smyth and the Board were as determined to retain Coranderrk as Green and the Kulin but their reasons were different. The recent criticisms of the Board's main station had touched Smyth's pride. The 1869 annual report had made much of the fact that Coranderrk, 'the most prosperous Aboriginal station in Victoria, or perhaps in Australia' was managed exclusively by the Board and its staff and owed nothing to 'extraneous assistance'. The next report, issued in August 1871, reiterated the Board's concern with the secular welfare of Aborigines according to the terms of its commission. It was, for those in the know, a rebuff to the church mission committee who had publicly and privately criticised Smyth's unfairness to their missions.

Ever since 1860 the Board had intermittently had trouble with the Melbourne Church of England Mission Committee which had staffed a series of mission stations with untrained volunteers and was chronically short of funds because there was little local sympathy for mission work among Aborigines. The Board paid all expenses except the missionary's salary but gained no credit for these stations. The committee had overextended itself in establishing the Framlingham station in 1865 and abandoned it to the Board, then sought another opportunity at Lake Condah. As the eastern Mara-speaking clans would not leave Framlingham the Board had to rebuild this station at government expense in 1869. Green's April 1871 report on his week's visit to Lake Condah shocked the Board. The missionary Joseph Shaw had sold the crops and taken stock for agistment without accounting to the Board for this income and spent it on goods for residents which the Board explicitly refused to supply. His requisitions for clothing were excessive (Green recommended that the women should dress themselves by the sale of baskets as they did at Coranderrk) and he was ordering flour at the rate of nine pounds (4.05 kg) weekly per head although the ration was five pounds (2.25 kg) weekly for adults. Shaw admitted the truth of the Aborigines' complaints that he had shot their fowls and struck a man with his riding whip; Green's report noted that 'at my request they said they would forgive him for all past things'.[23]

Shaw declined to account for his expenditure of station income. Instead the mission committee sent the Chief Secretary a distorted account of Shaw's dealings with Smyth, demanded Smyth's removal and criticised the 'arbitrary conduct' of him and Green. The Board was convened but the mission committee member Jennings stayed away, informing the vice-chairman that he had no hand in this complaint but wanted 'a fair secretary'. Green's report was sent for Shaw's comment but his reply was unsatisfactory. The Board halved Shaw's supplies, forbad agistment and censured him for misuse of government property and sending false returns. The Chief Secretary Duffy was satisfied with Smyth's explanation, which proved Shaw had lied, and declined to intervene.[24] This influential Anglican lobby did force an alteration of Board policy: all missionaries could expend station income as they chose so long as they accounted for it. Smyth would never concede this freedom to his subordinates at Coranderrk and Framlingham.

---

21 BPA – Annual Report 1871:9–10.
22 BPA – Annual Report 1872:10.
23 BPA – Annual Report 1871:7–8.
24 BPA – Minutes 3 May, 13 June, 4 August, 15 September 1871. CSIC 71/Z6229, 12 May 1871; 71/Z11616, 5 July 1871.

6. THE BOARD TAKES CONTROL

The Anglican protest had one more consequence. On 5 May the Board had asked the previous Minister to approve their nomination of two new members. Duffy instead instructed Smyth to obtain the resignations of the inactive members Henty and Embling and appointed his own three choices.[25] Two, members of the Legislative Assembly, had taken no previous interest in Aborigines and showed little during their membership. The wealthy Anglican pastoralist John Rout Hopkins (1828–1897) had come from Tasmania to the Western District in 1845; his father, a prominent merchant and philanthropist, had first visited Melbourne in 1837 and paid for the first missionary and church there. Hopkins attended only 13 meetings in his 23 years of membership. The Welsh pharmacist David Thomas (1826–1876) was also an Anglican; he attended 14 meetings before his death in 1876. The Scottish journalist George Alexander Syme (1822–1892) had been first a Presbyterian then Baptist clergyman and was always an advocate of radical causes. In 1862 he had joined the *Age* newspaper, published by his brother, and was now editor of its country weekly, the *Leader*. His attendance too was poor but he was well acquainted with Coranderrk. He had made visits from his brother's model farm at Woori Yalloak and once stayed with the Greens for a week. Syme admired both the young Scottish preacher and the Kulin men.

By the end of 1871 Green, Smyth, and the businessmen on the Board knew that no more reserves would be allotted for Aborigines and that annual appropriations would remain at the low level of the previous decade. Coranderrk was the only reserve containing valuable agricultural land in Victoria. Framlingham had little potential and the mission committees would retain any profit from the other four stations. The retention and development of Coranderrk was essential if the Board was ever to have an income to supplement the meagre funds approved by unsympathetic governments and uninterested Parliamentarians.

Sumner was elected vice-chairman to replace MacBain in 1871 and he, Syme and Smyth formed a sub-committee to choose a horticultural consultant to implement the agricultural development scheme drafted by Smyth and Green in January 1872. The estimated cost was £562: £32 for an aqueduct for irrigation, £80 for a sawmill so the men could cut timber to replace all dwellings; £263 to employ a horticultural consultant and skilled gardener for a year; and £187 for wages, at the rate of three to 10 shillings a week, for the 12 best workers. The Board again refused wages despite Smyth's insistence that they were essential and Green's warning that the pioneers felt it was unreasonable they should have to support so many newcomers 'to most of whom they are in no way related but as countrymen'.[26]

The agnostic scientist Smyth and the fundamentalist churchman Green had little in common except youth, stubbornness and a determination that all Aborigines should have decent homes, medical care and an opportunity to learn new skills. They had a genuine interest in the language and some aspects of the culture of the original inhabitants of Victoria. They felt great respect for many members of the Coranderrk community. But despite their sympathy they had no real understanding of Kulin marriage rules or political organisation. After his recent investigations Smyth was convinced of the residents' attachment to Coranderrk, but he interpreted this in European terms, as a fondness for a comfortable home in which they had invested much labour. He and Green had devoted 11 years to changing the habits of 'the blacks'; they did not understand that the Coranderrk pioneers still thought of themselves as Kulin. Smyth had no idea that until 1872 all residents were either Kulin, Pangerang who traced kinship from long-ago marriages to Kulin, or individuals incorporated as spouses of Kulin pioneers. His 1871 annual report had commented approvingly that:

> At Coranderrk there are men, women, and children, all living amicably with members of the Yarra and Goulburn tribes, who have been gathered from the Upper and Lower Murray, from Gippsland, and from the north and south-western parts of the colony.[27]

---

25 BPA – Minutes 3 May 1871; BPA – Secretary's Letter Book, 18 October 1871.
26 BPA – Annual Report 1872:5.
27 BPA – Annual Report 1871:4.

REBELLION AT CORANDERRK

From March 1872 the Board assumed responsibility for the agricultural development of Coranderrk. Their financial investment was a substantial proportion of their budget and they could not fail. They handed over the implementation of the scheme to two Europeans who had no knowledge of the Kulin and considered 'the blacks' an unsatisfactory labour force who must be coerced. Their own reputations as experts were at stake. The Kulin who owned and had managed this land for so long had new European bosses. The Board's horticultural consultant, given full executive authority to supervise the development scheme, was Frederick Search, then agricultural writer for the *Australasian*, a subsidiary of the *Argus* newspaper. Search advised concentration upon hops and the Board approved. The suggestion came in fact from Green, who had observed that the suitably light year-round cultivation tasks had proved congenial to the Kurnai of Gippsland. In July Search hired old Robert Burgess, who had some experience with Kurnai at Bairnsdale, as resident hopmaster and authorised him to take full control of the workers, without reference to Green.

Green, ordered away in March, June and July to fulfil his duties as Inspector, returned to find that he, like other workers, was now 'merely a tool' for the Board's development scheme. Even with 30 men (including eight Burapper newcomers) the labour force was inadequate. Search hired neighbours to speed the preparation of 10 acres (4 ha) of hops. All the new tasks of clearing and planting, cutting 26,000 hop poles, building an aqueduct, kiln and cooling house, and providing housing for the newcomers Green was ordered to collect, meant that the pioneers could not be spared for the usual farm work and general maintenance tasks. The grain acreage was cut from 130 to 10 acres (53 to 4 ha) and the garden from 20 to seven acres (8.1 to 2.8 ha), so the usual produce income was sharply reduced. The older dwellings grew dilapidated. Inevitably the pioneers grew resentful: they were working harder than ever for less direct return.

**John and Elizabeth Charles, c. 1876,
with children William and Henry.**

6. THE BOARD TAKES CONTROL

Mrs Louisa Briggs with her children (rear: William, Sarah, Jack [John Jr], Mrs Lizzie Briggs Charles; front: Caroline, Ellen, Louisa and grandson William Charles).

Despite Green's repeated pleas that the Board implement its June 1872 resolution to pay some wages when the produce income became available, most of this money was paid instead to Europeans. Green in fact had to reduce his usual distribution, providing only boots and clothes for workers. The men renewed their demand for cash wages. Smyth ordered Green to warn them that the Board was 'under no obligation to pay wages to Aborigines' and that 'they must be attentive and civil to all persons otherwise they will be sent away'. When the protests continued the Board exiled the main spokesmen. Smyth sent all residents a written warning that any who sheltered or fed the offenders would themselves be removed and persons using offensive or threatening language would be summonsed and dealt with by police.

The leader of this protest was the ploughman John Briggs Sr (c. 1825–1878), a Tasmanian 'half caste' admitted late in 1871 with his wife Louisa (1836–1925) who was the daughter of a Woiworung girl kidnapped by sealers in 1833. The Board recognised Louisa's claim to Victorian aid; the Woiworung clan-heads considered this family Kulin and acknowledged their role as spokesmen for the pioneers.[28] John and Louisa had spent their childhood in the Bass Strait sealing community and since 1853 had made a living independently on the goldfields and pastoral stations of western Victoria. They were not intimidated by officialdom. John Briggs immediately wrote to the Chief Secretary for 'pecuniary assistance' and Smyth was ordered to explain to the Minister. His report blamed the conduct of Briggs, his son Jack and the young Jajowrong John Charles (half-brother to Barak's aide Dunolly, and a future son-in-law of Briggs).

---

28 Barwick 1985.

Their exile continued, but the Minister's censure forced the Board to misuse the provisions of the Act to authorise further dismissals. When they wished to exile Wonga's speaker James 'Jemmy' Barker, leader of further protests, in May 1873 they ordered that a work certificate be issued for him. The Board continued to assert that these certificates (essential for lawful employment of Aborigines) prevented 'evil disposed persons from withdrawing willing and industrious Aboriginal labourers from the stations under false pretences'.[29] That was true, but officials also used them to limit the freedom of Aboriginal workers. The Minister questioned the morality of exiling station residents; in 1880 a successor challenged the legality of the Board's punitive dismissals. Crown law officers then gave an opinion that the Board apparently had no power to 'dismiss or prevent any Aboriginal from coming on any of the stations'.[30]

The Coranderrk people, already anxious about the European takeover of their farm, were dismayed by these unprecedented orders from the Board. Never before had any resident been punished by banishment unless this sanction was ordered by the unanimous judgment of their own court. They already had sufficient cause for anger and resentment: they feared further displacement by European neighbours hired to work their land; their useful food crops had been suddenly reduced; and they no longer had a voice in the management of their farm. Because hops demanded full-time labour for eight months of the year they were now forbidden to leave for their usual shearing and harvesting contracts and could not even be spared for boundary riding so that increased trespassing by neighbours' stock threatened their meat supply. Moreover, the Board reneged on the promised compensation for their extra labour. They had been assured that hops would provide funds for wages, boundary fencing, new homes and a hospital at Coranderrk. All were deferred or refused.

Green remained responsible for the general management, but had no control over the consultant Search and the hopmaster Burgess. This division of authority immediately caused difficulties. The Kulin men, resenting Burgess' harsh language and authoritarian direction, worked sullenly; Burgess consequently urged Search (in their hearing) to have the Board dismiss them and employ only European labourers. Green's warnings that the men were too few and too ill to be driven thus were ignored by Search who informed Smyth that they were merely lazy and Green unfit to control them.

The *Argus* employee Search was anxious that his government contract should enhance his reputation. When the rival *Age* published several articles giving Green credit for the introduction of hops and their successful cultivation – presumably using information supplied by Syme – he was angry and his criticisms of Green's general management grew ever more spiteful. The demands of hops caused Green, as Inspector, to delay his tours further annoying Smyth whose own reports depended on the inspection reports. Something of a despot, Smyth had never understood why Green did not manage these few Aborigines with the authoritarian efficiency he himself maintained in directing the massive Mines Department and he grew increasingly unsympathetic to Green's seemingly niggling plaints about the wishes and welfare of the Coranderrk men. Moreover, his reputation as Board secretary now depended upon the success of the hop plantation: the Anglican mission authorities had again complained to the Board and the government that Smyth unfairly favoured Coranderrk in distributing funds.[31]

These Anglican criticisms caused the Board to abandon their May 1873 resolution to 'place in Green's hands the hop income, to pay wages and procure necessities for the Aborigines'. They planned instead to share the new income among the six stations. In fact this scheme was forestalled. From June 1874 the hop income had to be paid into consolidated revenue to offset the Board's Parliamentary vote. The Board consequently lost all incentive for opposing abandonment: Coranderrk was no longer their only source of extra income, merely the most expensive station to maintain.

29 BPA – Annual Report 1874:4.
30 BPA – Secretary's Letter Book, 26 April and 11 May 1883; see also Secretary's Minute Book, 82/288, 25 November 1882.
31 BPA – Minutes, 7 August 1873.

6. THE BOARD TAKES CONTROL

Green was initially able to control dissatisfaction and keep the men at work by pledging that hops would ultimately provide larger family incomes since the women and children could be employed tying and picking for several months a year. But in fact the income distributed among the Kulin immediately decreased. All had shared the £180 income from other crops in 1870; in 1872 Green could distribute only £69 worth of clothing to workers. In 1873 Green estimated the value of their labour at £710 but wages were again refused and the men received only £82 worth of work clothing. The £983 net profit from the hop crop went to the Board and Treasury. The Board paid no wages until June 1874. The £93 owing to the Aboriginal pickers since January (at a penny a bushel, a third of the usual rate) was belatedly paid, at Green's insistence, after a quarrel which directly contributed to his removal.

Another of the Board's May 1873 resolutions – to fence Coranderrk when funds were available – lapsed without formal revocation in the minutes. Fencing had been urged in Smyth's January 1873 report which commended the improvements and warmly praised Green's management. But Search and Burgess instead took control of all workers to prepare another 10 acres (4 ha) for hops and build a drying kiln.

Smyth's report on his next visit in December 1873 was in sharp contrast to all other inspection reports of the previous decade: he complained of the station's new appearance of disorder and neglect. He queried the cessation of dairying and the reduction of the vegetable garden but did not mention the lack of progress at fencing. He was sufficiently aware of the labour shortage to suggest full-time employment of a European gardener. Green's own annual report declared that the demands of hop cultivation had been so great that much of the usual station work had to be left undone. Yet the medical officer's quarterly reports for February and June 1874 as usual praised the continuing good order and satisfactory management of Coranderrk.

The hop gardens at Coranderrk, c. 1877–1878.

Smyth valued efficiency above all else and he had always disapproved of Green's belief that the management of Coranderrk should be entrusted to the Kulin themselves. Ever since Search and Burgess had been appointed they had served as his main advisers, and all three were annoyed at Green's failure to discipline the Kulin labour force. When Green wrote at the end of 1873 asking approval of the residents' own court rules for punishing offenders Smyth did not submit his recommendation to the Board for three months, then replied that his own 'old rules' for discipline must be enforced.[32]

Green was necessarily away for much of 1873 and left again for lengthy tours the following January and June. In January 1874 he and Smyth had their first serious disagreement. The issues, according to Green's recollection, were the Board's delay in providing wages for residents and Search's proposal to hire European labour:

> He said, 'Mr Green, a gentleman has just been here, and has offered to rent Coranderrk from us, keep you and the blacks and bid you do nothing if we give him Coranderrk'. I said, 'I could do that, too, if you gave me Coranderrk; I do not want any such thing; Coranderrk will be self-supporting'. He said 'Why has it not been self-supporting?' I said, 'I do not want to employ anyone but the blacks to make it self-supporting, because I do not want to have it contaminated by the low white people we would have about'. He got in a great passion, and said he did not care whether it was black, white or blue labor [sic] – I ought to have it self-supporting, if it could be self-supporting.[33]

By March 1874 the Kulin men's discontent about wages and anxiety about Burgess' threats to replace them were so great that Green strongly urged dismissal of the hopmaster. But Search blamed Green for the friction. Smyth merely ordered Green to make the men work for Burgess and advised him to ignore the hopmaster's 'peculiarities of temper and manner'.

Fear of dispossession strengthened when the pioneers learned that the Board had approved Search's plan to employ 20 boys from the Industrial Schools as pickers. Green forestalled this by asking his new assistants the dormitory matron Miss Nina Robertson appointed in January 1874, and the teacher Rev. J. Heinrich Stähle who arrived in April, to bring the school children to work. The entire eight-ton crop was picked by the residents but they were not paid for months while Europeans earned £30 for cutting drains.

In June Burgess was given great praise and a £30 bonus. But Smyth now had to order the overseer Thomas Harris to work full time in the hop ground. He asked Harris to use his influence and the promise of a small wage to 'induce the Aborigines to give willing assistance to Burgess'. At the same time Smyth sent Green a spate of almost contradictory orders: to complete his tours and his delayed reports, to explain and rectify the neglect of general maintenance, to spend £30 for fencing and planting a hop nursery and, on 4 August, to work full time himself with the 15 best men digging the hop ground under Burgess' direction while sending all other men to prepare another four acres (1.6 ha) for hops.

Meanwhile, in May 1874, Search had presented an extremely critical report blaming Green's mismanagement for the lack of boundary fencing and the consequent presence of 177 trespassing cattle (36 of them reportedly owned by Green), the poor condition of the government cattle and the abandonment of dairying, the 'shamefully weedy' state of the garden and orchard, the poor output of the sawmill and the fouling of the unfenced aqueduct by wandering cattle. At their June meeting Smyth urged censure of Green but the Board instead decided to send 'extracts' from this report and ask for explanation. The secretary, already displeased because Green's delayed tours prevented completion of the annual report, grew ever more sympathetic to Search's complaints of his incompetence. In July Smyth

---

32 BPA – Minutes 6 February 1873, 13 March 1874; BPA – Letter Book, 9 October and 12 December 1872, 21 March 1874; BPA – Annual Report 1874:App.12.
33 Coranderrk Inquiry 1881:132.

urged all members to visit Coranderrk together, for the first time, to conduct an inquiry. Green was given one week's warning of this August visit, in order to muster the cattle; he was not told that the Board intended to investigate Search's criticisms which, he believed, he had rebutted satisfactorily in letters to Smyth a month earlier.

On 14 August 1874 five of the nine members came to Coranderrk. Jennings had inspected once and Mackenzie (vice-chairman 1872–74) twice but David Thomas and the recently elected vice-chairman Macredie had never visited although the latter, like Jennings, had been a Board member since 1860.

Gossip heard the previous day at Healesville apparently prompted their questions about the number and condition of the government cattle and the number of stock which occasionally trespassed from the adjoining property where Green paid for their agistment. Many local residents had been angered by Green's impounding of their stock and consequently hoped to discredit him. In fact Green's defence, that he had mustered 470 cattle in April and could not spare horses and men to muster again or act as full-time boundary riders controlling trespassing, seemed to satisfy the members. They acknowledged that the cattle's condition was usual for the district, that dairying was impossible at this season and that better breeding stock was needed.

As this was an official Board meeting Smyth wrote the minutes which were signed by the vice-chairman Macredie.[34] Smyth made much of the lack of vegetables in the station garden and the neglect of the orchard. Green testified that there were abundant potatoes in store and ample winter crops in the residents' private gardens. Harris, questioned privately, apparently contradicted Green's statement that there were always ample vegetables on the station. Harris was defensive, for vegetable production was his job as farm and stock overseer, but he had been ordered to work full time on the hops. He was anxious to please Smyth as this meeting would decide his claim for higher wages. Smyth was determined to censure Green and his minutes were misleading; there were 1,200 cabbages, and parsnips, onions, beans and cauliflowers at seedling stage in the main garden and the September–December report by Green's successor stated that the four acre (1.6 ha) garden had provided more than the station's requirements.[35] Harris later publicly contradicted Smyth's rendering of his evidence and confirmed that there were ample vegetables – but the opportunity did not come for seven years.[36]

In fact the visiting Board members spent most of the day investigating the petty complaints sent to Smyth by Search and Burgess: that the Kulin neglected the piggery and were incompetent to manage the sawmill, that their children urinated in the workshop and the buggy shed, and that Green 'bribed' workers with tobacco. There was 'no unpleasantness' that day until Smyth got excited about the children's habits and the insufficient number of privies at the houses. He knew very well, as Green had supplied information for his planned ethnographic volume since 1861 and was his major source of data on the Kulin after the former Guardian William Thomas died in 1867, that the Kulin still believed every death was caused by sorcery. So persistent was the Kulin fear of malevolent sorcerers that the elders, including Wonga and Barak, always insisted on burying their excrement secretly. No closets were built at Coranderrk until the visiting medical officer queried the residents 'cleanly and peculiar habits' in 1869. Green did not enforce new habits when Wonga and others objected: he commended the ancient practice (although he considered their rationale superstitious) because he believed the use of closets helped to spread disease. No more were built until after 1876 and in the 1880s some Kulin still refused to use them. Green did not attempt to interfere with Kulin beliefs which did not directly challenge Christian practice and so the Kulin continued the ancient rules about segregation of menstruating women, the ritualised avoidance by

---

34   BPA – Minutes 14 August 1874.
35   BPA – Annual Report 1875:App. 6.
36   Coranderrk Inquiry 1881:14, 131.

which men and women related in certain ways showed respect, and their interest in herbal and magical forms of healing.[37] But Smyth lacked Green's tolerance and was determined that the Kulin should adopt British notions of decency and propriety.

The main debate during the visit was about Search's criticism that Green had 'failed' to complete the boundary fencing. A good deal lay behind this dispute. Smyth had written to Green on 19 June saying the Board had considered 'a letter' complaining of conditions at Coranderrk and the Board wanted an explanation of why the reserve had not been fenced 'as it should have been'. Green knew that the anonymous complaints were prompted by the jealousy of Burgess and Search and was hurt by Smyth's peremptory letters treating him as a subordinate after 13 years of cooperation. He simply replied that he had been waiting 'some years' for approval and funds for fencing. Smyth demanded evidence. Green reminded him that he had applied in August 1872 for permission to fence and had asked for £250 for materials and wages but was merely told that the men should begin fencing in their spare time. He had also applied for a portion of the hop income in April 1874 to fence and build new houses. Green knew Smyth's denial was a lie for he had replied to other letters in the same envelope. Afterwards Smyth's clerk said he had seen the letter.[38] The implied criticism of his efficiency infuriated Smyth.

Seven years later Green saw Smyth's minutes and gave his own version of the Board's August 1874 inquiry conducted in his house at Coranderrk:

> Mr Smyth asked me if I had applied for money to erect the fence. I said I had. I do not know, but probably I was a little hot. He got in a great passion, and said, 'Sir, if you answer me that way I will order you out of the house'. I said, 'Mr Smyth, if I have said anything wrong I will be glad to apologise'. I said, 'I only said "Yes"'. 'But it is the tone of your speech, sir', he went on, until Mr Macredie insisted on his conducting himself right. He got up and said he would never sit on the Board any more, when he had been found fault with. The Board said Mr Green does not mean any offence. I said, 'No; I do not mean any offence; I might be a little hot'. I was really very sick at the time. I had been very ill with low fever typhoid, and had come back from long tour round the Wimmera district, and had all those letters waiting for me; and answering them, and one thing and another, had upset me. I kept my temper, and stood up and said, 'Well gentlemen, it appears to me that really I cannot give you satisfaction here, as I have really been trying all I can to do everything right. I must confess that there is much just now not done that I would have liked to have done, but I have been away so much and striving to get the hop garden in good order, I have had to neglect things I would otherwise have done; and, seeing there is an inclination in some of the members of the Board to think I have not been doing right, I wish you would relieve me of Coranderrk, and put somebody else here; I will do everything to help them'.[39]

Smyth's minutes were a biased account of the proceedings but, as the only record, they influenced the special meeting convened on 21 August 1874 to consider the future management of Coranderrk. It was the first meeting ever attended by all members. After hearing Smyth read his notes and extracts of reports from the hopmaster Burgess and the overseer Harris, nine members unanimously resolved that, as Green had 'expressed his inability from ill health and other causes to conduct the station satisfactorily', his wish to be relieved of the management would be accepted as a resignation. Although Syme protested, his dissent was not recorded.[40] Aside from Smyth himself, who had made inspections once or twice annually,

---

37 Coranderrk Inquiry 1881:131; Smyth 1878:I 64–5, 95, 110, 463–5; Royal Commission 1877:85–6.
38 BPA – Letter Book 10 June and 8 August 1874; Coranderrk Inquiry 1881:128; *Argus*, 30 November 1881.
39 Coranderrk Inquiry 1881:131.
40 Coranderrk Inquiry 1881:104.

6. THE BOARD TAKES CONTROL

the members' acquaintance with Green and the Kulin was negligible. To date Mackenzie had visited three times, Jennings twice, Thomas, MacBain and Macredie once. Syme had made only private visits, Sumner and Hopkins apparently had never bothered to make the journey to Coranderrk.

But six of the nine knew, although Green did not, that they had approved wages for some workers on 6 June 1872 then reversed their decision when they subsequently sought the Chief Secretary's approval for an additional £1,000 for their development scheme. He approved only on condition that they took steps to reduce costs and make Coranderrk self-supporting as early as practicable.[41] Mackenzie, Macredie, Jennings and Smyth had voted on 6 May 1873 to fence when funds were available and give Green the hop income for wages and other needs; the decision was reversed because of Anglican complaints before Green was informed. Green was still unaware that on 11 June 1874 Smyth had authorised Search – not him – to complete the necessary seven miles (11.2 km) of boundary fencing 'as soon after the first of July as possible' by hiring European contractors at £40 per mile. This decision, too, was cancelled when the Board was ordered to pay the hop income into the Treasury.[42]

The Board members had resolved that Green should remain in charge while they advertised for a successor. A week later Smyth obtained the vice-chairman's permission to place the teacher in charge and order Green to leave as soon as possible, explaining that he feared the hopmaster Burgess would leave if Green was not removed from the station.[43]

Nineteen months later a Parliamentary inquiry upheld complaints by members of the Mines Department about Smyth's 'tyrannical and overbearing' conduct towards his subordinates. He was found guilty of abusing, coercing and undermining his officers, of vindictiveness, inconsistency and failure to control his violent fits of temper. He was ultimately forced to resign all public offices on 4 May 1876. Meanwhile however, this 'half-mad bureaucrat' had forced Green from Coranderrk and ensured that the Kulin no longer had any rights of self-determination in the farming township they had built for themselves.[44]

41 BPA – Minutes 6 June and 2 July 1872.
42 BPA – Letter Book, 11 and 18 June 1874.
43 BPA – Letter Book, 27 August 1874; BPA – Minutes 21 August 1874.
44 Hoare 1974:33–40.

Chapter 7
LOSS OF A GOOD MASTER

> ... I think it would be cruel on the part of the Board to move the aborigines from Coranderrk, and that is why I refused to be a party to it. There is no data to show that it is unhealthy for the aborigines.
>
> John Green 1881[1]

The Kulin were stunned by Smyth's letter ordering Green to hand over control of Coranderrk to the young teacher appointed four months earlier. Rev. J. Heinrich Stähle, an ordained Moravian missionary who had left the Wimmera after five years work because of the death of his first wife, was equally surprised at Smyth's order that he was to take temporary charge of the station. He replied on 2 September 1874 and enclosed a petition against Green's removal that he had penned 'as requested by the black people'. His own letter reported that Green had told the Kulin he would not hand over the management until his appeal had been heard as he had not intended to resign and leave the station. Stähle asked Smyth to clarify his own position since he and Green had always worked 'in unity and peace'. At the Board meeting on 11 September after Smyth had read letters from Green and Stähle and his own notes on statements by the consultant Search, those present – old members Macredie, Sumner and MacBain and the two appointed in 1871, Thomas and Syme – refused to allow Green to withdraw his resignation and confirmed Stähle's temporary appointment. Syme complained once again that his dissent at the August meeting was not recorded.[2]

The advertisement specifying the needed qualifications for management of Coranderrk – 'a general knowledge of stock, farming and gardening' – attracted 10 applicants, but the nine members present on 2 October instead appointed Stähle as teacher/manager at £150 a year. Their decision to hire a gardener was never implemented. Green, promised £240 compensation for the house built at his own expense, removed his family to his Healesville property in early October and prepared to continue his duties as General Inspector.

MacBain, the Board's spokesman in the Legislative Assembly, had been one of the most conscientious and influential members ever since he was appointed president on Heales' death in 1864. He now requested leave of absence and was abroad until January 1876. No other member had sufficient authority or interest to curb Smyth's usurpation of power. Sumner, who had served as vice-president and vice-chairman for eight years and was now in the Legislative Council, had attended only a third of the meetings since 1872. The other members of Parliament, Thomas and Hopkins, rarely attended. Macredie and Jennings were preoccupied with the interests of the mission committees. Mackenzie and Syme, the members best acquainted with Coranderrk, found themselves helpless to alter majority decisions.

---

1   Coranderrk Inquiry 1881:136.
2   Coranderrk Inquiry 1881:104.

From 1874 onwards the weakness of a Board structure for policy making in Aboriginal affairs became apparent. The Board for the Protection of the Aborigines was not responsible to a clientele in the same way as the boards administering education, agriculture and land use, where consumer demand and public scrutiny had greater influence on decision-making. The vesting of control in such boards, neither executive nor wholly advisory, had served in the early days of the colony as a check on executive power and a means of ensuring a balanced representation on matters of public concern. But public and Parliamentary indifference decreased ministerial accountability in the case of Aboriginal affairs which was a minor item in any government's calendar of business.

The responsible Minister, the Chief Secretary, was usually also Premier and had many other duties. A sympathetic incumbent had sufficient political power to force relevant departments such as Lands, Education and Treasury to pay heed to Aboriginal needs, and the authority to secure Cabinet and Parliamentary support for Board policies, or to delay or reverse Board decisions. But the *ex officio* chairman had no first-hand knowledge of Board decision-making, for no Minister attended meetings between 1869 and 1913. Public criticism of policy was necessarily directed at the Minister but his replies relied on information supplied by the vice-chairman or secretary. Ministers could evade criticism by arguing that they were bound to abide by the decisions of the distinguished citizens serving in an honorary capacity as appointed Board members. Governments were always reluctant to challenge policy for fear of affronting the church groups involved in Aboriginal welfare work. No government would risk the scandal of a mass resignation of Board members thereby necessitating the establishment of a public service department.

As the Act made no provision for their removal, members served until they resigned or died. Thus policy making was left to a small group able to nominate like-minded men to replace those opponents who resigned because of disagreement with majority decisions. These busy men who met for a few hours a month had neither the expertise nor the opportunity to evaluate past policies and little control over the employees and missionaries who implemented their decisions. In fact, staff members could shape policy by their own control of information. Smyth and his successors as secretary decided the agenda for meetings, wrote the minutes and correspondence, and responded to ministerial requests for advice. Unchecked by the rules and hierarchy of normal departmental structure, they had virtual autonomy in administering the policy ostensibly framed by Board members.

The apolitical context of Aboriginal policy was both a weakness and a safeguard. Members from both sides of the House had pressed the claims of Aborigines as a matter of conscience since 1858 and by 1876 government leaders spoke piously of a Parliamentary tradition that the welfare of Aborigines was not a matter for party dispute.[3] But the Board ultimately depended upon the Minister, Cabinet and Parliament for the budget decisions and legislation needed to implement policy. This subordination discouraged long-term planning, as ministries changed constantly in colonial Victoria. Governments could delay or reverse Board decisions simply by refusing funds. Unstable governments were often ready to placate the lobby groups which wanted Aboriginal land or labour rather than the voteless Aborigines and the eccentric few who supported their interests.

In the 14 years since the Board's establishment, the Kulin had only once challenged their manager's authority and they had settled the matter with Green before the Board agreed to investigate. From 1875 onwards they had to go beyond the Board to appeal the decisions of the men appointed as their protectors.

Smyth's stubborn support for the irascible old hopmaster Burgess caused most of the trouble. Within weeks of Green's departure Stähle reported that the men refused to work under Burgess and that the hopmaster and overseer would not recognise his own authority as manager. On 19 October Smyth sent

---

3   Victorian Parliamentary Debates, Session 1876:975.

7. LOSS OF A GOOD MASTER

a formal warning that all men who remained disobedient would lose their rations. Macredie, Sumner, Jennings and Syme were asked to approve this retrospectively: they did so but Syme never attended again. Four days later Macredie, Jennings and Mackenzie met. They ordered the staff to cooperate, instructed Harris to work full time with the Kulin in the hop ground, and ordered Smyth to caution Burgess against using 'harsh or irritating language' to the men.[4] Mackenzie never attended again. Smyth instructed Burgess to moderate his language – and to bribe workers with tobacco.

The residents' growing discontent was not directed at Stähle: Green later said he had recommended this appointment because he was 'a very good man; the blacks liked him very well'.[5] Although he was temperamentally more authoritarian, Stähle did try to 'go with them and work with them' as Green had done. He did his best to prevent the employment of Europeans at Coranderrk, insisting that all work could be done by 'the people on the place'. He also begged for the regular wages which the Board had publicly announced in the last annual report, reporting that 'the blacks said to me when white people do these work they get paid for it but not we'.[6] By December 1874 the promise of cash wages had made all work 'more cheerfully and diligently'; but in fact they were paid only for hop picking and at a third of the rate given to Europeans. As a measles epidemic affected the whole community they were outnumbered by European pickers hired for the first time. The workers' resentment of the Board's broken promises increased when Search and Burgess insisted on hiring Europeans for making bricks and charcoal burning, fencing and construction of a second hop kiln costing £405, and hired Burgess' son as his assistant. Stähle disapproved, as Moravian missionaries were skilled tradesmen and had always taught their charges to master all the skills needed in their communities. Yet he, like Green, was ignored.

As the Board's correspondence for 1875 has been lost there are only hints of how the Kulin expressed their increasing discontent about the continuing recruitment of newcomers whose needs took precedence over their own, the delay in paying wages and their displacement by European labour on the land which they had cleared and made profitable. After the founder of Coranderrk, Simon Wonga, died of tuberculosis early in 1875 his cousin William Barak was the only Woiworung clan head left. All of the Kulin recognised his right to speak for the owning clan and he and his young speakers sent written complaints to the Board secretary. Smyth told Macredie and Sumner of their letters on 9 April, when the Board met for the first time in three months. They ordered Smyth to investigate, and Jennings was also present to hear his report in May. But the minutes record no decision on these protests. An unprecedented deputation of seven Kulin men attended the Board meeting on 7 July 1875. They were heard and ordered to return home; the members decided to defer all discussion of the management until their consultant Search could recommend a new manager.

Green had come daily to Coranderrk to help Stähle during the measles epidemic at hop picking time and no doubt Smyth believed he had incited the Kulin demands for his return. At this July meeting the Board suddenly resolved to send Green to form a station on the Murray, an idea debated and deferred ever since 1872. The wording of the resolution was insulting. The Board forbad Green to keep any stock of his own on the new reserve and warned that they planned to reduce his excessive salary but would pay him adequately if his services were retained after he reported on the feasibility of forming a new station.

This meeting which ignored the complaints of Barak's deputation and ordered Green to leave Healesville was attended by Smyth, the mission committee representatives Jennings and Macredie, the long-time vice-chairman Sumner, and the MLA Thomas who died the next year. It was also the first meeting attended by three new members Godfrey, Curr and LeSouef who soon dominated Board affairs. All of

---

4 BPA – Minutes 23 and 27 October 1874.
5 Coranderrk Inquiry 1881:131.
6 BPA – Stähle to Smyth, 21 September 1874.

the earlier members had been men of ability but few could claim to be well-born or well-educated. They were respectable middle-class men of substance but they were not 'gentlemen' by the canons of the time. The newcomers had entree to a level of colonial society which these self-made men, mostly Scottish nonconformists, could not penetrate.

All three had begun their careers on Victorian pastoral stations in the 1840s after being educated in England or Europe. They were or had been wealthy and their families had some claim to gentility. All three were 'establishment' figures, prominent in the public affairs of the colony, conservative in politics and strongly identified with the squatting interests which brought down Graham Berry's government in 1875. They were previously acquainted with each other through their membership of hospital management committees, the Old Colonists' Association (founded by Mackenzie) and the Zoological and Acclimatisation Society of which Sumner, Godfrey and LeSouef were executive members. The newcomers had a reputation as competent businessmen and an interest in scientific farming. They also had literary tastes plus pretensions to an authoritative knowledge of Aboriginal society.

The wealthy pastoralist and businessman Frederick Race Godfrey (1828–1910) had the surest claim to upper-class origins.[7] Son of an army officer, he had spent his childhood in India and joined his brother at Boort Station on the northern margin of Jajowrong territory from 1847 to 1863. He prided himself on his knowledge of 'the Loddon blacks' but had no contact with the Kulin after he moved to a pastoral property on the outskirts of Melbourne. He revealed his ignorance that Kulin social organisation differed from that of their neighbours when he challenged Green's description of their customs,[8] and made no contribution to the ethnographic studies later published by Smyth and Curr. Although accounted a man of principle and moderation during his three-year Parliamentary career which began in 1874, he proved dictatorial and bigoted during his 15-year Board membership. Godfrey had long been extremely prominent in Anglican church affairs and was largely responsible for altering the carefully non-denominational policy maintained by the founding members and later by the tolerant Presbyterian MacBain.[9]

Born in Tasmania, Edward Micklethwaite Curr (1820–1889) was the son of a wealthy merchant and pastoralist who first acquired Kulin land in 1839. He managed stations on the territory of Ngurai-illam-wurrung and Pangerang clans until 1851, travelled, was unsuccessful in various ventures in other colonies, then returned in 1862 and rose rapidly in the public service to become Chief Inspector of Stock from 1873. Various publications were already acclaimed and he had excellent political contacts because of his father's prominence in achieving separation from New South Wales. His social status was less certain than Godfrey's because of the family's loss of wealth (and perhaps because they were Catholics), and he was defensively insistent that only an 'educated gentleman' could command the 'obedience and confidence' of Aborigines.[10] In his eight-year career as a Board member he displayed the obstinacy, 'overbearing manner and pompous egotism' which had made his father unpopular.[11]

Other members disapproved of Green; Curr hated him from their first meeting and still continued his vendetta in his 1886–87 publication. It was partly snobbery which made him despise Green, who was neither gentleman nor businessman, and partly rivalry over their claims to ethnographic expertise. Curr offered no information for Smyth's compendium and his own reminiscences and ethnographic volumes reveal his profound ignorance of the social organisation of the Kulin and Pangerang.[12] He was scathing in

---

7   de Serville 1980:App. 1.
8   Royal Commission 1877:86.
9   Godfrey resigned in 1879 to go abroad but was re-appointed in 1896 and finally resigned in 1907. His bullying manner was also apparent in his cross examination of Ogilvie during the Royal Commission hearings (1877:1–12).
10   Royal Commission 1877:90.
11   de Serville 1980:122–3.
12   Curr 1883, 1886:I 36–142; Howitt MS:57.

his criticisms of the major contributors to Smyth's work, and of Smyth himself, condemning him because he was 'no bushman' and had no acquaintance with Aborigines 'in their savage state'. His criticisms in fact reveal his own ignorance of the differences between the Kulin and their neighbours, for the chapter he objected to came substantially from the unpublished accounts of the Woiworung Guardian William Thomas and the details are independently corroborated in Barak's descriptions for Howitt during the 1880s.[13]

Curr was particularly vain about his own proficiency as a linguist and singled out Green's translations for ridicule asserting that Green had no knowledge of 'any language but his own'.[14] Green's texts were speeches made by Simon Wonga and William Barak, and the Woiwurru vocabulary Green contributed in 1863 shows agreement with the material provided by Thomas despite the difference in transcription.[15] Green lacked the education to analyse grammatical structure but the surviving Board records suggest he had a fair comprehension of two Kulin dialects. In the early years this was a necessity, for the Taungurong had little English and Wonga and Barak always used Woiwurru in court deliberations and public speeches. To the end of his life Barak, a 'fluent and gifted' speaker in Woiwurru, was never able to express himself well in English.[16] Although Smyth's acknowledgment of Green's aid is scarcely fulsome – it was written in October 1876, after their quarrel – there is much evidence, in sections written earlier, that Green had been a valued collaborator and indeed a major contributor of demographic, linguistic and ethnographic data on the Kulin and other groups.[17]

Curr's own volumes repeat a fiction he later stated on oath at the 1881 inquiry: that the 'tribal' owners of Coranderrk and Melbourne had been extinct for 40 years. When forced to admit he had made only two or three brief visits and knew nothing of the station's history he supported his claim to expert knowledge of the Coranderrk residents by stating that he 'knew something of the language'. Probably it was to substantiate his claims that he later published his own word list labelled 'Healesville, Upper Yarra-Oorongir language', and reprinted portions of Bunce's vocabulary of the 1840s (a mixture obtained from Melbourne and Geelong Aborigines) for the 'Lower Yarra'. He provided his own 'Mordiyallook' (i.e. Bunurong) word list, possibly to challenge Smyth's conclusion that the dialects of the Woiworung and Bunurong were almost identical. Curr's publication also stressed his knowledge of 'Ngooraialum' (Ngurai-illam-wurrung), a fourth dialect of this unnamed language, although admitting he had not heard it spoken for '34 years'.[18]

Curr's authority for information on the names, numbers and locations of the 'tribes' speaking this language was the third member appointed to the Board in 1875. The quoted account, an incomplete list of Taungurong clans, stresses the author's 'considerable opportunity' for gaining accurate information. The writer's prejudice and ignorance of Kulin life had already been painfully revealed in his contribution to Smyth's book.[19]

The third new Board member, Albert A.C. LeSouef (1828-1902) had arrived at the Goulburn Protectorate Station in Ngurai-illam-wurrung territory as a 13-year-old in 1841 and left within two years when his father, William, was dismissed. He was subsequently employed overlanding cattle and as overseer on various pastoral properties mostly outside the Kulin area. From 1863 he served as Usher of the Black Rod in the Legislative Council, and from 1870 was also secretary of the Zoological and Acclimatisation

---

13 Curr 1886:I 52–5, 238–41; Howitt MS, 1904.
14 Curr 1886:I 243–4.
15 Smyth 1878:II 98–133.
16 Mrs Bon, in *Argus*, 28 November 1931.
17 Smyth 1878:I vi and *passim*.
18 Coranderrk Inquiry 1881:120–1, 126; Curr 1887:III 523–35; Smyth 1878:II 13–14.
19 Curr 1886:III 523–4, 566; Smyth 1878:II 289–99.

Society. LeSouef's family were accounted gentlefolk; his wife's kin were well connected (the late Peter Snodgrass was the least successful of her brothers-in-law); his work ensured a wide acquaintance with influential members of colonial society. LeSouef was widely respected and esteemed but to the Kulin his name was merely a reminder of his father's cruelty. He was a conscientious Board member for 27 years and an ardent opponent of the secular principles on which it was founded.[20]

Although affiliated with the Plymouth Brethren, LeSouef had been educated at a Moravian school and had a special sympathy for the Moravian missionaries. This led to friendship with Rev. F.A. Hagenauer, the colony's senior Moravian missionary, and their families were later linked by marriage. But Hagenauer, appointed superintending missionary of the Anglican and Presbyterian-Moravian mission stations in 1872, was no friend to Green whose influence with the Aborigines at his station had roused his jealousy in 1869.[21] The publication in the Board's annual reports of Green's advice on the allocation of funds to the missions, and his criticisms of their staff, had increased his enmity. This authoritarian old German missionary resented Green's rival authority and criticised his claim to be a missionary without being ordained. He particularly deplored the ethnographic research which Green conducted at Smyth's request, since he abhorred and forbad any persistence of Aboriginal language and custom at the stations he controlled. His views and those of the three new members shaped Board policy for the next decade. Their refusal to heed the opinions of the Coranderrk pioneers provoked protests which attracted the attention of press, public and Parliament.

The Minister who arranged the appointment of Godfrey, Curr and LeSouef at Smyth's request was Robert Ramsay, Postmaster General and acting Chief Secretary from July 1874 to August 1875. He had defended Green in 1870 and had continued to support the development of Coranderrk.[22] Smyth may have acted alone for the minutes, unusually, make no mention of a Board decision to nominate new members. MacBain later told Parliament that the MLA Godfrey solicited appointment for himself and his friends, and Godfrey retorted that Board affairs were in Smyth's hands at this time because other members would not attend.[23] In fact, MacBain was abroad and Mackenzie and Syme had withdrawn because of their disapproval of Smyth's treatment of Green. Curr later said he had refused the appointment but was persuaded by Ramsay. Although under oath he was lying: he, Godfrey and LeSouef had all asked the Minister for appointment.[24]

As a result of their actions the members who knew Green and the Kulin left the Board in 1874 and 1875. Three old pastoralists who knew nothing of Kulin history or social organisation – but prided themselves on their knowledge of 'the blacks' – began to dictate Board policy. Godfrey was elected vice-chairman at this July 1875 meeting, Curr succeeded him in 1877 and LeSouef held the office from 1879 to 1881. The occupations of the three new members permitted them to travel on Board business and with Smyth they formed a voting bloc.

The Board's opinions altered profoundly between 1874 and 1876. The secular emphasis of the founding members had been maintained by Syme, MacBain, Sumner and Smyth, but with their departure denominationalism became important. The original members, mostly urban and radical in politics, had been replaced by conservatives of pastoral background. Now a majority were Anglicans, well aware of the Melbourne mission committee's anger at Green's criticisms of their staff and Smyth's refusal to recognise missionaries as anything more than local guardians responsible for the secular welfare of station residents.[25]

---

20 de Serville 1980:78, App. 2 and 3.
21 Coranderrk Inquiry 1881:136.
22 BPA – Annual Report 1875.
23 CSIC 17 June 1875, 75/G6539; Victorian Parliamentary Debates, Session 1876:983–4.
24 Coranderrk Inquiry 1881:123–4; CSIC 75/G6539, G6827, H6805, 24–25 June 1875.
25 CSIC 71/711616, 5 July 1871.

7. LOSS OF A GOOD MASTER

At this July 1875 meeting, the members also discussed difficulties with the Moravian missionaries; the Board had censured them in the past but now declined to intervene. The annual report, published two months earlier, had included Green's proposal to merge the two Gippsland stations. He reported that the Kurnai and the missionaries had agreed to abandon the Anglican station and settle at Hagenauer's mission – if the Board paid £700 for the land needed to extend this reserve. Green had also recommended removing the Framlingham residents to Coranderrk and the Anglican mission in the Western District if the mission committee secured a Moravian missionary to replace their incompetent manager. None of this pleased the Anglican members and it was particularly offensive to the new vice-chairman Godfrey, an Anglican lay canon.

The next meeting on 4 August 1875 was attended only by Smyth and the three new members. Learning that Green had departed for the Murray, Godfrey, Curr and LeSouef constituted themselves a sub-committee to report on the future management of Coranderrk which they visited three days later. Curr said afterwards they knew nothing of the station's history, were not acquainted with the residents and did not even know the name of the manager.[26] After an afternoon's escorted tour they concluded that most residents were suffering from 'consumption' and must be removed to a warmer climate.

Emphasising that their own 'knowledge of the habits of the natives' extended over 30 years, they insisted that the climate and situation of Coranderrk were unsuitable for Aborigines. Their report asserted that '30 per cent' of residents had died in the first half of 1875.

The dwellings at Coranderrk, c. 1886.

---

26   Coranderrk Inquiry 1881:120.

Of the 21 deaths among 142 residents, 11 were caused by measles or resulting 'pleuropneumonia', during an epidemic which seriously reduced the Aboriginal population of Victoria and adjoining colonies. Tuberculosis (consumption or phthisis were the common terms) had killed many Kulin since the 1840s and most of the Woiworung families at Coranderrk were sufferers. This mortality rate was better than at other stations through the 1860s, mainly because the population was young. Green's analysis of the 51 deaths during his 14 years of service argued that a majority had died of untreated 'syphilis' or 'low fever' rather than respiratory complaints. He also pointed out that many were moribund when brought for treatment at this refuge for the sick.[27] Epidemics of 'low fever' and 'intermittent fever' (probably typhoid or paratyphoid spread by contaminated water) ceased when the protected aqueduct was built in 1873. Births exceeded deaths until that year, when 12 died of pleuropneumonia following an influenza epidemic. The worried medical officer conducted *post mortem* examinations and concluded in June 1874 that the 'chest disease' then prevalent was 'not in any way connected with the condition of the station'.

Venereal disease and tuberculosis were common complaints in the European population – Batman died of the first and Heales of the latter – although always under-stated because they were considered evidence of moral lapse or inherited weakness. Both were incurable owing to medical ignorance of the time. Laymen such as the new Board members, and most of the colony's doctors, believed that lung disease was caused by a cold, damp climate and particularly by 'miasmic humours' rising from the ground. Doctors were beginning to understand that the incidence of tuberculosis was linked to poor diet and overcrowding. It was not until the 1890s that the manner in which the tubercle bacillus was transmitted through infected milk and the contagious discharges of sufferers was clearly understood and acted upon by the colony's medical men.[28]

Godfrey, Curr and LeSouef were genuinely concerned about the death rate at Coranderrk. But their decision to abandon the station was also influenced by the fact that on 7 August, the day of their visit, the Chief Secretary had received a letter from Stähle. He wrote on behalf of the residents pleading for the dismissal of Burgess. He sent it to the Board's *ex officio* chairman by registered mail because Smyth had not replied to the complaints he and the Kulin had made over five months earlier. The senior public servants Smyth and Curr were outraged that a subordinate had complained directly to the Minister and vice-chairman Godfrey was embarrassed at having to provide an explanation for his political opponent Graham Berry, the new Chief Secretary. The sub-committee considered that the complaints were further reason to remove the Kulin to the hinterland and dismiss Stähle.

Only Smyth and Jennings joined the newcomers when they approved their own report, on 18 August. They then interviewed the horticultural consultant Search about a replacement for Stähle. A week later the same members, plus Macredie, voted to abandon Coranderrk. They planned to persuade the Minister by arguing that the sale of this valuable reserve would pay for a new station without additional appropriation. They also resolved to employ for two months an experienced pastoral station manager to inspect all stations and depots in company with Curr.

They chose one of their own kind. Christian Ogilvie claimed experience of 'managing the blacks' since about 1841, apparently with the Kurnai of Gippsland, and had the education and inclination, if not the wealth, to consider himself a 'gentleman'.[29] The next day Smyth sent him to report on Coranderrk. Ogilvie later recalled that his report led to Stähle's dismissal. At their next meeting on 7 September, the same

---

27 Royal Commission 1877:81. Hickson had reported that most residents of Acheron station were suffering from syphilis and Green argued that most newcomers to Coranderrk were also affected. Syphilis and gonorrhoea were not distinguished in the nineteenth-century reports on causes of death but the incidence of sterility and of children suffering from congenital syphilis suggests that both forms were present among the Kulin from the 1840s (Barwick 1971; Smith 1979:294–303).
28 Balfe 1951:150–1, Smith 1979:287–94; Barwick 1971.
29 Royal Commission 1877:1–12; Coranderrk Inquiry 1881:116–9. Christie (1979:191) says Ogilvie was manager of a sheep station near Omeo.

members appointed Ogilvie temporary manager. They suspended Stähle for his refusal to acknowledge Ogilvie as the Board's Inspector instead of Green and for his 'improper' letters to the Board and attempt to bypass them by appealing to the Minister. A week later the three new members and Macredie interviewed Stähle and voted to dismiss him. Smyth rejoined the meeting and they resolved to appoint Search's choice as manager. They also decided to warn Burgess that Ogilvie had complete control of the management, although he would be retained as hop grower. Curr later made public the fact that the new members considered Burgess incompetent;[30] but they did not dismiss him, presumably because they feared to lose face by seeming to heed the residents' complaints. Jennings, absent from this meeting, apparently disapproved of their treatment of Stähle. Through his intervention, the Anglican mission committee hired Stähle to take charge of Lake Condah as soon as he left Coranderrk in October 1875.

After this 14 September meeting, vice-chairman Godfrey wrote to the Minister nominating another old pastoralist to replace G.A. Syme who had resigned as a protest against the Board's treatment of Green and the decision to abandon Coranderrk. Syme later explained under oath that he had refused to join Smyth's 'fishing inquiry' to investigate Green's management in August 1874 because it was composed of members 'bent upon' Green's removal; their animus was, he said, indicated by the trivial nature of the complaints and their readiness to take Green's words as a formal resignation. He ceased to attend after the Board rejected Green's appeal to remain at Coranderrk because Smyth had refused to record his disagreement and his attempts to amend resolutions. Syme also declined to join the new members' August 1875 investigation, declaring their criticisms of the climate and management were ridiculous and that all of the troubles stemmed from Green's unjust removal.

Unlike others who withdrew because of disagreement with Board policy, Syme was prepared to make his disapproval public. He was largely responsible for the various *Age* and *Leader* articles championing Green in the ensuing years. The radical *Age* supported the reform policies of Premier and Chief Secretary Graham Berry and had five times the circulation of the ultraconservative *Argus* which was labelled 'The Squatter's Friend and Vested Interests' Guardian' by those antagonistic to its support for the Legislative Council and pastoral interests.[31] Syme asked Berry to intervene so Green's case could be examined during a subsequent Royal Commission inquiry and the *Age* journalists, who became Berry's political proteges, secured the board of inquiry which finally made public the Board's treatment of Green and the Coranderrk people. The Aboriginal protests received extraordinary publicity because they happened to coincide with a crisis in colonial politics. The fate of Coranderrk became almost a test case for issues then bitterly contested by the conservative establishment and Berry's supporters. Both newspapers were politically partisan and they took opposite sides in the debate over Coranderrk as in most other public controversies of the time.

Public criticism probably increased the new members' antagonism to Green and strengthened their determination to end the 'rebellion' at Coranderrk. As none of the new members had any acquaintance with the Kulin since the 1840s they found it impossible to believe that the Coranderrk people had adapted their traditional culture to a new kind of political expertise. Ignorance and a profound paternalism encouraged Godfrey, Curr and LeSouef to assume that Aborigines must be the pawns of agitators. Because they could not directly criticise various prominent sympathisers, Green became the scapegoat. The renegade action of the former member Syme, in publicising and politicising the policies and internal disputes of the Board, strengthened the intransigent attitudes of this conservative clique. Embarrassed by the favourable *Age* reports on Green, they used the *Argus* for their counter propaganda. The *Argus* published much information which could only have been obtained from the Board's members or secretary.

---

30 Coranderrk Inquiry 1881:124.
31 Coranderrk Inquiry 1881:104. For an account of the influence exerted by the Symes, and the rivalry between the *Age* and *Argus*, see Serle 1971:26–31.

The decisions of the new members were opposed by Board members who had a better acquaintance with the Kulin, by the Coranderrk people themselves and, most embarrassingly, by their own employee Ogilvie who also claimed a lifetime's experience of 'managing the blacks'. He too was blinkered by his views about discipline, temperance, the genetic superiority of 'half castes' and the causation of tuberculosis; but he was a fair-minded man. In his first report on 20 September 1875, he stated that the site was unsuitable for Aborigines because it was too cold and wet and too near the town although he found no evidence of drunkenness or prostitution. He warned that 'by far the larger proportion of the Aborigines at Coranderrk would prefer remaining there, partly because it is their country, or near it'.[32] He upheld the residents' attachment to this location in private reports to the Board, and publicly, and thus helped to defeat the abandonment scheme proposed by Godfrey, Curr and LeSouef.

Smyth and the founding members of the Board knew full well that there had been only one case of prostitution since Coranderrk was formed, and that drunkenness was virtually unknown before Green's departure.[33] The new members and their employee Ogilvie, knowing nothing of the deliberate recruitment of mostly 'half caste' children and young women for the Coranderrk school, ignorantly assumed these were the offspring of resident families and therefore queried the morality of the Kulin. Few European men believed the 'lubras' as chaste as their own womenfolk: Ogilvie and Curr were prepared to deny that the Kulin were 'virtuous' even without evidence.[34] Sniggering speculation about the parentage of 'half castes' became an increasing threat as young 'half caste' couples married and produced a second generation of mixed ancestry. Rumours of immorality were an effective weapon for interested parties who sought abandonment of Coranderrk so they could acquire the land. Such rumours could not be openly discussed and repudiated in annual reports and slanderous reports persisted in the district despite the proof of their falsity supplied by all witnesses at various inquiries.[35]

Ogilvie's report declared that he could remove the Coranderrk residents by autumn if the Board decided to send them to the Murray and providing a reserve were prepared immediately. The phrasing suggests he knew of Green's reports that there was no suitable site on the Murray.

But the minutes of the meeting the next day, 21 September, did not mention Ogilvie's report or Green's letters. Macredie, Smyth and the new members, and the MLA Hopkins (who had not attended since the 1874 removal of Green and never attended again), agreed to ask the Minister to restore the hop income to the Board. They resolved to notify the Anglican mission committee, which wanted to form a northern station, that the Board planned to collect all northern Aborigines at a new station somewhere on the Murray. They also voted to inform Green they had no further need for his services. As compensation for dismissal, they offered three months' work as relieving manager at the Wimmera mission station at the insultingly low rate of £50 a year – less than that paid a ploughman.

Six years later, under oath, Green recalled his perception of the events leading up to his dismissal as Inspector. Smyth's letter of 22 September dismissing him without explanation came, he said, two weeks after he reported that the Kulkyne site Smyth had chosen was under water and hopelessly unsuitable. Green had advised against forming any Murray station as all of the young Aborigines were willing to come with him to Coranderrk. Meanwhile, he had received a letter (probably from the teacher Stähle) warning him that Ogilvie had 'stated that it was the whole object to get the blacks removed from Coranderrk'.

---

32 BPA – Annual Report 1876:App. 2.
33 Royal Commission 1877:116 and BPA – Annual Reports 1861–74.
34 Coranderrk Inquiry 1881:124; BPA – Annual Report 1876:App. 2.
35 This issue was debated at length in later inquiries, yet the fiction endured (Royal Commission 1877; Coranderrk Inquiry 1881; Massola 1975).

7. LOSS OF A GOOD MASTER

Green believed that the Board had intended to use him as a 'decoy' in moving the Kulin to the Murray so their reserve could be sold and that he was dismissed because he 'would be no party' to removing the Kulin from Coranderrk.[36]

At the end of September, only Smyth and the new members met to approve measures to enforce discipline at Coranderrk. They decided to seek Orders-in-Council to control two Burapper men who wished to leave. They soon learned that Chief Secretary Berry would not condone this; nor would he consent to sell Coranderrk or restore the hop income to Board control. However, he did agree to advance money from the surrendered income for Board needs.

The same members, and Macredie, met again on 6 October to discuss Green's reports that there was no suitable site for a Murray station. They voted to send Curr and Ogilvie to the same areas Green had toured, although Smyth and Macredie were certainly aware that Green had reported ever since 1862 that drunkenness, prostitution and mortality from tuberculosis were serious problems on the Murray. They also resolved to have the Healesville constable visit regularly to assist the dormitory matron Miss Robertson and the overseer Harris in managing Coranderrk during Ogilvie's six weeks' absence.

The sudden dismissal of Stähle had disturbed those at Coranderrk. He, like Green, had recognised their capacity and their determination to manage their affairs for themselves. After his departure in October, they had no protection from the authoritarian direction of Search, Burgess and Ogilvie. The school was closed and religious services ceased. Every family was in mourning – 31 had died since Green's departure – and they missed his medical care and, apparently, the familiar Presbyterian rituals with which he had comforted the sick and mourners. The news that they would be removed and their land sold was openly discussed in the district but there was no staff member with sufficient authority to intercede for them.

Since Smyth and the Board had ignored their appeals, the Coranderrk pioneers took their complaints to other men of influence. Barak had some acquaintance with the old justice George Harker who had retired to Lilydale when he left Parliament in 1874. He had shown sympathy for their needs when Treasurer in 1859 and was well known to their friend Dr Embling, the former Board member, and to the Chief Secretary Berry. They went to Harker and he wrote on their behalf to the Minister on 23 October opposing abandonment of Coranderrk.[37] In fact, their protest was in vain, for Berry's government had been defeated on its land tax proposals three days earlier and vice-chairman Godfrey was easily able to reassure the new Chief Secretary, J.A. MacPherson (like himself a moderate from a pastoralist background) when he asked the Board for a report on Harker's letter.

The Kulin protest was not mentioned in the minutes of the Board meeting on 10 November. Only Godfrey, LeSouef and Smyth were present to discuss Green's requests to be reinstated. They decided to offer him one month's salary on condition he gave up all claims to compensation for dismissal without notice after 14 years service and to inform him that he could not continue as Inspector as 'another gentleman' had been appointed. They rejected his offer to return as manager of Coranderrk. The decisions were probably invalid as three did not constitute a quorum. They were also foolishly spiteful, as Search's nominee had refused the post and no suitable manager could be found. At this meeting, the members simply deferred for Ogilvie's return the serious complaints by Miss Robertson the dormitory matron left in charge of Coranderrk. She urged the dismissal of Burgess, his son and the three European labourers Ogilvie had hired for the hop plantation. She also reported that all the men had refused to work unless rations were increased, in other words, gone on strike, and that certain men were demanding payment of the wages promised almost a year earlier.

---

36 Coranderrk Inquiry 1881:132; *Leader*, 19 February 1876.
37 CSIC 75/Hl2439, 23 October 1875.

Burgess had succeeded in displacing the Kulin from their farm and he openly threatened further changes when he became manager, as he confidently expected. After three years of hop cultivation, the Kulin's living standard had worsened substantially as they no longer shared the income from sales of produce and could not be spared to go shearing and harvesting to earn cash wages. The Board had reneged on its promises to provide stock and funds for fencing, a hospital, new houses and regular wages.

After the 1 December 1875 Board meeting another of the founding members ceased to attend – although he did not formally resign. The prominent Methodist Sumner presumably disapproved of the decisions made by Godfrey, LeSouef, Macredie and Smyth. They simply deferred for Ogilvie's attention complaints by the Kulin, the dormitory matron and overseer, and the medical officer's report that Burgess' son, employed by the Board, was annoying the dormitory girls with 'improper attentions'. The main business was a decision to invite the Anglican church committee to form a new station, with Board support, 'in any part of the colony'. It was a tacit admission that the new members had made fools of themselves. Curr and Ogilvie had just returned with the information that there was no site on the Murray except at Kulkyne and they had located only 54 Aborigines. Their tour had cost the Board £210 in expenses plus Ogilvie's salary.

At their next meeting on 14 December the three new members, with Macredie and Smyth, grudgingly offered Green £20/12/0 for his expenses during three months work on the Murray on condition that he relinquished all further claims to compensation for his dismissal. At the same time they appointed Ogilvie 'General Superintendent of Stations' at a salary of £400 a year including expenses with full executive authority to hire, supervise and dismiss all staff on Board stations. He was to have complete control of their management but was explicitly instructed to 'refrain from interference' at the mission stations and to leave the missionaries 'free to act in their own way'.

To placate the striking Coranderrk workers their ration had meanwhile been increased by one-third.[38] Their anxiety was also lessened by Green's return to Healesville as he had resumed his regular religious services at the station and the sick visited him almost daily. Presumably he told them that removal to the Murray was unlikely. Soon after Ogilvie returned on 8 December, he distributed £125 in cash for the hop picking wages owed them since March but decided against a further increase in rations. He ordered Burgess' eldest son from the station, dismissed the European labourers and publicly rebuked the hopmaster for various actions, informing him that his authority would be greatly reduced when a new manager was appointed. Ogilvie confided to his diary his fear that Burgess would never cooperate with other staff and his intention to dismiss the hopmaster if he would not sign a new contract making him subordinate to the station manager.[39]

But by February 1876 the Kulin deeply distrusted Ogilvie and he had lost his sympathy for them. His ignorance of Kulin notions of proper behaviour created much of the trouble. It began in December 1875 when he threatened to prosecute the Taungurong Johnny Webster for horse theft. Green, who was there as usual to conduct Sunday services, explained why Webster believed he had an inherited right to the Board horse he had sold. He witnessed Webster's signature to the apology Ogilvie drafted, which asked the Board to take no action. But Ogilvie went ahead with the prosecution. In the eyes of the Kulin Green had fulfilled his kinship obligations (Webster's father had considered Green his brother) while Ogilvie had betrayed his word. He had already given offence by ridiculing the obligatory mourning behaviour of Kulin women when Eliza of Mount Franklin, now the wife of Barak's speaker Thomas Bamfield, 'damaged herself by beating her skull with a tomahawk' after the deaths of two children within a month.

---

38 Adults now received 6 lb (2.7 kg) meat, 7 lb (3.15 kg) flour, 2 lb (900 g) sugar and 1/4 lb (112 g) tea weekly, with half rations for children over two years: 10–12 pounds (4.5–5.4 kg) of meat and flour was the norm for European pastoral workers.
39 BPA – Journal of Christian Ogilvie, 8–28 December 1875.

Ogilvie's ignorance might have been pardoned but confrontation was inevitable when he decided to build Burgess a house down in the middle of their vegetable garden – away from the two parallel rows of houses where the Kulin and staff had always lived side by side. Green had lived among them, in a bark hut like theirs, until the Board insisted he move into the new dormitory buildings.

From the first the Kulin's own court had resolved, probably as a result of Green's persuasion, that all clans would live together and that the rigid code defining the placement and occupancy of shelters in a camp site would be changed. The dormitories could be accommodated to the Kulin belief system: they were simply a new form of camp for single young men and single women. This segregation of orphaned boys and girls was reconcilable with Kulin notions about propriety. The Coranderrk people kept their new rule despite the problems this caused for individuals in avoidance relationships. Yet one of the most persistent conventions of Kulin society was that the placement of dwellings was a symbolic statement about land ownership:[40] when people from different clans assembled, their dwellings were oriented according to the respective locations of the territories from which the occupiers came. The placement of Burgess' house on their first garden site was an affront. The Kulin opposed the decision not just because it was garden land, although the area they had so laboriously cleared and planted without tools probably had some historical significance for them, but because the siting of Burgess' house challenged an ancient convention about ownership and a new rule made by their court. By ignoring the protests Ogilvie and Burgess showed they had no respect for Kulin laws or for the people who made them.

Birdarak – Tommy Bamfield with his children David and Betsy.

---

40 William Thomas discovered the rule from his observations of assemblies at Melbourne in the 1840s; A.W. Howitt could map the appropriate placement of the Kulin clans and their Pangerang neighbours from the descriptions given by Barak in the 1880s (William Thomas, Journals, 1839–1847; Howitt MS:25–27). Marie Reay (pers. comm.) found in 1944 that some Kulin families from Coranderrk still preferred to camp at Barmah rather than on the Cumeroogunga Aboriginal Station, where the majority of residents were Joti-jota or Pangerang. For the old people this was a decision based on allegiance to 'country', not simply a matter of eligibility to reside on the reserve.

Only one European, John Green, had treated the Kulin as equals, had shown respect for their problems in adapting their notions of proper behaviour to a new kind of community life and had taken the trouble to explain the reasons for European rules and conventions. Early in 1876, there seemed hope for his return.

On 5 January 1876, the former Board vice-chairman MacBain resumed his seat after 14 months of absence overseas and immediately insisted that Ogilvie's powers be reduced. LeSouef backed him. On 12 January they, with Curr, Macredie and Smyth, severely limited Ogilvie's authority as 'General Inspector' and deferred the appointment of the police officer chosen to succeed Stähle as manager. But they accepted the report (written by Ogilvie and signed and submitted by Curr) describing their joint tour which urged the establishment of a new station at Kulkyne and a special medical inspection of Coranderrk.[41] On 31 January MacBain, Smyth and Jennings (who had attended only two meetings since the new members were appointed and had no part in Green's dismissal) met to consider a 'serious complaint about the management' sent directly to MacBain by his former Parliamentary colleague George Harker.

It was Smyth's last Board meeting, for it was the next day that his subordinates in the Mines Department petitioned their Minister to investigate his 'despotic conduct'. He was suspended from all public offices during the resulting inquiry and resigned his public service post on 4 May 1876 after being censured for his 'imperious irritability of disposition and want of self-control'.[42]

Harker's complaints were echoed by the visiting medical officer's January report which condemned the Board's negligence in failing to provide a teacher, so that the children received 'no attention' except for the few dormitory girls under Miss Robertson's care.[43] This complaint, and his denunciation of the Board's failure to renovate or replace the dilapidated huts despite his previous warnings that the occupants' health was threatened, was a grave embarrassment to the Board as his comments had always been published in their annual reports. This was his last report; a few months later the Board accepted advice that a local doctor should visit when needed and thereafter published no accounts of conditions at Coranderrk except for the manager's annual reports. Ogilvie himself was scandalised by the failure to improve residents' living conditions, for he knew that the Board could now draw on the hop income – and had done so to pay for his journey with Curr. He had specifically drawn the doctor's attention to the 'damp floors and generally inferior huts' and noted in his diary that:

> he seemed to agree with me – but how is it that no notice has been taken of this before either Dr Gibson has not reported it – or else he has – & consequently either he or the Board is to blame – palmam qui munit ferat.[44]

Harker's complaint was examined by all the members except Godfrey and Smyth on 3 February. Jennings then won a motion that Green's request to return as manager be considered provided he consented to relinquish all claims to compensation for his dismissal. A committee consisting of all members except LeSouef and Smyth, with Jennings as chairman, was named to examine Green's 'fitness' for appointment. The Board agreed that Smyth should supply relevant information about Green's past service.

The powers of the Board had long been personified by Smyth, the one member and official familiar to the Coranderrk people, and they gleefully celebrated this 'hitch in the Mining Department' when one of the men brought the news from Melbourne on 4 February. Ogilvie's journal recorded that he had to:

---

41 BPA – Minutes 12 January 1876; BPA – Journal of Christian Ogilvie, 20 December 1875.
42 Smyth had already informed the Board on 14 January that he would no longer serve as secretary unless the regulations were amended to relieve him of the duty of certifying Board accounts. With the Minister's approval this became the vice-chairman's responsibility. Smyth did not formally resign as secretary until June and retained his Board membership until June 1878, when he took a post in India (Hoare 1974:33–40; Serle 1949:30; Mennell 1892:425).
43 BPA – Annual Report 1876:App. 16.
44 BPA – Journal of Christian Ogilvie, 31 January 1876.

> explain to him and his admiring crowd – in language that they could understand that Mr Smyth was only temporarily suspended pending the decision of stronger men but that he might be able to justify himself and in that case he would be more powerful than previously but that under any circumstances his suspension did not in the least affect his position with reference to them.

Ogilvie feared that the loss of Smyth's support would further affect his own position already weakened by MacBain's intervention. He was also angry at the Board's decision to consider Green instead of appointing his nominee. He went to Melbourne 'principally about hiring hoppickers' on 8 February the day Green was to be interviewed. But the committee met at MacBain's office and he could not attend.

A few weeks earlier Ogilvie had tried to placate the Kulin by allowing the Taungurong leaders Thomas Bamfield, Peter Hunter and others to take their families for a shearing holiday with Mrs Bon and other friends about Yea and Mansfield for the first time since 1872. Ogilvie's diary entry for 11 February made much of the overseer Harris' report that hostility had increased during Ogilvie's absence in Melbourne. Harris mentioned rumours that certain employers had told these men that 'our object here is to make slaves of them'. Always ready to blame incitement by outsiders when the Kulin resisted his disciplinary measures, Ogilvie was seemingly oblivious of the fact that the whole community was angry about the way he had ridiculed their complaints about Burgess' house, his appointment of Burgess' second son as supervisor in the hop ground and his announced plans to hire 40 European pickers.

Ogilvie used the excuse of taking patients to hospital to return to Melbourne the day before the scheduled Board meeting on 16 February. He was excluded again. Jennings' committee had meanwhile satisfied themselves that Green should be rehired as manager and, after hearing the committee's report, all seven members interviewed Green. He accepted the immediate appointment, at £200 a year plus rations, 'subject to the instructions of the Board through their General Inspector'. Afterwards, Ogilvie saw Godfrey and offered his resignation because Green was not put wholly under his control.

Minor business had been adjourned until the next day and MacBain did not bother to attend. In his absence the other six members and Ogilvie approved altered terms for Green's appointment: he would be 'subject in all things to the instructions of the General Inspector'. Only Curr dissented, apparently because he opposed Green's appointment on any terms. When Green was called in to hear the new offer he refused the appointment. Godfrey's motion authorising Ogilvie to hire a manager and a teacher was then approved unanimously.[45] A teacher was essential because the school had been closed for five months to the dismay of the Kulin, as well as the medical officer and George Harker, a long-time member of the Board of Education.

Green's anxiety about the school was a major reason for his request to return at a lower salary and status and his sacrifice of the compensation due to him. The Coranderrk school was his life's work. He and his wife Mary had kept it open even when they had no assistance but that of senior pupils and had to neglect the other work of the station. It was the school that they and Wonga and Barak had fought for 15 years earlier; the school was what made the Taungurong and Kurung and Jajowrong elders leave their own country so that their children could master new skills. But Green refused to be subordinated to Ogilvie without right of appeal to the Board because he and the Kulin had learned in recent months to distrust Ogilvie's judgment. As Green later explained: 'I was willing to do anything through the Board … but I could not manage in that way … I would not go back if the Inspector could come and tell me, or any of the blacks, to do anything'.[46]

---

45   Ogilvie's diary records that 'the Board met four times and I attended; at the last meeting Mr Halliday was appointed …' (BPA – Journal of Christian Ogilvie, 15–23 February 1876; BPA – Minutes 16 and 17 February 1876).
46   Coranderrk Inquiry 1881:134.

Green's refusal was the result of principle, not pique, and was wholly consistent with his character. He wanted the post for the sake of the Kulin, not his own benefit. Although a practical farmer, enthusiastic scientist, successful preacher and experienced administrator, he was idealistic and naive, obstinate and incapable of tact, wholly ignorant of the meaning of expediency and compromise. He was an admirable man but an impossible public servant.

MacBain, who had successfully fought in January to deprive Ogilvie of complete executive power over the Board stations, was outraged that his colleagues had succumbed to the blackmail of Godfrey and Ogilvie in revising the terms of Green's appointment. When the adjourned Board meeting reconvened for a third session on 18 February MacBain seconded Macredie's motion that Green be offered the position on the original terms. Macredie's motivation is unclear, for he had taken part in all of the previous meetings concerning Green's resignation and dismissal. Perhaps he simply considered it improper that Green should have less freedom than the managers of the four mission stations. Although he was an Anglican his long association with the Presbyterian church committee which funded the Moravian missions had made him aware, like the prominent Presbyterian MacBain, that the Presbyterian committee's convener, Rev. Robert Hamilton, and other prominent churchmen thought highly of Green and considered Coranderrk an unofficial Presbyterian mission station because of Green's proselytising there. It seems likely that the three founding members of the Board were somewhat shaken by the current revelations about Smyth's abuse of his powers and thus doubtful of the wisdom of allotting Ogilvie the authority he demanded.

The Board divided on their motion. The old members MacBain, Macredie and Jennings, who had known Green's work for 15 years, voted for his return. The motion was opposed by Curr, LeSouef and the member appointed a month earlier, Sherbourne Sheppard, an old pastoralist acquaintance of Curr's who had occupied Pangerang territory in the 1840s.[47] Godfrey, as vice-chairman, gave his casting vote against Green's appointment. This majority, who knew of Green only from Smyth's hostile reports, then authorised Ogilvie to bring his nominee Hugh H. Halliday, the old police sergeant recommended as 'a good disciplinarian', for interview despite MacBain's objections that Halliday had no knowledge of farming, stock or Aborigines and was 'the last person who should be appointed'.

No doubt the new members were influenced by Ogilvie's complaints of 'outside interference', based on Harris' account of events during his absence from 8 to 11 February. Harris had failed to mention the influential visitor who arrived in that period whose *Age* and *Leader* reports of 19 February stunned Ogilvie and the Board members. The Mines Department scandal was naturally a major topic of conversation and the headline 'Coranderrk Hop Farm: Mr Green and Mr R. Brough Smyth' ensured that the Board's treatment of Green and the Kulin was quickly made known throughout the colony.

---

47 The new members had proposed Sheppard as Syme's replacement on 14 September 1875, but it was Graham Berry's successor who finally appointed him on 10 January 1876. He had seconded Jennings' motion for Green's reinstatement on 3 February, but presumably was later influenced by the hostile opinion of his old friend Curr. His attendance was good until 1881, but then lapsed, and he took no part in Board affairs after July 1882 although he remained a member until his death in December 1884.

Chapter 8
THE THREAT OF REMOVAL

> ... I am ngurungaeta from my father. When I go I shall leave the word that my sister's son [Robert Wandin] shall be ngurungaeta with him two others. Beside each of the ngurungaeta there was the man to whom he gave 'his words' ... Beside me are Robert Wandin, Tom Mansfield [Bamfield] who gets 'the word' from me, and Tom Dunolly.
>
> William Barak 1882[1]

The lengthy anonymous articles which appeared in the *Age* and *Leader* on 19 February 1876 were written by the agricultural editor John Lamont Dow whose lecture tours and articles on reform of land legislation and agricultural practice had immense influence. Dow shared the radical liberal views of the Syme brothers and Graham Berry and had ambitions to enter Parliament as their protege.[2]

This Scottish-born immigrant, reared in the Geelong district from 1847, had worked as shearer and miner in Victoria and had been an explorer and pastoralist in northern Queensland during the 1860s. He had real sympathy for Aborigines but only a superficial knowledge of them and had too little insight to question the contemporary European view that only 'fullbloods' who clung to their ancient customs were real Aborigines.

Dow had joined the *Age* in 1873 before the anonymous articles which gave Green all the credit for the development of hop growing were published. Probably Dow wrote them in collaboration with the *Leader* editor G.A. Syme whose friendship with Green preceded and outlasted his membership of the Board. Syme may have opposed the appointment of Frederick Search as horticultural consultant and been outvoted by the other members of the selection committee (Smyth and Sumner). Subsequent *Age* and *Leader* attacks on Search and Smyth were clearly influenced by intimate knowledge of Kulin views, as well as the open rivalry between the *Age* and *Argus* and their subsidiary publications on matters of agricultural development. The 1873 articles had so angered Search that he apparently threatened to resign. The next annual report dated July 1874 (when Smyth's quarrel with Green was at its height) had effusively praised Search and Burgess and omitted all reference to the efforts of Green and the Coranderrk residents.

Dow's articles describing his February 1876 visit quoted Harris and Burgess and emphasised that the acting manager Ogilvie was away hiring European labourers. The garbled dating of remarks attributed to Green (who was also absent in Melbourne) suggests Dow was reporting statements heard secondhand from Syme or recalling what Green had told him on earlier visits. The articles accurately recounted the history of Coranderrk and itemised the extensive improvements made by the Kulin in earlier years. Dow pointedly criticised the Board's failure to continue fencing, clearing and growing vegetables since Green's departure, and contrasted Green's success in making the station nearly self-supporting with the Board's

---
1   Howitt MS:34.
2   CSIC 78/N6789, 3 July 1878. J.L. Dow (1837–1923) was MLA for Kara Kara 1877–1893 and Victoria's leading agricultural journalist for 40 years.

current expenditure on European labour. He particularly questioned the economics of hiring pickers from Melbourne since there were 40 men 'able and willing to pick the whole harvest under those who understand how to work them' plus 50 women and girls 'ready as a reserve force'. Dow displayed little sympathy for Smyth, but his February 1876 account is probably a fair representation of the perceptions of Syme, Harris, Green and the Kulin pioneers:

> For some time back, but particularly since the hop growing experiment has been established as a success, Mr R. Brough Smyth has betrayed much anxiety to shift the Aborigines from Coranderrk. Out of the 4800 acres [1943 ha] of the station there are at least 1000 acres [405 ha] of alluvial flats equal in richness to the twenty acres [8.3 ha] already under hops, and for the most part much easier to clear than the present plantation. It is pretty well understood that certain officials and their friends in Melbourne have had their attention directed to the value of Coranderrk, and consequent thereupon there has sprung up in certain quarters a large amount of so-called interest in the welfare of the Coranderrk natives. It has been suggested that, for the benefit of their health, they ought to be shifted up to the Murray. A difficulty has occurred, however, in the positive objection on the part of the aborigines to be shifted, which objection they have conveyed to Mr Green, whom they look upon as their protector.

Dow published details, including the dates of Smyth's letters, of the events leading up to Green's dismissal 'without any cause being given', asserting that he had been subjected to 'a systematic course of persecution' because he would not cooperate in removing the Aborigines from Coranderrk. Dow concluded this masterful piece of propaganda with the comment that 'harassment' had seriously affected Green's health, then criticised hopmaster Burgess:

> Having got rid of Mr Green, the evident aim is now to make out that the blacks are useless, so that a plausible excuse may be obtained for clearing them out. Harris, the farm overseer, is now no longer allowed to enter the hop grounds to direct their labors. He has an order from Mr Smyth to supply Burgess with what blacks he wants at any time, and leave them under his care. Burgess either does not understand how to work the blacks or does not want to. They, the natives, complain that before they are at work long he pretends to be disgusted with them, tells them to drop their tools and leave. Burgess then reports to Melbourne that the blacks are no use, and asks for white labor.

At the end of his visit Dow had called a meeting of residents, identified himself and questioned them about Board policy. He quoted the views expressed by William Barak and others:

> To the question 'Do you or do you not want to leave Coranderrk?' William, who is king of the Yarra tribe, and who acted as spokesman said 'Me no leave it, Yarra, my father's country. There's no mountains for me on the Murray,' which sentiment met with the full approval of the meeting. A wish to have Mr Green back again was volunteered, and my attention particularly requested to what they evidently considered a serious grievance. Burgess, the hop manager had laid down stuff in the midst of their garden with the intention of building himself a new house. This garden they said they had cleared and planted, the land had been set apart for them, and it had always been their own. Burgess has made himself most unpopular with the natives, and this encroachment … was evidently filling their minds with the utmost resentment. The natives of Coranderrk are a fine, healthy-looking intelligent race, and their sympathy with Mr Green is openly shown, as if he were one of themselves, and Mr Smyth a common enemy. Some of them can read the papers, and it appears they became early acquainted with the action of the Mining department against their chief. 'Ha, ha,' one was heard to say, 'Mr Smyth sack Mr Green. Now Mr Smyth get sack "long umself"'.

8. THE THREAT OF REMOVAL

The hop kiln at Coranderrk.

Since Smyth's behaviour was already a *cause célèbre* these press accounts roused public interest in Coranderrk. The Board subsequently had to justify policy decisions in a way never necessary before. The newspaper description of their history and beliefs also heartened the Kulin, showing yet again that some men of influence would heed them even if officials did not. But the apparent leaks from their former employee, Green, probably united the Board members in opposition to him.

On 21 February 1876 the three new members, with Macredie and Jennings, appointed the police sergeant Halliday as manager. MacBain sent his resignation to the Chief Secretary the next day telling him, as he told Parliament a few months later, that he was disgusted by the unfitness of Halliday and by the tactics of the 'little family' of new members led by Godfrey. MacBain revealed that Godfrey had strongly protested Green's return, had been determined to obtain Green's submission to the terms demanded by Ogilvie and, failing in this, had 'stated at the board that if Mr Green were re-appointed he would resign his position'.[3] The minutes, written by Godfrey himself, do not mention these threats.

When Ogilvie returned to Coranderrk on 23 February he learned that a deputation had left 'to complain to some members of the Board of Burgess' House being built in their garden'. He wrote separately to those members he apparently considered his allies – Vice-Chairman Godfrey, Smyth, Sheppard, Macredie and LeSouef – to 'send them back at once without giving them any satisfaction'.[4]

---

3   Victorian Parliamentary Debates, Session 1876:983–5. BPA – Minutes 16, 17, 18, 21 February 1876.
4   BPA – Journal of Christian Ogilvie, 23 February 1876.

The deputation, which walked to Melbourne with the Woiworung clanhead William Barak, included only one of his speakers, his nephew Robert Wandin, for Dunolly and Bamfield were ill. With them were the Taungurong leaders James ('Jemmy') Barker and Peter Hunter, participants in so many earlier deputations, and the younger Jajowrong man William Parker (1845–1886) and Martin Simpson (Ra-ker-nun, 1854–908), orphans reared by Green ever since they were brought from Mount Franklin in 1864.

Owing to Smyth's suspension there was no one at the Board's office in the Mines Department. The relatively new local member E.H. Cameron saw them waiting in the lobbies of Parliament House on 23 February. Cameron had come to the Anderson's Creek goldfield in 1853 and was storekeeper and postmaster at Warrandyte for six years to 1863 when he began farming some 20 miles (32 km) from Coranderrk.[5] He thus had a long acquaintance with the Woiworung and the history of their attempt to secure the land. His sympathy was roused because the men were being loudly berated by the MLA Godfrey who 'threatened that if they dared to interview the authorities he would have them removed at once from Coranderrk'. Cameron thought it his duty as their local member to introduce the deputation to the Chief Secretary and later informed this Minister of Godfrey's threats as evidence that he would use 'any excuse' to achieve abandonment of Coranderrk.[6]

To the Board's chagrin, the next day's *Argus* gave a full account of the deputation's interview with the Chief Secretary on 23 February. Their only complaint, stated 'very respectfully and intelligently', was their 'long-standing grievance' at the removal of Green. They told the Minister of Green's work and asked him '"how would he like it himself" if he had lost a master who had been kind to him?' Godfrey, interjecting, explained Green's removal asserting that his dismissal was his own fault: Green had incessantly objected to necessary changes at the station and was 'one of the most impracticable men' Godfrey had ever met.

Godfrey suggested the deputation explain why Green had neglected the boundary fencing and was embarrassed by the reply: one retorted that Green had sent many letters to the Board but 'in the usual way' nothing was done. Godfrey falsely declared there was no correspondence on the matter and attempted to ridicule the deputation by asking them to explain rumours of drunkenness at Coranderrk. It was probably Jemmy Barker, the only deputation member who was not a staunch teetotaler, who replied: 'if a blackfellow stopped two or three months without ever tasting a nobbler, and then took one or two and lay down and had a sleep, what harm did that do to anybody?' Chief Secretary MacPherson, concluding the interview, said he wished to contradict the rumour that the government intended to remove the Coranderrk residents. He reassured them that the government had no such intention and would do its utmost to make their home comfortable. He promised to visit the station himself as soon as possible to inquire into any grievances or complaints.

The tone of the *Argus* article contrasted strangely with Dow's serious account of the grievances of the Coranderrk people, for the anonymous author attempted to ridicule the Aborigines with patronising comments about the 'uncivilized minds' of the 'simple-natured residents'. But the reasonableness of their requests was just as apparent. The deputation's action and the Minister's response had immobilised the Board: they could not remove residents and sell the reserve without his consent.

At Coranderrk, meanwhile, the overseer Harris was learning that his future as a Board employee was precarious because of Ogilvie's anger over Dow's press disclosures. His lack of education and marriage to a Taungurong girl discouraged acceptance by the new staff members. His residence on the station isolated him from other labourers in the district but he was unable to identify with his wife's relatives. He had shown no loyalty to Green when questioned at earlier inquiries and Ogilvie's journal shows that he was the

---

5 Ewen Hugh Cameron (1831–1915) was a Scottish farmer's son who had immigrated in 1853. He held the seat of Evelyn from 1874 to 1917.
6 CSIC 76/K20278, 19 September 1876.

8. THE THREAT OF REMOVAL

main source of rumours rousing official fears of outside interference. Harris exploited his special access to Aboriginal opinion for his own benefit; Ogilvie relied on him for information but despised him. Harris had helped Dow to obtain the views of the Kulin but, now that it was certain Green would not return, he was once more trying to curry favour with Ogilvie.

The Healesville court had dismissed Ogilvie's prosecution of the Taungurong man Webster for horse stealing on the day the *Argus* announced the result of the deputation. Ogilvie's journal blamed Green, who 'appeared as the friend of Johnny Webster and told some tame story about the Natives settling the rights of succession to property themselves Bah'. When Harris told him next day that Green had privately denied the Websters' ownership of the disputed horses Ogilvie angrily called the two brothers in to discuss their claims. His diary commented that:

> Bamfield came in with him – but as I object to this man as a lazy mischief maker I told him to leave the room – & on his refusing I put my hand on his shoulder and a slight scuffle ensued – he however remained outside & the door was closed on him.[7]

This was a serious affront to the dignity of the Taungurong leader who had an obligation to represent the Websters. Ogilvie was oblivious to how grievously he had offended Kulin etiquette by laying hands on a clan-head. But he should have known from the doctor's reports that Bamfield, once a famed shearer, was in constant pain from chronic rheumatism and for years had been intermittently unfit for work.[8]

Ogilvie's anger about the residents' insubordination increased that evening, when eight men:

> came in to tell me that they objected to white men having been engaged to press and to pole & pick – In fact they feel themselves quite masters of the situation since their deputation returned from visiting the Chief Secretary.[9]

Ogilvie hastily altered Burgess' arrangements so that the Kulin and Europeans would work as separate teams and then set off to interview the vice-chairman 'on the subject of the deputation'. His journal records that on 28 February he:

> Saw Messrs Godfrey & LeSouef and as I could not make either understand how destructive these deputations were to the authority of the Manager – especially when the Ch: Secretary gave the people to understand that Coranderrk was all but their own property – I gave in my resignation.

That morning's *Argus* contained a rejoinder to Dow's *Age* criticism, in the form of a lengthy letter by Frederick Search. His employment as horticultural consultant apparently ended with Ogilvie's appointment but his jealousy of his rival Dow may have prompted him to reply even without encouragement from Board members. His letter, dated a week after the *Age* and *Leader* articles appeared, described their content as 'a pretty romance' apparently written 'with the object of making capital for Mr John Green'. He quoted the Board's 1874 report to demonstrate that all credit belonged to himself and Burgess. This propaganda was in fact eclipsed by a prior article, with eye-catching engravings of the Coranderrk workers, in the Syme-owned *Illustrated Australian News* which gave all credit to Green and the Kulin, mentioned the 'rather harsh circumstances' of Green's dismissal and presented financial details of past and present crops and improvements to show that the current employment of European labour was unwise and unnecessary.[10]

---

7   BPA – Journal of Christian Ogilvie, 24 and 25 February 1876.
8   BPA – Annual Report 1872:12, 1873:8.
9   BPA – Journal of Christian Ogilvie, 25 February 1876.
10 *Argus* 28 February 1876; *Illustrated Australian News* 27 February 1876.

REBELLION AT CORANDERRK

The Board's appropriation was to be discussed in the Supply Debate next day and Godfrey had to work out the best means of salvaging the situation. Ogilvie had brought with him a face-saving memorandum written on 25 February which attempted to reconcile the views of the more intransigent members such as Curr with the political reality of the Minister's sympathy for the Kulin. Godfrey knew that the Board could not publicly oppose their Minister and as a loyal backbench member, he did not want the grievances of Coranderrk Aborigines cited by the reformers as an example of the misdeeds of the conservative government. Berry was already 'stumping the country' in anticipation of the next election and, as a moderate who believed in principle rather than party loyalty, Godfrey no doubt disapproved of the *Age* attempts to politicise events at Coranderrk.

Ogilvie's memorandum argued that Coranderrk should be retained despite the cold climate and the proximity of Healesville, 'as by far the greater number from long residence are very much attached to it', although a sanatorium somewhere on the Murray might be useful for sufferers from lung disease as well as a refuge for northern Aborigines. He specified the duties of the four couples necessary to supervise the station, hops, farm work and school. Obviously, Ogilvie was planning to replace all of the existing staff. He urged immediate completion of the boundary fencing and repair or replacement of all cottages. Arguing that the 20 best men could do all the work of the station, Ogilvie insisted that they be rewarded with cash wages and an increased meat ration. He suggested increasing the manager's powers to discipline residents by imposing 'small fines or other light punishment (of course not corporal)' but argued that more serious offences 'such as assaulting a white man' must be dealt with by magistrates. Godfrey immediately appropriated certain sentiments as his own in his Parliamentary speech, and these portions appeared in the 1876 annual report over his signature.

Ogilvie's next diary entry was made after the Board meeting on 1 March:

> Wrote a private letter to Sheppard today that if the Board would allow me to withdraw my resignation I would do so – they allowed me – my reason for resigning was to establish a principle – it seemed to me that this was gained by what Mr Godfrey & Mr Inglis said in the house on 29th February – & I offered to withdraw my resignation because I did not see why I should lose my salary & because the Age was making capital out of it & laying the blame on the Board.

Ogilvie had talked at length to the urban member Inglis when he made his sole visit to Coranderrk, and it was his opinion which was relayed to Parliament.[11] Inglis condemned the idea of Green's re-appointment asserting that residents 'did nothing towards their own support under his rule'. He blamed Ogilvie's loss of control and the previous manager's 'resignation' on the residents' freedom to correspond with 'a certain old gentleman in town' (presumably Harker). Another member retorted that interference with the Aborigines' letters was 'monstrous' and quoted at some length residents' complaints about the employment of Europeans and their anger and anxiety about plans to remove them from their home.

Godfrey reacted angrily to the charge that there had been no full-time school and few church services for two years. He objected to the interference of visitors questioning Coranderrk people who were 'pretty shrewd in discovering whether the persons who spoke to them possessed influence or not'. He asserted that the government knew nothing of plans to remove them; he and two other members had merely recommended the provision of winter quarters because of the incidence of pneumonia and the Aborigines would return in summer to 'pick hops and have their labour utilised in other ways'.[12] Godfrey concluded his disingenuous explanation with two false statements: that 'it was never intended to break up the station' and that Stähle had 'resigned because he was interfered with by two other officers who were

---

11   Victorian Parliamentary Debates, Session 1875–76:2329–31.
12   Ogilvie claimed he originated this idea as a means of avoiding the cruelty of removal (Royal Commission 1877:4–5).

8. THE THREAT OF REMOVAL

made independent of him'. He announced that Inspector Ogilvie, hired to control the stations ('except of course' the mission stations which the government 'did not interfere with'), had resigned because the Chief Secretary's reception of the deputation had rendered the Coranderrk men 'altogether beyond his control'. Others then told Parliament that the Coranderrk residents were justly aggrieved at the employment of Europeans and censured Godfrey's determination to treat them like convicts. They insisted that the Board must not interfere with their right to approach the Minister and correspond freely with friends.

Godfrey was somewhat chastened by his colleagues' criticisms but this had no effect on Ogilvie's paternalistic rule. He was, however, more responsive to the complaints of the Kulin. Both Harris and Burgess praised their work and conduct during his absence but Barak's nephew Wandin and the Jajowrong John Charles led 'very boisterous' protests when 20 more European pickers arrived; Ogilvie had to increase the workers' meat ration to 10 pounds (4.5 kg) a week to silence them. He may have felt some guilt: Godfrey had told Parliament they were paid threepence a bushel for hop picking, three times the actual rate in the past. Before the season finished he had to pay off five Europeans after amorous advances to the dormitory girls were bitterly protested by the Taungurong leaders Jemmy Barker and the eldest son of John and Louisa Briggs who had returned to Coranderrk in 1874.[13]

On 20 March 1876, the colony's Chief Medical Officer arrived to investigate the sanitary condition of the station at the Chief Secretary's request. He merely toured the 32 huts with Ogilvie and did not examine the sick. He condemned the draughty construction and damp clay floors of the 'wretched hovels' and deplored the over-crowding: between four and 10 adults and children slept in each two-roomed hut. Ogilvie supplied information on the death rate and incidence of 'lung disease'. Dr William McCrea, who had completed his medical training in the 1830s, upheld the idea that climate as well as poor housing conditions contributed to the spread of tuberculosis. When a colleague demonstrated the falsity of McCrea's statements five years later he retracted them, saying Ogilvie was the authority for his comments that the climate was unsuitable for Aborigines, who reportedly complained of the cold and damp. Explicitly relying on evidence from Ogilvie, McCrea advised the replacement of all dwellings, erection of a new school and hospital, improvement of the ration scale and increased use of the Lilydale doctor instead of quarterly medical inspections. Ogilvie had hoped this medical advice would force the Board to make the improvements he had long demanded; instead, McCrea's report was used in the new members' campaign for abandonment.[14]

Next morning Ogilvie went to Melbourne 'about money to pay hoppickers'. In fact, the Board was meeting on the day after, 22 March, to discuss the secretary's post and he hoped to attend. He had something else on his mind but the new members and Macredie were wary, resolving that it was 'not desirable for Ogilvie to interfere with Green's religious ministrations to the blacks at Coranderrk until after arrival of the school master'. It was a rebuff for Ogilvie and he had another rebuff two days later. Chief Secretary MacPherson fulfilled his promise to visit Coranderrk accompanied by another Minister, apparently Robert Ramsay (then Minister of Public Instruction), who had also visited in Green's time. The promised examination of residents' grievances was somewhat inhibited by the hurried return of Ogilvie who was indignant because the Minister had left him behind in Melbourne. But MacPherson did challenge the location of Burgess' house in the garden as well as the Board's refusal to let the Coranderrk men accept outside employment. He also rejected the Board's proposal that Curr should become secretary.[15]

13 BPA – Journal of Christian Ogilvie, 3–20 March 1876.
14 BPA – Annual Report 1876:App. 12; Coranderrk Inquiry 1881:33–7.
15 Coranderrk Inquiry 1881:117; BPA – Minutes 22 March and 5 April 1876.

Encouraged by the Minister's apparent sympathy for their complaints about wages, many of the Kulin left to work for neighbours as soon as their own harvest finished. When Burgess demanded their labour Ogilvie tried to stop the particularly embarrassing exodus because the new manager Hugh H. Halliday had arrived. When John Charles and others defied him Ogilvie wrote threatening to prosecute their employers, Guillaume de Pury and Paul de Castella, unless they sent the men without work certificates home at once. Ogilvie's action was purely punitive and contrary to his own stated views and Board policy on employment. He must have known the Board would not risk embarrassment by prosecuting the two most prominent men of the district who had sheltered and employed the Woiworung since 1850.[16]

Sergeant Halliday took charge from 1 April 1876 and within weeks some grievances were appeased. He and his family were more approachable than Ogilvie and he showed his sympathy by immediately recommending higher wages which the Board deferred. He did, however, supply more clothing, boots and meat, approve renovations to the dwellings and at last re-opened the school. The changes resulted from the Board's acceptance of Dr McCrea's report but residents naturally thought Halliday responsible and they warmed to him.

Bigotry and detestation of Green meanwhile prompted the Board members, and Ogilvie and Halliday, to foolish actions which renewed the anger of the Kulin and were interpreted as sectarian prejudice by the many Presbyterian residents of the district. Green's spiritual and medical care over nearly two decades had won him many friends and his concern for Coranderrk people was respected even by those who coveted the reserve and had little sympathy for Aborigines. The Anglican majority on the Board had formed the sub-committee which hired the new teachers, James Stewart Deans and his wife Laura. As soon as they arrived Ogilvie ordered the new manager Halliday to forbid Green to conduct services on the station, and requested the teacher to hold Anglican prayer services instead. The decision roused the ire of MacBain and Syme as well as Bamfield's friend Mrs Bon and Green's friend Rev. Robert Hamilton. The Board also risked offending the local member Cameron and the interested Ministers MacPherson and Ramsay, all of whom were Presbyterians.

The Kulin immediately planned a petition protesting Green's exclusion and apparently addressed it to a Melbourne sympathiser for presentation to the Chief Secretary. However, Halliday intercepted a draft and mailed it instead to Ogilvie. An angry memorandum from Ogilvie insisted the Minister must make the Aborigines understand he would only heed complaints relayed through the Board and urged presentation of the stolen draft petition as evidence that 'some well and some ill intentioned white people' were undermining the Board's authority. At their next meeting on 3 May 1876 the Anglicans Godfrey, Sheppard, Macredie and Jennings retrospectively approved Ogilvie's order forbidding Green entry to the station. They declined to return the draft as Halliday had asked, but resolved simply to 'investigate' the petition rather than present it to the Minister. Neither employee, Ogilvie or Halliday, was censured for actions likely to involve the Board in denominational conflict and bring further Parliamentary criticism of the Board's interference with residents' correspondence. In the end Ogilvie had to request the nearest Presbyterian clergyman, Rev. Alex Mackie at Lilydale, to conduct marriages for residents and everyone's face was saved when he volunteered to conduct monthly service throughout Halliday's tenure. Mackie was pleased by the invariably excellent attendance but had too little confidence in the residents' understanding to conduct baptisms and communion services as Rev. Hamilton and later Rev. Stähle had. Nor did he attend for funerals which were conducted by lay staff members to the dismay of the Kulin and many in the neighbourhood.[17]

---

16 BPA – Journal of Christian Ogilvie, 28–30 March 1876; Aveling 1972:16–19. Ogilvie's views on employment appear in BPA-Annual Report 1876:App. 2 and Royal Commission 1877:1–4, 10–11.
17 Royal Commission 1877:52–6; Coranderrk Inquiry 1881: 91–3.

8. THE THREAT OF REMOVAL

Only the four new members attended a special Board meeting on 17 May and on that day Godfrey, who had been acting as secretary on the Minister's instructions, wrote recommending Ogilvie for the position of secretary. He was appointed when Smyth formally resigned on 1 June but there is no record that the Board pursued its resolution to send a deputation to MacPherson on the secretaryship and 'other matters'. Treasury had just refunded the £806 hop profit for the Board's use but Ogilvie had calculated that McCrea's housing recommendations would cost £750 and another £240 was needed for boundary fencing. Ogilvie was determined that these improvements would be made; but a major scandal about the management of Coranderrk had erupted before the Board met again in July.

No debate on the annual report, dated 30 June, is mentioned in the 1876 minutes although this had been a major item of business in previous years. In Smyth's time, the detailed reports of station managers, inspector and medical officers were published in full but his successors censored or omitted all unfavourable comments. This first annual report compiled by vice chairman Godfrey and Ogilvie (now secretary and inspector) not only concealed months of dispute and the departure of half the Board's members but also the dismissal of two senior officers. The report merely commented that the 'temporary disorganization' resulting from staff changes at Coranderrk had now been remedied. Green's reports were omitted, but the Curr-Ogilvie report recommending a station at Kulkyne was included together with the September 1875 report by Ogilvie deploring the site and in which he was sanguine enough to offer general policy recommendations after three weeks' employment. He had urged 'purely paternal' care for aged and sick 'fullbloods', rigid discipline for other adults and training for young 'fullbloods' and 'half castes' of both sexes so they could be 'sent into the world to compete for employment with the white population, the station never being closed against them in periods of distress or sickness'.[18]

The main body of this 1876 report announced a new policy of closing depots and bringing Aborigines into stations. It also asked for legislative power to apprentice all youths who 'object to remaining on the stations', a suggestion made by the missionary Hagenauer in his own report for the year. None of this had been debated by the Board, although they had voted against hiring out girls.[19] The report explained that the Curr-Ogilvie recommendation for abandonment of Coranderrk had been rejected 'as, unfortunately the greater number of the people have a very decided and natural objection to leaving'. Instead, the Board planned to replace 20 huts and use the planned Anglican station at Kulkyne as a sanitorium for invalids. The report of course pointed out that these plans would necessitate additional funding.

The Board already had the hop funds released by the Treasury and thus had no excuse to defer erection of the new houses, hospital and fencing promised to the Kulin ever since 1872. Tenders for new dwellings were called in August 1876 but eight months later Ogilvie told a Royal Commission inquiry he had cancelled them on Godfrey's instructions when 'this wretched Parliamentary affair blew up'.[20] Board accounts show that £259 was expended on buildings and improvements in the first half of 1876 (most of it for Burgess' house) and another £302 in the next 12 months, mostly for new outbuildings. Halliday's annual report a year later complained that replacement of all dwellings was a matter of urgency although two men had built themselves new huts and minor repairs had been made.[21] Over the same period, hop growing expenses totalled £1,417. The Kulin were not paid wages except for picking until after June 1876; the total cash paid in the next 12 months was £88. The Board's funds were now consumed by the wages paid to Ogilvie and the staff of five at Coranderrk.

---

18 BPA – Annual Report 1876:App. 2.
19 BPA – Minutes, 17 May 1876.
20 Royal Commission 1877:4, 12.
21 BPA – Annual Report 1877:App. 2; only £336 was expended in 1876 (Royal Commission 1877:68–70).

Ogilvie made only one brief visit to check on the new manager he had chosen and simply ignored the complaints about him written by various residents and by Green. He suspected that the recently widowed overseer Harris carried gossip to the Greens who were rearing his children but needed him to make the men work for Burgess. He could, however, put a stop to the constant complaints about Halliday being made by the dormitory matron Miss Robertson. He ordered her to leave the station on 20 July. After interviewing her on 31 July the Board gave way to his angry demands for her dismissal and forbad her to return. Ogilvie had to send a written apology for the 'intemperate manner' in which he addressed the Board; she was not rehired as a teacher at the Board's other station until Ogilvie himself had resigned.[22]

At the same meeting, the members considered Halliday's report on a public meeting at Healesville, and Ogilvie's complaints about Green's allegations concerning the death of Mrs Harris. The local Parliamentary representative Cameron had ignored the 'grave charges' made at this meeting until the chairman, E.B. Henley, a 'respectable manufacturer', formally requested him to investigate on 11 August. He referred the matter to the Board vice-chairman Godfrey the next day and mentioned it privately to the Chief Secretary. The Board's only reply was an invitation to become a member, which Cameron declined.

On 19 August numerous 'respectable' townsfolk attended a second public meeting, this time convened by a former member of Parliament, John Sinclair who had long fought for the labour and temperance causes espoused by Heales and other founding members of the Board. Despite his retirement to Healesville this old radical still had considerable influence with opposition members of Parliament. Cameron's conservatism was being increasingly challenged in his own electorate and he could not ignore Sinclair's views. Those at the meeting were aware of the earlier complaints: that Mrs Harris had died in childbirth (just before Ogilvie left) attended only by the drunken wife of the hopmaster; that Barak's brother and sister-in-law had recently died without medical aid and the consumptive Webster brothers were neglected; and that Ogilvie and Halliday ignored increased drunkenness and fighting on the station. Bamfield and other Aborigines attended this meeting with Green and complained about a second childbirth fatality: Bamfield's niece had no medical attention and was buried without a certificate. After a letter from Halliday was read the meeting unanimously resolved to ask the Chief Secretary to investigate. The resolution was sent to the Minister and the press.

The *Argus* report of Sinclair's complaint that Coranderrk people were allowed to 'die like dogs' and were buried without ceremony, 'apparently nobody caring for their bodies or their souls', prompted a Parliamentary debate on 24 August.[23] A member who had previously criticised the Board questioned the Minister, MacPherson, who said he had only received the complaint that day and had ordered an inquiry. He read out the Board's reply: Halliday's routine report on the most recent death which suggested the Lilydale doctor had been called immediately but had been unable to come. Cameron rose to deplore the Minister's reliance on evidence from the man accused of mismanagement, then moved adjournment. Reminding members that his motion for appointment of a Select Committee on the management of Coranderrk had been on the notice paper for a fortnight, he read out the charges preferred at the first Healesville meeting. His demand for an impartial inquiry was supported by the former Board member MacBain, by John Gavan Duffy (son of the reforming Lands Minister who had shown sympathy for the Taungurong deputation in 1859) and five other speakers.

---

22   BPA – Minutes 31 July, 2 and 16 August 1876.
23   *Argus*, 23 August 1876; Victorian Parliamentary Debates, Session 1876:507–12.

8. THE THREAT OF REMOVAL

James Edgar.

The Premier rebuked charges by opposition members that the government was uninterested in Aborigines but suggested that it was improper to allow a Parliamentary inquiry before the Board had an opportunity to investigate allegations against its servants. He pledged that he would defer government business to allow Cameron to put his motion for a Select Committee in a week's time if the Board's report was satisfactory.

The Board's vice chairman, Godfrey, told the House that the charges were false and unsubstantiated, then admitted he had just received the manager's letter and had made no other inquiry. Objecting that 'discipline would be wholly lost' if the Board was subject to investigation, he insisted that:

> the whole of this disturbance had been caused by an officer who was formerly employed in a position at the station which the board thought he was not fit for. The board proposed to place him in a position he was fit for, but he did not choose to accept the offer of the board and he had since raised all kinds of allegations and had endeavoured to bring the board into disrepute.

Chief Secretary MacPherson, relying on Ogilvie's statements, then told the House that the new manager was exposed to constant agitation and opposition. Without naming Green he supported Godfrey's accusations:

> Until a short time ago the Coranderrk station was in charge of a person who had been there for years, under whose rule nothing was known about the station, everything being supposed to be going on right. No doubt persons drank and died then as persons drink and die now. The board, finding the management unsatisfactory, offered that person the position of superintendent, with the same salary, but subject to an inspector. The offer was declined;

121

> the person left the station; and since then nothing but intrigue had been going on; and he [Mr MacPherson] had been moved in all directions and on all sorts of grounds – on religious, social, and all the other grounds the man's friends could think of – to have him back in charge of the station.

There is no evidence in the Chief Secretary's official correspondence that he had been plagued with representations on Green's behalf, merely two letters written by Rev. Robert Hamilton in February and June 1876 which urged Green's reinstatement.[24] But another influential sympathiser had written to MacPherson that day.

Mrs Anne Fraser Bon was the widow of a self-made man who had acquired great wealth as a pastoralist. The Delatite River clan of Taungurong had been sheltered at his station near Mansfield since 1846 and this Scottish doctor's daughter had shown a compassionate interest in their welfare ever since her arrival in the colony in 1858. Her letter offered detailed criticisms of the Board's neglect of those Taungurong who still preferred to spend much of their time in the Mansfield area and complained of their treatment at Coranderrk. She asserted that the Board's failure to provide medical care, food and clothing had indeed caused the death of Bamfield's niece.[25]

Mrs Bon was a critic who could not be ignored. She was a wealthy philanthropist who had great influence in the Presbyterian Church and was associated with old Dr Embling and his wife on the ladies' committees of several Melbourne hospitals. Her sympathies were not with the conservative squatters but rather the nonconformist churchmen and reforming politicians who were attempting to improve the condition of the poor in the colony by their advocacy of temperance, improved medical care and alterations of labour and land legislation. These were the major issues of Victorian politics in the 1870s and the complaints of the Coranderrk people received new attention as a result of the intervention of sympathisers able to lobby for press and Parliamentary support.

The removal of Miss Robertson, the last of the staff members from Green's time who had the inclination or influence to act as advocate for the Kulin, meant that they had to find allies elsewhere. They knew Ogilvie was unsympathetic and they had no acquaintance with the remaining Board members –all old pastoralists except for the lawyer Jennings, whose business interests also allied him with the conservative establishment. The sympathy of Mrs Bon had a special importance because she had for years managed one of the colony's major pastoral holdings and had as much experience of employing Aborigines as any Board member. Her advice was thus taken seriously by practical men like MacPherson who had a jaundiced view of idealistic reformers ignorant of rural realities. MacPherson was a conscientious administrator of his department's 'lepers, lunatics, police, prisons, culture and Aboriginals', but he had reason to distrust any campaign conducted by the *Age*. The Minister's view of affairs at Coranderrk was perhaps as much influenced by an independent critic like Mrs Bon as the report delivered by Godfrey on 30 August 1876.[26]

Godfrey's report of his investigation explained that the one-week time limit had precluded convening the Board. Instead, he had invited the lawyer Jennings and the critics Cameron and Duffy (also a lawyer) to sit with him on a board of inquiry. Before Cameron joined them they had spent a day inspecting Coranderrk. The minutes of evidence for the 12-hour hearing at Healesville on 28 August, in Godfrey's hand, were signed by 13 Aboriginal witnesses most of them with a mark. Only those closely involved in the disputed incidents had been questioned.

---

24 CSIC 76/Kl658, 76/K6780, 18 February and 29 June 1876.
25 CSIC 76/J9204, 24 August 1876; Sutherland 1888:II 324–5.
26 *Australian Dictionary of Biography*, v.6:196; CSIC 76/J9507, 30 August 1876.

8. THE THREAT OF REMOVAL

None of them criticised Halliday's management. The other witnesses – Harris, the new teacher Deans, Rev. Alex Mackie of Lilydale, and the publican accused of supplying drink – upheld their statements that only a handful of residents drank. Most of the charges related to a cricket match at Coranderrk on 4 August when Ogilvie was at the station. The captain of the team, James Edgar (1847–c. 1885), was one of the Burapper men who came to Coranderrk in 1872. He explained that he had authorised Halliday to deduct from the team's wages the cost of the lunch and supper provided for them and their gentlemen guests from Melbourne. All agreed that the publican had not provided alcohol, although the Callithumpian team had liquor with them. That evening a few had celebrated their victory in Healesville drinking lemonade and brandy. On their return a man and wife had fought but all denied that John Briggs had frightened the children in the dormitory when he visited his wife who was acting dormitory matron. He was 'very merry and dancing' but 'able to walk and doing no harm to anyone'. His impressive wife Louisa was questioned at length about the care of the sick since she had been nurse and midwife since her arrival. She and Mrs Green had attended all previous confinements and never needed a doctor; the two recent cases were the first childbirth fatalities. Other staff members warmly praised her care of the dormitory children and she was entirely composed when answering charges that the children were 'verminous': head lice were not a new thing and she used soda as a cure.

Rev. Mackie, who like Green had some medical qualifications, pointed out that residents now frequently called him from Lilydale when the doctor was not available. Green, of course, had been forbidden to enter the station. Mackie's examination was brief but the point was not lost on residents of the district who also knew that religious funerals had ceased with Green's exclusion, as Sinclair had pointed out.

The staff members had been prepared for the inquiry by Ogilvie who went to Coranderrk in advance and was present throughout the hearings. He had obviously primed Godfrey with information to help discredit the Aboriginal witnesses. This was particularly apparent with the leading witness Bamfield who was cross-examined about an irrelevant matter. Bamfield firmly denied that he had any 'fight with any official' although once Ogilvie 'ordered me out of his office and pushed me out when I swung him round & we went out together'.

Harris was a frightened witness, defensively eager to prove his own identification with the staff rather than the Kulin, and full of gossip about the few who drank.

The old policeman-cum manager Halliday was matter-of-fact and his honesty about his unpreparedness and Ogilvie's lack of supervision was in itself a telling criticism of the Board. He said he had no written instructions or rules to help him manage the station and had left the care of the sick to Miss Robertson and the Aboriginal women who were experienced nurses. He admitted he had not called the doctor promptly for the three who died although Bamfield and Wandin had made urgent requests. He believed half the station suffered from lung disease; as the doctor had treated these patients earlier their deaths were not unexpected and he had approved their burial without certification. No birth or death had been registered for some time, and he had informed the doctor and police of Mrs Harris' death only because 'she was married to a white man'.

The last witness was John Green who explained that all births and deaths in his time had been recorded and reported to the Board and that he had been bound by written instructions which defined the duties of all employees. It had always been his practice to send a man for the doctor, 'even to Melbourne if necessary', when a death seemed imminent but he had only requested an inquest or *post mortem* in three cases of sudden death.

The covering report signed by Godfrey, Jennings, Cameron and Duffy was strongly critical of Halliday's negligence in merely sending a letter to the doctor when Bamfield reported his niece's state and censured his 'peculiar conduct' over the burial of Wandin's aunt. They considered that the charge concerning Mrs Harris needed no answer as she was a 'half caste' married to a European and acquitted Mrs Burgess of drunkenness when attending her (although noting that her appearance at the hearing 'would favour the belief that she drinks at times'). They concluded that reports of drunkenness at Coranderrk had been greatly exaggerated and absolved Halliday of the charges of negligence, although they found the system of treatment faulty and the supply of medical comforts admittedly inadequate.[27]

Board affairs were still newsworthy because of the Dow–Search exchanges and the acrimonious Parliamentary debate. The *Argus* on 25 and 26 August had published the gist of the Board's annual report and the full content of Chief Medical Officer McCrea's report and both *Argus* and *Age* sent reporters to the inquiry. Some 50 Aborigines and most of the district's residents also attended. The latter had a special interest in the outcome, for the town was too small and poor to support a doctor. They would benefit if, as the former Parliamentarian Sinclair had suggested at the public meeting, the Board was forced to provide adequate care by appointing a resident medical officer. An *Argus* reporter's lively account, headlined 'by electric telegraph', appeared the day after the hearing. This account made much of the fact that Green:

> took a prominent part in the inquiry, cross-examining all the witnesses, and acting, apparently, as the spokesman for the person who preferred the complaint, as Mr Henley himself, although he was present, made no remarks during the hearing of the evidence.

Temperance advocates must have been disturbed by witnesses' testimony that liquor was freely available at Healesville and brandy and wine were the main medical comforts distributed by the manager. Old James 'Jemmy' Barker had already 'impressed on Mr Godfrey the desirability of the blacks having a nobbler now and again'. The publican, however, had piously asserted that when the Callithumpian team asked for gin 'for those poor devils as they were tired and weary' he had replied that he 'would not give one drop of drink to the blacks if he received £50 for it'.

On subsequent days, 29 and 31 August and 1 September, the *Argus* devoted half a page to detailed descriptions of the comfortable living conditions afforded the 146 residents of Coranderrk. The anonymous reporter did not mention Green and reported Harris absent but gave detailed accounts of interviews with the teachers, Burgess and the Halliday family. Halliday's management was described as 'patriarchal in the best sense' and the friendly relations between residents and his wife and daughters were the subject of extended comment. Burgess, however, was described as tactless, unpopular and frequently in dispute with the Aborigines. The journalist mentioned none of them by name except Mrs Louisa Briggs – a 'handy and vigorous all-round administrator' who was paid 10 shillings a week to care for the 22 children in the dormitory. His comments about the residents were patronising and his facetious description of their physical appearance gave a false impression of promiscuity. He strongly condemned the retention of 'half caste' children insisting that they were eager to imitate Europeans and should have a chance to make their way in the general community.

He exaggerated the liberality of the ration scale and pointed out that residents also had free tobacco, firewood and clothing as well as the produce of the communal garden and orchard and milk from the station herd. He commented that most households had their own gardens containing fruit trees, vegetables and flowers and all kept a variety of fowls for their own use. Many also owned horses which grazed at the station's expense. Nearly all had guns and still hunted to supplement their diet and to obtain skins for the manufacture of rugs. The women sold eggs and made baskets and mats which were traded to pedlars

---

27   CSIC 76/J9507, 31 August 1876.

8. THE THREAT OF REMOVAL

for clothes, ornaments and pretty crockery to replace the tinware, now provided by the Board, which they disdained. Pictures cut from illustrated newspapers, and photographs of their families, decorated the walls of the dwellings, which were all neatly furnished with tables, chairs, beds and a meat-safe.

He reported that the working men were paid a shilling per five-hour day but their earnings averaged only £3 to £3/1/0 per quarter as they worked irregularly. This, he suggested, was due to their laziness and he made no mention of the fact that they were not paid in bad weather. No more than 30 hours a week of constant work was expected of the men and the women did little except at picking time. He conveniently ignored the fact that men were still expected to hunt for meat and the women were fully occupied with home duties. He reiterated his point that only about 28 men worked 'and those not regularly' – a list of residents in 1876 shows that this was the adult male population of working age. Not all of these were able-bodied.[28]

Although most of the 4,850 acre (1,963 ha) reserve (now divided by a public road) consisted of scrubby ranges which provided pasture for only part of the year, it included 640 acres (259 ha) of swamp land which had been fenced as a seasonal fattening paddock. As the reserve was unfenced trespassing stock outnumbered the 400 cattle, 16 working bullocks and 10 horses owned by the Board. The reporter emphasised that the cultivated area described as 'one of the richest pieces of country in the colony', totalled only 45 acres (18.2 ha) of hay, eight acres (3.2 ha) of potatoes, six acres (2.4 ha) of vegetables and five acres (2 ha) of orchard and vineyard plus 20 acres (8.1 ha) of hops. His jocular style gave the impression that the Coranderrk community consisted of lazy wastrels with loose morals who lived in unearned luxury and had little claim to be called Aborigines because of their mixed ancestry.

He did report that medical care was inadequate, mainly because there was no doctor nearer than Lilydale, but his description of the residents' dwellings contrasted ludicrously with the abject poverty described by the Chief Medical Officer six months earlier and Ogilvie's description of their huts in the current annual report. He was escorted round by Halliday. Although the day was rainy he found most huts warm and dry but draughty. Most were now floored with bricks or boards – only a few with clay. All were now lined with canvas and some were papered. All had two main rooms, each about 12 feet square (3.65 m square), and the larger families had lean-to additions. It was dinner time and the reporter commented that 'two camp ovens hung over every fire, while there was a steaming kettle on the hob and a well-laid table awaiting'. The homes equalled those of peasants the world over and he had seen 'overseers' and even squatters' huts in Australia that were no better'. The residents were healthy, well fed and tastefully dressed; the children better educated than many eminent members of Parliament. Indeed, the only defect at Coranderrk was that too many residents were 'nearly white'.

The *Argus* was able to publish a summary of Godfrey's inquiry report two days after it was submitted and promised a full report as soon as Chief Secretary MacPherson had time to consider it. To Godfrey's dismay, the *Argus* also leaked the contents of separate reports submitted by Cameron and Duffy.[29] All three reports were published before Godfrey had convened the Board to discuss the inquiry. Cameron argued that the witnesses had been intimidated and his report demanded a fuller inquiry into the Board's negligence. Duffy, too, thought the evidence unsatisfactory and urged the appointment of an impartial tribunal to examine the Board's administration of all Aborigines.

---

28 CSIC 76/J9682, 'List of Natives belonging to Coranderrk …', 21 August 1876.
29 *Argus*, 2 and 5 September 1876; CSIC 76/J9578, 76/J9507, 31 August 1876.

Duffy had toured Coranderrk escorted by Godfrey and Ogilvie, the day before the *Argus* reporter. He had seen only clay floors in the huts and deplored the failure of the 'previous manager' (i.e. Green) to remedy this and provide boundary fencing. He had seen only four gardens round the homes and commented on the lack of flowers even though the reporter had seen 'wallflowers, polyanthuses and narcissi in abundance'. He too considered Dr McCrea's complaints exaggerated and described the dwellings as ordinary bush huts like those of shepherds and selectors but cleaner and better kept than he had expected:

> Indeed, the supply of cooking utensils and little luxuries, such as fresh eggs, and the efforts made to brighten the walls with pictures and little presents, here and there, of a few books and artificial flowers, were specially noticeable …

Although he was impressed with Mrs Briggs' care of the dormitory children he argued that they should be under the care of a 'trained white woman' or boarded out with European families. The reporter had emphasised the religious services provided by the teacher and visiting clergyman: Duffy deplored the lack of religious training. Duffy informed the Minister that only about 30 of the 146 residents were 'unmixed blacks' (a gross distortion) and most of the children were 'almost white'. He expressed fear that the state would soon be supporting only 'quadroons and octoroons well able to take care of themselves'. He concluded that Coranderrk must be abandoned as 'unsuitable in climate and position' and the residents dispersed among the mission stations. But he pointed out that the present staff and Board members had been in control only a year, were eager to remedy defects and planned to erect 18 new cottages. Duffy's report was virtually a paraphrase of views expressed elsewhere by Godfrey and Ogilvie. He had no previous acquaintance with the Kulin and no opportunity to speak to them on this hurried visit.

Meanwhile, the *Age* on 30 August and 4 September had questioned the propriety of Godfrey's inquiry into Board administration and suggested that the abandonment decision might have been influenced by the many district residents anxious to acquire the reserve. Godfrey could ignore press opinion but he later criticised the dissenting views of Cameron and Duffy in his own supplementary report to Chief Secretary MacPherson. This letter, never published, made capital of Green's role as prosecutor, insisted witnesses had not been intimidated and again urged the Minister to approve abandonment. Godfrey offered a new rationale – proximity to Melbourne – insisting that discipline was now seriously undermined by visitors who taught the Aborigines to go over the manager's head to the Board, Chief Secretary and Parliament.[30]

Although Cameron did not publicly correct the *Argus* suggestion that Green had led this attack on the Board, he wrote to the Chief Secretary explaining that it was he who asked Green to serve as complainant when Henley, unprepared on only 12-hours notice and disapproving of Godfrey's acting as a judge in his own cause, had declined. As evidence that the residents' fears of Godfrey's plans for their removal were well founded, he reminded MacPherson how Godfrey had bullied the deputation within the precincts of Parliament House. Cameron pledged his strenuous opposition to any forced removal from Coranderrk because the site was ideal; all that was needed for the happiness and well-being of the Aborigines was replacement of the Board members and officers.[31] His letter was not published.

The Board had no opportunity to consider Godfrey's handling of the inquiry until 6 September. The four new members plus Macredie and Jennings were now the only ones who attended. The five old pastoralists and their chosen secretary Ogilvie approached Aboriginal affairs as a problem in efficient and economic station management. They were now determined to end the complaints which had brought the Board into disrepute, by putting the Aborigines under firm control. There had been protests lately at most of the stations but these had been kept from the press. The Board congratulated Godfrey and Jennings on their handling of the inquiry and resolved to take no further notice of Cameron's complaints

---

30   CSIC 76/K9896, 12 September 1876.
31   CSIC 76/K10278, 19 September 1876.

since he had refused membership. Their main business was a decision to ask the Minister to gazette an Order-in-Council prescribing the residence of all Aborigines at their home stations. By this means the Board, which had no power to control their movements, could request police to bring or restore named persons to the prescribed place. Ogilvie had recommended similar action, utilising the vagrancy laws, in his angry memorandum on the Coranderrk residents' petition and he had already obtained lists of all who 'belonged' to the stations from the managers. The Coranderrk list was dated 21 August 1876.

When he submitted the lists to the Chief Secretary for gazettal Godfrey offered the explanation that 'the Board's object was not to coerce the Aborigines or prevent them visiting their friends and relatives when desirable but to make it necessary for them to obtain permission before absenting themselves'.[32] But MacPherson was a lawyer and had been Premier and Chief Secretary at the time the 1869 Act was passed. He was aware that this disciplinary use was a perversion of the Act's intention and knew very well that it was a device to control the Coranderrk people. His minute in reply said that the matter could wait until their permanent residence was decided. Godfrey wrote again arguing that this power would strengthen the hands of all managers and need not interfere with the future of Coranderrk. His letter ended with a complaint that many residents of that station were absent without leave.

On 8 September Godfrey again convened the six effective members for a special meeting. They unanimously approved resolutions supporting Halliday's management despite the inquiry's criticisms. Then LeSouef moved, and Curr seconded, a resolution that Coranderrk was not a fit locality for Aborigines. Only Jennings dissented. The motion was prompted by a minute the Chief Secretary wrote to accompany the inquiry's papers when he forwarded them for the Board's comments. He asked the Board to decide, before incurring further expenditure, whether the Aborigines should remain permanently at Coranderrk or should be removed in the next few months. MacPherson himself felt that:

> the wishes of the people themselves should be met as far as reasonable. If they have hunting grounds for which they long or cherish with affection any particular spot of country I do not see why they should not be allowed there to end their days. The half caste children to go to our schools, mix with other children & be absorbed in the community.[33]

On 12 September Godfrey sent off the Board's official reply and Jennings' letter of dissent. The reply ignored the criticisms of Halliday made in the inquiry report and said that, as the government had granted only £325 for medical attendance at six stations, adequate care for the sick was impossible. Reminding the Minister that the Board had adopted the sub-committee's advice on abandonment a year earlier, Godfrey now demanded removal of all Aborigines from Coranderrk, insisting that the location promoted chest disease and drunkenness. The Board promised to postpone all improvements until their abandonment decision received the consent of the government and the 'concurrence of the Legislature'. The members would then decide whether to form a new station in a more congenial climate or disperse residents to existing stations. Godfrey suggested that Coranderrk might be retained as a summer resort if it could be profitably managed for the benefit of Aborigines.[34]

The Board had priorities more important than the wishes of the Kulin. As businessmen, the members were reluctant to give up the hop income, their only measure of independence from the stingy annual appropriations. Coranderrk could be more profitably operated by a small European labour force. The members had other uses for the money. The Anglican and Moravian–Presbyterian mission committees

---

32   CSIC 76/J9682, 6 September 1876.
33   CSIC 76/J9507, 6 September 1876.
34   CSIC 76/K9898, 12 September 1876.

had long protested that an undue proportion of Board funds was spent on hop cultivation and were urgently demanding improvement of the four neglected mission stations. The Board's other station, with no external support and few visitors, would remain neglected.

Three days later the *Argus* published MacPherson's confidential minutes and the Board's reply. Jennings' enclosed counter-proposal was not made public. A unanimous declaration by the Coranderrk residents, opposing Board plans for their removal, was also withheld from the press.

A cricket match at Coranderrk, c. 1879.

Chapter 9
WHO OWNS THE LAND?

> … have gone on the idea from the beginning that those natives are children, and in anything I have recommended I have inferred that they would be treated as children – made to go to those places and kept there – and if I am asked my advice, I recommend that this should be done; that the blacks should, when necessary, be coerced just as we coerce children and lunatics who cannot take care of themselves.
>
> E.M. Curr 1877[1]

The Coranderrk residents became acquainted with the proposals for their removal by reading the *Age* and *Argus*. The ideas of the Board, Duffy and the authors of various letters to the editor roused dismay. They had been aware since their troubles with the pastoralist Hugh Glass at the Acheron Station some 15 years before that they needed European witnesses to ensure officialdom would credit their sincerity. The legalistic proceedings of Godfrey's tribunal provided a precedent for a new kind of protest.

On 11 September 1876 Halliday wrote to Ogilvie that earlier in the evening he had been asked to ring the bell for a general meeting. When all the men assembled they said they required another witness and the teacher was called to record their resolutions. The first motion, put by the Taungurong leader James 'Jemmy' Barker and the Jajowrong John Charles, begged the Board to inform the government that they were well satisfied with their treatment by the Board and present manager and asked not to be removed from Coranderrk. Six Burapper who came in 1872 did say they would go to a new station on the Loddon (their home area) but there was unanimous support for the motion put by John Briggs (the half-Tasmanian husband of a Woiworung Louisa) and the Jajowrong Martin Simpson: 'that if the station at Coranderrk is broken up they will not proceed to any other mission station in the colony'. They also carried unanimously the resolution put by two young newcomers, the Pangerang Robert Bains and the Burapper James Edgar: that 'this meeting approves of Mr Halliday's management of the station'.[2] The teacher witnessed the signature or mark of the 27 men attending. Twenty were Kulin pioneers and included Barak and all who had taken part in previous protests and deputations. Only five old Kulin men usually away at Yea or Mansfield and three Pangerang youths were omitted. Probably all were absent. All of the authors of resolutions were 'half castes' except Barker: that fact was irrelevant to the Kulin.

The Coranderrk court had made a consensus decision in the old way and devised a new means of convincing sceptical Europeans of the authenticity of their protests. Although Godfrey had derided previous petitions, insisting that the Coranderrk people had been incited or manipulated by outsiders, he could not ignore this because staff members had participated. And of course, the expressed support for the manager could be used as a weapon against Green. Godfrey thought the resolutions proved the residents no longer wanted Green.

---

1 Royal Commission 1877:78.
2 CSIC 76/K9992, 14 September 1876.

The Kulin perception of the situation was more sophisticated. They had been made well aware of the fact that Ogilvie and Godfrey distrusted and detested Green; he himself had probably told them that he would not return on Ogilvie's terms. But the possession of this land mattered more to them than any European master. Halliday, unlike Ogilvie, showed some respect for Kulin laws and the residents' ambition to regulate their own lives. Of course the improvement of their economic condition since Halliday's appointment strengthened his position. Workers received 10 pounds (4.5 kg) of flour weekly, picking rates tripled to threepence a bushel and from June 1876 cash wages of two and one-quarter pence per hour were paid for all work. Moreover, Halliday accepted residents' tenders for contract pole cutting, fencing and other tasks which had formerly been allotted to Europeans. They were paid for the labour and materials needed for renovating their huts and Halliday renewed their freedom to go shearing and take harvesting jobs when they were not needed at home. This old police sergeant would not tolerate any demands by Burgess and made no secret of the fact that he wished to get rid of the hopmaster and considered that Harris and the Kulin could manage the hop ground themselves.

Godfrey had to forward this petition to the Chief Secretary; but at their next meeting on 4 October the four new members had a long debate about the Aborigines' protests against removal. Ogilvie of course realised the strength of the residents' sentiments although he had no real understanding of the reasons for their attachment to this land. Godfrey, Curr, LeSouef and Sheppard knew also that Macredie and Jennings had voted for Green's return, and that Jennings' counter-proposal had made nonsense of their main argument for removal. Jennings, with a lawyer's logic, had taken the trouble to review the mortality rates for all stations. His submission to the Chief Secretary proved that the location of Coranderrk was not at fault, citing medical evidence and statistics from past years. Jennings argued that new dwellings would overcome any disadvantage and said that he opposed abandonment 'above all' because most residents were attached to the site and would consider it a great hardship to be removed.

Jennings recommended that the Board transfer control of Coranderrk to the Anglican mission committee and named the unemployed missionary Joseph Shaw[3] as a suitable manager. He urged the dismissal of Burgess as Harris was sufficiently skilled at hop growing. If the Board paid the wages of Harris and the teachers the mission committee would refund all profits from hops and other crops. This solution would benefit everyone but the current manager Halliday, and Jennings pointed out that he had been hired on the understanding that his employment could cease at any time on one month's notice. The new members' demand that Coranderrk be abandoned was indefensible. Godfrey and Curr, in particular, would not lose face by giving way to the demands of either the Aborigines, Green or the urban 'do-gooders' they despised.

The fate of Coranderrk, and the future of the Board, were also debated by Parliament on 4 October.[4] When the Board's appropriation came up in the Supply Debate opposition members immediately asked if the government intended to remove the Coranderrk residents. They challenged the Minister to explain why the Board's estimates had climbed from £6,000 to £7,500 and why a lump sum was requested rather than the usual subdivisions. The Chief Secretary temporised saying he favoured an impartial inquiry to recommend future policy for all Aborigines and 'half castes'. MacBain criticised the validity of the Healesville inquiry and demanded a full investigation of the management of Coranderrk – and an opportunity to debate the matter when the House was not half empty. After strong criticism of MacPherson's abandonment of Ministerial responsibility, Godfrey was allowed to reply on the Board's behalf.

---

3   CSIC 76/K8996, 12 September 1876. Shaw had resigned from Lake Condah in 1872 after an Anglican inquiry had acquitted him of a resident's charge of immoral behaviour.
4   Victorian Parliamentary Debates, Session 1876:974–86.

9. WHO OWNS THE LAND?

Godfrey lost his temper and gave a thoroughly unconvincing defence of Board policy. First, he argued that the extra £1,500 was needed to provide houses, fencing and stock for Coranderrk and the existing mission stations. Later in the debate, he said that the use of this sum was purposely left vague so it could be used either for Coranderrk or a new station on the Murray. Finally, in a fury, he pledged that not one penny would be spent on improvements at Coranderrk until the government decided the fate of this station. He criticised everyone involved in recent events even declaring that Dr McCrea's reforms were excessive: Coranderrk was not a Melbourne sanatorium and he had lived in huts worse than those occupied by the Aborigines.

The debate grew more and more acrimonious, despite the insistence of the Premier and Chief Secretary that Aboriginal welfare should not be a matter of political dispute. Godfrey angrily recounted the attempts made since August 1875 by his subcommittee of new members to remove the 'unfortunate' Aborigines from this unhealthy site. Every move, he complained, had been 'checkmated, either by some of the members themselves or, more generally, by people outside who brought pressure to bear through the Chief Secretary'. Denying the rumours that some members sought possession of this reserve for themselves, he insisted that the Board would not forcibly remove all residents – merely draft off some to a warmer climate or the care of missionaries and encourage young 'half castes' to seek their own living. The Coranderrk Aborigines would not work, he said; he feared they were exposed to evil influences from the city who taught that it was the duty of the State to support them.

Duffy, who had a negligible acquaintance with Aborigines and no knowledge of the Kulin, agreed with Godfrey's criticisms declaring that Aborigines were 'notoriously unreliable witnesses'. Indeed, on his visit to Coranderrk he had been told they did little but hold meetings to discuss their grievances. He argued that dispersing the 'half castes' would reduce the cost to the government; the rest could go to mission stations and would not object as most 'had come from a warmer climate'. He had little good to say of the Board: it was difficult to convene and 'the fact that the books were kept by some clerk in the Mining department, or the Chief Secretary's office, whilst it met in a room in Temple-court and its inspector lived somewhere else, showed how its affairs were managed'. Duffy obviously had some doubts about Godfrey's bullying of witnesses at the inquiry: he insisted that the Board's administration should be thoroughly investigated and suggested that reconstitution of the membership might be necessary.

Cameron, the local member, agreed with the last point but flatly contradicted the statements that the site was unsuitable. Coranderrk was selected for a station 'because it was a camping-place of the blacks' and a large majority were natives of the district. He had known many of them for the last 23 years. Another member who had long been Local Guardian for the Wathaurung survivors near Geelong pointed out that governments had ignored pleas for increased funding for Aborigines for 16 years. He proposed that the Electoral Bill currently before the House be amended to provide a representative for the Aborigines who were more numerous than the University of Melbourne alumni demanding representation. It was a serious suggestion by a man who had great knowledge of the Kulin. Godfrey had requested his appointment three weeks earlier but he was never appointed to the Board.

MacBain, angered by Godfrey's suggestion that the indifference of long-time Board members had allowed Smyth sole management, retorted that Godfrey had usurped control with a new board constituted at his own request and that Aborigines were worse off than they had ever been. He too demanded an inquiry, explaining that he had no confidence in the new members. He insisted Coranderrk was a healthy and productive site and most residents were natives of the area. He ridiculed Godfrey's proposal to remove them to the Murray where the Aborigines were 'decimated by consumption'. No site there would produce sufficient vegetables or livestock to feed an Aboriginal station, whereas Coranderrk could pay half the Board's expenses if properly managed. Naming the persons involved, MacBain then described at length

Godfrey's efforts to prevent Green's re-appointment when no manager could be found following the dismissal of Stähle. He had supported the Board members who wanted Green though he had 'never thought him the most suitable man for the position'.

MacBain said he had been shocked at Godfrey's vendetta against Green. He told the House Godfrey had used every tactic possible to prevent his reinstatement, including threats of resignation, and had then appointed Halliday whom MacBain considered totally unqualified. Because MacBain found himself a minority of one, helpless to change decisions by the clique of newcomers, he had resigned from the Board. He concluded this exposure of the Board's internal difficulties by reporting that the 'little family' of new members had hired an unnecessary inspector, at £400 a year plus expenses, who did nothing useful.

Godfrey had provoked these disclosures by taunting MacBain to explain why he had resigned; he now announced that MacBain's expressed reason was that his church was not represented in the new appointments. MacBain said this was a lie; he had always taken care to ensure that no church was recognised in Board affairs 'and that was why some of the present members of the Board found fault with their predecessors'. Godfrey called him a liar in return asserting that MacBain had questioned him about members' denominational allegiance.

The accusations exchanged by these two staunch Tories were serious, for sectarian conflict had been exacerbated by the political crisis over government aid to the churches. Many members of the Legislative Assembly knew that Godfrey was chairman of various Anglican church committees but probably few knew that MacBain had been criticising his participation in earlier Anglican complaints about the Board's unfairness in allotting funds to their missions. The many Scots Presbyterians in the House must have been aware that MacBain had been prominent in church affairs since 1853. The Premier and Chief Secretary had long been associated with him as trustees of church property. Yet he was widely esteemed for his tolerance and honesty and the government could not dismiss his criticisms of the Board as opposition sensationalism.

Members from both sides of the House were dismayed by these exchanges; there was sufficient guilt about the treatment of Aborigines in the colony to make members of every political persuasion feel the survivors should be well cared for – if it did not cost too much. MacPherson, of course, was particularly vulnerable to criticism from the radical opposition members who had considered him a turncoat since 1870. Also, the coalition government's support was crumbling. To silence criticism that he had abdicated his ministerial responsibility for Aboriginal affairs, MacPherson announced that he would arrange an independent investigation of the Board administration within the month.

But several opposition members thought the Minister's action inadequate. Graham Berry, who had twice been Treasurer and had gained some acquaintance with Board affairs during his brief term as Chief Secretary, shrewdly pointed out that Godfrey had misled the House in explaining the requested increase in funds. The amount for medical care was in fact reduced and the new sum was primarily for salaries at Coranderrk rather than buildings. Berry argued that the Board should be abolished immediately by repeal of the 1869 Act if necessary. He condemned MacPherson's neglect, declared the 'present' Board an irresponsible failure and asserted that the Aboriginal stations should be under the direct charge of the government.

The two members were irreconcilably opposed on the issues of the day. The pastoralist-lawyer MacPherson was a moderate reformer and still shaken by the way his short-lived government had displeased the pastoralists, merchants and senior civil servants who represented conservative interests in the colony. It had fallen because of Berry's budget and he had subsequently helped to destroy Berry's ministry. Berry had scores to settle, an election was imminent and the scandalous mismanagement of Coranderrk was opportune for his campaign against the squatter establishment which the remaining Board members represented. He could count on *Age* support on this issue because of the involvement of Syme and Dow. Berry, who had immigrated in 1852 and spent his life as a Melbourne storekeeper, newspaper publisher and politician, had no first-hand knowledge of the Kulin and their history. But perhaps what he said was not just the expectable invective of an opposition leader. His democratic sympathies probably inclined him to believe that the handful of surviving Aborigines should be left unmolested on their scrap of land. The Kulin read his views about the Board in the next edition of the newspapers – and remembered them. When Berry became Minister they asked him to make good his words.

It was a month before the four new members, Godfrey, Curr, LeSouef and Sheppard, met at the regular Board meeting on 1 November 1876. They made plans for a deputation to ask the Chief Secretary about extensions and leases of various reserves and to learn his intentions about the commission of inquiry. Parliament had granted an extra £1,500 but because of Godfrey's pledge it could not be spent on improvements until future policy had been settled. As they had no reply, they met twice in December, with Jennings, to discuss the Board's position *vis-a-vis* the Minister. The other business dealt with was the dismissal of the hopmaster Burgess, urgently requested by Halliday. The correspondence revealing their reasons apparently does not survive but the minutes show that they gave in to his demands for two months pay in lieu of notice and three months later were still debating his demands for compensation.[5]

Godfrey's December request for an interview with the Minister outlined the new policy approved by a 'majority' of the Board. Jennings of course dissented and Macredie was absent for six months from September 1876. Godfrey sought authority to fence and stock all stations. He recommended the removal of 'most' Coranderrk residents to a new station on the Murray and the compulsory settlement at stations of all wanderers. He also renewed his bid to enforce Board control by prescribing the residence of all Aborigines.[6] Jennings wrote separately, still urging the retention of Coranderrk. He suggested Halliday be transferred to the Board's proposed new station on the Murray. He begged the Minister to make a rapid decision, pointing out that none of the improvements considered essential by the Chief Medical Officer McCrea had begun at Coranderrk. Five months later Jennings tried to interview the Minister about Anglican control of Coranderrk and a Murray mission, but in vain.[7]

MacPherson, no doubt thoroughly confused, received the Board deputation on 18 December. He ordered them not to implement any part of their new policy until he had received the report of a Royal Commission to be appointed in a fortnight's time. He and Premier Sir James McCulloch had promised Parliament that the inquiry into the Board's administration of Aboriginal affairs would be conducted by gentlemen both eminent and impartial. The Royal Commissioners appointed to 'inquire into the present condition of the Aborigines of this colony and to advise as to the best means of caring for, and dealing with them, in the future' were distinguished public figures. But all were extreme conservatives, strongly opposed to many policies of the radical government led by Graham Berry which gained a massive majority in the election of May 1877. Further, the leading figures were openly biased in favour of missionary control of Aborigines.

Commissions and boards of inquiry were commonplace and often used as a device to postpone or evade government responsibility for action on difficult questions. Membership was a recognition of social status, and there was some manoeuvring for appointment to this Royal Commission. The old reformer Dr John Singleton offered his services and probably others did too. But apparently, the government had some trouble securing the members it wanted. MacPherson's letter of 13 January inviting the Board vice-chairman Godfrey to serve as a commissioner said that the government also intended to appoint

---

5 BPA – Minutes, 6 and 12 December 1876, 14 February and 14 March 1877.
6 CSIC 76/K14822, 11 December 1876.
7 CSIC 76/Kl5113, 12 December 1876; CSIC 77/15169, 1 May 1877.

the Chief Justice, Sir William Stawell, and the Bairnsdale police magistrate and hop grower A.W. Howitt who had gained fame as explorer and geologist and had cooperated in Smyth's ethnographic research. There were two more members of Parliament invited: the Board's chief critic, E.H. Cameron, and J.G. Francis, conservative Premier and Chief Secretary 1872–74. Godfrey's pencilled note on the back of this letter suggests that he and other Board members had some doubts about the impartiality of the chosen commissioners:

> Jennings thinks that it would not be safe if Cameron is put on it for me not to be and suggests that as it is a Board to enquire generally into the management of the Aborigines it can't be said to be an inquiry into the conduct of the Board, 'AW.' says Godfrey ought to be on; 'Sheppard' – if Godfrey on Board has no objection to Cameron being member.

Five days later Godfrey wrote the Minister declining to serve. But he was appointed with the others on 29 January, although Francis had been replaced by G.W. Rusden, Clerk of the Legislative Council. Rusden had drafted the Anglican report and petition for relief measures in 1856 and participated in the 1858 Select Committee. He had shown sympathy for Aborigines in his histories. But he had none for Robert Brough Smyth, whom he had publicly called a liar during the Mines Department investigation the previous year.[8] Rusden may have hoped to learn more about Smyth and the past history of the Board, but he was disappointed. The commissioners were instructed to focus on current conditions and future policy.

Very likely Godfrey had made the disintegrating government pledge that the commission would not examine the Board's past conduct before he finally accepted appointment. Cabinet owed him a favour: his own seat had been abolished in the recent electoral redistribution but Godfrey decided not to stand against Robert Ramsay, a Minister, lest he weaken the government's chance for re-election. Thus Godfrey had time on his hands. He and Rusden became the most important participants, each attending 14 of the 15 public hearings held in Melbourne from 24 April to 31 July. Godfrey missed only the evidence given by Stähle at the beginning and his successor as Board vice-chairman, Curr, at the end. Rusden was absent when Rev. Robert Hamilton first tried to present his evidence about Smyth's treatment of Green on 21 May which was the day of Graham Berry's landslide election victory.

The rest of the commissioners attended only half the hearings. The appointed chairman, Stawell, who had shown no previous interest in Aborigines, attended eight sessions. Howitt, the only commissioner who had any understanding of the land tenure systems and marriage rules of Victorian Aborigines, was also present at eight hearings. His knowledge was still limited to the Kurnai of Gippsland, for he had not begun the sessions with Barak which provide the only anthropological record of Kulin custom. He missed the last four hearings concerning Coranderrk; these were the only ones attended by E.H. Cameron. Cameron's lack of participation was not necessarily the result of negligence or preoccupation with the election; perhaps he had decided that an adequate examination of Aboriginal administration was precluded by the terms of the commission and Godfrey's prominent role. After the election, the new Premier and Chief Secretary Graham Berry appointed a sixth commissioner, John Gavan Duffy, perhaps as a recognition of his interest and perhaps as a mark of gratitude for the Catholic support which had helped to win the election. Duffy attended only two of the three concluding sessions, when Green and Miss Robertson, Harris and the teacher Deans were questioned about affairs at Coranderrk.

Before the hearings, an unspecified number of commissioners also visited all six stations and sent detailed questionnaires to Local Guardians and other knowledgeable persons throughout the colony. These reaped 36 replies. The Board had not troubled to obtain a detailed enumeration of Aborigines since Green updated his 1863 count in 1869 and, as Ogilvie had made only brief visits to the six stations, there had been no reports on the condition of the Aborigines using the ration depots since his dismissal.

---

8 Legislative Council 1858–59:41–3; Hoare 1974:35.

The census conducted by police in February 1877 showed that the 1863 population of 1,920 had declined to 1,067. Of these 297 were children. There had in fact been a loss of 1,150 persons, 60 per cent of the 1863 total, within 14 years. The total number listed as residents of the six stations was 486, or 45 per cent of the total, but the managers' reports showed that average monthly attendance in that year fluctuated between 432 and 617 persons. At every station except Coranderrk the able-bodied males, often accompanied by their families, were absent for much of the year doing seasonal work in the vicinity. There had been 200 'half castes' in 1863, now there were 293; but this classification included persons whose ancestry was actually one-quarter to three-quarters Aboriginal as well as first- and second-generation 'half castes'.[9] Future policy for 'half castes' was a major concern of the commission and all of the 24 witnesses were questioned intensively about the differences between 'fullbloods' and 'half castes' and asked whether differential treatment was advisable. They and the questionnaire respondents were also asked to comment on the boarding out of orphans, the apprenticeship of youths and outside employment of adults and whether the stations should be self-supporting communities.

The recommendations of the Royal Commission report were predictable enough since it was largely written by Godfrey, substantially the same as his statement of the Board's 'new policy' 11 months earlier. The report insisted all Aborigines be settled at the stations for training. Missionary management was declared essential. In careful phrases designed not to offend local churches, the report recommended importing 'trained missionaries from Europe' – in other words Moravians. They, as Ogilvie had pointed out, were cheaper as they were paid by a wealthy international mission society. They were also immeasurably better qualified than any colonial amateurs.[10]

The report declared that funds for fencing, stock and the development of industries were essential to make the stations self-supporting. Ogilvie and Halliday had argued for outside employment and the encouragement of assimilation. The commissioners, however, concluded that Aborigines, and 'half castes', lacked sufficient moral fibre to live independently and assimilation was at present impossible because of the overwhelming evidence that persons of Aboriginal ancestry would be 'shunned' by Europeans whose strong prejudice forbad absorption. The commission report, not surprisingly, defended the Board structure of administration, but argued that the membership (ostensibly '13') should be reduced to seven and non-attendance made cause for removal. The report recommended that at least one member of Parliament should be a member but insisted that the Minister, who 'rarely' attended, should not be chairman.

Godfrey was defeated on one point: the report opposed any new station on the Murray. The few Aborigines there could be dispersed on existing stations. The report argued that all attachment to tribal lands had vanished and Aborigines could be grouped at the stations without regard for their traditional ties. Nearly every witness who knew the Aborigines well had contradicted this argument. Even Ogilvie, despite Godfrey's bullying cross-examination, had insisted on the residents' attachment to Coranderrk. But he still had no idea of the principles which enabled the Kulin and some neighbouring groups to settle together but made them unwilling to go elsewhere. Ogilvie mentioned that some women and children from Ulupna on the Murray had recently wanted to come to Coranderrk but now refused to go to Hagenauer's station in Gippsland: he blamed 'this affair in Parliament', oblivious of the fact that these Pangerang had kinsmen in Kulin clans but no ties at all with the distant Kurnai.[11]

9   Barwick 1971:298–9.
10   BPA-Annual Report 1877:App. 1.
11   Royal Commission 1877:4–5.

REBELLION AT CORANDERRK

The commissioners concluded that Coranderrk was not well managed and strongly criticised the neglected dwellings (many still with clay floors) but did not support the Board's contention that the location was unsuitable. Seventeen witnesses had been questioned about Coranderrk, and the former medical officer and the Lilydale doctor had made reports. All but the Board member Curr, who insisted Coranderrk be sold to pay for a new station, maintained that the climate and proximity to a township had no adverse effects and argued that the only change needed was a missionary manager. Ogilvie still regretted that its proximity to Melbourne encouraged 'Parliamentary interference' but although he admittedly had no great affection for the residents he opposed abandonment because of their 'love of the place'. To indicate the 'spirit that prevails there' he read excerpts from residents' letters to the Board: 'All the men are anxious to know who owns the land – the people or the Board', and 'We would like Mr J. Green back. That is all'. Ogilvie insisted that 'to remove the people from Coranderrk you would have to send up twenty or thirty police'.[12]

Ogilvie could speak relatively freely because he had resigned for 'a better billet' on 4 April 1877, a month before the hearings began. His evidence contrasted with the proposals for future policy contained in his letter of resignation which was entered in Board minutes and presented to the Royal Commission. This letter reminded the Board of its plan for a sanatorium station on the Murray. The final portion, excised from the Royal Commission report and crossed out in the minutes, suggests that his resignation was largely motivated by resentment of interference:

> It is, however, much to be deplored that degrading exigencies of Parliamentary life should not only have prevented the Board from carrying out necessary reforms but should have had such a bad effect on the people that they are now hardly amenable to any discipline at all. I have therefore no hesitation in saying that should in future the Parliament still interfere with the legitimate authority of the Board the sooner Coranderrk is broken up the better.[13]

The Board's affairs had been in chaos ever since Smyth had been suspended 14 months earlier. Their records had been moved from the Mines Department, where a clerk had been employed for some years to handle accounts, to the Chief Secretary's Department, while they now met at the Acclimatisation Society offices. The Board was effectively immobilised for another 13 months, from the government's first announcement of a Royal Commission until its report was received in November 1877. Ogilvie was discreet about the Board's administration at the hearing but later commented that only three or four members attended regularly and 'the secretary, in a great measure, was the Board'.[14]

Indeed, six meetings had lapsed without a quorum in the three months before Ogilvie resigned. But Godfrey, Curr, LeSouef and Macredie met four days later to consider two applications for the post. They awarded it immediately to Captain A.M.A. Page. His application, dated the day before, said he had held a station on the Murray and was always interested in Aborigines; he had also been commissioned as an army officer and was 'accustomed to discipline and control'. LeSouef had proposed him as a 'fit person'.

Page's appointment in May 1877 markedly increased LeSouef's influence in Board affairs. It also gave rise to charges of nepotism as they had been partners in a farming property, and Page subsequently employed LeSouef's son as his clerk and their farm servant as hop dryer at Coranderrk.[15]

Page, one of the colony's gentlemanly failures, was previously manager of small farms and stations in the Gembrook district to the east of Melbourne.[16] He was elderly, often ill, concerned with the petty details of correspondence and accounts and apparently unwilling to travel on journeys of inspection. He was also vain,

---

12 Royal Commission 1877:6, 11.
13 Royal Commission 1877:1; BPA – Minutes 11 April 1877.
14 Coranderrk Inquiry 1881:119.
15 BPA – Minutes 4 and 11 April 1877; Coranderrk Inquiry 1881:81, 125, 140; *Argus*, 15 December 1881.
16 Coranderrk Inquiry 1881:48–54.

authoritarian and vindictive when he was opposed. He suited the Board members who had found Ogilvie's decided views on policy a challenge to their own authority; he suited Hagenauer and the other missionaries because he made no attempt to interfere with their management and responded promptly to their requests for money and supplies. Although he succeeded Ogilvie in May 1877 the government did not approve his appointment as Acting Secretary until the end of June. Page, advised by Hagenauer, indirectly controlled Board policy until his death in 1889. The Kulin found him a greater threat than his predecessors because he made no effort to check on the management of Coranderrk. He visited only once or twice a year for a few hours and refused to heed any protests or complaints unless relayed through the manager.

This kind of managerial autonomy was what Ogilvie, Curr and the Royal Commission report recommended. But since Green's dismissal, the Kulin had found that their managers could not be trusted with this kind of power. There was growing dissatisfaction with Halliday's sincerity, although they did not yet realise he had secretly opposed their pleas – led by John Briggs – for independent 40-acre (16 ha) farms on the reserve despite his promises of support.[17]

Halliday naturally tended to favour the newcomers and the Kulin pioneers who accepted him, rather than those who openly showed their loyalty to Green. He found an ally in the discontented old Jajowrong Tommy Farmer, who had always blamed Green for the loss of his farm at Mount Franklin which he had in fact abandoned in 1864. Despite his age Farmer had little status in Kulin society for he had lived with Europeans since childhood and had none of the ritual knowledge proper to an elder.

William Parker (1847–1886), his wife Mary and children.

---

17   BPA – Minutes 3 January 1877; Royal Commission 1877:11.

Halliday had also won over the younger Jajowrong Martin Simpson, a participant in Barak's September 1876 deputation to the Chief Secretary, by awarding him a coveted pole cutting contract. Both of these pioneers had been absent for long periods in recent years, working in their home territory for Europeans who were old friends – and friends of Godfrey. Halliday's favouritism to two other men, non-Kulin newcomers, had caused much dissension in recent months. The Kulin bitterly resented the fact that James Edgar had replaced Harris as 'overseer' of the hop ground and Alick Campbell (1851–c. 1933) had been made stockman in place of Robert Wandin who had held the post for years. Both these men were Burapper who had formed no ties to the Kulin community, for they had married the women they followed from Mount Hope Station in 1872. But Harris was related by marriage to a large number of Taungurong, and Wandin was not only Barak's nephew but his speaker and thus responsible for this land and all who lived on it.

Apparently, no Aborigines had been formally questioned during the Royal Commissioners' visits to stations and none were invited as witnesses. It seems no coincidence that it was these four proteges who accompanied Halliday to the hearing on 22 May the day after Rev. Robert Hamilton, now the influential Moderator of the Presbyterian General Assembly, asked the commissioners to examine Green's treatment. Godfrey, who once held a station in their home area, was primed with details of each man's history. In an extraordinary series of leading questions he tried to elicit their grievances against Green and obtain statements that Coranderrk was an unsuitable location.[18] When asked why they had come the men said they had organised a brief meeting that morning, attended by 'every man on' (old James 'Jemmy' Barker and Jajowrong William Parker, members of the previous deputation, were absent) and were chosen to tell the commissioners that most residents were quite satisfied with Halliday's management and wanted only better houses and more meat. When cross-examined about attitudes to Green all said some residents still wanted him back but they said they 'did not know' why others felt thus. They were abiding by Kulin etiquette which held that no man could speak for another unless he was a clan-head representing his group. But the commissioners concluded that there was no real support for Green. Their impression was encouraged by Farmer's comment that 'we are getting more clothing from this manager'.

When Rusden, Stawell and Howitt joined Godfrey in cross-examining them about their attachment to Coranderrk the four said it was their home and they would prefer to remain there. They insisted few would leave Coranderrk. The two Burapper men who declared Green had forced them to come or kept them there did finally say they would be willing to return to their original home near the Murray but Godfrey had to work hard for this answer. Godfrey also tried to suggest that drunkenness was rife because of the station's location, but the witnesses' statements that the Coranderrk people were sober, hard-working and well-conducted were supported by Halliday (who also said they were peaceable and amenable to his discipline), Ogilvie, the teacher Deans, the overseer Harris and all former staff members. They also testified that all but a 'very few' residents were determined to remain at Coranderrk.

The community was united in opposing removal but dissension between the Kulin pioneers and the newcomers was being fostered by Halliday's favouritism. The 1877 correspondence is lost, but hints of how the pioneers felt about Halliday's decision to give positions of authority to non-Kulin appear in the Healesville court records published in the Board's annual report. On 1 May 1877, Halliday had called the constable to quell a 'row', and John Briggs Jr was subsequently gaoled for 'obstructing and assaulting the manager' while James Edgar and the Jajowrong pioneer John Charles were fined for mutual assault. In July Harris told the commissioners he had been 'in the hop garden (but not in charge) the last fortnight because the men refused to work under Edgar'.[19] Halliday's own annual report, dated 24 July, noted the factionalism but misinterpreted its cause: he concluded that 'fullbloods' and 'half castes' should be

---

18 Royal Commission 1877:26–33, 91–2, 94.
19 Royal Commission 1877:94.

9. WHO OWNS THE LAND?

separated as 'they do not agree too well together on the same station and when any dispute arises the ill-feeling shows itself'. He had argued ever since his appointment that the 'half castes' should be treated as Europeans and encouraged to seek assimilation off the station.[20]

Green's supporters naturally expected the commissioners would examine the circumstances of his dismissal, for this had been implicit in the government's pledges made during the 1876 Parliamentary debate. Rev. Robert Hamilton, as co-convener of the Presbyterian missions committee, prepared their official submission and when called as a witness on 21 May also presented his own report on Coranderrk, based on his acquaintance with Green and the Woiworung since 1860. However, he was ordered to revise his comments and Green, whose reply to the Board questionnaire was dated that day, was not called for examination. The exclusion of the former officer who knew more about the depots and six stations than anyone else in the colony was purely spiteful.

Over the week following the election of Berry's government the missionary Hagenauer was questioned at length about past policy and Coranderrk (which he had never visited). Other churchmen who had a negligible acquaintance with Aborigines were invited to give their views. While these witnesses were encouraged to comment on past policy Hamilton's defence of Green was rejected twice more. No reference to his removal remained in the final transcript. Curr, as acting vice-chairman, was cross-examined by Godfrey, Rusden and Cameron (who took the chair) on 1 June. Curr could not remember the date of his appointment but was led to speak of his intensive study of the 'habits and language' of the Aborigines since 1841. As he admitted he had not seen all stations, questioning concentrated on Coranderrk. Arguing that Aborigines must be coerced for their own good, for they were no more than children, he insisted all residents must be removed from this station. Despite all the evidence to the contrary he asserted that the site was injurious to the residents because it encouraged lung disease, drunkenness and Parliamentary interference. He said the Aborigines had told him this was never a camping place for them 'before the time of the whites'; he did not explain that his contact with the Kulin totalled a few hours during two visits in 1875 and 1876. Curr concluded his evidence with a demand for managerial authority without right of appeal, and a defence of the Board. Their authority must be increased, he told the commissioners: 'As it is, the board can inspect, devise measures, talk and recommend – anything but act'.[21]

Apparently this was to be the concluding session. But Berry's indebtedness for *Age* support in his election victory enabled G.A. Syme to gain an interview for himself and Green on 6 June; the next day Green and the former dormitory matron Miss Robertson were examined by all the commissioners except Howitt. Green's written submission was restricted by the terms of the printed questionnaire. His examination was confined to the recruitment of the Coranderrk residents, particularly the Burapper witnesses (whose former employer had meanwhile testified that he requested Green to remove them), and generalisations about future policy. His opinion of other stations was not sought and his removal and final dismissal were not mentioned. Green later informed Berry that Stawell had insisted the Royal Commission was limited to present conditions, and reminded the new Minister of his promise to arrange a fuller investigation. Green asserted that MacBain and Syme, who had 'resigned owing to my unjust removal and treatment' were, with several other Board members, 'anxious to have the whole investigated'.[22]

The commission concluded at the end of July 1877 after another interview with Curr and a final session with the Coranderrk overseer and teacher. But Stawell's refusal to give Green a hearing ensured Berry's sympathy. When acting governor in 1875 Stawell had refused Berry a dissolution so his government could seek popular support for its reforms. In Berry's view, Stawell personified the conservative forces ranged

---

20 BPA – Annual Report 1878:App. l; for evidence of Halliday's views see Royal Commission 1877:32–3, 112–3 and BPA-Minutes, 3 May 1876.
21 Royal Commission 1877:76–9.
22 CSIC 77/M7066, 18 June 1877.

against him. The problems of the Coranderrk people probably had roused some sympathy before; now Berry saw them and Green as victims of the colony's immoral, land-hungry establishment. The fate of Coranderrk was another cause for his moral crusade.

Meanwhile, public opinion had been influenced by a vicious article in the *Argus*, written by the popular correspondent 'The Vagabond'.[23] Recalling an afternoon's visit during the hop harvest four months before, he compared Coranderrk to a 'free negro settlement' in the American south. He blamed the squalid housing on the 'neglect and shiftlessness' of the inhabitants and said Chinese pickers had to do all the work because the residents were too lazy. He deplored the number of 'half castes' maintained in idleness as a result of the prostitution of the women to whom 'chastity was unknown'. He said this land must be given to Europeans. The antagonistic rumours 'The Vagabond' reported represented the views of district residents who coveted the reserve but he gave the impression that the criticisms were the opinions of staff. Even the Board were outraged and their 1877 annual report included statistics showing that the Aboriginal pickers performed better than Chinese or Europeans and court records disproving his lies about large numbers being charged for drunkenness. Aside from Halliday's insistence that morality had improved since his appointment, no attempt was made to defend the good name of the Aboriginal women.

The Board members were in a quandary about Coranderrk. The previous government had returned the profit from one hop crop but objected to the Board's retention of the income from the current crop. If the protracted negotiations with Berry's ministry failed and Treasury kept all hop profits the Board would have no incentive for maintaining this costly station. Curr, Godfrey and LeSouef still favoured abandonment but Jennings and the commission witnesses had destroyed their main argument against this location. If they defended the morality of the residents as Halliday demanded they would lose their last argument for removal. If they did not defend the morality of the station under Halliday's management their critics might secure Green's reinstatement.

Halliday's July 1877 annual report covered the 15 months since his appointment. The men had repaired 12 cottages, erected five outbuildings and completed five miles (8 km) of paddock fencing. He estimated it would take them two years to complete the needed nine miles (14.4 km) of boundary fencing as the hop crop monopolised their labour for most of the year. He too condemned the neglected dwellings and insisted all must be replaced. In this report the Board asked for an additional appropriation of £3,000 for necessary buildings, fencing and stock for all stations. Ogilvie had told the Royal Commission that the fencing at Coranderrk would cost £750–1,000 and the 20 huts needed would cost £30 each.[24] After receiving the Royal Commission report in November 1877 the Board renewed their request for funds to improve other stations but did not mention Coranderrk. Berry declined pending a Cabinet decision on the commissioners' recommendations.[25] In fact, the Legislative Council had refused to pass Berry's budget and the political crisis over his retaliatory action, a decision to 'retrench' 200 senior public servants, was at its height. The Anglican mission committee had renewed its offer to take charge of Coranderrk but this too had to be deferred for Cabinet approval.[26]

The policy changes the Board were able to implement meanwhile had merely exacerbated the discontent of the Kulin. Instead of increasing rations, they resolved that residents must purchase any extra tea and sugar required, and at the end of 1877 ceased to issue meat at Coranderrk. Halliday had advised the commissioners that the men were 'too independent of work, and to bring them more under subjection

---

23 *Argus*, 7 July 1877; BPA – Annual Report 1877:App. 2.
24 Royal Commission 1877:12.
25 BPA – Minutes 26 November 1877, 1 April 1878; Secretary's Minute Book 78/14, 14 November 1877, 9 May 1878.
26 BPA – Minutes 2 January 1878.

I would recommend that the meat ration be stopped, and that the pay for labour be increased one penny per hour as an equivalent'.[27] The Board allowed this increase only to married men with children and half this rate to men without dependents.

Back in September 1877 the new secretary Captain Page had asked for Board support to discourage the many deputations coming down to complain of Halliday's management. When the Board members refused to heed them, residents began writing directly to Berry reminding him of his well-publicised expressions of sympathy. After Berry had repeatedly bypassed the Board in granting certain wishes Godfrey was sent to rebuke the 'interference' of the *ex officio* chairman in February 1878.[28]

However, Berry could not ignore the complaint made two days later by his former Parliamentary ally John Sinclair. His public criticisms of the lack of religious and medical care at Coranderrk had led to the Royal Commission investigation, and Healesville now had a doctor as a result of a government subsidy. The Kulin leaders frequently visited the 70-year-old reformer Sinclair at his Healesville home – he was, as an ill-educated former builder, probably the most approachable of the local justices – to seek advice. Berry immediately asked the Board to report on the petition Sinclair had written for three unnamed pioneers on 11 February. They complained they were short of potatoes and milk and had to pay threepence a pound for beef purchased at the station:

> althow [sic] the cattle are there [sic] own as they worked at several stations shearing & harvesting & brought the money to Mr Green & he laid it out in purchasing cattle for them and they cannot get any hay for there [sic] horses.

Reporting that Sergeant Halliday had taunted one of these men to come into the bush if he wanted to fight the manager, Sinclair deplored the increased use of police control and the lack of religious instruction. The petition asserted:

> that they [sic] have been badly treated ever since Mr and Mrs Green left. Mr Green looked after there bodys & souls and went always to work with them and showed them how to work and they want him back again and they will keep themselfs [sic] without any money from the state.[29]

The complaints came from the Woiworung clan-head Barak, his speaker Bamfield and James 'Jemmy' Barker who had been Wonga's speaker. These were the men who had a right to represent the owners of this land. But the ignorant Board members, determined to emphasise the manager's authority, sent the petition for Halliday's report without further investigation. Vice-Chairman Curr's reply to the Chief Secretary merely quoted Halliday's contradiction of all complaints.[30] Berry forwarded this to Sinclair who replied on 16 April declaring that the Aborigines were dissatisfied with the statements of the Board and manager and intended to visit the Minister to make their own report.[31]

Two weeks earlier Curr, Godfrey, LeSouef and Jennings had empowered the secretary Page to decide whether the services of the farm overseer were required. They, like Halliday, suspected that Harris was supporting the renewed agitation for the return of the Greens. The Board had also authorised Page to send notice to all stations that he had full authority to exile, with a work certificate, any resident guilty of insubordination. Both of these threats dismayed the Kulin. No improvements had been made at the station as a result of the Royal Commission; there was in fact less cultivation than before as Halliday had no experience of farming and Harris now had to do Burgess' work in the hop ground as well as his previous tasks. The Board's failure to develop Coranderrk lent weight to the rumours the Kulin heard constantly in the township – that they would be removed to mission stations and the reserve would be sold.

---

27 Royal Commission 1877:112; BPA – Minutes 12 September and 3 December 1877.
28 BPA – Minutes, 5 September 1877; Secretary's Minute Book 78/7, 1 and 9 February 1878.
29 CSIC 78/01477, 11 February 1878.
30 CSIC 78/03291, 2 April 1878.
31 CSIC 78/N4130, 16 April 1878.

Jemmy Barker with his wife Jeannie (Rowan) and their children, Aaron and Israel, c. 1876.

Sinclair's second letter to the Minister indicated that he was aware of plans for a meeting that day. The manager Halliday could learn only that it had been convened by Bamfield and Barker and attended by 21 men. There were now only 27 men: eight were Burapper newcomers. On 30 April 1878, Halliday telegraphed to warn the Board secretary that 'the blacks' were walking to Melbourne to complain that their wages and clothing were overdue, after 'disputes between them and the half castes' in which Bamfield and Barker were the principals. The Board members next day made plans to visit without warning to discover the origin of the complaints. They also confirmed Page's order that the 'malcontents' Bamfield and Barker be expelled from Coranderrk.[32]

The deputation had walked most of the night and did not wait on the Board as expected. Instead they went to Parliament House, where Dow, the *Age* and *Leader* journalist who had been elected as a Berry protege, introduced them to the Chief Secretary. The *Age* account next day, 2 May, probably written by Dow, quoted their criticisms of Halliday's management but maintained that the real cause of complaint was still Green's removal. Berry pledged himself to 'do what he could to meet their views' and asked Dow to investigate the management on his behalf. Berry questioned the deputation about Green's knowledge of their plans (presumably because of the incessant Board complaints that Green was inciting the Aborigines); the men said they had told him and many others that they intended to interview the Minister. In fact, the Lilydale clergyman Rev. Alex Mackie later said he had suggested this deputation:

> They came to me on one occasion, when the station was threatened to be taken from them. I told them if they did not manage themselves better it probably would be … They asked what they should do. It was at the time that the country was in a state of excitement about embassies and so on. I advised them to go to Mr. Berry on an embassy to protest against the

---

32   BPA – Minutes 1 May 1878, Secretary's Minute Book, 78/15, 30 April and 1 May 1878.

> station being sold. A man was almost in tears. He said, 'The white people have only left us a miserable spadeful of ground, and now they want to take that away from us'. I said, 'Is there anyone who wants to leave?' He said 'No'. I visited the station and I could not find anyone who wanted to leave.[33]

The ten men in the deputation led by Barak were all Kulin pioneers. Four of them were 'half castes': his speakers Robert Wandin and the Jajowrong Thomas Dunolly, the latter's half-brother John Charles, and the Taungurong William Hamilton (Talgium, 1850–c. 1900), brother-in-law to the overseer Harris. With them were the Taungurong men Thomas Bamfield and Dick Richards of Kilmore, husband of Dunolly's sister Ellen and the two Jajowrong, Martin Simpson and the dying Tommy Farmer, who had been members of the previous deputation to a Minister and witnesses at the Royal Commission. Farmer's opinion had changed as Halliday's behaviour grew more coercive; later the European friend who had reared him informed the Board that Farmer had 'never been easy in his mind since the removal of Mr Green although he makes no complaint against any person over him'.[34]

The *Age* report provoked LeSouef to convene a special Board meeting. The four angry old pastoralists who attended resolved to send the absent Jennings and Macredie to protest their chairman's reception of the deputation without Board observers and his 'interference' in appointing Dow. But since 'Berry was not to be seen' vice-chairman Curr finally had to write asking the Minister not to act on Dow's report before the Board conducted an investigation.[35]

On 15 May Curr visited with the solicitor Jennings and the secretary, Page. On 31 May all six Board members heard Curr present his own and Jennings' reports. Despite the formal reticence of the minutes it is clear that there was an angry dispute:

> As Jennings' report recommended re-appointment of Green to the managership of Coranderrk in Halliday's place, a warm discussion took place on the subject; Le Souef, Sheppard, Godfrey and Curr, vice-chairman, expressed themselves as strongly opposed to the re-appointment of Green under any circumstances – in consequence of which Jennings took back his report that the passages objected to might be erased. It was also suggested that Curr should erase from his report a passage referring to Green which he declined to do, stating that in his opinion the question of the re-appointment of Green was at the bottom of the disorders complained of at Coranderrk and could not consistently be ignored by him. As the reports differed in several essential particulars, Mr Godfrey was asked to look over the two reports and the evidence taken at Coranderrk and endeavour to produce a report to be forwarded to the Minister which should be confined to facts concerning which the Board was unanimous.

Only Curr's report (minus Godfrey's excisions) remains in the Board archives.[36] Ironically, he had to report that drunkenness was less prevalent than among European labourers. He ridiculed complaints that there was less food and religious instruction and more card playing and Sabbath-breaking under Halliday's rule. He said that the residents had been 'split into two sections': lazy drunken 'fullbloods' and orderly 'half castes' who did most of the work. He dismissed the leader Barker as a drunkard and ridiculed Bamfield, 'the organiser and spokesman of the discontented party', as a man with a liking for 'stray drinks and frequent prayer'. He falsely declared that Bamfield had frequently been in court for drunkenness and cruelty to animals under the former managers Green and Stähle and had 'assaulted' Ogilvie. Halliday had said Bamfield had also tried to fight an 'orderly, well-conducted' 'half caste'; these facts, Curr held, contradicted Green's evidence that Bamfield was a 'good trustworthy man'.

---

33 Coranderrk Inquiry 1881:92.
34 BPA – James Bodkin to A.M.A. Page, 13 July 1879.
35 BPA – Minutes, 2 May 1878; Secretary's Minute Book 78/15, 2 and 3 May 1878; CSIC 78/N4652, 3 May 1878.
36 BPA – Curr to Board, 30 May 1878.

The Board's 1878 annual report pointed out that although the populations of Healesville and Coranderrk were nearly equal, Europeans had been charged with 19 offences and Aborigines with two. It also revealed that both charges against Bamfield had been made by Halliday's protege James Edgar.[37] Both charges were malicious and that was why Bamfield had wanted to fight this 'half caste'. Curr, making his third brief visit, had no inkling of the division between the Kulin pioneers and the younger Burapper and Pangerang men to whom Halliday had given positions of authority. They had, in Kulin eyes, no rightful claim to control or speak for the owners of this land. Curr was oblivious of Kulin rules and confident that he understood 'the blacks'; he was able to speak to some residents 'in their own language' on his visits.[38] Of course, he spoke to the Pangerang intruders, not the owners.

Jennings was not present at the next meeting on 2 July 1878 when he was elected vice-chairman. Curr's intransigence had so alarmed his colleagues that they would not allow him a second term. Jennings thus had to sign the report Godfrey concocted for the Minister. It said only that the grievances were trivial, vexatious and confined to one or two disaffected individuals. It asked him to implement the Royal Commission recommendation for missionary management.[39]

Dow's report, submitted a day later, was more informative.[40] Dow meant well, but his misinterpretation of the divisions in the Coranderrk community decisively shaped Berry's reaction to the Board's future policy proposals. His report was accepted as the view of a sympathetic observer to whom Aborigines spoke freely. They had done so in 1876; but the information conveyed to him in this meeting was shaped by the presence of Board staff. Halliday and the Board secretary – who was making one of his rare visits – escorted him round the station and attended his meeting with the men. Although Dow told Berry that his experience as an explorer and pastoralist in Queensland had shaped his views of 'blacks and half castes', Dow himself did not realise that his ignorance of Kulin social boundaries and his beliefs about differential treatment shaped his perception of the factionalism at Coranderrk. He depicted their disagreement on the basis of 'caste' antagonism; but details in his lengthy report clearly indicate that the opposition was actually that of Kulin pioneers versus the alien newcomers led by James Edgar. Dow did understand that 'the old blacks' disapproved of the appointment of this 'half caste overseer' because he had displaced Harris, who was 'identified with Mr Green' but he had no inkling that Harris had been incorporated into the kinship system or that his children had a birth right to use this Woiworung territory.

Although Dow misinterpreted the factionalism he did perceive its cause and criticised Halliday for siding openly with 'newcomer half castes' throughout the day. Of the 27 male household heads and youths at Coranderrk, 17 were Kulin and eight of these were 'half castes'. There were also two Pangerang and the other eight were Burapper who had arrived since 1871. Dow's report informed Berry that the 'pure blacks' (i.e. a majority of Kulin pioneers) and the 'half castes' (the newcomers) had lined up on opposite sides of the room and exchanged recriminations, the 'spokesmen from the pure blacks' (the deputation members) reiterating their criticisms of the management, while the:

> half castes retorted by stating that the pure blacks (Jemmy Barker was particularly mentioned) were promoting a bad feeling by spreading reports invidious to the half castes, such as that the half castes had no business in the station at all … when one half caste referred in a sneering manner to the alleged inferior work of the blacks in the hop plantation, one of the blacks waved his hand over toward the half castes in the most majestic manner and replyed addressing them, 'Why you fellows, who are you, who are you anyhow, why you came here like a lot of scotch thistles!' As showing the feelings actuating the pure blacks in this matter also a rather pertinent

---

37   BPA – Annual Report 1878:App. 10.
38   Coranderrk Inquiry 1881:126.
39   BPA – Minutes 2 July 1878; CSIC 78/06738, 2 July 1878.
40   CSIC 78/N6789, 3 July 1878.

9. WHO OWNS THE LAND?

question was addressed to me by one of the blacks. 'Look here, Mr Dow', he said, 'suppose the time come when the last blackfellow dead, who will this station belong to. Sir Henry Barkly gave this station to Mr Green for the <u>blacks</u>, not for the half castes.'

Reminding Berry that he had known the station in Green's time, Dow particularly lamented the loss of Mary Green, for whom all residents felt 'sincere affection'. He insisted that 'all the trouble has originated in the summary, unexplained, and in the opinion of many impartial observers most unjust dismissal of Mr Green'. Enclosing his 1876 *Leader* article as evidence, Dow advised Berry to reinstate Green as inspector and manager, disband the Board by asking present members to resign and assume direct control of Aboriginal affairs. He urged Berry to consult MacBain, who had resigned over the Board's treatment of Green and would corroborate his own statements.

Berry probably had little inclination for the sort of intervention Dow demanded. Removal of the well-connected Board members would certainly revive the local antagonism roused by his dismissal of the 200 senior public servants. Dow's advice was the exact opposite of the Royal Commission's recommendation for retention of the Board without a ministerial chairman. A realisation that the Colonial Office might still be concerned about the colony's sorry record of 'native' administration may have played some part in Berry's decision to place the requested £3,000 special grant on the current Estimates in mid-1878, despite his government's financial problems. Certainly he was not moved by the Board's letters, and had ignored all requests for an interview.[41]

The Board members, too, were constrained by the recommendations of the Royal Commission. LeSouef immediately urged that £1,000 of the special grant be spent on a new station in the Murray region but when Godfrey cited the evidence received by the commissioners against a station in that locality (thus belatedly vindicating Green) the Board instead resolved to disperse the Murray Aborigines on existing stations.[42] The residents' protests, Berry's sympathy and the commissioners' advice made it impossible to abandon Coranderrk. Moreover, the Board dared not implement their decision to exile the leaders Bamfield and Barker because of the repercussions which followed the banishment of insubordinate Aborigines from Stähle's and Hagenauer's stations. The Board had long been dissatisfied with Halliday's management (as Curr later admitted) but it was not until 14 August that Godfrey and Macredie put a motion 'not to defer any longer' his dismissal.[43] Some members had fought the change because they did not wish to appear to succumb to the Aborigines' protests; but now they feared that Berry would be influenced to select Green as the missionary manager they had advised.

Their secretary was pressing for appointment of an Anglican clergyman who claimed 20 years of experience as a 'missionary' – apparently among Europeans. Without advertising the post the Board, on the motion of Curr and Sheppard, appointed Page's choice, Rev. Frederick Strickland, to take charge of Coranderrk from 20 September 1878. Strickland was kindly, ineffectual, ignorant of farming and a chronic alcoholic given to fits of violent rage when drunk; but Page was able to hide his friend's deficiencies. The public service clerk employed for years had resigned within weeks of Page's arrival. The Board authorised him to keep the salary and find his own clerical assistance. Thus no one but Page, and LeSouef's son saw the Board correspondence and there was no vestige of the normal public service controls in Board affairs except for the Audit Commissioners' constant criticisms. Page could ignore the complaints of Coranderrk residents, for the Board was determined to uphold the manager's authority, and their own. But he learned that he could not ignore the powerful sympathisers whom he offended.

---

41 BPA – Secretary's Minute Book 78/22, 25 May and 3 June 1878.
42 BPA – Minutes, 1 August and 4 September 1878.
43 Coranderrk Inquiry 1881:120–1; BPA – Minutes 14 and 26 August 1878.

Chapter 10
CAUSE FOR REBELLION

> Barak was also a statesman. His house was the council chamber in which the elders met to discuss their affairs, which were connected chiefly with what they considered the injustice and want of sympathy shown them by the Aborigines Board. Barak had two intelligent half-castes as secretaries, whose letters were well composed, neatly written, and honoured by receiving space in the columns of 'The Argus' and other newspapers. Barak had many political friends among whom were Sir Graham Berry, Mr Alfred Deakin, Messrs. E. Zox, J.L. Dow, R. Murray Smith, J. MacPherson Grant, Robert Stirling Anderson, Sir James Patterson, Mr W.A. Watt, Sir Henry Wrixon, Sir Bryan O'Loghlen, Messrs F. Longmore, R. Richardson, and many others.
>
> Anne F. Bon 1931[1]

At the end of 1878 the future of Coranderrk seemed secure. The Board had earmarked £720 for improvements, including £450 for the boundary fence, and requested public service architects to design improved housing.[2] A majority of Board members however still favoured the removal of the Coranderrk residents. The next annual report announced that a number had been transferred to the Wimmera mission station 'for their health'. Only two were tuberculosis sufferers. The widowed Louisa Briggs and her five single children were transferred largely because she had made complaints about the new manager Strickland's neglect of the sick. In November 1878 the Board ended their contract with the local doctor because of his quarrels with the manager, and soon afterwards he left the district leaving the residents once more dependent on the distant Lilydale doctor and John Green.

Strickland's behaviour antagonised the residents, other staff and many townsfolk. The clergyman's 'outrageous' conduct on his first August visit brought a complaint from Halliday even before he had news of his own dismissal. He immediately sent the secretary numerous warnings about the residents' reaction, asserting that the best workers were planning to leave 'and never intend to return' and the remainder, also dissatisfied, were not numerous enough to save the hop crop. The Halliday family moved to Healesville when Strickland took charge in September and for the next few years were more of a nuisance to the Board than Green had ever been. The Board punished Halliday's defiance in removing a girl servant, with a summons. He was fined for employing an Aboriginal without a work certificate. They withheld a promised gratuity and reference because of his complaints about his unjust dismissal and demands for reinstatement. They could not silence his complaints that Strickland was drunk on duty and maltreated the dormitory children, for the old policeman knew enough of the law to get sworn affidavits and enlist witnesses.[3]

---

1   *Argus*, 28 November 1931.
2   BPA – Minutes, 13 November 1878.
3   BPA – Secretary's Minute Book, 78/52, 72, 75, 76, 80, 85, 91 – August to 21 December 1878.

Still unable to believe that Coranderrk residents were capable of organising protests, the Board blamed Halliday when James Edgar and Alick Campbell sent complaints to Jennings that Edgar's young sister had been neglected before and after her death in October 1878. After a brief investigation Page dismissed their letters, suspecting incitement by Halliday although both he and his son denied any involvement. Page even enlisted detectives to try to prove that members of the family were abetting or forging complaints by residents and were the authors of anonymous letters, but in vain.[4]

The balance of power within the Board altered in 1879 when Godfrey resigned in March to go abroad. But LeSouef had already begun to take a newly dominant role. This was partly because his friend Page and his son, the Board clerk, had been installed in the Acclimatisation Society offices where he presided, and partly because LeSouef was sympathetic to the policy alterations demanded by his friend Rev. Hagenauer, the senior Moravian missionary. Despite the Royal Commission verdict against sending 'half castes' out to service, Hagenauer had wanted such a policy and LeSouef proposed the change in December 1878. Curr dissented and Godfrey demanded amendment of the scheme, but LeSouef's proposal that boys should be 'encouraged' to leave the stations was passed by the Board in January 1879.[5] The resulting pressure to consent to apprenticeship of their children, the transfer of their friends to the Wimmera mission station and finally Page's dismissal of four young 'half caste' men (two of them Kulin pioneers) for 'insubordination' in March 1879 increased the insecurity of Coranderrk residents. Resentment of Board policy encouraged a new solidarity of interest among 'half castes' whatever their origins and the Kulin pioneers who had 'half caste' kinsmen.

Although Jennings was vice-chairman until the end of June 1879, when LeSouef succeeded him, the fate of Coranderrk was meanwhile decided by others. Curr later revealed how this had occurred: because he had contradicted Jennings' testimony that the Board met monthly for an hour, he was cross-examined on the length of Board meetings and explained that 'Some leave early, after the formal business is done. Mr Jennings is one of them. Others stop later'.[6] The Board, which subsequently complained of 'Chief Secretary "misrule" i.e. hearing deputations, in force for years except when Sir B. O'Loghlen was acting' also took advantage of Berry's absence on his constitutional mission to England for the first half of 1879.

Sir Bryan O'Loghlen, who was Attorney General and acting Chief Secretary, immediately ordered the Board to investigate the complaints about Halliday's management made by three residents at the end of April. The Board deputed vice-chairman Jennings and the secretary to investigate the residents' 'unrest'. Curr, clearly distrusting Jennings' sympathies, accompanied them to Coranderrk on 2 May. They concluded that the complaint was a forgery but took evidence nevertheless. Five Board members interviewed O'Loghlen on 12 May, requesting him to send a detective to find the writer, alleging that 'the blacks are being used as a catspaw for certain ill-disposed persons'. The Board suspected the Halliday daughters, previously in charge of the dormitory, especially when further anonymous criticisms were received. They ignored the corroborating evidence about the neglect of Edgar's sister received from the teacher, other residents, and Louisa Briggs, now at the Wimmera station.[7]

Meanwhile, at a special Board meeting on 7 May Jennings, Macredie and LeSouef heard Curr demand a deputation to convince the Chief Secretary of 'the necessity of breaking up Coranderrk'. He obstinately revived his 1875 scheme for a station at Kulkyne and insisted that the Board seek the necessary land and funds in exchange for Coranderrk. Two months earlier the Board had paid for a tour by the two Moravian missionaries who reported that the few survivors on the Murray would come to the Wimmera. Yet the Board had been unable to obtain an extension of this reserve and the land was too poor to support a larger

---

4   BPA – Secretary's Minute Book 78/85 – 29 October to 20 November 1878; 79/111, 116, 136 – 30 April to 30 October 1879.
5   BPA – Minutes, 4 December 1878, 15 January 1879.
6   Coranderrk Inquiry 1881:123.
7   BPA – Secretary's Minute Book 79/111, 30 April – 15 May 1879; 79/136, 13 August – 30 October 1879; CSIC 79/P3890, 29 April 1879.

population. Mindful of this, and the repeated Anglican offers to take control of Coranderrk, LeSouef suggested Curr defer his motion until the two of them had made a hasty visit to determine whether the existing Anglican missions could absorb the Aborigines of the Murray and Coranderrk. In fact they did not go to Stähle's station in the Western District but only to Gippsland to interview the Lake Tyers missionary and Hagenauer who supervised all four mission stations. The report by Curr and LeSouef, published in the Board's 1879 report, declared that the two longest-serving missionaries (neither of whom had visited) said that Coranderrk was 'utterly impossible to manage satisfactorily'. As they had 'always held the same opinion' Curr and LeSouef urged that the inhabitants of Coranderrk and Framlingham be transferred to the Wimmera and Lake Tyers mission stations. Both were remote, neglected and at risk of closing because of depopulation. The choice was no doubt suggested by Hagenauer, always concerned for Moravian interests, although he later publicly denied that he had been consulted by Curr and LeSouef and admitted that he did not want the Coranderrk people at his own station because 'their demands are so great'.[8]

Jennings' final duty as vice-chairman was to sign two submissions drafted by LeSouef and Curr which urged the acting Chief Secretary to sell Coranderrk and Framlingham and announced that the Wimmera and Lake Tyers stations would eventually house all surviving Aborigines. The authors offered no reason for closing Framlingham and merely reiterated the objections to Coranderrk that Jennings, and Curr himself, had already disproved in letters to the Minister:

> Several of the present members of the Board have always held that Coranderrk was originally badly selected … being too cold and wet; and so far back as August 1875 Messrs Curr, Godfrey and LeSouef recommended that it should be abandoned … Other and grave reasons, namely its close proximity to the township of Healesville and other surroundings … make it, in the unanimous opinion of the Board, extremely desirable to break this station up.

The second submission of 12 June 1879, also immediately published in the annual report, asked for specialist investigation of the lung disease 'peculiar to the natives'. LeSouef, Curr and Godfrey's replacement on the Board formed the deputation who interviewed O'Loghlen five days before Berry's expected return. The new member, George H. Bennett, was a Scottish Catholic brewer who attended only four Board meetings.[9] He was O'Loghlen's choice: the Board, at Godfrey's request, had nominated the former critic John Gavan Duffy. The carefully chosen deputation stressed the advantages of their proposal to a financially embarrassed government: the two reserves offered, now 'of great commercial value', would sell for at least £33,200. In return, the Board asked only extension of the Wimmera and Lake Tyers reserves and £2,000 for rehousing transferred Aborigines.

However they had mistaken the sympathies of O'Loghlen who was a leading Irish Catholic spokesman, and had over-reached themselves by suggesting abandonment of Framlingham. Although O'Loghlen did not become the Parliamentary representative of this district for another decade, he apparently knew that the mostly Irish selectors who were near neighbours of the Framlingham people were on cordial terms with them and warmly supported their possession of the small reserve now coveted by powerful landowners of the region. O'Loghlen knew nothing of the Kulin and little of the beliefs of the Mara-speakers at Framlingham. But he had an intuitive understanding of how the dispossessed felt about the land that remained to them. His reply the next day urged further consideration, insisting that the feelings of the Aborigines must be considered. Instead he suggested giving each family tenure of a portion of the reserves,

---

8   Coranderrk Inquiry 1881:45–8.
9   George Henry Bennett (1850–1908) immigrated as a child in 1855, and was first a brewer then cordial manufacturer. The Board minutes record no resignation, but he was no longer listed as a member in 1881. After a term as mayor and urban Parliamentary representative he was apparently re-appointed in 1904 and served as a Board member until his death.

mentioning that the Framlingham residents had proposed such a scheme and wanted to choose their own superintendent. The Board's attempt to subvert Berry's opposition failed, for O'Loghlen insisted they must defer action for the Minister's decision.[10]

Berry, the London tradesman's son, lacked O'Loghlen's sensitivity about attachment to land; but his concern for injustice probably caused him to ignore LeSouef's renewed plea for the sale of two stations, despite the economic recession and disintegrating support for his government. LeSouef's letter was prompted by the advance notice given to Dow's August 1879 Parliamentary motion on the unsatisfactory state of Coranderrk which drew attention to the special inquiry he had conducted at Berry's request. The Board now had no member in the House except Hopkins who had not attended meetings for four years. Dow tabled his report, so all members could read it, in October 1879. The ensuing *Age* publicity prompted the former manager Halliday to vindicate himself in a letter to the *Argus* which ended by urging abandonment of the station because:

> so long as members of Parliament allow blacks to interview them in Melbourne with senseless complaints, and step between the board and them by introducing their deputations ... so long as the Coranderrk blacks are encouraged by having private inquiry agents who speak their language sent up to meet them by roadsides and hear what reports they have to make, so long will it be impossible for even an angel from Heaven to manage Coranderrk and preserve discipline.[11]

The complaints of the Lilydale doctor about the lack of medicines and neglect of the sick were ignored throughout 1879 and his advice on the necessity for a surgery and hospital at Coranderrk was rejected in June in favour of abandonment. Having decided to give up the station, the Board spent no money on improvements, despite a reproof from the Chief Medical Officer. O'Loghlen had asked him to investigate in response to the Board's request for medical advice on lung disease. The Board consulted another specialist but his hypothesis about contagion merely roused scepticism in members such as Curr who were determined to blame the climate at Coranderrk.[12]

In August 1879 Page won Board approval to spend all available funds on making the mission stations more attractive 'as an inducement to many to leave Coranderrk'. It was a disastrous move, for the Coranderrk people were already annoyed by Strickland's lack of interest in their farm and his failure to work beside them as Green and Halliday had done. They now blamed him for the cessation of building, clearing, fencing and necessary repairs. Correspondence between separated members of Louisa Briggs' family undermined the Board's propaganda; their comparisons of conditions at the two stations roused discontent at the Wimmera station and alarm back at Coranderrk.[13]

Page had repeatedly rebuked the teacher and his wife for complaints about Strickland, but by July the staff members' quarrels were a matter for Board debate. The complaints made by Mrs Anne Bon about the neglected state of the dying Jemmy Webster also came to the Board's attention; in October 1879 they formally objected to 'any interference whatever' in their affairs.[14] Page, something of a misogynist, had written a surly letter a year earlier ordering Mrs Bon to send all future 'communications regarding the blacks in writing to the Board'. He refused to allow Bamfield to shear at her station, describing him as a lazy trouble-maker, and reminded her of the cause of his antagonism.

10   CSIC 79/P5308, 13 June 1879.
11   *Argus* 1 November 1879.
12   BPA – Minutes, 4 June, 2 and 23 July 1879.
13   BPA – Strickland to Page, 10 September 1880.
14   BPA – Minutes, 2 July and 1 October 1879.

10. CAUSE FOR REBELLION

In October 1878 Mrs Bon had escorted her lifelong protege Bamfield to the Board office to obtain his overdue clothing issue. Page refused because Bamfield was absent without permission: 'you replied then "we will go and see the Chief Secretary about it"; that would to Punch sound like a threat to me – such remarks should not be made without reason in the presence of the aborigines'.[15] Page's unreasonableness in demanding the return of Bamfield, John Charles and other shearers from her station and his rudeness in rebuking her interference alienated a useful ally and provoked her to go beyond the Board. In November 1879 she petitioned Berry to prevent the closure of Coranderrk.[16]

Page had under-estimated the determination of the 42-year-old Scottish widow who had owned and managed one of the largest pastoral stations in the colony for more than a decade. Anne Bon was shy and retiring but she had a Presbyterian conscience; when championing the needy she was never cowed. As a 'lady visitor' at the Melbourne hospitals where most of the sick from Coranderrk were brought when terminally ill she observed their lack of clothing and learned of their anguish when taken from home to die. From visiting relatives, she heard a great deal about conditions at the station and the attachment of the Kulin to this land. Her sense of decency was outraged at the apparent negligence of the highly paid government officer who rarely visited the sick and never attended their pauper burials. Page had initially encouraged her concern and still notified her when patients arrived. But when he rebuffed her practical criticisms of their needs Mrs Bon's stern conscience rebelled at doing Page's work for him.[17]

The detectives sent up on O'Loghlen's authority had failed to prove that any outsider had aided or incited the protests of the Coranderrk residents, although they too were more inclined to accept the opinion of the manager than the word of the Aborigines.[18] Page's suspicion of incitement verged on paranoia: his own reputation was involved for he had chosen this manager. He had vice-chairman LeSouef sign his letter censuring the Board employee William Goodall when Strickland complained that he had publicly sympathised with the residents and deplored their removal. Goodall, the popular and successful manager of Framlingham since 1869, shared John Green's views about the Aborigines' capacity to manage their own affairs and had been a welcome visitor to Coranderrk over the years. As a lay preacher, he was always invited to give a sermon.

The teacher assured the Board that Goodall's sermon on this occasion had not urged rebellion, and winningly reported that Goodall had expressed hope that Green would not be made inspector as Page was better qualified. Goodall's forthright reply said he had merely advised residents that the Board might reconsider their abandonment plans if the men would 'work instead of running to Melbourne every week with a lot of complaints'. He insisted that:

> Strickland told me before requesting me to address his people that disorganisation had existed for some time; ever since they heard of the recommendation of the Board to remove the station, & that it was impossible to get them to do anything as they were constantly gathering in groups & declaring it was almost useless to do any work if the government were going to remove them ... He knows perfectly well (at least he told me so) that great discontent has been manifested for years ... & ascribed the cause to the bad influence of his neighbours & Parliamentary interference. He will find the true cause much nearer home if he will only look for it.[19]

---

15   BPA – Page to Mrs Anne Bon, 14 October 1878.
16   BPA – Minutes, 1 October 1879; Mrs Bon to Page, 3 October 1879; Charles Sweetapple to Page, 11 November 1879; CSIC 79/Q10589, 20 November 1879.
17   Coranderrk Inquiry 1881:59, 93.
18   BPA – Secretary's Minute Book, 79 /136, 13 August – 30 October 1879.
19   BPA – Secretary's Minute Book, 79/148, 14 November 1879 – 8 January 1880; Goodall to Page, 11 December 1879, 2 January 1880.

REBELLION AT CORANDERRK

There were incessant protests at Coranderrk throughout 1880. Strickland was fighting with everyone. On 8 January he reported that Bamfield had organised a strike by 'all hands' because the sugar was inedible; Tommy Farmer, on his deathbed, was 'the only man not in rebellion'. Page and Strickland found the sugar was unfit for consumption, but stopped the rations of the 'insolent' Bamfield anyhow. Suspecting incitement, Page inquired whether any outsiders had visited; Strickland then recalled that four weeks earlier:

> on the 17 December the man Lacy again visited the station and went from house to house ... I found him at Barak's ... he said Berry asked him to come and report on the station ... told him he could not remain unless he produced some written authority. He then said well Dow and Jennings both authorised him to come. I ordered him off at once ... the men were only restrained by me from dogging him off ... his visit kept the station in uneasiness until after midnight. I hope the gentlemen named will reprove him.[20]

The station was already a popular tourist resort, visited by large numbers each week, yet the improbability of Strickland's tale did not seem to strike Page. The manager's letters grew more and more hysterical through the year, and Page's response to criticisms grew more vindictive, but there was little control over their actions. LeSouef went abroad from February to October and the acting vice-chairman was Curr, the busy public servant who was determined to end the protests at Coranderrk. Moreover, Berry's majority had fragmented during 1879 and he was narrowly defeated at the elections of February 1880.

His successor as Chief Secretary was Robert Ramsay, whose earlier sympathy had altered because of the Board's propaganda against Green. During his five months in office, the Board had little fear of ministerial interference.

Barak broke his leg in January and was not able to work again. The protests of the younger men, mostly 'half castes', were conducted under his direction. As Page and Strickland did not understand the principles of Kulin political organisation which made these men serve Barak, they – and Mrs Bon – were blamed. On 22 March Strickland reported that John Charles and Alick Campbell had been 'abusive' to him and the overseer about the employment of Europeans; Campbell had refused to work with Harris and when told he would be replaced by a European had complained that Harris was always trying to 'employ the – whites'. A Pangerang pioneer who had beaten his Kulin wife was to leave 'by the sentence of the old men'; but Strickland's own threat to exile a Burapper newcomer had brought a challenge from the Kulin pioneer John Charles, who told him in front of the assembled men that neither he, Page nor the Board 'could or should' remove residents – 'he defied you to try it on'. Almost every letter complained of riot, insubordination, rebellion and repeated strikes, as well as the gratuitous advice offered by 'meddling white people' – but Strickland nevertheless considered that 'an equal number of British labourers would not behave so well'.[21] He had no complaint to make about the first visit of Mrs Bon, whom he had invited to stay overnight. She was escorted by Rev. Mackie of Lilydale, and the convener of the Presbyterian missions committee, on 19 May and was 'much surprised and pleased' by what she saw. But afterwards he complained that her sympathy encouraged Bamfield's 'impudence' and wished she would mind her own business.[22]

On 22 May 1880 Strickland whipped Phinnimore Jackson one of the dormitory boys and injured him severely, apparently by accident; next morning close relatives led by John Charles and Alick Campbell released four boys he had locked up, and 'threatened' him. The five men took the injured lad to Green when they could not find the constable. Worried by the hostile gossip in Healesville (but still unaware

---

20 BPA – Strickland to Page, 13 January 1880; Secretary's Minute Book 80/154, 14–16 January 1880. Lacy's position is not recorded.
21 BPA – Strickland to Page, 22 March and 19 April 1880.
22 BPA – Strickland to Page, 20 May and 19 June 1880.

that the Coranderrk residents had immediately petitioned the Chief Secretary to investigate his cruelty),[23] Strickland went to Page. He convened the Board on 27 May so Strickland could report the men's insubordination. Curr, Sheppard and Macredie agreed that Page should discover whether the men could be charged under the 1869 Act and if not obtain Orders-in-Council to exile them from the station. They did not know that Green had written to vice-chairman Jennings (the only member he knew) advising against prosecuting the men because of the boy's injury. Strickland went home to prepare the written report demanded. It explained that the punishment occurred because the dormitory girls were on strike, demanding wages, and had encouraged the boys to 'rebel', and said he had 'delayed' reporting events in hope that the men would apologise. As they remained defiant he proposed to summons all five for obstructing him in his duty.

At the Board meeting on 2 June Curr, Sheppard and Macredie were cautious. They authorised Strickland to summons only one man for 'assault' (a verbal threat to fight). They found his report unconvincing. Moreover, in Parliament the day before, Dow had again queried conditions at Coranderrk and asked for remedial action based on his 1878 report to Berry. The Minister, Ramsay, had agreed that the management was unsatisfactory. He announced that he had read the Royal Commission report and other documents and promised immediate action. The Board was worried: Ramsay had not mentioned Page's letter demanding removal of the Coranderrk residents.[24]

Despite the press publicity given this pledge Ramsay did not reveal any decision to Parliament. He was a conservative lawyer who had little taste for the clamour about Aboriginal affairs, and because of the precarious state of the government, was mainly concerned to silence criticism. The Board of course interpreted his reluctance to intervene as sympathy for their views. Ramsay had appointed the members whose decisions had caused all the trouble since 1875; all he did now was appoint a new member. This was William Anderson, a wealthy Presbyterian farmer in the Western District who had been petitioning the Minister about the plight of those exiled from Lake Condah ever since his election to Parliament in May.[25]

Strickland complained incessantly of the impertinence of the residents and finally, without Board authority, announced that 'in self defence' he had the local constable summons all 'inciters to rebellion'. The five, all but Campbell, resident since the 1860s, were tried on 2 July. Three were acquitted and two given minimal fines by two local justices who had little sympathy for Aborigines. Strickland thought it a victory, informing Page that Green had been forbidden to testify. He had borne with Christian fortitude Green's condemnation afterwards. He warned Page 'there was little done on the station that was not reported to him'. The manager did not mention that another Healesville resident was charged with contempt of court for protesting Strickland's interference with the Aboriginal witnesses.[26]

The Board's plans for abandonment were in fact frustrated throughout 1880 despite the changes of government. Ever since 1869 Lands Department officials had opposed extension of the Wimmera reserve but now a number of leaseholds were due to expire. In January 1880 the departmental head advised his Minister to approve the Board's request for extension – on condition that Coranderrk, Framlingham and the Anglican mission at Lake Condah were given up for sale. The Board was aware that neighbours had long been lobbying for subdivision of these reserves. But the mission representatives Jennings and Macredie, together with LeSouef (perennial spokesman for Hagenauer) had always pointed out that the

---

23 CSIC 80/S5352, 23 May 1880.
24 BPA – Strickland to Page, 31 May 1880, Minutes 27 May and 2 June 1880; Victorian Parliamentary Debates, Session 1880:262; CSIC 80/S5367, 1 June 1880.
25 William Anderson (1828–1909) immigrated from Scotland to Tasmania in 1842 and arrived at Port Fairy in 1844. He was a member of Parliament until 1892 and a Board member for 29 years.
26 BPA – Strickland to Page, 7 and 25 June, 3 July 1880; Coranderrk Inquiry 1881:61, 75, 129, Argus 21 November 1881.

mission stations could not be closed without consultation, compensation for improvements and a risk of offending the sponsoring sects. Discovering that the Wimmera reserve could not support an increased population, however big the extension, because of the poor quality land and the rabbit plague, the Board revived Curr's discredited Kulkyne scheme, only to learn that the Wimmera Aborigines refused to go there and the Moravian authorities refused to close their station.[27] They could not be forced because this land, unlike the other reserves, was vested in mission trustees. An alternative proposal by Page was approved by Curr, Sheppard and Jennings and sent to Chief Secretary Ramsay on 17 June 1880. The scheme took advantage of the absence of LeSouef and Macredie who would not have condoned any interference with the Moravian missions. It was likely to be accepted by the Lands Minister, currently John Gavan Duffy, whom Godfrey had persuaded to support Board policy.

Page's scheme rejected the Lands Department's argument that all surviving 'natives' should be amalgamated on one station. Page asserted that this would increase management difficulties without reducing costs. Instead the Board offered to give up Coranderrk, Framlingham and Hagenauer's Gippsland station in return for a large reserve at Kulkyne and £8,000 for needed dwellings at the two Anglican stations and the Moravian mission in the Wimmera. Noting that the Board did not 'anticipate any permanent objection from the blacks unless they are encouraged thereto by white people whose interests are affected by their removal'. Page's letter emphasised the financial advantage to the government: the three improved reserves would cost £42,200.[28] The price of £4 an acre was what Curr and LeSouef had suggested earlier for Coranderrk but, by this time, neighbours were offering £15–£20 an acre for hop-growing land on the river flats.[29]

Ramsay agreed to receive a deputation to discuss this proposal after the elections – but in July Berry was returned with a narrow majority, heading a deeply divided party. The '£1,000,000 debt' incurred by his former ministry had been a major election issue and retrenchment was a major topic of debate. O'Loghlen and other Catholic supporters formed a 'corner party' which Berry had to placate and Curr – the Catholic public servant with excellent political connections – was lobbying for acceptance of the Board proposal, knowing that the financial incentive was opportune. Berry made his decision on 10 September; a minute in his own hand ordered the under secretary to write to the Board:

> to the effect that complaints have reached me as to the efficiency of the management of Coranderrk and to say further that these complaints have been continuous almost from the period of the dismissal of Mr Green and to suggest to the B.P.A. the propriety of reinstating that gentleman in his former office.

A draft of the required letter was prepared. Yet Board records do not mention it; instead the Board replied to the under secretary's letter of 17 September asking if Coranderrk residents could be resettled 'without any great expense' if Berry approved immediate abandonment. Presumably his advisers had persuaded Berry he could not afford to be sentimental.[30]

He may also have been influenced by Board propaganda about the residents' protests during that week. On 10 September Strickland had reported a 'panic among the people' as a result of a letter from John Charles giving a 'deplorable description' of the Wimmera station. Barak and Bamfield came to complain to Mrs Bon about clothing issues and her report to LeSouef, who had recently returned, made him write directly to the manager on 11 September. Strickland's angry reply said the complaints were false and the men were absent without permission:

27   BPA – Minutes, January–October 1880; CSIC 80/R6077, 26 January 1880.
28   CSIC 80/R6077, 17 June 1880.
29   BPA – Strickland to Page, 10 September 1880.
30   CSIC 80/S9115, 10 and 13 September 1880; BPA – Secretary's Minute Book 80/181, 18 September – 20 October 1880.

> The object of their visit was to learn the best way of selling their colts but they thoughtfully made use of Mrs Bon without informing her of the real object of their journey; I do wish she would not encourage them in their scheming.

On 16 September he reported more men had gone to Melbourne without permission and complained that Bamfield had organised a meeting of the men a week earlier 'and none of them will tell the object'.[31] Page had already written censuring Mrs Bon for encouraging such visitors and demanded that she 'not interfere again' in Board affairs.[32] He justified this by spreading rumours that Mrs Bon had incited the protests. Unfortunately for Page the manager later reported that the meeting was provoked by the news that the Board intended to sell Coranderrk and remove residents to distant mission stations. Page had ordered the staff to ensure that the Aborigines remained ignorant and blamed the popular teacher for the leak, but he retorted that the men had learned of the proposed sale in Healesville.[33]

Page replied to Berry on 22 September, before the Board met again. But as a result of LeSouef's return, no more was heard of selling Hagenauer's station. Page's letter offered to give up Coranderrk in return for an extension at the Anglican station in Gippsland plus £1,500 for rehousing and £800 a year additional funding to compensate for the hop profits. A second letter that day offered to forego the increased annual funding to win the Minister's consent.[34] The minutes for 6 October merely note that the Moravian authorities had refused to send the Wimmera people to Kulkyne. A week later the under secretary asked the Board to map the extensions needed in Gippsland and the Wimmera; Page instead asked for land at Kulkyne. On 20 October he learned that Berry would approve the requests for land but was 'not prepared at present' to include the needed £1,500 in the budget he was preparing for a hostile Parliament.[35]

At Coranderrk resentment of the Board's underhand scheme to sell their home united the Kulin pioneers and the newcomers. This was the only reserve within the territory of the Kulin, Pangerang and Burapper clans. At the end of October Strickland reported that 'not a man on the station' would do anything when ordered. What was the use of making improvements when they would be exiled? The manager notified the secretary that 'they say that Captain Page may get the white men to make up the fence, they would not'. Some of the Kulin pioneers were seeking jobs with sympathetic former employers in their home districts: they might be forced to leave Coranderrk but they would not go to the distant mission stations in the territory of the Kurnai and Wotjo-speakers. Berry, their last hope, had failed them.

Meanwhile, the Coranderrk people had gained new sympathisers. In recent years most victims of tuberculosis and hydatid tumours of the lung had been sent to Melbourne hospitals. Their distress about their home, and their neglected state, shocked the clergymen and charitable ladies who visited patients. In July 1880 two hospitals refused to accept any more terminally ill patients as they were not intended to serve 'incurables'.[36] Largely through the efforts of Mrs Bon and the former Board member Dr Embling, the decision was reversed by the hospital management committees, as there was no alternative care at Coranderrk. Their lobbying influenced many prominent colonists, including members of Parliament, who had previously been unconcerned about Aboriginal affairs.

31 BPA – Strickland to Page, 10, 14 and 16 September 1880.
32 Coranderrk Inquiry 1881:59.
33 BPA – J. S. Deans to Page, 30 October 1880.
34 CSIC 80/R9457, 80/T9455, 22 September 1880.
35 CSIC 80/R9844, 13 October 1880; BPA – Secretary's Minute Book, 80/181, 20 October 1880.
36 BPA – Alfred Hospital to Page, 17 July 1880; Strickland to Page 25 July 1880.

The reformers' concern probably penetrated to the Chief Secretary. On 13 November the under secretary informed the Board that Berry had decided not to give up Coranderrk 'at present'. Berry himself told Parliament this on 7 December. Cameron, now in opposition, had asked if the reports of abandonment were true. Neither said any more, but J.H. Graves, who represented an adjoining electorate, complained of the large number of 'half castes' and insisted they be made of use to the colony.[37]

A week after the Parliamentary debate Strickland worriedly reported that G.A. Syme and his wife had visited; 'some of the people knew him' and he had talked to Harris. Afterwards, they had gone to visit the Greens. Strickland also mentioned that Mrs Dunolly had begged him to let Green enter the station to prescribe for her dying child but he had refused as Green was not a doctor. A year earlier Thomas Dunolly had told detectives investigating the anonymous complaints about the management that: 'If we work and behave ourselves Mr Strickland is kind'. But the vindictiveness of Strickland and Page had destroyed the residents' confidence. Dunolly explained to a later inquiry how the exclusion of Green had roused his distrust of Strickland and the Board:

> He said he could not let Mr Green come to see her. I told Mr Strickland I would go up and see Mr Green, whether he would come; and Mr Strickland told me, that if he came here he would be sent off; so I went up and told Mr Green that and he told me to never mind; I was to report it to the Board. So I told him I would not report it to the Board, for they would not take any steps in it for me, because they always against us.[38]

The continuing neglected state of the Coranderrk patients brought to Melbourne hospitals had meanwhile roused widespread criticism. On 21 December 1880 the philanthropist E.L. Zox, a leader of the Melbourne Jewish community, interrupted the Supply Debate to comment on the incompetence of the management and asked the Minister to investigate. Berry replied that the troubles stemmed entirely from the Board's senseless and unjust removal of Green, who was loved 'almost as a father'. He had been urged to reinstate Green but was disinclined to interfere with the Board without asking Parliament to repeal the Act. He planned to visit soon and then would ask the House to authorise action. When the conservative Duffy derisively blamed all difficulties on Green and his friends both Zox and Dow reproached him. Finally Duffy, too, urged an inquiry into the present management. Even Graves, who had previously demanded the removal of the 'half castes', defended the residents' attachment to this site. The former Chief Secretary Ramsay also warmly defended Green, reminding the House that he had made several visits in Green's time. He argued that Green had been harassed into resigning and urged his reinstatement; but he warned that a railway planned for Lilydale might render the site unsuitable.

Dow, the only speaker from the government side of the House, then criticised his leader's reluctance to interfere with the Board. He condemned their harsh treatment of Green, and opposed abandonment because residents 'declared that they would not leave Coranderrk; that the land there was given them by Sir Henry Barkly; that there they had been brought up, and that there they wished to die'. Yet he argued that all 'half castes' should be removed. The new Board member Anderson, himself a recent critic, hastened to dissociate himself from Board policies and agreed that Parliament should investigate the management of Coranderrk.[39]

Thoroughly embarrassed by the press coverage of the debate, vice-chairman LeSouef convened six Board members two days later to plan a rejoinder to the Parliamentary criticisms. He and Anderson were sent to 'interview Berry and explain the facts of Green's dismissal'.[40] On 13 January 1881, the *Age* condemned the

---

37   BPA – Secretary's Minute Book, 80/207, 13 November 1880; Victorian Parliamentary Debates, Session 1880:262. Graves was also closely associated with LeSouef in the Acclimatisation Society.
38   BPA – Strickland to Page, 9 and 16 December 1880; Secretary's Minute Book 79/136, 26 September 1879: Coranderrk Inquiry 1881:18.
39   Victorian Parliamentary Debates, Session 1880–81:1261–2.
40   BPA – Minutes, 23 December 1880.

'sanitary state' of the station, obviously utilising Syme's observations on his recent visit. Four days later two Cabinet members, Richardson and Vale arrived. Strickland complained of the conduct of 'Berry's sons' on their two-day visit and hastened to Melbourne to prepare a defence. No Board member had visited for years and Page had accepted Strickland's explanations without bothering to inspect. The Ministers they despised had more first hand knowledge of Coranderrk and the Kulin than the Board and their staff. The Lands and Agriculture Minister, Richard Richardson, was an engineer, farmer and Methodist lay preacher who used to buy grain from the Mount Franklin farmers before their removal in 1864. He had attacked the Board during the 1876 Parliamentary debate. The Attorney General, W.M.K. Vale, was a barrister and Congregational lay preacher who had defended Green's management against local criticism back in 1870. Their criticisms of Strickland's management appeared in an *Age* article written by Alfred Deakin, the young barrister and journalist elected to Parliament in 1879 as a Syme protege. The article commented on Strickland's offensive manner; he later pretended he had assumed the ministerial party 'belonged to the Press' but was forced to admit the visitors had identified themselves on arrival.[41]

LeSouef, Curr and Macredie could do little but instruct their secretary to write to Berry demanding a decision on abandonment before they made any improvements. Berry replied that he must visit the station before deciding its fate.[42]

During February Strickland's reports on the station grew more and more hysterical. The wily leader Bamfield conducted an ingenious campaign challenging Strickland's interference with Kulin decisions about the allocation of dwellings; after the constable was brought to evict him from the contested hut Bamfield spread his belongings on the road and – so Strickland complained – made 'the place as dirty as he could to disgrace me when visitors came'. Strickland was furious that the overseer Harris and a son of the former manager Halliday were checking wage payments to 'see the people had their rights'. He was also feuding with the teacher Deans. He reported that residents came and went as they pleased and constantly complained of his failure to make improvements. This, he reproached Page, was not his fault: the Board had ordered the cessation of building because they intended to sell the station.[43]

There was no excuse for the Board's negligence. Their best defence was to divert criticism by alleging that the Aborigines' protests were incited by others. They provided confidential documents for an *Argus* journalist's report, which praised conditions at Coranderrk yet advocated abandonment because of the unhealthy climate and outside interference. The anonymous journalist attempted to ridicule *Age* comment on the inhabitants' attachment to the site with a false assertion that only two Aborigines were born in the district. To the Board's discomfort, he also attacked their policy of accommodating 'half castes' at the stations, asserting that most of the Coranderrk people were 'almost white'. Anyhow the article did not appear until 19 March, two weeks after the opposition member Zox again questioned Berry about the management. Berry still declined to give Parliament his decision, admitting that he was unwilling to overrule the Board. Because proximity to the township encouraged 'demoralization' Berry now thought removal the proper course if the Aborigines' fondness for their home 'could be overcome'.[44]

---

41 BPA – Strickland to Page, 17 and 28 January, 3 December 1881. Richardson said the party were pressed to identify themselves but had wished to remain anonymous to get a better idea of the normal running of the station (Coranderrk Inquiry 1881;109–12).
42 BPA – Minutes 19 January and 16 February 1881; CSIC 81/V780, 21 January and 11 February 1881.
43 BPA – Strickland to Page, 28 January, 15, 21 and 24 February 1881.
44 Victorian Parliamentary Debates, Session 1880–81:2612.

**Coranderrk pioneers Martin and Matilda Simpson,
later 'native missionaries' at Maloga Mission.**

This is also what Ramsay had said in the previous debate when the local member Cameron was conspicuously silent. Both leaders, Berry and Ramsay had a genuine concern for Aboriginal welfare: but in the present political climate they were more concerned to woo the conservative local member Cameron and placate his radical electorate. The voters wanted the reserve and Aboriginal labour. They also wanted the Lilydale railway extended to Healesville; but they did not want to pay for it. Cameron had been strongly opposed in recent elections because of his antagonism to Berry's reform programs, and he was now chairman of the Railways Standing Committee. He was a determined advocate of rail expansion and the sale of Coranderrk to pay for a spur line to Healesville would please his electorate and solve his problems. Now that Berry was the responsible Minister the criticisms of Coranderrk by the opposition and his own party were an embarrassment; he could win votes by selling Coranderrk and escape reproof by blaming the advice of the Board.

By March 1881, therefore, the imminent closure of Coranderrk seemed certain. The resulting press rumours about their removal had united the Kulin pioneers and the newcomers. The recent deaths of James 'Jemmy' Barker, Peter Hunter, Jemmy Webster, Tommy Farmer and other pioneers, and the emigration of a few such as Martin Simpson for employment meant that there were now only 22 men. They planned a unanimous protest under the leadership of Barak and Bamfield. On 28 March 1881, the manager telegraphed a warning that 22 men were walking to Melbourne to ask Berry to 'do away with the Board'. Page immediately contacted the Chief Secretary's department to demand that the Board be represented at the interview, asserting that they knew of no cause for complaint. As usual, he asserted that the deputation must have been 'urged and induced' by some troublesome person.[45]

---

45   BPA – Secretary's Letter Book, 28 March 1881; CSIC 81/U3179, 28 March 1881.

10. CAUSE FOR REBELLION

Barak's last deputation had made the 42-mile (67 km) journey in 18 hours, walking through the night. None had the 10 shilling coach fare, so they walked again. This journey was even slower, for Barak's broken leg had healed badly, Bamfield was always crippled with rheumatism and other men were suffering from tuberculosis or hydatid tumours. They had eaten nothing for 24 hours by the time they reached the orchard owned by John Norris on the outskirts of Melbourne. Norris later testified under oath about his own chance involvement: he had been surprised to see so many Aborigines and therefore questioned 'the chief man, whom I had known for many years'.[46] With some reluctance Barak had eventually authorised one of his aides to explain, and Norris had been impressed by their account of the mismanagement of their farm and their dismay at its impending loss. Learning that they had told no one of their intentions, he had offered them food and driven ahead of them to Melbourne to try to make arrangements so the lame 'old chief' would not be disappointed. He had found Berry at the Treasury in time to make an appointment then went to tell Mrs Bon, whom he had never met, that they hoped to camp at her house overnight. The next morning he went to Parliament House, where he knew no one, hoping to find some member willing to sponsor the deputation. He and Mrs Bon were present when the Coranderrk men were introduced to Berry by the opposition members Zox and Graves, and Berry's protege Deakin. The Board's vice-chairman and secretary, and the new member Anderson, also attended. The *Argus* provided a detailed account of the proceedings. To the Board's embarrassment, this conservative newspaper gave a sympathetic account of the deputation's aims. The men had come to protest against being removed, to complain that they were no longer employed in improving the land and to ask Berry to abolish the Board and allow them to manage the station for themselves under Green's guidance. In reply:

> Mr Berry expressed the opinion that Mr Green had been got rid of on insufficient grounds, and that his successor had been injudiciously selected. Were it not for interfering with the Aboriginal Board, he would make the alterations the men asked, and he very much questioned the utility of a board. There was no intention at present of changing the site of the station. Mr Berry then saw the black-fellows one by one, and questioned them privately as to the state of affairs at the station. They all agreed in asking for the re-appointment of Mr Green, and in complaining that the present manager exercised no control over them.

The Board had asserted that individual questioning of the men would prove them 'utterly unable to assign any reason for their coming'. Later in the day, Berry informed the deputation, through their sponsor Zox, that he did not intend to remove them and would ask the Board to 'consider the propriety of re-appointing Mr Green'.[47]

According to Norris' account, Berry told the deputation he could not alter the management as his 'hands were tied' by the Board, and he forced LeSouef and Anderson to admit they had no complaint against Green except his refusal to accept their terms for reinstatement. Finally, Berry assured the men 'I will give you that promise, you shall not be removed'.[48] According to Barak's nephew Robert Wandin the pledge came after he had intensively questioned LeSouef about the planned removal to Lake Tyers.[49] LeSouef's account to Curr and Jennings, the only members present at the next Board meeting, focussed on the demand for Green's return and ridiculed the complaints made by Zox and Deakin about Strickland's management. Ignoring the role of Norris, LeSouef blamed Mrs Bon for the deputation and asserted that this example of rebellion should convince Berry that 'continual interference' made abandonment a necessity.

---

46   Coranderrk Inquiry 1881:114–6.
47   *Argus*, 30 March 1881.
48   Coranderrk Inquiry 1881:115.
49   Coranderrk Inquiry 1881:17.

The minutes were of course written by Page, whose resentment of Mrs Bon verged on hatred. Page had no inkling that she had forwarded a petition from the Coranderrk people asking for Green's reinstatement a week before the deputation. The accompanying letter soliciting Berry's sympathy made it clear that she was in touch with certain politicians, for she anticipated that 'Coranderrk will be again before the House tonight'.[50] Page had just obtained information from the former manager Halliday, now in Melbourne, confirming their earlier conversation about interference. Page was not credulous enough to believe Halliday's assurance that the extracts from a Healesville letter (presumably from his son) were sent 'in confidence and not for any official use, as I have no desire to mix myself up with either the blacks or their wire pullers'. Strickland had complained of frequent visits by Halliday's son, who had asked Harris to check the wage payments, saying he 'would see the people had their rights'; Halliday himself had sent numerous reports about Strickland's cruelty and drunkenness and repeated requests to be reinstated as manager. But the somewhat garbled hearsay information he provided could be used to challenge the authenticity of the Aborigines' complaints about Page and Strickland:

> Harris was called down to attend a Board meeting last Thursday. Harris says Page told him he did not blame Green for this row at all, that it was Mrs Bon and Hamilton, he also says they have got no suspicion that Green was down at Hamilton's all the time & is not back yet (Sat. evening). He also says that 3 members of the Bd voted for Green and 3 against, & that the Board will have to satisfy the Blacks or there will be another 'kickup', so you can see who is at the bottom of it. I heard Green made all sorts of promises to the blacks as to what he would do if he got back. When the Blacks left Mrs Bon's for Melbourne a gardener named Norris was sent with them to introduce them to Mr Zox.[51]

Evidence presented at the ensuing inquiry however proved false the Board's contention that Mrs Bon and other 'interfering whites' had incited this 'rising'. The Aboriginal witnesses emphatically denied all suggestions that outsiders had encouraged their deputation; they insisted that 'we got it up ourselves' for sufficient cause: 'we saw it in the paper they were going to send us to Lake Tyer', 'we heard that the station was going to be sold and shifted and we did not want it, so we went down to see Mr Berry'.[52]

The manager sourly reported to Page that the men had returned from their interview with Berry 'in great glee, marching in order by twos & carrying flags or handkerchiefs on poles'. Their unanimous protest had forced Berry to promise them security. When Page tried to gain further extensions at Lake Tyers in April the wary under secretary warned Berry that the request was 'connected with that of purpose of abandonment of Coranderrk' and Berry refused to act. The chagrined Board members reluctantly authorised expenditure of £400 on improvements at their May 1881 meeting as Berry 'had decided the station was not to be broken up'.[53] But the contractors were ordered to cease construction in July. Page had devised a new means of circumventing the Minister's wishes. After securing the approval of four Board members Page wrote to the Chief Secretary on 8 June asking Berry's consent for his plan to 'get rid of all the "half castes" who are capable of providing for themselves'. He recommended the dismissal of three families, mentioning that 'two of the men selected you particularly noticed (when they formed part of a deputation to you) and remarked that they should not be living on a Black Station'. Berry replied that adult male 'half castes' 'should be allowed to leave' if they could earn an honest living. This was 'not so satisfactory' as they had hoped but the five Board members assembled at the July meeting interpreted the letter as ministerial consent to exile three couples on work certificates, giving them the option of leaving their children at Coranderrk.[54]

---

50 BPA – Minutes 6 April 1881; CSIC 81/V2688, 23 March 1881.
51 BPA – Strickland to Page, 28 January and 28 February 1881; Halliday to Page, 5 April 1881.
52 Coranderrk Inquiry 1881:9, 13, 17.
53 BPA – Strickland to Page, 31 March 1881; Minutes 11 May 1881; CSIC 81/U3600, 27 April – 11 June 1881.
54 BPA – Minutes 1 June and 6 July 1881; Secretary's Minute Book 81/229, 8 and 16 June 1881.

10. CAUSE FOR REBELLION

William Barak (1818/24–1903) with his second wife Annie and their son David.

Page clearly intended the scheme to increase his control over the young leaders of the protests and, perhaps, saw it as an alternative means of ensuring the eventual closure of Coranderrk. The Board's opposition to the dispersal of the 'half castes' had been emphasised in the *Argus* article in March 1881, and their annual report (dated July 1881 but submitted to Parliament in December after a bitter dispute) declared that 'half castes' could not be turned adrift from the stations because the Board considered them 'unreliable, untruthful, and sadly wanting in energy, perseverance, self-reliance …'.[55]

On 9 July Berry was defeated on a motion put by O'Loghlen, who became the next Premier. He and Chief Secretary J.M. Grant (who had resisted subdivision of Coranderrk while Lands Minister 1864–69), and their Cabinet colleagues Graves and MacBain had shown sympathy for the Kulin. But Cabinet was now dominated by a Railways Minister known as an untrustworthy intriguer, and extravagant railway expansion was considered crucial to the colony's development.[56]

The Coranderrk residents were already distressed about Page's orders exiling three families, and were mourning Barak's wife Annie, who had died that week. Green defied Strickland's order and came to pray for her because the manager had not done so. The old leader was grieving for her and in despair about their only child, a ten-year-old son also obviously dying of tuberculosis. By the rule of patrilineal descent, this lad was Barak's last hope for the continuity of the Woiworung clans, although his sister's son, Robert Wandin, had a thriving family. Barak made up his mind to take his son to a Melbourne hospital. Strickland gave him a coach pass and wrote Page to meet them and arrange for the boy's admission to hospital. Barak waited in vain until nightfall and then carried his son on his back to Mrs Bon's home at Kew, as they had no money for food or shelter.[57] Outraged, Mrs Bon took them to Dow at the *Age* office on their way to the hospital. An *Age* article on 14 July described the case as a typical example of neglect

---

55 BPA – Minutes, 15 and 17 November 1881; Annual Report 1881; *Argus* 19 March 1881.
56 Deakin 1957:55–6, 78–80; Serle 1971:1–13.
57 *Argus*, 19 October 1881; Coranderrk Inquiry 1881:99.

which made reform of the Board essential. Strickland indignantly tried to clear himself by reporting that he had written to Page and anyhow Barak had money from the sale of his horses.[58] Barak returned home to seek comfort from Thomas Bamfield who, like himself, had some training as a sorcerer and had acquired the power to find knowledge in dreams like the famed *wirrarap* who had guided the Kulin clans in their youth:

> When I got home from taking my poor fellow to the hospital (David, his son who died there) Tommy Punch and I were crying about him all evening. Then Tommy went to sleep and when he woke he said 'I saw the poorfeller – he was here – he said stand there. There were two strings hanging down and he said we will go up them – don't be afraid – you won't fall down. I climbed up after him and we came to a square hole – and a lot of people looking down at us. The boy went through and said to me, "I am only waiting here for you and my father". One of the girls said "How is my mother". I said "Why it looks like our Minney." Then I went up also and I saw a lot of people there.'[59]

This was a time of crisis for the two clan-heads. They had adopted Christianity without forswearing an older faith and were conscious of the obligations of their heritage. When the older Kulin were dead who would care for the land? Bamfield himself had only one surviving son; he too was consumptive and would die at the age of 17.[60] The question still obsessed Barak a year later, when he enunciated the principles of Kulin social and political organisation for the amateur ethnographer Howitt. In response to Howitt's sympathetic questioning he named the clan heads and speakers of the past and present and spoke of his plans for the future:

> When I go I shall leave the word that my sister's son [Robert Wandin] shall be ngurungaeta, with him two others … If a ngurungaeta had a son who was all right and who did good to the people would be ngurungaeta. If he was a bad man or people did not like him they would get someone else – some relation of the old ngurungaeta – his uncle ~~brother son~~; ~~sister son~~.

Howitt's manuscript notes indicate some confusion about the choice of sister's son; his later book transcribed this information as 'most likely a relative of some former Headman, such as his brother or brother's son'.[61] Barak was the last of the Woiworung clansmen by patrilineal reckoning, although Robert Wandin ('half caste' son of his sister), the Briggs family and, indeed, most of the Kulin residents could trace their descent from Woiworung women. Since only males could transmit membership, a patrilineal clan ostensibly became extinct on the death of its last male member. Yet throughout Australia linkages through female clan members were utilised to ensure that clan land was protected and ritual knowledge was retained. In some areas adoption was possible: the famed Woiworung clan-head Ninggollobin, 'Captain Turnbull', acquired an eight-year-old son after the loss of his own children, in a formal adoption ceremony witnessed by William Thomas in 1844.[62] There are hints in Howitt's notes that some such mechanism was used to make Barak himself heir to the Wurunjerri-balluk clan-head after the death of his father Bebejan, for the senior Kurnaje-berreing leader Billibellary had many sons, including Wonga.[63]

However, while the Kulin elders debated the future guardianship of this land the Board made plans to lobby the new Chief Secretary to remove them from it. The minutes declare that the next meeting on 31 August 1881 was convened at LeSouef's suggestion to discuss an article published by the *Argus* two days earlier. This argued that the subdivision and sale of Coranderrk (now worth £25,000) would pay

---

58 *Age*, 14 July 1881; BPA – Strickland to Page, 15 July 1881.
59 Howitt MS:15. David Barak died at the Melbourne hospital in August 1881. The Minnie mentioned by Bamfield was his eldest child, who had died age 10 in April 1875.
60 David Bamfield, born in 1868, died of 'consumption' on 17 August 1885.
61 Howitt MS:34; Howitt 1904:308.
62 William Thomas, Journal, 6 July 1844.
63 Howitt MS:2, 8, 33–4, 34a–b, 38, 46.

for the extension to Healesville of the Lilydale railway at no cost to the government or the European electors of the Healesville district. The article emphasised the Board's long-standing desire to remove the Aborigines to the Wimmera where they would enjoy a more congenial climate and be free of the 'contaminating influence' of the township. The *Argus* article (and a similar one in the *Age*) summarised arguments put to the touring Minister of Railways by the local member Cameron and his constituents at a public meeting in Healesville.[64]

Page's minutes do not mention this, nor the fact that the new Minister had, on 19 August 1881, appointed Cameron chairman of a board of inquiry to investigate the management of Coranderrk. At this meeting, LeSouef and Macredie put a motion requesting the Minister to approve abandonment. It passed, of course, since Curr and Jennings were the only others present. The Board were confident that local lobbying for the railway and the financial incentive would quickly induce the government to consent. Page's letter, signed by the new vice-chairman Anderson, reiterated old arguments that the location was unhealthy and encouraged discipline problems.[65] Page's second argument for removal, that only one of 22 adult 'fullbloods' belonged to the district, was both ignorant and spurious. The population of 106 included 38 Kulin adults and their 48 children born at Coranderrk. Only the three remaining Burapper households were not linked by kinship or marriage to the Kulin and their children born at Coranderrk had, by Kulin custom, lifetime rights to use this Woiworung clan territory. None of the young people had known any other home.

LeSouef and his protege Page were urging abandonment because of their fear and anger about the board of inquiry. Mrs Bon, and perhaps other appointees, would certainly press for Green's reinstatement. Her criticisms of Page's negligence were unanswerable. They knew that the Board's own members, notably the influential public servant Curr, were alarmed by reports of Strickland's conduct. Strickland could be eased out without scandal if Coranderrk were closed, but another dismissal would delight the Board's opponents and make Green's return inevitable. Above all, they were bitterly angry at the Minister's disloyalty to the Board. On 29 July, two weeks after Dow's *Age* attack, Page, LeSouef and vice-chairman Anderson had interviewed Chief Secretary Grant to ask for appointment of a Local Committee, a supervisory mechanism included in the 1869 Act by request of Cameron's predecessor but never utilised because the Board's founding members remembered the disastrous consequences of such trusteeship at Acheron station. Page's notes of the interview say they told Grant that Berry had intended to appoint three members: Cameron and two local justices who were prominent land-holders: Guillaume de Pury (who had employed Woiworung at his Yering property since 1855), and Thomas Armstrong. Page also noted that 'Mr Grant said he had heard something about the matter but that Mrs Bon he understood had interfered'.[66] Grant was prepared to agree, although he could find no record of Berry's promise, for the new Lands Minister had also urged him to appoint these three to please Cameron.[67] Then the MLA Alfred Deakin, a fellow lawyer, sent him written evidence contradicting the Board's version of Berry's intentions:

> Just prior to the retirement of the late Ministry Mr Berry promised a deputation which I had the honor of introducing that he would appoint a local Board to report on the present management of Coranderrk with a view to taking it out of the hands of the Central Board and reorganising it ... In accordance with his request I supplied him with the names ... Berry was perfectly willing to appoint them but as by this time he had placed his resignation in the hands of the Governor he thought it best to leave the formal appointment of the Board to his successor.

---

64 *Argus* and *Age*, 29 August 1881; BPA – Minutes 31 August 1881.
65 CSIC 81/U8199, 7 September 1881.
66 BPA – Secretary's Minute Book, 81/234, 29 July 1881.
67 CSIC 81/U6701, 29 July 1881 (letters from W. Anderson, A. Page and D. Gaunson).

Those named were Mrs Bon, Cameron, the former Board member Dr Embling, and two Lilydale farmers, Duncan McNab and John Kerr.[68]

Grant had recommended these five as a Local Committee under the Act before receiving Cameron's objection that Berry had agreed to appoint himself, Armstrong and de Pury. Grant's suspicion of this disagreement was natural enough. He no doubt recalled the local lobbying to secure this land during his five-year term as Lands Minister and his final promise to protect the Kulin from their covetous neighbours, and he had heard his Cabinet colleagues Graves and MacBain advocate an inquiry in Parliamentary speeches. Grant had all seven nominees commissioned for a different purpose: they were to serve as a 'board to inquire into and report upon the present condition and management' of Coranderrk, under Cameron's chairmanship.[69]

Infuriated by this reinterpretation of their request, LeSouef, Macredie, Curr and Anderson met on 7 September to discuss the inquiry. They sent Anderson to protest, and to urge immediate abandonment, but in vain. O'Loghlen's Cabinet dared not risk more scandal. All that the Board could do was ask to be represented at the hearings and obtain advance copies of the transcripts of evidence.[70] In fact, they had little to fear: Cameron, de Pury, Armstrong and Kerr had a vested interest in securing the railway extension and according to the *Age* on 29 August, the latter two and de Pury's partner had offered to give land for this purpose. Moreover, de Pury and McNab had already declined to serve as commissioners.[71] Only two people threatened the plans of the Board and the hopes of the majority of district residents: 67-year-old Dr Thomas Embling, a notorious eccentric, and a stubborn woman, Mrs Anne Fraser Bon.

---

68 CSIC 81/U6701, 1 August 1881.
69 CSIC 81/U7577, 9, 18, 19 August 1881; *Victorian Government Gazette*, 26 August 1881:2483.
70 BPA – Minutes, 7 September 1881.
71 CSIC 81/U7577, 30 August 1881.

Chapter 11
MRS BON INTERVENES

> The blacks are neither slaves nor criminals, then why are they treated as such? You have power to re-appoint the manager they love, to whom they always repair when invaded by sickness or death and by doing so you will have the assistance of the House, the thanks of the outside public, and the approval of Heaven …
>
> Anne F. Bon 1881[1]

Whatever the reasons for his poor attendance, the performance of E.H. Cameron as a member of the 1877 Royal Commission had scarcely been impressive. Yet O'Loghlen's Cabinet could not overlook his claim to be chairman of the 1881 board of inquiry since he represented the district in Parliament. The new ministry was a collection of factions held together by little more than dislike of Berry's policies and any hope of retaining power depended on the support of moderates such as Cameron, who had been asked to serve as a government whip. His prospects of political advancement – even his chances of re-election – depended on his management of this controversial inquiry. Like the Board, Cameron wanted the fate of Coranderrk settled rapidly and discreetly. But he had underestimated the interest of the Melbourne press.

The *Age* and *Leader* journalist Dow knew enough about recent lobbying for subdivision of Coranderrk to be suspicious of the impartiality of local members of the inquiry. Since Dow had already conducted an inquiry for Berry, Chief Secretary Grant could not ignore his claim to take part in this investigation. Anyhow the government could not afford to antagonise this radical agricultural reformer who had considerable influence on public opinion. But Dow's appointment was not formally gazetted however until 29 September, a month after the other commissioners.[2]

Cameron held the first hearings at Coranderrk on 29 and 30 September 1881 although Dr Embling and Mrs Bon urged postponement because they had received insufficient notice and Dow's appointment was expected. Cameron was in a hurry to have the railway extension settled. To ensure that a majority of commissioners could be counted on to support local interests he had persuaded Guillaume de Pury, the socially prominent vineyard owner who was Swiss consul and chairman of the Healesville bench of Justices, to withdraw his resignation.

Only Cameron, the local justices de Pury and Armstrong and, on the second day, the Lilydale farmer John Kerr took part in the first hearings. Mindful, perhaps, of his 1876 protest that residents could not speak freely before the manager, Cameron would not allow Strickland to be present. After touring all 21 households the investigators examined the manager and Mrs Strickland (now dormitory matron) and the overseer Harris. Finally, 15 residents, some at their own request, testified.

---

1 CSIC 81/V2688, Anne F. Bon to Chief Secretary Graham Berry, 23 March 1881.
2 *Victorian Government Gazette*, 29 September 1881:2713.

Mrs Ann Briggs (1824–1884).

Cameron aimed to prove that the Coranderrk people had little attachment to the area, that few were natives of the district and that most were 'half castes' who (in his eyes) had no entitlement to government aid. Strickland was immediately questioned on these points. He had the evidence ready as he had prepared it for the Board's submission on abandonment. He said the population of 94 included only 30 'pure blacks', seven of them children; 21 adults and 34 children were 'half castes' and two adults and seven children were 'quadroons'. When asked where they came from, Strickland said there were only two adult 'blacks' of 'the distinct Yarra tribe' (Barak and Ann Briggs) and listed 16 distant places of origin for the remaining adults.[3]

In fact 38 adults and 48 children were Kulin. Eleven of the Aboriginal witnesses were Kulin pioneers and the newcomers George and John Briggs were of Woiworung descent. The Pangerang Alfred Morgan, brought from Echuca in 1866, had married the Kri-balluk widow Caroline Ferguson nearly a decade earlier. Only one witness, the Burapper Alick Campbell, could not trace some connection with Barak's clan.

Many of Cameron's questions had to do with the differences between 'blacks' and 'half castes'. The Kulin witnesses, who invariably referred to members of the Coranderrk community as 'natives', 'blacks' or 'blackfellows' in their testimony, did not consider this a relevant distinction.[4] The investigators' questions were phrased in such a way that the Kulin found it almost impossible to explain their own understanding

---

3   Coranderrk Inquiry 1881:1 Ann Briggs (1823/4–1884), aunt of Louisa Briggs, had been kidnapped from Port Phillip in 1833. John Briggs Sr borrowed the fare to fetch her from Tasmania shortly before his own death early in 1878. She was the mother of his eldest son George who testified at this inquiry but was never a permanent resident of Coranderrk.
4   Coranderrk Inquiry, 1881:6–28.

of who had rights to share Barak's country. What mattered to them was clan membership, not place of birth. The old Nira-balluk Taungurong Dick Richards tried to make this distinction explicit when he, like all other witnesses, was asked where he was born: 'I do not know where I was born. My country is Kilmore'.[5] Cameron's party heard what they wanted to hear: of the 15 witnesses only Barak and his nephew Wandin had been born in the vicinity.

The investigators did not understand that young men born at distant places – Bamfield at Benalla, Dunolly on the Loddon – had an obligation to serve Barak and care for this land as descendants of Woiworung women who had been members of the owning clan but had married into clans far away. Morgan said he had been born at Wharparilla on the Murray; he had no chance to explain how he and his wife were identified with the pioneers and why he served as a 'talker' for Bamfield, whose mother had belonged to a Pangerang clan and whose 'aunty' was still living at the Maloga Mission across the Murray from Echuca where Morgan's Wollithiga clan and other Pangerang remnants had found refuge since 1874. Unfortunately, the investigators were blind to such rights and obligations. Their own culture emphasised exclusive ownership of land and resources. They were accustomed to tracing family membership by the father's surname and regional identification by place of birth. Europeans had occupied Kulin land for nearly half a century yet still failed to comprehend the principles of ownership and guardianship tenaciously upheld by the surviving Kulin.

Cameron's party questioned each witness about his willingness to leave Coranderrk for a warmer climate. All were adamant that they would not leave as it was their home. The Kulin denied that the climate was unsuitable: the Jajowrong pioneer William Parker (1845/49–1886) pointed out that 'my country is as cold as this'.

Kulin witnesses were not overawed, nor did they answer to please as Europeans so often assumed. They were familiar with the European habit of direct questioning – an unimaginable discourtesy in their own society – and dealt patiently with the investigators' leading queries according to their own notions of propriety. Their brief answers were frequently misunderstood because they used different rhetorical conventions and politely assumed a degree of background knowledge which Cameron's party did not possess. European preconceptions influenced the questions about Strickland's management; Kulin replies were shaped by an ancient convention that one should not claim to know and speak for the sentiments of others. When the investigators urged them to state their complaints and asked whether Strickland was unkind they expected the witnesses to draw conclusions about his character and motivations. Instead they merely mentioned specific examples of his behaviour. All reported that Strickland 'kept a distance'. He never visited their homes or worked with them. He had no interest in the farm and did not trouble to visit the sick. He did not supervise the distribution of rations and clothing and was impatient with their requests or complaints. His religious ministrations were considered inadequate by the Kulin (apparently by other churchmen also). Dunolly reported that Strickland held 'Service on Sunday, and once every evening lately, since Mr Brown's report was about' but these were poorly attended as he only invited 'a few of us, such as he thinks would come'.[6] The investigators thought the complaints petty; the Kulin thought they had given a comprehensive indictment of a man unfit to be their master.

They were unanimous in complaining that their dwellings were dilapidated and their wages and rations so inadequate that they had to borrow from each other and sell baskets and fish to purchase food. Now that they had to buy meat all were in debt to the butcher; their wages were intermittent as they could not work in bad weather and the payments were often months overdue. The clothing issue of one outfit per

---

5   Coranderrk Inquiry, 1881:24.
6   Brown was perhaps the hospital chaplain Rev. James Brown who told the inquiry that all Coranderrk residents 'call themselves Presbyterians' (Coranderrk Inquiry 1881:8–28, 44).

year was inadequate and they could no longer buy good clothing and household furnishings. Harris had already corroborated their complaints, reporting that Strickland had blamed the Board for not sending sufficient supplies.

In a patronising manner Cameron's party asked witnesses whether they would be contented at some other place where they would receive free food and clothing without working. This and other questions about the farm work revealed their preconception that the residents were lazy and shiftless. Strickland had already told them so, although Harris contradicted him in his evidence and blamed Strickland's failure to work with them. Strickland found the 'pure blacks' obedient but not the 'half castes' and complained that the ploughman (now John Charles – Page had exiled James Edgar, and John Briggs Sr and Tommy Farmer had died) had refused to plough for potatoes 'unless I am paid the full price a white man is paid'.[7]

Barak and the other elders – fluent in all the Kulin dialects but never at ease in English – struggled to explain what they meant when they complained of the mismanagement of Coranderrk. All witnesses insisted they wanted to work, wanted to grow food for themselves, wanted to clear more land for pasture and fence out the neighbours' trespassing stock so their land would again produce meat. Strickland, Page and the Board were in fact a hindrance to Kulin ambitions. Barak summed up their wishes:

> If they had everything right and the Government leave us here, give us this ground and let us manage here and get all the money. Why do not the people do it themselves – do what they like, and go on and do the work.[8]

Barak's 'talker' Bamfield had made detailed criticisms when examined the day before and Barak had approved the letter Bamfield had just handed in summing up the residents' complaints about the management since Green's removal seven years before:

> I report this matter for the welfare of the station. The station has never been improved since the old manager left. No clearing or grubbing done; no potatoes, cabbages, or other vegetables have been grown, and no fencing done since he left. Last time we mustered we counted 300 cattle and horses belonging to the township and cockatoo farmers. Nothing has been put in the orchard, and vegetables have not been grown for the good of our health. Mr Green was very neighbourly, and used to gather young men and women, and old people, and teach them like children, saving them from drinking and fighting; and every year he used to have a gathering. Mrs Green was like a mother to all the natives, and was good to the women when they were confined, and she used to look after the sick. Under Mr Green we used to kill our own cattle, and grow our own potatoes, cabbages, onions, carrots and pumpkins – everything we could grow. We had plenty of milk, butter and cheese. We get nothing like that now. Nothing has improved since the manager took charge of the station. I do not know what he was put here for. He ought to look around the run and get it made into four or five paddocks for the spring, a paddock for weaners, and a paddock for fat cattle, and kill our own cattle. Clearing and grubbing should be done. The manager is ruining the station. He is not doing his work … Why should they take advantage of a poor black because he cannot read and write? I think they have done enough in this country to ruin the natives without taking it from us any more …[9]

---

7 Coranderrk Inquiry 1881:3–4, 79.
8 Coranderrk Inquiry 1881:9–10.
9 Coranderrk Inquiry 1881:8–9.

Deardjoo Warramin – Tommy Avoca (1834–1894).

When asked to state their principal complaint the witnesses said they wanted Green back. When asked why, each made a brief statement about Green's behaviour. The laconic reply of the old Jajowrong Tommy Avoca (Deardjoo Warramin, c. 1834–1894) was typical. He had made his home here because, on his arrival, he had seen Green and Harris assisting one of the Kulin to put up a fence.[10] To the Kulin listening, the old man had said all that was necessary about the kind of man Green was. He had reminded his hearers that he had seen the pastoralists and the goldseekers usurp his own clan territory. Avoca had come voluntarily to look over the new 'blackfellows' township'. He remained for 16 years because, for the first time, he saw Kulin and European men work side by side as equals to care for land which belonged to the Kulin. But the history of the Kulin and the conventions of Kulin rhetoric were unknown to those who questioned him.

Cameron intended this to be the major hearing of his hasty inquiry and he excluded the press. Page had interviewed him beforehand about Board representation then, satisfied that Cameron was sympathetic to the Board's views, went to Sydney on sick leave. He was still absent on 5 October when the *Argus* reported that the inquiry members who had not been present complained they had been 'unfairly treated' and were planning a formal protest against Cameron's proceedings.

---

10   Coranderrk Inquiry 1881:28.

Strickland informed Page on 10 October that he did not know what complaints had been made as Cameron had thought he should not attend the hearing. He reported that the hop crop would be lost as the men had been on strike and 'not one on the station will put a potato seed in the ground'. He feared the seed potatoes (hastily sent up by Page to conceal the fact that no food crops were grown) would be wasted unless European labour was hired to plant them, as:

> the men are in a state of revolt; they say they are waiting to hear if they are to have the place to themselves, that the Board in Melbourne is to be done away with, that I am to go about my business, that you will not be required, in fact they are all confederate to run the station … All this disaffection has been increased by, and is the result of the late extraordinary Board Meeting; in saying this I am not censuring the gentlemen who visited the Station, but those who called the Board into existence. Punch, Barak, Dunolly and Morgan are the leaders.[11]

Infuriated, Page authorised Strickland to hire a local labourer. It was a risky move as the wages were two months overdue because of his negligence and the employment of another European (previously servant to Page and LeSouef) had provoked these four leaders to organise the deputation to Berry earlier in the year. It seemed safe enough, however, with the inquiry concluded. But on 17 October the *Argus* announced that Mrs Bon, Dr Embling and Dow were conducting a second hearing at Coranderrk. Page hastily convened the Board to discuss Strickland's letter but it was only after 'long discussion' that Anderson, Jennings, Curr and LeSouef retrospectively approved his action. They agreed to send Strickland's complaint to the Minister as proof that the residents' rebellion made abandonment a necessity but decided to meet again to scrutinise Page's covering letter.[12] Meanwhile, the *Argus* coverage of the second hearing suggested that their manager was a liar and their secretary was irresponsible.

Although all members were invited, the farmer Kerr was the only local man to join Embling, Mrs Bon and Dow for the visit of 18 October. The account on 19 October by the *Argus* reporter who accompanied them said the men were at work when the investigators arrived. The evidence of the staff members Strickland, Harris and Mrs Deans (teaching alone while her sick husband was abroad for four months) confirmed the complaints of the Aborigines.

Strickland and Harris testified, as they had to Cameron's party, that there had been no vegetables and few potatoes grown for three years as priority was given to hop cultivation. The staff agreed that families with many young children were short of food as children received half rations or none according to age. The men accumulated debts for meat because they were paid by the hour and had no income in long spells of wet weather. The only point on which Strickland disagreed with other witnesses was the adequacy of the clothing issue. Harris explained that residents had received 'abundance lately – in the last month' but they were used to buy clothes 'as good as anybody in the district' and resented the Board policy which forced them to purchase meat and dress like paupers.

The staff also blamed Board policy for the fact that trespassing cattle had outnumbered station stock for 18 months: Page had stopped the men from completing the needed few miles of boundary fencing and had dismissed the boundary riders Robert Wandin and his successor Alick Campbell. There was labour enough for fencing and rebuilding the huts, some of which were unfit for habitation, but Page had ordered such work stopped because the station was to be abandoned. Strickland tried to defend Page by saying abandonment was recommended by the 1877 Royal Commission but Mrs Bon corrected him.[13]

---

11 BPA – Strickland to Page, 10 October 1881, in CSIC 81/U9612, 28 October 1881.
12 BPA – Minutes, 19 October 1881.
13 *Argus* 19 October 1881; Coranderrk Inquiry 1881:1–6, 12, 14, 28–30.

The *Argus* reporter also gave a sympathetic account of the residents' main complaint: 'that their station, which, in the words of William, king of the Yarra Yarra tribe, was "given them by Sir Henry Barkly, in the name of the Queen" was being mismanaged'. He noted that only two households had meat that day, and it was native game; the rest had dined on dry bread and tea. They had no vegetables for a long while – except the seed potatoes issued in the last two weeks. He mentioned that a wash-house and extensions to several houses had been built recently. Although residents believed this was the result of their deputation to Berry, he had been 'informed' that the contracts were signed before that date. He reported that the teacher's wife upheld the justice of residents' complaints and had announced that Page had forbidden her husband to make any reports against Strickland. The same *Argus* account quoted Harris' evidence that the station should be self-supporting if Page had not forbidden completion of the boundary fence a year earlier, that Strickland opposed all suggestions for development of the farming and that he and Page had never 'been over the run'. Harris confirmed the manager's negligence: 'Mr Strickland has no sympathy with the blacks; he never visits them at their work, and passes them without speaking. He never makes a general inspection.'

The *Age* of 19 October devoted only a paragraph to this hearing, but that was sufficient to worry the Board. The report, presumably provided by Dow, said that the management was unsatisfactory and residents were unanimous in seeking the reinstatement of Green. It also said that witnesses 'from the station and elsewhere' would be examined by the board of inquiry in the coming week. There was no hope now of a brief and discreet inquiry. Worse still the *Argus* had announced on 17 October that the inquiry was due 'chiefly to the importunities of Mrs Bon' and argued that the really important question was not the management but whether the station would be broken up on the Board's advice. With considerable relish the *Argus* noted two days later that the inquiry members were divided into two factions and speculated about the future participation of the Lilydale farmer Duncan McNab whose resignation had not been accepted.

On 20 October Anderson, Jennings and Curr met to approve the letter demanding abandonment which Page had prepared to accompany Strickland's complaint of 10 October. No doubt Page used the manager's angry report on the unauthorised hearing to alarm Board members. Strickland's letter of 18 October said he had been excluded when Mrs Bon's party toured the huts to collect complaints. He was present when all men and the dormitory girls were assembled for the hearing and had heard Mrs Bon and Dr Embling summarise the grievances – all of them 'extorted and exaggerated'. He blamed Bamfield for inciting complaints and insisted that Harris and Mrs Deans had lied in corroborating them. He was outraged that he and his wife had been 'insolently catechised before a room full of Aborigines and they were appealed to as to whether what I said was true or not'. He blamed Embling for the subsequent impertinence of the four dormitory girls who were his house servants and the sulkiness of the men: the 'kind doctor' had insisted that the girls should be paid 10 shillings a week wages or be allowed to take service elsewhere and had been shocked that the men were forbidden to go out shearing this year. Moreover, Mrs Bon had dwelt upon 'her favourite theme' that their land had been taken from them and 'in a martial manner' had obtained a unanimous declaration that they would never leave Coranderrk. Dow had concluded the hearing with a promise (already reported by the *Argus*) that 'they should be removed'.[14]

At this meeting on 20 October Page was an angry and badly frightened man. He believed the members, except for Jennings, would ignore the complaints of Barak and Bamfield (the only Aboriginal witnesses quoted by the *Argus*). He could persuade them to dismiss Mrs Deans' testimony because of her known antagonism to the manager. But Harris' revelations about negligent supervision of the farm work would seriously embarrass his patron LeSouef, as well as Curr, Macredie and Anderson who were famed for the

---

14   BPA – Strickland to Page, 18 October 1881; on 29 May 1882 he wrote Page that Dow had asked permission for him to be present throughout but Mrs Bon had objected.

interest in agricultural development. Those members who had hired Page would probably support him but he could not count on the current vice-chairman, the MLA Anderson, appointed to stop his criticisms of Page's treatment of Aborigines in the Western District. He and the Minister might well use Page as a scapegoat to save themselves embarrassment. The only possible tactic for Page was to draw attention to Harris' evidence in the *Argus*, call him a liar and demand that he be brought to town and forced to recant. The Board agreed.

Page and Curr cross-examined Harris on 21 October. As in every other inquiry since 1874 he tried to protect himself, torn between the demands of his employers and loyalty to the Aboriginal community which had given him both friendship and a wife. In his evidence, repeated before the vice-chairman Anderson, Harris insisted the men were working well although John Charles still refused to plough the potato paddock. Their week-long strike before the inquiry began was not the result of interference: their wages, usually paid quarterly, were two months overdue and they had no meat. Page was wholly at fault but, instead of censuring him, Curr angrily accused Harris of disloyalty to the Board. Fearing dismissal, Harris wrote to Mrs Bon who subsequently produced his letter as evidence that the Board had tried to intimidate inquiry witnesses.[15]

Harris was so obviously surprised at Strickland's complaints about Coranderrk workers that Page dared not send his letter to the Minister. He immediately wrote questioning the manager's report that the hop crop would be lost because of the men's rebellion. It crossed with Strickland's letter of 20 October saying the men were working well and a European was planting potatoes. Strickland's reply of 24 October simply called Harris a liar. A day later he reported that he had withheld the clothing issue because the men objected to Page's order that they must sign for what they received and, later, had come in a body to protest his order that they could not go shearing without Page's permission. Strickland also sent Page his resignation. Two days later he asked Page to withhold this from the Board. Page had meanwhile sent him copies of the evidence taken at both hearings and Strickland declared that:

> the authorised report is contradictory and the unauthorised a combination of lies; I regret to say that Harris is under covert a partisan in all the mischief, he holds with the hare and runs with the hounds, is often at Mr Green's; Mr Green's man [Harris' farm partner] is often here …[16]

Strickland and Page desperately needed a scapegoat: comparison of the transcripts of Cameron's hearings and the *Argus* report had shown that the residents and staff had explained the reasons for the strike and general dissatisfaction in almost identical terms to the rival parties of commissioners. The Board had obtained the transcripts from Cameron, the affronted chairman of the inquiry. He had immediately proclaimed the second, 17 October, hearing conducted by Mrs Bon's party 'unauthorised' and refused to include this evidence in the official transcript.

The *Argus* publicity encouraged collusion between Cameron and the Board. They were already angry about the political intervention (as they saw it) which had transformed the Local Committee scheme into an investigation of Board affairs. Board members feared for their own reputations, as the board of inquiry had power to demand access to files and examine witnesses under oath. Page perhaps showed Cameron the manager's account of how Mrs Bon, Dow and Embling had conducted their investigation. Page could no longer control his detestation of Mrs Bon and had made sure the Board members shared his resentment of her interference. She provided an easy scapegoat for them, and for Cameron, as she was unprotected by the public reputation possessed by Embling and Dow. As past and present members of Parliament they could claim some right to examine affairs at Coranderrk. She was only an interfering woman.

---

15 BPA Minutes, 20 October and 15 November 1881; Coranderrk Inquiry 1881:53, 80, 83–4.
16 BPA – Secretary's Letter Book, 21 October 1881; Strickland to Page 24, 25 and 27 October 1881.

11. MRS BON INTERVENES

On 24 October the Board urged Grant to appoint an additional member to the board of inquiry. It was done immediately, as Cameron made the same recommendation. All but the Board newcomer Anderson must have been aware that John C. Steel's nomination by gentlemen appointed to protect the interests of the Aborigines was somewhat questionable. Steel, a Coranderrk neighbour, had tried every possible tactic to acquire portions of the reserve over the years and owned most of the currently trespassing cattle. He had served as chairman of the August 1881 Healesville meeting when Cameron brought the Railways Minister to hear pleas for railway extension, and was a leader of the local lobby for subdivision of Coranderrk.[17] With Steel's appointment Cameron and the Board could again be confident that local interests would prevail. On the same day Strickland's complaint of 10 October and Page's covering letter were at last sent to the Minister. Page informed Grant that the Board had approved the hiring of European labour in order to save the hop crop and demanded that he uphold Board authority and 'abolish' this station because outside interference had rendered 'discipline and management' impossible.[18]

Strickland had complained to Cameron's party on 29 September that the dormitory girls corresponded with 'outside influence'. In a private letter two months later he urged Page to cross-examine Mrs Bon on her letter exhorting Bamfield to 'get all the blacks together, that they were to be earnest in prayer that they may be delivered from the oppressor'. Months later Strickland made a sworn declaration that he had read the letter before giving it to Bamfield on 29 September.[19] Yet on 21 October he only reported to Page that a letter in Mrs Bon's writing, addressed to Bamfield in care of Green, had arrived in the station bag by mistake and complained that 'her communications keep the whole station in constant ferment'. The old army officer Page, who had begun to think of the inquiry as a kind of war, had no scruples about spying on the enemy. No doubt he and Strickland considered they had a right to examine the correspondence of those under their paternal care. He apparently encouraged Strickland to read residents' letters and confiscate any which provided evidence of incitement. Strickland stole a letter written on 26 October by Sophia Deddrick, a Mount Franklin orphan who was servant to Rev. Robert Hamilton, addressed to the Taungurong girl Alice Sapora Grant who had been a pupil-teacher at the school for several years and had just become engaged to the widowed overseer Harris.[20] Sophia's comments on preparations for the inquiry hearings in November show that the Kulin themselves were organising further testimony about the mismanagement of their station. But Page and Strickland kept her letter because it seemed to implicate Mrs Bon and Green.

> Give the flowers to Mr Green, he will be staying with us while he is down … Mrs Bon was here yesterday and she asked me to let her take my letter home that you wrote to me, she wanted to take down the names of those that are coming down, she said that she must have Finnimore down, too, she said that she didn't know what they want with [three Healesville labourers who had worked on the station], she said what evidence can they give.[21]

The Kulin would certainly have expected Green to appear as a witness for them, especially if Strickland's beating of the boy Phinnimore Jackson was examined. But Green was probably going to Melbourne for the Presbyterian General Assembly being held at the same time; he had built a 'chapel' in Healesville since his dismissal and resumed his old career as a lay preacher. The Kulin still preferred to 'call themselves Scotchmen' and drive in to his services. This infuriated Page, who publicly derided their denominational preference at a subsequent hearing and insisted they were merely 'spiting the manager'. Green, when questioned on this point, reported that they said they disliked the Anglican service and preferred the

---

17 *Argus*, 29 August 1881; CSIC 81/U9678, 24 October 1881, 81/V8903, 26 October 1881; *Victorian Government Gazette*, 28 October 1881:2936.
18 CSIC 81/U9612, 28 October 1881.
19 BPA – Strickland to Page, 28 November 1881; 29 May 1882.
20 BPA – Strickland to Page, 29 August 1881.
21 BPA – Sophia Deddrick to 'Zippy' [Alice Grant], 26 October 1881. Both were 'half castes' reared in the dormitory. Sophia (1857–1884) died in childbirth at a Melbourne institution; Alice, born in 1861, outlived her husband Harris and was still at Healesville in 1921.

familiar forms he had always used. He quoted one man's view that 'Mr Green knows our inside – he speaks inside to us'. This understanding was what Tommy Avoca had tried to explain at the first hearing. When asked whether Green was kind, Avoca replied: 'Yes, he said he was once a blackfellow himself'. Green had probably made a joking reference to Jemmy Webster Sr's belief that Green was his brother reincarnated, but to old Avoca the words meant that Green understood he was a *Ngamajet* and was therefore loyal to his Kulin kinsmen.[22]

Strickland's spying was soon checked. Mrs Deans had told Mrs Bon's party that her mail was tampered with and on 1 November Strickland complained that her 'example of forbidding her letters to be sent in our bag has spread over the station'. Page used the information Strickland had obtained to influence opinion behind the scenes although he dared not mention the source at the public hearings.

The inquiry chairman Cameron did not call the witnesses named in Sophia's letter to the three hearings conducted in Melbourne from 2 to 4 November. Essentially conservative, and ill-acquainted with the Kulin despite his long residence on their land, he was inclined to trust the opinions of the gentlemen charged with their care. He had intervened when a former vice-chairman Godfrey bullied the Coranderrk men but he could not approve of their continuing protests and the *Age* campaign against the Board. He had, after all, signed the Royal Commission report vindicating the Board and hoped to avoid examination of the Board's treatment of Green. He had been instructed to limit the scope of his inquiry to 'present conditions' and he had to consider the sentiments of his constituents. Many of them had known Green since 1858, were grateful for his medical and religious services, and considered he had been badly treated. Others were more concerned about removing the Aborigines to some distant place so their reserve could be subdivided and sold. Cameron did not want to be embarrassed by questions about the change in his own views on the fate of Coranderrk and the Aborigines' wishes.

Cameron was motivated by more than a selfish concern for his own political future; the development of this district by means of the railway extension mattered to him because he had struggled on 100 acres (40.5 ha) himself. But he could not, if his inquiry was to have any credibility, exclude the clergymen and medical experts recruited by Dr Embling and Mrs Bon to report on the care of the sick. After these impartial witnesses had exposed the negligence and bigotry of the Board members and their staff, Cameron conceded the necessity for further hearings – political expediency could not silence the Presbyterian conscience of this son of an Inverness farmer.

The official transcript of Cameron's inquiry was nearly twice the length of the earlier Royal Commission report. It included evidence from 69 witnesses who testified at 10 full days' hearings lasting until 8 December 1881. Tempers grew so hot and suspicion so great that the last 34 witnesses were examined under oath. Because the Board demanded representation Page attended every session, frequently interjecting and even being allowed to cross-examine witnesses. Cameron approved every request to call witnesses and submit written evidence in the Board's defence; he excised large portions of the shorthand transcript; he did everything he could to protect the Board. But he could not stop them from displaying their ignorance. Every member of the inquiry had more knowledge of Coranderrk and its residents; Mrs Bon, Embling and Dow also had greater knowledge of the Board's past policy and administration because they had carefully prepared themselves by reading the annual reports of the last 20 years. And neither Cameron nor the Board could control the press. The factionalism of the inquiry members and the overt antagonism to Mrs Bon delighted journalists and encouraged publicity for the hearings. The *Age* coverage was typically brief and atypically impartial, perhaps to avoid embarrassment to Dow who was still an employee. The *Argus* published the venomous criticisms of Mrs Bon uttered by Page, Strickland, Curr and Jennings, and much else that Cameron had deleted from the transcript.

---

22   Coranderrk Inquiry 1881:28, 59, 137.

11. MRS BON INTERVENES

All nine members, now including McNab, were present when the board of inquiry was convened in Melbourne on 2 November. Rev. Robert Hamilton was the first witness called. He had visited Coranderrk regularly to marry and baptise residents until the manager Stähle was dismissed late in 1875. He visited all of the Coranderrk patients in city hospitals and many came to his home for help. He was questioned intensively about the servant he had employed since 1874 on a work certificate originally recommended by Green. Sophia Deddrick was the only girl in service: the Board's recent annual reports had opposed the hiring out of Aboriginal females because of their supposed proneness to immorality. Hamilton praised her as trustworthy and competent and argued that girls should be free to take service with respectable families; but he also pointed out that the 'half castes' and 'blacks' all had 'a hankering to be allowed to live in one community'.

Hamilton argued that a hospital should be built at Coranderrk because the patients said they wished to die among their friends and dreaded the distant institutions where no one could speak their language. Four more Presbyterian clergymen who visited city hospitals, three doctors and three hospital officials supported his demand for a local hospital because of the anguish these patients suffered. They confirmed that the Aborigines were poorly clothed and appeared neglected on arrival.

The clergymen reported that all the Coranderrk patients 'call themselves Presbyterians'. The riven Presbyterian Church was much in the news that week because of the bitter debates at their Assembly and the press took note of a hospital official's detailed account of an unseemly squabble over the religious affiliation of Barak's dying son. His father had declared him a Presbyterian on admission. Page had scratched out the entry, insisting that all Coranderrk patients were Anglicans because that was their manager's denomination. Hospital officials finally overruled Page because Barak said he had been married, and the boy had been christened, by a Presbyterian minister.[23] This denial of religious freedom embarrassed and annoyed the Board vice-chairman Anderson and Cameron, themselves Presbyterians. Page's bigotry also antagonised another witness – the current convener of the Presbyterian missions committee. He had visited Coranderrk in 1876 and accompanied Mrs Bon there in 1880. He now embarrassed the Board by pointing out that the Coranderrk people currently lived in much worse conditions than residents of the mission stations. He considered their complaints were justified and that Halliday and Strickland had grievously neglected the sick.

Three doctors demolished Board arguments that the site was unhealthy. Medical Officer William McCrea blamed the former inspector, Ogilvie, for hearsay evidence contained in his 1876 report and read out his June 1878 protest to the Chief Secretary criticising the Board's negligence in replacing only six of the 32 huts and undertaking minimal renovation of the remainder. He again blamed the mortality from lung disease on the Board's failure to provide adequate housing, sufficient clothing and a nutritious diet. Dr William Thomson, a medical specialist commissioned by the Board to undertake a study of lung disease in 1879, gave similar evidence and condemned the Board's failure to provide a hospital where the sick could be isolated. He argued that the disease had spread because sufferers were not taught to dispose of their infectious discharges which impregnated the dwellings. He reported that he had traced one death to a gift of second-hand clothing once worn by a tuberculosis victim. He explained the new hypothesis of contagion gaining favour among pathologists: 'there are some germs or organisms, whether animal or vegetable I do not exactly know, that, multiplying in the lungs, destroy the tissues'.[24] He repeated the assurance he had given the Board in 1879 – the climate at Coranderrk had nothing to do with the incidents of 'tubercular phthisis' or the mortality from pleuropneumonia following the 1875 measles epidemic. The death rate had been just as high in warmer localities such as Queensland.

---

23 Coranderrk Inquiry 1881:42.
24 Coranderrk Inquiry 1881:35. Thomson had published volumes on the subject in 1876 and 1879.

Jennings, a founding member of the Board, had testified briefly before the medical experts were called. Their evidence was especially humiliating for him because he had vainly opposed his colleagues' policy, and now had to defend them. He claimed to be unprepared and said he had no recollection of most of the matters he was questioned about, including details of the legislation under which the Board operated. It was an extraordinarily unimpressive performance by one of the colony's most experienced solicitors who had been active in community affairs for decades. He blamed Mrs Bon for the discontent but, when she read out the Royal Commission evidence showing that residents had been upset about the Board's removal policy long before she visited, he apologetically withdrew his remarks. When asked how often he had visited Coranderrk he skirted the question, admitting that he had last visited in 1879 and knew 'very few of the Aboriginals personally'. Page had recommended he testify, as the member best acquainted with Coranderrk: he had made five visits in 21 years. Curr made three visits between 1875 and 1879; LeSouef inspected in 1875 and was there on Acclimatisation Society business in 1876; Macredie went up once for the 1874 meeting which led to Green's removal. The remaining Board members, Anderson, Sheppard, Sumner and Hopkins, had never visited Coranderrk. Their lack of contact was painfully revealed at a later hearing when Page had to name the eight Board members because the staff at Coranderrk could not do so.

The next day the Moravian missionary Rev. F.A. Hagenauer was called to testify in the Board's defence. Page led the questioning and asked Hagenauer to give an opinion on reports that Aborigines considered the Board secretary an enemy. Hagenauer merely praised his promptness in answering correspondence and said the missionaries preferred Page to 'Mr Brough Smyth and his iron rule'. Hagenauer had to admit he had never visited Coranderrk and knew nothing of Green's management, but asserted that neither his Moravian colleague Stähle nor 'the angel Gabriel' could manage this station.

Hagenauer in fact weakened the Board's case for abandonment by saying he had refused to accept Aborigines from Coranderrk 'because they would unsettle mine'. Only one family had gone there. The man was one of the Brataualung Kurnai who had given a wife to Barak, and his own wife was a member of Bamfield's clan. He was the link which had made it possible for the Kulin to solicit Kurnai support in 1878. Hagenauer had told this inquiry 'There came deputations from the Coranderrk men to get my men to join them in making some demands on the Government … They did not want to leave Coranderrk'; he did not explain that the Kurnai at both Gippsland stations had subsequently complained to the Board about their own treatment but he had forced them to apologise and exiled the leaders.[25] There had been a series of protests at every station except Framlingham since Page's appointment. Page had visited Lake Condah to examine complaints but no news of residents' letters to the Board had reached the press. The missionaries would not complain of the negligence of Page and the Board: they had resented the careful supervision of Smyth and Green.

Hagenauer denied that Curr and LeSouef had really 'consulted' him about closing Coranderrk in 1879 and showed some sympathy for the attachment residents felt for their site. Perhaps, now aware that the Board had offered to sell his own Ramahyuck station in 1880, he emphasised that even the non-Kurnai residents loved the place as their home and argued that it 'would be a great punishment to send them away'. He made it clear that he did not favour dispersal of those at Coranderrk:

> we are afraid of them on the other stations. The natives read the newspapers and say, 'The Coranderrk people get this and this allowed; we want that too. What is right to one is fair to another'. It unsettles them on the whole.[26]

---

25 Coranderrk Inquiry 1881:46; BPA – Hagenauer to Page, 20, 25 and 29 July 1878.
26 Coranderrk Inquiry 1881:45–8.

11. MRS BON INTERVENES

The inquiry members de Pury, Kerr and McNab were absent when Hagenauer and Page were examined that day; they and Armstrong and Dow missed the rest of Page's testimony on 4 November although Board vice-chairman Anderson took care to attend. Page tended to blame Strickland and Harris for any defects in management which were challenged by the inquiry members. He said the Board stopped repairing dwellings because they expected the Minister to approve abandonment. He had stopped the boundary fencing because it was a waste of labour: the neighbours were determined to use the reserve as a town common and incessantly cut and broke the fences as fast as they were erected. He argued that the Board wished to reduce the hop acreage because it took up all the workers' time and disclaimed responsibility for the absence of vegetables, milk and butter. Page insisted that the Board had no legal authority to control Aborigines over the age of 18 and they did as they pleased. They could only be punished by a court summons, like Europeans. He deplored this as the Coranderrk residents were uncontrollable: they could not be compared with the residents of other stations because they were 'nearly all half-castes and know so much'.

The *Argus* account on 4 November of Page's testimony was unsympathetic. His professions of ignorance and angry disclaimers in reply to nearly every question put to him by Cameron, Steel, Embling and Mrs Bon made a poor impression. The *Argus*, 5 November, also revealed that Page had read out a document 'casting serious reflections on Mr Green's management'.

Page had read two documents but the *Argus* naturally ignored the *Leader* article which prompted Page to produce Smyth's minutes of the 1874 meeting criticising Green's management. Cameron insisted the minutes be excised from the transcript as irrelevant to present conditions but he included the *Leader* summary of Kulin protests since 1875. This article, probably written by G.A. Syme, pointed out that the Coranderrk people had consistently fought for two things: the right to remain in their home and the return of 'their friend, Mr Green'. It was cleverly phrased and Cameron could not deny the truth of arguments he had put himself in earlier years. He was already annoyed about the Board's apparent intimidation of the witness Harris and somewhat shaken by the medical evidence. He could scarcely approve of the evasive tactics adopted by the witnesses Jennings and Page. Nor could he ignore the letters tabled by Mrs Bon which included Strickland's unctuous invitation to visit the station and Page's requests to visit hospital patients and objections to her 'interference' when she offered practical help. Cameron agreed that a further hearing should be held at Coranderrk on 17 November.

The Board and Page were disturbed by this continuation of the inquiry. They knew, of course, that removal could not be justified as essential for the residents' health: that argument had been disproved two years earlier when Dr Thomson first gave them his views. They knew from the leaked transcript that Strickland had admitted the death rate was low in recent years. But they could not reverse the policy of abandonment they had upheld for six years without casting doubt on the expertise of its authors, Curr and LeSouef. They also feared that discipline on other stations would be affected if they were seen to succumb to the demands of the Aborigines and the urban sympathisers they despised.

Only one rationale for removal – that the location encouraged subversion by ill-intentioned agitators – was likely to be acceptable to Parliament, press and public. Most immigrants to the colony were prone to believe that Aborigines were a 'childlike race' in need of discipline and protection. They were unlikely to probe too deeply if the removal of the Coranderrk people for their better protection made a valuable reserve available for development by others. The eccentric few who took the complaints of the Aborigines seriously were either members of the board of inquiry or would be called as witnesses. They had to be discredited. The Board's most plausible defence was the argument that all the trouble had been fomented by their dismissed former employee Green. His influential supporters, who could not be attacked directly, would thus lose all credibility. Curr, LeSouef and perhaps some other Board members already believed that Green was wholly responsible for the Coranderrk protests. It was inconceivable to them that Aborigines had the mental or political capacity to organise the protest campaign of the last six years unaided. Further because they knew nothing of Kulin social organisation they could not accept that the apparent leaders of the protests – young men born at distant places – had any attachment to this land or any right to oppose its sale. They knew Cameron's party had asked Harris who was the leader; he had replied 'Barak'. They did not know that these others spoke for Barak.

The Board was publicly attacked during the Supply Debate on 10 November. Richardson, who had visited Coranderrk as one of Berry's ministers, asked the new Premier whether he would remodel the Board if the inquiry recommended this. Berry's appointment of this leading Orangeman was one of the reasons O'Loghlen had crossed the floor but he did not treat the question as an opposition attack. For both men, the treatment of Aborigines was a matter of conscience. O'Loghlen assured the House his government was as concerned about Coranderrk as the previous Cabinet which had recommended an inquiry. He promised Zox and others who expressed anxiety about future policy that Parliament could debate the issue when Cameron submitted his report.[27]

Five days later Anderson, Curr, LeSouef and Macredie fought so bitterly over Page's draft of the 1881 annual report that the meeting had to be adjourned 'to think the matter over'. The report began by blaming outside interference for the insubordination and discontent at Coranderrk and demanded that the reserve be sold and a portion of the profit be used by the government to rehouse residents elsewhere. It was the final section which caused dispute. In the version passed by Jennings, Macredie, Curr and LeSouef in the absence of Page and vice-chairman Anderson on 17 November they dared make only the mildest complaint about the Minister's rejection of the Board's advice and the frequency of recent inquiries. But they firmly rebuked the ignorant critics who opposed the Board policy of retaining 'half castes' (now a majority at Coranderrk), arguing that:

> Were they turned adrift to shift for themselves, family ties would be broken, and much unhappiness would ensue; the men would inevitably, with few exceptions, become loafers and vagabonds, and the women prostitutes; for, although sharp and cunning enough in small matters, they are, as a rule, unreliable, untruthful, and sadly wanting in energy, perseverance, self-reliance, and other qualities which fit men to successfully compete with their fellows in the battle of life.[28]

The Board's derogatory opinion was, as they must have known from the transcripts supplied by Cameron, contradicted by the evidence already collected. At Coranderrk that day the Kulin were convincing the inquiry members that the Board had no understanding of, or sympathy for, their community. Only de Pury and Dow were absent from the proceedings.

The Coranderrk residents had talked about the prior hearings and followed the press accounts of the sessions in Melbourne. They had learned that the chairman could exclude witnesses and that directed questioning could prevent witnesses from saying what they wanted to say. More sensitive to differences in cultural conventions than their interrogators, they knew that Europeans had great faith in the written word. Six men and three women had therefore prepared carefully witnessed statements detailing their complaints. Citing press accounts of Page's testimony, they showed he had lied about various matters. They gave examples of the negligence of the Stricklands and the punitive attitude of Page, mentioning his threats to exile individuals who made complaints or suggestions about the work of their station. When the

---

27 Victorian Parliamentary Debates, Session 1881:703–4.
28 BPA – Minutes, 15 and 17 November 1881; BPA – Annual Report 1881.

11. MRS BON INTERVENES

17 November session opened at Coranderrk Barak handed in a petition signed by the 15 senior men. Its shrewd argument was a direct reply to Page's statements at the Melbourne hearing. The *Argus* reporter, seeing its relevance to the current debate about reform of the public service, published it in full.[29]

> The only complaint we have is this, we all wish Mr Green back here in Mr Strickland's position. Mr Strickland is not a fit man here in regard to work and also to the sick people; he has no idea of tilling the ground or making any improvements on the station, or doing any good for the welfare of the black there; no potatoes or hay here on the station, and the station ought [to] keep itself in meat, but it does not; we all have to buy meat. When Mr Green was here he used to be doing what Mr Strickland is doing now, that is, he used to preach the gospel and also do the farming work, and also do what Mr Capt. Page is doing now as inspector, and made a good improvement; and now it takes three men and there is no improvement. If Mr Green had the use of the money what is laid now since he left, there would [be] something what the station would be able to pay back. We are all sure if we had Mr Green back the station would self-support itself. No wonder the visitors that come here and go away and say the station ought to be sold, when we won't be allowed to clear the ground; the Central Board, and the manager too, are only leaving this open for to give room to the white people to have something to say about it. The only thing we wish is Mr Green removed back here, and then they will see that [the] station will [be] improved better, and will also see that those who speak against us will also see we have a head manager of us …

Annie Hamilton and her infant son.

William and Annie Hamilton and children.

---

29   *Argus*, 19 November 1881; Coranderrk Inquiry 1881:60.

The main business of this hearing was an examination of Strickland's beating of Phinnimore Jackson and other dormitory boys in May 1880 and the subsequent trial of the men who had intervened. The witnesses' testimony embarrassed not only Strickland but the inquiry member Armstrong, who had been one of the justices involved. After this Mrs William Hamilton[30] and Mrs Caroline Morgan testified about their problems in obtaining sufficient food and clothing for their families since the Stricklands took charge. Mrs Morgan handed in detailed complaints written out for her by Barak's aide Dunolly.

Bamfield's niece Eda Brangy,[31] cook for the dormitory children, also submitted written evidence which ended with a report that Barak's little son David had been taunted by the Strickland daughters who told him 'you and your father are leading the people astray'.

She and Alice Grant, who served as washerwoman and pupil-teacher, were questioned about their unpaid duties for the manager's family and the treatment of the dormitory children under the Stricklands' regime. The lad Phinnimore Jackson had already revealed that he was kept from school as servant to Strickland as none of the men would work for him. The girls, too, said they would no longer work as his servants without pay. Such remarks contrasted with the warm praise of Mary Green volunteered by many witnesses. She had treated them as family, not as servants.

The evidence of the final witness, the teacher Mrs Deans, was continually interrupted by Page, but he could not shake her insistence that he had written forbidding her husband to complain about the manager. She confirmed the Aborigines' testimony, reported another severe beating of a little girl, criticised Strickland's religious ministrations and gave details of the frequency with which he was drunk and 'unaccountable for his actions'. Cameron excised a good deal from the transcript but not the comments about Strickland's drinking. It had been the talk of the township since his arrival and Halliday had sent Page sworn statements about it within months of Strickland's arrival in 1878.

Argus coverage of the day's evidence included exchanges with Dr Embling and Mrs Bon which had provoked Strickland to stalk out shouting 'you wicked woman'. Cameron excised these from the transcript. At the end of the day Barak, Bamfield and five others handed in more written submissions plus another petition signed by all 46 adult residents, men and women, which said:

> We want the Board and the Inspector, Captain Page, to be no longer over us. We want only one man here, and that is Mr John Green, and the station to be under the Chief Secretary; then we will show the country that the station could self-support itself.[32]

But these statements were omitted by the *Argus*.

When the hearing re-convened at Healesville next day, 18 November, all witnesses were sworn. Ten townsfolk who had some acquaintance with the station testified that the Coranderrk people were moral, sober, hard working and always reluctant to complain to outsiders about their treatment. Their evidence, like that of Rev. Mackie and the Lilydale doctor, effectively contradicted Board allegations that this location encouraged sickness, immorality and 'incitement' by agitators. The four called by Strickland to disprove Mrs Deans' charges about his drinking considered residents well fed, well clad and satisfied with his management. The comments of several hop growers were solicited yet Green, who had developed a thriving hop plantation on his neighbouring selection, was not invited to testify.

---

30 Annie Johnson Hamilton (c. 1858–1935) and her 'quadroon' daughter Agnes were brought from the Swan Hill district in 1874 but Annie was born in the Euston area like Barak's wife.
31 Eda Brangy (born 1865) and her younger sisters came from the Wangaratta district in 1873. Bamfield continued to visit the clan remnants on the Upper Murray, a mixture of Kwatkwat, Ballung-kara-mittung (Minjambuta) and Yajtmathang, to the end of his days. Eda also retained contact with these kinsmen and in 1894 settled at Warangesda Mission Station, NSW where she married Ned Davis on 7 January 1896.
32 Coranderrk Inquiry 1881:98.

The overseer Harris was then cross-examined about his evidence at previous hearings. Page interrupted incessantly and angrily contradicted Harris' account of how he had been bullied by Page and Curr. At the Melbourne hearings Page had asserted that he regularly rode over the run; Harris now demolished this lie by saying 'I do not know what horse he would have'. Harris said every man on the station denied that Page had ever inspected their farm. Barak's nephew Wandin publicly rebuked Page's negligence:

> You do not know half what goes on in your absence. We do not know what Mr Strickland is writing down to you. You only just come up there about half-past four or five o'clock and go round and are off the next morning. You have no time to see what is going on.[33]

When Page himself was sworn he said Harris was solely responsible for the crops grown. Page was forced to admit that he had 'not a great deal' of knowledge about farming. His evidence under oath was cautious but he lied when explaining why Rev. Hamilton's servant Sophia Deddrick was an exception to the Board's policy against female employment; he said she had left her post and was such an embarrassment at the station that he had 'gladly' renewed her certificate. In fact the Board had forbidden her to return to Hamilton when she came home for a brief visit in 1879; she left anyhow and her certificate was renewed for fear of Berry's intervention.[34]

Wandin had asked to be sworn as a witness to explain his dismissal from the stockman's post. Page had said he took bribes and spent his time at a public house. Wandin said Green had taught him not to drink and he was dismissed (as Harris had said) after threatening to take Strickland to court over money owed to him. He confirmed what other residents had told the inquiry: it was useless to report problems to Strickland or Page and the Board because 'I thought they would not take any notice of me. Like everything else when you tell them – no money to do this or that'.[35] He said residents were unanimous in wanting 'our station to be under the Chief Secretary' with only Green and Harris to help them manage it.

The commissioners questioned Wandin at length about his insistence that all residents wanted Green as 'head man over us'. Some were genuinely puzzled about the need for a European presence on the station if, as witnesses had vehemently insisted, they wished to manage for themselves. They were more at ease with this personable young 'half caste' reared in Green's household because he could adopt the European conventions of speech and argument which they understood. But Wandin was also – by ancestry, speech and allegiance – Woiworung. He could not, by Kulin standards of good manners, bluntly say what his people had learned, long before the troubles with Hugh Glass in his boyhood: they needed a sympathetic European to live with them and serve as witness and representative in their dealings with avaricious Europeans who would not deal honestly with black men, and uncaring Europeans who would not believe their complaints.

Wandin, more accustomed to the style of persistent questioning which older Kulin found so uncouth, gave detailed responses that the interrogators could not misunderstand. To the repeated question 'Is there no man but Mr Green?' he replied 'No; if you were to go all over the country you would not find a better man that Mr Green'. When they asked why Green was liked, Wandin replied that he 'looked after me as if I was one of his own sons; and Mrs Green was very good too'. This they could understand but they argued with Wandin about his assertions that Green had never brought people to the station against their will. They presumably had in mind the statements Godfrey had elicited from the Burapper men Edgar and Campbell at the 1877 commission; Wandin remembered that these men had come at their own expense after their womenfolk had consented to move to Coranderrk.

---

33 Coranderrk Inquiry 1881:88–9.
34 Coranderrk Inquiry 1881:96; BPA – Minutes 3 December 1879.
35 Coranderrk Inquiry 1881:88.

Most witnesses that day were questioned about Strickland's drinking. There was no lack of evidence although an eyewitness, called by Strickland, cleared him of the most recent of the incidents reported by Mrs Deans. The transcript of this session was heavily censored. The *Argus*, however, on 21 November quoted Strickland's blasphemous condemnation of Coranderrk and his assertions that he would drink when he saw fit in this 'hell upon earth' and published evidence (excised from the report by Cameron) that the inquiry member Steel owned most of the stock now trespassing on the reserve. At the end of this article, the *Argus* also published, 'for the information of the public', the 1874 Board minutes which had been 'rejected as evidence' when Page read them at a previous hearing. The anonymous journalist's action frustrated Cameron's intention to limit his inquiry to present conditions.

The former Board member G.A. Syme came to Healesville for the next hearing on 25 November and on oath described the 'animus' shown by colleagues who had used trivial complaints by Smyth and Search as an excuse to harass Green into resigning. He pointed out that the Aborigines and the Board had been satisfied with Green's management for 14 years. He explained that he had left the Board in disgust on learning that certain members were determined to get rid of Green on any pretext. He flatly denied that the protests of the Coranderrk people were provoked by 'outside influence'. In discussions with many of them over the years he had found them genuinely attached to their home and devoted to the former manager. They invariably said: 'We trusted Mr Green, we looked up to him as a father'. In his cross-examination Page contradicted Syme's statement that Green had led by kindness, suggesting that Green had ruled by enlisting police aid and by 'tying men up to a post and flogging them'. The *Argus*, aware that the *Leader* editor had published numerous articles defending Green, solemnly reported these ludicrous charges.

Argus coverage of this hearing further embarrassed the inquiry chairman by revealing his willingness to placate the Board. Four of the seven witnesses heard that day appeared to defend Strickland, and Page was allowed to lead their examination. The *Argus* quoted Mrs Bon's pointed queries about who had called them and Cameron's blustering reply – both were excised from the transcript. Page's intervention did him little good as Mrs Bon quickly demonstrated the ignorance of the builder hired by Page for recent renovations and the friend who had once accompanied him to Coranderrk. The third defence witness was the constable who had served at Healesville for six years and had become very friendly with the manager's family. He had copied from the Case List Book of the Healesville Court all charges concerning Aborigines since 1876. He was forced to admit that Coranderrk residents were 'very respectful to the law' and that 13 of the 25 charges had been dismissed. When cross-examined about Strickland's prosecution of the men who had intervened in Phinnimore's case 18 months earlier he was evasive to the point of lying about Strickland's role. The *Argus* account omitted this evidence but emphasised his comments about drinking, antagonism between 'blacks' and the 'half castes' they considered 'intruders', and assertions that discontent was altogether due to recent inquiries.

Page's fourth witness was the Healesville publican and store-keeper who made a large part of his income supplying groceries to the station and driving visitors there. He reported that the Aborigines made no complaints and were so well fed that they no longer brought fish for sale. His insistence that residents were sincerely attached to their home and his condemnation of Board policy forbidding outside employment did not please the Board. His assertion that under former managers Aborigines frequently visited Healesville to beg and 'tempt the whites' also antagonised one of Page's allies.[36]

36   Coranderrk Inquiry 1881:100–8; *Argus* 26 November 1881.

This was the former manager Halliday, once more with the Melbourne police, who indignantly refuted the publican's 'gross misrepresentation' about begging and prostitution in a letter to the *Argus*. He said 'The Coranderrk blacks would starve before they would beg' and the chastity of their women was maintained 'with great strictness'. None had ever disputed his orders or declined to work. He criticised the Board's use of outdated legislation to prevent a 'quadroon' girl from taking service with his family; the 1869 Act by which they were made slaves 'was a disgrace on the Statute book of Victoria'. He blamed the Board's determination to remove residents for all discontent:

> Some of the evidence before this commission has surprised me. In my time, instead of the natives leaving the station during hop-picking ... they would make it a point to be back in time for it, and would bring any of their black friends they could induce to accompany them, as they took a pride in showing natives from other places their station and their crop of hops ... One of the great objections they have to leaving Coranderrk is that there lie the bones of their relatives and friends, and they fear to die on any of the mission stations, in consequence of the mode of burial they believe to be practised at some of them ... It is a mistake to consider the aborigines of the present day in the same light as they were viewed 30 years ago ...[37]

Halliday's remark was a deliberate reproof for the Board members who had no close association with Aborigines for 30 years and had barely laid eyes on the people of Coranderrk.

But the five old pastoralists who controlled the Board were much more worried by John Green's letter published in the *Argus* of 30 November which gave a detailed rebuttal of Smyth's 1874 minutes. Jennings was absent when they met that day for 'a long discussion' of the propriety of replying in the press. Instead, on the motion of Macredie and LeSouef, they decided to ask the inquiry chairman to call Green and re-call Syme so both could be cross-examined 'on evidence in the Board's possession'. Macredie who had signed Smyth's minutes as vice-chairman, was worried by Green's statement that publication of Smyth's criticisms, to which he had never had an opportunity to reply, was cause for 'an action for damages against the board'. Green's letter told how Macredie had reproved Smyth at the time and reported that when he was offered re-appointment a majority of members had told him they blamed Smyth's animosity for his removal. Green said he would explain to the inquiry if called and mentioned that Harris would provide a written statement correcting Smyth's version of his 1874 remarks about Green's management. Macredie knew that Green's letter was accurate and that MacBain, Syme and probably Jennings would publicly say so if Green was denied a hearing. Perhaps Macredie himself felt some concern, for he too had once supported Green against Godfrey, Curr and LeSouef. Page's unauthorised use of records had at last forced the board to face a humiliating public examination of their treatment of Green.

Page was obviously confident that he could find evidence in Board files to discredit Green. The only other tactic possible was to destroy the credibility of the Aborigines and their sympathisers by arguing that the protests at Coranderrk were simply fomented by 'outside agitators'. Strickland had just written urging Page to question Mrs Bon about her letter to Bamfield at the start of this inquiry and had advised him to have a look at the papers describing Bamfield's previous conduct which the constable had left with Cameron. He said the constable did not wish to read these at the hearing 'because Bon and Syme were present'.[38] Page was probably aware that Cameron had in fact rejected the constable's evidence as hearsay pre-dating his appointment. But the correspondence which Strickland had stolen or steamed open could be used to reinforce Board members' prejudice against Mrs Bon.

---

37 *Argus* 5 December 1881. Halliday reported that bodies were buried wrapped in blankets and bark elsewhere. Wooden coffins and Christian ritual had been adopted at Coranderrk in 1861 by agreement between Green and the residents' court.
38 BPA – Strickland to Page, 28 November 1881.

Only Cameron, Steel, Mrs Bon and Embling attended the inquiry hearing in Melbourne next day, 1 December 1881. They – and Page – examined the rest of the eight merchants called (apparently by Mrs Bon) to give opinions on Page's suspect accounts for clothing supplied at Coranderrk. The fruitgrower John Norris was called to explain his chance involvement in Barak's deputation to Berry. Then the former Cabinet member Richardson described his January 1881 inspection of Coranderrk and gave his opinion of Strickland's management. Finally the Board's former inspector, Ogilvie, testified about his 18 months' service. He said little about his visit to Coranderrk that week. He annoyed Cameron by naming him and the former Chief Secretary, MacPherson, as 'irresponsible people' who had encouraged earlier complaints. Ogilvie also annoyed the Board by arguing that station residents should be encouraged to take outside employment and girls should be apprenticed as servants. He reported that the Aborigines were genuinely attached to Coranderrk and the Board had been divided about the policy of abandonment. He offered the embarrassing comment that only three or four members attended and the 'secretary, in a great measure, was the Board'. The *Argus*'s 2 December account of the hearing, however, emphasised Ogilvie's opinion that Coranderrk should now be broken up, and gave more space to the angry exchanges between Page, Mrs Bon and Norris concerning Barak's deputation to Berry. Both of them denied Page's accusation that two men had been 'drunk on Mrs Bon's verandah' afterwards.

Alfred Morgan, c. 1876.

11. MRS BON INTERVENES

Page had apparently obtained this information from the Burapper Alick Campbell, still considered an intruder by the Kulin, who had been in town for medical treatment. Two days after this Strickland reported he had told Campbell that Page wanted him back in Melbourne – and warned Page that Campbell had visited Green as soon as he returned. Later he wrote that others wanted clothing like Page had given Campbell (apparently as a bribe). Two weeks afterward he informed Page that Campbell wanted to visit the Murray: 'the people he says are very angry with him and charge him with having told you about two drunken men who slept on Mrs Bon's verandah'. Strickland complained that the people were sullen and anticipating Green's return, that Harris was 'as hoggish as he can be, quite one with the people', and that Mrs Deans spent her time visiting the homes of the 'malcontents' Dunolly and Morgan 'doing much to help the "Bon" woman carry out her mischievous designs'. He thanked Page for sending wine and brandy in demijohns labelled vinegar but ruefully reported that when he collected them in Healesville some loungers in the bar called out 'vinegar is brandy on the sly'.[39]

Cameron and the local men Steel and Kerr, with Mrs Bon and Dr Embling, were the only members present for the final hearing on 8 December 1881. They had played the major part in the inquiry as the other four members had missed half the sessions. The first witness called was the Board member Curr. His frightened colleagues had presumably chosen him to defend the disputed abandonment policy which he had originated. He bore a famous name and was an acknowledged authority on pastoral station management. He could claim some ethnographic expertise because he was a colonist of 1839 and had been collecting data on Aboriginal languages at Board expense since 1878. He was the only member who had visited all six stations. He was the Board's expert. His truculent ignorance was probably decisive in determining the result of the inquiry.

Although on oath, Curr proved an elusive and dishonest witness. Like the earlier witness Jennings he pleaded that he could not remember when closely questioned about uncomfortable aspects of Board's decision-making. He said he had visited Coranderrk 'two or three times' in his seven years on the Board and knew nothing of the station's history or past management. He vehemently asserted that it was not the 'native ground' of present residents and had never been 'the head-quarters of a tribe'. When forced to admit it had been a favoured camp site for generations he insisted that 'the tribe to which Coranderrk belonged died out nearly forty years ago'. He said he would not accept medical evidence that the site was healthy but later declared his studies had shown consumption existed everywhere. When challenged on his opinion that discontent was due to 'outside influence' rather than the Board's persistent pressure for removal he repeatedly asserted that 'There have been no persistent efforts. We have recommended it several times'. He then argued that residents must be forced to go to an isolated site on the Murray because tourist parties encouraged behaviour he 'could not state before a lady'.

Mrs Bon was not so mealy mouthed. She had reminded an earlier witness that the 1877 Royal Commission report had confirmed that 'the people of Coranderrk are a virtuous people, and insinuations of prostitution are delusions'.[40] All staff members and residents had been questioned about morality: all had said drinking was negligible and prostitution and illegitimate birth were unknown.

Curr was forced to admit that he had no actual knowledge of any immorality – but still denied that Aborigines were virtuous. He considered them merely children, incapable of real attachment to any place or person, and insisted it was for their good that they had never been consulted about removal. Curr blamed all of the difficulties of management on Green, a 'dismissed servant' who had been 'plotting these seven years to keep us in hot water'. He insinuated that Green was the author of the anonymous letters which a detective had been sent to investigate. Curr insisted he had remained on the Board only to

---

39   BPA – Strickland to Page, 1, 3, 7, 8, 12, 15 December 1881.
40   Coranderrk Inquiry 1881:40.

prevent the Aborigines from falling into the hands of Green, 'who would not treat them well'. He had to admit he had no 'direct knowledge' of any interference by Green. He then contradicted his own argument by saying he had already made plans to dismiss Strickland, whose management was bad, and by criticising the competence of the former manager Halliday and the hopmaster Burgess.[41]

Curr contradicted Ogilvie's earlier statement that the secretary effectively controlled policy then excused his own ignorance of Board administration by saying the members had great confidence in Page. He blustered even more when questioned about the absence of inspection reports since Page's appointment – he could not reveal that Page had visited only three stations and most Board members had made only one trip to Coranderrk and had never inspected the other stations.

When questioned about the Board's failure to fence and farm Coranderrk Curr admitted he did not know whether Page had any knowledge of farming and said fencing had been stopped because it would add nothing to the value of the land when it was sold and subdivided. Curr's statement that Board policy was opposed by neighbours, who would lose their free grazing if the station was sold, embarrassed commissioner Steel, who then complained about the Board's refusal to share the cost of fencing the boundary between his run and Coranderrk. Prompted by Cameron, Steel explicitly contradicted previous testimony that he coveted the reserve: hints of land speculation in anticipation of the railway extension were newsworthy. The *Argus* also quoted Page's angry taunt about a 'very improper letter' which Strickland said had upset the Coranderrk people, together with Mrs Bon's proud retort that all of her correspondence could be 'published in the *Argus*'. Curr's evidence concluded with a demand that the inquiry members end the 'degradation and misery' of the Coranderrk residents by supporting the Board's policy of removal.[42] The belligerent falsehoods uttered by this professed authority annoyed all the commissioners, especially the conservative local landholders who hoped to profit by eviction of the Kulin they had known and employed for decades.

John Green was a restrained and patient witness. He declined to pronounce on the present management as he had made only a few brief visits when called to the sick in recent years. He agreed that as many as a dozen residents at a time came to him almost daily for medical aid but would not specify their complaints, saying only that they told him it was useless to protest to Page or the Board. His only criticisms concerned Strickland's 'astonishing' falsehoods and interference with witnesses when Phinnimore Jackson's protectors were tried by the Healesville bench and the frequency with which Aborigines had been taken to court for trivial offences in recent years. He gave detailed replies to all criticisms made in Smyth's 1874 minutes and said Harris should be allowed to explain the comments attributed to him as he had given Green a written statement saying the minutes were distorted. Green was encouraged to describe the history of the Board's attempt to 'decoy' the Coranderrk people to the Murray and his dismissal. He said he disapproved of abandonment because there was no medical evidence that the site was unhealthy and because residents had 'been taught that it would be their home if they would stay and work'.

Page led the cross-examination, but could defend his assertion that Green had controlled the Coranderrk people by using police with only one document – written by Mary Green when Green was touring. He offered no evidence for his assertions that Green showed 'photographs of young fellows' to 'seduce' girls away from other stations. Hagenauer says that 26 were taken away from his station. The only document Page could produce was an 1869 letter Hagenauer had written to the Presbyterian mission committee complaining that 'the man seeks his own glory' and his inspections were harmful. Green, aware of Hagenauer's enmity, replied with some sadness, 'He says I did a great deal of evil'. The inquiry members were unimpressed by Page's efforts. Hagenauer's jealousy and pompous self-consequence had

---

41 Coranderrk Inquiry 1881:120–7.
42 Coranderrk Inquiry 1881:123; *Argus* 9 December 1881.

been apparent in his earlier testimony. The Presbyterian mission committee's support for Green was well known, and Mrs Bon and Embling had reminded the inquiry that the Board's annual reports from 1861 to 1874 were 'all favourable' to Green. Green himself mentioned that he had seen the former Board secretary Smyth again (late in 1878):

> before he went to India, and he expressed himself sorry that anything had happened. I saw him the day after this deputation of Aborigines was down [29 March 1881], and he said, 'I congratulate you on the prospect of going back to Coranderrk; it has only been a mess since you left.' I said, 'I am not going back.' I tell you this to show that he seems sorry for what has transpired since.[43]

In conclusion, Green was asked whether he had 'in any way incited the blacks to move on your behalf'; his denial, on oath, satisfied everyone but Page who angrily pressed the question. The *Argus* account emphasised that Green had 'combated' the charges of immorality at Coranderrk, reporting that there had only been one illegitimate birth there in his time. Green was not newsworthy and the *Argus* account on 9 December of the final hearing gave more space to the inquiry members' struggle with the unsatisfactory evidence provided by Page on disputed accounts, his rudeness to Mrs Bon and Dr Embling, and his refusal to answer questions about his business connection with LeSouef. A second *Argus* article that day announced that the chairman would draw up a draft report or submission to other members.

Over the next few days the *Argus* published Page's statement on the accounts and Embling's rejoinder saying that the inquiry members were still dissatisfied but had to cut short Page's examination in order to prepare their report before the Parliamentary recess. Page meanwhile obtained assurance from Strickland that the disputed clothing had not been for his own family and sent the *Argus* a statement by the merchants involved, and a copy of LeSouef's letter to the inquiry chairman denying that he was connected with Page in any business transaction.[44]

The *Age* was the first to announce the result of the inquiry. Strickland angrily wrote to Page on 15 December 1881 describing the effect of the brief paragraph announcing that the inquiry report would oppose abandonment and recommend 'more practical management':

> Mrs Deans was flourishing the 'Age' about the station yesterday; there was great shouting and firing of guns through the evening in token of Victory over the Board.[45]

---

43   Coranderrk Inquiry 1881:132.
44   *Argus* 10, 12, 14, 15 December 1881; BPA – Strickland to Page, 12 December 1881.
45   *Age* 5 December 1881; BPA – Strickland to Page, 15 December 1881.

Chapter 12
A BRIEF VICTORY

> Numbers of them that I know are sensible men and Christian men and have a right to protection from the Government against mismanagement and wrong. They believe they are in danger of losing the little piece of country which they say they have received from the Queen. The remedy for all this worry and trouble is the reappointment of Mr Green ...
>
> Rev. Robert Hamilton 1882[1]

Victory was not as near as the *Age* had suggested on 14 December 1881. Parliament went into recess on 24 December but the report of the board of inquiry was not sent to the Chief Secretary until 2 March 1882, after 10 weeks of bitter wrangling by the members. On 19 December the *Age* predicted that the final report was unlikely to be unanimous. Announcing that Cameron had not yet convened the commissioners to discuss his draft report which was expected to oppose abandonment and advise a change of management, the *Age* leaked the news that a majority now opposed their chairman. Dr Embling, Mrs Bon, the MLA Dow and the Lilydale farmers Kerr and McNab had already drawn up a separate report demanding removal of the incompetent Board and abolition of Page's 'sinecure'.

This leak infuriated and united the Minister, Board and Cameron. The criticism of Page was alarming because his supernumerary appointment to fill an unadvertised post, and his inflated salary, would be difficult to defend if the opposition cited his case in their increasingly frequent attacks on patronage and poor discipline in the public service. As Embling had publicly announced that Page's final cross-examination had been cut short so the commissioners could submit their report before the end of the Parliamentary session, the news also raised questions about Cameron's competence as chairman of the inquiry. Cameron's failure to convene his colleagues in December may have been motivated by chagrin. The Minister's decision not to table the Board's annual report until the last day of the session was doubtless due to a desire to forestall opposition questions. Only the *Age*, on Christmas Eve, commented on the Board's argument that 'long-continued systematic interference of irresponsible people' made abandonment of Coranderrk a necessity.

Smarting under the *Age* criticism, Page sought a scapegoat. He sent Strickland's recent complaints about Harris and Mrs Deans to the vice-chairman in a 'private' letter urging their dismissal as Strickland would resign if they remained. Anderson, a naive newcomer to the Board who had not yet visited Coranderrk agreed that 'these worthies' must be 'cleared off the station; as for what may be said by the public we shouldn't regard ... Mrs Bon is going too far, her conduct is becoming transparent'.[2] Despite this vindictive outburst Page took no further steps to remove the overseer and teachers. Even he realised that Strickland

---

1 CSTC 82/X2934, 23 March 1882.
2 BPA – Anderson to Page, 27 December 1881.

had to go as Curr had told the inquiry that his management was bad and announced plans to remove him. A wholesale dismissal of staff would merely confirm the accusations that Page and the Board had been negligent.

The minutes of the 18 January Board meeting suggest that Jennings, Macredie and Curr discussed nothing but Page's report of his (first) inspection of Framlingham and the two Gippsland mission stations. Presumably they were informed of Strickland's letter of 10 January complaining that all residents were 'defiant', that Harris was sending further evidence to Cameron and that Rev. Hamilton was now visiting weekly to conduct services in the Presbyterian form. He told Page he would resign 'whenever you suggest'. Three days later Page wrote urging the Minister to close Coranderrk immediately. Abandonment would conceal the humiliation of Strickland's removal, get rid of other staff considered disloyal to the Board and render the inquiry report irrelevant. Page should have known the Minister could not consent, but this and other actions during January 1882 suggest that he was somewhat unbalanced by his obsessive dislike of Mrs Bon. Three times the *Argus*[3] publicised the fact that Cameron had postponed meetings to discuss his draft report: each delay encouraged Page to try another tactic to defeat what he saw as her machinations.

On 1 February Cameron convened the inquiry members; on the same day five Board members approved Page's request to send Strickland's 'explanation' of his resignation to the Minister with an assurance that they were seeking a suitable replacement. It went to the Minister the next day when the *Argus* published a summary of Cameron's draft report. The *Age* was able, presumably because of the journalist Dow's involvement, to print the amended version just approved by all inquiry members, plus additional clauses proposed by the majority spokesman Dr Embling. These – because Cameron rejected them – eventually appeared as 'Addendum A' to the main report, over the names of the five commissioners (Mrs Bon, Dow, Embling, Kerr and McNab) who signed Cameron's report 'subject to protest'.[4]

The *Argus* immediately published Strickland's letter explaining his resignation which argued that the frequent brawls and 'murderous attacks' necessitating police surveillance of Coranderrk had ceased soon after his arrival; all was peaceful until Mrs Bon and Dr Embling interfered. Strickland 'deliberately and positively' charged them with being the cause of all discontent and insubordination. It seems likely that this propaganda was leaked by the Board rather than the Minister since Strickland wrote a 'private' letter three days later thanking Page and the members for their kind words and promise of compensation. The *Argus* then published replies by Mrs Bon (who quoted Strickland's cordial invitation to make her first visit in 1880) and by Dr Embling, who pointed out that he had never visited before the inquiry. Both loftily said the public would be able to judge who was at fault when the inquiry report was released.[5] Meanwhile, Page was burrowing desperately through Board files to find some evidence against these critics, even asking the Framlingham manager to report whether Embling had been paid for his medical services there while a Board member, but in vain.[6]

Although the full text of the inquiry report and its addenda was not published until 3 March and the minutes of evidence were not printed in Parliamentary records until late in 1882, the press had long since revealed that the report was an indictment of Strickland, Page and the Board. The commissioners misunderstood or misinterpreted much that the Kulin had said. But their attachment to their farm and their criticisms of its management were accepted not only by the three urban sympathisers who had long championed the Kulin but also by six farmers who considered the existence of Coranderrk a handicap to development of their district. They upheld the justice of the Aborigines' complaints at some cost to

---

3 *Argus* 6, 21, 26 January 1882.
4 CSIC 82/X2072, 2 February 1882; BPA – Minutes 1 February 1882; *Argus* 2 February 1882; *Age* 2, 3 February 1882; Coranderrk Inquiry 1881:iii–vi.
5 BPA – Strickland to Page, 27 January and 6 February 1882; *Argus* 3, 6 February 1882.
6 BPA – Goodall to Page, 9 February 1882.

12. A BRIEF VICTORY

themselves since disapproval of the Board's plan to sell the reserve meant that the railway extension to Healesville was unlikely to be built. Their sympathies – as the *Age* had hinted – had been altered by the evasions, falsehoods and accusations of interference which Curr, Jennings, Page and Strickland had used to protect themselves and by the dignity of the Kulin witnesses who had spoken in defence of their land. But local support was not wholehearted: the wealthy landowners of Healesville and their Parliamentary representative Cameron soon revealed that they cared more for their own prosperity than the wishes of the Kulin. The Kulin owed their brief victory to two farmers, John Kerr and Duncan McNab, who showed a disinterested concern for the civil liberties of black men they scarcely knew. Press reports of the commissioners' meetings suggest that their votes created the majority which forced Cameron to excise his proposal that Coranderrk be supervised by a local committee: they disapproved of further 'filtration' of complaints and considered the Aborigines were entitled to approach their Minister.[7]

All nine commissioners supported certain basic points in the main report. They argued that the station should be fenced, that vegetables should be grown and the hop acreage should be reduced to an area manageable by residents without importing labour. They agreed that requiring residents to purchase meat caused hardship. They questioned existing methods of distributing clothing and insisted that wages should be paid monthly and punctually. They recommended provision of adequate medical attendance and erection of better housing and a hospital. They advised engagement of a manager who understood Aborigines and was skilled at farming, reporting that the Coranderrk people wished to be rid of the Board and have Green as manager under the direct control of the Chief Secretary.

The commissioners unanimously recommended that 'full-blooded Blacks' should be maintained in comfort whether or not they worked (with small wages to encourage industry), while both female and male 'half castes and quadroons' should be 'encouraged to hire themselves out'. The majority's Addendum A merely qualified this point by specifying that the latter should be specially trained for employment and insisting that the station would 'still be considered their home'. Cameron's party had revealed their preconceptions about the differential entitlement, morality and capacity for work of 'pure blacks' and 'half castes' at the first hearing. Other evidence shows that the remaining commissioners shared these preconceptions. The recommendations of their final report ignored the sentiments of the Kulin witnesses. They had made no such distinction when explaining their wish to possess and farm this land and be free (as in Green's time) to take well-paid shearing and harvesting work when they were not needed at home or place their girls with friendly employers who would train them to manage a household in European style.

Some commissioners believed that the Coranderrk workers were as capable as Europeans and were objecting to the disparaging comments in the Board's recent annual reports. A variety of less generous motives underlay their unanimity in suggesting a redefinition of Aboriginal identity and a consequent restriction of eligibility for government aid. Mercenary considerations played some part in their thinking. The authors of Addendum A explicitly queried the increasing cost of Aboriginal welfare despite the rapid decline in numbers, although they did emphasise that the Coranderrk people subsidised the Board's operation by their profitable cultivation of hops. Arguments that 'half castes' should earn their living off the stations had gained strength recently because of the chronic shortage of domestic servants, despite high wages, in a colony short of labour.[8]

---

7 *Age* 3 March 1882; see also *Argus* 9 February 1882.
8 *Argus* 8 May 1882; see also Serle 1971:83–4.

**David Barak (1867–1881), son of William and Annie;
he died of consumption in August 1881.**

The main report suggested reform without attributing blame. But Mrs Bon, Embling, Dow, Kerr and McNab were determined to express their righteous anger about the ignorance and lack of sympathy of the official protectors. Their Addendum A explicitly blamed all mismanagement on the 'incompetency or culpable negligence of the Board and its officers' and condemned their heartless indifference toward the sick. Page's treatment of Barak and his son was specifically cited. The majority opposed Cameron's recommendation that the Education Department should take over the school and a European overseer and stockrider should be hired. They obviously interpreted this advice as an attack on the staff members who had shown sympathy for the residents. They argued that Harris had proved a capable overseer for 18 years and that the Aborigines themselves were good stockriders. They also strongly opposed Cameron's advice that residents should be forbidden to keep stock.

Addendum A emphasised that the Board's charges about Aborigines' 'immorality and untruthfulness' were not proven. It recommended that the Board be relieved of the management of Coranderrk. It pointedly opposed supervision by a local committee, explaining that the Coranderrk residents 'earnestly desire to be free of Boards, and to be under the direct control of the Chief Secretary'. Arguing that they were all strongly attached to the home where a hundred of their relatives and friends were buried, the Addendum recommended permanent reservation of the land and insisted that:

> The natives appear to have been chiefly stirred into a state of active discontent by the pertinacity of the Central Board in pressing upon successive Governments the gratuitous advice that the Blacks should be removed from Coranderrk. The natives also bitterly complained of the removal of Mr Green, who appears to have won their confidence and respect. On these points the evidence is very full.[9]

The main report said nothing about Page but Addendum A condemned his administration and his inability to explain accounts. It directly questioned the lack of inspection reports since his appointment and deplored his refusal to heed complaints from Aborigines. It recommended that his 'sinecure' be abolished, arguing that his work could be done by the better qualified inspector of charitable institutions, at a saving of £500 a year. Addendum A also insisted that the clerical work (currently done by LeSouef's son) be assigned to a public servant. These comments by a majority of commissioners were utterly damning, both as an assessment of Page and a comment on patronage in the public service. However, Cameron and the three Healesville justices de Pury, Armstrong and Steel (who perhaps considered that such Calvinistic criticism of a gentleman was intolerable) had meanwhile drafted a rejoinder which became Addendum B of the final report.

Forgetting the Premier's assurances during the recent Parliamentary debate, they declared that advice on the restructuring of Aboriginal administration was beyond the scope of their inquiry. This minority asserted that the Board had supplied full information on Coranderrk and said they also had 'ample testimony' on the contentment prevailing at all other stations. They argued that interference, rather than the Board, was the cause of discontent. These four local men declared that the station's proximity to Healesville made it impossible to prevent residents from 'making complaints, which may be well or ill founded – to credulous sympathisers'. They insisted that the Aborigines 'must be the least capable of all persons in deciding how or by whom the station should be managed'. They in fact contradicted the main report by advising that the reserve should be sold and its occupants sent to 'an isolated part of the colony' if discontent persisted after a trial of the reforms on which the inquiry members had unanimously agreed.[10]

The main report drafted by Cameron was an official document expressing group opinion; Addendum B may represent a stance imposed by Cameron's electors rather than his own views. In his original report he may have adopted a deliberate strategy of reporting without blame in the belief that concerned Cabinet members would quietly alter Board membership and press for staff changes, thus achieving reform without political embarrassment. Press accounts of the inquiry members' meetings suggest, however, that the majority showed distrust of Cameron's sympathies and had good reason for their obstinacy in arguing that reform would be impossible so long as the Board and Page retained control.[11] It was public knowledge that Cameron was under pressure from his electors to continue his campaign for the Healesville railway and other services promised by the incumbent ministry.[12] As a government whip Cameron was also obliged to help forestall the return to power of Graham Berry – a likelihood as soon as Parliament resumed if Berry's Liberal supporters could find common cause with the Constitutional party to defeat O'Loghlen's minority 'Ministerial' government. The *Age* and *Argus* were for once in agreement in condemning the scandalous maladministration of the railways and education departments and the political patronage shown in the appointment of many magistrates and petty officials. A concerted opposition attack on the public service was being planned. The Addendum A criticisms were opportune to embarrass not only the responsible Minister, the Board's Parliamentary representative Anderson and Cameron himself,

9   Coranderrk Inquiry 1881:vi.
10 Coranderrk Inquiry 1881:vii.
11 *Age* 3 February 1882; *Argus* 3 and 9 February 1882.
12 *Argus* 17 April 1882.

but also the senior public servants Curr and LeSouef. This political threat could best be counteracted by discrediting the Addendum A authors; anyhow Cameron already distrusted the liberal identification and influence of Dow, Embling and Mrs Bon.

For Cameron and his electors, as well as the Board and their employees, there was only one effective defence against the inquiry verdict for the retention of Coranderrk. By arguing that lawful authority was threatened by outside interference they could challenge the authenticity of the Aborigines' complaints and the credibility of their supporters. Addendum B had a political purpose. Yet it is likely that Cameron believed his own propaganda. His acquaintance with Coranderrk Aborigines was slight and his attitude towards them patronising.[13] He had intervened on their behalf only when prominent constituents pressed him to do so and, most noticeably, they had never sent a petition or deputation to him despite his prominent role as the region's Parliamentary representative. The contested recommendations in the main report, and the arguments in Addendum B, were clearly contradicted by the Aborigines' evidence at the first hearing when there was no press coverage. Only inquiry members and the Board had seen this transcript. For another three weeks Cameron delayed sending the report, addenda and minutes of evidence to the Chief Secretary.

This was despite the fact that the *Age* and *Argus* had announced on 9 February that a subcommittee composed of Cameron, Dow and Embling (the three members with Parliamentary experience) had checked the final report. Mrs Bon was also present. Only the *Argus* published the minority rejoinder Addendum B.

Meanwhile, the Coranderrk leaders, distressed by comments in the newspapers, decided to reply. Their letter was published by the *Argus* on 11 February. Barak with his aides Bamfield, Dunolly and Wandin and the Jajowrong men John Charles and William Parker proved the authenticity of the Addendum A comments by objecting to Cameron's recommendations forbidding ownership of stock and employment of a European stockrider. They reiterated their refusal to have 'any boards over us'. They also contradicted the allegations in Strickland's published letter explaining his resignation:

> Since Mr Strickland took superandent [sic] on this station he was never liked by us, because he never had no interest in us, and never helped us in our wants, and we can also prove that there was no bad language or murderous attack have been here, but since Mr Strickland been here there has been more drinking and disorderly … We can also say that Mrs Bon and Dr Embling has cause no unpleasantness, but pleasantness on the station, those two, and their comrades have strived had for the good of us, and we hope that they will succeed.

Another Strickland letter, which attempted to discredit Barak and praise Page, was published by the *Argus* on 15 February. Two days later a third and more vicious letter from Strickland appeared. He argued that the youth of Coranderrk were headed for 'prison or the lash' as a result of the evil suggestions of the 'venerable Doctor' and the colleague who 'forgets her sex and enters the arena of public life and dons the unmentionables or the kilt'. He asserted that Mrs Bon's meddling was prompted by concern for Green and her liberality to Aborigines depended on money obtained from the Board.

Page told every applicant for Strickland's position there was no vacancy. Meanwhile, he negotiated privately with William Goodall, the experienced manager of the Board's other station Framlingham, to take charge temporarily. The Board's confidence that the Minister could uphold their recommendations was shaken by his 14 February reply to Page's 'letter of 21 January expecting abandonment': Chief Secretary J.M. Grant

---

13   See *Argus* 2 September 1876.

said he must visit before deciding the fate of Coranderrk. Goodall was persuaded to inspect Coranderrk a few days later, although he continued to insist he did not want a permanent transfer because of his affection for the Framlingham Aborigines with whom he had been associated 'almost since infancy'.[14]

Annoyed by Strickland's attacks in the *Argus* and alerted to the Board's intentions by Goodall's visit, the Coranderrk people planned a unanimous protest. On 19 February all 21 men signed a petition to Grant declaring 'we don't want a stranger manger here only the wone [sic] we ask for please. We also don't want the Central Boards, and the present Inspector, to be no longer over us'. All put their names on the covering letter to the influential young politician Alfred Deakin, a sponsor of their last deputation to the then Chief Secretary Berry, asking him to introduce them to Berry's successor Grant so they could explain their wish for Green's return. Arguing that 'we are not children for the board to do as they like with us any longer. They have done it long enough', the men urged Deakin to 'help Mrs Bon and Dr Embling' to carry out their wishes.[15]

Deakin published this evidence that 'the blacks themselves desire' in the *Age* as a deliberate reply to a petition for retention of the Board and Page presented by the Anglican mission committee in a well-publicised deputation to Grant on 22 February. The Board member Jennings was present when his committee made their plans (as the *Age* had noted) but was discreetly absent from the actual deputation. It was a more partisan venture than even the press realised: the quoted letters from four missionaries had been solicited earlier by Page. It was also premature as Grant merely told the deputation that the government had not received Cameron's report.[16]

The inquiry's report ultimately went to Grant on 2 March 1882. Page also wrote to him that day attempting to cast doubt on the authenticity of both of the recently published letters by the Aborigines. Insisting that these were composed by 'some white person', he urged the Minister to quell such interference by sending up a detective.[17] Grant agreed to investigate Page's complaint; he was also taking action on a complaint about Page's own correspondence.

The *Argus* published the final version of the inquiry's report and addenda in full the next day. A lengthy editorial reviewed the recommendations and the minutes of evidence on 6 March. This supported most of the Addendum A criticisms and argued that Coranderrk should be retained. It also said the inefficient Board needed new members and called for removal of Page who was 'practically irresponsible'. But the *Argus* concluded that the support given by the minority Addendum B precluded abolition of the Board as:

> It is scarcely likely that the Government will incur the unpopularity which would undoubtedly attach to any interference with gentlemen who are discharging honorary duties in a way which meets with a measure of approbation.

The editorial ended with an announcement that Chief Secretary Grant had asked the Board to investigate a complaint about Page's comments on Mrs Bon.

The complaint was forwarded by Grant's staff next day and Page began to draft an explanation. Anxious to defend himself, he also sent a note to the detective whom he had briefed that morning on his suspicions about the letters sent by the Kulin to Dow and the *Argus*. Page said he would like to possess one of the letters 'urging them to rebel' which he believed they frequently received.[18] The Board meeting that day was devoted to discussion and amendment of Page's draft reply to the inquiry's report.

---

14 BPA – Goodall to Page, 30 January, 6 February, 2 March 1882; Strickland to Page, 20 February 1882.
15 CSIC 82/Xl587, 19 February 1882; *Age* 25 February 1882.
16 *Age* 21, 23, 25 February 1882; *Daily Telegraph* 24 February 1882.
17 CSIC 82/W2082, 2 March 1882.
18 CSIC 82/W2858, 7 March 1882.

On 8 March a second *Argus* editorial offered further criticism of the Board's niggardly treatment of the 'original proprietors' of the colony, condemned Page's administration and described Strickland as a most unsuitable manager. The *Argus* acknowledged that Mrs Bon deserved the thanks of the public for provoking this much-needed inquiry but hoped that when the management had been reformed she would 'use her undoubted influence over the blacks for the purpose of allaying agitation and maintaining discipline'.

Sherbourne Sheppard, whose 11-month absence from Board meetings had occasioned comment during the inquiry, was chairman for the special meeting convened the next day to deal with the complaint made to the Minister by the authors of Addendum A. They had asked Grant to take action on a serious breach of discipline by an officer of his department 'whose administration has been impeached before us'. They enclosed a letter written by Page in January 1882 to Mrs Jeannie Rowan (c. 1844–1910) in which he promised 'My dear Jenny' a Persian cord dress. They queried the necessity for this letter since Page had assured the inquiry that the manager had sole responsibility for clothing issues and demanded that Grant protect the investigators he had appointed from Page's insults.[19]

The commissioners had devoted much time to Page's inflated accounts for clothing sent to Coranderrk and press reports had noted their dissatisfaction even before Addendum A's censure was made public. Mrs Bon's cross-examination of merchants and suspicious queries about the destination of expensive dresses had infuriated Page. Confident of his own innocence, he had worriedly sought Strickland's assurance that these items were not for his own family and to hastily institute a clothing register. This evidence of distrust annoyed both Strickland and the Coranderrk people who had read the press reports and shrewdly concluded that Page was demanding their signatures to protect himself. Their honesty, praised by all previous managers, had been impugned. They had few opportunities to show their disdain for authority but despite the inconvenience they unanimously refused to sign and the 1882 clothing issue remained untouched in the store until Strickland left the station. Their tattered appearance of course lent weight to visitors' suspicions about clothing accounts, to the embarrassment of Page and Strickland.

Page perhaps hoped to bribe Mrs Rowan with his promise of mourning garments: he considered this Lake Condah woman a virago (and thought her new husband Rowan a disreputable loafer) but had some inkling that she had acquired considerable influence within the Coranderrk community while married to Jemmy Barker. Page's malicious letter was meant to ensure that Mrs Bon was blamed for the clothing register. It was to be read to the illiterate recipient by Strickland. Page did not anticipate that Mrs Rowan would gain possession of his indiscreet criticisms:

> … your friend Mrs Bon said the last Persian cord I sent up was not for the blacks. Of course you and I know that it is an infamous lie, but a lie, even out of the mouth of a person like Mrs Bon, is believed by some people – those who don't know her. You have that woman to thank for all the signing business …[20]

In the explanation demanded by the Board Page said he had written this 'private' letter to console Mrs Rowan for the loss of a child by her first husband. No doubt he was moved by her grief, although he was not aware that the death of this eldest son of Wonga's speaker Barker was a tragedy to all the Kulin as it signalled the near extinction of yet another of their clans.

At their 9 March meeting Sheppard, Curr, LeSouef and Jennings rejected this explanation, declaring that their secretary's letters to Aborigines were not private. They forced him to write a grudging apology to Mrs Bon (which, like his explanation, complained of her provocation) and sent both documents to their

---

19   BPA – Minutes, 9 March 1882; CSIC 82/W2083, 24 February 1882.
20   BPA – Page to Mrs Jeannie Rowan, 24 January 1882; Page to Wm. Anderson, 23 May 1882; CSIC 82/W2083, 9 and 10 March 1882.

12. A BRIEF VICTORY

Minister, Grant, with letters proving they had gravely censured Page for insulting and ungentlemanly remarks. They acknowledged the gross impropriety of his letter yet asked Grant to take account of Page's 'well-known trustworthy conduct and courteous behaviour'. Presumably, they were unaware of Page's February circular to all station managers criticising the 'shameful remarks' of Mrs Bon in equally spiteful terms.[21] This censure of Page was sent over Sheppard's signature. Perhaps disapproval of the secretary's conduct was the cause of Sheppard's withdrawal from Board meetings as he attended only two more before his death in 1884.

Only Curr, LeSouef and Jennings attended a special meeting called to discuss the nomination of new members on 16 March. Decision was deferred and the minutes do not explain why Page immediately wrote asking Grant for an interview about abandoning Coranderrk. Page and his patrons were now confident that their views would prevail. Rev. Hagenauer, supervisor of the four mission stations, had requested the Presbyterian mission committee to support the Anglican committee's petition for retention of the Board. The *Argus* had published yet another letter from Strickland which praised Page and suggested both Barak and Mrs Bon were liars, as well as a letter from Page's predecessor Ogilvie which defended the Board and insisted the secretary's job was no sinecure.[22] Grant had taken no further action on Page's breach of public service discipline.

The next morning, 17 March, the Board members found that the whole file of embarrassing correspondence about Page had been published by the *Argus* and summarised by the *Age*. No one but their Minister Grant could have released it.

There would be no real victor for the Coranderrk Aborigines until the government accepted and implemented the recommendations of the inquiry report. The three-month delay since the *Age* first leaked the commissioners' sentiments had made them anxious and angry but they knew nothing of the political considerations which influenced the eventual Cabinet verdict on their future. Aside from MacBain, Cabinet members knew little of Aboriginal administration and nothing of the Kulin. The fate of this station was a minor issue, relevant only to the Kulin and (as a former resident of the district had informed Grant) those neighbours who had 'assisted in the disturbance' in order to remove the occupants and make the reserve available for selection or proclamation as a public common for their own use.[23] But criticism of the Board secretary's administration had transformed the political importance of the Coranderrk 'rebellion'. The Board had wider responsibilities and 'Verax', on 13 June, was probably not the only *Argus* reader who wondered about the other five stations and concluded that 'Coranderrk is not the shocking example – merely a case of mismanagement found out'.

Aboriginal affairs was one of the few non-partisan issues on which conservatives and liberals could unite to castigate any government. The 1877 Royal Commission had received negligible press attention, so the public image of the Board was determined by press coverage of the recent hearings and subsequent criticisms of the questionable policies of the Board and the reprehensible conduct of their staff. Press and Parliament were united in a continuing demand for reform of an overstaffed, undisciplined and inefficient public service in which recruitment and promotion were largely determined by patronage.[24] This long-standing problem had a new importance as a focus for general antagonism to an unpopular and inexperienced minority government.

---

21 CSIC 82/W2083, 9 and 10 March 1882; BPA – Secretary's Letter Book, 10 February 1882.
22 *Argus* 7 and 15 March; BPA – Hagenauer to Page, 28 February 1882.
23 CSIC 82/X2624, 16 March 1882.
24 Serle 1971:33; see also Turner 1904:II242.

Grant was the most experienced politician in a ministry composed of 'Catholics, party rebels and opportunists'.[25] He had been one of the original guarantors when David Syme purchased the *Age* and was an early contributor; he had gained fame as a champion of legislative and land reforms during the 1860s and '70s. But in 1880, while Berry's Justice Minister, he had broken with the Liberal leader and helped O'Loghlen defeat him. Thus he was specially subject to attack by his former colleagues of the left who considered he had betrayed his principles and his friends in joining a stopgap Cabinet. This ageing radical thinker was a poor man, defensive about his acceptance of a well-paid Cabinet post in his declining years; he was aware that he had no political future if this ministry fell; he was less able than before to control his ferocious temper and fondness for drink. The multitudinous duties of the Chief Secretary's portfolio were of little use in rebuilding the popular image and electoral support he had once possessed.

Grant was willing to give a hearing to the reformers who were the Board's major critics – he had supported some of them in past crusades for other causes – but he had little sympathy for indigenous land ownership. In 1868 he had told Parliament that Aborigines had too much land and should be dispersed and made of use to the colony. He subsequently defended Coranderrk, but probably only to please the fellow reformers who had founded the Board. Grant had little sympathy for the conservatives now dominating the Board, who in turn distrusted and despised him.

Confrontation was now inevitable. If Cameron had reported promptly, it would perhaps have been possible for Premier O'Loghlen to act as mediator. In private negotiations with Curr, a fellow Catholic, and other members impressed by his unassailable social status he might have pressed the Board to accept reforms without loss of face. But it was too late now, and O'Loghlen was probably too indolent and indecisive, too uncertain of his own electoral and Parliamentary support, to risk censure for the sake of a handful of voteless Aborigines, especially after the Anglican church had publicly declared its support for the Board.[26]

Already, by March 1882, the inquiry commissioned by Grant had become an embarrassment to his Cabinet colleagues. Some of them had expressed sympathy for Coranderrk Aborigines in the past, but the ministry ridden with scandal was itself a victim of sectarian prejudice and unlikely to take decisive action on any issue which might offend the major Protestant churches. O'Loghlen's government deferred its decision until June 1882; meanwhile it became increasingly apparent that the mission committees, the press, even the Board members themselves, disagreed about the future of Coranderrk and the necessity and propriety of dismantling the existing system of administration. The hapless Minister could not control the Board nor silence their critics. He could not count on public support for the administrative changes the reformers demanded. Yet he was unable to ignore the evidence that Kulin complaints were justified.

The worried Minister derived little comfort from the police investigation of Page's charge that recent letters from Coranderrk were forged by some European. The detective reported that after a fortnight 'constantly with the blacks' he could not obtain the slightest information about any letters inciting rebellion and had confirmed the authenticity of the documents forwarded by Deakin. He had proved that Barak's petition was penned by his aide Dunolly, in his nephew Wandin's house, and had learned 'why' it was signed by all 21 men:

> I ascertained that the whole of the Blacks wish for a Mr Green a former Superintendent to be reinstated and the removal of Mr Strickland whom they appear to dislike and if Mr Green was reinstated they say they would be contented.

---

25 Serle 1971:17.
26 See Deakin 1957:63ff; *Australian Dictionary of Biography* entries on Grant, O'Loghlen and Berry; and particularly Serle 1971 for an account of the political situation at this time.

12. A BRIEF VICTORY

The remainder of the detective's report was unsubstantiated hearsay. It seems likely that Strickland was the source as identical phrases occur in his letters to Page. This was the portion emphasised in the summary prepared by departmental officials to guide the Cabinet decision of June:

> I may also add that Mr Green is aware of what the Blacks desire & from what I ascertained he wishes to get back again ... the blacks I hear visit him very often and he then no doubt posts them up in every thing connected with the station as he and Mr Strickland ... are not on good terms with each other. Further I have no doubt that Mr Green is at the bottom of all the letter writing; at present things appear to be in a confused state on the station in consequence of the dislike the Blacks have to Mr Strickland who I find to be a kind man ... Punch alias Thos Mickie [Bamfield] appears to be the leader of the others and what he says is always carried out by the others. This man is a great friend of Mrs Bon's and is known to have left the station of a Sunday to attend Mr Green's church at Healesville.[27]

Ever since December the Board had repeatedly requested Grant to give them copies of the inquiry evidence and an opportunity to reply. Cameron had of course supplied transcripts of evidence from the beginning. Four members had approved Page's reply weeks before Grant finally approved their request on 23 March. Certain comments on Rev. Hamilton were probably added to the final version after that date, when Grant received an influential deputation whose statements humiliated and divided the Board.

It was a curious deputation, comprising four members of Parliament of varied religious and political persuasions, and the colony's four senior Presbyterian clergymen, all former Moderators or conveners of the missions committee. It was led by Alfred Deakin, an Anglican turned spiritualist, whose written petition declared that the deputation had come to protest against the defence of the Board presented earlier by a 'deputation from a denominational mission'. Deakin questioned Anglican support for rule by 'men at a distance' who made no attempt to learn Aboriginal opinions. He cruelly satirised the old pastoralists on the Board suggesting that they aimed to manage Aborigines like cattle. His petition also deliberately rebuked the Addendum B authors, insisting that Coranderrk residents were 'the first persons' who must be consulted about the management. The deputation urged Grant to end the Board's 'unjust despotism' by assuming direct control, reinstating Green and safeguarding the residents' tenure of Coranderrk.[28]

In a separate petition, Rev. Robert Hamilton also cast doubt on the Board's complaints of outside interference, explaining that the real cause of discontent was the Board's continuing campaign to sell the land. He provided a lengthy history of Green's 'missionary' work, reminded Grant that the Board had praised Green for 14 years and had invited him to return as manager. Hamilton said he had the authority of one of the Board's longest serving members (presumably Macredie) for his suggested compromise: although the Board 'could not consistently re-appoint Mr Green themselves after all that had transpired', they would accept his reinstatement under direct control by the Chief Secretary. He said the Presbyterian mission committee would be happy to supervise Green's missionary work and Coranderrk would thus become a mission station independent of Board control. Finally he demolished Grant's arguments against ministerial intervention by showing that the 1869 Act gave the power of appointing staff to the Governor-in-Council, not the Board.[29]

Deakin's verbal summary of the Aborigines' complaints, emphasised in the *Age* and *Argus* accounts of the deputation, could be dismissed as mere 'back door additions' to the inquiry evidence. But the publicity given to the views of the Presbyterian church spokesmen mortified Jennings and Page, who had organised the Anglican petition, and Hagenauer, whose employers had rejected his advice. The Board never publicly commented on Hamilton's proposal. His hints of sectarian factionalism were, however, confirmed by

---

27 CSIC 82/W2082, 2, 7 and 21 March 1882.
28 CSIC 82/W2872, 23 March 1882.
29 CSIC 82/X2934, 23 and 24 March 1882.

subsequent events. Only the Presbyterian Anderson and Macredie a Presbyterian sympathiser joined LeSouef for the monthly meeting on 5 April. Discussion of new members was scheduled but the minutes record only their approval of Page's reply to the inquiry report. Yet when this went to the Minister on 11 April 1882 it was accompanied by a request for appointment of two members, both Presbyterian members of Parliament who were fervently opposed to Graham Berry. One was the inquiry chairman E.H. Cameron who had previously refused appointment. The other, associated with LeSouef and the former member Godfrey on the council of the Acclimatisation Society, was C.M. Officer, a pastoralist born in Tasmania who had immigrated to the Wimmera in 1847 and had once been a Local Guardian for the Board.[30]

A day later the *Argus* announced both nominations and leaked the name of a third nominee whose consent had not yet been obtained. This was the educational reformer Dr Alexander Morrison whose financial expertise had strengthened the local Presbyterian church. His conservatism was reassuring to adherents disturbed by the dispute on dogma which had caused rifts at the recent Assembly.[31] He had shown no previous interest in Aborigines. The reasons for the Board's hasty decision were partially revealed in a 'private' letter which vice-chairman Anderson sent to Grant (himself a Presbyterian) before the official nomination. Anderson named these three 'as I hear Mrs Bon and Dr Embling are taking steps to have themselves appointed'. He warned Grant that 'from what Mr Cameron tells me I fear I could not hold by such should she be appointed'.[32] The leak may have come from Macredie, a regular contributor to the *Argus*. But news of the nominations appeared in a summary of the Board's official reply which could scarcely have pleased the members or their secretary. The *Argus* on 12 April ignored Page's attack on his critics and emphasised that the Board had admitted recent management was bad and had agreed to the suggested reforms.

Page's draft reply had been altered by Curr, Sheppard, LeSouef and Macredie on 7 March and approved by the latter two and Anderson on 5 April. Jennings was absent from both meetings. The final version sent to Grant bore little resemblance to Page's wrathful draft. Board members had excised a good deal of polemic, notably Page's complaints about 'Chief Secretary misrule', most of his bitter criticisms of Barak, his allegation that Green was 'an utter failure and thoroughly demoralised the people', and his argument that farm development was impossible because most Coranderrk workers 'spit blood when they work hard for long periods'.[33] The version approved and signed by vice-chairman Anderson blamed all deficiencies on past governments which had failed to heed Board advice. The Board still urged immediate abandonment of Coranderrk but agreed to undertake the suggested reforms 'if' the present ministry provided extra funds. Page's attempt to rebut the Addendum A criticisms was feeble, relying on assertions about lack of evidence and the 'gross untruthfulness' of Aboriginal witnesses and citing the minority comments on interference. Page dared not object openly to the inquiry's recommendation about encouraging visits by clergymen but tried to discredit Rev. Hamilton by falsely asserting that he had demanded £200 for past services. The Board members who had trusted Page to deal with correspondence had no idea that Hamilton had in fact asked only £25 for marriage fees owed to him over 12 years as an explicit protest against the Board's abandonment policy.[34]

---

30   CSIC 82/W3291, 11 April 1882. Charles Myles Officer (1827–1904) had begun a medical degree in Scotland before rejoining his family in Victoria. He was a conscientious member of the Board for 22 years, resigning a month before his death.
31   *Argus* 12 April 1882; CSIC 82/W3548, 18 April 1882; Serle 1971:134–40. Alexander Morrison (1829–1903), head of Melbourne's Scotch College, had immigrated in 1857. He too served the Board until his death.
32   CSIC 82/W3548, 10 April 1882.
33   BPA – Annotated draft notes for reply to board of inquiry, n.d.
34   BPA – Hamilton to Page, 31 May 1880; Minutes, 13 December 1881; Coranderrk Inquiry 1881:[preface], 1–4.

12. A BRIEF VICTORY

The official reply was primarily a defence of the Board secretary. Strickland was expendable but the members had to vindicate Page or else concede the Addendum A charges about their own negligence. The element of patronage in Page's appointment would not bear investigation. Curr had made statements on oath defending Page's competence and asserting that he regularly inspected all stations. The reply stated that Page inspected Coranderrk at least six times a year. Evidence given by staff and residents was that Page had visited only once or twice annually before the inquiry. His first inspection of three other stations was made after the inquiry concluded and Lake Condah missionaries (who had found his four visits to quell protests most helpful) had just reproved his failure to inspect for two years.[35] Page's journey to the Wimmera for his second inspection in four years was the reason for the delay in presenting the Board's reply.

Since the publication of the inquiry verdict hostility to the Coranderrk people had increased in the district. Some Europeans publicly displayed their antagonism at a local race meeting on 10 April. Cameron was well aware that he was in trouble with his electors and on 14 April, two days after the *Argus* summarised the Board's reply, he escorted a Cabinet member to a public meeting at Healesville. Sinclair (Barak's old ally), and John Green, increasingly prominent in township affairs, were among the main speakers. The *Argus* account on 17 April made no mention of Coranderrk. Cameron had to apologise for the absence of the Minister for Railways but announced that the government would keep its promise to provide a rail extension. The Minister for Public Works then expressed regret that government policy forbad the provision of roads for people who paid no rates and urged district residents to join some adjacent shire.

Neither Cameron nor the *Argus* spelled out the implications but these were clear enough to district residents: the retention of Coranderrk, a large area of unrateable government property, threatened local development. If the government would not provide direct subsidies for roads, the small European population of this district would have to bear the cost of providing services for themselves and the Aboriginal community in their midst. Cameron's visit was a propaganda exercise, intended to reassure his electors and force O'Loghlen's Cabinet to take account of their needs when making decisions about the inquiry report and the railway extension.

The inquiry report was tabled immediately after Parliament resumed on 25 April. Two days later, after Graham Berry's address-in-reply developed into a want-of-confidence motion condemning ministerial incompetence in administering various departments during the long Parliamentary recess, Grant also tabled the Board's reply. It was ignored by the *Age* but published in full by the *Argus* on 28 April. Its content angered many people and prompted three letters which influenced subsequent events.

The Coranderrk people were annoyed by the comments aimed at discrediting them and their leader Barak and alarmed by Board arguments that their station should be abandoned and the 'half castes' should support themselves by working elsewhere. The three families Page had sent away on work certificates in July 1881 had suffered such hardship that they had taken refuge at the impoverished Maloga Mission across the Murray. Letters telling of their trials had shocked the Coranderrk community. Page had recently told John Briggs Jr and other Kulin men that he 'would like to see them away earning their own living and being independent'. Briggs had a temporary job with a neighbouring landholder and Page had told him to remove his family from the station. Briggs and three other men, well aware of the insecurity facing rural labourers with large families and indignant at the idea of being removed from their home, now wrote asking for help to establish their own 50 acre (20 ha) farm blocks adjoining Green's selection on the reserve's Healesville boundary.[36]

---

35 BPA – Mary Stähle to Page, 6 February 1882.
36 BPA – Secretary's Letter Book, 26 April 1882; Jack Briggs to Page, 1 May 1882.

The second letter went to the *Argus* on 6 May instead of the Board. Rev. Mackie of Lilydale wrote challenging the veracity of Anderson, ostensible author of the Board's reply. He gave details of Page's neglect of Mrs Bamfield and other patients sent to Melbourne hospital and pointedly suggested that a recent death, and the drunkenness at the local races on 10 April, confirmed the inquiry's evidence of Strickland's negligence. The third angry letter was written by Strickland. He was distressed that the reply made little attempt to exonerate him and, perhaps, annoyed that Page had recently paid scant attention to his complaints of persecution by Bamfield and other residents. Page, himself annoyed by Bamfield's 'impudence', used this letter as a weapon in a deliberate attempt to discredit the other leader associated with Mrs Bon.

Briggs' impressive letter was considered at the Board meeting on 3 May. Jennings and Macredie of course remembered that Briggs' father had first made such a proposal in 1876; LeSouef was equally sympathetic. They ordered Page to obtain more information on the aid requested. Page must have been appalled, understanding only too well that a permanent settlement of such farmers would subvert his own plans to disperse the 'half castes' and abandon the station. He then read Strickland's letter, a belated and distorted report on a disturbance at Coranderrk on 10 April. The members retrospectively approved Page's instruction to summons the principal offenders and agreed to renew their request for an interview with Grant about abandonment.[37]

**Birdarak – Thomas Bamfield and his wife Eliza
with their children, Betsy and David, c. 1876
(lady on left is not identified).**

37 BPA – Minutes, 3 May 1882; Strickland to Page, 28 April 1882.

Normal Parliamentary business was suspended while the marathon opposition attack on ministerial responsibility and public service reform continued. The inquiry report was relevant and that night Zox and Deakin tackled the Chief Secretary. Grant announced that the report had been circulated to Cabinet, promised a rapid verdict and pledged time for Parliamentary discussion before any decision was implemented.[38] The press reports showed the urgency of a Board interview with the Minister and Page wrote the necessary letter before setting off on an unprecedented two-day visit to Coranderrk, the day before Bamfield's trial for drunkenness at the local races. No doubt he had qualms about his use of Strickland's long delayed and improbable account of Bamfield's conduct, as the manager had frequently been guilty of hysterical exaggeration. He had to ensure that he and the Board were not embarrassed by this prosecution. He could count on the cooperation of the venal constable who had lied to support Strickland during the inquiry; he could also be confident that de Pury, chairman of the Healesville bench of justices, would understand the necessity of upholding the authority of the manager and the Board. Page left Healesville on 5 May, as soon as de Pury, Armstrong and another justice had given Bamfield the maximum sentence of 30 days gaol with hard labour for being 'drunk and disorderly' on 10 April.[39]

The quick tempered Board secretary had acted with his usual thoughtless vindictiveness in punishing Bamfield: there was little likelihood that his manoeuvre would influence the Cabinet decision or discourage opposition use of the inquiry's findings. His attempt to discredit Mrs Bon's protege had unexpected consequences. The 'case of the blackfellow Punch' provoked unparalleled correspondence in the press and a major Parliamentary debate. Bamfield, Strickland and Page were briefly the central figures in a public controversy about the ministerial responsibilities of an unpopular government.

All that had happened on 10 April was that Bamfield and five other men had gone to the Easter races three miles (4.8 km) from Coranderrk. They were given liquor by acquaintances including members of the board of inquiry. The pioneer Martin Simpson and three Burapper newcomers – including John 'Sambo' Rowan (1841–1907), husband of 'Jeannie' and recipient of Page's notorious letter – had fought with Europeans who apparently taunted them about recent events.

There was a brief disturbance when they returned home late at night angry and noisy. Strickland sent for the Healesville constable, although the only 'brawler' he actually saw was Bamfield who was quarrelling with his wife. She was taken home by William Parker (whom she had brought from Mount Franklin in 1864), while Bamfield was put to bed by his Pangerang aide Alfred Morgan. He roundly cursed Strickland then and again when woken by the constable during the night. Next morning he made 'insolent' remarks (about Strickland's negligence and drinking habits) then penitently offered the manager a spoken and written apology. They shook hands in the presence of Robert Wandin.

Strickland's daily letters to Page made no mention of these events until 22 April when in an aside concerning Bamfield's insolence, he asked whether Page had seen a press account of Bamfield's conduct. Unperturbed, Page replied four days later that he had seen nothing. Next day he queried a local newspaper's version of 'disgraceful proceedings' at the races and advised Strickland to summons all offenders if these reports were not exaggerated.[40] Strickland's first report on Bamfield's behaviour was written 18 days after the offence. His angry letter of 28 April admitted he had only hearsay evidence of fights at and after the races but said he had seen Alfred Morgan restraining Bamfield from threatening his equally 'muddled' wife: 'when let loose he took his gun and swore he would shoot her ... Morgan took the gun and I threw it under the house ... Punch then got a knife and swore he would cut her throat'. Strickland had sent for the constable and gone to bed but 'returned because I could hear him calling "where is Strickland, I'll have his – heart

---

38 Victorian Parliamentary Debates, Session 1882:134.
39 BPA – Strickland to Page, 5 May 1882; *Argus* 10 May 1882.
40 BPA – Secretary's Letter Book, 26 and 27 April 1882; *Booroondara Standard* 13 and 20 April 1882.

out this night". It took three men to keep him from me, he shouted he would shoot me'. Strickland said Bamfield had begged forgiveness next day, and enclosed his written apology.[41] He did not explain why Bamfield and the other men had not been arrested or summonsed by the constable.

On 2 May Strickland reported that he had now summonsed Bamfield to appear at the next monthly court but Bamfield had since left for Melbourne probably 'to consult Mrs Bon' and perhaps to evade his trial. He also sent a brief report on a recent death and replied to Page's demand for information on Rowan's written complaint of neglect. Strickland admitted he had refused to call a doctor and had told Rowan that the injuries resulting from a 'very severe beating' by a European were his own fault.[42] In his letters, Strickland mentioned the departure of Morgan, Wandin, Mrs Bamfield and Parker, who had medical reasons for visiting Melbourne before and after Bamfield's removal to a Melbourne gaol on 5 May.

These witnesses, angry about the belated summons and even more disturbed by the exceptional punishment, went to Mrs Bon. They signed statutory declarations that Bamfield had never threatened his wife and that Morgan alone:

> took him to his hut and left him there asleep and took away his gun; that Mr Strickland, who saw him drunk, sent for a Policeman who came and roused Punch up, and when he heard Mr Strickland was going to give him in charge and have him locked up, he used some threatening language to him but used no weapon, and then when he alone went to sleep again.[43]

Any triumph Page felt when he left the Healesville court on Friday 5 May was short-lived; the next morning's *Argus* contained Mackie's letter which, among other charges, detailed Page's neglect of Mrs Bamfield. On Monday Mrs Bon used the witnesses' statements to persuade the former Board member Syme, two prominent temperance spokesmen and seven members of Parliament – from both Houses and all parties – to sponsor her petition asking the Chief Secretary to arrange for reduction of Bamfield's sentence to one week. Grant obtained his release that day by means of a Governor-in-Council order annulling the sentence. On Tuesday the released prisoner was at Page's office.

On Wednesday the *Argus* quoted from Strickland's report on the recent death to answer one of Rev. Mackie's criticisms, acknowledging that the information came from the Board. No source was cited for the following paragraph which contained a false report that the local constable had arrested and gaoled 'Punch' immediately after he threatened the manager with violence but released him after 48 hours 'to save the inconvenience of sending him to the Melbourne gaol'. The *Argus* announced that the justices who tried Punch on 5 May had said he deserved a sentence considerably longer than a month yet he had been freed after three days because of Mrs Bon's intervention.[44]

The impact of this report was marred by a letter signed 'Humanitarian' published by the *Argus* on 11 May. It noted that Strickland had summonsed Bamfield weeks after forgiving him in front of witnesses. It reported that Page had refused to give the penniless prisoner his fare home and told him to go to the friends who had got him out of gaol. The writer condemned the inhumanity and 'want of judgment' of the Board's employees and declared the Board would quickly be abolished if their dealings with Aborigines were 'regularly and publicly reported'. The *Argus* editor agreed with this 'gentleman of high standing' that Strickland's retention required immediate explanation by the Board.

---

41 BPA – Strickland to Page, 28 April 1882.
42 BPA – Strickland to Page, 2, 3 March 1882; Samuel Rowan to Page, 30 April 1882.
43 CSIC 82/W4402, 18 May 1882, Anne F. Bon to Chief Secretary.
44 *Argus* 10 May 1882; (The 'recent death' was that of an Aboriginal woman called Lizzie who had come from Geelong six weeks previously. She died at Lilydale and the *post mortem* showed the cause of death was apoplexy. According to the *Argus* report she had been well cared for both at Coranderrk and at the home where she died. S. A.-R.) Victorian Parliamentary Debates, Session 1882:360.

12. A BRIEF VICTORY

The Board was immediately convened to plan action on the letter from 'Humanitarian' and a rebuke for the Minister. Anderson's questions for the Parliamentary notice-paper were in the next day's *Argus*. Two of them were now redundant: accounts of the previous night's Parliamentary debate revealed that Dow had already forced Grant to promise an immediate decision on the inquiry report.[45] Anderson also asked whether Grant was aware that the released prisoner Bamfield was 'with great difficulty, prevented from murdering his wife and shooting the manager' and had previously 'seized, used violence and threatening language' to the former manager Ogilvie.

These comments on Bamfield, and a letter by 'Justice' which also appeared in the *Argus* on 12 May, provoked an angry correspondence.[46] The use of pseudonyms merely confirmed the public impression that the well-informed writers must be the people most closely involved in the recent investigation of Board affairs. 'Justice' (probably the inquiry member Steel, defending his fellow justices) described Bamfield's behaviour on 10 April in hostile terms and managed to suggest he had been an eyewitness. He contradicted the *Argus* report that Bamfield had been gaoled immediately, admitting that Strickland's 'forgiving disposition' had condoned the offence but argued that Bamfield had been justly punished for 'attempted murder' at the next monthly court. 'Justice' deplored the release of this 'ringleader of the discontented blacks' by the people who had encouraged 'rebellion' for the last two years, then ended his letter by asking why gentlemen who were otherwise trustworthy 'dare not allow their deeds at the board be made known'.

'Humanitarian' retorted that the writer had answered none of his criticisms of Page and Strickland and announced that Ogilvie had admitted provocation and exonerated Bamfield of Anderson's charge. A letter from Dr Embling questioned the fairness of Bamfield's trial by two inquiry members who had proved themselves 'against the blacks' and ridiculed the charge by 'Justice' of interference: the inquiry had discovered none although friends of the Board 'earnestly did their best'. He pointed out that Ogilvie, one of those who had volunteered evidence as a supporter of the Board, had mentioned no violence when questioned at length about Bamfield. 'Justice' in reply, offered no factual proof of his charges and merely demanded that this 'savage gentleman' be confined in a lunatic asylum before he killed those members of the 'highest society' with whom he was on visiting terms.

Page drafted his own reply to 'Humanitarian' but presumably the vice-chairman considered his intemperate correspondence had caused enough trouble. Anderson's official reply declined to answer anonymous allegations and focussed on the *Argus* editor's challenge. He explained that Strickland had reluctantly remained pending a decision on abandonment when the post would be abolished. Anderson alleged that Grant had privately said 'he would not advise' but thought in the circumstances the Board should delay an appointment.[47] Anderson's letter (like his questions) was a blatant attempt to force the Minister to heed Board's advice on abandonment. The conservative Board members had always mistrusted Grant's political sympathies. At odds with their Minister since he commissioned the inquiry, they felt betrayed by his apparent willingness to give a hearing to liberal critics they despised and were now determined to embarrass him. Bamfield's case had given them new allies.

Bamfield's prosecution and release had an unforeseen importance. Grant had asked the Governor to exercise the prerogative of mercy without the usual consultation of the committing magistrates. Therefore Bamfield's release was seen as an insult to the Healesville bench who had tried him as well as the Board who had ordered this prosecution. The colony's courts, inadequately staffed by police magistrates on circuit duty, relied on the unpaid services of appointed justices of the peace. These gentlemen of good

---

45 BPA – Minutes, 11 May 1882; Victorian Parliamentary Debates, Session 1882:246; *Age* and *Argus* 12 May 1882.
46 CSIC 82/W4402, 16 May 1882; *Argus* 12, 13, 15 May 1882.
47 BPA – Page to *Argus* (draft), 15 May 1882; Secretary's Letter Book, 14 May 1882; *Argus* 13 May 1882.

repute, who rarely had any formal legal training, served as magistrates for most trials. Any criticism of their impartiality was disturbing, not merely because O'Loghlen's government was being attacked for appointing 'partisan' magistrates, but because many rural courts could not be maintained if the justices withheld their voluntary services.

On 16 May, the day that Anderson's questions were scheduled, the *Age*, *Argus* and *Daily Telegraph*, as the Legislative Assembly was to vote on Berry's censure motion, devoted their editorials to the topic of public service reform. They also published a letter quoting the resolutions of a public meeting at Healesville. The resolutions condemned Grant's insult to the justices, regretted their consequent decision from the bench and requested Cameron, the district's Parliamentary representative, to cooperate with the Board's vice-chairman in demanding an explanation from the Minister. The newspapers simultaneously published a letter by the justices. They complained that the release of Bamfield was extraordinary 'even in this land of Ministerial wrongdoing' and expressed fear that this leader 'and the rest of the blacks will now set all law and order at defiance'. They described Bamfield (crippled for a decade by chronic rheumatism, probably a misdiagnosis of the spinal tuberculosis which caused his agonised death) as 'a big powerful fellow in robust health'. They expressed dismay that Grant was risking the lives of Strickland and other Europeans by freeing this 'most dangerous man'. They assured the public that the account of Bamfield's behaviour by 'Justice' was accurate and added the 'important fact' that this was his third violent offence. They cited earlier charges for 'threatening to take the life' of James Edgar and assaulting Alfred Morgan. This was deliberate distortion, for de Pury and Armstrong had heard the constable tell the inquiry that Edgar's malicious charge of threatening language had been dismissed and also that Morgan had been gaoled for fighting Bamfield.[48] Page no doubt welcomed the justices' support. But he was aware that the falsity of their allegations would be apparent to Mrs Bon and anyone else who checked the Healesville court records published in the Board's annual reports. That morning Page was ordered to provide information for the Minister's reply to Anderson's questions. He had to make a convincing case that would protect himself and Strickland, the Board and the justices who had shown their support for the Board in signing Addendum B of the inquiry report and in punishing Bamfield. The only documentation he had was Ogilvie's 1876 journal entry describing the incident with Bamfield and the Webster brothers as 'a slight scuffle' and Ogilvie's reply to Page's telegraphed plea for more evidence which merely said he had given provocation by forcing Bamfield out of the room and 'the whole affair lasted only a quarter minute'. Nevertheless Page informed the Minister that Ogilvie had been seized and pinned down until released by two men while Bamfield swore he had 'settled many a policeman and would settle old Ogilvie yet'. Page also embroidered his description of Bamfield's current offence, insisting 'it was proved in the Healesville court' that he had threatened his wife and Strickland with gun and knife and would have killed both if not forcibly disarmed by two men.[49]

In Parliament that night although Anderson announced he would postpone his questions he read out the one concerning Bamfield. The *Age* and *Argus* next day publicised Deakin's demand that Anderson retract his allegations of attempted murder since two witnesses declared them false and the Speaker's suggestion that the question, 'already altered in a wholesale manner' should be withdrawn altogether. But Page was probably comforted by press reports of further public meetings condemning Grant's insult to the three justices. The *Argus* also published Halliday's letter acquitting himself and Page of negligence in caring for Mrs Bamfield. The semi-literate former manager was moved to an atypical elegance of expression in describing his regard for Page and his sorrow at the deceptions practised by the Bamfields. He quoted much detail from the records of the Lying-In Hospital to support his regretful conclusion that Mackie was a liar and managed to hint delicately that Mrs Bon was the source of Mackie's unjust accusation.[50]

---

48   Coranderrk Inquiry 1881:106–7; BPA – Annual Report 1878:App. 10.
49   BPA – Journal of Christian Ogilvie, 25 February 1876; Ogilvie to Page, 13 and 15 May 1882; CSIC 82/W4402, 16 May 1882.
50   *Age* and *Argus* 17 May 1882; Victorian Parliamentary Debates, Session 1882:278.

12. A BRIEF VICTORY

The Board's propaganda campaign had received a severe check for all 'debatable matter' was excised from Anderson's questions rescheduled for 18 May. That morning's *Argus* announced, however, that Grant would discuss Bamfield's release. The news appeared in a report that the three justices had interviewed the Solicitor General. They had been assured that he intended no insult in accepting the petitioners' representations on Bamfield's behalf, although the facts were now contradicted by other persons. Mrs Bon immediately informed Grant, who had acted without seeing any documentation, that her petition was supported, 'in addition to other evidence', by witnesses' written statements proving that the charges made at Bamfield's trial were false.[51]

---

51 CSIC 82/W4402, 18 May 1882.

Chapter 13
FINAL DEFEAT

> Coranderrk, they state, they received from the Queen at the hands of Sir Henry Barkly, as a small substitute for the country they had lost. They regard it as their own property and are exceedingly attached – I may say wedded to it – then why send them from it? … why punish them for the bad management of their Protectors? They are neither paupers, lunatics nor criminals – then why treat them as such? … Are they to be driven from place to place like cattle by the white usurper?
>
> Anne F. Bon 1882[1]

The two-hour 'Coranderrk Debate' provoked by Anderson's questions on 18 May 1882 was the longest Parliamentary examination of Aboriginal affairs during the Board's century of existence. It began with an adjournment motion on another matter and ended with a reproof from the Speaker who condemned opposition tactics in wasting time on irrelevant issues. The Hansard record was not a verbatim account but the detailed *Argus* transcript of the speeches and interjections shows that discussion degenerated into rowdy farce. After three weeks of debate, Berry's censure motion had been defeated when the conservatives rallied to support O'Loghlen's ministry. The House was half empty. The victors were in high spirits, the defeated Liberals were bitter. Berry and O'Loghlen were absent, Ramsay was on his deathbed and others who had visited Coranderrk and defended the Kulin in previous debates – MacBain, MacPherson and Vale – had left the Legislative Assembly. Ten of the 20 members who spoke or interjected had shown no previous interest in Aborigines. The *Age* described the irregular debate as spirited but unprofitable; an *Argus* editorial declared that the exchanges of the 'furious partisans' cast doubt upon the manners, morals and common sense of the colony's elected representatives.[2]

Anderson read his truncated questions to the Minister then angrily elaborated upon the excised allegations and condemned Grant's gross insult to the Healesville justices and the Board. He subsided when Dow and the Speaker objected, saying he was unwilling to move adjournment of the House to press his case. Grant gracefully took full responsibility for Bamfield's hasty release to save the Solicitor General embarrassment. He read Mrs Bon's petition which spoke of the Aborigines' horror of incarceration and blamed those who gave Bamfield liquor. He named the 10 prominent supporters. He extolled the Healesville justices (de Pury, Armstrong and his own former legal partner) and promised a decision on the inquiry report within two weeks.

The Speaker then cut short Deakin's argument that two justices, those involved in the inquiry, were motivated by animus and one of them had supplied Bamfield with liquor on 10 April. An adjournment motion on a railways scandal permitted Deakin to continue his statement as a personal explanation. He, and later Dow, declared that they could produce documentary evidence from witnesses proving

---

1   CSIC 82/X4907, Anne F. Bon to Mr Wilson, 29 May 1882.
2   Victorian Parliamentary Debates, Session 1882:359–69; *Age* 19 May 1882; *Argus* 19 and 23 May 1882.

that another justice associated with the inquiry (Steel) had supplied drink to Aborigines at the races and had encouraged a European fighting a young Kulin, Martin Simpson, with shouts of 'Give it to the black bastard!' But the immediate cries of 'Shame' and reproaches by government speakers seemed to be directed at Deakin's attack on the character of a justice rather than expressions of dismay at this evidence of worsening race relations in the Healesville district.

One by one others who had supported Bamfield's release rose to explain their reasons. Zox, a justice himself, explained that he had signed after a thorough investigation. He had seen both the summons and information and hinted that the manager had concocted the charge three weeks after publicly pardoning Bamfield. He criticised the exceptional sentence and urged the government to examine the decisions made by certain 'cliques' on the Board. Cameron, who had repeatedly interjected, reproached Zox for making such statements after receiving his explanation of the case. He said Zox had admitted being 'misled by a certain lady'. Cameron also reproved Deakin for attacking the justices he had originally nominated for the inquiry. He then gave an exaggerated account of Bamfield's 'crimes' and insisted that the manager had, on his own responsibility, delayed action until the normal court day.

Dow, always the shrewd showman, transformed the debate by announcing that he suspected Anderson's questions had been dictated by Page whose persecution of Bamfield 'because he would not hold his tongue under oppression' had worsened since the inquiry report was made public. He reminded the House that the Board had campaigned to sell Coranderrk since the days of secretary R. Brough Smyth; Bamfield a 'leading man among his tribe', had been subject to constant harassment because he had fought from the beginning against removal. Dow challenged Anderson's scandalous falsehoods about Bamfield whose wife had made a statutory declaration that no woman could have a better husband. Dow himself had found him, over eight years' acquaintance, to be the mildest of men. He condemned the retention of Page – whom 'even the *Argus*' had declared unfit for his position – and read out Page's 'My Dear Jenny' letter to show how this incompetent officer, 'who was the Board', had tried to discredit the philanthropic lady who was 'the real protector' of the Aborigines.

Members of all parties warmly defended the character and good works of Mrs Bon and acknowledged that she had been known for her interest in Aborigines since her arrival in the colony a quarter of a century earlier. Several demanded that the Chief Secretary immediately dismiss Page whose 'ruffianly' behaviour had proved him unfit to be a public servant. But others were more interested in supporting Dow's argument that 'half castes' should be drafted off the station to work for Europeans. He had insisted that the 'pure blacks' should retain possession of Coranderrk; others suggested they be removed to Gippsland so this valuable reserve could be used by others.

Humiliation apparently drove the Board's vice-chairman, Anderson, to abandon his usual rectitude. He asserted that there was no trouble at any other station, gave a false account of Green's dealings with the Board, insisted abandonment was essential for the Aborigines' health and said Page's letter was the result of Mrs Bon's 'persecution'. He explained that he had once been prejudiced by interviews with Mrs Bon and 'letters from aborigines complaining of Captain Page' (actually protests from Lake Condah residents) but since joining the Board he had visited several stations and learned that Page was the best officer the Board had ever had. He did not admit that he had never visited Coranderrk. He gave a fanciful description of the murderous frenzy of the dangerous maniac Bamfield and a false chronology of the prosecution. Anderson ended his tirade by asserting that Deakin and Dow were 'chivied by the *Age* and the *Age* was chivied by Mrs Bon'. Dow retorted that his interest in Aborigines pre-dated his association with the *Age*. Other members echoed Dow's demand for a thorough Parliamentary discussion of the inquiry report and further investigation of the Board's administration.

Richardson, who had visited Coranderrk as a Cabinet member early in 1881 and condemned its administration when a witness at the inquiry, then rebuked Anderson for succumbing to Page's influence instead of dismissing him. He also attempted to reprove the lack of interest shown by 'the Ministerial side' whose jeering interjections had continually interrupted the debate. For nearly 30 years this Methodist lay preacher had shown an unostentatious sympathy for Aborigines, but the House was more familiar with his belligerent and bigoted attacks on O'Loghlen's ministry. His blundering argument that 'half castes' should be supported by their genitors rather than the state was disrupted by derisive heckling. Provoked by Cameron's sniggering suggestion that many of those at Coranderrk came from his own Mount Franklin electorate, Richardson angrily retorted that he could table a list of the putative fathers of Coranderrk residents – many of them members of the House. Further criticisms of the Coranderrk management by members who had visited were consequently so interrupted by lewd remarks and laughter that the Speaker closed the debate.

As reported in the *Argus* on 19 May, Richardson had stated an uncomfortable truth in his accusation that 'faces colour whenever the question of the blacks is discussed'. Persistent gossip, he contended, about the concubinage openly acknowledged in earlier decades, and the facts of physical resemblance, did not support the reassuring fiction that Aboriginal women had been exploited only by the lower orders of immigrant males.[3] Prudery and fear of further revelations played some part in ensuring that this was the last extended debate on Aboriginal policy by the Victorian Legislative Assembly in the nineteenth century. The propertied gentlemen of the Legislative Council had ignored Aborigines completely after their 1858 Select Committee report.

Differential treatment of 'pure blacks' and 'half castes' had been strongly recommended in 1858. The pioneer pastoralists who were the main advisers took a robust view of the consequences of frontier morality – they had to, in a colony where 'the incidence of bastardy was high'[4] – and their argument that 'half castes' should be encouraged to make their way as equals in society was based largely on their ethnocentric belief in the superiority of Caucasoid genetic endowment, their total ignorance of cultural influences on behaviour and their desire to keep welfare costs to a minimum by requiring the indigent to support themselves. These considerations had influenced Board policy ever since, particularly at Coranderrk, which Europeans saw as a training institution for young 'half castes' rather than a home for those who identified themselves as Kulin. The 1877 Royal Commission had not rejected the goal of 'absorption' for persons of mixed ancestry, merely postponed its implementation because of pessimism about the efficacy of the training so far given and an anxious awareness that the strength of popular prejudice forbad real assimilation.

In 1882 the Board, their critics, the government, Parliament and the press almost unanimously favoured differential treatment of the people they distinguished as 'fullbloods' and 'half castes'. Continuing immigration and changes in the colonists' own notions of morality had, of course, made their attitudes to the original owners of this land more complex. Statements that the immigrants owed compensation only to the 'dying race' of 'pure blacks' had become increasingly common since 1877. This idea was fostered by the lobbies which coveted Aboriginal land and labour. Its acceptance was encouraged by recent publicity about the cost of Board administration as well as information about the declining size and altered composition of the 'native' population. The idea that 'half castes' could make their own way and earn acceptance was supported by the buoyant economy and 'boom mentality' of Victoria in the 1880s: the colonists felt proud that they had transformed the land and were euphorically confident that they could transform their society to achieve a good life for all.

---

3   Kiddle (1961:119–22) provides evidence for the Western District supporting Richardson's contention.
4   Kiddle 1962:505.

Times had changed. The invaders responsible for the atrocities of the 1830s and '40s were mostly dead. The evangelical reformers now prescribing future policy had no personal responsibility for the theft of land and women from the Kulin and their neighbours, and no real understanding of the bitterness of the landowners who still survived. After half a century of triumphant dispossession, colonists could acknowledge with propriety a generalised guilt about the expropriation of land. Liberality would not be costly now that the disinherited were apparently near extinction.

These mid-Victorian moralists, however, did not consider the state responsible for the private sins revealed by the existence of 'half castes'. The 'wowsers' who sought to improve colonial society by imposing their own puritanical views implicitly accepted the Biblical statement that descendants should suffer for the iniquity of their fathers and explicitly demanded that 'the offspring of white immorality' should not share the scanty compensation afforded the Aboriginal community from which their mothers came.[5] Even those sympathisers who demanded the retention of Coranderrk for the Aborigines – Deakin, Dow, Rev. Hamilton and Mrs Bon – argued that their extinction was near and suggested that their reserve would eventually be available to Europeans.[6]

During the Parliamentary debate, Dow had revealed the thinking of some inquiry members when he demanded an end to the 'system of white propagation' which would 'render necessary the maintenance of the station for ever and ever'.[7] Addendum A had specifically insisted that the station was 'still to be considered the home' of 'half castes' who found work elsewhere; this was certainly the view of the main authors, Mrs Bon and Dr Embling.[8] But even they did not see the 'half castes' as heirs of this land. No one but the Coranderrk people themselves proposed that the families who considered themselves Kulin should have permanent tenure of farms on the reserve. They considered they had a right to go on farming the land on which their children had been born, which they had developed and which their maternal ancestors had owned. Their claims to use this land were recognised by Kulin law and acknowledged by Barak head of the owning clan. But the European intruders were primarily concerned with their own claims to possession, based on an alien law.

The fate of Coranderrk and the families who lived there was decided by others in 1882. The decision-makers – Parliament, press, government, Board and inquiry members – were blinkered by their ignorance of the Kulin. Their decisions were shaped by a prurient concern with sexual morality and a punitive notion of retributive justice, a variety of mercenary ambitions and a wholly mistaken fear that the 'half caste' population of the colony was rapidly growing. This last anxiety was based on a false impression that Coranderrk was typical of the Board's six stations.

Board enumerations did not distinguish 'half castes' until 1877 when 293 persons of mixed ancestry (27 per cent of 1,067) were counted. They formed a fifth of the Gippsland population, a third of the number at the Wimmera and Western District stations but almost two-thirds of the population at Coranderrk because of the peculiar history of recruitment to this central school. Miscegenation was negligible. Surviving records show that there had been 200 persons of hybrid ancestry in 1863 when the 60 adults, marrying within their own communities, had already begun to produce a second generation of 'half castes'. By the 1880s second- and third-generation 'half castes' were being born to young couples who had married at the stations. Page himself did not know the size of the Aboriginal population in

---

5   Exodus 20:5. References to the illegitimate status of 'half castes' were common at this period. Christie (1979:201) reports that Anne Bon used this phrase in a letter to the Chief Secretary dated 9 December 1882 which apparently influenced the Parliamentary Draftsman in the preparation of the 1886 Act. For an account of 'wowserism' at this period see Serle 1971:127–78.
6   Such statements were more or less explicit in their petitions to government, and were made by others in letters to the press (CSIC 82/W2872, 82/X2934, 23 and 24 March 1882; 82/X4907, 29 May 1882; *Argus* 10–23 May 1882).
7   Victorian Parliamentary Debates, Session 1882:364.
8   Coranderrk Inquiry 1881:v. The importance of Mrs Bon's authorship is suggested by the many similar phrases used in her letters, written before and after its publication.

June 1882; when the Government Statist reported that his figure from the 1881 census was '780' and asked for the correct total, Page had to reply that his records suggested the correct number was '870' but migration across the Murray made it difficult to keep records. Migration to the Maloga Mission in New South Wales, a consequence of the Board's policy of exiling families from Coranderrk, had the effect by 1887 of reducing the number of 'half castes' in Victoria to 256 (31 per cent of 806).[9]

Victorian colonists throughout the nineteenth century had a profound fear of interacial marriage and the growth of minorities unable to be assimilated. Legal marriage between Aborigines and Europeans remained a rarity. The dogmatic views of the dominant Protestant churches played some part in this: the old Guardian, William Thomas, had commented in 1858 on the plight of one couple who could not find a clergyman willing to marry them. Colonists' xenophobia was not limited to the indigenous population. Antagonism to Chinese immigration had been evident since the gold rush days but became more overt and cruel during the 1880s. The predominantly British colonists of course perceived the Chinese and Aborigines differently; neither group was a serious economic threat; yet intermarriage with either was considered an abomination.[10]

This inexplicable 'inherited British certainty of racial superiority over lesser breeds'[11], not the follies of either Bamfield or Page, was the real subject of the Parliamentary debate of 18 May 1882. And it was the puritanical prejudice of the Parliamentary critics who sincerely deplored Page's regime which gave him and the Board their ultimate victory – the unchallenged right to determine future policy.

Certainly Page, reading the press reports next morning, could see that his propaganda campaign had been challenged. But the debate was not a rout. It was clear that most speakers, including his opponents Dow and Deakin, in fact favoured permanent dispersal of 'half castes' from Coranderrk and other stations. This was the policy which he, with LeSouef and Hagenauer, had been pressing upon the Board for years. It was humiliating to read the criticisms of his own behaviour which figured so prominently in the columns of the *Argus* and *Age* and galling that so many members had spoken admiringly of Mrs Bon. Still, Cameron and Anderson had ably presented the evidence he had provided about Bamfield's misdeeds and prosecution. Strickland and the justices would maintain the fiction to protect themselves. Since only Page and LeSouef's son saw the Board correspondence he need not fear that his manipulation of the facts would ever become known.

Page was no doubt disconcerted by Dow's comments on an anticipated illegitimate birth, an embarrassing scandal not yet revealed to the Board. When they returned from Bamfield's trial on 5 May a deputation of angry men led by Dunolly, Wandin and Morgan had asked the manager if he 'also' intended to send away Bella Lee (1867–1885). This 'half caste' orphan from Yackandandah had been reared in the dormitory since her arrival in 1878. Rumours about her prolonged illness and the medicines administered (seven kinds of homeopathic remedies and purgatives) were circulating among the women of the station including the teacher's wife. The Stricklands denied that she was pregnant, but when questioned, Bella confessed she had spent a night in the bush with a young newcomer, Thomas Spider (1860–1886). He was a police tracker[12] from Queensland who was admitted to Coranderrk when tuberculosis rendered him unfit for duty. It was he who reported the pregnancy to Dunolly who mentioned it in a letter to Mrs Bon next day. On 8 May John Green went to the Healesville constable to report that the teacher Mr Deans and his wife had told him the girl had been given drugs to procure an abortion. Strickland informed Page of the pregnancy two days later but was absent when constables from Healesville and Lilydale investigated on 11 May.

---

9   See Barwick 1963, 1971, 1972 for details of the Victorian Aboriginal population and the migration to Maloga and Cumeroogunga.
10 Serle 1971:295–302; see Curthoys 1973 and Markus 1977, 1979 for discussions of colonists' attitudes to racial and ethnic minorities.
11 Serle 1971:338.
12 The practice of hiring 'black trackers' from Queensland to assist Victorian police endured until the 1970s.

REBELLION AT CORANDERRK

Bella Lee and Lizzie, and their infants.

Tommy Dunolly (1856/57–1923), woman on left unidentified, on right Eda Brangy.

When confronted, the teacher upheld Mrs Strickland's ignorance of the pregnancy when dosing Bella and said Green had already heard the rumours from residents. Mrs Deans, who was not on speaking terms with Mrs Strickland who was the dormitory matron, blamed gossip heard from Mrs Caroline Morgan, Mrs Jessie Dunolly and dormitory resident Eda Brangy. Eda said she had not known of the pregnancy when she told these three women that Bella was given castor oil and wine daily for months 'to bring on her courses'. Mrs Strickland admitted giving unspecified 'simple medicines' to Bella, explaining that she had blamed the absence of menses on Bella's lasting 'cold on the chest' (probably the onset of tuberculosis, which had killed her whole family). The police accepted Mrs Strickland's account and informed their superiors that a slander had been 'got up amongst the blacks' because of their 'great dislike to Mr Strickland and his family'.[13]

Rev. Mackie's private reply to the vice-chairman's *Argus* letter, expressing dissatisfaction with Strickland's report on Lizzie's recent death and dismay about Bella's case, alerted Page to the police investigation, which Strickland had not yet mentioned.[14] He obtained the police report on 17 May and immediately telegraphed the Lilydale constable inquiring about suspicious circumstances as well as asking him to check on Strickland's report of the death. The eventual replies declared the Stricklands innocent.

Dow's knowledge of the scandal, and further press criticisms, made Page fear for his own job. On 20 May he telegraphed the Framlingham manager to come immediately without revealing that he was wanted to replace Strickland.[15] That morning the *Argus* had published a comprehensive indictment by 'Sympathiser' of the incompetence, unsympathetic attitudes and drinking habits of Board staff, as well as Mrs Bon's

---

13 BPA – Secretary's Letter Book, 82/276, 10–25 May 1882; BPA – File '1882 correspondence re Bella Lee' [CSIC 82/X4705, 8–23 May 1882].
14 BPA – Rev. A. Mackie to vice-chairman, 15 May 1882.
15 BPA – Framlingham Manager's Letter Book, William Goodall to J.H. Stähle, 21 May 1882.

letter repudiating a Cabinet member's statement to Parliament that she was satisfied with Page's apology. The *Argus* editor censured the Board and Minister for retaining Page, an officer whose 'utter want of judgment and discretion' proclaimed him unfit for his post. In the same issue 'Veritas' rebutted Halliday's letter with detailed proof of the necessity for Mrs Bon's charitable care of Mrs Bamfield and other patients and provided evidence that Bamfield was a most affectionate and responsible husband and father.

The *Argus* subsequently published Mackie's own reply to Halliday's letter which made it perfectly clear that Page had been the real author and that Page was wholly to blame for neglecting Mrs Bamfield and other patients. Mackie drew attention to the inexplicable replacement of Halliday as manager quoting a resident's complaint that 'When we get used to a man, and begin to like him, then the Board takes him away'. Two letters from 'Fair Play', who described himself as Page's friend for 16 years, insisted that Page's unique lapse from courtesy was the result of persecution by Mrs Bon. Editorial comment appended to each letter ridiculed the attempt by 'Fair Play' to prove Mrs Bon's animus and defended her obligation as a member of the inquiry to question Page's dubious accounts. The *Argus* contemptuously noted that Page showed no contrition for his offensive letter and had been forced to apologise to save his job. On 23 May a long editorial advised members of Parliament to demand a thorough investigation of the Board's administration.[16]

Later that day a special Board meeting was called to 'appoint somebody in place of Strickland'. Page presented two reports which the worried vice-chairman had demanded the previous day: one was an 'explanation' of his notorious letter, the other a statement of the number of illegitimate births at Coranderrk. Page said there had been none 'for six years'; there had been only one in 19 years as Green and others had told the inquiry.[17] The minutes record that it was Anderson who put the motion to send the Framlingham manager Goodall to Coranderrk for a fortnight as the Minister had promised to decide the station's fate within the week. Page's minutes did not mention the reason Goodall was ordered to 'go at once': Strickland had sent word of Bella's miscarriage early on 22 May. Because of the debate comments and police investigation, the Board dared not withhold the news from their Minister. With Strickland's report went the police file dismissing the abortion allegations and a covering note from Page asking Grant to take note that Green was 'the author of this scandalous report'.[18]

Meanwhile, the father, Spider, well acquainted with police procedures, had called the Healesville constable to examine the foetus, explaining that he and others believed the medicines had killed Bella's child. The constable (who had lied to defend the Stricklands at the 1881 inquiry and Bamfield's trial) reported that Mrs Strickland said she had only once dosed Bella with castor oil since his last inquiry. He dismissed the abortion rumours and once more blamed 'a section of the Blacks who are dissatisfied with Mr Strickland's management'.[19] Dunolly anxiously wrote to Mrs Bon asking whether the drugs named had killed the five-month foetus. It was an innocent query to a trusted friend known to have considerable medical knowledge. Aghast at Dunolly's letter, Mrs Bon advised him to collect written evidence from Bella and her closest friend, Eda Brangy, about the medicines administered. She also asked Bamfield to make sure his niece Eda wrote to her about what she knew.[20]

Grant tabled the letters of Page and Strickland and the report of the first police investigation in Parliament on 31 May. Richardson's request for all papers on the Bella Lee case was prompted by insinuations in local newspapers rather than information from Mrs Bon.[21] Certainly, she had made no mention of this matter,

---

16   *Argus*, 20, 22 and 23 May 1882.
17   BPA – W. Anderson to Page, 22 May 1882; A.M.A. Page to W. Anderson, 23 May 1882.
18   BPA – Minutes, 23 May 1882; File '1882 Correspondence re Bella Lee' [CSIC 82/X4705, 23 May 1882].
19   BPA – File '1882 Correspondence re Bella Lee' [CSIC 82/X5826, 24 May 1882].
20   BPA – File '1882 Correspondence re Bella Lee' [82/X5826] Declarations by Eda Brangy, Bella Lee and Thomas Dunolly, 14–15 June 1882.
21   Victorian Parliamentary Debates, Session 1882:474.

and no intemperate criticisms of public servants, in letters sent to the Chief Secretary's office on 29 May. One letter urged the Minister to take direct control and permit the four senior dormitory girls to take paid employment elsewhere. Her lengthy submission to the permanent head of Grant's department proved a more effective form of lobbying. Page's superior officer (well aware of the administrative deficiencies of a board structure) circulated copies with the inquiry report in mid-June although other correspondence was merely summarised for Cabinet members.[22]

Mrs Bon's depiction of Coranderrk Aborigines as businesslike Christians anxious to make their station self-supporting was influential because her canny management of her own vast estate was well known. Her role as a major employer of rural labour gave weight to her description of the Coranderrk workers as good shearers who spent their earnings 'on decent clothing and furniture for their houses'. Her criticisms of their deprivation and suggestions for better management were factual and shrewd. Mrs Bon's analysis of the mistaken or disreputable arguments for abandonment of Coranderrk added to the moral force of her well-known exposition of the reasons why its retention was important to the Aborigines. She reported that as a regular hospital visitor, she saw all Coranderrk patients whose dying request had 'invariably been "take me home to die among my own people"', yet they were 'put into paupers graves wherever convenient, without even Christian burial'.

These facts, and her discovery of 45 unbaptised children at Coranderrk, were a reproach to a government much concerned with the niceties of Christian doctrine. Her reminder that Aborigines taken to court by the Board were undefended by counsel perhaps did as much to redeem Bamfield's character as her explanation that his mother, 'the Chiefess of the tribe, gave him to me many years ago'. Bamfield, she said, earned 12 shillings a day with food and lodging when able to shear for her and was 'a superior black – too much so for his "protectors"'. Mrs Bon's reputation for practicality and philanthropy and her advice as a landholder with wealth and influence, equalled by none of the active Board members except perhaps Macredie, could not be wholly ignored by Cabinet.

Page probably had no inkling that the head of the Chief Secretary's department was impressed by Mrs Bon's criticisms, but he was well aware that his job was at risk, and busied himself collecting evidence against the critics he feared. Strickland supplied him with a statutory declaration that he had 'read' Mrs Bon's letter inciting Bamfield at the time of the inquiry. But there is no evidence that the former Board secretary Smyth, just returned from India, answered Page's request for a rejoinder to the criticisms made by Green and Syme of the 1874 minutes which caused Green's removal from Coranderrk.[23]

Others were lobbying too. The Chief Secretary had already received a copy of Rev. Hagenauer's letter to his local member that both Gippsland missionaries opposed the abolition of the Board. Hagenauer reported that he:

> could very easily get up a petition in favour of the Board and Inspector signed by all the blacks in this district and even from the other stations, but you are well aware that even the best of the Aborigines are not competent to form an opinion on the subject.[24]

Hagenauer's view that Aborigines should have no voice in their management was shared by the Stähles, now Moravian missionaries in Anderson's electorate. The protests provoked by their authoritarian rule at Lake Condah were nearly as enduring as the rebellion at Coranderrk but so severely repressed by Page that no hint of complaint had reached the press. The Stähles sent letters defending the Board to several concerned members of Parliament. Ambitious Mary Stähle, who had reproved Page's negligence a few

---

22 CSIC 82/X4879, 82/X4907, 29 May 1882.
23 BPA – Strickland to Page, 29 May 1882; Secretary's Letter Book, 5 June 1882.
24 CSIC 82/X4926, Rev. A Hagenauer to A. McLean, MLA, 26 May 1882.

months earlier, forwarded copies of the correspondence to the Board secretary.[25] She now warmly defended him and offered spiteful criticisms of Mrs Bon's unwomanly actions in letters to the politician (Francis Longmore) who had most strongly urged Page's dismissal in the recent debate. Page perhaps felt some gratitude that Mrs Stähle had influenced Berry's former Lands Minister, but it was disturbing to learn from his letter that there was:

> very strong feeling among politicians that there has been gross mismanagement of the blacks at Coranderrk and two or three Boards have reported this; the feeling of the House is that the Aboriginal Board must be done away with and the management placed in the hands of the Chief Secretary – I lean to that view.

It was clear from Mrs Stähle's earlier letter that Page need have no illusions about her motive for this ostentatious display of loyalty. Her assurances that her husband shared her detestation of Green and Mrs Bon, her wistful hints about wishing to see Coranderrk again and her delicate innuendoes about the Framlingham manager's competence for his rumoured promotion as its manager had clearly revealed her furious jealousy that her husband's claim to reinstatement was not recognised.[26] No doubt Page felt there were far too many former managers of Coranderrk waiting in the wings. Neither Stähle nor Green asked for reinstatement, then or later. But Halliday had declared himself an applicant for Strickland's post and had written to express his gratitude for Page's professed support. The teacher Deans was another 'aspirant to the throne of Coranderrk' according to William Goodall who took charge on 26 May. A Healesville resident had warned that Deans spoke openly of his umbrage that the Board had appointed Goodall, 'his junior and even inferior', as temporary manager. As Deans and his wife spent most of their time gossiping in the cottages 'to no good purpose and certainly not for the love they have for the people' Goodall suggested Deans be replaced by a female teacher who could serve as dormitory matron.[27]

Of course, Page had briefed Goodall, before sending the only qualified manager who did not covet the post, on his own distrust of staff and residents. Page simply wanted him there to silence criticism until Cabinet approved abandonment. He sent non-committal replies to all Goodall's outraged letters about the 'uninhabitable' dwellings, pleas for other urgently needed improvements and suggestions for future management. Page was displeased by Goodall's support for residents' 'justified complaints'. He was even more embarrassed by Goodall's euphoric reports that Coranderrk people were kind, cooperative, well-behaved, obedient and – under the leadership of Bamfield – eager to work. Page's replies were pessimistic: such comments undermined his own plans to remove unruly Aborigines and confirmed the incompetence of the protege he had maintained in office for four years. Page did not realise that Coranderrk residents genuinely welcomed the arrival of an experienced farmer, teacher and preacher who consulted them about the management of their farm and came to work beside them. They of course knew Goodall of old for he had visited regularly as a trusted friend of the Greens. Goodall's family had come from Tasmania to farm in the Warrnambool district when he was a child. He had taught for three years at a local school before he was hired at the age of 23 (at the request of the Aborigines and with Green's warm recommendation) to take charge of Framlingham in 1869. Although the Board's niggardly funding had always discouraged farm development, Framlingham had been the home of a loyal and contented community ever since.[28]

---

25   BPA – H.J. Wrixon to Rev. J.H. Stähle, 2 June 1882; Francis Longmore to Dr Johnstone, 16 June 1882; Mary Stähle to Francis Longmore, 22 June 1882. (It is assumed that Rev. Stähle had remarried).
26   BPA – Mary Stähle to Page, 6 February 1882.
27   BPA – William Goodall to Page, 6 June 1882.
28   Barwick 1981; Critchett 1980.

Page did not understand why Goodall was so well received at Coranderrk but he did know that his advice on future management was relatively disinterested. Goodall wanted to return to his family and lifelong friends at Framlingham. On 6 June he suggested taking with him the 'nice looking sensible' girl Bella Lee as Strickland had repeatedly refused to marry her to Spider and would not let them meet. Goodall himself favoured the marriage as the couple were 'very much attached' but there was no house available.

Only Jennings and Macredie, Curr and LeSouef attended the regular Board meeting on 7 June 1882. Page's minutes mentioned his report that Goodall expected to have the station 'in working order' within the fortnight but offered no explanation of ensuing resolutions. Page was instructed to inform Briggs and other men wanting farm blocks that the Board could not consider their request as the future of Coranderrk was in the government's hands. He was also ordered to write the Chief Secretary 'repeating' the Board's request for abandonment of Coranderrk plus the Moravian missions in Gippsland and the Wimmera, in exchange for a reserve on the Murray. This had been the Curr–Page scheme in June 1880, approved when Macredie and LeSouef, the main supporters of the Presbyterian–Moravian missions, were absent.

Page wrote to the Coranderrk men on 8 June. But a scandal erupted that day which precluded sending the Minister a proposal which would antagonise the Presbyterians in Cabinet and Parliament. The wife of the inquiry member Steel, calling to farewell her friend Mrs Strickland, reported that the police had received another complaint signed by many residents including Bella. Questioned in front of Mrs Steel and the Strickland daughters, and thoroughly frightened by Mrs Strickland's reproach that 'you would put me in prison by signing such letters', 16-year-old Bella tearfully denied knowledge of the contents of the complaint (drafted by Mrs Deans). Bella subsequently assured Goodall that Mrs Strickland had not known of her pregnancy. Goodall hastily completed the report Page had instructed him to prepare on Bella's case. He was convinced of Bella's obvious affection for the family who had reared her and impressed by their assiduous care of the dormitory children.

Sympathetic to Mrs Strickland's anxiety about the insinuations in local newspaper reports, Goodall strongly supported her plea that the Board 'bring the instigators of this foul slander to justice'. But later in the day, Deans produced a letter written by Bella which listed all the drugs given, including purgative 'salts', hours before the miscarriage.

Goodall hastily rode to Healesville. He telegraphed Page to come at once because new evidence confirmed an abortion attempt and brought the police for a third investigation. The constable again derided the complaint but his superiors disagreed and advised further inquiry.[29] Goodall's telegram meanwhile sent the Board secretary and vice-chairman to seek ministerial approval for a full investigation. Failing to find Grant, they approached O'Loghlen who was Attorney General as well as Premier. He ordered the district police magistrate J.A. Panton to investigate. After a thorough briefing by Page, Panton went alone to Coranderrk for his inquiry of 14–15 June. He had already made a few unofficial visits during his long association with the Healesville bench and Grant's rejection of his offer to serve on the 1881 board of inquiry probably still rankled for he prided himself on his 'intimate knowledge of the character of the Aborigines'. The justices' letter defending their sentencing of Bamfield had mentioned Panton's stern warning when acquitting Bamfield of an earlier (and equally malicious) charge. Magistrate Panton had an urgent reason for censuring the Aborigines and Mrs Bon: the monthly court at Healesville had just been cancelled because the justices refused to attend. The *Daily Telegraph* on 5 June reported that their boycott was due to resentment of Bamfield's release a month earlier.

---

29   BPA – File '1882 Correspondence re Bella Lee' [CSIC 82/X5826, Goodall to Page, 8 June 1882, Constable Tevlin to Superintendent of Police, Bourke District, 8 June 1882; Superintendent to Chief Commissioner of Police, 12 June 1882].

The magistrate's bullying treatment of witnesses was apparent in the transcripts of evidence; his prejudice was obvious in his report. He believed firm control was needed to 'discourage underhand outside interference' and check the 'mutinous temper' of residents; he advised monthly visits by the district police magistrate who would 'parade the inmates', deal with all complaints and punish those who made frivolous or false charges. His report seriously distorted much of what the Aboriginal witnesses said partly through ignorance but mainly by selective emphasis.[30]

Panton ignored the clear evidence that in their mother's absence, the Strickland daughters (possibly aware of Bella's plight) had dosed her intensively to restore menses; Mrs Strickland, called home because the sickly girl became seriously ill, continued to administer the purgatives and hot mustard baths, which were the popular home remedies of the time, right up to the day Bella miscarried. None of the Stricklands were examined by the magistrate.

Eda Brangy was the main witness as she had carried the news of Bella's treatment outside the dormitory. Panton branded this nervous 17-year-old a liar because she contradicted herself and described her as 'a low type of pure Aboriginal young woman and, I understand, a niece of Punch'. He misinterpreted Dunolly's attempt to get accurate information from Bella and Eda implying that Dunolly had fomented a scandal at Mrs Bon's direction. Panton's report deliberately minimised the role of the teachers, ignoring Dunolly's testimony that Deans had told him 'he was going to put an action up against Mr Strickland. He said "Tush what's the use of getting Bella's evidence in a case like this she has been cuddled and bought over by Mrs Strickland"'. Panton emphasised Deans' own attempts to blame Green and Mrs Bon but ignored his statement that, over six years, he had found Coranderrk people strictly truthful. Panton's report omitted or distorted the evidence – emphasised in Goodall's private report to Page about his own role as assistant in the inquiry – that Mrs Deans originated the suspicions of abortion, wrote the complaint to the police and collected signatures for it and (because Eda and Bella had refused to write complaints for the teachers) stole the letters the girls wrote for Barak's aide Dunolly. Mrs Deans sent copies to the addressee, Mrs Bon, but kept the originals for her husband's planned lawsuit.

Goodall's report blamed the teachers, not Mrs Bon and the Kulin, but warned Page that the Deans could not be proven guilty.[31] He praised the Kulin witnesses, except for spiteful Eda, but wondered at their enmity to the Stricklands; he did not know that Eda had bravely protested the Stricklands' persecution of little David Barak at the 1881 inquiry, or how bitterly she and others resented the false prosecution of the Taungurong clan-head Bamfield. Goodall's report and further letters to Page explained what the magistrate had known but deliberately omitted from his report: Deans was suing Strickland for malicious slander because the manager had told the 1881 inquiry that Mrs Deans had criticised the morality of the Strickland daughters and described their home as 'little more than a house of common resort'.[32] The magistrate was no doubt inclined to protect the good name of these young women, and concerned that exposure of the jealous squabbling of European staff would lower their status in the eyes of the Aborigines. By depicting the Aboriginal witnesses as credulous simpletons led astray by Mrs Bon the magistrate could placate the Healesville justices and assist future managers to maintain law and order at Coranderrk. He too (to Page's dismay) assumed that the station would remain; as it was in his jurisdiction he had no wish to encourage the occupants to flout the authority of the manager and the Board.

News of Panton's inquiry did not reach the press and his verdict was not available when the inquiry report and other papers were at last circulated to Cabinet (contrary to Grant's statements in the House) between 9 and 16 June. On 8 June the *Argus* published a letter from 'Kawberr' of Healesville demanding

---

30 BPA – File '1882 Correspondence re Bella Lee' [CSIC 82/X5826], Report of J.A. Panton, P.M., 24 June 1882.
31 BPA – File 82/876, William Goodall to Page, 15 June 1882.
32 BPA – William Goodall to Page, 15, 17 and 23 June 1882.

that the Coranderrk residents be removed to Gippsland and on 13 June a reply from 'Verax' described their attachment to land which was their 'rightful possession'. 'Verax' (seemingly privy to decisions made at the last meeting) reported that the Board was 'even up till this date' pressing the government to sell the reserve. He, like previous writers, queried the Board's reasons for making all decisions in secret and pointed out that the public had seen no inspection report on any station since Page's appointment. Finally 'Verax' condemned Grant's 'possuming' to avoid Parliamentary debate: the prolonged delay was cruel, he argued, and it was doubtful that 'anything will "turn up" to help the poor Chief Secretary'.

Further criticisms of the Board's competence appeared in a report on neglected wanderers in the Western District. 'Amicus' urged Grant to abolish the Board in a letter to the *Argus* of 16 June and described the plight of three Coranderrk families camped under a bridge near Alexandra. Two families had left home to earn money to pay their butcher's bills, while an aged couple said they had come for a last glimpse of their own country as 'the Board is going to send us away from Coranderrk'. Strickland's explanation in the *Argus* of 24 June that they had left the station against his advice was an ineffective rejoinder to the heart-rending account of their sufferings by 'Amicus'.

Press debate on the reform of Aboriginal administration had continued for more than a year. It was now the middle of June and O'Loghlen's ministry could no longer defer a decision on the 1881 inquiry report. But the government had barely survived a challenge on its budget during the preceding week. The attack had come mainly from the conservatives, and Cabinet members were in no mood to take action which might provoke a confidence motion for the third time. Their options were few. Abolition of the Board was politically impossible because of the recommendations of the 1877 Royal Commission (written of course by the Board Vice-Chairman), the well-publicised defence provided by the Anglican mission committee and the opinions of a minority of the board of inquiry and the conservative *Argus*.

The 1869 *Aborigines Act* provided no means of dismissing Board members; in a stalemate over policy, the Minister could only repeal the legislation which served as the Board's charter or else swamp opposition by appointing additional members. Except for Grant himself, members of O'Loghlen's Cabinet had little ambition to be known as reformers and, by this time, their command of Parliament was too frail to ensure the passage of amending legislation. Direct control of Aboriginal affairs would add an unwanted, contentious and expensive responsibility to the already overburdened Chief Secretary's portfolio. Abandonment of Coranderrk was equally impossible because of the clear evidence against removal provided by the 1877 and 1881 inquiries, the opinion of the Presbyterian mission committee and the united opposition of the press. Closure of the station would please only the Board, its secretary and some of Cameron's electors. It would create enormous controversy and it would be costly as the residents would have to be rehoused elsewhere.

For O'Loghlen's government in June 1882, there was only one politically feasible way to end the embarrassment caused by Grant's sponsorship, 10 months earlier, of a public inquiry into the behaviour of his subordinates. They had to reform the Board which had openly challenged the Minister. They could only do so by altering the membership. They had to placate the critics by forbidding the sale of Coranderrk and ensuring that the unanimous recommendations of the board of inquiry were implemented. The three Presbyterians already nominated by the Board in April would probably be acceptable to the most prominent critics; they were also likely to be sensitive to the political problems of the Minister. Morrison, as headmaster of Scotch College a prestigious Melbourne school, was presumably sympathetic to the ministry's stance in the raging debate over aid to church schools, while Officer and Cameron could probably be manipulated by appealing to their party loyalties and their own Parliamentary ambitions. The Coranderrk land would be available to Cameron's electors soon enough: the 'pure blacks' were decreasing fast and all colonists agreed that 'half castes' should be dispersed to earn their keep. The government could trust Cameron to force the Board to implement his report and to placate his own electors. Behind the scenes the Minister could bargain with the new members; in public, he could continue to elude direct responsibility by blaming the Board for unpopular decisions. The only real problem for Cabinet was how best to silence the few noisy liberals who supported the Aborigines' complaints and how to persuade Parliament, the press and the public that the responsible Minister had acted responsibly in adopting this compromise. The Bella Lee case was providential.

The critical issue was Grant's ministerial responsibility for the behaviour of the public servants Page and Strickland who were officially employees of his department although never subject to normal departmental control. Grant could not ignore the evidence of negligence contained in the inquiry report, yet he could not censure these subordinates without embarrassing the Board who defended them and the superior officers responsible for them. The members of Cameron's inquiry had been partisan from the beginning and the two factions had canvassed their views in the press so long and so heatedly that neither Cabinet nor the public wholly trusted their opinions. The magistrate Panton's supposedly impartial assessment would provide an independent test of the negligence of Board staff, the veracity of the Aborigines' complaints and the interference of European sympathisers. His opinion was also important to the Attorney General and Solicitor General who had failed to placate the angry justices at Healesville. Panton was urged to hurry his report when the opposition member Richardson gave notice of his question asking Grant to investigate the Bella Lee case.

The permanent head of the Chief Secretary's department compiled extracts from Panton's summary for his Minister's reply on 27 June. It was a selective compilation (because the improper behaviour of public servants was still a major subject of debate) and made no mention of staff involvement or the magistrate's scathing criticisms of 'slovenly unsuitable management'. Parliamentary convention forced Grant to defend a besieged government and public service. He cared little for the Kulin but a great deal for justice. Showing a last glimmer of that idealism which had made him a forceful reformer, Grant made no attempt to hide his contempt for the magistrate Panton's opinions and his own subordinate's motives in choosing these excerpts. He identified the author and compiler before reading the prepared statement which said Panton had abandoned his investigation on concluding that a false and malicious scandal had been fomented by interested persons 'outside the station'. Grant then invited his Parliamentary colleagues to read 'the evidence taken' which he had brought to the House. There was no discussion. Perhaps the House was genuinely indifferent; perhaps even Grant's opponents were embarrassed by the old man's humiliation. The *Argus* merely mentioned the magistrate's conclusion about outside interference and devoted more space to a report that Strickland had been relieved of duty and the Board had installed Goodall temporarily until a permanent appointment could be made.[33]

The magistrate's report strongly urged that Goodall be retained as manager but the Board had not known this when Page offered him the post. On the day after Panton's visit Goodall agreed, on suitable terms, to assist the Board. But when Page wrote on 26 June offering only an extra £50 a year (and warning that Goodall might have less than a year's tenure as the Board was expecting abandonment) Goodall immediately declined. He was of course bargaining for a salary of £300 a year when he pointed out the drawbacks of this insecure promotion. He explained that, although all residents were kind and respectful, he felt an indefinable mistrust rather than the true sympathy he felt for 'my own people at Framlingham'. He urged deferral of any appointment 'to see how they take the news that Green is not coming back'. He was convinced that the majority would only be satisfied with Green's return. He reported that residents had told him a few days earlier that:

---

33 Victorian Parliamentary Debates, Session 1882:793; *Argus* 28 June 1882.

should any other be appointed they would at once repair to Melbourne and renew their agitation in his behalf and not cease until they got what they wanted. Of course I cautioned them … that I thought such behaviour would either result in their banishment or in all probability the abandonment of Coranderrk altogether, but of course you know better than I what talking to a Coranderrk half-caste means.[34]

The Board ignored Goodall's objections probably because the *Argus* comments on the Minister's speech and Strickland's removal made delay seem unwise. The five active members attended a special meeting on 28 June to appoint a permanent manager. LeSouef and Jennings proposed appointment of Goodall at £250 a year; LeSouef and Sheppard also won a motion to issue press releases on Board meetings. The first of these, published by the *Argus* on 30 June, announced that Goodall had been chosen from many candidates and pointedly remarked that the Board had not yet received Panton's report on Bella Lee. The terms of Goodall's appointment were not made public. Page had warned that he would have no claim to compensation if the Board's recommendation for abandonment succeeded, but his successor at Framlingham had been hired on the understanding that he would resign in Goodall's favour 'if you find you cannot succeed at Coranderrk'. The threat was clear: if Goodall could not subdue the protests at Coranderrk the Kulin would lose their home.[35]

O'Loghlen's government never publicly proclaimed a decision on the 1881 inquiry report but on 29 June Grant authorised gazettal of the four new members who were to reform the Board: the Board's nominees Cameron, Officer and Morrison, and Alfred Deakin. The *Argus*, publicising the appointments on 1 July, reported it was 'understood' that the government had decided not to abandon Coranderrk. The Board's dismay at their Minister's inclusion of the critic Deakin was short-lived. On 4 July he resigned as an explicit protest against the government's irresponsible decision. Grant accepted Deakin's resignation – 10 weeks later.[36] But it was not mentioned in Parliament that night, when Dow attempted to censure Grant for breaking his promise to allow debate before taking action on the inquiry report. Opposition indignation was not sufficient to muster the needed votes for an adjournment motion permitting debate.[37] Most members of Parliament probably accepted the political realities which dictated the Minister's decision. Some were influenced by the propaganda about outside influence; some assumed that Goodall's appointment indicated the Board's willingness to reform their administration; some were merely reluctant to offend Cameron, Officer and Anderson – all respected members of the House – by further criticism. Some, no doubt, cared nothing for Aboriginal welfare and were weary of the whole dispute.

Only the Coranderrk people were dissatisfied by the government's convenient compromise. Two days later the Kulin leaders once again waited upon the Chief Secretary. Grant received them but the brief *Argus* report did not describe the deputation's arguments for Green's reinstatement nor Grant's sentiments when he had to tell them he would not intervene. Grant declared that the government was determined to retain the Board which, the *Argus* reported on 7 July 'alone must decide questions affecting the management'. The Board issued no press release on their special meeting of 7 July which was called by Anderson because the Minister had promised to refer the deputation to them. Seven members, including the new appointees Cameron and Officer, waited in vain. They occupied themselves with a debate on Panton's report and the transcripts of evidence. Convinced of the teachers' guilt, they decided to dismiss Mr and Mrs Deans.

Knowing that appeal to the Board was useless, the Kulin men had walked home, accommodating their pace to the lameness of the old clan-head Barak. He had made this journey so many times with other men, all dead now. He alone remained of the deputation that had gone to the Governor's levee almost 20 years

---

34 BPA – Goodall to Page, 16 and 27 June 1882.
35 BPA – Minutes 28 June 1882; Secretary's Letter Book, 28 June 1882.
36 *Victorian Government Gazette*, 1882:1602, 1883:33.
37 Victorian Parliamentary Debates, Session 1882:885.

ago when Coranderrk was new. He could remember the earlier deputations with his cousin Wonga and John Green, to ask Smyth's help to form a school at the Yering camp; and, before that, the triumphant journey with Wonga and William Thomas to help the Taungurong clansmen mark out their reserve at the Acheron. The men who walked with him now could not remember the mournful journey to find a refuge in the mountains when the Woiworung clans were ordered to leave their land at Melbourne in the 1840s. None of them had been born when Barak first made the journey to the Coranderrk Creek, when all the land was owned by kinsmen, before the *Ngamajet* came.

Barak's deputation had knowingly risked the last of the Kulin land to champion Green. The new manager Goodall was more concerned with his own security than their despair when he reported that 'The answer they got from the Chief Secretary has evidently done them good. They came home rather crestfallen this time and no flags flying'. Reassured that they had no complaint against him, when all came cheerfully to work after the failed deputation (although 'things looked dark and stormy yesterday, they were gathered in knots about the village'), Goodall assured Page that all discontent stemmed from anxiety about their land. He urgently begged Page to 'get an assurance from the Government that the station will not be broken up'. Goodall naively reported that the Board's opponents had convinced the Aborigines that their protectors planned to abolish Coranderrk. He suggested Grant would give a prompt decision against abandonment if he understood that neither manager nor men could put their hearts into the work while the future remained uncertain.[38]

Goodall's ignorance was not feigned. Page was the only staff member aware of the secret endeavours to persuade a succession of Ministers to sell four of the six reserves the Board had been appointed to protect. Certainly the annual reports since 1875 had quoted the advice of Curr, Godfrey and LeSouef on removal of the Coranderrk residents. But the report released in December 1881 was the first to admit that the Board had recommended the sale of this reserve. Goodall and the missionary managers had been enlisted to defend the Board and ridicule the Coranderrk protests in total ignorance that the Board had repeatedly tried to close and sell their stations.

For seven years E.M. Curr and his friends had controlled Board policy and had allowed first Ogilvie, then Page, to administer Aboriginal affairs in secret without check. These gentlemen had caused the resignation of most of the founding members of the Board; from July 1882 they were in turn displaced by the three devout and influential Presbyterians they had nominated for membership. LeSouef and Curr won their motion to give Anderson a second term as vice-chairman in July 1882. But Officer, Cameron and Morrison held this office in turn until 1896.[39] Cameron was the main force for reform. He was determined to implement his own report and – having been involved in three investigations of the Board's affairs since 1876 was too knowledgeable to be fooled by Page. On 12 July he won a motion (passed unanimously) that in future Board meetings would be open to the press. He also insisted that the Board meet fortnightly until affairs at Coranderrk had been reorganised. He ensured that the members made regular visits to the stations.

Page's power, which had depended on his control of information, was severely checked. Under the new members' conscientious supervision he was galvanised into making tours of inspection and forced to provide detailed monthly reports. Soon most of the administrative reforms demanded by the Addendum A authors were implemented. Even the tone of Page's correspondence was marvellously transformed. Probably the Board never learned the full extent of Page's manipulation of information in the past but

---

38   BPA – Goodall to Page 10 July 1882.
39   BPA – Minutes 12 July 1882. Officer was vice-chairman 1883–84; Cameron 1884–87; Morrison 1887–90; then Officer 1890–96.

within months they discovered, and angrily forbad, his practice of encouraging managers (in this case Stähle) to read and confiscate residents' mail. At Cameron's insistence they ordered Page to publish separate accounts for each station in the annual reports.[40]

Page's rancour against Mrs Bon increased as each humiliating reform was forced upon him. There was no way he could resist without risking his job but he quickly realised that he could use the press scrutiny of Board meetings to disseminate propaganda in his own defence and embarrass her. Since old and new members shared his resentment of Mrs Bon's interference they did not check his attempts to make her a scapegoat for the Board's internal difficulties. When she sent Goodall a doctor's instructions for the care of Mrs Eliza Bamfield (suffering from a neglected abscess for 18 months) the members resolved to inform her that their staff took orders only from the Board. Anderson signed Page's letter. Mrs Bon retorted that the vice-chairman ought to visit the stations 'and make yourself acquainted with the people and their requirements' so she would not have to help them.[41]

Anderson had in fact delayed sending the letter until after he had made his first visit to Coranderrk on 14 July. He was accompanied by Cameron, who had made at least four visits since 1876; by Curr, who had last made the journey on his third visit in 1879; and by LeSouef, who had inspected in 1875 and gone up once on other business in 1876. The minutes noted that they reached no agreement on needed improvements. Their main task was to hear Deans defend himself against dismissal. As well as Magistrate Panton's transcripts the Board had Goodall's reports of Deans' 'reckless statements' about the Strickland girls. The teachers were dismissed from the end of July. Goodall reported that their departure after six years of service was marked by little or no demonstration; the *Argus* announced that the Coranderrk people had presented them with an engraved silver teapot as a 'token of esteem'.[42]

Press interest had not abated; neither had Grant's concern nor Mrs Bon's indignation. But the Board could not publicly admit their deadlock on the changes demanded by Cameron. Disagreement was apparent by mid-July when the old members apparently blocked Cameron's plans to rebuild Coranderrk. Curr's friend Sheppard ceased to attend after one meeting with the new members. By August Syme's *Leader* was gleefully publicising the Board's 'disunity'. Page's minutes rarely identified the sponsors of motions and never tallied votes but they nevertheless reveal that reform of the Board's policies and administrative practices was part of the agenda for all meetings from July 1882 until the newcomers effectively displaced the old guard a year later. Press releases and press attendance at meetings enabled the members and their secretary to present 'strategy statements' intended to influence press, public and Parliament as well as opponents within the Board.[43]

After Anderson's rebuff Mrs Bon apparently ceased to hope for internal reform of the Board. Subsequent complaints went directly to the Chief Secretary or the *Argus*. The first strategy was more effective. The sympathetic permanent head of this department used phrases from her letters (anonymously and sometimes within days) in his own queries to the Board.[44] He had ensured that her advice reached the Cabinet in June. On 13 July he wrote requesting the Board to provide Grant with a statement of policy on hiring out girls. This was one of the inquiry's unanimous recommendations. Addendum A had condemned the Board's inexplicable refusal to pay, or release for paid service, the four dormitory servants at Coranderrk. Mrs Bon had subsequently asked the Minister and the permanent head to intervene. Although Page may have resented his superior's inquiries, and perhaps suspected the source, he could not

---

40 BPA – Minutes 8 November 1882; *Age* 11 November 1882.
41 BPA – Minutes 12 July 1882; Secretary's Letter Book, 26 July 1882; Anne. F. Bon to William Anderson, 14 August 1882.
42 BPA – Goodall to Page, 23 June and 31 July 1882; *Argus* 16 August 1882.
43 Weaver 1981:x–xi.
44 BPA – Secretary's Letter Book, 3 August and 2 October 1882, 9 February 1883 (replies to Under Secretary's requests of 13 July and 15 December 1882); CSIC 82/X4879, 82/X11149, Anne F. Bon to Chief Secretary, 29 May and 9 December 1882.

ignore them. On 2 August the Presbyterian clergyman Morrison seconded LeSouef's compromise motion: to seek the views of the five experienced station managers on the disputed issues of future policy and the need for revision of the 1869 *Aborigines Act* as well as standardising disciplinary rules at all stations.

Journalists were present for the first time on 18 August 1882 when the Board heard the missions' supervisor Hagenauer, as chairman of the two-day conference, present the managers' advice. As their discussions were limited by the Board's instructions, most of their 17 resolutions concerned discipline at the stations. They agreed that men could work elsewhere so long as they paid for the support of their families and advised that all youths should be apprenticed or be compelled to work at home. But they strongly opposed outside employment of females and the removal of any children from the stations. Nevertheless, Hagenauer and another Moravian missionary won their motion that 'all lawful means should be adopted to raise the half castes to independence, and to merge into the general population'. They specified no method or timetable for achieving this goal. No one seconded Goodall's amendment substituting the word Aborigines. Only he and Green, of all the Victorian officials, had ever believed that the 'blacks' were as intelligent and capable as 'half castes'.

The managers considered revision of the 1869 Act unnecessary as discipline could be enforced by utilising the powers it afforded together with existing vagrancy and liquor laws. They gave formal support to the existing practice of withdrawing rations from able-bodied adults who would not work. They insisted residents must have written permission to leave the stations or obtain employment elsewhere. They supported one of Page's innovations: punishment of 'refractory' residents by banishment to another station or 'otherwise' as the Board directed. Other resolutions praised the existing administrative structure and insisted that all complaints to government must be relayed through the Board and 'no outside influence should be permitted'. The managers of the two Anglican stations sponsored most of the restrictive rules but Hagenauer's report mentioned no disagreement. At the Board meeting Hagenauer added his own lengthy statement on the need to protect girls from the advances of the 'class of white men' they would encounter as servants. He also argued that the stations held fewer than a dozen girls fit to be hired out and they were needed at home.[45]

The *Leader*, unimpressed by this attack on the inquiry's recommendations, retaliated with a scornful article (probably written by Dow or G.A. Syme himself) which suggested the conference was an attempt to bolster the Board's 'decaying reputation' and criticised the paternalistic sentiments of the managers. Hagenauer reappeared at the next meeting on 30 August with a pious rejoinder to the *Leader* attack which explained the benevolent intent of the new rules. The journalists ignored his defence of the Board in their reports. To the Board's dismay the *Argus* of 31 August also included criticism from Mrs Bon and the Coranderrk leaders.[46]

Press attendance at the August meetings had, for the first time, given the Kulin advance warning of Board plans. They were furious about announced decisions on the hiring of a dormitory matron and teacher and employment of European contractors for completion of the boundary fence. Goodall had successfully employed Kulin women to manage the dormitory and had urged re-appointment of their old friend Miss Nina Robertson, teacher at Framlingham since Ogilvie dismissed her for supporting their protests in 1876. The teacher, Joseph Shaw, named by the Board had been notorious for his cruelty to Lake Condah residents a decade earlier. Goodall had urged Page to pay residents for fencing. And for three months he had pleaded for replacement of most of the dwellings because the walls were falling and they had 'roofs like sieves'. He suggested the nine worth retaining could be repaired by the competent carpenter William Parker, a Jajowrong pioneer too weakened by tuberculosis for regular farm labour.

---

45 BPA – Minutes, 2 and 18 August 1882; *Age* and *Argus* 19 August 1882.
46 BPA – Report of F.A. Hagenauer, 30 August 1882; *Age* and *Argus* 31 August 1882.

REBELLION AT CORANDERRK

The government architect, sent up at Cameron's insistence in August, agreed with Goodall and the residents that all dwellings built before 1878 were uninhabitable. His report reminded the Board he had said so in 1878. To house residents decently the Board had to line and repair all huts and build 12 new cottages plus staff dwellings. To Page's chagrin he praised the transformation of the station under Goodall for whom residents now worked 'willingly and cheerfully'.[47]

The Coranderrk elders had learned a good deal about effective strategies in their experience of European-style politics during the various inquiries since 1876. They shrewdly imitated the emotive style of other letters to the editor in their own protest about decisions made without consultation. The letter published by the *Argus* on 31 August 1882 contained the signatures or marks of Barak and his speakers Wandin, Dunolly and Bamfield, plus Parker, Morgan and four more senior Kulin and Pangerang men:

> Sir, – We beg of you to put our little Column in you valuable paper please. We have seen and heard that the mangers of all the stations and the Central Board to have had a meeting about what to be done, so we have heard that there is going to be very strict rules on the station and those rules will be to much for us, it seems we are all going to be treated like slaves, far as we heard of it, – We wish to ask those Managor [sic] of the station Did we steal anything out of the colony or murdered any one or are we prisoners or convict. We should think we are all free as any white men of the colony. When we all heard of it, it made us very vex it enough to make us all go mad the way they are going to treat us, it seem very hard. We all working in peace and quiteness [sic] and happy, pleasing Mr Goodall, and also showing Mr Goodall that we could work if we had a good manager expecting our wishes to be carried out, what we ask for, but it seem it was the very oppisite [sic] way. So we don't know what to do since we heard those strict rules planned out. It has made us downhearted. We must all try again and go to the head of the Colony. We are all your Most Obedient Servants ...

Declaring it was 'monstrous that the Board can do nothing without that clique remonstrating', Page demanded a report from Goodall. He replied that the men 'knew very well what they were signing', but were now satisfied with his explanation that Board powers were unchanged. Page also obtained reports from Goodall and police on Mrs Bon's letter questioning the Board's failure to provide for aged Aborigines who delighted in periodic visits to their home territory. She published an Alexandra hotel-keeper's complaint about neglect of James and Violet Laidlaw, whose welfare had been debated by 'Amicus' and Strickland in June.

Journalists were not invited to the special meeting of 6 September and the press release did not mention that it had been called to 'deal with' Mrs Bon's letter, nor the resolution that Cameron must visit Coranderrk to soothe apprehension and explain that 'the Board would not tolerate such letters in future'. The press release emphasised that the buildings recommended by the government architect would cost £3,359 but the Board had only £1,000 for all stations and 'one or two members expressed the opinion that if the government insisted on keeping up the Coranderrk station they ought to maintain the buildings'. Page's minutes suggest that the three new members had been able to force LeSouef, Macredie and vice-chairman Anderson to approve rebuilding – on condition that Cameron organised a deputation to the Premier for the necessary funds.[48] The minutes also note that Page was authorised to publish a rejoinder to Mrs Bon's letter. Anderson, earlier in the year, had broken the Board's tradition of ignoring press criticism. The newcomers were accustomed to using the press to present their views on matters of public controversy. But the schoolmaster Morrison and the three farmers who had served a few years on the Parliamentary backbench had no experience of departmental administration and thus no comprehension of the power wielded by experienced bureaucrats such as Page. These busy men who met for a few hours

---

47   BPA – Report of A. Purchas, Government Architect, 29 August 1882.
48   BPA – Minutes, 6 September 1882; *Argus* 7 September 1882.

13. FINAL DEFEAT

a month had little opportunity, and perhaps felt they had no right, to examine public service files to check that Page's compilations were factual. The new members were, like most of their predecessors on the Board, naive and decent men who accepted this duty because of their benevolent concern for Aborigines. Their ignorance was disastrous for the Kulin.

Despite their religious differences the eight members now disputing Board policy had much in common. All were in their 50s or 60s, all stoutly conservative in politics and distrustful of reformers who wanted to alter the colonial society in which they had gained wealth and power. They were prone to interpret any challenge as criticism of their own expertise and were infuriated by the interference of their unreliable Minister. They found the unwomanly determination of Mrs Bon particularly exasperating and were prepared to believe their secretary's complaints of harassment. They acquiesced in Page's attacks on Mrs Bon because they trusted their secretary, they needed a scapegoat and, perhaps, because they hoped to silence Grant by discrediting this prominent adviser. Page's rejoinder in the *Argus* simply cited Strickland's previous defence plus a police report that Laidlaw worked for local farmers and Goodall's report that the Laidlaws and three other elderly visitors would not settle because Coranderrk was too cold.[49]

These few survivors of the Taungurong clan about Alexandra did not expect any European to understand the real reason for their reluctance to remain permanently at Coranderrk: these men were of the same moiety as the Woiwurung clan which owned this land and thus had no claim by marriage or descent to occupy it. Balliot – the woman now called Violet Laidlaw – had rights from her own clan ancestors. But like the Kulin wives of the past, she helped her husband keep his country.

Page's *Argus* rejoinder did not mention his order to remove the Laidlaws to a distant Gippsland mission and the constable's telegraphed refusal because they were so distressed. Nor did Page make public, even to the Board, the constable's report that the hotel-keeper was trying to exploit Mrs Bon's 'well-known Liberality charity and sympathy for the Aboriginals'. Press reports of the next meeting merely announced that Mrs Bon's statements 'were even more exaggerated than was at first supposed'.[50] The press were not informed when Mrs Laidlaw died 10 days later, before the Order-in-Council for removal to Gippsland could be enforced. The kindly constable assured Page that she died contented and 'while she had breath kept repeating the following lines of a hymn "Here we suffer grief and pain, here we part to meet again, in Heaven we part no more"'. Local farmers' wives sat with her to the end; their husbands followed the hearse to her pauper's grave. They gave her husband, the owner of the land they occupied, a horse and saddle to ride with them. They thought Mrs Laidlaw aged 70: she was at most 41. She and her husband had tried to build a home for the Taungurong clans at Acheron station two decades before. When he died two years later at Coranderrk yet another Kulin clan was extinct.[51]

The news of Balliot's death reached Coranderrk just as Barak and an aide set off to visit A.W. Howitt the learned *Ngamajet* who wished to write down Barak's knowledge of the Kulin. As the train jolted them on the long journey into Gippsland the last of the Woiwurung clan heads had time to remember the past, time to think of his plans for the future. Faintly ludicrous to European eyes in his worn suit and sandshoes, the old man carried with him his Bible and his memories. He could read a little and had memorised much of that Bible. The legends and beliefs of vanished tribes in a distant land had been read to him by Green and Hamilton since 1861. The people of the book were shepherds like the ancestors of the Scottish exiles who preached their words so passionately. Yet the care of flocks and herds and crops was easily learnt, so the Kulin had found, and much in that book was familiar, reconcilable with the teaching of the *ngurungaeta* whose wisdom had governed the Kulin in his youth.

---

49 BPA – Minutes, 6 September 1882; *Argus* 7 September 1882.
50 *Argus* 8 and 14 September 1882; BPA – Sr. Constable Irvine to Page, 7 and 8 September 1882.
51 BPA – Sr Constable Irvine to Page, 25 September 1882. Violet Laidlaw (Balliot, c. 1841–1882) and Jamie Laidlaw (Ballaganit, c. 1837–1884) were thought to be aged 20 and 24 in October 1861 (BPA – Acheron file).

Times had changed. In a lifetime of diplomacy Barak had learned to perceive and overcome cultural differences, and to adopt new ideas which could serve his people. In his youth the Murray tribes and the *berbira* of Gippsland were wild men beyond the Kulin pale; he had married a Kurnai woman and now journeyed farther into their territory than he had ever dared before. He had learned to think differently of the tribes on the Murray, too. They had been feared as sorcerers when he was young, but Pangerang, and later Burapper and finally a few Joti-jota had been sheltered on his land. They were now marrying Kulin. He had accepted their hospitality, in a last desperate effort to save his son by travelling to the warmer country at the Maloga Mission last winter. That missionary Daniel Matthews had brought their children to Coranderrk for refuge, as he and Green could never persuade the government to give them land. Matthews gave his own selection to make Maloga but it was not enough. Barak's boy had helped the Joti-jota and Pangerang petition the New South Wales governor for more land in July 1881. That bit of writing as all that was left now of his son, that signature 'David Berrick' on the July 1881 petition.[52] Still, there was his sister's son Wandin who had many children by Jemima, the Echuca girl Matthews had brought to Coranderrk on his first visit long ago. Barak had agreed to help Howitt write down the past; if this *Ngamajet* proved teachable maybe he could be trusted to write down Barak's thinking about future custodians for the land.

Daniel Matthews and his wife Janet of the Maloga Mission.

---

52 Matthews Papers, v. 2 part 2, petition by Maloga men, c. 5 July 1881. A.W. Howitt, notes on 'The Kulin Tribe', and Annie E. Whittaker's, 'Memories of King Berak', in Howitt Papers. See also *Australian Dictionary of Biography* entry on Barak.

13. FINAL DEFEAT

But if Cameron did not win his battle to reform the Board there would be no home at Coranderrk. The journalists who attended on 13 September 1882 to hear the Board debate the managers' advice on the inquiry's recommendations were deliberately misinformed about other matters besides Mrs Bon's letter. The minutes hint that the most important business was transacted after their departure. Page's explanation for the Board's decision to implement one inquiry recommendation was certainly false: the press (*Age* next day) were told that residents had originally requested the right to buy their own meat but as 'the men ran up bills at the butchers, and spent the money otherwise' the Board would now supply meat and reduce wages. The press reports did note that the Board modified the managers' advice on apprenticeship and female employment, but omitted Cameron's report that Premier O'Loghlen had told him the Board must seek extra funds from their own Minister, Grant. Battle lines were clearly drawn at this meeting: Curr and Jennings were again absent, and so was the newcomer Officer, so that Cameron and Morrison were pitted against Anderson, Macredie, LeSouef and the former member of Parliament J.R. Hopkins (who had attended only once since 1875).

The press announced that they were to meet again in a fortnight to continue debating the managers' resolutions. But on 27 September only Curr, Macredie and LeSouef attended and there were no press reports on their sole decision – to revert to monthly meetings. It was presumably on their authority that Page at last advised his public service superior that the Board 'strongly opposed' hiring out girls. The Board never did debate the rest of the managers' resolutions. Curr was in the chair on 4 October when Cameron told the old members that he and Anderson had seen the Premier and Treasurer, O'Loghlen, who said they could have the necessary £3,359 for rebuilding Coranderrk on condition that they asked for only half this year. Cameron had won, but the old guard and their secretary were not reconciled to defeat: Page's letter asking Grant to place the sum of £1,679 on the Supplementary Estimates specified that the Board made the request 'seeing that their recommendation to break up Coranderrk was not likely to be acted upon'.

The factionalism of the Board was hinted at in press reports of the next meeting on 1 November when debate on the annual report was deferred for a week. The *Age* account of the discussion on 8 November quoted Cameron's objections to the face-saving 1882 report, which explained that improvements would proceed because the government had repeatedly ignored Board advice to break up the station, and insisted that all discontent had been created by the inquiry and outside interference. Curr, LeSouef and Jennings refused to amend Page's draft.[53]

After a year of dispute on the 1881 inquiry report the Kulin could at last hope for the new homes and boundary fencing they had been promised when hop growing began in 1872. But their hopes were ill-founded. Another two years of dispute lay ahead and, by the time Graham Berry ensured that the Board could never sell their land, the Kulin were being driven from it.

---

53   BPA – Minutes, 13 and 27 September, 4 October, 1 and 8 November 1882; Secretary's Letter Book, 2 and 12 October 1882; *Age* 11 November 1882.

Chapter 14
THE END OF THE STORY

> We have taken away their inheritance, and virtually destroyed them by our presence, and we are bound in justice and honour to treat them with the utmost liberality and consideration.
>
> *Argus*, 1882[1]

The Board hastily contradicted a December 1882 press report that the Coranderrk residents were protesting Board decisions, the staff were quarrelling and the members were 'at daggers drawn' over censure of 'the celebrated "Bon" committee' in the annual report.[2] The falsity of Page's denial was apparent from press accounts of recent meetings, even though he successfully concealed the main sources of friction: the Board's failure to implement the most important inquiry recommendations and his own choice of a new teacher contrary to the wishes and advice of Goodall and the Coranderrk residents.

Forty-three-year-old Joseph Shaw, appointed on 4 September 1882, had twice been an unsuccessful candidate for the Coranderrk manager's post. He had 10 years of experience, dating back to 1862, as an untrained missionary and teacher at three Anglican stations. He also, as Page was well aware, had a grudge against Green who had forced him to make a humiliating apology for his cruelty to residents of Lake Condah and, with Smyth, had publicly criticised his competence and honesty as manager. He had resigned after a mission committee inquiry vindicated him of a resident's charge of immorality and had spent the intervening years in South Australia. Shaw, who had a low opinion of Aboriginal capacities, considered authoritarian control essential and made no secret of his disapproval of Goodall's less autocratic leadership. He was discontented with his housing, his salary of £120 a year (plus £20 for his wife Jessie's services as sewing mistress) and his subordinate position as 'second officer'. The school inspector repeatedly criticised Shaw's competence as a teacher, yet he was not only retained but promoted to manager within three years.[3]

Page encouraged the sycophantic private reports of Shaw and used his criticisms to secure the removal of Goodall whose sympathy for the Coranderrk people and incessant complaints on their behalf had become an embarrassment. Page had expected to control Goodall. By the end of 1882, he was so enraged by Goodall's opinions that virtually every letter challenged or reproved his decisions as manager.

Loneliness and exhaustion from overwork influenced Goodall's reaction to Coranderrk. Page's pessimistic warnings encouraged Goodall to distrust the Kulin leaders – his first letter spoke of Bamfield's 'very pleasant manner so far' – and he initially refused this promotion because he could not feel the trust and liking he considered essential for successful management. Even so, every letter and report commended the

---

1   *Argus*, third leader, 23 May 1882.
2   BPA – Minutes, 3 January 1883, Secretary's Letter Book, 5 January 1883 (reply to *Western Agriculturist* article of 23 December 1882).
3   Joseph Shaw (1839–1908) served at Yelta on the Lower Murray 1862–66, Lake Condah 1869–72, and Poonindie, South Australia, 1879–82, and had been a licensed state school teacher for four years (Shaw 1941, 1949; BPA – Secretary's Letter Book, 19, 20, 31 August 1872, 5 October and 12 November 1872; Shaw to Page, 9 August, 23 December 1882, 16 September 1884; Annual Report 1871:App. 1; CSIC 71/Z9073, Z11616, 2 June and 5 July 1871; 76/K8996, 12 September 1876; Royal Commission 1877:45; School Inspector's Report, 27 February, 10 September, 26 December 1884).

residents' kindness and insisted they deserved 'great praise for their good conduct and assiduous work', Goodall felt an alien at Coranderrk, despite his previous visits because the Kulin dialects were unrelated to the language used at Framlingham and only a few members of the westernmost Kulin clans had ever visited his station.

Yet the Kulin quickly accepted Goodall as a leader of Green's calibre. They showed him a protective loyalty, understanding that he had sacrificed his security at Framlingham for their sake and not for an extra £50 a year. He won their respect as temperance exemplar and religious leader as well as teacher and farmer. He was an experienced lay preacher, always invited to give sermons on his previous visits, and while manager was frequently invited to preach to European congregations in this strongly Presbyterian district. Goodall's religious activities had a good deal to do with his acceptance by the Kulin and the antagonism displayed by Shaw and Page who apparently hoped to make Coranderrk an Anglican station. But the Kulin, too, had by this time acquired a judicious appreciation of the differences in Christian doctrine and ritual and made plain their preference for the Presbyterian forms taught long ago by Green and Hamilton. They eagerly attended Goodall's services. Excellence in public oratory was one of the hallmarks of leadership in their society and they had always had a taste for ethical and philosophical discourse – when delivered with eloquence by men they respected.

Goodall also won allegiance by consulting and 'working beside' the men and supporting their 'justified complaints' about the neglected station. He could understand their bitterness: for 13 years the Board's failure to provide capital and wages had frustrated all attempts to develop farming at Framlingham. In mid-1882 both he and the Kulin were confident that the Board would quickly provide new housing, fence and stock the reserve and diversify the crops. Once the hop acreage was reduced they could do all necessary tasks themselves. They were defeated by Page's distrust (fuelled by jealous subordinates), by the Board's determination to retain the hop income employing European labour for other tasks and by the government's parsimony and procrastination in granting necessary funds for the long-delayed improvements.

For three months Goodall and Harris were the only Europeans on the station. They worked beside the Kulin men on the farm while first Mrs Maggie Parker then Mrs Louisa Briggs (back after four years exile at the Wimmera mission) supervised the dormitory. But they and the semi-literate overseer could not help with the school or the burden of paper work Page now imposed on managers. Two weeks after he took charge Bella Lee had mentioned in a letter that 'we leave prayers a little earlier because Mr Goodall gets so tired of running about so through the day'; by August Goodall admitted that he must have help as he could not sit down for two minutes.[4]

All of the men were driving themselves – and being driven by Page and Cameron – to renovate the hop ground and get on with subdivision fencing and clearing. If they did not succeed they would lose their land to covetous neighbours. But Goodall's first annual report complained, as Green had complained a decade earlier, that hop growing tasks monopolised the available labour leaving 'little time for any work outside the hop garden'.[5] The Kulin felt bitter resentment when Curr and Cameron hired European contractors at higher rates to fence their land in August 1882. Cameron's electors expected patronage in the allotment of government contracts; Curr argued that residents were not able or competent to do this work. The press was not informed of the reason why residents were allowed to complete one of the three contracts after November 1882. Goodall had rejected the shoddy work of a neighbouring selector

---

4   BPA – File '1882 Correspondence re Bella Lee' (Bella Lee to Mrs Strickland, 4 June 1882); Goodall to Page, 31 August 1882).
5   BPA – Annual Report 1883:App. l.

14. THE END OF THE STORY

(who had always been friendly and had wanted to hire skilled fencers from the station), reporting to the Board his 'hushworthy' admission that he could not 'get labour in the district because people are reluctant to see it fenced, saying where will we graze'.[6]

Local agitation for alienation of the obviously understocked reserve increased as the boundary fencing progressed. Neighbours made no secret of their ambitions. Their complaints were published anonymously in the *Australasian*, the *Argus* weekly, in March 1883. The agricultural correspondent 'Bruni', apparently escorted by the neighbour Steel on a 10-minute visit, had talked only with the new teacher Shaw. This article deplored the residents' failure to clear more pasture and condemned the management of the hop ground. 'Bruni' challenged the importation of fencers, but recommended dispersal of all 'half castes'. Noting that the reserve contained a 'larger area of hopland' than any other property in the district, he argued that this would 'pay well for cultivation if undertaken by intelligent farmers'. The angry vice-chairman ordered Page to obtain accurate reports from Goodall and Harris and take them to the editor. He denied any malicious intent, said 'Bruni' must have 'got information from a wrong source', but would not publish a correction.[7]

The criticisms were particularly annoying to the Kulin, Harris and Goodall because they had successfully harvested a record crop and managed the preparation by themselves for the first time since Green's departure. Goodall had resisted all of Page's orders to hire European labour and brought in only five pickers for the last two days. But his bitter protests about the workers' 'discouragement' because their wages were reduced by a halfpenny per hour and their tobacco issue ceased when a meat ration was reintroduced in January 1883 were ignored.

Goodall's reaction to Coranderrk was certainly influenced by the fact that he finally had to spend 22 months alone in the old manager's residence, long since condemned as uninhabitable. He was touched by the fumbling efforts of the dormitory girls to provide his meals and 'do what they can to make me comfortable' but he found life without his wife and children 'unendurable'. By the time a European matron took charge of the dormitory in early October 1882, he had been separated from them for four months. When he threatened to resign he was given leave to fetch his family to Healesville and house them at his own expense. On his return he found the new teacher and matron feuding. Apparently trusting the opinion of the Shaws, whom he had known since 1869, Goodall urged Page to dismiss the matron reporting that her authoritarian management of the dormitory was 'altogether wrong' and she was causing 'jealousy and estrangement' between him and the Shaws. Journalists attending the December 1882 Board meeting were given the impression that Goodall was wholly at fault. They did not have access to the matron's reply, which commented on Shaw's interest in the beer made by the dormitory girls and revealed all too clearly the ambitions of Page's new proteges. The matron's letter complained that Mrs Shaw had spitefully maligned her to Goodall and reported that:

> In Goodall's absence Shaw was always complaining and saying things were not well managed and that he had been the first to send in his application when the Stricklands were in trouble but Goodall was appointed and whatever he might say about not liking Coranderrk it was a lift for him to come here etc., he coveted the position. When Goodall returned he told me he hadn't made up his mind, I said I didn't care about staying either if Shaw was appointed in his place.

The matron was asked, then ordered, to resign. Page chose a replacement ignoring Goodall's suggestion that his wife serve without pay.[8]

---

6 BPA – Goodall to Page, 11 October 1882.
7 BPA – Secretary's Letter Book, 15 March 1883; Harris to Page, Goodall to Page, 12 March 1883.
8 BPA – Goodall to Page, 3 and 31 October 1882; D. Arelia Brand to Page, 13 November and 11 December 1882; *Argus* and *Age* 7 and 8 December 1882.

The 3 January 1883 Board meeting solemnly debated Goodall's protests about Page's ruling that he could visit his family two evenings a week but must not sleep off the station. No mention was made of Goodall's complaints about the residents' uninhabitable dwellings. For seven months he had warned that the Board's neglect would cause 'sickness and death'; in December he had demanded all huts be repaired, insisting that 'I can't ask men to go to work after spending the night in such a wretched condition, they are becoming very discontented and threatening to abandon work and build huts for themselves and I can't blame them'.[9]

Their discomfort and Goodall's enforced celibacy continued as the Board had no funds for buildings. O'Loghlen had reneged on his pledge to place half the needed sum on the Supplementary Estimates. When his government was defeated in the snap election of January 1883 Graham Berry was once more Chief Secretary in a powerful Liberal–Constitutionalist coalition which endured until 1886. O'Loghlen had lost his own seat and the Board discovered that Treasury officials had no record of his verbal promises to provide needed funds and allow the Board to retain the hop income. The Board was told no funds were available when the new government assumed office on 8 March 1883. But there were now two sympathisers in Cabinet: Berry himself and Alfred Deakin who had responsibility for public works. After much correspondence and several deputations to the new Premier and Chief Secretary, vice-chairman Anderson and Cameron secured £1,700 in July to cover existing contracts for lining nine dwellings and building four new cottages and a manager's residence of brick (which alone cost half the total expenditure of £2,308).[10]

Berry's return as Minister perhaps gave Coranderrk people hope that their wishes would at last be implemented. The conservative Board members had little sympathy for any radical politician and thought Berry little more than a mob leader. They had already had two-years experience of dealing with an antagonistic Minister and viewed the return of this critic with foreboding. But they needed his consent for legislation to implement their policies. There had been a stalemate on their plans for apprenticeship since November 1882: Crown law officers advised that the Board had no power to apprentice Aborigines except by the use of individual Orders-in-Council prescribing residence. They had asked Grant for a new regulation empowering them to apprentice any male (with his consent if over 21); instead the under secretary had replied on 15 December stating that the Minister wished the Board to reconsider its negative opinion on hiring out girls. He did not, of course, mention that Mrs Bon had written to Grant a week earlier but he did use a phrase from her letter questioning the justice of retaining so many 'half castes' at Coranderrk.

As there was no quorum at the next two meetings the matter was held over until 7 March 1883. Then LeSouef and Macredie, with the two Parliamentary members Anderson and Officer, resolved not to alter Board opinion on girls but to encourage 'half caste' youths and married couples to take service off the stations. Page's reply to the under secretary therefore aimed at prompting the new Minister to provide the needed legislation for the Board's change in policy. Page explained that if girls were hired out they would be victims of European immorality and the men left on the stations would have no one to marry. In reply to the under secretary's statement that 'to maintain half castes and quadroons with pure blacks is not just to the latter', Page pointed out that the 1869 Act made no distinction in defining Aboriginal status: 'every Aboriginal half caste or child of a half caste, such half caste or child habitually associating or living with Aboriginals, shall be deemed an Aboriginal'. Berry sent a peppery reply ridiculing the Board's fears about the morality of girls in service. The Board declined to change its views and Berry did nothing about the apprenticeship regulation.[11]

---

9   BPA – Goodall to Page, 6 and 14 December 1882.
10 BPA – Secretary's Letter Book, 15 May, c. 5 and 25 June 1883; File – 'Works at Coranderrk', April–September 1883; Secretary's Minute Book, 83/295, 12 October 1882 – 17 July 1883.
11 BPA – Secretary's Letter Book 13 November 1882, 13 March and 11 May 1883; Minutes, 7 March and 4 April 1883; CSIC 82/ X11149, Anne F. Bon to Chief Secretary, 9 December 1882.

14. THE END OF THE STORY

The new Minister did take action on another decision made at that March 1883 meeting: he approved an Order-in-Council for the removal of the leader Bamfield to the Gippsland mission station most remote from Coranderrk. No cause had been specified for this or a number of other recent transfers requested by Page. Berry, like his predecessor Grant, naturally assumed that such orders were used (as originally intended) to rescue individuals from unsatisfactory living conditions. In fact Page, with the approval of the managers' conference, had begun to implement his new scheme to punish refractory residents by banishment to distant stations. As he explained to the newly formed Aborigines Protection Board who had sought his advice on legislation for the neglected Aborigines of New South Wales, the Victorian Board had 'no power to punish an Aboriginal who misbehaves himself on the stations' except by transfer under an Order-in-Council 'as according to our law officers it appears doubtful if the Board or the Managers can dismiss or prevent any Aboriginal from coming on any of the stations'. Persistent idlers could be punished by withdrawal of rations but this was more hurtful to the family and friends who had to support them.[12]

Page's self-interest, rather than Bamfield's behaviour, motivated the banishment. Public service reform was still the main topic of Parliamentary debate, new review procedures were planned and Page's own job was not yet secure. He had not forgotten the humiliation he suffered over Bamfield's prosecution and release. By demolishing Bamfield's reputation he could vindicate his own actions and silence the critics who would certainly press the new Minister to abolish the Board and his own post. Although Goodall had never yet criticised Bamfield, Page's distrust had not abated. When Bamfield appeared at his office on 22 February requesting a certificate to work away as his meat ration had been stopped and he had to beg for his children, Page had LeSouef witness the complaint. He immediately asked the acting manager, Shaw, to advise whether Bamfield's removal would benefit the station. (Goodall was spending a week at Framlingham to sort out the problem of his kindly but inexperienced successor.) Just as he departed on 19 February Bamfield had come to demand restoration of his nephew's meat ration. This man usually lived near Wangaratta and only intermittently visited. Goodall, under pressure because of the coming hop harvest, was annoyed that Bamfield and his nephew had lately done little work and seemed more intent on organising protests against the Board. Angered by Bamfield's 'most insulting and overbearing manner', he ordered the overseer Harris to withhold his meat for a week but to supply his family. Other food had already been issued and women and children could always obtain meals in the dormitory. Goodall intended no further punishment. Two men had been exiled on three-month work certificates during his tenure but he had acted, on the unanimous advice of the residents' court, to punish cases of immorality that would otherwise have necessitated police action.

On his return a week later Goodall found that Shaw had written advising Bamfield's banishment, giving details of interference with Goodall and attempts to organise deputations to Melbourne. He had forwarded a file of Bamfield's letters to prove that this meddlesome leader was also interfering in his own management of the school. Harris, too, had provided evidence that Bamfield was 'saucy' to Goodall and was the 'fourman' at all meetings: 'when any meeting is called to go before Mr Goodall he is always the leading man. He has tried to get these newscomers [sic] to go down to Melbourne with him'. Goodall could not contradict his subordinates without increasing Page's suspicions of his own competence as manager and he was angry about Bamfield's 'untrue' complaint that his family was starving. Goodall explained that his meat was withheld:

> for his idleness and insolence and for endeavouring to prevent other men going to work and for stirring them up to rebellion. He also threatened unless he got what he wanted to leave the station and take others with him and also go to Melbourne and report me.

---

12   BPA – Secretary's Letter Book, 8 March, 8 April, 11 May 1883.

When Goodall was ordered to report on whether the station would benefit if Bamfield left, he replied that it would be an advantage if he were 'removed from it altogether' as he was 'continually stirring up strife between the half castes and the blacks'. Yet he expressed concern that giving Bamfield the desired work certificate would encourage others, unless he was ordered to take his family with him.[13] Having bitterly protested to Page about the reduced wages, he hardly needed to spell out his problems of keeping men on the poorly paid hop work while labour-hungry neighbours offered higher rates and the Board itself paid Europeans for fencing which residents were well qualified to do. But his remarks were taken out of context to justify Bamfield's banishment seven weeks later.

On 17 March Page ordered Goodall to tell Bamfield his complaint was not forgotten; he did not inform Goodall of the Order-in-Council until two days before the forcible removal and forbad him to mention it to anyone. Goodall, shocked that anything more than a work certificate was intended, remonstrated privately when Page arrived with two constables to arrest Bamfield on 6 April. Goodall knew there was already considerable tension at the station. As well as reducing wage rates Page had delayed payment of the hop picking money. Moreover, Page's decisions about siting the new cottages offended Kulin convention and his orders about allocation were considered unjust. Goodall had tried to explain their sentiments and vainly reported the 'murmuring' of the pioneers (including Dunolly and Morgan) to whom he had promised the houses. Page insisted they go to the largest families who happened to be non-Kulin newcomers. Earlier that week Goodall had written insisting residents must be rehoused before the manager; he was 'at least warm' and there was great discontent because no repairs had yet been made. But the *Argus* of 5 April had publicised the Board's approval of contracts for a manager's brick residence costing £936 and only four cottages.[14]

There were other reasons for tension which Goodall, Page and Shaw did not understand. Coranderrk was a far more complex community than the other five stations which mainly housed the survivors of clans belonging to one or two local language groups. The regional loyalties which divided Kulin clans and the marriage alliances and resulting kinship ties which bound them into a confederacy had been complicated by the recruitment of mostly 'half caste' children from distant areas, only some of whom had links with specific Kulin clans. Recent immigration from the Murray River had encouraged factional disputes. These resulted from regional loyalties and generational differences and were about individuals' entitlement. Goodall, knowing nothing of recruitment to Coranderrk and Kulin political authority, assumed that community divisions arose from 'caste' antagonism. His attitudes in fact encouraged factionalism. He believed he was punishing poor behaviour and rewarding the deserving as Christian values and good administrative practice demanded. But Bamfield and the faction he led perceived the new manager's decisions as favouritism to particular people.

The survivors of the Taungurong clans who had walked from the Acheron with John and Mary Green were mostly elderly and sick, mostly 'blacks' except for the Hamilton family and a few others. They were a minority now but they had greater knowledge of the old ways and could not forget the loyalties of the old days. They had settled at Coranderrk because of past marriages with Barak's clan. They did not, because they were of the same moiety, make marriages with those Kurung and Jajowrong clans who also came because of marital ties to Barak's clan. The eastern Kulin clans in the old days had little contact with the westernmost Kulin whose Jajowrong language was distinctly different. The kinship ties which did exist came from marriages with the geographically intermediate Woiworung, Taungurong, and Ngurai-

---

13 BPA – Shaw to Page 20, 23, 24, 26 February 1883; Harris to Page, 23 and 26 February 1883; Goodall to Page, 26 February 1883; Secretary's Letter Book, 22 and 23 February, 17 March, 17 April 1883.
14 BPA – Goodall to Page, 13 March and 2 April 1883; Secretary's Letter Book, 19 March and 16 April 1883.

illam-wurrung clans of the appropriate moiety. Now these elders felt themselves displaced by the young men and women, mostly Jajowrong or Kurung brought from Mount Franklin and Ballarat, they had supported as dependent children.

Bamfield felt this change most, for tuberculosis had killed the majority of his Taungurong relatives and friends. But his Taungurong clan had in the past formed alliances with Pangerang and Kwatkwat clans between Echuca and Wahgunyah. He had been responsible for bringing many of the survivors to Coranderrk. Most of the children brought from the Murray to be reared in the Coranderrk dormitory had died or moved to the Maloga Mission near Echuca, except for Mrs Jemima Wandin and Alfred Morgan – a member of Bamfield's mother's clan who served as his aide and spokesman. There was constant visiting now between the Burapper, Joti-jota, Kwatkwat and Pangerang assembled at Maloga and their relatives and friends at Coranderrk. Some of these links were old as Barak's clan had long ago made marriages with Pangerang and Kwatkwat clans of the appropriate moiety; some were the result of recent marriages. Most of the people exiled by Page since 1880 had found refuge at Maloga, while a number of older men from the Murray had settled there in recent years. Barak had welcomed them and the Board approved: it was now official policy to close the depots and settle wanderers at the stations. Two Murray men, 'Sambo' Rowan and Benjamin 'Lanky' Manton (1848–1929), had married widowed pioneers. But Goodall had little sympathy for these men who had spent their lives in camps and on pastoral stations. He considered them drunken and dissolute and misunderstood their close association with Bamfield, sadly concluding that this leader had a taste for bad company.

Goodall was not intolerant of indigenous belief. He never refused old people's requests for a holiday in their own country for he understood, however dimly, that they had responsibilities and rights which an immigrant to this land must not question. But when younger men like Bamfield and Morgan, whom he patronisingly considered more intelligent, revealed that they did not share his Calvinist notions about work and its rewards, he was both discouraged and angry. Goodall had great trouble understanding the old Kulin pioneers who preferred their own language. He did his best for them but was hurt by their seeming disloyalty. He could not share their memories and misunderstood the reasons why they still, with polite obstinacy, reminded Green's successors of their loyalty to the *Ngamajet* leader who had helped them build their home long ago. Goodall felt more at ease with the fit young 'half castes' of his own age who were now the best workers. He thought well of their farming skills and shared their enthusiasm for cricket. They spoke good English and because of their lifelong tuition in school or dormitory understood European expectations. He could talk to them as if they were Europeans; he forgot that they were also Kulin. Most of these young workers and householders had been children in Green's time eight years ago. The only managers they remembered had been distant, deceitful or drunken. Most were satisfied with Goodall and wondered at the loyalty of the older generation. Their relations with the new manager annoyed some of the elders who could trace out everyone's genealogical claims to reside on Barak's land and muttered that some of these uppity young folk had no right to be here.

Goodall had innocently exacerbated the tension in January when he took the cricket team and other deserving workers, mostly Jajowrong 'half castes', off to Framlingham for a week's holiday. He also took along the few old Kurung who had come long ago from Ballarat. In his homesickness he had become particularly close to these western Kulin, the only people at Coranderrk who could talk with him of the people and the country he had left behind. When it subsequently became known that he had promised the new houses to deserving young 'half caste' workers reared in the dormitory, Bamfield objected. The old pioneers had waited since 1872 for new houses but the few erected had gone to newcomers or newly wed youngsters. Bamfield's deputation on this matter led to bitter dispute: Goodall later reported to Berry that 'blacks' and 'half castes' had nearly come to blows. Goodall also misunderstood Bamfield's latest representation on behalf of his nephew who had said he would leave if he had no meat. The manager was, in Bamfield's eyes, usurping Barak's authority to decide who might share the produce of this land.

Bamfield had an obligation to represent this kinsman, and his own dignity as a clan-head was injured by Goodall's angry rejection and punishment. By Shaw's report, 'the other men disagreed with him' when he tried to organise a protest. Many approved Goodall's punishment of a poor worker. Bamfield then resolved to leave with his nephew. Only Page could issue work certificates. Bamfield's angry exaggeration was perhaps a necessary tactic with the unsympathetic Board secretary, but Page may well have incited the complaints against Goodall for his own purposes.

Officials had always misunderstood Bamfield's prominence in general protests and his championship of sectional interests and concluded that he was quarrelsome and troublesome by nature. They did not understand his dual responsibilities. Barak, ageing now and aware that his lack of fluency in English made a poor impression on Europeans, relied more and more on the skills of the younger men to whom he 'gave his words'. Bamfield, the oldest, was most prominent for he was a clan-head in his own right and accepted as successor to his father. Barak had made it known that Wandin and Dunolly would be *ngurungaeta* also when he died. But they were still in their late twenties, still being trained for their responsibilities. Bamfield served as Barak's spokesman in matters concerning the whole Coranderrk community; but in matters of internal dispute he often had to represent a factional interest to fulfil his own obligations as a Taungurong clan-head.

Mrs Lily Hamilton Harris (right) and daughters with Mrs Jessie Hamilton Dunolly, c. 1876.

14. THE END OF THE STORY

The behaviour of the Board and the manager had created a political crisis at Coranderrk. But it was not a leadership contest: all authority derived from Barak and no others challenged those whom he designated to care for this land. William Barak, Robert Wandin, Thomas Dunolly, Thomas Bamfield and Alfred Morgan were central figures in the disputes which officials did not understand. In Kulin society the arrangement of marriages had always been a means of furthering political ambitions. Marriage alliances in turn shaped political alliances. Past and present marriages had given these men a particular importance in the network of relationships that made Coranderrk a united community despite its internal divisions. Barak's clan had made marriages with only two of the many Jajowrong clans. Dunolly represented one; he had married Jessie Hamilton of the Kilmore clan of Taungurong. Caroline, daughter of the revered old healer Malcolm, belonged to the other; she had married Alfred Morgan. Mrs Eliza Bamfield, also of the Kilmore clan, had cared for all the Jajowrong children when she lived at Mount Franklin with her first Jajowrong husband. Wandin, Barak's nephew and nominated heir, had married Jemima Burns related to Bamfield's 'aunty' at Echuca. All but Bamfield and his wife were 'half castes'. When Bamfield was banished on the ground that he encouraged 'caste' antagonism, these ties (and similar links between other households) encouraged the Kulin and the Murray River people to unite in his defence.

The whole Coranderrk community was already bitterly angry that the Board had ignored or defeated the inquiry recommendations embodying their wishes. The unexpected arrest of Bamfield was the last straw. All of the men protested this injustice, pleading in vain that he should be allowed the 'honourable' alternative of leaving under a work certificate. Page revealed the vindictiveness which had inspired this punishment when he ordered Goodall to tell them that appeal to the Minister was useless as Berry himself had signed the warrant for Bamfield's removal.

Emily Hall and Jemima Burns Wandin Dunolly.

Nevertheless, 21 men again set off in April 1883 on the long walk to Melbourne hoping to intercede with Berry. Robert Wandin and Alfred Morgan were sent ahead, utilising the new Lilydale train service, to warn Bamfield's wife lying ill at Mrs Bon's home. Goodall, deeply disturbed by Page's antagonism and his manipulation of evidence so that residents blamed their manager's apparent treachery, reached Melbourne in time for another angry interview before Page left his office that Friday afternoon. Saturday's *Argus* gave a summary description of the disturbance following the arrest of 'Punch' and announced that the protesting men intended to seek out Berry at the Treasury building when they arrived. Goodall, unable to ignore the injustice of Page's action, and unhappily aware that the code binding all public servants forbad any public expression of his dissent, waited for them there.

Forewarned by Page that the men intended to see any Minister they could reach, Vice-Chairman Anderson interviewed Berry and the Premier. He sought an assurance they would not act without consulting the Board. Both said they were too busy to receive a deputation. Because Berry also told him the Board should be abolished. Anderson ordered Page to prepare a report for the Minister by Sunday. Page's careful defence asserted that 'whites, blacks and half castes' had long begged him to remove this dangerous man. He falsely declared that Bamfield had considerately been given advance notice, he inflated his previous offences and used extracts from Goodall's report to suggest he had initiated the banishment. On Monday morning three newspapers gave detailed reports of the deputation to Berry. Goodall's testimony had contradicted Page's report which was now before the Cabinet.[15]

Berry, accosted in the street by the deputation, could not ignore the request of Dr Embling, the former Board member who had been his political mentor, that he give the men a hearing. The whole party, including Goodall, Mrs Bon, Mrs Eliza Bamfield and a prominent temperance reformer, went to Berry's office for an extended interview which was recorded by several journalists. Embarrassed by the deputation's belief that he had condoned Bamfield's unjust removal without warning or stated cause, Berry called in the under secretary for an explanation. He said the Board had given no reasons for requesting this order. Berry then explained that such requests had to be approved because it was improper for a Minister to interfere with a board established by Act of Parliament. He assured the deputation he favoured direct ministerial control – and the sooner the better – but expressed doubt that Parliament would consent to repeal the Act and thereby abolish the Board.

The deputation's main spokesman was Alfred Morgan, Bamfield's aide. Arguing that all men had a right to earn an honest living, Morgan asked Berry to grant Bamfield's wish to leave the station and 'go on his own hook' like 'any other gentleman'. He denied that Bamfield would simply come home, explaining that 'if he does anything wrong we will assist to put him off the station'. When Mrs Bon interjected, 'He must not leave his home. You should not say that, Morgan', Berry shrewdly suggested that Bamfield was 'willing to do that rather than be sent from Coranderrk to an unknown country' and Morgan agreed. Goodall, called in to explain his original complaint in front of the Minister and permanent head of the department, could not say much without criticising Page. He insisted, however that the Board had not consulted him before ordering Bamfield's banishment. His account of recent events was fair and factual but he misinterpreted Bamfield's leadership of a recent deputation, suggesting that he was an 'agitator' against the 'half castes': 'He looked upon them as interlopers and thought they should be got rid of'. When Berry retorted that 'Most people think so', Goodall insisted they were not burdens on the state as their labour fully maintained them: 'the half castes as a whole and a large number of blacks were really good workmen and earned all that was given them'.

---

15   BPA – Minutes, 11 April 1883; Goodall to Page, 13 April 1883; Secretary's Letter Book, 8 and 13 April 1883; *Argus* 7, 9 and 12 April 1883; *Age* 9 April 1883; *Daily Telegraph* 9 April 1883; *Victorian Parliamentary Debates*, Session 1883:180.

When questioned directly, the Coranderrk men denied any animosity between 'blacks' and 'half castes', said the dispute was about a particular matter and unanimously declared that Bamfield was not quarrelsome. Berry then reproached the new manager for not encouraging self-government and advised him to limit his own power as much as possible. Stung by this injustice, Goodall agreed that the men were capable of deciding fit punishments. He explained that it was the manner of Bamfield's removal which they objected to and insisted that he had invariably obtained 'general consent' before exiling any resident. The men supported Goodall citing the recent exile of Manton. They explained that 'we asked him to go and not be rebellious'. Finally Berry agreed to rescind the order. He said he did so to uphold the deputation's dignity, understanding that they 'wanted to be treated as upright and honest men, and not as criminals'. But he insisted that Bamfield's release must not be regarded as a victory.[16]

Page saw it as a victory when the under secretary notified him that Cabinet had rescinded the order and instructed him to repatriate Bamfield immediately. He spent the day burrowing through his files and writing to his allies for more evidence against Bamfield. The Minister subsequently ordered the Board to find Bamfield suitable work if he wished to leave Coranderrk, and declared that henceforth full information must accompany any request for an Order-in-Council specifying residence.[17]

Anderson convened a special Board meeting on 11 April to deal with Berry's advice on hiring out girls and to censure their Minister for a decision 'certain to destroy all order and discipline'. For the benefit of the invited journalists he read out Page's report making Goodall the scapegoat, announcing that it had been before Cabinet when they rescinded the order. He, Curr and Macredie then approved a motion by Jennings and Cameron. It censured the Minister for acting upon 'the ex parte statements of some of the blacks' and instructed Anderson and Cameron to inform Parliament of the Board's views.

Both spoke in the Supply Debate that night. Anderson protested Berry's 'studied insult' at great length, again quoting Page's report to show that Goodall was culpable. Berry denied that he had promised not to intervene without consulting the Board. His statement that the Board would have restored Bamfield to his home if they had heard the 'further information' given by the deputation and manager was a deliberate reminder that the Board secretary had been proven untrustworthy. Berry argued that the general community could not support the Board's policy of transferring Aborigines like prisoners and exiling their families as punishment; they must be as free as other men. Cameron retorted that it was 'futile to argue with a gentleman who preferred to accept the word of a discontented lot of blacks'. He deplored the idea that the Board be abolished and sarcastically suggested that Berry, as *ex officio* chairman, should attend a few meetings.

Dow, supporting his party leader against these notorious conservatives, ridiculed the Board campaign to brand as a mischief-maker an intelligent man who 'would not be hunted from the land which belonged to him'. Reminding the House that he and the late member Ramsay had found Coranderrk a model of peace and orderliness under the management of Green, who 'talked the language of the aborigines, and was looked upon by them as their father', Dow insisted all discontent would end if the Coranderrk residents could have their old manager back. He again recounted the long history of the Board's attempts to break up the station. He also reminded the House that 'certain people in the adjoining township' still coveted this valuable land and were actively lobbying to secure it for building allotments and cultivation.

---

16 *Argus* 9 April 1883.
17 BPA – Wilson to Page, 9, 11 and 14 April 1883.

Dow, still agricultural editor of Syme's *Leader*, was well informed about the tactics of Cameron's electors. No doubt this was intended as a rebuttal of views expressed in the rival *Australasian* a month earlier. But any suggestion that members of Parliament were using their Board office for personal benefit was dangerous. In Parliament next day Dow announced that Cameron and Anderson had objected to the press rendering of his remarks. He declared these new members should not be blamed for the Board's long campaign to remove the Aborigines from Coranderrk. The *Argus*, always hostile to Berry, now forgot its campaign against Page. It gave detailed coverage of the Board meeting and debate and expressed editorial concern that this victory would render the Aborigines totally unmanageable. An unsigned article quoted Berry's own remarks to the deputation about the hazards of divided authority and the consequences of supporting a 'bush lawyer' like Bamfield. It concluded with a query about the willingness of Board members to 'continue to accept responsibility without power'.[18]

No one attended the May meeting; in June, Anderson, Officer, Macredie and Jennings retrospectively approved Page's letter of 17 April stating that the Board would not find employment for Bamfield as he was capable of looking after himself. Page had backed this with evidence he had assembled since the deputation. He aimed to protect himself and so ignored Green's sworn statements that for 14 years Bamfield had proved a 'good trustworthy man'. He had recopied the evidence from Strickland and the Healesville constable compiled to defend the 1882 prosecution but dared not re-use his version, publicly proven false, of the scuffle with Ogilvie. He had solicited reports from Strickland, Halliday and Stähle, who obligingly reported that Bamfield appeared pleasant and plausible to strangers but was actually lazy, quarrelsome, untruthful, discontented and dangerous. Stähle's bewildered reminiscence of his months as manager in 1875 complained that Bamfield was constantly 'setting caste against caste' yet when he intervened 'Punch in a most masterly manner managed to win both blacks and half castes to his side, and induced them to go unanimously against … the manager'.

Page had also solicited the opinion of the Lake Tyers manager who reported that in two days Bamfield had taught residents to look to Berry for help instead of the Board. Press accounts of the deputation had reached other stations and this June meeting was devoted to complaints from other banished men. Soon most were home. Alfred Morgan's shrewd appeal to a Minister who cared deeply about civil liberties had defeated Page's scheme to use protective laws for punitive purposes. It was a major victory, even though Page himself had survived another Parliamentary challenge, concealed Shaw's role and made Goodall the scapegoat for his authoritarian action.

The same June meeting deferred a decision on a piped water supply for Coranderrk even though typhoid had recurred. Goodall was suffering from it when he wrote a defensive letter on 13 April arguing that the press reports had distorted much of what he told Berry. Page's reply virtually called him a liar, said the Board would consider his statements and rebuked him for 'trying to serve two masters'. The minutes do not mention any censure of Goodall, but from this time on the new members clearly shared Page's distrust of the Board's senior employee. Goodall was on trial: if he showed further sympathy with protests or publicly dissented from Board policy he risked dismissal without compensation.[19]

Curr had not attended since April, probably as a protest against the Minister's intervention. But as his resignation was dated 4 July, the day of the next meeting, he may simply have been riled by news of the Board's decisions that day. Anderson, Cameron and LeSouef had elected the newcomer Officer as vice-chairman. All four then approved Cameron's motion that the Board had 'no cause whatever to complain of Strickland's conduct at Coranderrk' and agreed to supply a testimonial (which blamed Deans for

---

18   *Argus* 12 April 1883; *Victorian Parliamentary Debates*, Session 1883:179–81, 199.
19   BPA – Minutes, 2 May, 6 June, 4 July 1883; Secretary's Letter Book, 9 and 17 April 1883; Goodall to Page 13 April; Halliday to Page, 9 April 1883; Strickland to Page 10 April 1883; Stähle to Page, 13 April 1883; John Bulmer to Page, 30 April 1883.

14. THE END OF THE STORY

residents' unrest). They also accepted the resignation of Thomas Harris, submitted on 11 June. Page had long been determined to punish Harris for his disloyalty during the 1881 inquiry but every time he proposed dismissal Goodall defended the usefulness of the overseer. Page had effectively harassed him into resigning by burdening him with new duties, deferring his promised house and refusing to increase his wage, currently half a labourer's rate.[20] Harris settled on the selection, between those of Steel and Green on the Coranderrk boundary, he had purchased long ago.

The Coranderrk people now had no allies on the station or on the Board. But Mrs Bon's concern had not abated despite the vilification she had suffered. The apparent sympathy of Berry encouraged further lobbying for a government decision on the inquiry report. A week before the July Board meeting she had sent Berry detailed criticisms of Board policy and expenditure. She did not mention the word patronage. She showed how the most prominent supporters of the Board had benefited from it citing the gratuities paid to three missionaries and specifying their church salaries. She also questioned payments to Curr and LeSouef's son for tasks which were the responsibility of the over-paid secretary. She challenged the 'tyrannical' treatment of critics such as Mr and Mrs Deans, better qualified and better liked than the present teacher, while other inquiry witnesses who had supported the Board were rewarded. Ogilvie, for example, was housed by the Old Colonists' Association (dominated by Board members) and was 'now an inspector of stock under Mr Curr'. Two days earlier she, Embling, Dow and the two Lilydale farmers who had signed Addendum A had petitioned Berry to implement their recommendations and give the Coranderrk people 'immunity from official annoyance and oppression'. The Minister pledged action as soon as 'the pressure of other matters' would allow. He ordered his staff to make a summary of all the documentation on Coranderrk since he left office in 1880 for use at a Cabinet meeting in July.[21] Special funding for improvements was then granted but Cameron took all the credit.

Goodall had nothing but praise for Bamfield after his return, but he and particularly Page were annoyed by the behaviour of Bamfield's nephew and his cronies Alfred Morgan and 'Sambo' Rowan. In April Page had given orders that no Coranderrk resident could visit Melbourne without written permission and complained of Berry's 'interference' in giving railway passes to these men. The founder of Maloga had just written complaining that the immigrants and visitors from Coranderrk 'infuse a restless and independent spirit, such as to damage the management', and that the visitor Rowan was 'glorying in the fact that they had such a man at Coranderrk as Alfred Morgan who knew how to talk to the Chief Secretary'. Page replied that 'the Coranderrk half castes in particular can be led by any designing person male or female'. He lamented their ingratitude ('in the blood, I suppose') and expressed his determination to quench all 'rebellious spirit'.[22]

Mrs Morgan was hospitalised in Melbourne from May to August and her husband found work in town; he visited her but did not send money for his children's support. Mrs Bon's complaints about Page's neglect of Mrs Morgan and 'Sambo' Rowan brought immediate reproof from the under secretary. Learning that the men had also made complaints to Berry while 'loafing about' Melbourne, Page sent Goodall warrants for their arrest, instructing him on 26 July to prosecute both men for deserting their families. A week later he assured the suspicious new vice-chairman, Officer, that the prosecution was Goodall's idea. On 20 August Page sent the vice-chairman Goodall's request for Board authority to tell the Healesville court that Morgan should remove his family from Coranderrk. The gaol report showed he had contracted severe syphilis during his absence; moreover, he was 'always a disturbing element' and many men were 'very much against' his return. Officer replied that he, Cameron and Anderson wanted to see both men gaoled for a month but, 'after the way Goodall behaved in the Punch case, I am chary of

---

20 BPA – Secretary's Letter Book, 9 February, 3 March and 9 July 1883; Harris to Page, 11 June and 9 July 1883; BPA – Minutes, 4 July 1883.
21 CSIC 83/Y6176, 27 June 1883, Anne F. Bon to Chief Secretary; CSIC 83/Z6070, 25 and 27 June 1883.
22 BPA – Secretary's Letter Book, 16, 18, 20, 24 April 1883; Daniel Matthews to Page, 20 and 30 April 1883; Goodall to Page, 6 June 1883.

acting on any recommendation of his'. LeSouef and Hopkins (who had not attended for a year) joined them for the Board meeting of 5 September 1883. After Page reported that the court had acquitted Rowan and remanded Morgan so he could make arrangements for his family, the five old pastoralists decided they had better obtain Berry's approval before arranging permanent exclusion. On 26 September, the Officer informed Page of Berry's verdict: Morgan might leave to support himself but he would not exile the family. Berry had deplored the prosecution of these men by the 'manager' and said both should have been acquitted. He had also refused to fill the Board vacancy caused by Curr's resignation. The Officer regretted that Cameron had not taken part in this deputation as planned; he was well aware that the influential party whip could have dealt more effectively with the Minister. The Officer had no inkling that this revelation of Berry's distrust of the Board heralded an imminent crisis.[23]

Page sent Rowan and Morgan away on work certificates. These punishments of course angered the Coranderrk community. They already felt much indignation that the Board had used the new funds to hire many Europeans for building and renovating cottages and for fencing. Some of this they could have done themselves as in Green's day. Worse still, the Board had refused their September plea, through Goodall, for increased wages. Harris' departure had increased the insecurity of the pioneers: he was the last link from Green's time, and the only staff member who spoke their language. When he was not replaced, farm development was slowed and this revived neighbours' criticisms and residents' fear that their land would be given up. Goodall's work load was doubled when he assumed Harris' duties and he was grateful for Shaw's help with paper work. The teacher could not be expected to do manual work and anyway, Shaw knew little of farming. But shrewd residents noted the intimacy between Shaw and Page when the secretary visited more frequently to check on buildings. They understood that Goodall was out of favour and was being relegated to farm overseer although they were not, of course, aware how completely Shaw and Page now controlled information about affairs at Coranderrk. They, like the Board members, believed that Goodall had initiated the punishment of Bamfield, Morgan and Rowan. They felt Goodall had betrayed their trust; they feared the accession of Shaw who was obviously dominated by the unsympathetic Page.

On 30 September Dunolly penned a petition for Barak. All but Wandin and two elderly newcomers signed it. Barak took it to Melbourne himself and, with old Dr Embling, presented it to Berry on 2 October. Next morning's *Argus* quoted Berry's pledge that he would probably introduce a Bill next session to abolish the Board, and published the petition:

> Be pleased to accept our warmest thanks for the great kindest you have shown to us. We are again come to trouble you by sending this down as a Deputation in behalf of our selves as we are so busy with the Hopplantation.
>
> 1st We would like to hear when Coranderrk will be settled.
>
> 2nd We wish that the Board of Inquiry's report be carried through the House of your Assembly. We would like to know when Coranderrk will be settled. We would be very pleased to have our wishes granted to us, as far as it was promised to us. This is our wishes we want Mr Green back again and this station to be under your Department and the Board to be abolished from this station and that all we ask for.

The *Argus* of 3 October also gave details of a brief skirmish in Parliament the preceding evening. In a debate on public service reform, Richardson had asked when the inquiry report would be implemented. Berry replied that its adoption would involve the abolition of the Board and the re-appointment of Green. He promised a rapid Cabinet decision, regretting that there was no time this session to introduce the

---

23 BPA – Secretary's Letter Book, 7 May, 16, 19, 20, 23, and 24 July, 3 August 1883; Goodall to Page, 23, 25 and 26 July, 20 and 26 August 1883; Officer to Page, 21 August and 26 September 1883; Minutes, 5 September 1883.

necessary legislation. When Anderson and the former Minister Grant (still antagonistic to Berry although he supported the coalition) jeered his announcement that he had just received an Aboriginal deputation, Berry retorted that the Aborigines wanted Green and ministerial control, that the Board itself was divided into two factions on these issues and there were too many members of Parliament on the Board. Quoting the hostile interjections, the *Argus* concluded there were also two views in the House.[24]

Journalists were excluded from the regular Board meeting later that day. Only Anderson, Cameron and Jennings attended. Identical *Age* and *Daily Telegraph* accounts, obviously press releases, merely said 'nothing unusual had occurred on any of the stations' and conspicuously omitted to name those present. The brief minutes simply noted that Page had reported on the deputation to Berry. But Jennings, who had always defended Green, sent in his resignation the same day; presumably, he had quarrelled with the two newcomers, who both absented themselves from meetings for the next six months.

The names of the 23 petitioners had been omitted by the *Argus* and Goodall was ordered to discover them. He reported the residents' explanation for their unanimous petition:

> they had been informed that I was going to leave and Mr Shaw was to be appointed in my place and they were desirous in the event of my leaving to try and have Mr Green restored to them ... an impossibility as long as the Board existed because Mr Green would not come back under the Board ... They were also desirous of definitely knowing whether the station is to be continued or abolished.

Goodall insisted there was no apparent discontent and all were working hard and 'most kind and respectful to me'. He suspected outside influence as one man said his signature was for a book to be sent to Mrs Bon. The minutes and press accounts of Page's report to the November meeting show that he grossly distorted Goodall's account. The Board and public were informed that there was no cause for complaint and many did not know what they were signing. Only Officer, LeSouef and Macredie attended. These three made all Board decisions for the next six months.[25]

Goodall's first annual report, submitted in November but dated June 1883, was intended to be a vindication of the Coranderrk people, a reproof to Page and a public rejoinder to the criticisms of covetous neighbours. It was also, of course, a defence of his own performance but he did not, like most other managers, blame the delinquencies of unskilled or unruly workers for tasks undone. He genuinely admired the skills of the residents and had praised their enthusiasm for work in every letter to Page. His report proudly itemised their achievements during the year and pointedly remarked that theirs was 'the best piece of fencing in the district'. He emphasised that the residents had managed the harvesting and preparation of the hops by themselves and their product had been eulogised by judges at the Melbourne Exhibition. He gave full credit to Harris and his assistant John Charles. All annual reports since the departure of Smyth had deliberately covered up defects in administration. Goodall's report said nothing of his year-long protests about inadequate housing, wages and meat and did not indicate that the four new cottages and the renovations mentioned were not actually completed until September 1883. Goodall made no criticism of the Board, yet his praise of residents' eager development of their farm, his comments on their satisfaction with new homes and his gratification at their enthusiasm for church services were an indictment of past administration.

---

24   CSIC 83/Y10073, 3 October 1883; *Victorian Parliamentary Debates*, Session 1883:1248.
25   BPA – Minutes, 3 October 1883; Goodall to Page, 4 October 1883; *Age* 5 October and 8 November 1883; *Argus* 8 November 1883; *Daily Telegraph* 5 October 1883.

He said little about religion and named no sect. He merely noted that seating had to be extended to accommodate residents' 'remarkable attendance' at prayers and the regular communion services conducted by Rev. Robert Hamilton and Rev. Alex Mackie who had baptised 30 residents. Goodall only took credit for encouraging many men to become subscribing members of the Rechabite Tent of Healesville. These comments were an embarrassing repudiation of Page's 1881 statements that the sectarian preferences of the Coranderrk residents were simply a means of 'spiting' Strickland. The annual report did not mention that the Lilydale minister Mackie had been appointed, despite Page's objections, as the Presbyterian mission committee's official visitor from December 1882. With a Presbyterian majority on the Board, Page was unable to enforce his own religious preferences but he was largely responsible for Shaw's appointment and the Board's failure to transfer the school to the Education Department as the inquiry report recommended.[26] Shaw could thus ignore the inspector's request that he increase secular instruction beyond the legal minimum of four hours a day. He continued to emphasise religious doctrine in the school in which a third of the pupils was now European. No doubt peer group pressure from the children of Shaw, Goodall and nearby selectors, as well as the deliberate tuition of manager, teacher and matron, encouraged an increasing division between old and young at Coranderrk.

This caused a crisis in the last quarter of 1883 which was cleverly manipulated by Page for his own purposes. As a result of the withdrawal of Anderson and Cameron, no doubt offended by the Minister's objections to 'too many members of Parliament', the Board was once more dominated by Page's ally LeSouef. Vice-chairman Officer knew little of past administration; the last of the founding members, Macredie, was now 70 and less active.

Mrs Caroline Malcolm Ferguson Morgan (1845–1889) and sons Marcus (left), John (in front), Caleb (on mother's knee), and Augustus (right), c. 1876.

---

26 BPA – Annual Report 1883:App. 1, 1884:App. 2; Secretary's Letter Book, 15 December 1882; Rev. T.R. Wilson to Page, 4 December 1882.

14. THE END OF THE STORY

Goodall's reputation had suffered as a result of Barak's petition as Page had covered up the residents' unanimous opposition to Shaw. Goodall was in no mood for further protests. He was unusually short tempered from October to December because these were critical months in the hop ground and he and most of the men had to 'turn out at 4 am and work till late in the evening'. They were eight hands short as a result of Morgan's dismissal and the departure of other Kulin for situations on pastoral stations. Page was already implementing the new Board policy of encouraging the removal of 'half caste' lads and married couples. The departure of a number of long-established families affected alliances within the community and caused much anxiety. There had also been great ill feeling since the Board's September decision not to raise wages but instead authorise Goodall to adjust the hourly rate paid individuals to reward the best workers. It was a fair decision in European terms but it hurt the pride of the Kulin pioneers. Fit young men, mostly 'half castes', earned more at the expense of the old men, all 'blacks', who had laboured without wages to support these youngsters. Now they were punished for their age and infirmity.

The crisis at Coranderrk originated with protests from three middle-aged women, all pioneers, who could not be exiled without risking public outrage. These women could not be allowed to imitate the lamentable example of Mrs Bon. Mrs Caroline Morgan had returned from hospital in September 1883 to find her husband exiled and her promised house occupied by others. When she complained of Page's treatment, Goodall reproved her (or so he told Page); she then complained to Page about Goodall. As his new severity was impelled by Page's threat that he would be replaced if he could not put down rebellion, Goodall was incensed when the accuracy of his report was questioned in mid-October. Page had cleverly made him the scapegoat for previous punishments but now he was wary. He retorted that he already had more work than he could properly attend to and would resign from the management if he had to waste more time refuting criticisms.

**Annie Mclellan Reece Manton and her daughters,
Maryann Mclellan (left) and Charlotte Reece, c. 1876.**

REBELLION AT CORANDERRK

A week later Page demanded an explanation of complaints made by Mrs Annie Manton (c. 1852–1935), who asserted that her elder daughter in the dormitory was not protected from the attentions of Rowan's stepson. Goodall denied any misbehaviour and the matron angrily denied any negligence. Mrs Manton had been the previous matron until her new husband frightened the girls and was exiled in February 1883. Page knew there was more to her complaint than mere jealousy: 18 months earlier Strickland had reported that Mrs Manton wanted her daughter sent to service because of the boy's attentions and himself urged dismissal of a lad who was 'a great plague amongst our young girls'. When the newly arrived Goodall caught the boy at the dormitory window at night and ordered him off the station Page had approved, mentioning that he had exiled this 'thorough young blackguard' in 1880. In fact, Page had vainly sought an Order-in-Council to commit him to a reformatory for 12 months for leading other lads astray. But Goodall had since learned to distrust Page's opinions about Coranderrk people. The lad had proved a credit to the station and he saw no harm in the young couple's obvious attachment. But Mrs Manton went on protesting the courtship of her under-age daughter. Her vehemence on the matter over the next four years suggests that the youngsters (both second-generation 'half castes') were considered to be of the same moiety and their marriage was thus incestuous and utterly abhorrent in Kulin law. But she continued to phrase her opposition in terms of the lad's reputation which outraged Goodall. In 1884 the matron threatened to go to the Board because Goodall ignored his favourite's pursuit of the girl; Page exiled the suitor in 1886 when Mrs Manton still forbad marriage despite the couple's 'immorality'; finally they were married in 1887 as Shaw disapproved of the community's irrational objections.[27]

Goodall was annoyed by her complaints to Page and had little sympathy for her next tactic – a demand that her daughter leave the dormitory to help her at home. Mrs Manton had been bedridden since her recent operation for a chronic hydatid infection. As her younger daughter was with Mrs Bamfield, she had few household cares and he distrusted the intentions of the children's stepfather Manton. He felt little sympathy for the Manton–Morgan–Bamfield–Rowan clique whom he considered disloyal to him and too friendly with Mrs Bon.

On 28 October Goodall asked if Page had approved Bamfield's plans to go shearing, reporting that 'all' the men objected as none could be spared; the next day he asked permission to take the workers to the Agricultural Show as they were doing so well. As he no doubt suspected, Mrs Bon had obtained Berry's consent for four old shearers to go as usual to her station. Bamfield withdrew his application for a certificate but the rest were aggrieved when Page refused and he did not join the 18 men who went to the Show late in November. They paid their own expenses except for rail passes approved by Berry. As most of the old were short of cash they walked to Lilydale while most of the young paid coach fares. This rankled. To Goodall's humiliation, Manton, Rowan and another were gaoled for drunkenness in Melbourne. Press accounts of the 5 December Board meeting made much of their offence and Page's prosecution of the suppliers.[28]

Mrs Manton and Mrs Rowan were upset when the party returned saying their husbands could not be found and the angry manager merely said 'let them tramp it, let them feel it'. It was Page who refused their return passes as punishment. When Rowan returned Goodall rebuked him; both Rowan and his wife Jeannie were extremely abusive. Shaw and others were present but it was Dunolly who intervened. Mrs Rowan then had a bitter quarrel with Dunolly but Goodall intervened. Later she sent her husband to ask Goodall, in public, for a rail pass so she could visit her child's grave in Melbourne. Goodall acknowledged her right to a pass to visit and care for the grave: Kulin custom coincided with

---

27 BPA – Goodall to Page, 16 June 1882, 11 February, 14 September, 19 and 22 October 1883; Secretary's Letter Book 16 June 1882; C.M. Persse to Page, 22 October 1883 and 3 November 1884; Caroline Morgan to Page, 11 September 1883; Strickland to Page, 2 and 20 December 1880, 22 April 1882; Minutes, 3 November 1880, 7 April 1886; CSIC 80/T10814, 3 November 1880.

28 BPA – Goodall to Page, 28 and 29 October, 14 and 30 November, 3 December 1883; *Argus* 6 December 1883; *Daily Telegraph* 7 December 1883; CSIC 83/Y10002, 15 October 1883.

14. THE END OF THE STORY

mid-Victorian mourning behaviour. But he refused because he only had two passes for emergencies and she had visited Melbourne the previous week at her own expense without permission. He no doubt assumed she simply wanted to complain to Mrs Bon. But her request was probably a symbolic statement about her rights on this land. She had come from Lake Condah, where her remaining kin still lived, to marry Wonga's aide Barker; the eldest of the Hamilton girls, the sister of Dunolly's wife, had gone there in exchange. The grave was that of her eldest son, who should have been Barker's successor, who would now have stood beside Barak – as Dunolly and Wandin did – as aides and future *ngurungaeta*. Barker had been kinsman to, and bore the name of, the Mount Macedon clan head whom Barak had revered and through whom Dunolly's claim to live at Coranderrk was traced. The last of Barker's sons was only five; his mother Jeannie Rowan was reminding the whole Kulin community of past authority and present entitlements.

Goodall's refusal angered Mrs Rowan who perceived it as discriminatory. She knew that Dunolly's cricket team had passes for a lengthy tour. Her husband's stepson, the lad courting Annie Manton's daughter, was one of the 12. The team (all 'half castes') were Goodall's best workers and the leaders of his temperance campaign. Mrs Rowan was furious with these youngsters who dared to reprove her husband for shaming the community. She and Rowan had no inherited rights but – except for Dunolly, his brother John Charles, and Wandin – neither did the cricketers.

Annie Manton was even more infuriated when her husband was rebuked. He was one of the Hamiltons of Kilmore – Dunolly's children called her aunt – and had been a pioneer at Coranderrk with her first husband James Reece, one of the last Bunurong. In a fury, she went to retrieve her daughter from the dormitory. When Goodall pushed her out, she was bitterly abusive in front of Shaw and many residents. As she refused to apologise and her husband refused to work Goodall stopped their rations. It was the only available punishment but it had never been used on a woman.

Page and the three active Board members were alarmed by Goodall's report. The Minister would be outraged to learn that a sick woman was being punished because she wanted her daughter home and had protested an association with a lad the Board had tried to send to a reformatory. But they had to support Goodall or he would resign and then Berry would certainly insist they offer the post to Green. The Board members were aware that their expertise was being questioned by their critics and by the Minister – who did not know that the vice-chairman, Officer, had never visited Coranderrk, that Macredie had not been there since the 1874 inquiry which caused Green's removal and that LeSouef had made only four visits in 11 years. They had publicly announced plans for a Board visit on 8 December.

Three newspapers had agreed to send journalists. But Officer and Page went alone and their purpose was not mentioned in subsequent minutes or press reports. Apparently they approved this unprecedented punishment of a woman and forbad further complaints.

On 12 December Dr Embling and Mrs Bon escorted the two women to Berry's office. Mrs Manton had been without rations for 20 days. Berry was away and the Premier, James Service, declined to interfere despite Embling's warning that this deprivation threatened the health of a seriously ill woman. The under secretary interviewed them and demanded a report from Page who said he could not persuade Mrs Manton to apologise in order to get her rations – 'she is an intelligent woman but obstinate'. He forwarded reports by all staff members defending the punishment and the daughter's letter saying she would not leave the dormitory because her stepfather was 'a cruel bad man'.[29]

On 2 January 1884, Berry's protege Alfred Deakin asked him to investigate complaints made by two 'blacks'. He forwarded the lengthy statements written for Mrs Rowan and Mrs Manton by Embling on 13 December and said he possessed other letters. Both women were in fact 'half castes' married to 'black'

---

29 BPA – Minutes, 5 December 1883; CSIC 83/X11606, 83/X11656, 12 and 17 December 1883.

men but Embling's paraphrase of Mrs Rowan's words emphasised this opposition. He may have used the terms to avoid naming the individuals she criticised; she, knowing that Mrs Bon and Dr Embling felt that the pioneers were being crowded out by 'half castes', may have tried to win sympathy by emphasising the 'caste' identification. As evidence of Goodall's favouritism she cited his intervention in her quarrel with Dunolly and his allotment of the new houses to 'half castes although they have no real right to be there at all'. She complained that Goodall 'always acts like a brother with the half castes and sides with them against the blacks'.

Annie Manton complained that her daughter had to work without wages and was unprotected from a 'larrikin'. She had consulted Rev. Mackie and been assured that the two could not be married but feared a repetition of the Bella Lee case. She needed her daughter and her rations and believed Goodall should apologise for interfering with her rights as natural guardian of her child. She concluded by begging Berry to grant the petition those at Coranderrk had 'so often laid before him'. This plea for Green's reinstatement annoyed Page; so did Mrs Rowan's statement that Page would not help as he had never forgiven her 'for giving up the letter he had to apologise for'. The petitions reported that the women had twice borrowed money to see Berry and on the under secretary's advice, had asked friends to write for them. Mrs Rowan explained that:

> as the half castes and blacks are kept unfriendly with one another the blacks are unable to get their complaints put down in writing excepting by little children, whereas up till this time the half castes always did the writing for all the people at the station, and all the people worked happily together.

Officer and LeSouef met that day to consider Berry's demand for an immediate report. Only Officer and Macredie were present at the Board meeting on 8 January 1884. They informed attending journalists that they would proceed with their inquiry, despite the women's failure to attend, as Goodall was in town with the cricketers. Goodall's replies were detailed and on the whole just. He denied any animosity between 'castes', insisted that Mrs Rowan and Bamfield were 'the only blacks who were inclined to quarrel' and reminded his audience that the 'half castes joined the deputation and did all they could to get the sentence of banishment rescinded'. He was defensive about Mrs Manton's punishment, admitting that he had only stopped rations three times since 1869, and that the Mantons' friends could not assist as the ration was 'not too liberal'. But he argued that she was 'able to earn 1s.6d. per day' (presumably by hop-tying with other women) and could buy food two miles (3.2 km) away. He declared she was unfit to have charge of her daughter and had 'tried to debauch her'; he insisted the suitor was well conducted but agreed that the girl was too young for marriage. The vice-chairman had him read the girl's criticisms of her stepfather. Afterward five cricketers were brought in; only Goodall's proteges Dunolly and Spider (a loyal ally since Goodall enabled him to marry Bella Lee) were questioned by Officer. The Board's official report to Berry declared the charges 'trumped up and the outcome of evil influences outside the station'. Page lied in saying his letter had never been in Jeannie Rowan's possession and distorted the truth in stating that the new houses were fairly divided between 'half castes and blacks'.[30]

Goodall, Page, Officer and LeSouef had cooperated in turning the inquiry into an attack on the interference of Mrs Bon and Dr Embling. They had libelled the two women, but the extensive press reports were effective propaganda for the Board. On 12 January Shaw, acting manager in Goodall's absence, warned Page that the women had received an anonymous questionnaire, addressed to the Chief Secretary, which seemed 'a kind of "set off" against your inquiry the other day'; moreover, a great many had prepared and signed 'a petition of some kind' which he had not been able to see. He said he need not name the authors of the document, 'who took good care' that it did not come in the station mail bag.

---

30   BPA – Minutes, 2 and 8 January 1884; CSIC 84/ ASS, 2 January 1884, 84/B293, 9 January 1884; *Age, Argus, Daily Telegraph* 9 January 1884.

14. THE END OF THE STORY

Dr Alexander Morrison, the Presbyterian clergyman and schoolmaster who had attended only six of the 30 meetings since his appointment in 1882, made his first visit to Coranderrk on 17 January 1884. When Goodall returned on 21 January he informed Page that, although he was unable to learn the authorship of the questionnaire, Shaw had 'cleverly obtained a lot of information' for Morrison. Presumably Shaw cross-examined the dormitory child who had written letters for Annie Manton and Jeannie Rowan. Goodall told Page that Morrison would return that day. He also reported that a number of residents were 'highly displeased at the action taken by Mrs Bon and Dr Embling' and intended to send Page a protest: he would 'hurry it'. A letter dated that day was given to Morrison: it was in Dunolly's handwriting but totally different in style and spelling from all the other petitions he had penned as scribe for Barak.

Five days later Goodall informed Page that both the justice Steel and the Healesville constable were reluctant to 'inquire into the genuineness of the letter as requested by you'. On 31 January Page brought up a police magistrate who certified that Dunolly had written the letter and obtained the signatures. He had questioned 22 of the 29 who had signed; the rest, including Wandin, were absent from the station. The hapless Dunolly, pressed to prove his friendship for the manager, had mustered support from the 12 cricketers (some of them unmarried lads), nine women (wives or close kin of the cricketers) and eight of the dormitory children. Most were Jajowrong or Burapper. Except for Dunolly, his brother, Wandin and the members of the Briggs family who remained (presumably recruited because the eldest daughter was married to Dunolly's brother) none had inherited rights.

Dunolly's sister had not signed: she was married to the last elder of the Kilmore clan. Wandin's wife did not sign either: she had obligations to the Pangerang. Wandin's sudden departure was probably the result of a reproof from Barak, for this protest, unlike all others, lacked his imprimatur. None of the old Kulin and Pangerang had signed. Dunolly had mustered support from only 12 of the 26 adult males present, from only a quarter of the total population of 108. The Coranderrk community had shown 25-year-old Dunolly that he could not command their loyalty.

But the letter could be used as propaganda for the Board. The press had reported that a special meeting on 24 January had lapsed because only Officer and Macredie attended. Only Macredie, LeSouef and Morrison were present on 8 February when Morrison read out Dunolly's letter. The *Argus* published it – but omitted the '32' names Morrison said were attached to the letter. It answered only one of Jeannie Rowan's criticisms of Goodall, denying that he had neglected the men who went to the Show. It said nothing about Mrs Manton's tribulations. It merely declared that conditions were much improved since Goodall took charge and residents were 'never happier or better looked after' (the additional phrase 'in our lives' was crossed out with a different pen in the original). It concluded with a statement that the 'undersigned' were quite capable of making complaints for themselves and 'do not wish Mrs Bon or Dr Embling or anyone else to make them for us or in any way interfere with our Manager'.

The *Argus* also published Morrison's long report of his visit on 17 January when Goodall was absent. The tone was that of a hectoring schoolmaster. He ridiculed all complaints by the 'discontents' at the station and complained that 'the aborigines were pampered'. He recommended that future buildings should be cheaper but insisted Shaw must be properly housed: 'his present cottage might be utilised for the blacks'. Most of the report was devoted to his investigation of the document sent up to be answered 'for the Chief Secretary'. He said the Rowans had told him it was written by Dr Embling and sent up by Mrs Bon via Mrs Green. Rowan had obtained it from Mr Green on 11 January; the woman 'Bella Lee' had written the replies for Mrs Manton and Mrs Rowan and it was posted back next day in an envelope addressed to Embling (it seems that Shaw extracted the letter from the station bag, then questioned Bella's little sister who had done the writing). Morrison, however, waxed indignant about outside interference by 'mischievous' people in Melbourne and local 'agents', bitterly condemning the incitement of insubordination 'among the aborigines who are proverbially impressionable and easily led'.

REBELLION AT CORANDERRK

He had learned that Mrs Manton, Mrs Rowan and Bamfield 'were in the habit of going to Dr Embling and Mrs Bon with every little complaint, and boasted that they were encouraged to do so'; all had been in town just before the document was sent up. Probably Morrison, a defender of the conservative viewpoint in a bitter schism in his church, could believe any ill of liberal Presbyterians like Green and Mrs Bon and humanists like Embling. But Board files show that Shaw had deliberately misrepresented an approved visit by two of Embling's patients and the father of his stable boy who had simply brought his son back after the holidays.[31]

When the same three members met on 8 March Morrison publicly apologised for blaming Dr Embling and said the questionnaire was the work of Mrs Bon. Morrison then moved, and LeSouef seconded, a motion rising from his report, which had deplored the retention of so many 'nearly white' people at the expense of the state. Obviously Morrison had consulted Page, for his lengthy motion gave details of necessary steps for implementing as soon as practicable the policy announced to the Chief Secretary in the Board's letter of '8 June 1881'. He had no inkling that Page's 1881 letter had been a scheme to punish members of a deputation and circumvent Berry's decision to retain Coranderrk. Morrison's motion demanding that the 'half castes' be 'merged into the general population of the colony' did say the station managers must be consulted about how the policy could be implemented without 'manifest injustice' and should report on the practical consequences of withdrawing these labourers from the stations. The idea of consulting Aborigines did not occur to the three old men who decided the future of the Victorian Aboriginal population in their unanimous approval of this motion. They had not troubled to visit the stations in all their years on the Board.[32]

There is no record in Board files of how the Kulin received the Board's decision to exile their children. As only four new cottages had been completed so far because of the brickmaker's slowness, Morrison's motion to build cheaper wooden cottages perhaps seemed a good idea. But there was anger that Page had insisted on hiring numerous Europeans for hop picking and completion of the boundary fence. Of the £585 paid in wages that year, £200 went to European pickers. It was their largest crop and the product dried and pressed by the residents, under the supervision of the pioneer John Charles, won a gold medal and money prize at the Melbourne Exhibition. But Goodall had to send blistering letters when Page first delayed then reduced the wages owed to men who had worked 'often until midnight'. He complained that it was 'breaking faith not to pay the agreed rate, I could not engage white men for anything like the sum'.

The regular April meeting lapsed for want of a quorum but Cameron joined the same three members on 9 April. They debated the merging of 'half castes' and the related question of 'blacks' who wished to work off the stations. Page read out Berry's year-old advice on a work certificate for Bamfield which approved the release of any men capable of earning their living honestly. Cameron then seconded Morrison's motion that Page and Hagenauer should draft a detailed scheme for presentation to the government. He had not attended for six months; he now reported that he had just visited Coranderrk with Berry and Deakin and had agreed with most of their complaints about the allotment of the cottages, excessive cost of the manager's house and other unsatisfactory features of the management. Four days later the *Age* contained a letter from 'Civis' which sarcastically queried Berry's interference with 'the harmony of the board and its secretary', approved Berry's criticisms and recommended all orphans be transferred to orphanages and 'educated for the business of life among the whites'.[33]

---

31 BPA – Shaw to Page 8 and 12 January 1884; Goodall to Page, 5, 8, 9, 21 and 26 January 1884; *Argus*, 9 February and 9 May 1884; *Daily Telegraph* 11 February 1884.
32 *Age*, *Daily Telegraph* and *Argus* 6 March 1884; BPA – Minutes, 1 June and 6 July 1881, 5 March 1884; Secretary's Minute Book, 8 and 16 June 1881.
33 BPA – Goodall to Page, 9 and 24 April 1884; Annual Report 1884; App. 1 and XI; Minutes, 8 March 1884.

14. THE END OF THE STORY

Both Anderson and Cameron joined the other three active members for the meetings of 7 and 13 May when the proposals of Page and Hagenauer were unanimously adopted. All 'half castes' under the age of 35 would be forced to leave the stations. As it would be 'hard and unjust to cast them adrift without due notice', the scheme included discretionary power to supply the needy with rations, clothing and blankets for varying periods.

However, after seven years they would have no further claim on the government but be accounted 'free and equal citizens of the colony'. Other managers were not consulted: Page knew very well that all objected to his dispersal scheme. The policy reversed two decisions which Hagenauer had stoutly defended at the 1882 managers' conference. It required all girls as well as boys to leave the stations for apprenticeship as servants from the age of 13; all orphaned children would be transferred to public institutions in infancy so they would 'be accustomed to regard themselves as members of the community' and 'not be constrained to carry with them through life the impression of the indolent habits and manners of their original black friends'.

Hagenauer had opposed such proposals also at the 1877 and 1881 inquiries; now, full of self-consequence, he innocently revealed just how much of his previous opinion had been shaped by the Board's campaign against critics such as Mrs Bon, rather than his own convictions. The *Argus* quoted his lengthy speech claiming that he had persuaded Heales, the Board's founder, of 'the anomaly of classing these half castes as aborigines' but Heales' plans to remedy matters by legislative change had been cut short by his death. Since Heales died five years before the 1869 Act defining Aboriginal status was passed, the story was inaccurate; but Hagenauer had always glorified his own past role in policy-making.[34] The press lauded the scheme, quoting the Anglican mission committee's favourable opinion and Hagenauer's arguments. But although four members were prominent in Presbyterian affairs, and Morrison and Hagenauer were certainly attending the General Assembly sessions in Melbourne at this time, no evidence of Presbyterian mission committee support was proffered then or later. The authors of the new policy were confident that it would be cordially received: press, public and Parliament generally agreed that the 'half castes' should support themselves, and Berry, as well as the inquiry members, had publicly expressed similar views, although the Addendum A majority had insisted the station should 'always be the home' of those sent to service.

The Board proposals went much farther than the 1881 recommendations: Page and Hagenauer were prepared to divide families and communities by permanently exiling individuals from their homes. But there was no public debate on the morality of this racial classification or concern about the civil liberties of those affected. Most Victorian colonists complacently assumed that the 'half castes' wanted and would benefit from absorption in the society they had created. An *Argus* editorial of 19 May commended the 'long urged' plan to 'empty the Board's establishments', arguing that 'half castes' were usually intelligent although reportedly weak in moral character; the editor sanctimoniously urged humane and Christian families to free these 'semi-whites' from 'semi-captivity' on the stations and 'assist in the good work of raising the status of the half castes' by employing them as servants. Embling, annoyed by these criticisms of Aboriginal morality, reminded the public that there had been only one case of immorality in Green's tenure and praised Hamilton's 'irreproachable' servant. He expressed pleasure that the Coranderrk girls would no longer be forced to 'vegetate in detention'. He was certain that Christian ladies could 'safely' copy Hamilton's example and assist the 'hapless offsprings of the white man's reckless criminalities'.[35]

---

34 BPA – Minutes, 7 and 13 May 1884; *Age* 12, 14 and 15 May, 1884; *Argus* and *Daily Telegraph* 10 and 14 May 1884; Royal Commission 1877:37; Coranderrk Inquiry 1881:45.
35 *Argus* 10 and 14 May 1884.

Although support for the policy was expressed in moral terms, public acceptance was also motivated by self-interest: dispersal of the 'half castes' would benefit the colony by reducing the Board's £10,000 a year budget, easing the labour shortage and freeing for selection some coveted tracts of land. The disposal of Crown lands was once more a major political issue as the coalition government planned to introduce new selection legislation when Parliament resumed in June.[36] The disposal of some land at Coranderrk became a political issue following the 7 May meeting. The press had ignored the February debate on Steel's application to purchase 80 acres (32.4 ha) of Coranderrk. Cameron was absent when the Board resolved they had no power to sell the land. But all three newspapers gave details of Steel's interview on 7 May. He said the Lands Department had agreed to give him the area without payment, in exchange for land he owned in a distant area. On Cameron's motion that this land was useless to the station the Board approved its alienation.

Two days earlier the *Argus* had reported Cameron's speech at a dinner for Cabinet members who came to woo his electors with promises of railway construction: he admitted he had at first opposed the coalition but as they had acted 'so consistently in the interests of the country' he felt bound to give them his support. Cameron's new sympathy with Berry and Deakin had been apparent at the April meeting; the press made much of his comments on 7 May about Berry's order that all produce monies must be paid to Treasury from July 1884. He declared that he had no doubt this order was the result of dissatisfaction with Board accounts which still did not differentiate the stations. Cameron himself had demanded this be changed, back in November 1882 but Page had ignored the Board resolution. Cameron may also have been aware that Berry was perturbed about Mrs Bon's recent criticisms of Board accounts.[37]

The Board had to interview Berry about amendment of the 1869 *Aborigines Act* by which 'half castes' were deemed Aborigines. They also wanted him to reverse his decision on station income which offended the two church mission committees and made Coranderrk a financial liability instead of the Board's main source of income. Anderson and Page did not attend with the Board members; Hagenauer did and was the main spokesman. The next day the *Age* and *Argus* report on the Board deputation of 14 May were very different, although both noted that Berry had refused to cancel his order that produce income from all stations be paid into general revenue. The *Age* emphasised Hagenauer's argument for his policy: that dispersal would greatly reduce the cost to the government and allow amalgamation of stations; when vacated 'some of the estates would be useful, buildings included, for industrial and agricultural school purposes'. In fact, Hagenauer and Morrison were replying to Berry's criticisms of the expensive new cottages and staff dwellings at Coranderrk: he queried the erection of so many brick buildings for 'a decreasing race'. Hagenauer's plea for imitation of the new Queensland legislation 'by which all half caste children are to be removed to orphan houses' was a reply to Berry's query about the future of some Coranderrk children 'so white it was a shame to keep them there'. The *Age* noted that Berry jocularly objected that Parliament 'could not make a full black a half caste' when querying the clause stating that Aborigines who in future married 'half castes' would be treated as 'half castes' and excluded from care. Berry promised amendments 'generally in the direction suggested', but probably he had genuine qualms about this serious infringement of personal liberties. His successor Deakin excised this clause from the Bill, yet Page and Hagenauer nevertheless enforced their ruling without legal authority.

No promise to amend the Act was mentioned in the brief *Argus* report on 16 May, although Berry was reportedly in favour of 'gradual merging', remarking that 'when he was at Coranderrk the pure blacks seemed to complain that they were sacrificed to the half castes'. But he made various objections to the scheme, insisting that 'Aboriginals should be able to look on the station as a home or refuge' and 'enter its grounds and live in tents whenever they liked'. In fact, the *Argus* account emphasised Berry's challenge

---

36   *Argus* 4 July 1884.
37   BPA – Minutes 8 February and 7 May 1882; *Argus* 5 and 8 May 1884; *Age* 8 May 1884.

14. THE END OF THE STORY

to 'reports that the Board had allowed Mr Steel to take eighty acres', quoting Cameron's embarrassed explanation that excision of this 'worst part of the ground' had not been completed and would have to come before the Chief Secretary for approval.

Next day's *Argus* publicised another rebuke: Cameron's constituents had displayed 'considerable local feeling' at a Healesville protest meeting. They demanded that he introduce their deputation (to be led by Green) presenting a popular petition for sale by public auction if the Lands Department was determined to alienate this area. Green had condemned this confiscation of Aboriginal land 'promised to them 23 years ago by the then Governor'. The chairman and other prominent townsfolk (all sympathetic witnesses in 1881) had alleged with some warmth that 'there must have been some underhand and secret influence at work when Mr Steel could get a promise 'of this valuable cleared land 'in exchange for a rough selection'.

Cameron's naive support for the greedy inquiry member Steel revived Berry's suspicions of the Board. The correspondent's report that Green had said officials of the Board once 'tried to bribe him to assist them in having the whole of the reserve sold' was inaccurate; during a dispute over Berry's criticisms at the September Board meeting, Cameron called for explanations by Green and Smyth. Press reports of the next meeting quoted Green's reply that he had in fact referred to local lobbying to have the whole reserve opened for selection under a clause of the 1865 Land Act.

But Mrs Bon was lobbying too; her June suggestion that Berry obtain the original of Dunolly's letter to discover the names of those who had signed was immediately implemented. No doubt the discovery that most were children or women fuelled Berry's distrust. Green's deputation, his last recorded intervention in the affairs of Coranderrk, did save the reserve. Without informing the Board, Berry arranged in July for gazettal of the whole 4,850 acres (1,962 ha) as a permanent reservation, revocable only by Act of Parliament instead of a ministerial decision. On 6 October 1884 he thus at last fulfilled the most important recommendation of the Addendum A supporters.[38] Since Berry ignored the Board's subsequent request to make all reserves permanent it was clearly a response to the wishes of the old Kulin. After nine years of sustained protest, their land was safe. But their children were already being driven from it. It was none of Berry's doing. Twenty-two months after this deputation Page was still asking for amendment of the Act 'as promised by the Chief Secretary'. The policy was to begin on 1 January 1885 and Page did enforce it immediately at Coranderrk. But Berry's reluctance to introduce the necessary legislation delayed its full implementation until January 1887.

Cameron was not present at the 2 July 1884 Board meeting at which he was elected vice-chairman on LeSouef and Macredie's motion. It was no doubt a vote of confidence; it was also motivated by a realisation that the Board would not get their Bill without pressure from a Parliamentarian of long experience. Berry could not ignore the party whip Cameron while the coalition endured. But Officer and Anderson were deputed to interview Berry again about amending the Act and reversing his decision on produce monies. No journalists were present. The identical press releases in three newspapers merely reported that nothing unusual had happened on any station except that work at Coranderrk was less satisfactory than usual owing to the uncertainty of the 'half castes' about their future: the Board's recommendations 'not being altogether to their taste although they met with the approval of the pure blacks'. Page contrasted this with the reaction at Framlingham where the 'half castes' 'heartily approved' and the 'blacks' 'strongly denounced' the policy. He probably aimed to suggest that the reaction was irrational.

---

38 BPA – Minutes, 3 September 1884; *Argus* 4 September and 2 October 1884; *Daily Telegraph* 4 September 1884; CSIC 84/ A4821, 16 June 1884; CSIC 84/B5478, 3 and 25 July 1878; *Victorian Government Gazette*, 6 October 1884.

There was good reason for a difference in attitudes. Framlingham had been settled by local clans and the 'half castes' were close kin; as this station had never been developed all workers spent much of the year away on seasonal work and were keen to obtain the promised selections of land in the vicinity. But Page was deliberately distorting the situation at Coranderrk. He had forbidden a planned deputation to Berry by Wandin, Dunolly, his brother and another Jajowrong pioneer. They had intended to leave on 19 May but Goodall persuaded them to wait for permission. He begged Page to approve as they wished to ask Berry 'what was to be done with them' and wanted to put their case for raising the age limit for married 'half castes'. Goodall explained that many felt 'after such a long residence here at this station, which they have always been taught to look upon as their home, to turn them away would be to them a great hardship'. Goodall said he had assured them Page's permission 'would not be withheld'. It was. He had to forbid any contact with Berry who would certainly have informed the men Page did not yet have power to exile them. Goodall's June report noted that all were working well despite a considerable amount of dissatisfaction over the new policy. Two families had left (both Burapper who had signed Dunolly's petition); on Page's orders other families – including most of Louisa Briggs' family who were of Woiworung descent – were packing up. Goodall contradicted Page's statement that only 'half castes' had protested:

> The Blacks are also dissatisfied and express regret that they have made so many complaints regarding them and are anxious for them to remain on the station and would if they thought it would be of any use intercede on their behalf.[39]

Page's press releases for the 2 July meeting, published two days afterward, were intended as defensive propaganda. The *Argus* had meanwhile described a Parliamentary attack on the equivalent Central Board of Health and a demand for 'removal' of its secretary and chairman; Berry's reply showed that he was prepared to disband a body whose recent decisions had been much criticised. Berry had made no public statements about abolition since the resignations of Curr and Jennings but his refusal to replace them suggested that he might intend to dissolve the Board or let it lapse by attrition. This was a valid fear: none of the members were young, and both Sheppard and Sumner, still members although they had not attended for years, died in 1884. Berry was clearly annoyed about Cameron's display of patronage on Steel's behalf and had publicly questioned various features of the new policy. The introduction of a Bill for amendment of the Act would give Board critics a chance to demand a government decision on the inquiry report. Deakin and Dow would probably raise the issue – if only to defend their previous stance – and would certainly be supported by the opposition and those radical members who disliked the coalition and wanted an excuse to embarrass Berry. Page again had anxieties about his job now that the new Public Service Board had begun investigating the qualifications and performance of individuals. Cameron's reports to Berry's criticisms were not reassuring and the Minister was all too likely to heed any Aboriginal protest about Page's premature orders to find employment off the stations.

The press releases had deliberately mentioned Cameron's election as vice-chairman. For his own prestige, and as author of Addendum B of the inquiry report, Cameron would certainly oppose any move for abolition. It seems clear that during July 1884 Berry and Cameron reached some agreement about disciplining the Board and secretary. On July 20 Page wrote reminding Cameron to obtain written confirmation of Berry's statement 'at the meeting he had with you' that only the produce income from Coranderrk should be paid to Treasury and not that of the mission stations. When Cameron assumed the chair on 6 August for the first meeting of his three-year tenure as vice-chairman, he made it clear that Page was the servant of the Board by ordering him to visit Framlingham. The press recounted in detail events at the 3 September meeting when Page's ally LeSouef argued that the Board should pay all travelling expenses which now had to come out of his £500 salary. Cameron retorted that Berry believed

---

39 BPA – Goodall to Page, 19 May and 8 July 1884; Minutes, 2 July 1884; *Age*, *Argus* and *Daily Telegraph* 4 July 1884.

the secretarial duties 'ought to be discharged for £150 a year, and Captain Page could then occupy himself in visiting the stations oftener'. Page and LeSouef huffily defended the onerous duties of the secretary, correctly interpreting the remark as an attack on their patronage network. When Morrison insisted that Page could not afford to tour regularly Cameron reported that 'Mr Berry complains there is not enough inspection' although 'since his visit to Coranderrk he had changed his mind considerably about the board work'. He also reminded the members of their own negligence. He demanded a two-day inspection of Coranderrk, which must be made self-supporting now it was fenced. But only he, LeSouef and Page visited on 26 September.

Meanwhile the new vice-chairman Cameron had cast doubt on Board support for the new dispersal policy. On 11 September Premier Service asked him to state Board policy in reply to a question from the representative of the Lake Condah district about the Board's rules on releasing 'half castes' from the stations for employment. Everyone in the House knew he was one of Berry's old allies; most respected him greatly; few knew what lay behind his question. He had become acquainted with the Stähles when they defended Page's treatment of 'Punch' two years earlier. Now he was defending Stähle and the Lake Condah workers who had protested to him, the Anglican mission committee and the Board about Page's 'interference'. Cameron replied that it was the former practice to make workers pay for maintenance of their families but the rule had been neglected. Then he asserted that:

> Of late – in fact for the last twelve months – the board had been against allowing the half castes to leave the stations to get work. There was plenty of employment for them on the stations, and they were allowed a small payment – 2 1/2 d an hour – for pocket money. They were also provided with food, house accommodation and clothing. He was of opinion that it would be much better not to allow the half castes to go out to work at all.[40]

According to the *Argus* account, Cameron told the next meeting on 1 October that because half the reserve was covered with scrub and almost useless the men would be better employed clearing than tending hops. He was determined now to implement the inquiry recommendations on farming. His reputation as one of the district's champion farmers had been challenged by local criticisms of the undeveloped pasture and use of imported fencers at Coranderrk. He was also aware that most of the neighbours who supported Green's protest about Steel's ploy were seeking an opportunity to purchase this land rather than defending Aboriginal occupation. The decision was deferred, and the station was never fully stocked, although Goodall reported that the herd had been reduced by two-thirds since the meat ration was restored. The Board would not reduce the hop acreage while there was still hope that Berry would refund the income; this was finally refused in March 1885, although pressure from the mission committees forced the government to allow missionaries to retain the small income from other stations.[41]

Three of the Kulin families whom Page had ordered away were reprieved – by mischance and Goodall's intervention – late in 1884. Wandin was incapacitated by rheumatic fever, Dunolly's wife was seriously injured and John Charles' widow was allowed to remain after he was killed while searching for a neighbour's lost child. And Page could not prevent the lawful return of the Campbell family, 'to give the children schooling', when they found they were 'barely making a living' on a pastoral station. Stähle and two other missionaries were also questioning Page's hasty and illegal implementation of the new policy, reporting that the exiles could not obtain secure homes or sufficient wages to maintain their large families. But Goodall was the most serious threat. He made no secret of his sympathy with the

---

40   BPA – Page to Cameron, 20 July 1884; *Age* 7 August 1884; *Daily Telegraph* 4 September 1884; *Argus* 7 August, 4 and 12 September 1884; *Victorian Parliamentary Debates*, Session 1884:1367.
41   BPA – Minutes, 3 December 1884, 4 March 1885; *Argus* 2 October 1884, 4 January 1885.

problems of the reluctant emigrants and had opportunities to talk to Board members and the press. There would be no trouble installing Shaw as his successor: he had proved a loyal ally in rebuking interference. He was growing increasingly restive about his subordinate status, complaining when acting manager in September that as he was only 'second officer' residents would not obey him. This and other evidence that the residents disliked Shaw did not trouble Page; they must be taught to obey.

By October 1884 Goodall was well aware that Page would use any excuse to be rid of him. He openly challenged Page's prejudice ('in your opinion I am guilty of the charges before I have had opportunity of stating my case') when 'unfairly' rebuked over complaints made by the dormitory matron. Shaw's enclosed note defended Goodall – yet the matron's letters also cited his support. Her complaints were mainly about Goodall's wife – but Page's account led the Board members, who had never met Goodall, to blame him. It was Shaw, as acting manager, who objected when Mrs Bon asked for the usual shearers and 'interfered' on behalf of two dying lads. Although the minutes blamed Goodall, it was Shaw's complaints which earned Mrs Bon and Berry a formal rebuke from the Board in November 1884. They received another in December for trying to help old Barak. He had asked for aid to make the long journey to Lake Condah to bring back some orphaned children to their relatives. They were the fruit of the marriage between a Hamilton of Kilmore and John Green's namesake that Wonga had arranged in 1870. But the Board ruled that children could not be moved from station to station 'at the request of relatives'.[42]

In January 1885 the Board approved travel expenses for Page and a £504 house for Shaw. Press accounts of the February meeting quoted Page's criticisms of the neglected state of Coranderrk; Goodall had retorted that all his time and that of the men was engaged in looking after the hop crop. A decision to hire an overseer lapsed the following month because Berry refused to return the hop income. Goodall's annual report of July 1885 commended the 'hearty willingness' of the Coranderrk workers and noted that their number was 'much below any previous year' but did not explain that this was due to Page's unauthorised dispersal policy. The men had now completed all subdivision fencing and doubled the value of the reserve through extensive clearing, however, only 120 cattle were left and Goodall warned there would soon be no meat. But Cameron's pastoral development scheme ended in July 1885, when the purchase of cattle had to be delayed.

Stähle's complaints about Page's intervention in the management of his station had escalated into a formal protest by the Anglican mission committee in May. They objected to favouritism in allocating funds to Board stations and criticised Page's 'undue interference' with the missions, demanding that his powers be reduced to those of his predecessor Ogilvie. This was a reminder of the Board's 1875 directive that the secretary should 'refrain from interference' with missionaries. The mission committee, notified by Hagenauer that Page was aggrieved by their letter, volunteered to 'substitute another which will be more acceptable' and it was this version which appeared in press accounts of the June meeting. Press reports of the July meeting included a motion by Morrison denying any unfairness in funding and insisting that the Board was responsible for their secretary's actions. Morrison himself had presented an April memorandum condemning the 'inequitable' distribution of funds and nominating himself and Cameron to act 'with the Chief Secretary' to reduce expenditure on Coranderrk. He had also insisted that the schools at Coranderrk and other stations be put under the Education Department. None of this became public.

---

42   BPA – Shaw to Page, 10, 13, and 16 September 1884; Goodall to Page, 16 and 30 June, 8 July, 25, 27 and 29 October, 1 November 1884; File – Correspondence on dispute between Mr Goodall and Miss Persse; Minutes, 5 November and 3 December 1884.

Page, aware of the inspector's unfavourable reports on Shaw, feared the loss of his ally. Page had again survived public criticism of his job performance; he now used these complaints about Coranderrk to remove Goodall, arguing that transferring Goodall to Framlingham – where he could be paid less for lesser duties – would reduce management costs at Coranderrk from £544 to £270.[43] His calculations excluded the wage of the dormitory matron whom he now planned to dismiss.

There were no press accounts of the 28 August 1885 meeting when Page recommended Goodall's transfer to the newly vacant Framlingham post which the ambitious Shaw had refused. Page's minutes gave no explanation of the 'long discussion' by Cameron, Officer, LeSouef and Macredie which resulted in a motion to 'try to get Goodall permanently transferred'. The minutes declared that no definite decision was reached on future management of Coranderrk, yet Page quickly advised that staff costs could be halved by appointing the Shaws as manager and matron and handing over the school to the Education Department. Goodall agreed to visit Framlingham for a month, but family illness forced his return to Coranderrk by 12 September, when Mrs Jessie Shaw warned Page that Goodall had 'held a meeting with the men … trying to incite them against the wishes of the Board'.

On 18 September Shaw, who was relieving at Framlingham, informed Page of his wife's report that Goodall had:

> called a meeting of the men and told them that the Board wanted him to leave Coranderrk but that he would do all in his power not to do so, and incited them also to resist the wishes of the Board … such conduct can only be calculated to provoke insubordination and … would be practically ruling the Board. Everybody knows how childish the natives are and even the half castes, but it is unmanly to play upon their feelings for private purposes and there must be an absence of gentlemanly instincts in those who would allow themselves to do so. To stir up the feelings of the natives … is also an injustice to those who may be expected to succeed him.

But the effect was rather spoilt by a Framlingham resident's 15 September letter to Anderson which complained that Shaw had 'come round after Prayers to see if they would sign a petition for Mr W. Goodall … wanted us to sign and we wouldent [sic]'. Page rebuked Goodall for inciting rebellion at Coranderrk; his reply of 1 October insisted he had been 'unaware that a meeting was being held until I was sent for'. He had prevented an immediate deputation to enforce their protest only by explaining that 'nothing definite to my knowledge had been done to effect my removal' and assuring them he 'had no wish to leave seeing they were so much against it'. He deplored his subordinates' anonymous 'stab in the dark' and promised he would be no party to any agitation on the station one way or the other. But 'to carry out my promise to the Blacks', he urged the Board to avoid any change in management as he had not the slightest doubt it would cause trouble.

Meanwhile the Board had again been strongly criticised in Parliament during the budget debate of 23 September.[44] The opposition leader Thomas Bent, who had worked closely with Cameron as O'Loghlen's Railways Minister, challenged Berry to report on the treatment of Aborigines as there was considerable public dissatisfaction about affairs at Coranderrk. Berry retorted that he had not heard recently of any discontent except the feeling that existed about Green's removal: 'that appeared to be a chronic sentiment which time did not heal, but whatever wrong was done then could not be remedied now'. The *Age* and *Argus* accounts next day omitted Berry's comment and local members' criticisms of Page's 'very unbusinesslike and injurious' interference at Lake Condah and unjust neglect of the Gippsland missions. Instead the press emphasised other members' arguments for alienation of Ebenezer

---

43 BPA – Minutes, 14 December 1875; 4 March, 1 April, 18 June and 1 July 1885; W.E. Morris to Page, 22 May 1885; H. Macartney to Board, 9 May 1885; Page to Church of England Mission to Aborigines, 2 July 1885; Morrison memorandum, 25 April 1885; School Inspector to Page, 18 August 1885.
44 Victorian Parliamentary Debates, Session 1885:1210–12; *Age* and *Argus* 24 September 1885.

and Framlingham since their 'insolent and lazy' residents were not developing the land, and quoted their opinion that 'of all the barbarians of the world the blackfellow was about the most difficult to assimilate to the conditions of civilisation'. Berry seemed to agree that the 'pure blackfellows' should be 'treated as children' and the 'half castes' be made of use to the colony but reminded the House that as the law stood the latter could not be turned out of the stations. The debate was constantly interrupted by raucous gibes about the origins of the 'half castes'. Cameron said little.

But the Board vice-chairman was armed with statistics compiled by Page when his opponent renewed his demand for information about Board policy on 8 October.[45] Coranderrk had finally been gazetted as a permanent reserve. The opposition leader Bent opened the debate with a complaint (apparently from Green) that many residents of the Healesville district wanted Coranderrk broken up and the Aborigines removed to a more suitable locality. Cameron's reply, and particularly his interpretation of Page's statistics, was ludicrously inaccurate and totally unjust to the Coranderrk residents. In his summary of Board expenditure, he argued that Coranderrk residents cost £20 per head, three times that of other stations. A year earlier Page had told the New South Wales authorities the average cost per head at stations was £12 a year while the wanderers maintained at depots cost £5. Cameron was ignoring church funding elsewhere and the fact that Berry's recent special grant had been spent mainly on staff dwellings. He blamed the discrepancy on outside influence which had forced the Board to house Coranderrk people in 'little castles' and provide wages of '£26' a year as well as free housing, provisions and 'four' suits of clothing annually.

In fact, wages had declined since 1881 when the maximum possible was £14 a year; there was no meat; and only nine cottages were built between 1883 and 1886. Cameron's explanation of the £771 spent on the Melbourne district was even more farcical: the amount constituted Page's salary, that of his clerk and travel expenses for hospital patients, Board members and staff. Cameron declared it was:

> to a large extent accounted for by blacks being brought from Coranderrk to Melbourne to interview Ministers – an arrangement which was not only expensive but was calculated to break down discipline.

Cameron admitted the Coranderrk men worked as hard as any ordinary labourers but said they would be of more use off the station. Berry had already argued that the state should be relieved of its burden by dispersing the 'half castes' to areas where labour was scarce. He made no reply to Cameron's statement that he believed the Minister would have submitted a Bill authorising the Board's policy if time had allowed. Cameron himself made no comment on the abandonment of Coranderrk. His Board colleagues did. Anderson corrected the false statements on Coranderrk costs and admitted that rebuilding was necessary because the buildings had decayed, but he complained that 'owing to the pressure brought to bear on various Governments the Board had been compelled to continue Coranderrk'. The Officer assured the House that the Board would still be glad to remove the residents of this unsuitable station to a warmer climate but admitted that 'many of the blacks did not wish to be removed as they regarded the district as their own country'. Berry then interjected 'They have always been against removal' and when a Gippsland member, previously Hagenauer's supporter, rose to 'protest most emphatically against the removal of the Coranderrk blacks' Berry shouted 'Nobody thinks of removing them!' This was his last public statement on Aboriginal policy as Chief Secretary.

Opposition leader Bent ended the debate by announcing that he could no longer support the Board: he protested that 'a very large proportion of the vote of £10,000 was not being spent upon the blacks, but upon whites', querying recent salary increases and apparent 'political patronage'.

---

45 *Victorian Parliamentary Debates*, Session 1885:1386–90; *Argus* and *Age* 9 October 1885.

14. THE END OF THE STORY

The brief debate was the only serious discussion of Aboriginal affairs and Board policy between 1882 and 1890; it was repeatedly ruled out of order and many members complained that the opposition leader was wasting everyone's time. The press the next day suggested it was just a stonewalling tactic in an opposition campaign to block passage of the Estimates. The derisive remarks and interjections suggest that most members of Parliament had little sympathy for Aborigines but great interest in obtaining the reserves. Cameron had announced that only 849 Aborigines remained in Victoria and 261 of these were 'half castes'. They were cared for by respected citizens; the House need not waste time debating their welfare. Cameron had once again proved his political opportunism at the expense of Coranderrk Aborigines. His opinions about them and the future of their station had veered wildly over the last decade. They had never trusted him – never once sought his help. The young men who had helped them, Deakin and Dow, were probably absent from this debate. They were principled men, although young and ambitious. They were preoccupied now with plans for irrigation and talk of federalism. They were building a nation.

At Coranderrk two old men who also cared about the resources of this land, and understood the principles of sovereignty and federation, had just learned that Berry had made their land safe and arranged that it could not be taken from them without the consent of Parliament. But they heard the words of Parliament read from the newspapers by the young people. They knew that Parliament planned to take the children of their clans from this land. Their society of linked land-owning clans had long ago been described by the old Local Guardian, William Thomas, as a confederacy. Barak's new friend A.W. Howitt called it 'the Kulin Nation'. Their society had changed. They had helped to change it by sharing their land with other clans and with the *Ngamajet*. They had maintained the Kulin confederacy for a lifetime, had even extended it by new alliances and had admitted other clans to enjoy the resources of Coranderrk. Now their land was safe, but they had no sons.

Barak, always more patient than Bamfield, tried to comfort his wild grief. In August, Bamfield's only son had died at the age of 17, his young daughter too. Now his wife Eliza was also dying of tuberculosis and he had only one child left. He would take them to Mrs Bon's station in his own clan country this month, as it was shearing time. Let the Board try to stop him! Last May he had asked for the land that Steel wanted, the hundred acres (40.5 ha) cut off from Coranderrk by the new road which had been built for the neighbours' use. He had told them he would keep himself and his family on that block beside Mr Green, and ask no more aid. But the Board refused. Last January there was trouble too when he wanted to take his dying children to see their kin at Wahgunyah, and on to Maloga Mission. Old Dr Embling believed the air there might ease the chest sickness which the *Ngamajet* had brought to the Kulin. Bamfield's children, like Barak's son in 1881, had been kindly treated there before they came home to die. Most of the young people of the Kulin clans were going to Maloga now, since they had been told they must leave Coranderrk. He and Barak had built on old ties and formed new ties between the Kulin and the people of the Murray. Now the young Kulin were making marriages, making alliances, with the people there and helping to build their station on the scrap of land Daniel Matthews had given back to them. Matthews had learned about building a blackfellows' township when he brought the children to Green, long ago when Coranderrk was new. But he was not a teachable man like Green; he wanted to rule the people like all the other managers at Coranderrk since Green's time; he grew angry because the Kulin wanted to manage themselves. This new manager Shaw was the same.

Shaw was still at Framlingham on 6 October, as Goodall had remained at Coranderrk to care for his sick wife. There was no publicity for the Board meeting that day: it was convened to prepare a reply to the guardian Thomas' complaint, forwarded by the Anglican mission committee, about the management. Goodall was hastily ordered back to Framlingham. Page's press releases for the 18 November meeting, attended only by Cameron, Officer and LeSouef, did not mention the motion put by the latter two that Goodall be transferred permanently to Framlingham. They also resolved to make an inspection of Coranderrk. Reporters were invited to accompany Cameron, LeSouef, Officer – who was making his first visit – and Page. The *Age* and *Argus* reports of 24 November noted that the purpose of the inspection was to judge the success of Shaw's management as neither he nor Goodall was willing to be permanently stationed at Framlingham. The reporters quoted the Board members conclusion that residents were contented and Shaw was 'very popular'. The significance of Shaw's criticisms of workers' abilities, and his demand that wage and ration rates be reduced to force them to work on the station, was missed by the journalists. As they believed all Aborigines were lazy, they did not realise that men who were keen workers for Goodall were protesting Shaw's appointment. Even Goodall was apparently deceived by the Board's propaganda. A week later he offered to withdraw 'any objections I have had to my removal' because of this report that 'things go smoothly'.

The visit had a second propaganda aim; denunciation of the Minister's support for Mrs Bon's constant interference. She had asked Bamfield and other shearers to go as usual to her station and because Berry insisted 'the full blacks should have considerable license' Cameron had warned Page 'you better let those Darkies go – this time'. Press reports of the inspection made much of Board members' complaints about the lack of hands 'due to' the intervention of Mrs Bon and Berry, allegedly discouraging to those who remained behind to labour diligently. Shaw blamed the absence of these five shearers for the backward state of the hop ground, announced that he had to close the school so the boys could work and asked the Board either to import Chinese labour or reduce the hop acreage. To silence the press queries the embarrassed Board members explained that 'every year there were fewer hands to work'. They did not mention that Page had illegally exiled seven 'half caste' workers and their 20 dependents. The *Argus* noted that Shaw complained of trouble as a result of Officer's statement, in the recent Parliamentary debate, that the Board and their managers had 'no power to compel' station residents to labour. Shaw's mocking account of Bamfield's resulting protest was quoted:

> Punch, a full-blooded black who has waxed prodigiously fat on a liberal diet and laziness, showed himself to be an attentive reader of Parliamentary debates by triumphantly producing the report of the speech to Mr Shaw a day or two after it was delivered.

But Bamfield's physician, Dr Embling, wrote two letters to the *Argus* contradicting this ridicule.[46] Bamfield's fat was 'an infirmity' – not the result of over-eating. He was an excellent husband, father and worker, and a responsible political figure as 'last elected chief of the Broken River tribe'. As proof of Bamfield's work skills, Embling published the record of his current earnings: between 31 October and 8 December, he had earned £10/10/0 shearing 1,751 sheep, triple the number of his younger mates. He also explained that these proficient shearers went regularly to Mrs Bon's station where some were born. Their cheques were 'not spent in drink but go towards paying debts in Healesville for the many items which the Board does not supply'. He argued that the 'half castes ought to work and they are good workmen' and that their children and all orphans should be removed to institutions: 'this would solve the Coranderrk problem'. But he strongly opposed the 'forced industry' of hop cultivation and insisted that the 'few poor blacks' should be 'free commoners of Victoria':

> They complain, 'You have taken our lands and killed our game, and we are in hopeless beggary. We shan't be alive long, and all we ask is, let us live quietly and in peace'. William Barak, a devout Christian, the old chief of the Yarra tribe, has again and again said, 'I am an old man; all my people are dead – my wife and children are dead – why should I be obliged to work at hop picking? I know all the lands belonging to my people; you have got them. Let me have a little pension that I may pass my last days quietly'.

---

46 BPA – Goodall to Page 30 November 1885; Cameron to Page, 15 October 1885; *Age* 24 November 1885; *Argus* 24 and 26 November, 19 December 1885.

14. THE END OF THE STORY

**Betsy Bamfield Foster (1870–1898)
and David Bamfield (1868–1885).**

Embling's obvious sympathy for Aborigines, and his role as one of the founders of the Board and member of the 1881 inquiry, gave his opinions a spurious expertise. His advocacy of the popular sentiment that Aborigines were 'a dying race who have no white man's ambitions and no possible white man's hopes' lent weight to the new paternalism – already voiced in the 1885 Parliamentary debates – which would become a weapon for pressure groups demanding the reserves.

Ignoring an application from the former manager Halliday, Cameron, Officer, Anderson and LeSouef resolved on 1 December 1885 to ask the Minister to appoint Goodall permanently at Framlingham and Shaw at Coranderrk. Cameron, Officer and Page were deputed to suggest ways of reducing station expenditure 'particularly at Coranderrk'. To cover any possible criticism of the backward state of the hops Cameron publicly expressed regret for allowing 'the best men' to go shearing.

Page instructed Goodall to remove his family from Coranderrk as soon as his wife recovered. To secure approval of the necessary transfer Page wrote enthusiastically – if somewhat inaccurately – praising Shaw's skills and his 'twenty years' experience. But the Public Service Board declined to appoint Shaw as Goodall had a higher classification and could not be demoted. He was asked to 'return permanently' to Coranderrk in February 1886 but then Shaw refused to go to Framlingham and insisted on retaining his Coranderrk teaching post. Page therefore negotiated permission to allocate the stations without regard to qualifications. The Board did not meet between December 1885 and April 1886: the three members of Parliament were fighting an election. On 22 March Page informed the under secretary that his negotiations had succeeded and Shaw was now in permanent charge of Coranderrk. A fortnight later the matron resigned and Mrs Shaw was hired. In his original recommendations to the under secretary Page had planned to hire an overseer and hand over the school to the Education Department. Instead, he and Morrison selected John Mackie as teacher in July. Expenses did not in fact decrease, although no overseer was hired, for Shaw

REBELLION AT CORANDERRK

soon requested a higher salary.[47] Coranderrk did not become an Anglican station on Shaw's accession as manager. The Lilydale minister Rev. Alex Mackie continued to come for services and he conducted all marriages and baptisms: Wandin informed the Board of the residents' unanimous decision to have their children baptised 'only by a Presbyterian', and Page dared not intervene.

Joseph Shaw was an able, if authoritarian, manager of Coranderrk for 22 years. But the farm quickly declined. His June 1886 annual report explained the reason for demanding that the hop acreage be halved. By this time only 15 able-bodied men remained:

> so that the whole work of the establishment falls upon a very few, the half castes doing the lion's share of it, in fact if it were not for them, much white labour would have to be employed, or the hop industry and almost all farming operations abandoned.

Cameron's political influence was at its height at the end of 1885 as rumours of changes in the coalition ministry were rife. Both the Premier and Berry wished to retire. The *Argus* of 23 November, the day before the Board's last inspection of Coranderrk, had publicised a ministerial hint of Cameron's likely elevation to Cabinet. But his Healesville constituents took advantage of this visit to challenge him, at the public meeting chaired by John Green, on the delayed extension of the Lilydale railway. Cameron shrewdly countered this criticism by announcing that he had secured Deakin's ministerial promise of a special road subsidy to compensate for the unrateable Crown lands which greatly circumscribed the rate paying area. He was rewarded by vote of confidence. But Deakin was now involved in secret plans for a new coalition in which he replaced Berry as Liberal leader. Cameron did not achieve office when the government resigned in February and a March 1886 election confirmed public support for the new coalition. Deakin was also Chief Secretary; Dow was Lands Minister. Deakin had chosen most of his Cabinet colleagues from the left wing of his party. Cameron was unsympathetic to their views on most issues and perhaps felt slighted by his own party. These private sentiments inevitably shaped his relations with the new Minister. The coalition was to endure until November 1890 but Cameron's Board colleagues who recognised the importance of his 'representation in the House' had to press him to retain the vice-chairmanship until their Bill was passed.[48]

After the elections, Berry retired from Parliament in order to represent the colony as Agent General in London. The old Kulin leaders carefully planned a deputation and presentation: reciprocity was still important in their society. On 25 March 1886 the *Argus* published a detailed, rather mocking description of the 'somewhat rare compliment' offered Berry by a deputation of 15 men from Coranderrk. There were many ironies in this presentation. Barak had to leave behind some of the deputation members because Berry would 'not receive the women' and he did not know that Page had just defeated hopes for Goodall's return. Barak and Berry were men of similar age, similar grace, similar political and oratorical skills. Barak, Bamfield and the others came to thank the London tradesman's son who had listened to the Kulin, bringing baskets, weapons and an address composed by Barak which asked Berry to 'keep remembering the natives for the natives will remember you for doing good to Coranderrk':

> You do all that thing for the station when we were in trouble, when the board would not give us much food or clothes, and wanted to drive us off the land. We came to you and told you our trouble, and you gave us the land for our own as long as we live, and gave us more food and clothes and blankets and better houses, and the people all very thankful.[49]

---

47   BPA – Shaw to Page 10 February 1886; Secretary's Letter Book, 26 October 1885, 4 January, 9 February and 22 March 1886.
48   *Argus* 23 and 24 November 1885; *Age* 24 November 1885; Serle 1971:40–2.
49   BPA – Secretary's Letter Book, 22 March 1886; *Argus* 25 March 1886.

14. THE END OF THE STORY

The deputation was formally introduced by Zox and Deakin, but the *Argus* gave more space to the remarks of Mrs Bon who recounted the history of the pioneers' efforts to make a home for themselves. She pointed out that it was 23 years since the first deputation had left Coranderrk to attend a levee at Government House and beg the Governor to give them secure tenure of the Coranderrk land. Mrs Bon also:

> reminded Mr Deakin that, notwithstanding all that Mr Berry had done, there was yet plenty for him to do. The natives wished to be relieved of the board, and if the gentlemen composing it had not that sense of honour which should induce them to resign, they ought at feast to be relieved of their management of Coranderrk. A lot of money had been misspent in building a large house for the manager, which was locally known as the coffee palace.

Berry assured Barak and Bamfield and their followers that he would always be glad to hear from them, gracefully insisting that 'whatever he had been enabled to do for them was through the representations of Mrs Bon, than whom no people ever had a truer friend'. He also assured the deputation that their wishes would be studied by the present Chief Secretary, Deakin.

Barak's address to Berry expressed genuine grief and concern about the loss of a man he considered a loyal ally: 'you have done a great deal of work for the aborigines. I feel very sorrowful and the first time I hear you going home I was crying'.

Cameron and Page, on the other hand, felt considerable jubilation at the departure of this Minister they could not control. They had been notified in the previous April that a Bill embodying their recommendations would shortly be considered by Cabinet. Yet despite Cameron's challenge in the October debate Berry had eluded announcement of a decision on the new policy – or the inquiry report. Cameron and Page strongly censured the delay in their 1885 annual report, submitted just before Parliament was prorogued in December. Nothing of the planning for a new coalition leadership had been made public. As soon as the result of the elections was known Page wrote to the new Minister requesting action. On 2 June 1886 a 'rough draft' of the desired Bill was forwarded to the Board and on 23 June Deakin, without comment, introduced the Bill in Parliament.

To the considerable chagrin of Cameron and Page, who had expected that Berry's departure would end ministerial 'interference', Deakin had already begun to imitate Berry in heeding complaints from Mrs Bon and the Coranderrk people. In June Deakin challenged Board authority by over-ruling and rebuking Page's 'unwarranted' refusal to re-admit a recently exiled Taungurong family. Bamfield's niece Kate Brangy Friday (sister of Eda Brangy) had lived with his family in 1885; now Bamfield wanted her and her husband back from Maloga to care for his little girl as his wife Eliza had died in January 1886. Page had refused, but Mrs Bon put the case to Deakin enclosing Shaw's letter stating that he had advised Page to permit the family's return. Page had already submitted a careful defence when the Minister first challenged his decision. He had informed Deakin that there was no house at Coranderrk and enclosed letters from the missionary Daniel Matthews reporting that the Fridays were quite content at Maloga. Page did not mention that he had received letters from Kate Friday and her husband Jack begging to return as well as letters from Bamfield offering to house his niece. The evidence presented by Mrs Bon proved Page a liar.

The under secretary rebuked him by writing to Cameron direct; he said that Page's statement about the family's wishes was 'not strictly in accord with the facts'. Infuriated because 'it appears that a Black man's word is believed before mine', Page demanded Cameron's support to 'put a stop to this outside interference', insisting that 'it is time that either Mrs Bon or myself is put to one side; for years she has caused, as everybody knows, a great deal of trouble without doing any good'. He also berated Shaw for his interference and forbad any further correspondence with Mrs Bon.

Page's new policy was in danger of foundering even before the enabling legislation was passed: every station manager except Hagenauer was objecting to its hasty implementation and reporting that the exiled 'half castes' could not obtain housing and regular employment to support their large families. (The first girl sent to domestic service had died in childbirth at a Melbourne institution.) And although Daniel Matthews had accepted numerous Coranderrk 'half castes' 'because it seems to me a pity that they should roam about so', he had already offered support for various pleas to go 'home to Coranderrk'. In June 1885 he had urged Page to allow repatriation of Louisa Briggs' many descendants, explaining that 'they are an expense upon our limited means, and more than that, if we increase our numbers I should do so from those who are living in camps in New South Wales or Victoria and have no advantages'.

The Friday case was important to Page as the Minister's intervention seemed a victory for Bamfield's 'impudence' and set a precedent for other exiles. Page had been forced to re-admit the Jajowrong 'half castes' Alfred Davis (c. 1860–1933) and Henry Nelson (c. 1855–1920) late in 1885 because their families were in poor health. Their return had prompted a spate of pleading letters from the Briggs, Kerr and Morgan families who had taken refuge at Maloga. Page had refused, advising the exiles that Coranderrk was full. When Mrs Morgan appealed to Deakin for permission to return from Maloga, Page and Cameron had ignored the Minister's repatriation advice.

Page and Cameron, however, had learned that they could not ignore Mrs Bon's representations and, after all, the Fridays were 'pure blacks'. Cameron was as angry as Page at the Minister's second intervention: 'I was in hopes that Punch and Mrs Bon's influence would cease with Mr Berry's departure. I am strongly inclined to throw the thing up'. He agreed that this must be treated as a test case, to end 'the trouble and annoyance Mrs Bon and her protege give the Board' and force Deakin to acknowledge the Board's executive authority. By forbidding Page to re-admit the Fridays and threatening resignation in his own reproof to Deakin, Cameron deliberately challenged the new Minister's strength. All six Board members 'endorsed Cameron's action with cordial approval and thanks' at their meeting of 7 July 1886. Page arranged an August interview with Deakin for the Maloga missionary Daniel Matthews, who shared his own view that the Aborigines' freedom to come and go was 'prejudicial to authority' at the stations. Matthews urged the Minister to 'discourage the migratory habits of the Blacks and thus strengthen our hands'. He strongly supported Page's complaints about the interference of Bamfield, reporting that on one visit to Maloga Bamfield had 'influenced nearly thirty individuals; had I not returned in time he would have drafted them off to Coranderrk'. But at the Board's September meeting Officer, the only member of the Board who showed sympathy for Kulin attachment to Coranderrk – and had revealed it publicly in the 1885 Parliamentary debate – succumbed to Bamfield's continued pleas for repatriation of his closest kin and persuaded the Board to approve. Page still opposed it and falsely reported at the next meeting in November that the Fridays would now prefer Framlingham (where Jack Friday had lived before his marriage); instead the Fridays made their own way from Maloga to Coranderrk and were admitted. Bamfield had won.[50]

Thereafter Deakin's direct intervention almost ceased. The propaganda by Matthews and Page, and Cameron's resignation threat, had influenced his attitude toward the Board. There were other considerations, of course. The Anglican mission committee was once more publicly complaining about the Board's treatment of its Lake Condah mission and no one wanted more trouble about Coranderrk. Cameron's pressure probably influenced Deakin the most. The new coalition had numerous opponents, on both sides of the House, who might challenge the Chief Secretary's ministerial responsibility if the Board's vice-chairman resigned while Deakin was soliciting Parliamentary approval for legislation to

---

50 BPA – Secretary's Letter Book, 24, 25, 30 June 1886; Cameron to Page, 26 June 1886; Daniel Matthews to Page, 2 June 1885; Minutes, 7 July, 1 September and 17 November 1886. CSIC 86/F11591, 86/B6750, 86/E6827, 86/H5591, 86/E7888. BPA – Minutes, 7 July, 11 September, 17 November 1886.

implement a far-reaching alteration of Board policy. Yet probably this friction between the Board and the Minister contributed to the unusual delay in the processing of the Aborigines Protection Law Amendment Bill which almost lapsed from the notice-paper and was finally pushed through in the closing hours of the session.

The Bill was amended because of a deputation from Coranderrk. A punitive clause demanded by Hagenauer and Page – a legal validation of what they had recommended at the 1882 managers' conference – was altered, then excised by Deakin in response to their wishes. As Attorney General in the previous coalition, Deakin may also have had some part in excluding from the final Bill the provision which Berry had objected to when Hagenauer and the Board first brought him their recommendations in 1884. The Board's 1884 annual report had made public their intention to exclude from care any 'black' husband or wife who married an 'able-bodied half caste' after the policy came into operation, but this provision was omitted from the final Bill.

Chapter 15
DISPERSAL

> … a nation of robbers, robbing out of mere wantonness and not from the pressure of necessity.
>
> Alexander Harris 1847[1]

Barak and Bamfield, escorted by Mrs Bon and Zox, saw Deakin on 21 December 1886.[2] They asked him to ensure that they retained the right to appeal 'from the Board to the Chief Secretary' and objected to the new authority given by Clause 5 which enabled the Board, at its own discretion, to punish residents of stations by removal or forfeiture of rations. The petition asked for:

> our wishes, that is, could we get our freedom to go away shearing and harvesting and to come home when we wish, and also to go for the good of our health when we need it; and we aboriginals all wish and hope to have freedom, not to be bound down by the protection of the board, as it says in the bill (Clause 5). But we should be free like the white population. There is only few blacks now remaining in Victoria. We are all dying away now, and we blacks of aboriginal blood wish to have our freedom for all our lifetime, for the population is small and the increase is slow. For why does the board seek in these latter days more stronger authority over us aborigines than it has yet been. For there is only 27 aborigines on the station Coranderrk, including men and women.

The petition was signed by all the 15 'black' men – Kulin, Pangerang and Burapper – whom Barak had welcomed to his land. All were old, most were childless. The Board had not yet received legislative authority for its absorption policy, yet there were only six 'half caste' men left at Coranderrk: the Kulin pioneers Wandin, Dunolly, William Hamilton and Alfred Davis, the Burapper Alick Campbell and the Pangerang Bill Russell (a half-brother to Morgan and husband of a Taungurong pioneer). Their names were not included. The young Kulin had spent their lives there. They knew no other home. But the Board had said they must take their families away, must cease to be Kulin and try to be 'absorbed' among the *Ngamajet*. They could not ask for aid and had no right to remain. It was no use appealing. They had read the newspapers and knew what the men in Parliament believed. Their old friends Mrs Bon and Dr Embling said the same. The interview concluded with Zox's statement that 'he was desired by the Chief Barak to say that all the Coranderrk blacks wished was to be under the Queen, the Governor, the Chief Secretary, and the colony of Victoria'. Deakin promised to put their views to Cabinet.

He could not grant their wish for the abolition of the Board. But perhaps he did intend to allow the Bill to lapse, for when the opposition leader Bent challenged him on 7 October 1886, Deakin virtually disclaimed responsibility for the Board's expenditure and policy and set no date for the second reading

---

1   Harris 1847:421.
2   BPA – Annual Report 1884:4; CSIC 86/E2963; *Argus* 22 September 1886.

of their tabled Bill. But he finally did present it, as the last government Bill of the session, on 15 December 1886.[3] He explained that he 'would not have asked the House at that stage to pass the Bill if it were not specially recommended by the Aborigines Board'. He used the Board's own rationale for the Bill:

> its object was simply to enable those half castes who were connected with the mission stations to earn their own living, thus relieving the state of the burden of their maintenance, and preventing the Aboriginals from being crowded out of the station.

Deakin then announced that Clause 5, authorising removal and forfeiture of rations, would be amended so the Board required the consent of the Governor-in-Council before the authority was exercised. The conservative Catholic farmer Allan McLean interjected 'Clause 5 had better be omitted'. Deakin retorted that 'The Bill was not a Government Bill; it was the Bill of the Board'. Clause 5 was immediately struck out. It was the disreputable and always unsympathetic opposition leader Bent who objected to Clause 11 which made 'any able-bodied half caste found lodging, living or wandering in company with any Aboriginal' liable to 12 months imprisonment with hard labour as an 'idle and disorderly person'. It too was struck out. Clause 12 which empowered magistrates to decide, on their 'own view and judgment' (presumably on physical appearance) whether a person was Aboriginal or 'half caste' was also removed. The complex Bill was dealt with in ten minutes by three speakers on voice votes. Yet the Bill passed because, as McLean remarked, the Board's policy 'represented the unanimous wish of the people of the country with regard to half castes'. Two backbenchers did argue that the measure should have been postponed for full debate and condemned its hasty passage as 'indecent' – a 'travesty on legislation' and a 'disgrace to Parliament'. The next day's *Argus* made little of their objections in its editorial comment on the Parliamentary session:

> Members of the Legislative Assembly spent the last night of the session in a hilarious mood, as usual. The subjects before them changed so rapidly that fixed thought on any topic was out of the question, and time passed pleasantly in consequence … In the last 10 minutes left to the Government Mr Deakin scored by pushing the Aborigines Protection Bill through all its stages. Some members were irate, and protested against hasty legislation, just as some members protest on the last night of every session, but their voices were hardly heard in the din.

The *Age* that day probably summed up public opinion on the Aboriginal question. The editor considered the session memorable for the passage of new water supply legislation (largely prepared by Deakin and Dow) but concluded that:

> The other Bills which have been carried through their final stages are not merely of a minor character when compared with those relative to water supply and irrigation, but would not have stood out as important in any session.[4]

Now that he had legislative authority Page could ensure that the dispersal policy was fully implemented. All 'half castes' born after 1852 (i.e. 13 years and over) were ordered to find work and homes for themselves off the stations and the children of those 'over-age' 'half castes' still eligible to live on the stations were sent out as domestic servants and farm labourers from the age of 13. The sick and needy could be licensed to receive temporary refuge at the stations; but the government's new insistence on retrenchment, as the economic recession developed into the severe depression of the 1890s, limited aid to only the most desperate cases.

---

3 *Victorian Parliamentary Debates*, Session 1886:1810, 2912–13.
4 *Age* and *Argus* 16 December 1886.

15. DISPERSAL

Page never quite trusted Shaw's loyalty after the Friday case. He publicly defended Shaw's management when Bamfield, Jeannie Rowan and Barak made complaints to the Board over the next three years. But privately he berated Shaw for harsh treatment of various individuals. In 1887 he challenged Shaw's 'extraordinary proceeding' in refusing admission to Alfred Morgan whose visit from Maloga had been authorised by the Board; in January 1889 he insisted that Caroline Morgan, dying of typhoid, must be admitted: 'Nearly two years ago they begged me to let them return and at your request I said no – your comfort will be considered as much as possible but a woman and a large family cannot be punished for all time on your account'.[5]

Page also opposed Shaw's promotion demands until, embarrassed by an 1887 resignation threat, Chief Secretary Deakin and the Public Service Board, informed that the Board could not find an experienced replacement for this 'greatly underpaid and dissatisfied' manager, merely suggested Goodall's return. Shaw's application for promotion, minuted 'delayed until Goodall transferred to another branch', was not re-submitted until 1889.[6] Goodall had accompanied the Framlingham men on a deputation to Deakin to protest the closure of their station. He was quickly transferred to the Neglected Children's Department in Melbourne. By then Page was dying and Rev. F.A. Hagenauer became Board secretary-inspector in July 1889 and it was he who made the decisions.

Captain A.M.A. Page died on 5 March 1890. His 12-year rule had driven most of the Kulin from Coranderrk. He had failed to impose his authoritarian views because the Kulin had fought – and because they could enlist sympathisers. Public concern had lessened now that the 'half castes' were dispersed and the 'blacks' were dying.

Victorian Aboriginal administration became entirely authoritarian and paternalistic during Hagenauer's reign as secretary-inspector from 1889 to 1906 and during the subsequent regime of the clerk he trained as his successor. The last of the original Board members and mission representatives, Macredie, died in 1891. None of the newer members could challenge the expert authority of the colony's senior missionary who had begun work with Aborigines in 1858 and had, since 1872, controlled the administration of the four mission stations. The absorption policy was largely his scheme; he enforced it with ruthless benevolence. Having been a manager himself, he believed that the station managers' dignity and authority should be upheld at all costs. Hagenauer and Shaw had been acquainted since 1869; they shared a common background of missionary service, were both of autocratic temper and shared similar opinions on the necessity for the rigid discipline of wayward natives. In his 1888 annual report, Shaw had publicly requested the Board to strengthen the managers' control by means of new disciplinary powers. He complained that:

> when the natives were less enlightened there was little or no need of regulations, as they never thought of calling in question the authority of a manager; but now they are ready enough to do so ...[7]

Hagenauer felt that Aboriginal complaints, and questions by their sympathisers, were an affront to his dignity. He ensured that any complaints to higher authority were referred to the Board and the managers for report thus putting an end to ministerial intervention. Moreover, he provided only press releases instead of admitting journalists to Board meetings; when these were abandoned in 1894, the public, Parliament and the Aborigines themselves had no information on Board decisions except the annual reports. His successors published only two annual reports between 1912 and the dissolution of the Board in 1957.

---

5   BPA – Minutes, 7 July 1887, 5 September 1888, 6 March 1889; Secretary's Letter Book, 4 March 1887, 4 January 1889.
6   BPA – Secretary's Letter Book, 22 March, 5 May, 2 July and 14 November 1889.
7   BPA – Annual Report 1888:App. 1.

Fifteen 'fullblood' and 29 'half caste' Pangerang and Kulin adults and children had migrated from Coranderrk to the Maloga Mission between 1879 and 1886. A majority of the 50 'half castes' exiled after the passage of the 1886 *Aborigines Act* also sooner or later took refuge across the Murray, settling at or near Maloga, and, later, at the new government station, Cumeroogunga. Daniel Matthews' Maloga Mission seemed near collapse in 1888 when all buildings and most residents were forcibly removed to Cumeroogunga. In March 1889 Page had persuaded the New South Wales authorities to order the Cumeroogunga manager 'not to receive expellees or fugitives from Victoria'.[8] But Matthews continued to admit needy 'half caste' families and, even worse, solicited public subscriptions for their maintenance. In his published reports, letters to the press and speeches on fund raising tours, he ardently criticised the disastrous consequences of the Victorian absorption policy. As the Royal Commissioners had warned in 1877, the colonists' prejudice against Aborigines was too great for rapid absorption. The depression conditions of the 1890s further hindered equal opportunity in employment.

Hagenauer, as a professionally trained Moravian missionary, had always felt some disdain for laymen such as Green, Goodall and Daniel Matthews. He had long insisted that stations should be managed only by missionaries. Because Daniel Matthews' reception of Coranderrk Aborigines undermined Hagenauer's implementation of the dispersal policy, and Shaw's authority over rebellious Coranderrk residents, they both particularly disapproved the independent work of this amateur missionary. Matthews' writing and speeches argued that the exiles were necessarily reverting to the homeless, hungry, sick and uneducated condition which had prevailed before the establishment of the stations in the 1860s. This alarmed the Victorian church congregations he addressed and caused some concerned clergy and laymen to question the morality of the new policy and, by implication, the morality of its administrators. Hagenauer, with Shaw's support, retaliated with a public campaign to discredit Matthews. In a series of vicious letters to the influential church newspaper Southern Cross in 1890, they denied the necessity for his independent mission, queried his personal finances and warned the public against further donations to the Maloga Mission.[9] They could not silence Matthews, and they could not control the New South Wales authorities who continued to accept needy 'half caste' families. The names of many Coranderrk families – Barber, Brangy, Briggs, Campbell, Charles, Davis, Dunolly, Hamilton, Jackson, Kerr, Morgan, Nelson, Simpson and Wandin – became known across the Murray as they and their children helped to clear and farm yet another home for themselves.

Barak and his younger aides remained at Coranderrk. The ages of Dunolly and Wandin and their wives were close to the date (1852) that was the criterion for eligibility in the *Aborigines Act* 1886. In 1888 they were declared over-age and therefore eligible to remain although their children were sent to service. Page's notification pompously warned Dunolly that 'the Board expects him to behave properly and particularly not to act "letter-writer" any more'.[10] But Dunolly still had an obligation to Barak and this land and continued to be a 'trouble-maker'. In 1892 Hagenauer offered assistance to persuade him to take up his own farm somewhere else – preferably at the Wimmera! Instead Dunolly farmed land on the Victorian side of the Murray near Cumeroogunga until he returned, a frail old widower, as a 'licensed half caste' in 1905. Bamfield died in 1893, Barak in 1903, Wandin in 1908 – the same year as John Green. Finally, only Dunolly was left to fight for Coranderrk.

---

8   BPA – Minutes, 6 March 1889.
9   *Southern Cross* 12, 19 September, 17 October, 13 November 1890; Cato 1976, Barwick 1972.
10   BPA – Secretary's Letter Book, 15 December 1888.

Cottages at Coranderrk, c. 1891.

Meanwhile the Victorian government had pressed the Board to reduce costs during the depression of the 1890s; this and the lobbying of land hungry neighbours forced the Board to begin 'amalgamating' the six stations. Many eligible 'fullbloods' and elderly 'half castes' rendered homeless by the closing of Framlingham in 1890, the Wimmera mission in 1904, Ramahyuck in 1908 and Lake Condah in 1918 were forcibly resettled at Coranderrk, the one 'permanent' reserve. The displacement of the original Coranderrk population can be gauged from Board files: ten of the 41 adults resident in 1894 and 22 of 38 adults resident in 1909 had been transferred from other stations. When the Board planned to close Coranderrk in 1918 the secretary reported that 33 residents were willing to transfer to Lake Tyers and only 24 refused; but his own notes reveal that the 13 adults and 20 children who 'consented' were all recent arrivals. Certain families were immediately transferred to Lake Tyers. The Board's 1921 annual report announced that only 42 residents remained at Coranderrk; the secretary's unpublished enumeration named another 47 'half castes' ineligible for aid or residence who were camping in the vicinity. Descendants of the pioneers – the Davis, Franklin, Harris, Hunter, Manton, Patterson, Rowan, Russell, Terrick and Wandin families – plus exiled children of the recent immigrants, were camped in huts and tents to be near their 'old people'. But the manager who succeeded Shaw in 1907, C.A. Robarts, punctiliously maintained the Board's rule that 'the outside half castes are restricted to one day a week to visit their relatives and friends'.

The dispersal of the 'half castes' had ended farm development at Coranderrk. In 1890, Shaw, after repeated pleas, finally won consent to further reduce the hop ground to five acres (2 ha) 'on account of the half castes being sent away and only black children and old men being left to do the work'.[11] The Board did

---

11   *Daily Telegraph* 8 May 1890.

purchase stock after 1887 and, as a result of the population decline, there was a small annual surplus for sale. But two to five acres (0.8–2 ha) of vegetables and hay, five acres of hops and some 300 head of cattle did not constitute full exploitation of 4,850 acres (1,963 ha) of the reserve. Local agitation for alienation strengthened. Cameron's obligations to his constituents made him particularly susceptible to pressure from the Healesville Shire Council. Cameron had suggested the formation of this council in 1885, when he gave Deakin's promise of support to offset road building costs so Coranderrk would not burden the European community. Green had presided at that meeting; he was the Council's first president. He and the Coranderrk people remained friends to the end; they visited and worked for him at his Healesville home; they came to mourn at his funeral in 1908 and that of Mary Green in 1918. But he was not mentioned in Board records after 1885; presumably the old enmity of Shaw and Hagenauer discouraged any close association with the station.

The myth that Victorian Aborigines would not farm and could not use their reserves profitably began in the 1880s when the young were removed and the old despaired. The younger generation of Kulin who had helped to build the successful farm of the 1860s and 1870s were now building another home on the land of their Joti-jota and Pangerang allies in the north. The old Kulin now shared their home with reluctant immigrants from the Wimmera and Western District who had no claim to this land and mourned for their own homes now leased or sold to European farmers. The successful farming township which Green and the Kulin had built was destroyed in the 1880s by a handful of men who had rarely visited and never listened to the Kulin. The blackfellows' township which had been a source of pride to the clan-heads Wonga and Barak became a shabby zoo where thousands of idle tourists visited on Sunday afternoons. They came for a 'peep at the blacks'; they went away with their prejudices confirmed.

The Board members who presided over the destruction of Coranderrk in the last quarter of the nineteenth century were the old men appointed between 1876 and 1882: Anderson, Cameron, F.R. Godfrey (re-appointed in 1896), LeSouef, Morrison and Officer. With W.E. Morris, elected in 1887 as representative of the Church of England mission, they managed the Board affairs until the first decade of the twentieth century. LeSouef, Officer and Morrison had recently died; Cameron had ceased to attend in 1902 as a protest against the Board's refusal to relinquish the last of the land at Coranderrk. Coranderrk had one ally on the Board after 30 December 1904: Anne F. Bon was appointed. Anderson, Godfrey and their few younger colleagues obviously expected that this courteous gesture would end the incessant interference of the venerable philanthropist considered too aged to be an active participant. But to their poorly concealed chagrin she regularly attended Board meetings, harassed succeeding secretaries and maintained a voluminous private correspondence with Aborigines throughout Victoria until her death in 1936, aged 99.

Macredie and the five members who outlived him had initially rejected the Healesville Shire Council's 1889 applications to alienate land for a model dairy farm and to cut an access road through the reserve. The members finally consented to the latter proposal after Cameron led a Shire Council deputation to a Board meeting.

The Coranderrk residents had petitioned against the Shire Council's demand that their land become an agricultural college: Cameron publicly advised his colleagues that 'the acreage of the stations, and especially that of Coranderrk, should be curtailed, as there was more land there than could be profitably used by the Aborigines'.[12] In 1891 the Board gave retrospective approval for the road illegally cut across the reserve and granted the shire president a lease of the land they had offered to Steel and denied Bamfield.

---

12 BPA – Minutes, 3 June, 7 August, 2, 9 October 1889; Secretary's Letter Book 6 and 11 November 1891, 2 December 1891.

The new road neatly halved the reserve and in 1893 the Board, at a meeting in the Coranderrk manager's house, consented to relinquish the eastern half nearest Healesville for village settlement – when pressure was applied by Cameron and the Council, both directly and through the Lands Department. Hagenauer's press releases did not mention the Board decision to hand the acreage immediately to the Lands Department. The cancellation of 2,400 acres (971 ha), half the permanent reservation, by means of a clause in the omnibus 1893 *Crown Lands Reserve Act*, received no publicity until the Board's 1894 annual report, published 12 months later, announced that the excision 'at the request of the Minister of Lands and Agriculture' was *afait accompli*.[13]

Of course, the owners had protested: Barak and Wandin collected the signatures of all of the 17 men and 14 women residents for a 23 October 1893 petition to the vice-chairman Officer as soon as they heard the rumours:

> We heard little about our land going to be taken from us … They ought to leave us alone and not take the land from us it is not much. We are dying away by degree. There is plenty more land around the country without troubling about Coranderrk. We Aboriginals from Coranderrk wish to know if it's true about the land. Please we want to know. We got plenty of our own cattle and we want the run for them and if the White People take it away from us there will be no place to put them … We never forgot Mr Berry said to us in the Town Hall when we passed the native weapons to him he told us we can go away and come to our home here again any time to our station. We don't forget Mr Berry's word and also when we go into any of the White People's paddock to hunt or fish they soon clear us out of their private premises very quick and yet they are craving for Coranderrk.

The Board had in fact forbidden any publicity for the resumption scheme, well aware that any Aboriginal protest might be abetted by Berry. (Since his return from England two years earlier there had been repeated threats to appeal to him and he was currently leader of the opposition.) Shaw had known of the decision since the April meeting in his house. He had supported the excision as it would lessen his own responsibility for maintenance of fencing and pasture. Shaw's covering letter of 23 October merely noted that he had been asked to forward the petition to Board Secretary Hagenauer, as 'our people here are somewhat excited about the prospect of losing some of their land … I believe they have also sent one to Sir Graham Berry'. But the omnibus Bill was already before Parliament and the Board threatened punishment if the Coranderrk residents attempted any public protest; if Berry did challenge the excision clause hidden in the lengthy Bill, his protest was not recorded by Hansard or the press. Another protest against Shaw's management was firmly repressed in 1893: the Education Department teacher was removed 'in the public interest' because he had sent anonymous complaints to the press after the Board and the Chief Secretary refused to act on his criticisms of Shaw and Hagenauer. The Board had dismissed his predecessor John Mackie in 1890 for similar criticisms of Shaw's management and subsequently hired only 'more amenable' female teachers.[14]

Still the Healesville agitation continued but the Board's 1902 annual report, signed by vice-chairman Officer, actually rebuked the government's announced plans to sell Coranderrk and pointed out that half of this permanent reservation had already been alienated:

> and years ago the promise was made to the people that they should always occupy the same, and such promises ought to be kept; then again it has still a larger population than any of the other stations … and the people are attached to the place and look upon it as their home as long as they live, and much dissatisfaction would arise if an attempt was to be made to dispossess them.

---

13   BPA – Minutes 12, 21 April, 3 May, 1 November, 8 December 1893; CSIC 93/V3804, 17 May 1893.
14   BPA – Shaw to Hagenauer, 23 October 1893; Minutes, 5 March, 7 May, 2 July, 1890; 12, 21 April, 3 June 1893; Secretary's Letter Book, 8, 28 May 1890.

The retirement of Hagenauer in 1906 and Shaw in 1908 after nearly a quarter century of service was almost shocking. The young people at Coranderrk could not remember any other management. The Board had changed, too, in the last few years. Cameron was active again in 1907–08 but attended only two more meetings before his death in 1915. Mrs Bon attended regularly but a succession of members of Parliament served briefly and showed little interest. The most significant figure in reforming Board policy was John Murray, the brash new member for Warrnambool who had sneered at Aboriginal capabilities in the October 1885 debate. Disturbed by the plight of the Framlingham exiles, he conducted a campaign against Hagenauer's policy through the 1890s and when he became Premier and Chief Secretary emended the Act in 1910 so that needy 'half castes' could be licensed to reside on the stations and receive aid. He was the first *ex officio* chairman of the Board to attend meetings. Indeed, he assumed direct control of Aboriginal affairs as Graham Berry had never cared or dared to do. From 1913 until his death in 1916 Murray *was* the Board. He convened the members only once between December 1913 and May 1916, when it was reconstituted by his successor. Mrs Bon was the only continuing member: the Board was now composed of eight Parliamentary representatives of districts with sizeable Aboriginal populations.

In 1912, when there were still 66 residents, the Board refused to part with another 1,000 acres (405 ha) requested by the Lands Department. They also refused Dunolly's request for 50 acres (20 ha) as he could not acquire land elsewhere. In 1914 and 1915 Healesville residents petitioned the government to resume the reserve for a permanent military camp. Chief Secretary Murray refused, announcing that Coranderrk was the most suitable site for a central station housing all the surviving natives. The Healesville Shire Council then organised public protest meetings which complained that 'the congregation of a degenerate race a few miles from the township will ruin Healesville as a tourist resort'.

It was a ludicrous argument as the townsfolk had been touting tours of Coranderrk as a major tourist attraction for decades. In the postwar years, approximately 2,000 visitors a year went to Coranderrk. Cameron was succeeded briefly by James Rouget, as MLA for Evelyn. He was appointed to the reconstituted Board in 1916: his constituents' demands for resumption of the remaining reserve for soldier settlement provided the main business of the first meeting. Similar demands from other Parliamentary representatives led to a decision on 7 August 1917 to 'concentrate' all eligible Aborigines ('down to half caste standard') at the remote and impoverished Lake Tyers station in Gippsland. This was the only reserve not coveted by European neighbours. Any eligible Aborigines who refused to leave their homes would 'forego any future assistance'. Rouget's electors forced him to apply pressure to the Board and government as there were few other local properties suitable for subdivision for soldier settlement and all were defended by powerful interest groups. Valuations of Coranderrk were arranged in 1917: the Agriculture Department valuer's report said four six-roomed cottages were valueless because 'it is doubtful whether Europeans would care to inhabit them after Aborigines'. Rouget's own valuation of the reserve was also presented at the 7 August meeting: Coranderrk was worth £54,500 or an average £22 per acre (in 1879 the Board had offered it for sale at £4 per acre when neighbours were offering £15–20 per acre for hop land). Rouget's demand for a survey caused some embarrassment because it revealed that the 2,450 acres (992 ha) still permanently reserved had already been illegally reduced to only 1,780 acres (720 ha). At the same meeting Mrs Bon was censured because of the Coranderrk manager's complaints about residents 'interviewing Board members' and sending letters through 'outside channels'. The Board once again resolved that all Aboriginal complaints must be put in writing and go through the Board secretary or chairman.

W.H. Everard (MLA for Evelyn 1917–1950) persuaded the Board to consent to immediate abandonment of Coranderrk in 1917. The minutes of 7 May noted that, as a result of the appointment of election victors and retention of losers, the Board now had 'three members to represent the interests of Coranderrk', Cameron, Rouget, as well as Everard. On 28 May the Board was informed that all the Aborigines refused to leave Coranderrk because their relatives were buried there; the members resolved to reply that they must leave Coranderrk but, if they died at Lake Tyers, burial at Coranderrk would be arranged. But the residents were not moved in 1918. The Board had learned that selling Coranderrk would benefit only the Lands Department, although the Board could retain income from leases for the new Produce Fund established to subsidise the development of Lake Tyers. The manager's request for a portion of the reserve as compensation for the ending of his employment was refused. So was his January 1918 request that the Board leave 11 old people who objected to removal 'to such a distant place and among different tribes'. The Mantons, Terricks, Davises, Russells, Tom Dunolly (now married to Wandin's widow Jemima), and his sister Ellen Richards were now in their late fifties or sixties. In August 1918 the Healesville Shire Council supported this scheme, as residents had made a deputation to them.

At the meeting of 19 August 1919, Mrs Bon presented a petition by Dunolly and others urging the retention of Coranderrk; the secretary was ordered to reply that as the government had not dealt with the question of disposal the Board could not consider the petition. In 1920 the Board refused to consent to any excision while waiting for the government's decision on enabling legislation. Anne Bon, now aged 83 and growing frail, apologised for missing several meetings explaining that she was often at her station.

In 1921, overborne by Everard's consistent pressure on behalf of the Healesville Shire Council, the Repatriation Committee, the Patriotic League, the local branch of the powerful Returned Servicemen's League and six European soldiers who wanted blocks, the Board made definite plans for abandonment. In September Mrs Bon's colleagues passed a motion censuring her disloyalty in protesting to the Chief Secretary about plans for sale of three reserves. She insisted that her dissent on the removal of two families be recorded. The February 1921 minutes note that a 'petition to remain' sent by the surviving pioneers was merely 'received'. The secretary rebuked them. Once again they tried to enlist aid from sympathetic and influential people who would listen as the Board had never done. But those who had fought 40 years earlier to save Coranderrk were nearly all dead – only Anne Bon and John L. Dow remained. Dow published one of their letters in the *Age* on 8 July 1921:

> On 23rd last month three members of the Board visited Healesville and announced their intention of shifting us from our homes to Lake Tyers and we do not want to go. The proposal is totally against our wishes. Coranderrk is our home ... We wish you were again in power, so that you might help us in this trouble. You will remember, Sir, that a similar attempt to this was made some years ago, when we formed a deputation to Sir Graham Berry, who was then Premier of Victoria, at which deputation you were present. Sir Graham Berry assured us as long as there was 1 aborigine at Coranderrk our homes there would not be broken up. We hope, Mr Dow, you remember that. This assurance gave us the greatest satisfaction, and we returned home quite happy. Considering this settled the matter, we have been depending on that promise ever since.

On 13 September 1922 Board member John Bowser (Premier and Chief Secretary 1917–20) 'handed in protests from natives at Coranderrk against transfer to Lake Tyers' signed by all 44 residents. In May 1923 the Board 'received' Bowser's own protests against Board decisions, forwarded by the acting Premier for comment.

On 4 June 1923, the *Argus* published a letter from the Coranderrk residents. As the Board secretary had repeatedly warned them that public protest would merely hasten their removal, it was signed 'Sufferers'.

> We are very much in sad distress thinking of how the members of the board ... are breaking our homes up at Coranderrk, and trying to transfer us natives to Lake Tyers against our wish. About five years ago Sir Arthur Stanley [State Governor 1914–20] visited Coranderrk, and a member of the board, Mr Everard, MLA, came also and some others. We stated our case to Sir Arthur Stanley, that we do not wish to be removed from here to Lake Tyers ... we do wish to be here with our old people and be near our loved ones in the cemetry. Sir Arthur Stanley was full of compassion, and

… Mr Everard made the statement plainly that there was no compulsion to shift any of the natives against their wish; therefore we are standing on that, and also that this is an estate given as a home for the natives. Therefore we are not going to shift from here. Why, they are worse than the Germans, taking a poor blackfellow's piece of ground, which is only as large as a sixpenny bit to the whole of Australia. Remember, we are no more slaves because we are coloured. We are under the British flag, too. Our native boys went to fight for King, home, and country, and now this is how they are treating us – going to shift us from pillar to post. They might just as well shoot us all than shift us against our will. Will someone fight for us?

The *Argus* of 8 June contained a letter from 'D.M.' congratulating the editor on thus drawing community attention to the Aborigines' plight. The author was confident that their protests would be heeded, for 'In other countries, as New Zealand and America, the aborigines are protected with permanent titles and surely Victoria can afford to leave intact the small remnant of estate that hitherto has been conceded to the aborigines of the State'. A few more letters to the press, and several petitions to the Minister from prominent citizens prompted by letters from the old folk at Coranderrk, had little impact. Their friends were few. Public opinion – influenced by powerful pressure groups – was on the side of the six returned soldiers who would make this land profitable, rather than the 44 Aborigines who had spent a lifetime on it and their descendants who camped nearby because they were forbidden to live on an Aboriginal reserve.

'Throwing boomerangs at Coranderrk, the Aborigines station, Victoria'.
Source: The *Illustrated London News*, 12 January 1889, engraving by Melton Prior.

15. DISPERSAL

The Board minutes of 4 July 1923 record a decision to remove two families to Lake Tyers by Order-in-Council ('Mrs Bon protesting') as removal was the 'accepted policy of the Board'. The minutes note: 'in the event of the Wandin family refusing to go, they should be ejected from the station'. On 18 July Mrs Bon forwarded the protests of Annie and Lanky Manton and the newly widowed Mrs Jemima Dunolly (mother of the Wandins). At the next Board meeting on 1 August, the Parliamentary representatives again recorded a motion of censure for Mrs Bon's 'disloyal' behaviour in writing to the Acting Premier and objected that 'the natives' minds were poisoned regarding Lake Tyers which was a beautiful place and where natives were very contented'. The secretary reported that the Wandin family had 'left Coranderrk – they refused to go to Lake Tyers'.

The influential Australian Natives Association (which included no Aborigines) had immediately announced its support for 'Sufferers' in the next day's *Argus*. But the Board minutes of 5 September resolved to take 'no action' on their protest. The *Argus* of 28 August had already quoted an officer's report that the association's executive 'unfortunately met too late' to prevent the removal of several families under police escort. A planned Parliamentary protest did not eventuate. Only the *Evening Sun* of 22 August had deplored this 'land grab' by 'politicians whose interests lie with their white constituents and not with the voteless blacks'.

A new Chief Secretary now took office. On 5 September the Board censured him for interference and resolved to inform him that a Minister should not act on the representations of any person without first consulting the Board. They also resolved to obtain Orders-in-Council for removal of all Coranderrk residents except the Mantons. Apparently the Minister had different opinions. On 5 December 1923, the Board resolved that Annie and Lanky Manton, Mrs Dunolly, Alfred Davis and his family and William Russell might remain in their cottages. These nine were allowed the use of 50 acres (20 ha) which the next Board minutes described as 'poor land and not required'. At the same time the secretary instructed the constable appointed as Local Guardian to 'move on the colored folk' – the descendants of the old people who were camping on the 80 acre (32 ha) block outside the reserve fence. The Board had repeatedly offered to give it up but no one in the district wanted it. With Cabinet approval Coranderrk was 'closed' with the removal of the manager in February 1924.

From 1920 to 1927 there was no Parliamentary discussion of Aborigines whatsoever. But on 11 August 1927, Everard, speaking, he said, for his constituents rather than as a Board member, gave an angry resume of his campaign since 1918 to secure Coranderrk for soldier settlement. He demanded government acquisition of all remaining reserves: he was attacking a Lands Minister who was a fellow member of the Board. But the government fell before introducing the promised legislation to revoke the permanent reservation. Everard renewed his demands in 1928, 1929 and 1939 but the legislation that would enable the Board to profit from the sale of reserves was not passed. Meanwhile, the Board leased grazing and cultivation rights, receiving an annual income of £240–719 from 1925 to 1946. The money went to the Produce Fund to improve Lake Tyers. Nearly 100 descendants of the families who had built Coranderrk lived in substandard conditions in the vicinity. They were prevented from using any part of the reserve and discouraged from visiting their old people without Board approval. The last of the permitted residents died early in 1944. Mrs Jemima Burns Wandin Dunolly had gone Coranderrk in 1866 and had borne ten children to Barak's nephew. They had learned to speak Woiwurru from their great-uncle Barak but they were forbidden to live on his land.

The descendants of the Coranderrk people who had gone to Maloga and Cumeroogunga were also exiles. The New South Wales Aborigines Protection Board had imitated the Victorian policy for 'half castes' in their 1909 *Aborigines Act* and 1910 Regulations. Advised by Victorian officials, they had copied much from the Victorian Act – and added the punitive clauses which the Victorian Parliament had refused to pass in 1886. Because 'half castes' were required to leave, the population of Cumeroogunga decreased from 394 to 252 persons between 1909 and 1915. By 1924 the station had only 147 residents with 118 exiles camped across the Murray on the Victorian shore. Others had migrated back onto the lands of the Kulin and been forced to camp on riverbanks and rubbish tips in Victorian towns.

Small numbers of sympathisers had lobbied for change in Victorian policy through the 1930s with no result. The Board, now composed of three old members of Parliament and the under secretary, met only three or four times a year. Administration was wholly in the hands of the permanent head of the Chief Secretary's department and a clerk. Anne Bon had done what she could: she took up residence in a hotel across the street from the Board offices and attended all meetings until the end of 1935. She was 98 and still reproving Chief Secretaries and Board secretaries for their negligence and cruelty. Board minutes do not mention her death in 1936 and offer no tribute to her services. But the previous meeting was largely devoted to censure of her interference and complaints by the Lake Tyers manager that he scarcely dared reprove residents because they threatened to write to Mrs Bon.

Local lobbying to obtain the reserve for soldier settlement strengthened again after the Second World War. On 7 May 1947 Everard angrily pressed local claims in Parliament. When another member objected that Coranderrk should be turned over to Aboriginal ex-servicemen, Everard retorted that he did not wish this land occupied 'by men too lazy to work' and announced his resignation from the Board. His remarks were particularly offensive. After decades of pressure for reconstitution of the Board to provide greater expertise, the government had appointed four new members only two days before. One was the first Aboriginal member (Shadrach James). He had been born at Cumeroogunga, the son of one of the first girls to settle at Maloga (which was on her mother's clan land) and the Indian schoolmaster who taught there for 40 years. He was better educated than Everard.

His wife was the last of her family to be born at Coranderrk, just before her parents were ordered away. She was a daughter of Alick Campbell, a grand-daughter of Louisa Briggs.

Everard made a backhanded apology later in the debate, saying he did not criticise 'Shadrack James [sic], who is a fine man although he is of dark colour' – and went on to argue that nine Board members 'were not needed to care for the 24 fullbloods left in Victoria'. The next day he informed the *Age* that he could do more from the floor of the House to influence the government to resume the Coranderrk land for soldier settlement.

When the Coranderrk Lands Bill was passed on 6 July 1948 it was the Lands Department, not the Board or the Aborigines, who profited from the sale of Coranderrk. None of the Aboriginal ex-servicemen of the district acquired any portion of the land which their forebears had cleared and farmed.

Only the cemetery was still 'reserved from lease or sale'. The area where the Kulin were buried was all that was left of the 'black-fellows' township that they had built and for which they had fought. The one grave marked is that of Barak – and the tombstone was contributed by Anne Bon, not the Board:

> For theyr sakes shall their chyldren and seede continue for ever, and their prayse shall never be put downe.
>
> Their bodies are buried in peace, but theyr name liveth for evermore.

Appendix 1: The History of Farm Development at Coranderrk

Notes on Table 1

The table summarises the history of farm development at Coranderrk. The horizontal bars denote policy changes confirmed by legislation (the *Aborigines Acts* of 1869, 1886 and 1910). Some columns remain incomplete because the published annual reports omit the relevant figures.

The population columns show minimum and maximum attendance and numbers of adult males, including changes caused by births, deaths, immigration, dismissal or transfer. The 1869 Act empowered the Board to obtain Orders-in-Council prescribing residence. The resettlement of wanderers brought the Coranderrk population to a peak of 148 in 1878, but this was only a moiety of the group recruited – there were 51 deaths in Green's time and another 54 deaths in the ensuing three years. The population decline after 1878 was almost solely due to the dispersal policy for 'half castes', for birth rates were high and this was a young population. The exodus of more than 60 'half castes' between 1887 and 1895 is obscured in these returns, owing to the transfer in of 'fullbloods' and eligible older 'half castes' when the Board closed three of its six stations in 1890, 1904 and 1908.

The returns for adult males fluctuated from year to year as men went, or were sent away. The bracketed figure for 1908 is drawn from unpublished Board reports. Usually, only about half the number were able-bodied working men.

The rations column shows annual expenditure on provisions, detailed by station in the annual reports to 1891. These returns exclude the value of fruit, vegetables, grain and beef produced on the reserve, but show costs of imported food, clothing and necessities, including expenditure on livestock and meat for rations.

The stock numbers reported are those of annual musters, omitting numbers consumed during the year. The returns include station horses, working bullocks, dairy cows and beef cattle, but exclude the 20–100 pigs kept for use and sale from 1868 to 1872 and the small numbers of horses and cows owned by residents.

The crop acreage returns show the total area cultivated, excluding five acres (2 ha) of station orchard and the garden plots surrounding residents' dwellings which, according to the annual reports, provided a substantial harvest for private consumption. Wheat cultivation climbed to 130 acres (52.6 ha) but was replaced after 1872 by some 20 acres (8.1 ha) of hops forcing a reduction in grain and garden production. After 1872 only five to 30 acres (2–21 ha) of oats were sown for the subsistence needs of station stock; the area cleared for wheat was reseeded as 'grass paddock' and the remainder of the reserve was slowly cleared and reseeded as 'improved pasture'. The station garden of potatoes and other vegetables (27 acres [10.9 ha] in 1868) was reduced to 10 acres (4.1 ha) after 1872 because of the demands of hop cultivation. Because of the reduced population and shortage of labour, only two to five acres (0.8–2 ha) were maintained after 1884. The dispersal of able-bodied workers also necessitated a reduction of the hop ground to 10 acres (4.1 ha) in 1887, and five acres (2 ha) from 1882.

The columns reporting produce income are incomplete. As net returns from grain were not adequately reported during Green's tenure, the first column records only the sales of hides, meat and stock. The returns from 1868 to 1872 report cash sales of hides and pigs; from 1878 to 1884 the returns show purchases of meat by residents; after 1893 the returns record income from the sale of surplus cattle. These sales coincide with the population decline and the resumption of the better half of the reserve: a third to half of the remaining acreage was flooded every winter, so stock numbers were reduced by sale.

The other income column shows the actual net profit from hop sales after deducting all cultivation, harvest and handling expenses. The hop ground produced a substantial profit, but from 1875 to 1909 the hop income had to be paid directly to Treasury to offset the Board's Parliamentary grants.

The expenditure columns only roughly indicate the wages paid to residents, as annual returns for wages were not always distinguished. Wages paid for 'work outside the hop garden' were explicitly reported from 1874 to 1895, but afterwards merged with 'expenses and labour of cultivation'. 'Aboriginal wages for hop-growing' were distinguished for 1874, 1875 and 1885–91, but then merged into the general costs of cultivation. The bracketed returns in the column labelled 'hop work' are the figures given for total 'expenses and labour of hop-growing', including cartage, commissions, implements, wages to the hopmaster, farm overseer and other European contractors, and payments to European and Chinese pickers as well as Aborigines.

Wage rates varied over the years but were probably never higher than sixpence per hour plus rations. After 1874 residents received the same rate as Europeans for hop picking (threepence per bushel), but the hourly rate for farm labour was substantially lower. From 1878 to 1883 rates varied according to the number of dependents, with a maximum of sixpence an hour, but afterwards a fixed rate of two-and-a-quarter pence an hour was again supplemented by a meat ration.

APPENDIX 1

Table 1: Returns for population, rations issued, stock numbers, crop acreage and expenditure of farming at Coranderrk Aboriginal station, 1863–1910.

YEAR	POPULATION			RATIONS	STOCK	CROPS	INCOME (NET SALES)		EXPENDITURE (WAGES)		
	Minimum	Maximum	Males aged 14–17	Food, clothing, blankets etc., supplied by Board	Cattle & horses	Grain, garden (+ hops 1872–1910) area	Hides, meal & stocks	Net hop profit	Hop work	Not specified	Other tasks
	no.	no.	no.	£	no.	(hectares)	£	£	£	£	£
1863	40	40	12	200	5	5 (2.0)	0				0
1864	53	67	14	453		15 (6.1)	0				0
1865	80	105	35	477	76	15 (6.1)	0				0
1866	80	109	31	726		30 (12.1)	0				0
1867	76	105	21	472	72	53 (20.6)	0				0
1868	65	82	18	464	138	70 (28.3)	0				0
1869	74	91	26	472	174	95 (38.5)	28				0
1870	91	107	28	619	347	120 (48.6)	46				85
1871	105	116	23	531	400	140 (56.7)	0				0
1872	105	128	30	898	450	161 (65.2)	48	planted	0		0
1873	110	129	29	876	525	31 (12.6)		21	0		0
1874	125	144	36	1427	440	36 (14.6)		938	93		0
1875	137	142	43	1302	426	34 (13.8)		843	144		0
1876	137	147	43	767		43 (17.4)		1202	(440)		0
1876/77	129	147	37	1536		43 (17.4)		1587	(877)		84
1877/78	110	148	37	1596		40 (16.2)	105	1089	(795)		73
1878/79	95	113	39	1527	346	39 (15.8)	13	509	(519)		140
1879/80	90	105	35	1241	262	40 (16.2)	56	1118	(431)		275
1880/81	93	106	23	987	295	40 (16.2)	7	820	(351)		171
1881/82	90	101	30	753		40 (16.2)		680	(350)		155
1882/83	80	112	26	1329	260	37 (4.4)	24	1288	453		267
1883/84	85	108	25	1236	266	31 (12.6)	10	1277	585		178
1884/85	90	107	23	1361	131	27 (10.9)		706	457		163
1885/86	75	98	29	870	106	27 (10.9)		1047	376		170
1886/87	89	91	29	1025	180	18 (7.3)		876	266		168
1887/88	84	93	28	894	247	27 (10.9)		949	268		195
1888/89	75	84	26	847	272	27 (10.9)		940	200		123
1889/90	82	94	35	1006	280	26 (10.5)		314	303		121
1890/91	69	94	33	635	316	27 (10.9)		903	192		169
1891/92	73	95	30		319	22 (8.9)		1124	(265)		165
1892/93	55	79	24		366	25 (10.1)		476	(221)		187
1893/94	56	72	17		369	24 (9.7)	100	314	(214)		221
1894/95	57	67	16		270	25 (10.1)	154	406	(212)		265
1895/96	61	74	15		189	35 (14.2)	91	318		(295)	
1896/97	68	81			190	40 (16.2)	41	402		(291)	
1897/98	67	80			205	40 (16.2)	30	176		(264)	
1898/99	68	78			204	30 (12.1)	45	246		(241)	
1899/00	65	73			213	40 (16.2)	40	128		(216)	
1900/01	60	75			222	40 (16.2)	50	267		(217)	
1901/02	56	74			175	30 (12.1)	100	322		(301)	
1902/03	57	61				40 (16.2)	113	513		(297)	
1903/04	58	64			179	40 (16.2)	36	585		(333)	
1904/05	62	67			160	30 (12.1)	111	245		(273)	
1905/06	57	68			151	30 (12.1)	118	238		(296)	
1906/07	56	61			142	30 (12.1)	75	436		(314)	
1907/08	56	63			139	30 (12.1)	33	242		(284)	
1908/09	50	62		[19]	199	22 (8.9)	83	142		(240)	
1909/10	55	61			193	19 (7.7)	25	35			

Source: Annual Reports of the Victorian Board for the Protection of Aborigines 1861–1912. Modified from Barwick 1972.

Appendix 2: Membership of the Boards

Compiled from information supplied by Philip Felton.

A brief biography and terms of office of Board members mentioned in the text is given. Overt religious affiliations have been included as they often caused voting blocs. Membership of the Legislative Assembly or the Legislative Council is shown. In addition to Thomson and Serle's (1972) *A Biographical Register of the Victorian Parliament 1859–1900*, Browne's (1985) *Biographical Register of the Victorian Parliament 1900–84* contains biographical details for Victorian Parliamentary members. Extensive biographies of members marked with a (*) may be found in the *Australian Dictionary of Biography*.

The Boards:

1860–1869   **Central Board To Watch Over The Interests Of The Aborigines in the Colony of Victoria.** Members were appointed by the Governor of Victoria. The president was elected by the members and the Board was responsible to the Chief Secretary who, during that period, was also the Premier.

1869–1957   **Board For The Protection Of The Aborigines.** The Chief Secretary was *ex officio* chairman with the elected vice-chairman exercising effective control. The Chief Secretary was not always the Premier. Normal membership tenure was one year but the time was extended during the 1870s to two or more years.

1957–   **Aborigines Welfare Board.**

Members of the Boards referred to in Rebellion at Coranderrk:

1860–1864   ***Richard Heales (b.1821, d.1864)**, MLA East Bourke 1857–59, East Bourke Boroughs 1859–64, contested Melbourne 1856. Board president 1860–64. Coach builder, merchant, radical politician and temperance reformer. Chief Secretary 1860–61. Congregationalist.

1860–1871   ***Stephen George Henty (b.1811, d.1872)**, MLC Western Province 1856–70. Attendance of board meetings was poor, asked to resign. Merchant, pastoralist and banker. Anglican.

1860–1863   ***Henry Langlands (b.1794, d.1863)**, MLC Melbourne 1853, MLA Melbourne 1857–59, contested Melbourne 1856, Talbot 1856. Iron-founder, major employer and radical politician. Nonconformist, Baptist.

1860–1872   ***Thomas Embling (b.1814, d.1893)**, MLC North Bourke 1855–56, MLA Collingwood 1856–61, 1866–67, contested Collingwood 1861, 1864, Castlemaine 1871, South Province 1862. Apothecary, medical practitioner, and radical politician. Did not attend after 1868, asked to resign 1871. Congregationalist, Anglican and Independent.

1860–1884	***Theodatus John Sumner (b.1820, d.1884)**, MLC Central Province (later North Yarra Province) 1873–83. Pastoralist, merchant and philanthropist. Board Vice-president 1861–69, Vice-chairman 1871–72, did not attend after 1875. Son of a Methodist minister.
1860–1883	**Henry Jennings (d.1885)**, Practiced Law in Victoria 1849–83. Member Church of England Missions Committee. Board Vice-chairman 1878–79, resigned 1883. Anglican.
1860–1891	***William Macredie (b.1813, d.1891)**, Insurance manager, squatter, pastoralist, woolbroker, merchant and philanthropist. Wrote for the *Argus*. Trustee of Moravian Mission in the Wimmera. Vice-chairman 1874–75. Anglican.
1863–1878	**John Mckenzie**, Pastoralist. Vice-chairman 1872–74, ceased to attend 1874.
1863–1876	***Robert Brough Smyth (b.1830, d.1889)**, Civil servant, mining engineer, draughtsman, meteorologist. Secretary of Mines 1860. Board Secretary 1860–76, became voting member 1863, assumed role of Chairman 1874, resigned 1876. Agnostic.
1864–1876	*[Sir] **James MacBain (b.1828, d.1892)**, MLA Wimmera 1864–80, MLC Central Province 1880–92. Pastoralist, squatter, politician, and businessman including banking and insurance. Knighted 1886, KCMG 1889. President 1864–69, Vice-chairman 1869–71, absent 1874–76, resigned 1876. Presbyterian.
1871–1894	***John Rout Hopkins (b.1828, d.1897)**, MLA Grant 1864–67, 1871–77, Geelong 1892–94, contested South Grant, East Geelong 1868, West Geelong 1870, Grant 1877, 1880, Barwon 1880, South West Province 1882, Grant 1886, Geelong 1894. Pastoralist. Attended 13 meetings in 23 years, but only two meetings after 1875. Anglican.
1871–1876	***David Thomas (b.1826, d.1876)**, MLA Sandridge 1868–76. Apothecary, Doctor of Medicine. Attended 14 meetings. Anglican.
1871–1874	***George Alexander Syme (b.1822, d.1994)**, Journalist, editor of the *Age* newspaper 1866, and the *Leader* newspaper 1885, and newspaper proprietor. Resigned 1874. Presbyterian then Baptist minister.
1875–1879	***Frederick Race Godfrey**, contested East Bourke 1868, Kilmore and Anglesey 1877, South Province 1882. Squatter and pastoralist. Vice-chairman 1875–77, acting Secretary 1876, reappointed to the board in 1896–1907. Anglican.
1875–1883	***Edward Micklethwaite Curr (b.1820, d.1889)**, Squatter and pastoralist, public servant, Chief Inspector of Stock, author *The Australian Race*. Board Vice-chairman 1877–78, resigned 1883. Catholic.
1875–1902	***Albert Alexander Cochrane LeSouef (b.1828, d.1902)**, Pastoral overseer, Usher of the Black Rod of the Legislative Council 1863, Secretary of the Zoological and Acclimatisation Society 1870, director of the Zoological Gardens, Melbourne. Vice-chairman 1879–81, 1896–99. Moravian educated, affiliated with Plymouth Bretheren, Anglican and Presbyterian churches.
1876–1884	**Sherbourne Sheppard (d.1884)**, Pastoralist, occupied Pangerang territory in the 1840s. Attendance lapsed after 1881. Anglican.
1879–1881	***George S. Bennett (b.1850, d.1908)**, Brewer and cordial manufacturer, Mayor. Not listed as a Board member after 1881, re-appointed 1904–08. Catholic.

APPENDIX 2

1880–1909	***William Anderson (b.1828, d.1909)**, MLA Villiers and Heytesbury 1880–92, contested Warrnambool 1871, Villiers and Heytesbury 1892, 1894. Mercantile Bank, acquitted of fraud. Vice-chairman 1881–83, withdrew in 1883 for six months. Presbyterian.
1882–1914	***Ewen Hugh Cameron (b.1831, d.1915)**, MLA Evelyn 1874–1914. Postmaster, storekeeper, businessman and farmer. Vice-chairman 1884–87, withdrew in 1883 for six months, did not attend from 1902, but was active 1907–08, then only attended two meetings before his death. Presbyterian.
1882–1904	***Charles Myles Officer (b.1827, d.1904)**, MLA Dundas 1880–92. Pastoralist, Local Guardian. Member Zoological and Acclimatisation Society. Vice-chairman 1883–84, 1890–96, 1901–02. Presbyterian.
1882–1903	***Alexander Morrison (b.1829, d.1903)**, Schoolmaster, Principal Scotch College, Director National Mutual Life Association, Vice-chairman 1887–90. Presbyterian minister.
1882	***Alfred Deakin (b.1856, d.1919)**, MLA West Bourke 1879 (Resigned), 1880–89, Essendon and Flemington 1889–90, contested West Bourke 1879, 1880. Barrister, journalist, Prime Minister 1903–10. Appointed to the Board 1 July, resigned 4 July, attended no meetings. Presbyterian, Anglican, and Spiritualist.
1887–1910	**W.E. Morris**, Representative of the Church of England Mission Committee. Anglican.
1890–1916	***John Murray (b.1851, d.1916)**, MLA Warrnambool 1884–1916, contested Warrnambool 1883. Grazier, radical politician. Premier and Chief Secretary, *ex officio* Chairman 1913–15, convened only once between 1913–16. Presbyterian.
1896–1907	**Frederick Race Godfrey**, re-appointed.
1904–1908	**George S. Bennett**, re-appointed.
1904–1936	***Anne Fraser Bon (b.1838, d.1936)**, Pastoralist, major employer, philanthropist, author of verse and hymns as 'Sylvia', widow of John Bon. Presbyterian, Salvation Army.
1916–1919	***James Rouget (b.1866, d.1924)**, MLA Evelyn 1914–17, contested Evelyn 1908, 1911. Orchardist and secretary. Rechabite, Methodist.
1917–1947	***William Hugh Everard (b.1869, d.1950)**, MLA Evelyn 1917–50. Tea merchant, Anglican.
1917–1930	***[Sir] John Bowser, (b.1856, d.1936)**, MLA Wangaratta and Rutherglen 1894–1906, Wangaratta 1906–27, Wangaratta and Ovens 1927–29. Politician and Journalist. Chief Secretary 1917–20. Knighted 1927. Presbyterian.

REBELLION AT CORANDERRK

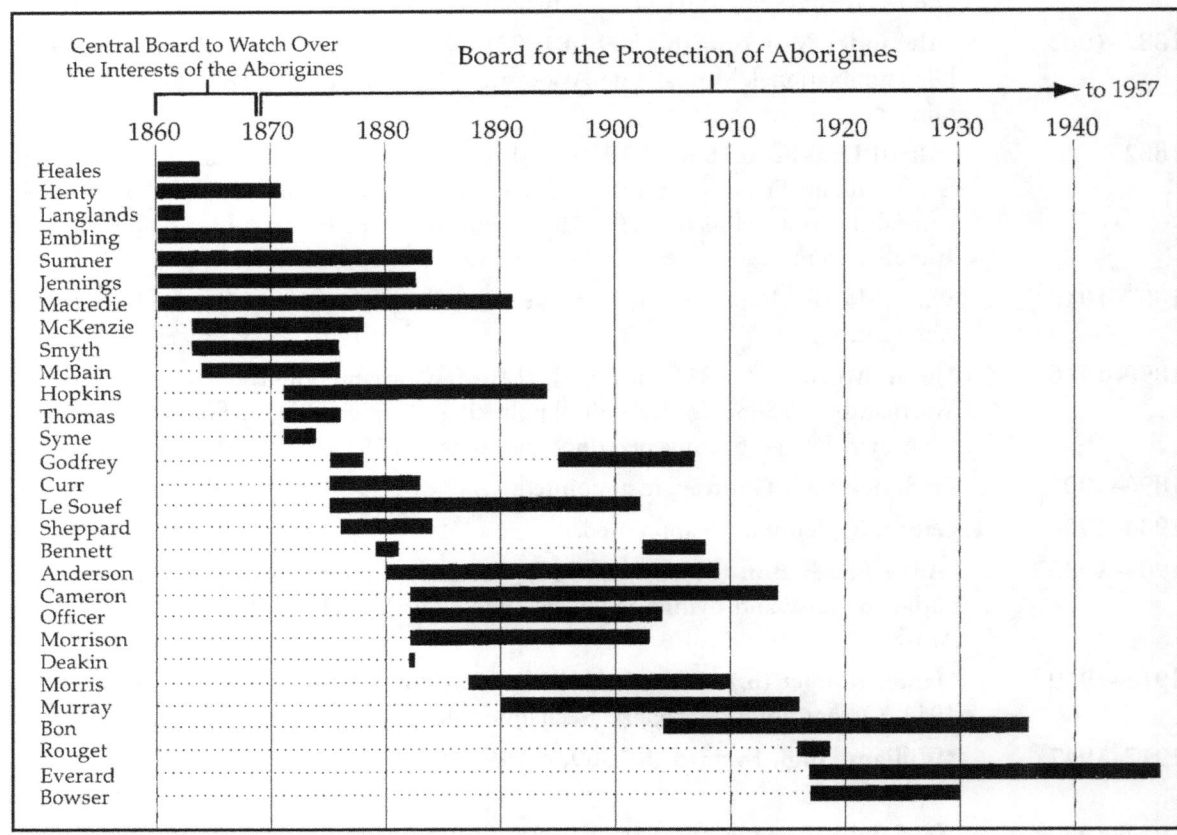

Histogram to show the periods of tenure of the individual Board members.

Bibliography

Age
> *The Age*, Melbourne.

Andrews, Arthur.
> 1920 *The first settlement of the upper Murray*. D.S. Ford, printers, Sydney.

Anon
> 1969 'Reminiscences of John Pascoe Fawkner', *La Trobe Library Journal*, 1(3):41–60.

Argus
> *The Argus*, Melbourne.

Australian Dictionary of Biography
> 1966–81 *Australian Dictionary of Biography*, vols. 1–8. Melbourne University Press, Melbourne.

Aveling, Marion.
> *1972 Lillydale: the Billanook country 1837–1972*. Gray Hunt and Associates Pty Ltd., Carlton.

[BPA – Annual Report]
> 1861–1912, 1922–25 Annual Report of the Board for the Protection of the Aborigines, nos. 1–51. *Papers Presented to both Houses of Parliament Victoria*. (Nos. 1–6 titled Annual Report of the Central Board to watch over the interests of the Aborigines in the colony of Victoria.)

[BPA – Files, Minutes, Correspondence etc.]
> 1860–1957 Archives of the Board for the Protection of the Aborigines Victoria 1860–1957 (titled Central Board ... 1860–69). Manuscript inward and outward correspondence concerning various Aboriginal stations; Minutes of Board meetings 1860–1957; Secretary's Letter Books and boxed correspondence; Secretary's Minute Book 1877–92; Journal of Christian Ogilvie 1875–77; Files (by various titles); Newspaper reports of Board meetings 1882–94. (Now deposited in Australian Archives, Brighton, Victoria. Catalogued as Series B312–B356.)

> 1882 Remarks of the Board for the Protection of the Aborigines, on the Report of the Board appointed to enquire into and report upon the condition and management of the Coranderrk Aboriginal Station. *Papers Presented to Both Houses of Parliament, Victoria*, Session 1882–83, vol. 2, no. 15.

Balfe, Harold.
> 1951 *The story of the century, 1851–1951*. Government Printer, Melbourne.

Barak, William.
> 1888 MS – Envelope 9: 'King Barak, king of the Yarry Tribe'. Archives, Public Library Melbourne.

Bareeba, Stephen.
> 1964 'How my grandfather killed Mr J. Green', *Australian Territories*, 4(3):15–18.

Bartlett, Geoffrey.
> 1964 *Political organisation and society in Victoria, 1864–83*. The Australian National University, PhD thesis.

Barwick, Diane E.
> 1963 *A little more than kin: regional affiliation and group identity among Aboriginal migrants in Melbourne*. The Australian National University, PhD thesis.

    1971 'Changes in the Aboriginal population of Victoria, 1863–1966', in Mulvaney, D.J. and J. Golson eds, *Aboriginal Man and Environment in Australia*. Australian National University Press, Canberra:288–315.

    1972 'Coranderrk and Cumeroogunga: pioneers and policy', in Epstein, T. Scarlet and D.H. Penny eds, *Opportunity and Response: case studies in economic development*. C. Hurst, London:10–68.

    1981 'Equity for Aborigines? The Framlingham case', in Troy P. ed., *A Just Society?* George Allen & Unwin, Sydney:173–218.

    1984 'Mapping the Past: An atlas of Victorian clans 1835–1904', *Aboriginal History*, 8(1–2):100–31.

    1985 'This most resolute lady: a biographical puzzle,' in Barwick D.E., Beckett J.R. and M.O. Reay eds, *Metaphors of interpretation: essays in honour of W.E.H. Stanner*. Australian National University Press, Sydney:185–239.

Barwick, Diane E., James Urry and David Bennett.

    1977 'A select bibliography of Aboriginal history and social change; theses and unpublished research to 1976', *Aboriginal History*, 1(2):111–69.

Baskett, Beverley A.

    1979 *The Aboriginal response to white settlement in the Port Phillip District 1835–1850*. University of Melbourne, M.A. Thesis.

Benson C. Irving.

    1935 *A Century of Victorian Methodism*. Spectator Publishing Co., Melbourne.

Berkhofer, Robert F.

    1971 'The political context of a new Indian history', *Pacific Historical Review*, 40:357–82.

Berndt, RM. and C.H. Berndt.

    1977 *The world of the first Australians*. Rue Smith, Sydney. First Published 1964.

Billot, C.P.

    1979 *John Batman: the story of John Batman and the founding of Melbourne*. Hyland House, Melbourne.

Blair, David.

    1881 *Cyclopedia of Australasia*. Fergusson & Moore, Melbourne.

Bonwick, James.

    1883 *Port Phillip settlement*. Sampson Low, Morrison, Searle & Rivington, London.

Bossence, William H.

    1965 *Murchison. The J.G. Kenny Memorial history*. The Hawthorn Press, Melbourne.

Bride, T.F. comp

    1969 *Letters from Victorian pioneers*. Heinemann, Melbourne. First published 1898 by Robert S. Brain, Government Printer, Melbourne.

Bridges, Barry.

    1966 *Aboriginal and white relations in New South Wales, 1788–1855*. University of Sydney, M.A. Thesis.

    1971 'The Native Police Corps, Port Phillip District and Victoria, 1837–1853', *Royal Australian Historical Society, Journal*, 57(2):113–42.

Bunce, Daniel.

    1979 *Travels with Dr Leichhardt in Australia*. Oxford University Press, Melbourne. First published 1859.

[CSIC-] Chief Secretary's Department, Victoria.

    1855–1900 Chief Secretary's inward correspondence, files and indexes. (Held by La Trobe Library, State Library of Victoria, Melbourne, in 1966–67; now in the care of the Public Record Office, Melbourne.)

Cannon, Michael.

    1978 *Life in the country: Australia in the Victorian Age 2*. Nelson, Melbourne.

Cannon, Michael ed.

    1982 *Historical records of Victoria. Vol 2A, The Aborigines of Port Phillip 1835–1839*. Victorian Government Printing Office, Melbourne.

Carris, Peter.

    1968 *Aborigines and Europeans in western Victoria*. Australian Institute of Aboriginal Studies, Canberra.

Cato, Nancy.

    1976 *Mister Maloga. Daniel Matthews and his mission, Murray River, 1864–1902*. University of Queensland Press, St Lucia.

Christie, M.F.

    1979 *Aborigines in colonial Victoria 1835–86*. Sydney University Press, Sydney.

[Coranderrk Inquiry]

    1881 'Report of the Board to enquire into and report upon the present condition and management of Coranderrk Aboriginal Station, together with the minutes of evidence', *Papers Presented to Both Houses of Parliament, Victoria*, Session 1882–83, vol. 2, no. 5.

Cranfield, L.R.

    1956 'The history of Warrandyte', *Victorian Historical Magazine*, 27(1):1–25.

Crawford, Ian M.

    1966 *William Thomas and the Port Phillip Protectorate 1838–4*. University of Melbourne, M.A. Thesis.

Critchett, Jan.

    1980 *Our land till we die: a history of the Framlingham Aborigines*. Warnambool Institute Press, Warnambool.

Curr, Edward M.

    1883 *Recollections of squatting in Victoria*. George Robertson, Melbourne.

    1886–87 *The Australian race*. 4 vols. John Ferres, Government Printer, Melbourne.

Curthoys, Ann.

    1973 *Race and ethnicity: a study of the response of British colonists to Aborigines, Chinese and non-British Europeans in New South Wales, 1856–1881*. Macquarie University, PhD thesis.

Deakin, Alfred.

    1957 *The crisis in Victorian politics 1879–81, a personal retrospect*, (J.A. LaNauze and R.M. Crawford eds), Melbourne University Press, Melbourne. Deverall, Myrna.

    1978 'Records of the administration of Aborigines in Victoria, c.1860–1968', *Aboriginal History*, 2(2):108–13.

Dibble, Vernon K.

    1964 'Four types of inference from documents to events', *History and Theory*, 3 (2):203–21.

Dredge, James.

    MS Journal 16 June 1841. (Typescript copy of Diary 1839–43) La Trobe Library, Melbourne.

Elkin, A.P.

    1964 *The Australian Aborigines*. Doubleday & Company, Inc., New York. First published 1938.

    1976 'R. H. Mathews: his contribution to Aboriginal studies, Part III', *Oceania*, 46(3):206–34.

Foxcroft, E.

    1941 *Australian native policy*. Melbourne University Press, Melbourne.

Giglioli, Erico Hillyer.

    1875 *Viaggia intorno al globo*. V. Miasner e Compagnia, Editori, Milan.

Great Britain, House of Commons.

    1844 *Aborigines (Australian Colonies). Return to an Address of the Hon. the House of Commons ... Copies of extracts from the despatches of the Governors of the Australian colonies*. House of Commons, Sessional Papers, vol. 34.

Grieg A.W. ed.
: 1928 'Some new documentary evidence concerning the foundation of Melbourne', *Victorian Historical Magazine*, 12(3):109–17; 12(4):172–81.

Gunson Niel.
: 1968 *The good country: Cranbourne Shire*. F.W. Cheshire, Melbourne.

Hagan, William T.
: 1976 'The reservation policy: too little and too late', in Smith, Jane F. and Robert M. Kvasnicka eds, *Indian-white relations*. Howard University Press Washington:157–69.

Hamilton, Robert.
: 1888 *A Jubilee history of the Presbyterian church of Victoria*. M. L. Hutchinson, Melbourne.

[Harris, Alexander]
: 1847 *Settlers and Convicts: or recollections of sixteen years labour in the Australian Backwoods by an Emigrant Mechanic*. London.

Haydon, G.H.
: 1846 *Five years experience in Australia Felix*. Hamilton, Adams & Co., London.

Henderson, Alexander.
: 1936 *Early pioneer families of Victoria and Riverina, a genealogical and biographical record*. McCarron, Bird & Co., Melbourne.
: 1941 *Henderson's Australian families, a genealogical and biographical record*, vol. 1, A. Henderson, Melbourne.

Hercus, Luise A.
: 1969 *The languages of Victoria: a late survey*. 2 vols. Australian Institute of Aboriginal Studies, Canberra.

Hoare, M.E.
: 1974 '"The half mad bureaucrat": Robert Brough Smyth (1830–1889)', *Records of the Australian Academy of Science*, 4(2):25–40.

Hopton, Arthur James.
: 1960 'A pioneer of two colonies: John Pascoe Fawkner, 1792–1869', *Victorian Historical Magazine*, 30(1):1–63, 30(2):67–99, 30(3):103–691, 30(4):175–250.

Howitt, A.W.
: MS *The Kulin tribe*. Manuscript, 73 pages. National Museum of Victoria Collections.
: 1904 *The native tribes of south-east Australia*. Macmillan and Co., Limited, London.

Kerr, J.H.
: 1872 *Glimpses of life in Victoria, by a resident*. Edmonston & Douglas, Edinburgh.

Kiddle, Margaret.
: 1961 *Men of yesterday: a social history of the Western District of Victoria*. Melbourne University Press, Melbourne.

Kolig, Erich.
: 1977 'Dialectics of Aboriginal life-space', in Howard, Michael C. ed., *'Whitefella business': Aborigines in Australian politics*. Institute for the study of Human Issues, Philadelphia:49–79.

Kruger, Frederick.
: c.1876–78 Album of 156 photographs taken by Frederick Kruger. Labelled as property of Board for the Protection of the Aborigines. National Museum of Victoria Collections.

Labilliere, Francis Peter de
: 1878 *Early history of the colony of Victoria*. 2 vols. Low, Marston, Searle & Rivington.

Legislative Assembly, Victoria.
: 1860 'Report from the Select Committee upon protection to the Aborigines, together with the proceedings of the Committee', *Votes and Proceedings of the Legislative Assembly of Victoria*, Session 59–60.

1956 *One hundred years of responsible government, 1856–1956*. W. M. Houston, Government Printer, Melbourne.

Legislative Council, Victoria.

1853 'Aborigines, Return to Address, MR Parker, 21st October 1853', *Votes and Proceedings of the Legislative Council of Victoria*, Session 1853–54.

1858–59 'Report of the Select Committee on the Aborigines, Together with the Proceedings of the Committee, Minutes of Evidence and Appendices', *Votes and Proceedings of the Legislative Council of Victoria*, Session 1858–59.

Lester, Geoffrey and Graham Parker.

1973 'Land Rights: the Australian Aborigines have lost a legal battle, but ...', *Alberta Law Review*, 11:189–237.

Long, J.P.M.

1970 *Aboriginal settlements: a survey of institutional communities in eastern Australia*. Australian National University Press, Canberra.

Lourandos, Harry.

1977 'Aboriginal spatial organization and population: south western Victoria reconsidered', *Archaeology and Physical Anthropology in Oceania*, 12(3):202–25.

McCrae, George Gordon.

1912 'Some recollections of Melbourne in the "Forties"', *Victorian Historical Magazine*, 2 (3):114–36.

McCulloch, Samuel Clyde.

1961 'Sir George Gipps and eastern Australia's policy toward the Aborigines, 1836–46', *Journal of Modern History*, 33(3):261–9.

McLean, Charles.

1957 *Report upon the operation of the Aborigines Act 1928 and the regulations and order made thereunder*. Government Printer, Melbourne.

Marcard, Patricia.

1964 'Early Victoria and the Aborigines', *Melbourne Historical Journal*, 4:23–29.

Markus, Andrew.

1977 'Through a glass, darkly: aspects of contact history', *Aboriginal History*, 1(2):170–81.

1979 *Fear and Hatred: purifying Australia and California 1850–1901*. Hale & Iremonger, Sydney.

Massola, Aldo.

1958 'Notes on the natives: formerly inhabiting the Goulburn Valley', *Victorian Historical Magazine*, 38(2):45–58.

1970 *Aboriginal missions stations in Victoria: Yelta – Ebenezer – Ramahyuck – Lake Condah*. Hawthorn Press, Melbourne.

1975 *Coranderrk: a history of the Aboriginal station*. Lowden Publishing Co., Kilmore.

Mathew, John.

MS Letter from Joseph Shaw to John Mathew, 29 June 1898, John Mathew Papers Box 3. Australian Institute of Aboriginal Studies, Canberra.

Matthews, Daniel.

1866–1902 Diaries, correspondence, newspaper clipping, Daniel Matthew's Papers. Mitchell Library, Sydney.

1876–95 *Annual Report of the Maloga Mission School*, nos. 1–20. (Various printers), Echuca.

Mennell, P.

1892 *Dictionary of Australasian biography, comprising notices of eminent colonists from the inauguration of responsible government down to the present time, 1855–1892*. Hutchinson, London.

Monckton, Captain C.A.W.

1921 *Some experiences of a New Guinea Resident Magistrate*. John Lane, The Bodley Head, London.

Morgan, John.
>1967 *The life and adventures of William Buckley,* (C.E. Sayers ed.), Heinemann, London. First published 1852.

Morrison, Edgar.
>1967a *Early days in the Loddon valley. Memoirs of Edward Stone Parker, 1802–1865.* 'Advocate' Press. Daylesford. (2nd ed.)

>1967b *Frontier life in the Loddon Protectorate, Episodes from early days, 1837–1842.* 'Advocate' Press, Daylesford.

Mulvaney, D.J.
>1976 '"The chain of connection": the material evidence', in Peterson, Nicholas ed., *Tribes and boundaries in Australia*. Australian Institute of Aboriginal Studies, Canberra:72–94.

Nance, Beverley.
>1981 'The level of violence: Europeans and Aborigines in Port Phillip, 1835–1850', *Historical Studies*, 19(77):532–52.

Nelson, H.N.
>1966 *Early attempts to civilize the Aborigines of the Port Phillip District.* Melbourne University, M.Ed. Thesis.

O'Donnell, N.M.
>1917 'The Australian career of Henry Fysche Gisborne', *Victorian Historical Magazine*, 5(3):112–36.

Parker, Edward Stone.
>1840 Periodical Reports, 29 February, 1 April and 3 August 1840. MSS. Victorian Public Record Series II, Public Record Office of Victoria, Melbourne.

>1841 Census of the Jajowrong tribe or nation, 23 February 1841. MS. Victorian Public Record Series II, Public Record Office of Victoria, Melbourne.

>1854 *The Aborigines of Australia, A Lecture.* Hugh McColl, Melbourne. (Reprinted in: Morrison, Edgar, Frontier life in the Loddon Protectorate, 1967.)

Parris, H.S.
>1950 'Early Mitchellstown and Nagambie', *Victorian Historical Magazine*, 23(3):126–60.

Pilling, Arnold R.
>1968 'Southeastern Australia: level of social organization', in Lee, Richard B. and Irven DeVore eds, *Man the Hunter*. Aldine Publishing Company, Chicago:138–45.

Presland, Gary ed.
>1977–80 *Journals of George Augustus Robinson, January–March 1840.* (Records of the Victorian Archaeological Survey, 5) Ministry of Conservation, Melbourne.

Robinson, George Augustus.
>1836–1837 Journals Flinders Island, vol. 12, pts 1–3, 21 December 1836 – 19 August 1837 G.A. Robinson Papers, Mitchell Library, Sydney. MS ML A7032, 7033, 7034.

>1839–49 Correspondence, censuses, journals, reports, Victoria. G.A. Robinson Papers, Mitchell Library, Sydney. MSS AL A7079-7088.

Rowley, C.D.
>1970 *The destruction of Aboriginal society: Aboriginal policy and practice – volume I.* Australian National University Press, Canberra.

>1971a *Outcasts in white Australia: Aboriginal policy and practice – volume II.* Australian National University Press, Canberra.

>1971b *The remote Aborigines: Aboriginal policy and practice – volume III.* Australian National University Press, Canberra.

Royal Commission on the Aborigines of Victoria.

    1877 'Report of the Commissioners appointed to enquire into the present condition of the Aborigines of the colony, and to advise as to the best means of caring for and dealing with them in the future, together with Minutes of Evidence and Appendices', Papers Presented to Both Houses of Parliament, Victoria, Session 1877–78, vol. 3.

Sayers, C.E.

    1956 'Leaders of the century: brief biographies', in Legislative Assembly of Victoria, *One hundred years of responsible government, 1856–1956*. W.M. Houston, Government Printer, Melbourne.

    1969 'Peter Snodgrass', in Bride, Thomas Francis, *Letters from Victorian Pioneers*, (C.E. Sayers ed.), Heinemann, Melbourne:213–15.

Scott, Ernest.

    1917 'The early history of Western Port – Part I', *Victorian Historical Magazine*, 6(1):1–18.

Selby, Isaac.

    1935 'The Hon. George Frederick Belcher and his reminiscences of early Victoria', *Victorian Historical Magazine*, 15(3):83–92.

Serle, Geoffrey.

    1963 *The golden age: a history of the colony of Victoria 1851–1861*. Melbourne University Press, Melbourne.

    1971 *The rush to be rich: a history of the colony of Victoria 1883–1889*. Melbourne University Press, Melbourne.

Serle, Percival.

    1949 *Dictionary of Australian biography*. 2 vols. Angus and Robertson, Sydney.

Serville, Paul de

    1980 *Port Phillip gentlemen and good society in Melbourne before the gold rushes*. Oxford University Press, Melbourne.

Shaw, Ethel.

    1941 'The history of Coranderrk Aboriginal Station', in Victorian Aboriginal Group. *Ninth Annual Report*. Melbourne.

    1949 *Early days among the Aborigines: the story of Yelta and Coranderrk missions*. W. & J. Barr, Melbourne.

Smith, F.B.

    1979 *The people's health*. Australian National University Press, Canberra.

Smyth, R. Brough.

    1878 *The Aborigines of Victoria*. 2 vols. John Ferres, Government Printer, Melbourne.

Stanner, W.E.H.

    1965 'Aboriginal territorial organization: estate, range domain and regime', *Oceania*, 36(1):1–26.

    1969 *After the dreaming: black and white Australians – an anthropologist's view*. (The Boyer Lectures: 1968) Australian Broadcasting Commission, Sydney.

Stanner, W.E.H. and Diane E. Barwick.

    1979 'Not by eastern windows only: anthropological advice to Australian governments in 1938', *Aboriginal History*, 3(1):37–61.

Sutherland, Alexander.

    1888 *Victoria and its metropolis: Past and present. Vol. 2 The colony and its people*. McCarron, Bird & Co., Melbourne.

Thomas, William.

    1838–67 Correspondence, censuses, journals and returns. William Thomas Papers. Mitchell Library, Sydney. Uncatalogued MSS, Set 214, Items 1–24.

    [1852/54] 'Brief account of the Aborigines of Australia Felix', and 'Account of the Aborigines', in Bride, T.F. ed., *Letters from Victorian Pioneers*. Heinemann, Melbourne, 1969:398–437.

1858 'Replies to questionnaire', in Legislative Council of Victoria. 'Report of the Select Committee on the Aborigines', *Votes and Proceedings of the Legislative Council of Victoria*, Session 1858–59.

1859 *The Guardian of Aborigines to the Honorable the Commissioner of Land and Survey, submitting a plan to Provide for the whole Aboriginal population of the colony of Victoria, 20th July 1859*. Government Printer, Melbourne.

1861 'Replies to questionnaire', 'Reports on the diseases of the Aborigines'; 'Returns of births and deaths of natives in the Yarra and Western Port Districts, April 1839–41 December 1859', in *First Report of the Central Board Appointed to Watch Over the Interests of Aborigines in the Colony of Victoria; Appendices 2 and 3. Papers Presented to Both Houses of Parliament, Victoria*, Session 1861–62, vol. 3, no. 39.

Thomson, Kathleen and Geoffrey Serle.

1972 *A biographical register of the Victorian Parliament 1859–1900* ... Australian National University Press, Canberra.

Thomson, William.

1876 *The histochemistry and pathology of tubercle*. Stillwell & Knight, Melbourne.

1879 *On phthisis and the supposed influence of climate being an analysis of statistics of consumption in this part of Australia with remarks on the cause of that disease in Melbourne*. Stillwell & Co., Melbourne.

Tindale, Norman B.

1974 *Aboriginal tribes of Australia: their terrain, environmental controls, distribution, limits and proper names*. Australian National University Press, Canberra.

Tudehope, Cecily M.

1963 'Derrimut: an Aborigine of the Yarra tribe', *Victorian Naturalist*, 79(10):288–92.

Turrler, Henry Gyles.

1904 *A history of the colony of Victoria*, 2 vols. Longmans, Green and Co., London.

Urry, James.

1972 'Notes and queries on anthropology and the development of field methods in British anthropology. 1870–1920', *Royal Anthropological Institute, Proceedings*, 1972:45–57.

Victorian Hansard.

1858–65 Parliament of Victoria, *Hansard*, Government Printer, Melbourne.

Victorian Parliamentary Debates.

1866–1948 *Victorian Parliament Debates*. Government Printer, Melbourne.

Waiko, John Douglas.

1970 'A payback murder: the Green bloodbath', *Journal of the Papua and New Guinea Society* 4:27–35.

Walter, Charles.

c.1867 Album of 108 photographs taken by Charles Walter and annotated by John Green. Original in possession of John Green Parkinson, Melbourne; copies in National Museum of Victoria Collection. An identical album, with different annotations, is held by the Pitt Rivers Museum, Oxford.

Weaver, Sally M.

1981 *Making Canadian Indian Policy: the hidden agenda 1968–1970*. University of Toronto Press, Toronto.

Williams, Nancy M.

1985 'On Aboriginal decision-making', in Barwick, D.E., Beckett, J.R. and M.O. Reay eds, *Metaphors of interpretation: essays in honour of W.E.H. Stanner*. Australian National University Press, Canberra:240–69.

1986 *The Yolngu and their land: a system of land tenure and the fight for its recognition*. Australian Institute of Aboriginal Studies, Canberra.

Index

The names used in the index are in the form most frequently used in the book. Other forms, or alternative names are cross referenced. The figures and appendices are listed separately.

Aboriginal 'half castes' 3, 51, 55, 69, 71, 73, 74, 81, 87, 104, 119, 129, 130–31, 135, 138–39, 140, 142, 143, 144, 145, 148, 152, 156, 157, 160, 166, 168, 173, 175, 178, 184, 191, 202, 210, 211, 212, 213, 220, 225, 233, 234, 236, 237, 239, 240–41, 242, 243, 247, 248, 249, 250, 252, 253, 254, 256, 257, 260, 262, 264, 266, 267, 270, 271, 272, 273, 276, 279

Aboriginal population of Victoria 16, 135, 212–13, 261

Aboriginal Reserves 39
    European opposition 42
    Funding 39–40

Aborigines Act (1869) 43, 81, 82, 127, 199, 225, 234, 253, 254

Aborigines Act (1886) 272

Aborigines Act (1909) 279

Aborigines Protection Board 235, 279

Aborigines Protection Law Amendment Bill 267, 269–70, 275

Acheron Station 53, 102, 129, 163, 223, 227, 236
    Abandonment 60, 62
    Alienation 39, 44, 45, 54
    Founding 38, 39
    Gazettal 44, 46, 54
    Members 66
    Rations 39, 43
    Return 54, 57
    School 43

Administration studies 4

Age newspaper 115, 122, 164, 165, 171, 174, 197, 199, 201, 206, 209, 210, 213, 228
    Alienation of Ebenezer and Framlingham Stations 259
    Articles on Hop cultivation 88
    Board of Inquiry (1876) 124, 126
    Board of Inquiry (1881) 187, 189, 190, 191, 193
    Coranderrk 129
    Coranderrk Hop Farm – Mr Green and Mr R. Brough Smyth 110
    Criticism of Halliday's management 142, 150
    Criticism of Strickland's management 157
    Deputation to Grant 194
    Gaoling of Bamfield, Tommy 206
    Healesville railway extension 163
    Inspection of Coranderrk 262
    Living conditions at Coranderrk 157
    Neglect of Barak's son 161
    Page's corruption 197
    Petition to Berry, Graham for Abolition of the Board 244
    Protest against abandonment 277
    Removal of 'half castes' from stations 252, 254
    Soldier settlement 280
    Support for Berry, Graham 133
    Syme, George Alexander 85, 103, 111

Alexandra 65

Amott, Ellen 62

Amott, Thomas 62

Anderson, Robert Stirling
    Influence of Barak, William 147

Anderson, William 170, 171, 172, 175, 176, 178, 193, 200, 209, 215, 216, 222, 226, 229, 234, 241, 242, 246, 254, 255, 259, 263
    Abandonment of Coranderrk 162
    Accusations against Green, John 159
    Appointment 153
    Board of Inquiry (1881) 157, 163
    Censure of Bon, Anne Fraser 224
    Closure of Coranderrk 274
    Coranderrk Debate 205
    Employment of Aboriginal women 241
    Gaoling of Bamfield, Tommy 205, 206, 210, 213
    Interview with Chief Secretary and Premier 240
    Letter to Grant, J. MacPherson 200
    Prosecution of Morgan, Alfred and Rowan, John 243
    Removal of 'half castes' from stations 234, 252
    Vice chairman 163, 175, 223
    Visits to Coranderrk 224

Anderson's Creek 51
Anderson's Inlet 32
Andrew, *see* Pondy-yaweet
Anglican mission committee 34, 79, 83, 127, 140, 253, 257, 258, 262, 266
Anglican missions 154
Argus newspaper 34, 169, 171, 172, 174, 177, 179, 180, 182, 183, 184, 186, 187, 193, 194, 197, 200, 206, 213, 214, 215, 255, 256
    Abandonment of Coranderrk 219, 220
    Abolition of the Board 220, 244
    Aborigines Protection Law Amendment Bill 270
    Alienation of Coranderrk 233, 255
    Alienation of Ebenezer and Framlingham Stations 259
    Appointment of Goodall, William to Coranderrk 221
    Bamfield's exile 240
    Barak, William 147
    Board leak of confidential documents 157
    Board of Inquiry (1876) 124, 125, 126
    Board of Inquiry (1881) report Addendum B 194
    Coranderrk 129, 139
    Coranderrk Debate 209, 210
    Coranderrk living conditions 125, 126
    Counter propaganda 104
    Criticism of Page, A.M.A., and Strickland, Frederick 196
    Deputation to the Chief Secretary 114, 115
    Dismissal of the Deans 224
    Gaoling of Bamfield, Tommy 204, 205, 206, 207
    Healesville Public Meetings 201
    Healesville railway extension 163
    Inquiry into attempted abortion 221
    Inspection of Coranderrk 262
    Journalist
        Search, Frederick 85–86, 88
    Kulin deputation to farewell Berry, Graham 265
    Kulin protest about living conditions 226
    Kulin protest against the Board 159
    Letter from Halliday, Hugh H. 150
    Letter from Rev. Mackie 202
    Letters from Dr. Embling defending Bamfield 262
    Letters from Strickland, Frederick 197
    Living conditions at Coranderrk 236
    MacPherson's minute 128
    Morrison's visit to Coranderrk 252
    Postponement of Board meetings 190
    Protest against abandonment of Coranderrk 277, 279
    Railway extension 264
    Reform of the Board 222, 242
    Removal of 'half castes' from stations 160, 253
    Removal of Laidlaw family 227
    Sale of Coranderrk to fund Healesville railway extension 163, 254
    Sinclair's complaint about Coranderrk deaths 120
    Ultraconservative views 103
    Visits to Coranderrk 262
Armstrong, Thomas 165, 180
    Board of Inquiry (1881) report Addendum B 193
    Gaoling of Bamfield, Tommy 203, 206, 209
    Local Committee on management of Coranderrk 163, 164
Arthur's Seat 28
Assimilation policy 3, 4
Atkinson, Ellen Campbell 3
Australasian newspaper 242
    Alienation of Coranderrk 233
    Search, Frederick 85–86
Australian Natives Association 279
Avoca, Tommy 169, 174

Baalwick 66
Bacchus Marsh 47
Bain, Robert
    Motion on Halliday's management 129
Ballaganit, *see* Laidlaw, Jamie
Ballarat 68
Balliot, *see* Laidlaw, Violet
Ballung-kara-mittung 202
Balybalip 68
Bamfield, Eliza 106, 204, 224, 239
    Death 261, 265
    Neglect 202, 204, 206
    Protest against Bamfield's exile 240
Bamfield, Thomas (Tommy) 66, 83, 107, 141, 167, 168, 171, 173, 180, 183, 213, 231, 240, 241, 248, 250, 266, 274
    Accusations against 235, 242
    Board of Inquiry (1881) report Addendum A 194
    Character 216, 262
    Complaints against Shaw, Joseph 271
    Death 272
    Death of children 162, 261
    Deputation to farewell Berry, Graham 265
    Exile 142, 145, 244, 245
    Family 120, 265
    Gaol 202, 203, 204, 205, 206, 207, 209, 210, 219
    Income 77
    Leadership 152, 171, 217, 237, 238, 239
    Letters 226
    Ngurungaeta 111
    Orders-in-Council 234, 235, 239
    Overdue clothing ration 151, 154
    Petition against Aborigines Protection Law Amendment Bill 269

INDEX

Protest about attempted abortion 215
Protest against allocation of dwellings 157
Protest against conditions at Coranderrk 142, 143
Protest against the Board 159
Protests about lack of rations 152, 235
Request for a doctor 124
Scuffle with Ogilvie, Christian 115, 122, 143, 206
Shearing 109, 262
Trip to Melbourne 155
Wirrarap 162
Banadruk, *see* Webster, Johnny
Band 15
Baptist Church 30
Barak, Annie 69, 71
   Death 161
Barak, David 69, 180, 219
   Death 161, 192
Barak, Lizzie 51, 58
Barak, William 57, 58, 61, 194, 237, 272, 274
   Abandonment of Coranderrk 112
   Aides 66, 68, 138, 249, 251, 272
   Beliefs about sorcery 91
   Board of Inquiry (1881) report Addendum A 191, 193, 194
   Clan 48, 71, 176
   Complaints against Page, AM.A. 178, 180
   Complaints against Shaw, Joseph 271
   Conversion to Christianity 51, 58, 227
   Country 166, 167
   Death 272, 280
   Deputation to Barkly, Sir Henry 61
   Deputation to farewell Berry, Graham 265
   Deputation to the Board 114
   Deputation to the Government 223
   Ethnographic studies 18, 99, 162, 227, 228, 261
   Family 15, 28, 32–33, 51, 67, 69, 175, 257, 279
   Founding of Coranderrk 25, 47
   Friendship with Harker, George 105
   Illness 152
   Income 77
   Initiation 68
   Leadership 9, 16, 48, 69, 97, 109, 129, 141, 147, 168, 171, 178, 197, 201, 212, 228, 262
   Life 223, 228
   Meeting with Batman, John 22–23
   Ngurungaeta 9, 111, 237
   Overdue clothing ration 154
   Petition 198
   Petition against Aborigines Protection Law Amendment Bill 269
   Petition against alienation (1893) 275
   Petition for abolition of the Board 244, 245
   Protest against Green's management 80
   Protest against the Board 159, 172

Remarriage 69, 70
Schooling 51
Wirrarap 52
Barber family 272
Barber, Jemmy, *see* Barker, Jemmy
Barker, Jeannie, *see* Rowan, Jeannie
Barker, Jemmy (James) 63, 80, 114, 124, 138, 141, 196, 249
   Death 158
   Exile 88, 142, 145
   Family 69
   Marriage 70
   Protest against abandonment 129
   Protest against conditions at Coranderrk 143
   Protest against Green's management 80
Barkly, Henry 47, 145, 156, 171
   Governor 40
   Grant of land to the Kulin 61
Barla
   Family 69
Barrabools, *see* Wudthaurung, *see also* Bengalat-bulluk
Batman, John 15, 19, 20, 22, 23
   'Purchase' of Kulin land 19–23
Baundaurrong 65
Bearringa 37
Bebejan 162
Beembarmin, *see* Tommy Farmer
Benalla 70
Benbow 29, 32
Bengalat-bulluk 18, 20
Bennett, George H.
   Appointment to the Board 149
Bent, Thomas
   Aborigines Protection Law Amendment Bill 270
   Criticism of the Board 259, 260
Berbira 228
Berrick, David, *see* Barak, David
Berry, Graham 2, 156, 160, 170, 193, 194, 200, 201, 209, 229, 242, 243, 244, 254, 255, 256, 257, 259, 260, 262, 275, 276
   Abandonment of Coranderrk 105, 150, 151, 155, 156, 157, 158
   Chief Secretary 102
   Criticism of MacPherson, J.A. 132–33
   Election 133, 134, 139, 234
   Fall of Government 98, 105
   Gazettal of Coranderrk 255, 261
   Influence of Barak, William 147
   Letters from Coranderrk 141
   Local Committee on management of Coranderrk 163, 164
   Meeting with Norris, John and Coranderrk residents 159
   Opposition to removal from Coranderrk 159

Orders-in-Council 234
Parliamentary debate on conditions at Coranderrk 157
Petition against alienation (1893) 275
Petition for abolition of the Board 244
Policy decisions 145
Politics 111
Promises to the Kulin 142
Protest against Bamfield's exile 240
Reappointment of Green, John 145
Removal of 'half castes' from stations 160, 252, 253
Retirement 264, 265, 266
Return 275
Royal Commission (1877) 103, 139
Visits to Coranderrk 252
Beruk, *see* Barak, William
Biebie, *see* Werry, Eliza
Billibellary 22, 28, 29, 30, 68, 162
   Clan 31
   Death 30
   Family 15, 37, 69
   Ngurungaeta 9
Birdarak, *see* Bamfield, Tommy
Board for the Protection of the Aborigines 187
   Abandonment of reserves 154
   Abolition 220, 241, 244, 255, 256
   Aboriginal 'half castes' 212, 270
   Aborigines Protection Law Amendment Bill 269
   Administration 136
   Amalgamation of stations 273
   Annual Reports 119
   Archives 1
   Assimilation 224, 272
   Attendance of Journalists 225
   Attitude to missionaries 272
   Board of Inquiry (1881) 120, 133
   Deputation to the Chief Secretary about abandonment of Coranderrk 149
   Employment of Aboriginal women 225, 229, 234, 241, 265
   Employment of Aborigines 225
   Employment of detectives 148, 151, 156, 195, 198
   Exile of individuals 141, 225
   Flouting of Ministerial authority 266
   Founding of a reserve on the Murray 97, 105
   Funding 75, 89, 93, 119, 127, 130, 131, 140, 154, 155, 160, 192, 226, 229, 234, 254, 255, 256, 258, 259, 260
   General Superintendent of Stations 106
   Government criticism 163, 164, 259, 261, 265
   Hop income 127, 128
   Inauguration 81
   Inspection 256
   Meeting on the reinstatement of Green, John 106
   Membership 40, 77, 81, 85, 96, 100, 103, 113, 118, 120, 130, 131, 133, 136, 137, 148, 149, 176, 200, 223, 226, 249, 271, 275, 280
   Mismanagement 191
   Orders-in-Council 81, 82, 105, 127, 153, 227, 234, 235, 241, 248, 278
   Patronage and corruption 85, 183, 187, 196, 215, 242, 243, 255, 256
   Policy 7, 84, 96, 97, 100, 102, 119, 126, 127, 131, 132, 133, 140, 145, 148, 150, 156, 157, 185, 210, 213, 223, 226, 234, 252, 257, 258, 260, 265, 266, 270, 271, 272, 275
   Punishment of Halliday, Hugh H. 147
   Reappointment of Green, John 109
   Reform 220, 224, 225
   Regulations (1871) 81
   Removal of 'half castes' from stations 234, 252, 253, 254, 255, 256, 257, 260, 266, 267, 269, 270, 274
   Removal of Coranderrk residents to Lake Tyers Station 276, 277, 279
   Reservations 85
   Residence at stations 126, 127
   Resignation of clerk 145
   Royal Commission (1877) 133, 134
   Sale of reserves 153, 223
   Secretary 53, 57, 71, 77, 85, 88, 96, 108, 117, 119, 126, 136, 137, 141, 176, 183, 186, 187, 196, 197, 200, 203, 218, 227, 238, 244, 257, 258, 271, 273, 276, 277, 278
   Sectarian conflict 83, 100, 118, 132, 246, 272
   Select Committee on the management of Coranderrk 120
   Vice chairman 81, 82, 85, 91, 96, 97, 101, 102, 107, 108, 119, 121, 134, 139, 143, 148, 149, 152, 157, 163, 172, 174, 183, 189, 200, 210, 218, 220, 223, 229, 233, 234, 240, 243, 244, 246, 250, 255, 256, 264, 266, 275
   Visits to Coranderrk 93
   Work certificates 88
Board of Inquiry (1876) 121, 124
Board of Inquiry (1881) 2, 165, 167, 168, 171, 174, 175, 176, 177, 180, 186, 187, 190, 198
   Report 191, 192, 193, 195, 197, 220, 222, 223, 229
   Report Addendum A 191, 192, 193, 194, 201, 211, 223, 224, 243, 253, 255
   Report Addendum B 193, 194, 195, 199, 206, 256
Bon, Anne Fraser 163, 165, 170, 171, 172, 173, 174, 176, 177, 180, 182, 183, 185, 186, 194, 195, 196, 200, 202, 204, 206, 209, 213, 214, 215, 216, 217, 218, 219, 228, 231, 240, 245, 249, 250, 262, 265, 266, 279, 280
   Accusations against 155, 159, 224, 250, 277

Appointment to the Board 274, 276
Attitude to Aborigines 212, 227
Board of Inquiry (1881) report Addendum A 189,
    190, 192, 193, 194
Censure 196, 279
Complaints about the neglect of the sick 150, 243
Coranderrk residents protest against the Board 159
Criticism of the Board 224, 225, 243, 247
Death 274, 280
Deputation to farewell Berry, Graham 265
Employment of Aborigines 109, 248, 257, 261,
    262
Gaoling of Bamfield, Tommy 206
Influence of Barak, William 147
Letter about Laidlaw family 226
Letters to the Chief Secretary 122, 224
Local Committee on the management of
    Coranderrk 163, 164
Petition against Aborigines Protection Law
    Amendment Bill 269
Petition to Berry, Graham against closure of
    Coranderrk 151
Petition to Morrison, Alexander 251, 255
Protest about attempted abortion 215
Protest against lack of rations 151, 154
Protest over sectarian conflict 118
Questionnaire and petition for Chief Secretary 251
Reform of the Board 224
Relationship with Bamfield, Tommy 66
Removal of 'half castes' from stations 234, 250, 253
Shelter for Barak, William and son 161
Visit to Coranderrk 152
Bon, John 66
Bonwick 16
Booringurmin 27
Boort Station 98
Borat 51, 70
    Family 69
Boronuptune 31
Bourke, Governor 21
Bowen, Lieutenant
    Contact with Bunurong 16, 17
Bowser, John
    Appointment 277
Brangy family 272
Brangy Friday, Kate 265
Brangy, Eda 180, 265
    Protest about attempted abortion 214, 215, 219
Brataualung 32, 51, 176
    Movement to Coranderrk 71
Briggs family 162, 251, 256, 266, 272
Briggs, Ann 166
Briggs, George 166
Briggs, Jack 87

Briggs, John Jr 117
    Assault 138
    Request for land 201, 218
Briggs, John Sr 166
    Accusations against 122
    Exile 168
    Protest against abandonment 129
    Protest against lack of rations 87
    Request for land 137
    Return to Coranderrk 117
Briggs, Louisa 19, 87, 256, 266, 280
    Board of Inquiry (1876) 122
    Care of dormitory children 126, 232
    Complaints about Strickland's neglect of the sick
        147
    Letters 150
    Newspaper reports 124
    Return to Coranderrk 117
    Transfer to Wimmera Mission 148
Broken River 27, 31
Buckley, William 17, 18, 20, 26, 63
Budgery Tom 18
Bumbang Station 69
Bungarim 27
    Ngurungaeta 9
Bungeleen family 30, 32
Bungeleen, Thomas 47
    Employment 57
Bungett, Joe 20
Buntingdale mission 27
Bunurong 12, 13, 15, 16, 17, 19, 22, 26, 28, 29, 31,
    32, 33, 37, 43, 48, 61, 68, 249
    Alienation of land 17, 59, 61
    Dispersal 29
    First contact 16, 17
    Language 12, 99
    Population 28
    Religious assemblies 30
Burapper 105, 123, 138, 139, 144, 152, 155, 163,
    166, 228, 237, 251, 256
    Movement to Coranderrk 71, 72
    Movement to Loddon 129
    Petition against Aborigines Protection Law
        Amendment Bill 269
Burgess, Robert 88, 89, 90–91, 107, 141, 186
    Appointment as Hopmaster 86
    Authoritarian discipline 105
    Complaints about Green, John 92
    Dismissal 102, 130, 133
    Dismissal of son 105, 106, 107
    House 107
    Newspaper reports 112, 124
    Relationship with Halliday, Hugh H. 130
    Relationship with the Kulin 90, 97

Warning from the Board 104
Wife 124
Burns, Jemima 279
Family 228, 236
Marriage 69, 239, 277
Burruppin, *see* Webster, Jemmy Jr
Buthera-ballu 43

Callithumpian cricket team 123, 124
Cameron, Ewan Hugh 120, 139, 165, 166, 167, 169, 170, 172, 174, 175, 177, 178, 180, 182, 183, 186, 191, 198, 200, 201, 220, 226, 232, 234, 241, 242, 244, 246, 254, 255, 256, 258, 259, 261, 263, 264, 265, 266, 274, 275, 276
Abandonment of Coranderrk 131, 156
Appointment to the Board 200, 222, 276
Board expenditure 260
Board of Inquiry (1876) 120, 122, 124, 125
Board of Inquiry (1881) 163, 189, 190, 192, 193, 194
Censure of Minister 241
Closure of Coranderrk 274
Coranderrk Debate 210, 211
Coranderrk deputation to the Chief Secretary at Parliament House 114
Death 276
Gaoling of Bamfield, Tommy 206, 210, 213
Healesville Railway extension 163, 264
Invitation to join the Board 120
Letter defending Green's role in Board of Inquiry (1876) 126
Local Committee on the management of Coranderrk 163, 164
Parliamentary debate on conditions at Coranderrk 157
Prosecution of Morgan, Alfred and Rowan, John 243
Reform of the Board 228
Resignation threat 266
Royal Commission (1877) 133, 134
Transfer of Goodall, William to Framlingham Station 259, 262
Vice chairman 223, 255, 256
Visits to Coranderrk 224, 226, 252, 262
Campaspe River 26, 28
Campbell family 272
Exile 257
Campbell, Alick 166, 170, 182, 183, 280
Accusations by Strickland, Frederick 152, 153
Complaints of Strickland's neglect of the sick 148
Petition against Aborigines Protection Law Amendment Bill 269
Relationship with Halliday, Hugh H. 138

Captain Turnbull 27, 29, 67, 69, 162
Family 69
Ngurungaeta 9
Central Board to Watch Over the Interests of the Aborigines 77
Aborigines Act (1869) 81
Bill for the protection of Aborigines 59
Change of name to Board for the Protection of the Aborigines 81
First report 55
Founding 40, 42
Funding 47, 59, 60, 77
Gazetting of reserves 54
Honorary Correspondents 42
Kulin request for land on the upper Yarra 48, 49
Legislation (1861–1863) 43
Medical aid 60
Membership 40, 41, 77
Misappropriation of supplies 60
Policy 42, 48, 49, 55, 56, 57, 59, 60
Powers 41
Reports (1864) and (1866) 72
Schools 47
Secretary 41, 47
Vice chairman 40
Charles family 272
Charles, John 87, 151, 168, 172, 245, 249, 252
Accusations by Strickland, Frederick 152
Arrival at Coranderrk 67
Assault 138
Board of Inquiry (1881) report Addendum A 193, 194
Death 257
Employment by Europeans 118
Letter about the Wimmera Mission 154
Protest against abandonment 129
Protest against conditions at Coranderrk 142
Protest against European labour 117
Chepstowe reserve 68
Chief Secretary
Role in Board decision making 96
Church of England Mission Committee 41, 83
Clan
Names 14
Right of land use 15, 167
Territories 14
Clarke, Adam 69
Coralcurke, *see* Wolmudging
Coranderrk
'Half castes' 104, 126, 178, 191
Abandonment 102, 104, 115, 119, 126, 127, 129, 133, 136, 138, 140, 145, 149, 150, 151, 153, 155, 156, 157, 159, 160, 163, 171, 173, 177, 183, 186, 187, 189, 190, 200, 201, 218, 219, 220, 222, 223, 229, 276, 277

INDEX

Advertisement for manager 96
Agriculture 73, 74, 75, 82, 85, 274
Alienation 77, 80, 81, 233, 254, 274, 275, 276, 277
Anglican criticism 88
Appointment of a horticultural consultant 85
Assault by Strickland, Frederick 152
Assemblies 63, 129, 141, 155, 259
Attempted abortion 215, 218, 219
Banishment of individuals 234
Chief Medical Officer's inspection 117
Closure 273, 279, 280
Complaints about Halliday, Hugh H. 120
Complaints against Strickland's management 149
Complaints against the residents 92
Confiscation of letters 173
Cricket team 123, 237, 249
Deaths 102, 105, 120, 123, 148, 158, 161, 176, 177, 183, 201, 204, 214, 216, 261
Deputation to the Board 98
Disease 102, 149–50, 155, 243
Dismissal of the Johnsons 82
Distribution of goods 80
Disturbance 201
Dormitory matron 233, 234
Drunkenness 63, 104, 124, 127, 143, 185, 203
European hostility 201
European labour 81, 86, 97, 105, 111, 114, 130, 232, 233, 243, 252, 262
Exile of individuals 88, 152, 201, 219, 234, 239, 262
Extension of the reserve 77
Extramarital liaisons 64, 81
Farm production, expenditure and income 77, 81
Fencing 74, 93
Founding 16, 25, 48, 51, 61, 62, 65, 66
Funding 91, 92
Gazettal 61, 255, 260
Grain production 74–75
Hop growing 85, 86, 88, 89, 90, 96–97, 105, 112, 130, 170, 191, 232, 233, 246, 257, 258, 262, 264, 274
Hop income 89, 104, 106, 108, 127, 128, 158
Horse breeding 77
Hunting 75
Illegitimate births 215
Inspections 176
Lands Bill 280
Leadership 239
Living conditions 76, 79, 89, 102, 105, 106, 108, 117, 119, 120, 125, 126, 139, 140, 153, 157, 167, 168, 171, 191, 217, 226, 229, 234, 236, 237, 243, 251, 254
Management 74, 194, 217, 221
Marriages 69
Movement to Malaga Mission 272
Neglect 91, 171, 186, 226
Origin of name 62
Parliamentary debate on abandonment 130, 131, 132, 133, 134, 209
Petition against abandonment 276, 277
Petition against Aborigines Protection Law Amendment Bill 266, 269
Petition against Green's removal 96
Petition to Morrison, Alexander 250
Petition to Sinclair, John and Berry, Graham 141
Petition to the Chief Secretary against abandonment, and in support of Halliday, Hugh H. 129, 130
Population 102, 166, 269, 273
Presbyterian services 232
Prostitution 104, 185
Protest about appointment of a new manager 194
Protest against abandonment 129
Protest against Bamfield's exile 240, 241, 243
Protest against European labour 117
Protest against Green's management 80
Protest against lack of rations 83
Protest against lack of wages 87, 98
Protest against removal 152
Protest against the Board 159
Public controversy 103
Questionnaire and petition for Chief Secretary 250, 251
Rations 75, 82, 91, 106, 115, 116, 125, 130, 140, 152, 154, 167, 171, 177, 180, 191, 229, 233, 235, 237, 262
Relationship between Kulin and non-Kulin newcomers 71, 137, 138, 143, 144, 236, 237, 239, 242, 250
Religion 69, 118, 245
Removal of 'half castes' from stations 157, 160, 247, 255
Repatriation of Bamfield's kin 266
Reserve size 125
Resettlement 273
Royal Commission (1877) 103, 138
Sale 162, 163, 254, 255
School 72, 73, 104, 108, 109, 116, 263
Self government 63
Shearing 262
Soldier settlement 279, 280
Strike by dormitory girls 153
Supplementary income 74, 76, 80, 82, 88, 109
Transfer to the Wimmera and Lake Tyers mission stations 149
Trespassing stock 90–91
Valuation of land 276
Violence 190

Visit to Agricultural Show 248
　　　Wages 83, 87, 88, 89, 90, 97, 116, 119, 125, 130, 181, 191, 229, 236, 243, 247, 250, 252, 260, 262
　　　Working population 74, 124, 264
Coranderrk Creek 61, 223
Corownang, see Warren, Jemmy
Cotton, Mr, see Baundaurrong
Cranbourne 62
Crown Lands Reserve Act (1893) 275
Culgorine 20
Cumeroogunga Station 3, 107, 272, 279, 280
　　　Population 279
Curr, Edward Micklethwaite 22, 129, 143, 148, 153, 159, 170, 171, 172, 174, 176, 177, 178, 180, 183, 185, 186, 190, 191, 218, 229, 232, 233, 242
　　　Abandonment of Coranderrk 102, 140, 149, 157, 163, 223
　　　Appointment of Halliday, Hugh H. as manager 113
　　　Appointment of Page, A.M.A. 136
　　　Appointment to the Board 97, 98, 100
　　　Attitude to Green, John 109
　　　Board of Inquiry (1881) 164, 200
　　　Board secretary's position 117
　　　Censure of Minister 241
　　　Censure of Page, A.M.A. 196
　　　Charges against Charles, John and Campbell, Alick 152
　　　Chief Inspector of Stock 98
　　　Deputation to the Chief Secretary about Coranderrk 142
　　　Reduction of Ogilvie's powers 108
　　　Relationship with Green, John 99
　　　Reply to the Chief Secretary 141
　　　Resignation 242
　　　Resolution that Coranderrk was not a fit locality for Aborigines 127
　　　Sub-committee on the future management of Coranderrk 102
　　　Tour of the Murray 104, 105, 108
　　　Vice chairman 101, 134, 139, 143, 152
　　　Visit to Lake Tyers Station 149
　　　Visits to Coranderrk 224

Daily Telegraph newspaper
　　　Gaoling of Bamfield, Tommy 206, 218
　　　Petition to Berry for Abolition of the Board 244
Davis family 272, 273, 279
Davis, Alfred 266, 279
　　　Petition against Aborigines Protection Law Amendment Bill 269
Davis, Ned 180
Davy, see Hunter, David

de Castella, Paul 33
　　　Employment of Coranderrk folk 118
de Labilliere 16
de Pury, Guillaume 33, 165, 177, 178
　　　Board of Inquiry (1881) report, Addendum B 193
　　　Employment of Coranderrk folk 118
　　　Gaoling of Bamfield, Tommy 203, 206, 209
　　　Local Committee on the management of Coranderrk 163, 164
De Villiers 18
Ngurungaeta 9
Deakin, Alfred 195, 213, 254, 256, 261, 269, 270, 271, 274
　　　Aborigines Protection Law Amendment Bill 267, 269, 270
　　　Appointment to the Board 222
　　　Attitude to Aborigines 212
　　　Chief Secretary 264
　　　Coranderrk Debate 203, 209, 211
　　　Criticism of Strickland's management 157
　　　Deputation to farewell Berry, Graham 265
　　　Deputation to the Board 199
　　　Gaoling of Bamfield, Tommy 206
　　　Healesville Railway extension 264
　　　Influence of Barak, William 147
　　　Local Committee on the management of Coranderrk 163, 164
　　　Meeting with Norris, John and Coranderrk residents 159
　　　Over ruling of the Board 266
　　　Petition from Coranderrk 198
　　　Public works 234
　　　Punishment of Manton, Annie 250
　　　Removal of 'half castes' from stations 255
　　　Resignation from the Board 222
　　　Visits to Coranderrk 252
Deans, James Stewart 217
　　　Appointment as teacher 118
　　　Argument with Strickland, Frederick 157
　　　Dismissal 222, 224, 242
　　　Evidence at Royal Commission (1877) 134, 138
　　　Lawsuit against Strickland, Frederick 219
　　　Protest about attempted abortion 215, 218
Deans, Laura 170, 171, 174, 180, 182, 183, 189
　　　Appointment as teacher 118
　　　Dismissal 222
　　　Protest about attempted abortion 218, 219
Deardjoo Warrami, see Avoca, Tommy
Deddrick, Sophia 173, 174, 175, 181
Delatite River 27, 31
Derrimut 26, 59
　　　Death 61
Devil's River 31
Dhudhuroa 12

INDEX

Dicky, *see* Yerrebulluk
Dindarmin, *see* Malcolm
Disease
   Diphtheria 82
   Goulburn and Devil's river people 31
   Hydatid infection 248
   Influenza 31, 46
   Introduction by Europeans 16
   Measles 97, 102
   Pneumonia 116
   Syphilis 102, 243
   Tuberculosis 69, 97, 102, 155, 175, 213, 225, 237
   Typhoid 80, 81, 102, 242
   Venereal disease 102
   Whooping cough 81
Doncaster 51
Dow, John Lamont 104, 156, 161, 163, 165, 170, 172, 174, 178, 222, 225, 256, 261, 270, 277
   Articles on Coranderrk 112
   Attitude to Aborigines 212
   Biography 111
   Board of Inquiry (1881) report Addendum A 189, 190, 192, 193, 205
   Coranderrk Debate 209, 210, 211, 213
   Criticism of the Board 243
   Influence of Barak, William 147
   Introduction of the Kulin to the Chief Secretary 142
   Lands Minister 264
   Parliamentary debate on conditions at Coranderrk 150, 152, 242
   Protest about attempted abortion 215
   Reappointment of Green, John 241
   Report on Coranderrk deputation to the Chief Secretary 114
   Report to the Minister 143
   Visits to Coranderrk 111
Dredge, James 27
Duffy, Charles Gavan 42, 54, 55, 61
   Kulin Deputation to the Board of Land and Works 38
   Lands Minister 39
Duffy, John Gavan
   Accusations against Green, John 156
   Appointment to the Board 149
   Board of Inquiry (1876) 121, 122, 124, 125
   Comments to Minister 126
   Royal Commission (1877) 134
   Visit to Coranderrk 126, 131
Dunolly family 272
Dunolly, Jemima, see Burns, Jemima
Dunolly, Jessie
   Exclusion of the Greens 156
   Protest about attempted abortion 215

Dunolly, Tommy (Thomas) 73, 87, 167, 170, 183, 256, 272, 276
   Arrival at Coranderrk 67
   Board of Inquiry (1881) report Addendum A 193
   Exile 257
   Gaoling of Manton, Benjamin, and Rowan, John 249, 250, 251
   Housing 236
   Leadership 170
   Letters 226
   Marriage 239
   Ngurungaeta 67, 111, 238, 249
   Petition 198
   Petition against Aborigines Protection Law Amendment Bill 269
   Petition to Berry for abolition of the Board 244
   Petition to Morrison, Alexander 250, 255
   Protest against attempted abortion 213, 215, 218
   Protest against conditions at Coranderrk 142
   Request for land 276
Dutigalla 22

Eastern Kulin Language, *see* Kulin Language
Ebenezer Mission 48
   Alienation 259
Echuca 59, 166, 237
Edgar, James 182
   Assault 138, 206
   Captain of Cricket team 123
   Charges against Bamfield, Tommy 144
   Complaints about Strickland's neglect of the sick 148
   Conflict between Kulin pioneers and the non-Kulin newcomers 144
   Exile 168
   Motion on Halliday's management 129
   Relationship with Halliday, Hugh H. 138
Electoral Bill representation for Aborigines 132
Embling, Thomas 54, 77, 105, 122, 155, 165, 170, 172, 174, 177, 180, 183, 185, 187, 194, 195, 200, 205, 212, 261, 262, 263
   Board of Inquiry (1881) report Addendum A 189, 190, 192, 193
   Central Board to Watch Over the Interests of the Aborigines 40
   Criticism of the Board 243
   Legislative Assembly Select Committee 40
   Local Committee on the management of Coranderrk 163, 164
   Medical treatments 59
   Petition against Aborigines Protection Law Amendment Bill 269
   Petition to Berry for abolition of the Board 244
   Petition to Morrison, Alexander 251

Protest against Bamfield's exile 240
Punishment of Manton, Annie 250
Questionnaire and petition for Chief Secretary 250
Removal of 'half castes' from stations 253
Resignation from Board 85
Enfeoffment 19, 22
see also Batman's 'purchase' of Kulin land
European
    Attitudes to Aborigines 34, 55, 56, 62, 77, 212
    Contact 16–23
    Disease 16
    Occupation of land 16, 25, 32
    Violence 17, 33
Evelyn county 32, 79, 81, 83
Evening Sun newspaper
    Protest against abandonment of Coranderrk 279
Everard, W.H. 279, 280
    Abandonment of Coranderrk 276, 277
Exogamy, *see* Kulin Marriage

Farmer, Norah 67
Farmer, Tommy 47, 67, 75, 168
    Death 152, 158
    Protest against conditions at Coranderrk 142
    Relationship with Halliday, Hugh H. 138
Fawkner, J.P. 20, 21
Ferguson, Caroline 68, 166
Ferguson, John 68
Framlingham Station 41, 48, 84, 85, 101, 176, 190, 194, 214, 215, 217, 218, 221, 225, 232, 235, 255, 256, 259, 260, 261, 262, 263, 266, 276
    Abandonment 149, 150, 153
    Alienation 259
    Closure 271, 273
    Transfer to the Wimmera and Lake Tyers mission stations 149
Francis, J.G.
    Royal Commission (1877) 133
Franklin family 273
Friday, Jack 266

Gal-gal-bulluk 13, 27, 67
Geelong 26, 47, 68
Glass, Hugh 31, 129, 181
    Alienation of Acheron Station 46, 54
    Compensation for land 44
    Corruption 44
Godfrey, Frederick Race 109, 129, 133, 138, 141, 148, 149, 174, 183, 274
    Abandonment of Coranderrk 102, 140, 223
    Appointment of Halliday, Hugh H. as manager 113
    Appointment of Page, A.M.A. 136
    Appointment to the Board 97, 100

    Appropriation of Ogilvie's recommendations 115
    Attendance at Board meetings 108
    Attitude to Green, John 130
    Board of Inquiry (1876) 121, 122, 124
    Closure of Coranderrk 274
    Defence of Board policy to Parliament 131
    Deputation to the Chief Secretary about reserves 133
    Encounter with Coranderrk deputation to the Chief Secretary at Parliament House 114
    Interview with the Minister 133
    Kulin complaints about Burgess' son 105
    Kulin petitions 129–30
    Meeting over protests against removal 130
    Membership of other committees 98
    Mission on the Murray 145
    Nominations for Board membership 103
    Opposition to Green's re-appointment 110, 142
    Presbyterian services forbidden 118
    Reaction to criticism of Coranderrk management 117
    Re-appointment 274
    Recommendation of Ogilvie, Christian as secretary 119
    Recommendations on Coranderrk 133
    Relationship with Green, John 132
    Report on Barker's letter 105
    Report to the Minister 143
    Residence at stations 127
    Resignation 148
    Royal Commission (1877) 133, 134, 135, 139
    Subcommittee on the future management of Coranderrk 102
    Supplementary report to MacPherson, J.A. 126
    Usurpation of Board control 132
    Vice chairman 101, 102, 119, 134
Goldfields 33, 51, 77
Goodall, William 194, 217, 223, 231, 234, 243, 245, 250, 251, 256, 257, 259
    Accusations against 238
    Appointment to Coranderrk 194, 215, 217, 221, 222
    Care of the sick 224
    Censure 151
    Comments on the problems at Coranderrk 151
    Defence of Coranderrk people 245
    Dormitory supervision 225, 233, 246, 248
    European labour 233
    Exile of Bamfield, Tommy 235
    Farm overseer 244, 258
    Gaoling of Manton, Benjamin, and Rowan, John 243, 249, 250
    Letters to Page 252
    Letters to Page, A.M.A. 223

Living conditions at Coranderrk 233, 234, 236
Policy 224
Protest against attempted abortion 218, 219
Protest against Bamfield's exile 239, 240, 241
Reappointment 271
Relationship with the Kulin 232, 236, 237, 248
Report on Laidlaw family 226, 227
Transfer to Framlingham Station 259, 261, 262, 263
Goona, Yanem 22
Goulburn depot 31
Goulburn Protectorate Station 99
Goulburn river 27
Aboriginal population 27
Grant, Alice Sapara 173, 180
Grant, J. MacPherson 77, 81, 161, 165, 173, 194, 195, 220
Abandonment of Coranderrk 205, 223
Age newspaper 197
Attitude to Aborigines 80
Board funding 229
Board of Inquiry (1881) 198, 200, 201, 202
Censure of Page, A.M.A. for corruption 196, 197
Censure of subordinates 220
Gaoling of Bamfield, Tommy 204, 206, 207, 209
Influence of Barak, William 147
Inquiry into attempted abortion 219, 221
Justice Minister 197
Local Committee on the management of Coranderrk 163, 164
Petition to Berry for abolition of the Board 244
Protest against abortion attempt 215
Reform of the Board 199, 222
Removal of 'half castes' from stations 234
Graves, J.H. 156, 161, 164
Meeting with Norris, John and Coranderrk residents 159
Green, John 13, 48, 59, 71, 72, 80, 90, 130, 153, 173, 177, 180, 183, 185, 186, 199, 201, 216, 217, 219, 223, 255
Accusations against 82, 83, 88, 90, 92, 114, 122
Appointment as General Inspector 49
Argument with Smyth, Robert Brough 90, 92
Arrival 51
Attitude to Aborigines 55, 62, 72
Board of Inquiry (1876) 124
Character 110
Death 272
Dismissal 105, 138, 159
Disputes with the Johnsons 82
Evidence at Royal Commission (1877) 134, 139
Exclusion from Coranderrk 118
Expectations of Coranderrk 72
Expenditure of own money on Coranderrk 74

Extension to Coranderrk 77
Forced resignation 92, 93, 96, 103, 105
General Inspector 53, 60, 86
Guardian of the Aborigines 48
Healesville Public Meetings 201, 264, 274
Hop growing 86
Influence at Coranderrk 79
Inspection of Gippsland and Western District 57, 59, 71
Inspection of Lake Condah Station 85
Inspection of Mohican Station 53, 57
Inspection of the Murray and Western District 60
Interview with Berry, Graham 139
Linguistics 99
Management 89
Medical knowledge 59, 147
Newspaper articles 111, 112
Ngurungaeta 63
Opposition by Godfrey to reinstatement 113
Orders from the Board 98
Ownership of land adjacent to Coranderrk 82
Preaching 51, 161, 227
Problems with Search, Frederick and Burgess, Robert 88
Protest against attempted abortion 215
Reappointment 109, 143, 154, 159, 244
Recommendations on Framlingham 101
Recruitment to Coranderrk 66
Relationship to Webster, Jemmy 65
Relationship with Shaw, Joseph 231
Relationship with the Board 77
Relationship with the Kulin 2, 62, 77, 81, 181, 237, 242
Royal Commission (1877) 138
School 72
Settlement at Coranderrk 62, 65
Struggles with the Board 98
Tour of the Murray 104, 105, 106
Visit from Syme, George Alexander 156
Green, John Jr 57
Green, Mary 57, 58, 59, 82, 180, 186
Arrival in Australia 51
Care of the sick 123
Death 274
Dormitory matron 73
Questionnaire and petition for Chief Secretary 251
Relationship with the Kulin 144
School 48, 59, 72, 109
Green, William 83
Grey, Earl 32
Guardian of the Aborigines 23, 32
Gunditjmara 48
Gunung-willam-balluk 27

Hagenauer, F.A. 135, 176, 177, 186, 197, 216, 225, 266, 272, 273
   Accusations against Matthews, Daniel 272
   Alienation of Coranderrk 275, 276
   Board Policy 148, 149, 254
   Closure of stations 154, 155
   Evidence at Royal Commission (1877) 139
   Exile of individuals 145
   Mission 101
   Relationship to LeSouef, Albert A.C. 100
   Relationship with Green, John 100
   Removal of 'half castes' from stations 213, 252, 253, 266, 276
   Retirement 276
   Secretary Inspector 271
   Superintending missionary 100
Halliday, Hugh H. 118, 138, 141, 144, 175, 180, 183, 186, 263
   Accusations against Bamfield, Tommy 143
   Accusations of interference 242
   Annual report (1877) 140
   Appointment as manager 110, 113, 118
   Assimilation 135
   Attitude to Kulin 130
   Board of Inquiry (1876) 124
   Checking of wage payments 157
   Complaints against Strickland, Frederick 147, 159
   Coranderrk living conditions 118
   Dismissal 147
   Dismissal of Burgess, Robert 133
   Favouritism 138
   Incitement of protests 148
   Letters 129, 150, 206, 215, 217
   Management 122, 127, 145
   Newspaper reports 124
   Report of Coranderrk deaths 120
   Royal Commission (1877) 138
   Transfer 133
   Views on 'half castes' 138
Hamilton family 236, 272
Hamilton, Agnes 180
Hamilton, Annie Johnson 180
Hamilton, Jessie 239
Hamilton, Lily
   Marriage 73
Hamilton, Robert 72, 110, 173, 175, 181, 189, 199, 200
   Attitude to Aborigines 212
   Evidence at Royal Commission (1877) 134, 138
   Letters to Chief Secretary suggesting Green's reinstatement 122
   Moderator of the Presbyterian General Assembly 138
   Petition to the Board 199
   Preaching 53, 69, 190, 227, 232, 245
   Protest over sectarianism 118
Hamilton, William 73, 180
   Petition against Aborigines Protection Law Amendment Bill 269
   Protest against conditions at Coranderrk 142
Harker, George 39
   Board of Education 109
   Complaint to MacBain, James 108
   Letter to the Minister 105
Harriet 64
Harris family 273
Harris, Thomas 80, 105, 110, 141, 152, 156, 157, 160, 165, 168, 169, 170, 172, 173, 177, 180, 183, 186, 189, 193, 232, 233, 235, 245
   Appointment as farm overseer 73
   Appointment as servant to Green, John 58
   Board of Inquiry (1876) 122, 124
   Comments on farm production 90
   Complaints against Strickland, Frederick 190
   Death of wife 120, 124
   Dismissal 144
   Evidence at Royal Commission (1877) 134
   Friendship with the Greens 120
   Hop growing 130
   Marriage 73
   Ownership of land adjacent to Coranderrk 82
   Relationship to Taungurong 138
   Replacement as overseer of hop ground 138
   Reports of Kulin hostility 109
   Resignation 243, 244
   Role at Coranderrk 114, 115
   Work in hop ground 90–91
Haydon 26
Heales, Richard 37, 54, 56, 59, 60, 61, 77, 253
   Central Board to Watch Over the Interests of the Aborigines 40
   Land Minister 61
   Legislative Assembly Select Committee 40
   Premier of Victoria 46
Healesville 82, 91, 141, 152, 158, 180, 182, 203, 276
   Agriculture 74
   Court records 138
   Growth 74
   Offences 144
   Public Meetings 120, 201, 206, 255
   Railway extension 163, 164, 173, 174, 191, 201, 254, 255, 264
   Rechabite Tent 245
   Residents 83, 233, 260
   Shire Council 274, 275, 276, 277
Heathen Missions Committee 53
Henley, E.B. 120
   Board of Inquiry (1876) 126

INDEX

Henty, Stephen George
  Central Board to Watch Over the Interests of the Aborigines 40
  Resignation 85
Hickson, Emily 39
Hickson, Robert 40, 43, 44, 46, 53
  Acheron Station Superintendent 39
  Resignation 57
Hobson, Maggie, *see* Miller, Maggie
Hobson, Tommy 69
Hodgkinson, Mr 60
Hopkins, John Rout 150, 176, 229
  Appointment to the Board 85
  Attendance at meetings 96
  Restoration of the hop income 104
  Visits to Coranderrk 93
Howitt, A.W. 10, 23, 52, 67
  Ethnographic studies 162, 227, 261
  Royal Commission (1877) 133, 134, 138
Hunter family 273
Hunter, David 53, 63
Hunter, Peter 37
  Death 158
  Deputation to the Board 114
  Shearing 109

Illustrated Australian News
  Article on Coranderrk 115
Indented Head 19, 20
Inglis, Mr
  Visit to Coranderrk 116

Jaara, *see* Jajowrong
Jackson family 272
Jackson, Phinnimore 173, 180, 182, 186
  Assault by Strickland, Frederick 152
Jagajaga 20
Jajowrong 9–10, 14, 15, 26, 27, 27, 34, 62, 68, 71, 87, 98, 109, 129, 236, 239, 251, 256, 266
  -*bulluk* 14
  Farming 47
  Gifts to the Queen 62
  -*goondeet* 14
  Language 12
  -*lar* 14
  Movement to Coranderrk 66
  Population 27
Jarcoort 12, 22
Jato-wara-wara
  Marriage 32
Jellebyook, *see* Miller, Harry
Jennings, Henry 43, 59, 96, 97, 133, 141, 148, 153, 154, 159, 170, 171, 174, 176, 177, 178, 183, 185, 190, 191, 195, 200, 202, 218, 222, 229, 244
  Abandonment of Coranderrk 102, 163
  Appointment of Halliday, Hugh H. as manager 113
  Board of Inquiry (1876) 122, 124, 126
  Board Regulations (1871) 81
  Censure of Minister 241
  Censure of Page, AM.A. 196
  Central Board to Watch Over the Interests of the Aborigines 42
  Counter proposal against abandonment 128, 130, 133, 140
  Disapproval of Stähle's treatment 103
  Exile of Bamfield, Tommy 242
  Meeting over protests against removal 130
  Motion to consider Green's reappointment 108
  Orders to Green, John 98
  Presbyterian services forbidden 118
  Protest against conditions at Coranderrk 142
  Resignation 244
  Resolution that Coranderrk was not a fit locality for Aborigines 127
  Role in Green's dismissal 108
  Vice chairman 144, 148, 149
  Visits to Coranderrk 83, 91, 93
  Vote for Green's return 110
Johnson, Burril
  Teacher 82
Jones, Stephen
  Compensation for land 44
  Mohican Station 44
  Sale of land 60
Joti-jota 228, 237, 274

Karkom, *see* Nelson, Harry
Katubanuut 22
Keilumbete 26
Kerr family 266, 272
Kerr, John 165, 170, 177, 185, 191
  Board of Inquiry (1881) report Addendum A 189, 190, 192
  Local Committee on the management of Coranderrk 163, 164
Kidnapping of Aboriginal women 18, 20
Kilmore 77
King Billy of Ballarat, *see* Balybalip
King Bobby, *see* Booringurmin
King, Charley, *see* Parnegean
King, Kitty 65
King, Mr 12, 65
King, Sarah 65
Kinship ties 13, 14, 69, 162
Kirrae-Wurrung 48
Kolakgnat 12, 22
Kooyan *see* Hunter, Peter

Kri-balluk 166
Kulin 48, 60, 155, 166, 272
    -(w)illam 12, 14
    -(w)urrung 9–10, 14
    Assemblies 26, 63
    Attendance of the Governor's Levee 61
    Attitude to 'half castes' 55, 129
    Attitude to Green, John 74
    Attitude to Halliday, Hugh H. 129
    -balluk 12, 14
    Brawl 203
    -bulluk 14
    Clan 14
    Clan head 9–10
    Confederacy 12
    Conversion to Christianity 65, 227
    Deputation to farewell Berry, Graham 265
    Deputation to the Board of Land and Works 38
    Deputation to the Board to complain over the location of Burgess' house and appointment of Halliday, Hugh H. 114
    Deputation to the Chief Secretary 114, 222
    Deputation to Thomas, William asking for land 37–38
    Dialects 99
    Disputes with the Johnsons 82
    Economy 26
    Ethnographic studies 98, 99, 100, 163, 227
    Etiquette 17, 20, 106, 138, 167
    European exploitation 33
    European occupation of land 16
    European violence 17, 18, 26
    Expectations about Coranderrk 72
    First contact 17, 18
    Gifts to the Queen and Prince Albert 62
    Identity 85
    Land tenure 12, 15, 162
    Language 12, 14
    Letter from the Queen 62
    Letters to the press 226
    Literacy 72
    Marriage 12, 13, 14, 69, 70, 239, 248
    Meaning of word 9
    Mourning 106, 249
    Movement to Coranderrk 66
    Nation 261
    Pastoral work 33
    Patrifiliation 14
    Petition against Aborigines Protection Law Amendment Bill 269
    Petition against alienation (1893) 275
    Petition against Green's exclusion from Coranderrk 118
    Petition for abolition of the Board 244
    Petition for the reinstatement of Green 160
    Petition to Berry for Abolishment of the Board 246
    Petition to Government 179
    Placement of dwellings 106
    Protest about allocation of dwellings 157
    Protest against conditions at Coranderrk 142
    Protest over Green's removal 97, 136, 168
    Protests against the dismissal of Green, John 136
    Protests against the sale of Coranderrk 155
    Reincarnation beliefs 65
    Relationship with Green, John 58
    Religion 29, 68
    Self government 64, 89
    Social and political organisation 162
    Social structure 10–15
    Sorcery 91, 162
    Subsistence hunting 33
    Territory 9
    Working for Europeans 63, 262
Kulkyne 104, 106, 108, 148, 154, 155
Kurnai 12, 22, 29, 32, 47, 48, 51, 57, 69, 86, 134, 176
    Aid 32
    Relationship with Kulin 70
Kurnaje-berreing 162
Kurung 27, 47, 71, 109, 237
    Movement to Coranderrk 66, 68
    Also see Woiworung
Kurung-jang-balluk 27
    Reserve 47
Kwatkwat 70, 180, 237
Kyneton 27

La Trobe, Lieutenant Governor 27, 32
Lacy, Mr
    Visit to Coranderrk 152
Laidlaw, James 226, 227
Laidlaw, Violet 226, 227
    Death 227
Lake Condah Station 48, 79, 85, 103, 176, 196, 201, 210, 225, 231, 249, 257, 258, 259, 266
    Abandonment 154
    Closure 273
    Protests against Stähle, J. Heinrich 216
Lake Hindmarsh 48
Lake Tyers Station 48, 242, 273, 276, 277, 279, 280
    Dispersal 3
    Extension to reserve 160
    Visit by LeSouef and Curr 149
Land rights 1, 3, 5
Lands Department Staff 33
Langhorne, George 28, 51
Langlands, Henry 59, 77
    Central Board to Watch Over the Interests of the Aborigines 40

Leader newspaper 165, 177, 182, 242
    Coranderrk (1876) 145
    Coranderrk article by Dow and Syme 111
    Coranderrk Hop Farm – Mr Green and Mr R. Brough Smyth 110
    Criticism of the Board 224
    Editor – Syme, G.A. 85
    Kulin criticisms of Halliday's management 142
    Reform of the Board 225
    Syme, G.A. article on Green, John 103
Learka-bulluk 27
Lee, Bella 218, 221, 222, 232
    Abortion attempt 215, 218
    Pregnancy 213
    Questionnaire and petition for Chief Secretary 251
Legislative Assembly
    Select Committee on Aboriginal reserves 40
    Select Committee to inquire into improving the present condition of the Aborigines 60
Legislative Council
    Select Committee 55
LeSouef, Albert A.C. 141, 149, 150, 154, 155, 163, 170, 176, 177, 178, 183, 187, 200, 202, 218, 226, 229, 243, 245, 246, 255, 256, 263
    Abandonment of Coranderrk 102, 127, 140, 157, 163, 223
    Absence abroad 152
    Account of protest against the Board 159
    Accusations against Green, John 159
    Appointment of Goodall, William 222
    Appointment of Halliday, Hugh H. as manager 113
    Appointment of Page, A.M.A. 136
    Appointment to the Board 97, 99, 100
    Attendance at Board meetings 108
    Board of Inquiry (1881) 164
    Board of Inquiry (1881) report 200
    Censure of Goodall, William 151
    Censure of Page, A.M.A. 196
    Closure of Coranderrk 274
    Deputation to the Chief Secretary about reserves 133
    Dominance of Board politics 148
    Gaoling of Manton, Benjamin, and Rowan, John 250, 251
    Kulin complaints about Burgess' son 105
    Meeting over protests against removal 130
    Membership of other committees 98
    Mission on the Murray 145
    Motion to get station managers advice on policy 225
    Nepotism 136
    Opposition to Green's return 110, 142
    Parliamentary criticisms 157
    Petition to Morrison, Alexander 251
    Protest against conditions at Coranderrk 142
    Reduction of Ogilvie's powers 108
    Relationship to Hagenauer, F.A. 100
    Relationship to Snodgrass, Peter 100
    Removal of 'half castes' from stations 213, 234
    Sub-committee on the future management of Coranderrk 102
    Transfer of Goodall, William to Framlingham Station 259, 262
    Usher of the Black Rod 99
    Vice chairman 100, 148
    Visit to Lake Tyers Station 149
    Visits to Coranderrk 224, 249, 262
LeSouef, William
    Assistant Protector 27
    Dismissal 28, 99
Lilydale 51, 123, 125
    Agriculture 74
Little Mr Green 58, 71, 257
Little River reserve 47
Lizzie
    Death 204
Local Guardians
    Evidence at Royal Commission (1877) 134
    Locket 63
Loddon River 27
Longmore, Frances 217
    Influence of Barak, William 147
Lonsdale, Billy 18, 68
    Ngurungaeta 9

MacBain, James 77, 81, 82, 85, 161, 164, 183, 197, 209
    Appointment of Godfrey, Frederick Race to the Board 100
    Call for inquiry 131, 132
    Chair of the Board 81
    Defence of Coranderrk 82
    Forced resignation of Green, John 96
    Inquiry into Coranderrk deaths 121
    Leave of Absence from Board (1875) 96
    Population figures for stations 80
    Protest over sectarianism 118
    Resignation 113, 132, 139, 145
    Return (1876), and reduction of Ogilvie's powers 108, 109, 110
    Vice chairman 108
    Visits to Coranderrk 83, 93
    Vote for Green's return 110
Mackenzie, David 22
Mackenzie, John 77, 105
    Membership of other committees 98
    Resignation from the Board 97, 100
    Visits to Coranderrk 79, 83, 91, 93

Mackie, Alex 180, 206
   Board of Inquiry (1876) 122
   Kulin protest against conditions at Coranderrk 142
   Letters 202, 204
   Preaching 118, 245, 250, 264
   Protest about attempted abortion 215
   Visits to Coranderrk 152
Mackie, John
   Appointment as teacher 263
   Dismissal 275
MacPherson, J.A. 130, 209
   Aborigines Act (1869) 127
   Board deputation 133
   Board of Inquiry (1876) 125
   Chief Secretary 105
   Inquiry into Coranderrk deaths 120
   Kulin deputation to the Chief Secretary 114
   Minute to the Board 128
   Relationship with Bon, Anne Fraser 122
   Residence at stations 127
   Visit to Coranderrk 118
Macredie, William 54, 96, 97, 110, 148, 154, 171, 178, 183, 190, 200, 202, 216, 218, 226, 229, 245, 246, 255
   Abandonment of Coranderrk 102, 157, 163
   Absence from Board (1876) 133
   Appointment of Halliday, Hugh H. as manager 113
   Appointment of Page, A.M.A. 136
   Board of Inquiry (1876) 126
   Board of Inquiry (1881) 164, 200
   Censure of Minister 241
   Central Board to Watch Over the Interests of the Aborigines 42
   Charges against Charles, John and Campbell, Alick 152
   Closure of Coranderrk 275
   Death 271
   Dismissal of Halliday, Hugh H. 145
   Exile of Bamfield, Tommy 242
   Forced resignation of Green, John 96
   Gaoling of Manton, Benjamin, and Rowan, John 250
   Kulin complaints about Burgess' son 105
   Meeting over protests against removal 130
   Motion that Green, John be reappointed on original terms 110
   Orders to Green, John 98
   Petition to Morrison, Alexander 251
   Presbyterian services forbidden 118
   Protest against conditions at Coranderrk 142
   Reduction of Ogilvie's powers 108
   Removal of 'half castes' from stations 234
   Restoration of the hop income 104
   Transfer of Goodall, William to Framlingham Station 259
   Visits to Coranderrk 91, 93, 249
Malcolm 31, 68, 239
   Wirrarap 68
Maloga Mission 167, 201, 213, 228, 237, 243, 261, 266, 271, 272, 279
   Founding 70
Mambulla 22
Mansfield 65, 129
Mansfield, Tommy, *see* Bamfield, Tommy
Manton family 273, 277
Manton, Annie 249, 251, 279
   Gaoling of Manton, Benjamin, and Rowan, John 249
   Protest against poor dormitory supervision 248, 250
   Punishment 249, 250, 251
   Questionnaire and petition for Chief Secretary 251
Manton, Benjamin 'Lanky' 237, 279
   Exile 241
   Gaol for drunkenness 248
Mara speaking 71, 85
Matthews, Daniel 70, 228, 261, 266, 272
   Letters about Friday family 266
   Removal of 'half castes' from stations 266
Matthews, R.H. 15
Mayyum, *see* Amott, Thomas
McCombie, Thomas 38
   Select committee on Aboriginal welfare 34
McCrea, William 175
   Chief Medical Officer 117, 118, 125, 130, 133
   Comments on the location of Coranderrk and tuberculosis 117
McCulloch, James
   Royal Commission (1877) 133
McLean, Allan
   Aborigines Protection Law Amendment Bill 270
McNab, Duncan 171, 175, 177, 191
   Board of Inquiry (1881) report Addendum A 189, 190, 192
   Local Committee on the management of Coranderrk 163, 164
Melbourne Exhibition 245, 252
Melbourne hospitals 155, 156, 161
Merri Creek School 30, 32, 47–48, 57
Methodist Church 27
Meymet-mainmeet 12
Michie, Tommy, *see* Bamfield, Tommy
Miller, Harry
   Family 69
Miller, Maggie 69
Millius, Captain
   Contact with Kulin 17
Minyambuta 70, 180

INDEX

Mitchelltown 27
Mogullumbitch, *see* Minyambuta
Mogullumbuk 10
Mohican Station 44–46, 57
    Farming 53
    Living conditions 54
    Purchase 45
    Rations 46
    School 46
Moiety 10, 15
    Bunjil 12, 13, 70
    Matrilineal 71
    Waa 12, 13
Mongara, *see* Clarke, Adam
Moorabool River 47
Moornalook 58, 65
Moravian missions 34, 35, 41, 53, 60, 96, 97, 100, 101, 110, 127, 148, 149, 154, 155, 176, 216, 218, 225, 272
Mordialloc Reserve 32, 68
    Alienation 48, 59, 61
Mordiyallook 99
Morgan family 266, 272
Morgan, Alfred 63, 166, 167, 183, 204, 213, 236, 237, 271
    Accusations against 243
    Assault 206
    Exile 243, 244
    Housing 237
    Leadership 170
    Letters 226
    Marriage 238
    Petition against Aborigines Protection Law Amendment Bill 269
    Protest against Bamfield's exile 240, 242
    Visit to Melbourne 203
Morgan, Caroline 180, 239
    Death 271
    Illness 243
    Protest about attempted abortion 215
    Protest against the exile of her husband 247
Morris, W.E.
    Appointment 274
Morrison, Alexander 220, 226, 229, 253, 254, 257
    Appointment 200, 222
    Closure of Coranderrk 274
    Living conditions at Coranderrk 252
    Motion to get station managers advice on policy 225
    Petition to Morrison, Alexander 251
    Removal of 'half castes' from stations 252
    Vice chairman 223
    Visits to Coranderrk 251
Mount Cole 68

Mount Emu 68
Mount Franklin Station 27, 32, 33, 34, 47, 62, 66, 67, 157, 203, 239
Mount Hope Station 71, 138
Mount Macedon 249
Mount Rouse 27
Munangabum 9, 27
Munnering, Tommy (Thomas) 29, 30
    Death 37
    Illness 37
Murchison Station 28, 68
Murradonnanuke 20
Murrangalk, *see* Buckley, William
Murray River 9
Murray, John
    Reform of the Board 276
Murrum-Murrum 37
Murup 10

Narre Warren depot 29
Nash, Henry 65
Nash, William 65
Native Police Corps 28, 29, 30, 37
Native title 22
Nelson family 272
Nelson, Harry 67
Nelson, Henry 266
Nevers, Charles 57
New South Wales
    Dispersal of Aboriginal 'half castes' 279
Neyernneyernne 27
Ngamajet 10, 16, 22, 174, 223, 269
Ngurai-illam-wurrung (Ngurelban) 12, 13, 14, 15, 26, 28, 65, 68, 99, 236, 237
    Language 12
    Population 27
Ngurungaeta 9, 10, 15, 16, 20, 23, 162, 227, 238, 249
Ningerranow 29
Ninggollobin, *see* Captain Turnbull
Ninggullabull *see* Barker, Jemmy
Nira-balluk Clan 66, 167
Norris, John 183
    Protest against the Board 159

O'Loghlen, Bryan 149, 154, 165, 178, 193, 201, 206, 209, 229, 259
    Attitude to abandonment 149
    Board of Inquiry (1881) 164, 198, 220, 222
    Coranderrk Debate 211
    Defeat 234
    Election 197
    Election as Premier 161
    Employment of detectives 151
    Influence of Barak, William 147

Interview with the Board 149
Investigation into abortion attempt 218
Investigation into Halliday's management 148
Reform of the Board 220
O'Shanassy, John 59
Officer, Charles Myles 220, 229, 243, 245, 246, 251, 255, 263, 266
  Alienation 276
  Appointment 200, 222
  Closure of Coranderrk 274
  Exile of Bamfield, Tommy 242
  Gaoling of Manton, Benjamin, and Rowan, John 250
  Petition against alienation (1893) 275
  Prosecution of Morgan, Alfred and Rowan, John 243
  Removal of 'half castes' from stations 234
  Transfer of Goodall, William to Framlingham Station 259, 262
  Vice chairman 223, 243, 275
  Visits to Coranderrk 249, 262
Ogilvie, Christian 105, 108, 109, 118, 122, 123, 126, 175, 183, 186, 197, 223, 225
  Abandonment of Coranderrk 104, 136
  Anger at press reports 115
  Appointment as Board Secretary 119
  Appointment as manager and Inspector 103
  Assimilation 135
  Attitude to Coranderrk living conditions 108
  Attitude to Green, John 130
  Attitude to the Kulin 104, 106
  Authoritarian discipline 104
  Board of Inquiry (1876) 126
  Comments on Smyth's suspension from the mines department 109
  Destruction of vegetable garden 106
  Dispute with Robertson, Nina 120
  European labourers 111
  Evidence at Royal Commission (1877) 138, 140
  General Inspector of Stock 243
  General Superintendent of Stations 106, 134
  Letter to allies on the Board 113
  Opposition to Board decisions 104
  Recommendations to the Board 115
  Reduction of powers 110
  Reports of outside influence 110
  Resignation 115, 116, 136
  Scuffle with Bamfield, Tommy 115, 205, 206, 242
  Secretary, Inspector 119
  Threat to prosecute de Castella, Paul and de Fury, Guillaume 118
  Tour of the Murray 104, 105, 108
  Trips to Melbourne 109
  Vagrancy laws 127

Old Colonists' Association 41, 98, 243
Old George *see* Tuolwing
Old Man Billy, *see* Goona, Yanem
Orders-in-Council 153, 227, 234, 241, 248, 279, 281

Page, A.M.A. 141, 150, 151, 152, 163, 168, 170, 171, 172, 173, 174, 175, 176, 177, 178, 179, 180, 181, 182, 183, 186, 189, 191, 194, 195, 196, 200, 202, 203, 205, 210, 215, 216, 217, 223, 224, 225, 226, 227, 228, 231, 233, 235, 238, 239, 240, 246, 248, 251, 252, 254, 256, 257, 258, 259, 260, 263, 264, 265, 266, 271
  Abandonment of Coranderrk 150, 154, 155, 190
  Accusations against Bamfield, Tommy 204
  Acting Secretary 137
  Appointment 136
  Appointment of Goodall, William 221
  Board of Inquiry (1881) 200
  Censure of Bon, Anne Fraser 224
  Censure of Goodall, William 151, 242
  Charges against Charles, John and Campbell, Alick 152
  Coranderrk Debate 210
  Corruption 183, 187, 196, 201, 213, 218, 220, 224, 234, 240, 242, 243, 245, 255, 262, 265
  Criticism 193
  Death 271
  Dismissal of complaints against Strickland, Frederick 148
  Exile of Bamfield, Tommy 242
  Exile of individuals 201, 237, 248
  Gaoling of Bamfield, Tommy 206, 207
  Gaoling of Manton, Benjamin, and Rowan, John 249
  Housing 237
  Inspection of the Wimmera 201
  Kulkyne site 154
  Letter about Laidlaw family 226
  Orders-in-Council 241
  Petition to Berry for abolition of the Board 244
  Prosecution of Morgan, Alfred and Rowan, John 243
  Protest about attempted abortion 215
  Punishment of Manton, Annie 250
  Relationship with Bon, Anne Fraser 160
  Relationship with Goodall, William 232
  Relationship with Kulin 156
  Relationship with Shaw, Joseph 244, 270
  Relationship with Strickland, Frederick 145
  Removal of 'half castes' from stations 160, 212, 234, 249, 256, 266, 271
  Secretary 141

Transfer of Goodall, William to Framlingham Station 259, 262
  Visits to Coranderrk 157, 250, 262
Pangerang 12, 61, 69, 98, 129, 144, 152, 155, 166, 228, 237, 251, 272, 274
  Petition against Aborigines Protection Law Amendment Bill 269
Panton, J.A.
  Inquiry into attempted abortion 218, 219, 221, 222, 224
Parker, E.S. 14, 25, 27, 34, 35, 66
Parker, Maggie
  Dormitory matron 232
Parker, William 138, 167
  Board of Inquiry (1881) report Addendum A 193
  Carpenter 225
  Deputation to the Board 114
  Letters 226
  Visit to Melbourne 204
Parnegean 37, 65
Patterson family 273
Patterson, James
  Influence of Barak, William 147
Peacock, Edward 30
Peeruk-el-moom-bulluk 10
Phillips, Billy, *see* Balybalip
Phillips, Johnny 83
Plenty River 19, 23
Pondy-yaweet 51, 63
Port Phillip 16, 21
Presbyterian Church 122, 175
Presbyterian mission committee 110, 127, 139, 152, 186, 197, 200, 220, 245, 253
Protectorate system 25, 27
  Dismissal of staff 32
  Failure 26, 32, 34
  Petition for land 32
  Port Phillip Protectorate 15, 25
  Rations 25, 28
Punch *see* Bamfield, Tommy

Ra-gun *see* Barak, Annie
Railway extension 191
Railways Standing Committee 158
Ra-ker-nun, *see* Simpson, Martin
Ramahyuck Station 48, 176
  Closure 273
Ramsay, Robert 154, 156, 242
  Chief Secretary 152
  Death 209
  Defence of Green, John 82
  Election 134, 153
  Parliamentary debate on conditions at Coranderrk 154, 157
  Postmaster General and acting Chief Secretary 100
  Visit to Coranderrk 117
Reece, James 249
Reservation of land for Aborigines 34, 35
Richards, Dick 63, 67, 167
  Protest against conditions at Coranderrk 142
Richards, Ellen 67, 143, 277
Richardson, Richard 178, 183
  Coranderrk Debate 211
  Influence of Barak, William 147
  Inquiry into attempted abortion 221
  Visit to Coranderrk 157
Robarts, C.A.
  Appointment 274
Robertson, Nina 105, 108
  Appointment as dormitory matron 90
  Care of the sick 124
  Complaints against Burgess, Robert and other Europeans 105
  Dismissal 120, 122
  Evidence at Royal Commission (1877) 134, 139
  Re-appointment 225
Robinson, George Augustus 15, 22, 25, 28
Rouget, James 276
  Appointment 276
Rowan family 273
Rowan, Jeannie 196, 204, 249, 250, 251
  Complaints against Shaw, Joseph 271
  Gaoling of Manton, Benjamin, and Rowan, John 249
  Questionnaire and petition for Chief Secretary 251
Rowan, John 'Sambo' 204, 237
  Exile 243, 244
  Gaol for Drunkenness 248
  Prosecution 243
Royal Commission (1877) 1, 119, 133, 134, 135, 136, 137, 138, 139, 140, 141, 144, 145, 148, 153, 165, 171, 174, 185, 197, 211, 220, 272
Rusden, G.W.
  Royal Commission (1877) 134, 139
Russell family 273, 277
Russell, William 279
  Petition against Aborigines Protection Law Amendment Bill 269
Ryrie brothers 32, 61

Saltwater River 19
Search, Frederick 86, 88, 89, 90, 105, 182
  Appointment as horticultural consultant 85, 111
  Criticism of Green, John 88, 91, 92, 96
  Letter to the *Argus* 115
  Recommendations for new manager 97
  Usurpation of Green's role 93

Service, James
    Punishment of Manton, Annie 250
    Removal of 'half castes' from stations 256
Seymours, see Buthera-balluk
Shaw, Jessie 231, 259
Shaw, Joseph 233, 236, 237, 245, 248, 249, 251, 259, 261, 271
    Accusations against Goodall, William 258, 259
    Appointment as manager 258, 263
    Appointment as teacher 231
    Cruelty 225
    Dormitory supervision 246
    Exile of Bamfield, Tommy 235
    Inquiry into Manton, Annie and Rowan, Jeannie protests 250
    Letters 266
    Management 262, 263, 271
    Misappropriation of supplies 85
    Petition against alienation (1893) 275
    Problems at Lake Condah Station 85
    Recommendation as manager 130
    Relationship with Goodall, William 232, 234
    Relationship with Page, A.M.A. 244
    Resignation threat 271
    Retirement 273, 276
Sheppard, Sherbourne 153, 154, 176, 222
    Appointment to the Board 110
    Board of Inquiry (1881) report 200
    Ceased to attend 224
    Censure of Page, A.M.A. 196, 197
    Charges against Charles, John and Campbell, Alick 152
    Death 256
    Deputation to the Chief Secretary about reserves 133
    Meeting over protests against removal 130
    Opposition to Green's re-appointment 110, 142
    Presbyterian services forbidden 118
Sievewright, C.W. 26, 27
Simon, see Murrum-Murrum
Simpson family 272
Simpson, Martin 203
    Deputation to the Board 114
    Emigration 158
    Fighting 210
    Protest against abandonment 129
    Protest against conditions at Coranderrk 142
    Relationship with Halliday, Hugh H. 138
Sinclair, John 120
    Healesville Public Meetings 120, 201
    Petition to Berry, Graham 141
    Proposed Board medical officer 124
Singleton, John
    Royal Commission (1877) 133

Smith, R. Murray
    Influence of Barak, William 147
Smyth, Robert Brough 14, 49, 59, 60, 62, 77, 79, 80, 82, 93, 111, 113, 131, 176, 177, 182, 183, 186, 210, 216, 223, 231
    Abandonment of Coranderrk 81, 102
    Attendance at Board meetings 108
    Attitude to Green, John 79, 96, 108
    Board administration 136
    Board Regulations (1871) 81
    Control over Board income 80
    Criticism by Anglican missions committee 85
    Discipline at Coranderrk 105
    Ethnographic studies 99
    Inspection of goldfields 66
    Kulin complaints about Burgess' son 105
    Letters from the Kulin 97
    Ownership of land adjacent to Coranderrk 82
    Recommendations on gazettal and wages 82
    Reduction of Ogilvie's powers 108
    Relationship with Green, John 58, 77, 91, 92, 97
    Relationship with Rusden, G.W. 134
    Religious beliefs 71
    Removal of Kulin from Coranderrk 112
    Resignation 119
    Restoration of the hop income 104
    Secretary 43, 108
    Secretary for Mines 42
    Secretary of the Central Board to Watch Over the Interests of the Aborigines 42
    Support of Burgess, Robert 90, 97, 102
    Suspension from Mines Department 93, 108
    Threats to the Kulin 87, 97
    Usurpation of power 96
    Visits to Coranderrk 79, 83, 89
    Voting member 43, 79
Snodgrass, Peter 53, 60, 100
    Acheron Station Trustee 39
    Alienation of Acheron Station 39, 44, 46, 54
    Corruption 45, 46, 49, 55
    Legislative Assembly Select Committee 40
Southern Cross newspaper
    Maloga Mission 272
Spider, Thomas 213, 215, 218
    Inquiry into Mrs Manton's and Mrs Rowan's protests 250
Stähle, J. Heinrich 96, 97, 149, 175, 176, 216, 257, 258
    Accusations against Bamfield, Tommy 242
    Appointment as teacher manager 90, 96
    Complaints against Page, AM.A. 258
    Confiscation of mail 224
    Dismissal 102, 105
    Evidence at Royal Commission (1877) 134

INDEX

Exile of individuals 145
Letter to Chief Secretary asking for the dismissal of Burgess, Robert 102
Relationship with the Kulin 97
Removal from Coranderrk 103
Resignation 116
Stähle, Mary 216
Letters 216
Stanley, Arthur
Visit to Coranderrk 277
Stawell, William 139
Royal Commission (1877) 133, 134, 139
Steel, John C. 173, 177, 182, 183, 185, 186, 218
Board of Inquiry (1881) report Addendum B 193
Gaoling of Bamfield, Tommy 205
Petition to Morrison, Alexander 251
Purchase of Coranderrk land 254, 255, 257, 261, 275
Sentence of Bamfield, Tommy 209
Visit to Coranderrk 233
Strickland, Frederick 153, 156, 157, 162, 165, 166, 167, 168, 170, 171, 173, 173, 174, 177, 178, 180, 182, 183, 186, 187, 190, 196, 197, 199, 201, 213, 216, 217, 218, 220, 226, 245
Accusations against Bamfield, Tommy 203, 204, 205, 206, 242
Accusations of interference 159
Appointment 145
Assault on Jackson, Phinnimore 152
Attempted abortion 215
Censure of Goodall, William 151
Charges against Charles, John and Campbell, Alick 152
Complaints about Harris, Thomas and Deans, Laura 189
Cruelty 180
Dismissal 221
Dormitory supervision 248
Drunkenness 180, 182
Letters 194, 197, 202, 219
Management 160
Neglect of the farm 150
Neglect of the sick 147
Praise by the Board 242
Replacement 215
Residents protests 154, 155
Resignation 173, 190, 194
Strickland, Mrs
Abortion attempt 218, 219
Sumner, Theodatus 97, 176
Attendance at Board meetings 96, 106
Central Board to Watch Over the Interests of the Aborigines 40
Death 256

Forced resignation of Green, John 96
Membership of other committees 98
Vice chairman 97
Vice chairman of the Board 85
Visits to Coranderrk 93
Supply Debate 116, 130, 156, 241
Syme, David 197
Syme, George Alexander 96, 177, 182, 183, 216, 224, 225, 242
Appointment to the Board 85
Disagreement with Board Policy 103
Dissent at forced resignation of Green, John 96
Editor of the *Leader* newspaper 111
Gaoling of Bamfield, Tommy 204
Interview with Berry, Graham 139
Protest over sectarianism 118
Resignation from the Board 97, 100, 103, 139
Visits to Coranderrk 93, 156

Talgium, *see* Hamilton, William
Tall Boy, *see* Bearringa
Tanderrum ceremony 22
Tarringower 27
Taungurong 12, 13, 14, 15, 18, 26, 27, 28, 31, 37, 43, 45, 46, 54, 55, 57, 58, 62, 65, 106, 109, 122, 129, 167, 223, 227, 237, 265, 269
Acheron Station 44, 54
Alienation of land 60
Ethnographic studies 99
Language 12, 99
Mohican Station 45, 53
Movement to Coranderrk 66
Protest over the alienation of Acheron Station 45
Removal from Watts River Reserve 61
Request for land 38
Territory 65
Terang 26
Terrick family 273, 277
Thomas, David
Appointment to the Board 85
Visits to Coranderrk 91
Thomas, William 12, 22, 23, 25, 26, 32, 35, 37, 42, 45, 46, 47, 49, 53, 57, 58, 59, 60, 61, 62, 97, 213, 223
Aboriginal Guardianship and reserves 39
Acheron Station 39
Assistant Protector 28, 29
Board attendance 96
Death 91
Ethnographic studies 71, 99, 107, 162, 261
Forced resignation of Green, John 96
Guardian of the Aborigines 32
Journal 31
Recommendations to the Central Board to Watch Over the Interests of the Aborigines 43

REBELLION AT CORANDERRK

    Recruitment to Coranderrk 66
    Request for reserves 33
    Visits to Coranderrk 93
Thomson, William 177
    Comments on lung disease 175
Timothy 63
Tooterrie 13, 28
Treaties 21, 22
Tribe 14, 16
Tuolwing 18

Ulupna 135

Vale, W.M.K. 209
    Defence of Green, John 82
    Visit to Coranderrk 157
Victoria
    Population 16
Victorian Legislative Council 32, 34
    Reserves 38
    Select Committee on Aboriginal welfare 34, 35

Wahgunyah 237
Wandin family 272, 273, 279
Wandin, Jemima, *see* Burns, Jemima
Wandin, Robert 159, 167, 170, 181, 198, 203, 228, 244, 251, 256, 264, 272
    'Half caste' 162
    Board of Inquiry (1881) report Addendum A 194
    Death 272
    Deputation to the Board 114
    Exile 257
    Family 51, 69, 161
    Income 77
    Letters 226
    Ngurungaeta 111, 162, 238, 249
    Petition against Aborigines Protection Law Amendment Bill 269
    Petition against alienation (1893) 275
    Protest about attempted abortion 213
    Protest against conditions at Coranderrk 142
    Protest against European labour 116
    Replacement as stockman 138
    Request for a doctor 124
    Visit to Melbourne 204
Wandyallock 68
Wangaratta 70
Wappan run 66
Warangesda Mission Station 180
Waring-illam-balluk 39, 65
Warrandyte Reserve 32, 47
Warren, Harriet 67
Warren, Jemmy 67

Wathaurung 12, 13, 14, 15, 16, 17, 18, 19, 20, 22, 26, 27, 47, 68, 131
    Language 12
    Movement to Coranderrk 66, 68
    Population 27
    Territory 19
Watt, W.A.
    Influence of Barak, William 147
Watts River Reserve 58, 61
Waveroo 12
Webster, Jemmy 174, 206
    Death 150, 158
    Family 65
Webster, Jemmy Jr 37, 63
    Family 66
Webster, Johnny (John) 63
    Family 66
    Prosecution 106, 115
Wedge, J.H. 20
Weragoondeet, *see* Werry, Peter
Werribee River 26
Werry, Eliza
    Daughter Ellen 66
    Family 66
    Marriage to Peter Werry 69
    Marriage to Yerrebulluk 66
Werry, Peter 67, 69
Western Kulin Language, *see* Kulin Language
Westernport 17
Westernport Bay Sealers 18
Wildgung, *see* Webster, Jemmy
Wimmera Mission 34, 71, 154, 155, 163
    Closure 273
    Discontent 150
    Green, John – relieving manager 104
    Transfer of Coranderrk residents 148
Winberi 9
Wirrarap 162
Woiworung 10, 12, 13, 14, 15, 16, 18, 19, 22, 25, 27, 28, 29, 31, 32, 33, 37, 43, 47, 48, 51, 53, 58, 59, 61, 65, 69, 71, 97, 144, 162, 163, 166, 181, 223, 227, 236, 256
    Acheron Station 54
    Contact with Batman, John 20
    Dispersal 30
    Language 12, 90
    Movement to Coranderrk 66
    Population 28, 69
    Religious assemblies 31
    Removal from Watts River Reserve 61
Woiwurru language 69, 99, 279
Wollithiga 167
Wolmudging 20
Wonga, Currie 51

Wonga, Maria 51, 69
Wonga, (Simon) 29, 31, 37, 48, 49, 51, 53, 57, 58, 59, 61, 64, 67, 71, 162, 223, 274
    Beliefs about sorcery 91
    Clan head 31
    Conversion to Christianity 58
    Death 97
    Deputation to Thomas, William 38
    Ethnographic studies 99
    Family 16, 69
    Founding of Coranderrk 25
    Income 77
    Initiation 68
    Leadership 69, 109
    Protest against Green's management 80
Wonga, Simon Jr 69
Woori Yalloak Reserve 58, 61, 85
Wornbulluk clan 47
Wortherly, Jack 9
Wotjo speakers 71
Wrixon, Henry
    Influence of Barak, William 147
Wudthaurung-bulluk 18, 20
Wudthowrung Territory 18
Wurundjeri, *see* Woiworung
Wurundjeri-balluk 9, 12, 16, 18, 22, 61
    Assembly 19
    Marriage 32
Wurung-hura-gerung-bulluk Clan 67
Wurunjerri-balluk 162
Wyerdierum, *see* Richards, Dick

Yackandandah 213
Yaitmathang 180
Yallukit-willam, *see* Bunurong
Yalukit-willani 22
Yarra Mission 51, 58, 61, 62
    School 28
Yea 65, 81, 129
Yeerun-illam-balluk 31, 39
    Clan heads 66
Yering 32, 33, 47, 48, 51, 53, 61, 223
    Goulburn River Trail 57
Yerrebulluk 66
    Daughter Ellen 62
    Farming 47
You Yangs district 20
Yowung-illam-balluk 37, 39, 58, 65

Zoological and Acclimatisation Society 41, 98, 99, 200
Zox, E.L. 178
    Coranderrk Debate 203
    Deputation to farewell Berry, Graham 265
    Gaoling of Bamfield, Tommy 210
    Influence of Barak, William 147
    Meeting with Norris, John and Coranderrk residents 159
    Parliamentary debate on conditions at Coranderrk 156, 157
    Petition against Aborigines Protection Law Amendment Bill 269

www.ingramcontent.com/pod-product-compliance
Lightning Source LLC
Chambersburg PA
CBHW081824230426
43668CB00017B/2364